LOVING CHICAGO IS LIKE LOVING A WOMAN
WITH A BROKEN NOSE…
NELSON ALGREN

BOOKS BY TROY TAYLOR

DEAD MEN SO TELL TALES SERIES
Dead Men Do Tell Tales (2008)
Bloody Chicago (2006)
Bloody Illinois (2008)

HAUNTED ILLINOIS BOOKS
Haunted Illinois (1999 / 2001 / 2004)
Haunted Decatur (1995)
More Haunted Decatur (1996)
Ghosts of Millikin (1996 / 2001)
Where the Dead Walk (1997 / 2002)
Dark Harvest (1997)
Haunted Decatur Revisited (2000)
Flickering Images (2001)
Haunted Decatur: 13th Anniversary Edition (2006)
Haunted Alton (2000 / 2003 / 2008)
Haunted Chicago (2003)
The Haunted President (2005)
Mysterious Illinois (2005)
Resurrection Mary (2007)
The Possessed (2007)
Weird Chicago (2008)

HAUNTED FIELD GUIDE BOOKS
The Ghost Hunters Guidebook
(1997/ 1999 / 2001/ 2004 / 2007)
Confessions of a Ghost Hunter (2002)
Field Guide to Haunted Graveyards (2003)
Ghosts on Film (2005)
So, There I Was (with Len Adams) (2006)

HISTORY & HAUNTINGS SERIES
The Haunting of America (2001)
Into the Shadows (2002)
Down in the Darkness (2003)
Out Past the Campfire Light (2004)
Ghosts by Gaslight (2007)

OTHER GHOSTLY TITLES
Spirits of the Civil War (1999)
Season of the Witch (1999/ 2002)
Haunted New Orleans (2000)
Beyond the Grave (2001)
No Rest for the Wicked (2001)
Haunted St. Louis (2002)
The Devil Came to St. Louis (2006)

BARNES & NOBLE PRESS TITLES
Haunting of America (2006)
Spirits of the Civil War (2007)
Into the Shadows (2007)

STERLING PUBLICATIONS TITLES
Weird U.S. (Co-Author) (2004)
Weird Illinois (Barnes & Noble Press) (2005)
Weird Virginia (Co-Author) (2007)
Weird Indiana (Co-Author) (2008)

HISTORY PRESS TITLES
Wicked Washington (2007)

STACKPOLE BOOKS TITLES
Haunted Illinois (2008)

BOOKS BY ADAM SELZER

How To Get Suspended and Influence People (2007)
Pirates of the Retail Wasteland (2008)
I Put a Spell On You, (2008)
Weird Chicago (2008)
Weird Chicago Presents: The Murder Castle of H.H. Holmes (editor) (2008)

COMING SOON
Ghost Hunting For Skeptics (Llewellyn Press)
I Put a Spell On You, Also (Delacorte Press)
The Wisenheimer's Guide to U.S. History (Delacorte)
Lost and Found (Delacorte Press)

BOOKS BY KEN MELVOIN-BERG

Thrilling Tales: Lost Temple of the Incan Blood God (2006)
Santeria and Palo Mayombe (2005)
Vodoun in Theory and Practice (2003)
I Wanna Iguana! (2002)
Sex Magic for Beginners (2001)
Jewish Mysticism and the Cthulhu Cult (1997)

WEIRD CHICAGO

Forgotten History, Strange Legends &
Mysterious Hauntings of the Windy City

BY TROY TAYLOR, ADAM SELZER
& KEN MELVOIN-BERG

- A Dark Haven Entertainment Book from Whitechapel Press -

DEDICATIONS:

From Troy: This book is for Haven, without whom it could not have been written and this entire grand scheme could not have taken place. I love you!

From Adam: This is for Ronni - who I first met on a tour that Ken, Willy and I ran two years ago. She puts up with staring at my back while I do research at all hours, makes me tea when my voice is gone, and never seems to worry that I'm going to get sucked into the Netherworld in the basement of Old Town Tatu.

From Ken: For Wendy --You were my one and only sibling and now my spirit guide. Your passing set you free and you have no more pain. For we are never promised tomorrow let us enjoy today.

From all of us goes a special thanks to "Ray & Olga" -- without your pettiness, jealousy, untold lies & bizarre, alcohol-fueled brand of insanity, none of this would have been possible. Thanks!

ORIGINAL COVER ARTWORK DESIGNED BY
©Copyright 2008 by Michael Schwab, Troy Taylor & Adam Selzer
Visit M & S Graphics at http://www.manyhorses.com/msgraphics.htm

Cover Photograph Courtesy of Ronni-Davis Selzer

THIS BOOK IS PUBLISHED BY:
Whitechapel Press
A Division of Dark Haven Entertainment, Inc.
15 Forest Knolls Estates - Decatur, Illinois - 62521
(217) 422-1002 / 1-888-GHOSTLY
Visit us on the internet at http://www. dark haven entertainment. com

First Printing -- July 2008
ISBN: 1-892523-59-0

Printed in the United States of America

CAST OF CHARACTERS

TROY TAYLOR

Troy Taylor is the author of more than 55 books about American hauntings and the unexplained. He has appeared in hundreds of newspaper and magazine articles, on radio and television broadcasts, in dozens of documentary films, and in one feature horror film. Critics called him "the best actor in the film", which wasn't saying much since he was playing himself. When not pounding away on a typewriter or chasing ghosts, Taylor started running ghost tours in 1993 and now has companies all over Illinois. He and his wife, Haven, currently live in downstate Illinois.

ADAM SELZER

Adam Selzer is an author, Chicago historian and part-time rock star with a lifelong interest in things that go bump in the night. Adam got his start in the "weird" business by hosting a public access paranormal TV show in Des Moines at the age of 12, which very few people ever saw. Later, he hosted a folk music radio show, which very few people heard. Undaunted, he is now a noted expert on Chicago-style hot dogs and a scholar of the city's "historical bohemia". Adam is the author of a number of subversive young adult novels, which have been banned in several school libraries -- a fact he is particularly proud of. Adam and his wife, Ronni, reside in Chicago and Adam can occasionally be found berating people who put ketchup on their hot dogs.

KEN MELVOIN-BERG

Ken Berg is a professional psychic, and expert on the supernatural and a widely known authority on Chicago's secret places. Ken got his start with the "weird" as a child, when it was not uncommon for him to regularly predict the deaths of family members before they occurred. This made him especially popular at family gatherings. He has also been a bouncer at the Metro, a medic in the Air Force, a game designer, and Kreamy the Cllown. As Kreamy, Ken opened for the Smashing Pumpkins during their final show. He is also a long-time Chicago tour guide and a psychic detective who has worked with numerous law enforcement agencies. Ken currently lives in a secret location on Chicago's west side.

WILLIE WILLIAMS

Willie Williams grew up in Chicago's Cabrini Green and is the official, full-time driver for the Weird Chicago Tours. He has been with the company from the beginning and has been given the coveted "Employee of the Month" award every month since Weird Chicago's inception. Willie's insightful comments about the tours, and about Chicago locations, appear throughout the book.

TABLE OF CONTENTS

WEIRD CHICAGO

I have struck a city - a real city - and they call it Chicago. The other places do not count. This is first real American city that I have encountered. Having seen it, I urgently desire to never see it again. It is inhabited by savages.
RUDYARD KIPLING

Chicago is, and always has been, a lusty, brawling, violent city; a polyglot city, a rich city, a city powerful and unafraid. In a curious, oblique manner, Chicago is proud of her reputation.
SEWELL PEASLEE WRIGHT

They tell me you are wicked and I believe them, for I have seen your painted women under the gas lamps, luring the farm boys.
CARL SANDBURG, "CHICAGO"

Chicago is a city of contradictions, of private visions haphazardly overlaid and linked together. If the city was unhappy with itself yesterday-and invariably it was-it will reinvent itself today.
PAT COLANDER

Chicago is unique. It is the only completely corrupt city in America.
CHARLES MERRIMAN, UNSUCCESSFUL MAYORAL CANDIDATE IN 1911

You can get much further with a smile, a kind word and a gun than you can get with just a smile and a kind word.
AL CAPONE

INTRODUCTION

Every street you walk down in Chicago has a history of its own.

Sometimes it's easy to find; you can see historical markers for most of the more famous stories, and even the gangster sites that aren't commemorated can be identified by the number of tour buses that drive by.

Other times, you have to look a little bit closer and see the faded signs on the sides of the buildings, or the old streetcar tracks peeking out from under the potholes.

Or, sometimes, you just have to see the ghosts.

At Weird Chicago Tours, research is a full-time job. When we started the company, we committed ourselves to providing not just the best ghost tours in town but the best, and most accurate, tours in the city of any sort. We jumped headfirst into the research - not just into new stories and locations, but into the famous Chicago stories that we knew by heart, in an attempt to separate history from legend.

We were amazed at how much we discovered. We found buildings that were thought to have burned to the ground a century ago still standing. We found stories of H.H. Holmes and his Murder Castle that have never been repeated since they were first in the newspapers. And we found other stories - amazing stories - that other books have left out altogether.

Lots of people know about Captain Streeter, Al Capone, the Dil Pickle Club, and other such Chicago icons, but others, such as Peter Nissen, The Chicken Man and The Wind Blew Inn were just as famous in their day. Inexplicably, they've since vanished into the ether. Some of the stories presented on our tours and in this book are being told for the first time in over a century.

Others are being told more accurately than ever before. The story of the Fool Killer submarine, for instance, has made its way into several books, but only as a brief mention. The full story - and the full mystery - has never before been explored.

And, of course, there are the ghosts.

Chicago is home to some of the most fantastic ghost stories in the world and new ones are being told all the time. But the pantheon of venerable haunted spots in any city will change over time. A century ago people told stories about the Robey House and the ghost of the Stockyards police station. A decade ago it was The Red Lion and That Steak Joynt. Today, it's time for places such as The Congress Hotel and Old Town Tatu to take their place. Our investigations into these locations have been extensive and sometimes the ghost stories are the least of what we find!

The tours alone weren't enough to cover all of the stories we unearthed; even the Weird Chicago blog and the Weird Chicago Radio podcast haven't been enough to cover everything.

Come along as we dig through the pages of history, through legend, myth and the footprints of the city as it was a century ago or more. You won't believe what you'll find!

Troy Taylor
Adam Selzer
Ken Melvoin-Berg
Summer 2008

1. BORN IN BLOOD: WEIRD CHICAGO HISTORY

The city of Chicago was started with confusion and bloodshed. No one really planned Chicago in the way that other great American cities were planned, with their sites carefully chosen and their streets laid out with care. The land on both sides of the Chicago River was low and wet, a brackish area of swamp and mud. The location that would someday become the Loop was only a few inches above Lake Michigan in those days and it spent the greater part of the year under water. The mouth of the river was choked with sand, allowing passage by nothing larger than a canoe, while most of the stream was filled with wild rice and its banks covered by wild onion. This aromatic vegetation would give Chicago its first name. Or maybe not....

Nobody really knows for sure why the city was called Chicago. On the banks of the river was wild onion - or maybe it was garlic - that the Indians allegedly called "Chickagou." Or, others claim, the name of the city came from an Indian word for "playful waters," which was "Sheecaugo," or from the word "Chocago," meaning "destitute," or from "Shegahg," which meant "skunk," or from an Indian chief named "Chicagou." And the list goes on. In general, though, most just interpreted the name to mean "bad smell" and, for some reason, the moniker stuck.

The only real dispute for this explanation came from poet Edgar Lee Masters, who tried to convince everyone that "Chicago" actually meant "strength." However, Masters, who was a regular customer of the Everleigh sisters' magnificent brothel in the South Side Levee district, was hardly an expert on Native American names.

Chicago began as empty wilderness and open prairie, an isolated region on the shore of a great lake. French explorers passed through without stopping for more than a century before settlers finally decided to put down roots.

A FORT IN THE WILDERNESS

It may not have been a cold morning in April 1803, when Captain John Whistler climbed a sand dune around which the sluggish Chicago River tried to reach Lake Michigan - but chances are, it was. A chilling wind would have been a characteristic greeting from the landscape that Whistler had come to change. His orders had been to take six soldiers from the 1st U.S. Infantry, survey a road from Detroit to the mouth of the river, and draw up plans for a fort at this location. Whistler managed to beat the British to the site. The British had also planned to build a fort at the entrance to the Chicago River and one has to wonder how the city might be different today if they had managed to show up first.

After claiming the site, Captain Whistler returned to Detroit to get his garrison and his family. He was 45 years old and neither his poor Army pay nor the dangers of the frontier stopped him from living a full and domesticated life. Eventually, he fathered 15 children.

Captain Whistler brought his entire family with him to the Chicago frontier, including his grown son, Lieutenant William Whistler, as well as 3-year-old George Washington Whistler. The names of both are of later importance. Lieutenant Whistler would command the fort that his father built during the Black Hawk War in 1832 and 1833, thus becoming the last military officer in charge there. George, who would later build railroads for the tsar of Russia, became the father of artist James A. McNeill Whistler. (That means he was married to the lady who became famous as "Whistler's Mother.")

Fort Dearborn in 1803

WHERE IS IT NOW?

The site of Fort Dearborn was at the present intersection of Wacker Drive and Michigan Avenue. The actual boundaries are marked with plaques on the sidewalk. Nearby stands a statue that makes it look like the settlers are killing the Potawatomi!

Captain Whistler's family was spared the arduous trek over erratic Indian trails to the Chicago River. While the troops marched on foot, the captain and his brood boarded the U.S. schooner Tracy, which also carried artillery and camp equipment. It sailed to the mouth of the St. Joseph River, where it met the troops. The Whistler family took one of the Tracy's rowboats to the Chicago River, while the troops marched around the lake.

There were 69 officers and men in the contingent that had the task of building Fort Dearborn, which was named in honor of Secretary of War Henry Dearborn, a man who would go on to be considered one of the most inept leaders in American history. During the War of 1812, Dearborn was placed in command of all of the American troops between Lake Erie and the Atlantic. He tried to capture Montreal, but his troops were so disorganized that they never even made it across the Canadian border. Dearborn was finally relieved of his command by President James Madison in 1813 after he narrowly avoided being court-martialed. In spite of this, a number of Chicago parks and developments were named for him, leading author Norman Mark to refer to him as "an example of one of history's most successful failures."

The hill on which Fort Dearborn was built was eight feet above the river, which curved around it and stopped from flowing into a lake by a sandbar, flowed south until it found an outlet. To this spot, the soldiers hauled the logs they had made from trees cut on the north bank. The fort was a simple stockade of logs. They were placed in the ground and then sharpened along the upper end. The outer stockade was a solid wall with an entrance in the southern section that was blocked with heavy gates. Another exit, this one underground, was located on the north side. As time went on, they built barracks, officers' quarters, a guardhouse and a small powder magazine made from brick. West of the fort, they constructed a two-story log building, with split-oak siding, to serve as an Indian agency, and between this structure and the fort they placed root cellars. South of the fort, the land was enclosed for a garden. Blockhouses were added at two corners of the fort and three pieces of light artillery were mounted at the walls. The fort offered substantial protection for the soldiers garrisoned there but they would later learn that it was not protection enough.

CHICAGO'S FIRST "BOSS"

The history of the first settlers in Chicago was purposely shrouded in mystery for many years. For nearly a century, Chicagoans were led to believe that the first settler was a runaway slave who lived along the Chicago River for a short time and then faded into oblivion. However, Jean Baptiste Point du Sable was a trader who had been born to a Frenchman and a black woman on the Caribbean island of Santo Domingo. He was never a slave. He was well educated and he went on to develop a trading post and farm that paid him handsomely.

For many decades, John Kinzie, the influential trader of the early 1800s, was lauded as the so-called "Father of Chicago." Although he offered many great services, including saving some of the troops from Fort Dearborn from being killed, he was also selfish and troublesome and his bickering with Captain John Whistler eventually led to the officer being removed from Fort Dearborn. Although tradition calls Kinzie the successor to Point du Sable's trading post, he actually took it over from a man named Jean Lalime --- Chicago's first murder victim. The killer? The "Father of Chicago" himself!

Jean Baptiste du Sable built a cabin on the north bank of the Chicago River in 1779. His wife was an Indian woman named Catherine, who he married in Cahokia in 1788. They had two children together, a boy and a girl. In 1795, the land around the Chicago River was acquired from the Native Americans by treaty and, in 1800 the first commercial transaction took place on the banks of the Chicago. For unknown reasons (some claim that he failed in a bid to become the head of the Potawatomi Indians), du Sable sold his trading post to Jean Lalime, a trader who

The site of Chicago with the Cabin of Jean Baptiste Point du Sable

had been active on the St. Joseph River.

Du Sable moved on to Peoria and then St. Charles, Missouri, where he died and was buried, but two men associated with the sale of the trading post became an integral part of Chicago's early history. Those men are Jean Lalime and the man who witnessed the sale, John Kinzie.

Kinzie became the first "boss" of Chicago, the self-appointed civilian leader of the settlement. He was known for his sharp dealings with the local Indians over trade goods and furs. He also established close ties with the Potawatomi Indians and even sold them liquor, which created tension among the other settlers.

Kinzie was born in Quebec in 1763, the son of a surgeon in the British army named Mackenzie. He allegedly worked as a silversmith before establishing himself as a fur trader in Detroit, in Ohio, and later, along the Chicago River. Kinzie's relationship with the local Native American populace was so close that his first wife was a white woman who had been taken captive by them. Margaret Mackenzie had been captured by Indians in Virginia, along with her sister Elizabeth when she was just 10 years old. She was taken to Detroit, where she met and married the Indian trader. Years later, Margaret and Elizabeth's father found them and persuaded them to return with him to Virginia. Both women left their husbands, took their children, and later remarried in Virginia. Kinzie had three children with Margaret and two of them eventually joined their father in Chicago.

Kinzie later married Eleanor Little, the widow of Daniel McKillip, who supported the British during the American Revolution and who was killed at the Battle of Fallen Timbers. Eleanor's father was also a British loyalist and narrowly escaped being hanged in Pittsburgh in 1783. Kinzie had four children with Eleanor and in 1804; they arrived in Chicago, where Kinzie took over the trading post that had belonged to Jean Lalime.

Jean Lalime was Chicago's original "man of mystery." As the second owner of the trading post that was started by du Sable, he played an important part in the development of the city, but he has been all but ignored by historians. Oddly, when John Kinzie took over the trading post a few years later, there is nothing to show that Lalime was paid anything for it. Did he purchase the post from du Sable as a front man for Kinzie? Some believe so, for there is evidence that the two men knew one another before Kinzie came to Chicago, dating back to a contract that Lalime witnessed for Kinzie and his half-brother, Thomas Forsyth.

Regardless, Lalime took up residence in the du Sable cabin and in 1803 Dr. William C. Smith, the first surgeon at Fort Dearborn, called him "a very decent man and a good companion." The following year, Kinzie moved to Chicago and took over the trading post. Lalime moved into a nearby cabin. There is no record to say what happened between the two men or what became of the goods that Lalime purchased from du Sable. Lalime is never mentioned again as the owner of the post. He became an Indian interpreter for Fort Dearborn, which suggests that he earned little income, but he was still a respected man, for Charles Jouett, the government Indian agent, named his son after him.

Kinzie's business prospered, but it was not without problems. A conflict that he had with Captain Whistler's son, John Whistler, Jr., deteriorated so badly that it caused a major rift within the community. Whistler had demanded that Kinzie stop giving liquor to the Indians, but Kinzie refused. The disagreement became so heated that word of it reached officials in Detroit. Whistler, along with all of the other officers at the fort, were recalled and assigned to various posts across the frontier.

In 1810, Captain Nathan Heald replaced Captain Whistler at Fort Dearborn. Heald brought with him Lieutenant Linus T. Helm, an officer, like Heald, who was experienced in the ways of the frontier. Not long after arriving, Helm met and married the stepdaughter of John Kinzie. In addition to her and Captain Heald's wife, there were a number of women at the fort, all wives of the men stationed there. More families arrived and within two years there were 12 women and 20 children at Fort Dearborn.

CHICAGO'S FIRST MURDER VICTIM

As time passed, it became evident that the split that occurred between John Kinzie and Jean Lalime was not a friendly matter. The two men became bitter enemies and were in constant conflict with one another. Lalime had likely sided with the Captain Whistler and the other officers at the fort during the disagreements with Kinzie, further complicating matters with the civilian populace. Then, finally, in April 1812, the animosity between Kinzie and Lalime boiled over into violence.

One afternoon, Lieutenant Helm warned Kinzie that Lalime was looking for him. A few moments later, Lalime confronted him outside of the fort and the two men exchanged heated words. A brief struggle ensued, leading to Kinzie being shot in the shoulder and to Lalime being stabbed to death. Kinzie fled to Milwaukee and remained in hiding there until word came that the murder had been ruled as "justifiable homicide." Kinzie soon returned to Chicago, only to find that some of the officers at the fort who had been friends of Lalime had buried the dead man in Kinzie's own yard. Rather than be angry, though, Kinzie erected a fence around the gravesite and tended it until his own death. After he died, Lalime's bones were forgotten until they were accidentally disturbed during a construction project many years later at the southwest corner of Cass and Illinois streets.

The bones were later "presented" to the Chicago Historical Society by the author Joseph Kirkland. They were placed in a glass case and put on display until the historical society building was destroyed by the Great Fire of 1871. After that, the remains vanished into history, along with just about everything we know about Jean Lalime, Chicago's first "mystery man" and first murder victim.

THE FORT DEARBORN MASSACRE

When the War of 1812 unleashed the fury of the Native Americans on the Western frontier, the city of Chicago almost ceased to exist before it got a chance to get started. On August 15, 1812, the garrison at Fort Dearborn evacuated its post and, with women in children in tow, attempted to march to safety. But it was overwhelmed and wiped out, in a wave of bloodshed and fire, after traveling less than a mile. The story of the massacre will be repeated for as long as Chicago continues to stand and marks the deadliest event in the history of the city.

At the start of the War of 1812, tensions in the wilderness began to rise. British troops came to the American frontier, spreading liquor and discontent among the Indian tribes, especially the Potawatomi, the Wyandot and the Winnebago, near Fort Dearborn. In April, an Indian raid occurred on the Lee farm, near the bend in the river (where present-day Racine Avenue meets the river) and two men were killed. After that, the fort became a refuge for many of the settlers and a growing cause of unrest for the local Indians. When war was declared that summer, and the British captured the American garrison at Mackinac, it was decided that Fort Dearborn could not be held and that the fort should be evacuated.

Monument to the slain settlers of Fort Dearborn

General William Hull, the American commander in the Northwest, issued orders to Captain Nathan Heald through Indian agent officers. He was told that the fort was to be abandoned; arms and ammunition destroyed and all goods were to be distributed to friendly Indians. Hull also sent a message to Fort Wayne, which sent Captain William Wells and a contingent of allied Miami Indians toward Fort Dearborn to assist with the evacuation.

There is no dispute about whether or not General Hull gave the order, nor that Captain Heald received it, but some have wondered if perhaps his instruction, or his handwriting, was not clear because Heald waited eight days before acting on it. During that time, Heald argued with his officers, with John Kinzie, who opposed the evacuation, and with local Indians, one of whom fired off a rifle in the commanding officer's quarters.

The delay managed to give the hostile Indians time to gather outside the fort. They assembled there in an almost siege-like state and Heald realized that he was going to have to bargain with them if the occupants of Fort Dearborn were going to safely reach Fort Wayne. On August 13, all of the blankets, trading items and calico cloth were given out and Heald held several councils with Indian leaders, which his junior officers refused to attend.

Eventually, an agreement was reached that had the Indians

providing safe conduct for the soldiers and settlers to Fort Wayne in Indiana. Part of the agreement was that Heald would leave the arms and ammunition in the fort for the Indians, but his officers disagreed. Alarmed, they questioned the wisdom of handing out guns and ammunition that could easily be turned against them. Heald reluctantly went along with them and the extra weapons and ammunition were broken apart and dumped into an abandoned well. Only 25 rounds of ammunition were saved for each man. As an added bit of insurance, all of the liquor barrels were smashed and the contents were poured into the river during the night.

On August 14, Captain William Wells and his Miami allies arrived at the fort. Wells was a frontier legend among early soldiers and settlers in the Illinois territory. He was also the uncle of Captain Heald's wife, Rebekah, and after receiving the request for assistance from General Hull, he headed straight to Fort Dearborn to aid in the evacuation. But even the arrival of the frontiersman and his loyal Miami warriors would not save the lives of those trapped inside Fort Dearborn.

Throughout the night of August 14, wagons were loaded for travel and the reserve ammunition was distributed. Early the next morning, the procession of soldiers, civilians, women, and children left the fort. The infantry soldiers led the way, followed by a caravan of wagons and mounted men. A portion of the Miami who had accompanied Wells guarded the rear of the column. It was reported that musicians played the "dead march," a slow, solemn funeral march that would be a foreboding of the disaster that followed.

The column of soldiers and settlers was escorted by nearly 500 Potawatomi Indians. As they marched southward and into a low range of sand hills that separated the beaches of Lake Michigan from the prairie, the Potawatomi moved silently to the right, placing an elevation of sand between them and the white men. The act was carried out with such subtlety that no one noticed it as the column trudged along the shoreline.

The column traveled to an area where 16th Street and Indiana Avenue are now located. There was a sudden milling about of the scouts at the front of the line and suddenly a shout came back from Captain Wells that the Indians were attacking. A line of Potawatomi appeared over the edge of the ridge and fired down at the column. Totally surprised, the officers nevertheless managed to rally the men into a battle line, but it was of little use. Soldiers fell immediately and the line collapsed. The Indians overwhelmed them with sheer numbers, flanking the line and snatching the wagons and horses.

What followed was butchery. Officers were slain with tomahawks and the fort's surgeon was cut down by gunfire and then literally chopped into pieces. Rebekah Heald was wounded by gunfire but was spared when she was captured by a sympathetic Indian chief. The wife of one soldier fought so bravely and savagely that she was hacked into pieces before she fell. In the end, reduced to less than half their original number, the garrison surrendered under the promise of safe conduct. In all, 148 members of the column were killed; 86 adults and 12 children were slaughtered in the initial attack. The children had been loaded onto a single wagon for safety and were killed in one frenzied attack.

Captain Wells managed to kill eight Indians with his bare hands before he was felled and pinned down by his horse. Warriors pounced on him and killed him, then cut out his heart and ate it, hoping to ingest some of his ferocious bravery.

In the battle, Captain Heald was wounded twice, while his wife was wounded seven times. They were later released and a St. Joseph Indian named Chaudonaire took them to Mackinac, where they were turned over to the British commander there. He sent them to Detroit where they were exchanged with the American authorities.

The surrender that was arranged by Captain Heald did not apply to the wounded and it is said that the Indians tortured them throughout the night and then left their bodies on the sand next to those who had already fallen. Many of the other survivors suffered terribly. One man was tomahawked when he could not keep pace with the rest of the group being marched away from the massacre site. A baby who cried too

Decades later, some of the descendants of the Potawatomi warriors who took place in the massacre were put on "display" as part of the midway at the 1893 Columbian Exposition.

By that time, Prairie Avenue, between 16th and 18th streets, was known as the home of the richest people in town. Those few mansions that still stand remain pictures of elegance, especially since the South Loop began to turn itself around in recent years.

Years ago, outside the now-demolished Pullman mansion (by many accounts the fanciest of the lot) stood the Massacre Tree, a tree that still contained bullet holes from the Fort Dearborn Massacre.

The tree stood until August of 1894, when it fell in a storm. Crowds gathered to dig up chunks of the roots as keepsakes.

GHOST ALERT!

The horrific Fort Dearborn Massacre is believed to have spawned its share of ghostly tales. The actual site of the massacre was quiet for many years, long after Chicago grew into a sizable city. However, construction in the early 1980s unearthed a number of human bones around 16th Street and Indiana Avenue.

First thought to be victims of a cholera epidemic in the 1840s, the remains were later dated more closely to the early 1800s. Thanks to their location, they were believed to be the bones of massacre victims.

The remains were reburied elsewhere but within a few weeks, people began to report the semi-transparent figures of people wearing pioneer clothing and outdated military uniforms wandering around an empty lot that was just north of 16th Street.

The apparitions reportedly ran about in terror, silently screaming. The most frequent witnesses to these nocturnal wanderings were bus drivers who returned their vehicles to a garage that was located nearby, prompting rumors and stories to spread throughout the city. In recent times, the area has been largely filled with new homes and condominiums and the once- empty lot where the remains were discovered is no longer vacant. But this does not seem to keep the victims of the massacre in their graves. Current paranormal reports from the immediate area often tell of specters dressed in period clothing, suggesting that the unlucky settlers of early Chicago do not rest in peace.

much during the march was tied to a tree and left to starve. Mrs. Isabella Cooper was actually scalped before being rescued by an Indian woman. She had a small bald spot on her head for the rest of her life. Another man froze to death that winter, while Mrs. John Simmons and her daughter were forced to run a gauntlet, which both survived. In fact, the girl turned out to be the last survivor of the massacre, dying in 1900.

John Kinzie and his family were spared in the slaughter. He and his family were supposed to travel by boat to a trading post on the St. Joseph River, but, because of the attack, they never departed. Appealing to the Potawatomi chiefs, they were taken away from the massacre site and returned to the Kinzie cabin. There they were joined by Mrs. Helm, the wife of Lieutenant Helm, and Mrs. Kinzie's daughter from her previous marriage. She had been shot and Kinzie removed the bullet with a penknife. After presenting gifts to the Indians, the Kinzies later escaped to the trading post.

The war ruined Kinzie. He was now deeply in debt and had lost a fortune during the attack on Fort Dearborn. Though in no danger from the Indians, he was captured by the British and accused of high treason since he was a British subject. He was placed in irons and held on a prison ship off Quebec for seven weeks. He was freed in 1814 and re-joined in family. Two years later, he returned to Chicago, but found that much had changed. He failed in re-starting his business, thanks to a bad loan, and soon was working for his largest competitor, the American Fur Company. In time, the fur trade ended and Kinzie worked as a trader and Indian interpreter until his death in 1828. Thirty years later, his daughter-in-law would write a book that named Kinzie as the founding settler of Chicago. The book would overlook Kinzie's questionable business practices and the murder of Jean Lalime and would be accepted as fact for many years. Later, it would be seen as evidence of Juliette Kinzie's affinity for social climbing and her need to be part of a Chicago dynasty. At that point, her historical "facts" were called into question.

After the carnage, the victorious Indians burned Fort Dearborn to the ground and the bodies of the massacre victims were left where they had fallen, scattered to decay on the sand dunes of Lake Michigan. When replacement troops arrived at the site a year later, they were greeted with not only the burned-out shell of the fort, but also the grinning skeletons of their predecessors. The bodies were given proper burial and the fort was rebuilt in 1816, only to be abandoned again in 1836, when the city was able to fend for itself.

CHICAGO: "MUDHOLE OF THE PRAIRIE"

After the Fort Dearborn Massacre and the end of the war, many things changed in Chicago, but if there is one thing to which the city owes its very existence, it is the Illinois & Michigan Canal.

Commercial demands for a waterway to connect the eastern states, the Great Lakes and the Mississippi River began before Chicago was ever dreamed into existence. Only the war slowed down the demand and in 1814, a campaign for the construction of the canal began. President James Madison asked Congress to authorize the building of the canal but his requests were ignored. In spite of this, the route was investigated by army engineers and in January 1819, John C. Calhoun, then secretary of war, submitted a report to Congress urging that the canal be built. Once again, Congress ignored the recommendations but the canal plan was kept alive by supporters for the next 13 years.

Chicago in those days was merely a collection of wooden cabins, but in 1827 Congress granted land to the new state of Illinois for the canal and began financing it. In the summer of 1830, building lots in Chicago were offered at auction to the public. Chicago had already existed for some years along the sheltering walls of the original Fort Dearborn and the replacements that followed it. The small collection of buildings that made up the settlement grew larger as time passed, but it was still nothing to look at. A visitor in 1823 noted, "The village presents no cheering prospect... it consists of a few huts, inhabited by a miserable race of men, scarcely equal to the Indians from whom they are descended. Their log or bark houses are low, filthy and disgusting, displaying not the least trace of comfort."

Chicago grew slowly at first but when the canal project finally began to get underway, the normal population of 100 or so souls swelled to more than five times that number. Then, in 1832, came the Blackhawk War and the arrival of hundreds of soldiers. There was no room, and little food, for the residents and soldiers, but the people managed to make do until the arrival of General Winfield Scott in July.

Scott came west to Chicago and brought several hundred soldiers along with him. He also brought a cholera epidemic, causing the Indian peril to be forgotten. Townspeople and newly arrived settlers alike took flight and almost overnight, Chicago was emptied of its civilian population. Only the military men remained behind, compelled by orders and a sense of duty, and they spent weeks fighting the epidemic and digging hasty graves for those who died. By autumn, the war had ended and the soldiers and the epidemic had departed. The townspeople returned to their abandoned homes and life in Chicago resumed.

For Chicago, the Blackhawk War was important for two reasons. First, it brought about the removal of the Native Americans to lands farther west. Secondly, it caused hundreds of men to take a forced excursion through the wilderness of northern Illinois and southern Wisconsin. They returned to their homes with marvelous tales of the area's beauty and of the forests, mill sites and farmland that waited for the coming of settlers. In scores of eastern communities, these reports were heard with great interest and soon, homesteaders began traveling to Illinois --- and to Chicago.

The first wave of the tide of immigration reached Chicago in the spring of 1833. Most of the settlers passed through on their way to points farther west but some, attracted by the city's potential, ended their journey there. The city was still a village of log huts in 1833, with only one frame building, the warehouse of George W. Dole, which had been erected the summer before. The summer was a time of great activity and dozens of frame homes and structures were built. They were of flimsy and haphazard construction, to be sure, but their presence provided convincing evidence that civilization was coming to the shores of Lake Michigan.

As Chicago grew, it earned at least two of its many nicknames. The first, "Slab Town," came from the method used to nail weatherboards to standing posts to create structures. The second, less affectionate nickname was "The Mud Hole of the Prairie." This came from the fact that there were few sidewalks and no paving of any kind in the city at that time. Heavy traffic and frequent rains transformed the roads and footpaths into murky quagmires that were both impassable and dangerous. One frequently circulated story of those days told of a resident who spotted a man's head and shoulders sticking out of the mud. He asked the man if he could be of assistance but the man replied, "No thanks. I have a horse under me."

Chicago's street problems continued for many years. In 1849, planks were laid on several of the downtown streets and an experiment was conducted that graded Lake Street down to the level of the lake and then covered it with wooden planks. It was thought that the sewage would settle into the gutters that had been created and be carried off, but the opposite actually occurred. Soon, the stench in the streets made travel unbearable. Engineers advised the city council that the only way that Chicago could be drained was to raise the

The task of raising the Briggs House, a hotel at Randolph and Wells Streets, out of the mud in 1857 involved the coordinated efforts of hundreds of workers. During the raising, the hotel remained open for business.
(Chicago Historical Society)

Work on the Illinois & Michigan Canal Begin (Illinois State Historical Library)

grade of the streets by 12 feet. This monumental task, which consisted of filling 1,200 acres and lifting almost every building in the city was started in 1855 and completed in the middle 1860s. While the work was in progress, pedestrian travel in the city was strange, and often dangerous, with sidewalks running at erratic levels and staircases that had to be used to travel just one block.

The canal project finally got underway in 1833 with the construction of a harbor at Chicago, but this would not be the most significant event to occur. That historic moment was the incorporation of Chicago as a city in August of that year. There is no record as to how many people actually lived in Chicago at the time but it is thought that this might have been the first incident of voter fraud in her history. The incorporation began a tradition that has stained Chicago's reputation ever since.

A preliminary vote was held on August 5, but only 13 actual voters turned out. Only one of them voted against incorporating but since he lived up the South Branch, outside of the proposed city limits, his vote didn't count anyway. The voters were invited to return to the polling place, known as Jolly Mark's Tavern, on August 10 and this time, 28 people showed up and 13 of them became candidates for office. The rule of thumb in those days was that each voter represented five, non-voting people, meaning that Chicago had about 140 residents at most. Unfortunately, 150 people were legally required to reside in a city before it could become incorporated. In spite of this, the vote somehow went through and Chicago became an official city. It's no wonder that "vote early and vote often" became a slogan used to ridicule Chicago's voting habits in years to come.

Regardless of these great strides, the city was still seen by most as an "Indian town." Fur pelts, knives, guns, blankets and whiskey were still being sold and traded on the streets and Native Americans were both the consumers and suppliers of these frontier goods. The Potawatomi were so important to the early years of the city that they contributed $200 of the $486 needed to construct the first bridge over the Chicago River. Even so, they were becoming an embarrassment to the leaders of the new city and steps were taken to try and bring an end to this era in Chicago history.

That period came to an end by late summer of 1833. In the waning days of July, nearly 8,000 Chippewa, Ottawa and Potawatomi Indians assembled on the outskirts of the village and on September 28, their leaders signed a treaty that relinquished their claim on any lands east of the Mississippi River. In return, the government paid them about $1 million in cash and supplies (spread out over a 25-year period) and transported them west to new lands that were roughly the size of present-day Kansas. A down payment of about $150,000 in cash and goods was made on that night but according to reports; no less than $20,000 of it was stolen, after the Indians had been plied with whiskey.

By August of 1835, the Native Americans had been completely removed from Chicago and the rest of Illinois. With the Indian presence gone, hordes of new immigrants began swarming in from the east to claim the territory that had now been opened for occupation. Chicago was now the gateway to the "promised land" and the city began to overflow with land-hungry settlers. With all of these new arrivals and eager workers came the men who had been so desperately needed to begin work on the Illinois & Michigan Canal.

BUILDING THE ILLINOIS & MICHIGAN CANAL

On July 4, 1836, the small city of Chicago, which now boasted a population of about 4,000, celebrated Independence Day. Amid the celebratory shouting, booms of cannons and wildly fired pistols, a group of townspeople crowded aboard two small schooners and a steamboat and traveled up the Chicago River to the spot where the South Fork joined the South Branch to see the first spade of earth turned for the new Illinois & Michigan Canal. The passengers aboard the boats were joined by a crowd that had come from miles around. They were merchants who hoped to sell more flour, tools and lumber; boatmen who hired out heavy draft horses to pull barges and land lawyers who were piling up more than $500 a day in fees. They firmly believed that the canal would be the road to wealth and prosperity for Chicago and eventually, they were right.

The southwest bank of this confluence was the place where the waterway was to start and it was called Canalport. This area had a long history, even in those days, and would eventually become the Bridgeport neighborhood. On that day in 1836, this piece of land became the focus of national attention and remained in the spotlight for many years afterward.

From where the crowd was standing at Canalport, they could look to the west and see the head of navigation of the Chicago, the beginning of the long-used portage and the eastern end of Mud Lake, which the canal would displace as a route of water travel. The first shovel was plunged into the earth and the crowd erupted with delight. It was a day of great celebration and years later, participants would recall how, as they refreshed themselves at a nearby spring, revelers poured whiskey and lemons into the water.

Work soon began on the canal, although labor was scarce in northern Illinois at the time and consequently, advertisements touting high wages were placed in newspapers and on handbills distributed in eastern cities and overseas, especially in Ireland where most spoke English and lived in poverty. In late 1836, about 350 laborers had been hired to build shanties to house the work crews. By the end of 1838, over 2,000 men were shoveling dirt on the canal line.

Laborers on the Illinois & Michigan Canal included white Americans, Native Americans, black slaves, Germans, but mainly Irish immigrants. Most of the Irish were Catholic, unskilled, unmarried and desperately poor. They had come to Chicago with the dream of high wages from working on the canal but found brutal, and often deadly, working conditions. During the years of construction, there was no record kept of just how many workers died but estimates have ranged into the hundreds, or perhaps even the thousands. Life was harsh and diseases ran rampant. The workers lived in rough shanties that had been hastily thrown up along the route of the canal. They were often infested with insects and when it rained, the shanties were usually flooded. The food the men were provided with was barely edible and usually spoiled, since the construction sites were often some distance from proper settlements.

The average worker earned between $16 and $20 each month, with the food and shelter supplied by his employer often deducted from that small amount. Needless to say, the horrible conditions and low wages festered with the men and created a volatile situation. In the winter of 1838, it boiled over when workers were paid with bank notes that were worth less than their face value. Riots followed, shutting down the canal project.

And this would not be the only time the work was shut down. In 1837, a national bank panic, and the depression that followed, wreaked havoc with the financial state of Chicago. By the spring of that year, the economy of the entire region was in shambles. The state of Illinois was bankrupt and only Chicago's mayor, William Ogden, kept the city from the same fate. Ogden was on the verge of personal financial disaster himself but appealing to civic pride, he urged Chicago not to place a moratorium on city debts. Instead, he convinced the city council to issue $5,000 in scrip, which was receivable for taxes and carrying an interest rate of one cent per month. The plan was backed by merchants and bankers and using this paper money, along with certificates issued by banks and trade tickets given out by stores, Chicago was able to transact what little business it had without destroying the city's credit.

Over the course of the next several years, Chicago remained broken and stagnant. Business and industry refused to grow and while settlers still passed through the city, there was nothing in Chicago to keep them. The population failed to increase until the 1840s, when Chicago began to stir once more. Real estate prices slowly rose and new stores and factories started up.

It took 12 years to complete the Illinois & Michigan Canal and when it opened in 1848, Chicago had a population of nearly 20,000 people, making it a city to be reckoned with.

The fortunes of the Illinois & Michigan Canal rose and fell. Before the coming of the railroads, it was on its way to prosperity but by the late 1860s, it was

Illinois & Michigan Canal in Bridgeport

fighting a losing battle. Even so, tolls and land sales made it possible for the canal to pay off its debts as early as 1871. It was one of the only canals constructed in the country that was able to do so. By the 1870s, steamboats had replaced horses and mules as a method of moving barges along the canal but navigation became increasingly more difficult as the state stopped spending money to maintain the waterway. By the late 1890s, commercial traffic on the canal had greatly decreased and by 1914, it had largely ceased altogether.

The achievement that so many men had hoped and slaved for --- to make possible the passage of boats from the Great Lakes to the Gulf of Mexico --- seemed successful when a boat loaded with sugar from New Orleans reached Chicago in 1848. But the canal's depth of only six feet turned out to be inadequate for all but the most shallow of barges. Barge captains and shippers complained that the canal was not big enough to carry goods at a profit and they demanded more depth and more water. It was impossible to pump more water; it would have to reach the canal by flow from the Chicago River. In February 1865, the state legislature authorized the Board of Public Works of Chicago to lower the bed of the canal at Summit and dredge the river to reverse the current and force the sewage down the Illinois.

Boats on the Chicago River

The operation was completed in July 1871, when the river's current was reversed and its mouth became the source. The main reason for providing this new flow of water into the canal was not to help traffic, but to expedite the flow of Chicago's sewage. For this reason, the interests of Chicago overshadowed the interests of those who wanted to continue the use of the canal as a commercial artery. Within 10 years, the canal was judged a menace to the general health and completely inadequate for the huge task that was required of it. Soon, the railroads that had seemed so unnecessary decades before were now seen as the new lifeline for Chicago.

The canal continued to fade into oblivion but the greatest decline came just before 1900. A few years later, interest in the canal shifted from commercial to recreational use. Canal excursion boats began serving a number of amusement parks, like Rock Run outside of Joliet, but this period also passed. In 1935, the Civilian Corps of Engineers in conjunction with the National Park Service restored some of the locks and started other historic preservation projects. Although these plans faltered during World War II, efforts to reuse the old canal right-of-way for this purpose were later revived, culminating in 1984 with the creation of the Illinois & Michigan Canal National Heritage Corridor. The canal trails, parks and recreation areas provide a lasting legacy to the history that once was, offering memories of the canal that left an indelible mark on the landscape of Chicago.

CHICAGO GOES TO WAR

In October 1848, Chicago saw the arrival of the railroads. On October 25, the first train locomotive, with a tender and two cars, began its first run along a five-mile stretch of the Galena & Chicago Union Railroad tracks and by 1855, Chicago was the terminus of 10 railroad trunk lines and 11 branch lines. The city had also become the country's greatest meat packing center and one of the world's greatest grain ports, shipping millions of bushels each year to New York and points beyond. The population had now grown to over 80,000 with hundreds of bustling factories, hundreds of new buildings being erected, gas lights and a land boom that was as spectacular as the one in the 1830s. The city was no longer sneered at for being the "Mud Hole of the Prairie." As historian Lloyd Lewis wrote, "Chicago had become Chicago."

In 1860, Chicago was a city firmly entrenched in the ideals of the northern states. For all of its rowdy nightlife, gambling and crime, it was loyal to the Union and in the South was sneered at as "Abolitionist Chicago." Among its other drawbacks, southerners believed, was that a number of lines of the Underground Railroad, which moved many runaway slaves into Canada, terminated in Chicago. By the beginning of the 1860s, there were at least 1,500 free blacks in the city and at least 20 newly escaped slaves arrived each day to be aided by Chicago abolitionists, who put them across the border.

Chicago responded immediately when war broke out between the north and the south in April 1861. War fever ran high in the city and businessmen quickly saw profits from the spending of soldiers' pay, as did the criminal element, which operated the brothels, gambling parlors and saloons. Men and boys from all over the Chicago region quickly came to the defense of the Union. In the first 10 weeks after the start of the war, 38 companies were formed and 35,000 men enlisted. All sorts of uniforms were designed and men from every class and culture joined up to fight the Confederacy. The local Jewish community raised their own company, as did the Germans, and prepared to fight side-by-side with farmers and city dwellers.

In 1860, Abraham Lincoln had lost most of the Irish vote in the city to Stephen Douglas, as the little senator had spoken out against bigots who wanted to "protect their jobs" from immigrants. The Irish were discriminated against as a lower class of citizens. "Hit him again, he's Irish" was a popular Chicago saying and signs reading "No Irish Need Apply" were often encountered by those seeking work. But when President Lincoln's call came to preserve the Union, an Irish Brigade was quickly formed in

A Chicago Sanitary Commission Fair during the Civil War. The Sanitary Fairs were organized to provide relief for Union soldiers. President Abraham Lincoln donated his draft of the Emancipation Proclamation to the 1863 Sanitary Fair in Chicago, where it sold for $3,000.

Chicago. Congressman John A. Logan, who ancestors hailed from Ireland, was made the general.

By the time the fighting actually began, the state of Illinois had over 73,000 men in service and by the time it all ended, at least 231,000 had answered the call to arms. Few men were ever drafted in Chicago, although many of the wealthier citizens hired substitutes. Chicago had a population of 100,000 at the start of the war and yet sent 15,000 men into battle. By war's end, every third man in the city had enlisted in the military.

The Civil War was a boom time for Chicago, gaining nearly 70,000 residents during the four years of conflict. The city saw more than its share of excitement during the war with the drinking, rioting, burning of saloons, shooting of gamblers and wrecking of whorehouses. But even these activities hardly compared with the wild speculation in land, the shipments of prairie grain and the deals negotiated for southern cotton that had been smuggled over enemy lines. The tavern owners, criminals and shysters all speculated and made enormous amounts of money. Even the bakers, meat packers and solid citizens made money as soldiers died on the distant battlefields. Men who had come to Chicago with nothing were soon driving splendid carriages and living in new homes. Jobs were plentiful and Canadians swarmed across the border to find higher wartime pay. By the end of the war, the city's population had increased by huge percentages, but real estate values had risen even more. By 1863, Chicago had grown to the point that another 24 square miles were added to the city limits. Over 6,000 new buildings were constructed during the war and the overworked railroads hauled hogs, steers and grain into the city in record numbers of boxcars.

But the railroads brought other things as well, like drifters, vagrants, lawbreakers, hoodlums, whores and no-good types who were looking for a lucky break. These confidence men, counterfeiters, pickpockets and thieves joined the outlaws and killers who already roamed the Chicago streets. These new arrivals were also looking for their share of the pie. As a result, crime took over entire districts of the city, creating a problem that would plague Chicago for many decades to come.

"EIGHTY ACRES OF HELL"

The misery of the Civil War's prison camps came to Chicago in February 1862 when a training camp for federal soldiers was converted into place of brutal misery for Confederate prisoners. Rumors of crowded and unhealthy conditions, along with death and disease, were widely circulated in the southern press during the war. The camp

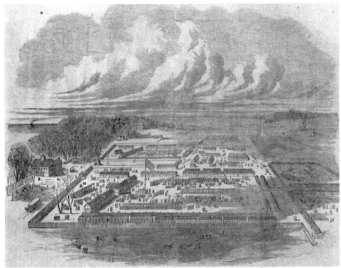

(Above) Camp Douglas on the south side of Chicago
(Below) Rebel prisoners at the infamous camp
Illustrations from Harper's Weekly Magazine

WHERE IT IS NOW?

Today, the Lake Meadows condominiums are located on the site and a short distance away is a monument to Stephen Douglas that is located on the remains of Okenwald. The burial crypt is located between Lake Park Avenue and the Illinois Central Railroad tracks. The tomb was not completed until 1881 because of the failure to produce backers who would give private funds for its completion. The tomb was eventually funded by the state of Illinois and remains today as the last visible reminder of Chicago's "Eighty Acres of Hell."

soon earned what many people would consider a fitting nickname -- "Eighty Acres of Hell."

Camp Douglas was named in honor of Stephen A. Douglas, the famed Illinois legislator and Lincoln rival, who died in Chicago in June 1861. Douglas was well known for his recent Democratic presidential nomination, which he had lost to Lincoln the year before, as well as his previous 25 years in Illinois politics. During the last years of his life, Douglas and his wife had resided at Okenwald, their South Side estate. It was located just east of the present-day intersection of Cottage Grove Avenue and 35th Street. Following Douglas' death, the government took control of his property and constructed a training camp that was named in his honor. The camp enclosed about 60 acres, which were further divided by interior partitions to create compounds of various sizes. Each of the compounds, or squares, was named according to the purpose that it was used for.

Garrison Square, which was about 20 acres in size, was lined on all four sides by the officers' quarters and the enlisted men's barracks and had a flat parade ground in the center. Hospital Square was about 10 acres in size and served as a medical facility. Whiteoak Square, which was another 10 acres, originally served as the post's prison. When orders were received to prepare the camp for Confederate prisoners, Whiteoak was merged with portions of other squares, creating Prison Square, a compound of 20 acres.

In the early months of the war, the outpost trained thousands of Union troops under the command of General Joseph H. Tucker. Soon, however, the camp became a place of misery for the Confederate prisoners. The camp received its first prisoners in February 1862, after the Battle of Fort Donelson, and soon overcrowding, starvation, scurvy and a lack of medical attention made the place a living hell. The death toll for the camp during the last three years of the war has been estimated at as many as 6,129 men, which is slightly less than one-third of the entire prison population at the camp. Most perished from scurvy and smallpox, despite the best intentions of relief workers, who organized a fund to care for the men in 1862.

While many left the camp as corpses, others managed to escape. In November 1863, 75 ragged prisoners managed to tunnel their way beneath the walls. In response, eight companies of the Veteran Reserve Corps and a regiment of Michigan sharpshooters were ordered to the camp for additional protection. There were no more tunnels dug out of the camp.

The arrival of additional guards did not bring an end to the fear of insurrection that concerned Chicago city officials. The city was filled with "copperheads," spies and southern sympathizers, who might attempt to arm the prisoners at the camp. The compound was guarded by only 450 Union enlisted men and officers. This was not a number large enough to make most Chicago citizens feel safe. Somehow, though, the camp managed to make it through the war without serious incident and it was closed down in the summer of 1865. The remaining prisoners were asked to take a loyalty oath to the United States and were then set free. For a short time, the post was used as a rendezvous point for returning federal troops, but by fall, it was deserted. In November, the government sold the property and Camp Douglas ceased to exist. The remaining buildings were demolished a short time later.

THE GREAT CHICAGO FIRE

According to the legend, the Great Chicago Fire was started by a cow belonging to an Irishwoman named Catherine O'Leary. She ran a neighborhood milk business from the barn behind her home. She carelessly left a kerosene lantern in the barn after her evening milking and a cow kicked it over and ignited the hay on the floor. Whether fact or fancy, the legend of Mrs. O'Leary's cow became an often-told tale in Chicago and eventually spread all over the world. However the fire started, on Sunday evening, October 8, 1871, Chicago became a city in flames.

In 1871, Chicago was truly a boomtown. It had become one of the fastest growing cities in America and because of this, construction standards had been "loose," to say the least. Beyond the downtown area, the city was miles and miles of rickety wooden structures. Most of the working-class neighborhoods consisted of wooden cottages and tenements, all of which made for dangerous fuel in the event of a fire.

And fire was always a possibility. "The absence of rain for three weeks," reported the *Chicago Tribune* in the fall of 1871, "has left everything in so flammable a condition that a spark might set a fire that would sweep from end to end of the city."

On the night of October 8, the Patrick O'Leary home, a small frame dwelling at 137 De Koven Street, was a lively place. O'Leary, his wife and five children were already in bed, but the two front rooms of the house were rented to Patrick McLaughlin, a fiddler, who, with his family and friends, was entertaining his wife's cousin, who had recently arrived from Ireland. The rooms were filled with music and drinking

The O'Leary Cottage after the 1871 Fire

and at some point, a few of the young men who were present went out to get another half-gallon of beer --- or so Mrs. McLaughlin would later swear.

Gossips in the neighborhood told a different story. They claimed that at some time in the evening (likely between 8:00 and 9:00 p.m.), some of the McLaughlin clan decided to prepare an oyster stew for their party and a couple of the young men were sent to get some milk from the cow that the O'Learys stabled in a barn at the rear of the house. A broken lamp found among the ashes of the stable a few days later gave rise to the legend that the cow, or a careless milker, had started the fire that destroyed Chicago.

No matter what the cause --- and no one had time to hunt for clues or blame anyone on the night of October 8 - the Great Chicago Fire did break out near the O'Leary barn on De Koven Street on the west side. The home and barn were located in what was then called the "West Division," an area of the city that was west of the south branch of the river. Whether the cow kicked over the lantern or not, conditions were perfect for a fire. The summer had been dry and less than three inches of rain had fallen between

> The tail of the O'Leary cow was served up as oxtail soup in a fancy Chicago restaurant the month after the fire. Mrs. O'Leary herself developed a lifelong bitterness towards reporters.

July and October.

By 10:00 that evening, the fire had spread from the O'Learys' across the West Side in two swaths so wide that all of the engines in town were clanging on the streets and the courthouse bell, in the downtown section, pealed incessantly. Many things conspired to give the flames such headway in such a short amount of time. The watchman on the City Hall tower had misjudged the blaze's location and called for a fire company that was located a mile and a half out of the way, causing a terrible delay. In addition, a strong, dry wind from the southwest was blowing. Furthermore, most of Chicago's fire companies had been exhausted by a fire on the West Side the day before and had celebrated the defeat of the blaze by getting drunk. The firemen had been working almost day and night all summer, battling one conflagration after another, and had needed to relax. The residents of "the city of shams and shingles," had believed that it would never burn. Fires might damage small neighborhoods, but not the great city.

THE O'LEARY COMET?

Could a comet from space have started the Great Chicago Fire? Aside from the O'Learys' unfortunate cow, there have been other causes suggested for the fire, including one that was first brought up in 1882. The Chicago Fire was not the worst conflagration to sweep through the Midwest; it was not even the worst one to start on October 8, 1871!

On that hot and windy autumn night, three other major fires occurred along the shores of Lake Michigan. About 400 miles to the north, a forest fire consumed the town of Peshtigo, Wis., along with a dozen other villages, killing 1,200 to 2,500 people and charring approximately 1.5 million acres. The Peshtigo Fire remains the deadliest in American history, but the remoteness of the region meant it was little noticed at the time. Across the lake to the east, the town of Holland, Mich., and other nearby areas burned to the ground. Some 100 miles to the north of Holland, the lumbering community of Manistee, Mich., also went up in flames. Farther east, along the shore of Lake Huron, another tremendous fire swept through Port Huron, Mich., and much of Michigan's "thumb."

That four large fires occurred all on the same day, all on the shores of Lake Michigan, suggests a common root cause and some believe that cause was Biela's Comet, which broke up and rained down over the Midwest at that time. It has been theorized that the eyewitness accounts of spontaneous ignitions, a lack of smoke from all of the fires, and flames falling from the sky could have been the result of pieces of the comet falling to earth.

Could one of these sparks have landed on the O'Leary

Within half an hour, all of Chicago was on the streets, running for the river. Most could not believe what they were seeing as a wall of flames, miles wide and hundreds of feet high, devoured the West Side and was carried on the wind toward the very heart of the city. By 10:30 p.m., it was officially out of control and soon the mills and factories along the river were on fire. Buildings, even across the river, were hit by fiery missiles from the main blaze, and began to burn. Owners of downtown buildings began throwing water on roofs and walls as the air filled with sparks and cinders that contemporary accounts described as resembling red rain.

Even then, the crowds were sure that the flames would die out when they struck the blackened, four-block area that had been burned during the previous night's fire. But with the force of hundreds of burning homes and buildings behind it, the blaze passed over the burned-out path, attacked the grain elevators along the river, and fell upon the Union Station.

From the West Side, a mob poured into the downtown section, jamming the bridges and flooding the streets. It was believed that the river would stop the fire in its path, but a blazing board that was carried on the wind settled on the roof of a tenement building at Adams and Franklin, one-third of a mile from any burning building. The fire hungrily jumped the river and began pushing toward the center of the city. Fire engines, frantic to save the more valuable property of the business district, pushed back over the bridges from the West Side.

Among the first downtown buildings to be engulfed was the new Parmalee Omnibus & Stage Company at the southeast corner of Jackson and Franklin streets. A flying brand also struck the South Side Gas Works and soon this structure burst into flames, creating a new and larger center for the fire. At this point, even the grease- and oil-covered river caught fire and the surface of the water shimmered with heat and flames.

In moments, the fire also spread to the banks and office buildings along LaSalle Street. Soon, the inferno became impossible to battle with more than a dozen different locations burning at once. The fire swept through Wells, Market and Franklin streets, igniting more than 500 different buildings. One by one, these great structures fell. The Tribune building, long vaunted as "fireproof," was turned into a smoking ruin as was Marshall Field's grand department store, along with hundreds of other businesses.

Many of the great hotels, like the Palmer House and the Sherman, were reduced to blazing ash. The Grand Pacific Hotel, which had just been completed and was not yet open, crashed down in flames. Another new hotel, the Bigelow, with its art gallery, Turkish carpets and carved wood furniture, was also consumed. The Tremont House burned for the fourth time in its history and the manager, John Drake, left the place in a hurry, carrying the contents of the hotel safe in a pillowcase. Unshaken, though, Drake passed by the Avenue Hotel on Congress Street and noting that it was untouched by fire, entered and approached the distracted owner with a startling offer to buy the place, right then and there with $1,000 from the Tremont's safe as a down payment. The deal was made and a hasty bill of sale was written, witnessed by fleeing guests. Drake then departed and went home with his pillowcase full of silver. He knew that he had an even chance of being a hotel owner the next morning. As it turned out, the Avenue Hotel survived, but Drake had to insist on his ownership rights with a pistol.

In the early morning hours of Monday, the fire reached the courthouse, which stood in a block surrounded by LaSalle, Clark, Randolph and Washington streets. A burning timber landed on the building's wooden cupola and the soon turned into a fire that blazed out of control. The building was ordered evacuated. The prisoners, who had begun to scream and shake the bars of their cells as smoke filled the air, were released. Most of them were allowed to simply go free, but the most dangerous of them were shackled and taken away under guard. Just after 2:00 a.m., the bell of the courthouse tolled for the last time before crashing through the remains of the building to the ground beneath it. The roaring sound made by the building's collapse was reportedly heard more than a mile away.

Around this same time, the State Street Bridge, leading to the north side, also caught fire and the inferno began to

Contemporary illustrations, like these from Harper's Weekly, show the madness and panic that was described in first-hand accounts of the Fire

GHOST ALERT:

By 3:00 on the morning of October 9, 1871, the pumps at the waterworks on Pine Street had been destroyed and by Monday evening, the only intact structure for blocks was the gothic stone Water Tower. Somehow, it managed to survive the devastation.

Legend has it that this structure is haunted by the ghost of a man who stayed on the job during the fire, continuing to pump the water as the fire got closer. The story goes that this heroic city worker waited until the last possible minute and then took his own life rather than be engulfed in the flames. His ghost has reportedly been seen through an upper window of the tower, dangling from the end of a rope, and his footsteps are said to have been heard inside as he scrambles away from the approaching flames.

devour the area on the north side of the river. Soon, stables, warehouse and breweries were also burning. The lumber mills and wood storage yards on the riverbanks were eaten by the fire and many people who were dunking themselves in the water had to flee again to keep from being strangled by the black smoke. Some people threw chairs and sofas into the river and sat with just their heads and shoulders visible. Many of them stayed in the river for up to 14 hours.

Then, the fire swept into the luxurious residential district surrounding Cass, Huron, Ontario, Rush and Dearborn streets. Here stood the mansions of some of Chicago's oldest and most prominent families. By daylight, these beautiful homes were nothing but ruins. The servants of the rich desperately buried the contents of the mansions in hidden places on the grounds. Oddly enough, at least a dozen pianos were later unearthed in gardens. Also discovered were family silver collections that, despite being buried, had melted into twisted masses.

Members of the Chicago Club, the expensive enclave of the rich, never dreamed that the fire would dare to affect them. Many of them had breakfast while the city burned and they toasted their defiance of the fire. The building burned, though, almost as the men lifted their glasses, and they ran for their lives, after having stuffed their coats with wine bottles from the best years' vintages and fine Havana cigars. The club's celebrated red satin lobby sofas were carried in grand fashion down to the lake.

The flames were not the only threat that the city's residents of the cit had to worry about. In the early hours of the fire, looting and violence had broken out. Saloonkeepers, hoping that it might prevent their taverns from being destroyed, had foolishly rolled barrels of whiskey out into the streets. Soon, men and women from all classes were staggering in the streets, thoroughly intoxicated. The drunks and the looters did not comprehend the danger they were in and many were trampled in the streets. Plundered goods were also tossed aside and were lost in the fire, abandoned by the looters as the fire drew near.

One observer later stated, "The rogues smashed windows reckless of the severe wounds inflicted on their naked hands and with bloodied fingers rifled impartially till, shelf, and cellar, fighting viciously for the spoils. Women, hollow-eyed and brazen-faced, moved here and there stealing, scolding shrilly, and laughing with one another at some particularly 'splendid' gush of flame or 'beautiful' falling-in of a roof."

Alexander Frear, a New York alderman, who was caught in the fire, remembered seeing Wabash Avenue choked

Chicagoans took refuge in any safe place they could find, both during and after the fire, including among the open graves of the City Cemetery in what is now Lincoln Park.

with crowds and bundles.

"Valuable oil paintings, books, pets, musical instruments, toys, mirrors and bedding were trampled under foot. Goods from stores had been hauled out and had taken fire, and the crowd, breaking into a liquor establishment, was yelling with the fury of demons. A fellow standing on a piano declared that the fire was the friend of the poor man. In this chaos were hundreds of children, wailing and crying for their parents. One little girl in particular I saw, whose golden hair was loose down her back and caught fire. She ran screaming past me and somebody three a glass of liquor upon her, which flared up and covered her with a blue flame," Frear later wrote.

On Lake Street, Frear saw a man loading a wagon with loot that he had stolen from Shay's, a dry-goods store. Someone with a revolver shouted at him not to drive away and the thief replied, "Fire and be damned!" The man put the pistol back into his pocket.

Frear recalled that everyone seemed to be shouting at the top of his lungs. He saw people pushed off bridges and into the river to drown, while boat crews fought to keep crowds from clambering onto their decks.

Frear also wrote that rough-looking men carried women and children to safety and then went back into danger to find more. Police officers saved countless lives as fireman dashed into the flames and carried out unconscious victims. Horses broke out of stables, or fought loose from their handlers, and ran frenziedly through the streets. Rats, smoked out from under houses and wooden sidewalks, died squealing under the feet of the fleeing masses.

During the early morning hours, the flames jumped the river to the north and the panicked residents ran ahead of the fire, edging eastward, toward the lakefront and Lincoln Park. Women's dresses caught on fire. Sick and injured people, carried on mattresses, stretchers, and chairs, were knocked to the ground and trampled. Some of the fugitives, insane with fear, plunged into blazing alleyways and were burned alive. Many of the elderly were crushed under the feet of the frantic crowds and a number of housewives, rushing into their homes for cherished possessions, perished in the inferno. The Chicago Historical Society was destroyed, losing city records of incalculable value and the original draft of the Emancipation Proclamation, which Abraham Lincoln had written during the Civil War.

Lincoln Park became a macabre location during the fire as it served as a gathering place for uprooted families and fleeing fire victims. Graves

Devastation of Chicago after the Great Fire

(Left to Right) Ruins of the Courthouse; Monroe & Dearborn Streets; Remains of Trinity Church

in what had once been the old City Cemetery had been opened so that their occupants could be moved and now the yawning pits and the haphazardly stacked tombstones were being used to shelter huddled masses of adults and children.

On the lakefront, thousands took refuge away from any buildings that might burn but they were still tortured by the heat and the storm of falling embers. Men buried their wives and children in the sand, with a hole for air, and splashed water over them. Many fled to stand chin-deep in the waters of Lake Michigan, breathing through handkerchiefs.

Throughout the day on Monday, the fire kept to its wind-driven task, finishing the business section and the north side. The wind blew so hard that firefighters could get water no more than 10 feet past the nozzles of their hoses. Streams of water could not carry above two stories. Fire engines were destroyed in the flames and companies were separated from their officers. The fire department, like the city of Chicago, was destroyed.

CHICAGO ON FIRE!
10,000 BUILDINGS BURNED.
FIRE STILL RAGING.
MASS MEETING
WILL BE HELD AT THE
CENTRAL RINK
At 3 O'clock To-Day,
TO TAKE ACTION TO AID
Chicago's Suffering People
HELP, HELP, HELP
CITIZENS, TURN OUT!
F. W. PELTON, Mayor.
Monday, October 9th, 1871.

Thankfully, the fire began to die on the morning of October 10, when steady and soaking rains began to fall.

The Great Fire, as it was called from then on, was to be the most disastrous event in America until the San Francisco earthquake and fire of 1906. The people of the city were devastated, as was the city itself. Over 300 people were dead and the fate of many more was never reported or their bodies were never found. Another 100,000 were without homes or shelter. The fire had cut a swath through the city that was four miles long and about two-thirds of a mile wide. Over $200 million in property had been destroyed. Records, deeds, archives, libraries and priceless artwork were lost although a little of it had survived in public and private vaults. In the destruction of the Federal Building, which, among other things, housed the post office, more than $100,000 in currency was burned.

Chicago had become a blasted and charred wasteland.

On Tuesday, sightseers poured into town and among them were hundreds of criminals from neighboring regions, eager for pillage.

General Phillip Sheridan

Local business owners hired Allan Pinkerton to assign his detectives positions around the remains of stores and banks and soon, six companies of Federal troops were deployed under the command of General Phillip Sheridan to assist in maintaining order. Two days later, Chicago's Mayor Roswell Mason placed the city under martial law, entrusting Sheridan and his troops to watch over it.

Sheridan recruited a volunteer home guard of about 1,000 men to patrol unburned areas of the city. He also enforced a curfew, much to the chagrin of Illinois governor John M. Palmer, who felt that martial law was uncalled for and unnecessary. Mayor Mason was heavily influenced by local business leaders, however, and ignored Palmer's order to withdraw the troops.

The state of martial law didn't last long. A few days after it went into effect, a local businessman -one of those responsible for pushing Mason into enacting martial law - was accidentally killed by a member of the volunteer home guard. In spite of this, Sheridan received orders from President Grant that left four companies of men on active duty in the city through the end of the year.

As terrible as the disaster was, Chicago was not dead but merely shaken and stunned. Within days of the fire, rebuilding began on a grand scale. The vigor of the city's rebirth amazed the rest of the nation and within three years, it once again dominated the western United States. It soared from the ashes like the fabled phoenix and became the home of the nation's first skyscraper in 1885. The city then passed the one million mark in population five years later. The Great Chicago Fire marked the beginning of a new metropolis, much greater than it could have ever become if the horrific fire had never happened.

CHICAGO BUSINESS: THE RICH GET RICHER

In the years after the Great Fire, wealth and prosperity returned to Chicago. According to many reformers and activists, that wealth remained in the hands of a privileged few. These included men like Marshall Field, Potter Palmer, George Pullman, Cyrus McCormick and others, most of whom had made fortunes in the city even before the fire and the Civil War.

"GIVE THE LADY WHAT SHE WANTS"

Marshall Field

Marshall Field's is considered a Chicago icon today and is known as the founder of America's greatest mercantile firm, Marshall Field & Company. Renowned in his day as the "merchant prince," Field was then commonly regarded as one of the richest men in the world. After his death in 1906, Field's estate was estimated at over $100 million, according to one authority, much of it consisting of Chicago real estate. While he made a fortune from the city of Chicago, he also gave much of it back, including the lakefront museum that was established and named in his honor. He was also largely responsible for the founding of the Art Institute and laid the groundwork for the University of Chicago. Field was undoubtedly a great philanthropist, but charitable or not, he was not always well liked.

Field came to Chicago in 1856 and went to work as a clerk in a dry goods store with a salary of $400 a year, half of which he saved. A pioneer of new merchandising methods, he went on to coin the ultimate customer service slogan of "Give the Lady What She Wants." He and a partner, Levi Z. Leiter, purchased a store in 1865 that became Marshall Field & Company. Even before becoming the premiere dry goods merchant in the country, Field looked for other ways to make money and discovered real estate investment. He was known for being a serious, mild-looking man and was famous for never praising his employees and paying them low wages --- never a cent more than he had agreed to pay them, no matter how well they performed. At each year's end, he held a dinner in his home for partners and members of upper

Marshall Field & Co. on State Street -- America's Original Department Store

management. Over after-dinner brandy, he would make simple announcements to the assembled group as to which of them would not be celebrating the holidays with the company the following year. If an employee had not measured up, his presence would no longer be required by Marshall Field & Company.

In 1876, Field constructed a luxurious mansion with a prestigious address on Prairie Street. The house cost over $2 million to build and was the first home in Chicago to have electric lights. Field lived here with his wife, the former Nannie Scott of Ironton, Ohio, who became known as the social queen of the city. Here, the Fields reared a son, Marshall Field, Jr. and a daughter, Ethel.

The family entertained both famous and infamous American and European personages and held many notable parties and balls. Perhaps the most noteworthy party was staged in January 1886 in honor of the two Field children. More than 500 guests were present and because Gilbert and Sullivan's operetta Mikado was then all the rage in the fashionable world, the gathering was designated as a "Mikado Ball." Wealthy children and their parents attended the party in colorful, Oriental costumes. Their carriages passed beneath special calcium lights that had been erected for the evening. The ball, said to have cost $75,000, was talked about for years afterward.

Field died at 71 in New York City from pneumonia contracted while playing golf on New Year's Day with his nephew, his secretary, and Abraham Lincoln's eldest son, Robert.

His legacies, from the Field Museum to Chicago University, are still a part of the city today, as is his single-handed renovation of the retail sales industry. Field took an early 1800s consumer landscape that was centered on the idea of caveat emptor, or " let the buyer beware," and transformed it into a shopping experience that was fit for the gilded age. Unconditional refunds, consistent pricing and international imports are among the Field innovations that are considered standard in the retail business today.

CHICAGO'S CASTLE BUILDER

Potter Palmer

Potter Palmer was another of Chicago's industrial pioneers, shaping more of the city that most of us can begin to imagine today. No man worked harder to develop the portion of the city that followed the northbound edge of the lake, although he is best recalled for his wonderful hotel, the Palmer House, which continues to provide luxurious accommodations to this day.

Palmer had been a daring merchant in the 1850s, who had sold out to Marshall Field, and who then shocked Chicago in 1865 by announcing that he was retiring from business on the advice of his doctor. He then left for Europe and New York City and the quiet bachelor learned to enjoy his money before returning to Chicago in 1868. Shortly after he came back, he helped to build a baseball park for the Chicago White Stockings, the city's most successful team, and embarked on a new business plan, one that was so secret that even his closest friends had no idea what he was up to. Palmer's plan was to move the city's main commercial district from Lake Street, which ran east and west, to State Street, which ran north and south and parallel with the lake. Chicago only learned of his plan when he approached the city council with a request to widen State Street, where, he explained, he had quietly bought almost a mile of frontage.

The council told him that the idea of moving the business district was ridiculous. State Street was little more than a muddy alley, narrow and lined with pawnshops, saloons and boarding houses. Merchants on Lake Street also fought the proposed street widening, as did property owners on State Street, who did not want to have to move their buildings. But Palmer was absolutely fixed on the idea and he pushed the bill through the city council without ever resorting to threats or bribery. He was simply a very determined man and he was

The Palmer House Hotel -- One of Chicago's Finest

able to accomplish just about anything that he set his mind to.

But all did not go smoothly. Many of the owners of older buildings along State Street decided to ignore the ordinance and refused to move their buildings. Palmer simply bypassed them, tearing down the old structures that he had purchased along the street and erecting handsome new stores and business buildings. He placed all of them on the new building line so there would be plenty of parking spaces for the carriage trade and for trolley car tracks. Until all of the main streets were widened to a standard width after the Great Fire, State Street, with its irregular building line, was one of the strangest looking streets in the city. Soon, Lake Street merchants began moving into Palmer's new buildings, despite the higher rents, so that their business rivals could not take possession of the "splendid quarters."

In the summer of 1870, Potter Palmer surprised Chicago again by announcing his engagement to beautiful socialite Bertha Honore, the daughter of the late real estate magnate, H.H. Honore of Louisville, Ky. She was 21 years old at the time of their engagement and Palmer was 44. The two of them had met eight years earlier when Bertha was shopping in Palmer's Lake Street store with her mother. Bertha would become known as an outspoken feminist, the grande dame of Chicago society and later, the official hostess of the World's Columbian Exposition. She was likely better known than her husband, who returned to his quiet ways after their marriage. At the time of her engagement, though, Bertha was more than satisfied to have a loving husband and to be the wife of an "innkeeper.".

The "inn" in question was the much-praised Palmer House, which was just nearing completion on State Street. The hotel was designed to be Palmer's wedding present to his wife. Even by Chicago standards, a city that was used to extravagant hotels, it was an impressive place. It was eight stories tall and boasted 225 rooms, making it one of the largest hotels in the country. It was decorated with expensive marble, hand-woven rugs, antiques, and furniture imported from Europe. It would be staffed, Palmer proudly announced, by several hundred uniformed blacks. The hotel was also billed as the only fireproof hotel in America, with alarms in every room, fire hoses on every floor and a large water tank on the roof. Unfortunately, the hotel would prove these claims to be untrue during the inferno of 1871.

In the years after the Great Fire, Chicagoans would date their past with two simple phrases: "before the fire" or "after the fire." The Great Fire would define the city's history as both a major dividing point and a transforming event. A new and modern city was built on the scorched ruins of what was little more than a western boomtown. Many tremendous changes came to Chicago "after the fire" and Potter Palmer was responsible for at least one more of them.

In addition to the new State Street shopping district, Palmer was also the creator of the lavish residential district known as the "Gold Coast." As mentioned earlier, Palmer was a determined man and he dreamed up an idea of turning the low, treacherous dunes of the lakeside into a housing area for the privileged members of Chicago society. The project was helped by the ambitions of the Lincoln Park commissioners, who were in the early stages of developing Lake Shore Drive. Palmer quitclaimed the land where the drive would run and the park commissioners, who controlled the eastern strip of land, quitclaimed a portion of their property to Palmer. The land itself was developed by bringing in soil and fill to level out the area. Much of it came from a great distance so that no marsh soil would be included, which was thought to cause malaria. The property was then parceled out to purchasers, who began constructing new homes. The quiet thoroughfare, shaded by rows of trees, paralleled the lake for almost a half-mile before reaching Lincoln Park. It was an ideal residential street, fronting an inland sea, and was lined by

Potter Palmer's Famous Castle in the city's Gold Coast

solid, handsome dwellings and strong iron fences.

Potter Palmer himself constructed a huge dwelling that captured the imagination of Chicagoans and visitors alike. The Palmer house has long been referred to as a "castle" and it was certainly designed to look the part with imposing heights and battlements that would more befit a medieval fortress than a Chicago residence. The house was designed and built in the early 1880s by prominent architects Henry Ives Cobb and Charles Sumner Frost. The style was "English Gothic" with square windows and the exterior covered with ivy, thus recreating the look of a British manor house.

The house was built at a cost of nearly $1 million and almost instantly became the showplace of the city. During the 1893 World's Columbian Exposition, it was one of the leading sights for tourists, outside of the fairgrounds themselves. It was during this period of time that the stone castle by the lake was at the peak of its glory. Here, Bertha Palmer ruled as the social queen of America's second-largest city and as president of the Board of Lady Managers of the World's Fair, she was the dominant figure of all social events at which American and European celebrities were entertained. Guests included Presidents Grant and McKinley, the Infanta Eulalia of Spain, the Duke and Duchess of Veragua (the duke was a descendant of Columbus), various Russian princes and princesses and many other leaders of the era.

In the years that followed the fair, the house continued to be the social center of Chicago and Mrs. Palmer also maintained homes in both Paris and London. She remained a resident in the house until her death in 1918. Potter Palmer himself died in 1902 and with his passing, a great era in Chicago history came to an end. And whether beloved or hated, it cannot be denied that he left a permanent mark on the city.

CHICAGO'S MOST NOTORIOUS "RAPIST"

Charles Tyson Yerkes

Charles Tyson Yerkes came to Chicago in the 1880s for no other reason than to pillage the growing city. The street transit mogul began his business empire at the age of 8 when he borrowed $18 from his father and made a deal with a local grocer to sell a certain soap to the grocery at nine cents a pound. Yerkes bought the soap at six cents a pound and started his fortune.

Yerkes was born in Philadelphia as the son of a bank president and left home at 15 to work as an office boy in a grain commission house. He started his own stock brokerage at 22, went into banking three years later and by 34, found himself in prison. A panic at the Philadelphia stock exchange -- started by market confusion in the aftermath of the Chicago Fire -- left him overextended and unable to deliver the money that he had received from selling City of Philadelphia securities. He was pardoned after seven months and after speculating successfully during the Panic of 1873, he seized control of Philadelphia's Continental Passenger Railway Company. With his profits, he paid off his criminal shortfall to the city, even though the city council had already forgiven his debt.

Within a few years, Yerkes found himself divorced and he relocated to Fargo, N.D. He remarried but found that small town life did not suit him. In 1881, he and his wife, with just $40,000 of his own capital, moved to Chicago. Thanks to connections that he maintained in Philadelphia, he managed to establish credentials with the local financial community. After some initial ventures into gas and electricity stocks, he took an option on the North Chicago Street Railway. A year later, he also acquired the West Division Railway Company and his object became clear: he planned to gain a monopoly of all Chicago transit.

Yerkes devoted the next 12 years to his plan, starting in 1886. During this time, he irrevocably wrecked the pattern of Chicago mass transit. The service was poor and at rush hours, there were always fewer seats than passengers. Yerkes didn't care and in fact, relished the idea of the overcrowded cars. "The strap hangers pay the dividends," he explained.

With shrewdness, cunning, the force of his personality and of course, the ever-present Chicago methods of bribery and back-door political dealing, Yerkes built a tangled maze of companies that managed to finance his business maneuvering so that he had to invest very little capital of his own. Even so, he was always able to rake in millions. Not only did he control the companies that contracted for his projects (which billed at astronomical rates) but he also took kickbacks from the contractors who were hired.

His clever business dealings not only enriched his pocketbook, but they also brought about a change in Chicago transit from horse-drawn cars to cable cars and by the middle 1890s, he was introducing trolley systems to the city and building an elevated transit system as well. The downtown branch of the system was called "The Loop," after the smaller streetcar route that had been there earlier.

He built a magnificent Chicago mansion for himself and his wife, but they were never admitted to the city's high society, which rankled the second Mrs. Yerkes. Although the couple was unacceptable to Bertha Palmer and the rest of the city's elite, this did not prevent the social register husbands from joining Yerkes in his predatory business forays whenever they smelled a profit.

The other Chicago titans used Yerkes for a time but in 1896, they decided to try

Yerkes' maze of businesses would create the original Chicago elevated train system

and force him into bankruptcy. A number of merchants and bankers, including meatpacker Phillip D. Armour, decided to try and rid the city of Yerkes by calling in his loans, for which he had pledged most of his holdings as collateral. But in the eagerness to destroy the man, they never considered that he could retaliate against their banks and business with the strength of the transit system, virtually bringing Chicago to a screeching halt. Yerkes was given a reprieve on the advice of Marshall Field. "Leave Mr. Yerkes alone," he reportedly told the others, "and he will come to his own end."

Yerkes dealt through any dirty politicians that he could find and bought favors constantly. In fact, his Chicago mansion, his collection of fine jewelry, his racing stable and his art collection (which had been bought in Europe and contained works by the masters) were assessed at a worth of only $7,000 when tax time rolled around. The Chicago Tribune called this the "Chicago system of taxation." It would not be the only time that the newspaper attacked Yerkes and his business operations. Much of this came from not only disapproval of the way that he did business, but personal animosity, as well. Yerkes' methods were not so different from those of other Chicago businessmen, but something about the man (perhaps because his connections were all in the East) was just completely unlikable. For his part, Yerkes returned the editor's dislike. On one occasion, after learning that an article was going to be published about his private life, including innuendoes about his wife, he called on the editor of the paper in question.

"The publication of this article will hurt me," he allegedly said as he stood in the man's office, "and I shall be down and out. There will be nothing for me to do. But I'll also inform you that if you publish it, I, myself, personally, will kill you for sure!" He wished the editor a good morning than then walked out the door. The article was never published.

Thanks to money that was spread throughout the Chicago City Council and the state legislature in Springfield, Yerkes was given 12 transit renewals that would have permitted him use of the streets of Chicago for the next 99 years without any sort of payment! Illinois Governor John Peter Altgeld vetoed these bills, in spite of Yerkes' offer of a half-million dollar bribe to sign them. Altgeld's successor, John R. Tanner, was not so principled and he signed a bill that authorized the city council to extend Yerkes' franchises for another 50 years without payment. But this did not go unnoticed by Yerkes' enemies. Banding together with the usually ineffectual Municipal Voters League, they forced Yerkes to mount an expensive defense of his 50-year bill after the first one was defeated.

Yerkes did everything he could to win the public's trust, including the donation of an electrically lighted fountain in Lincoln Park and the construction of the world's largest refracting telescope (later installed at Yerkes Observatory on Lake Geneva in Wisconsin) but the citizens rallied against him anyway. The Municipal Voter's League posted thousands of placards condemning him throughout the city. The newspapers elaborated on charges that he was using public money for private gain, causing ministers to rail against him from church pulpits and mass meetings to be held, where it was half-seriously proposed that he be hanged. Mayor Carter Harrison, Jr., then in his first of five terms, vowed that he would "eat my fedora hat" before he would allow Yerkes to win. When the second bill (for the additional 50 years) reached the city council, a mob carrying guns and nooses marched on City Hall to monitor the voting. Not surprisingly, the bill was soundly defeated.

The vote in 1898 ended Yerkes' pillaging of Chicago for good. He gave a stirring farewell speech to his transit workers and then left Chicago after disposing of his personal holdings, which were rumored to have put over $20 million in his pockets. He moved to New York and then to London, where he moved socially in the king's circle and headed the syndicate that dug the London Underground transit system.

Yerkes died, at 68, in December 1905 while living sick and alone in New York City hotels. He was estranged from his second wife because of his involvement with a married woman -- and her daughter. His fortune, which had been worth anywhere between $30 million and $70 million, had dwindled to around $2 million at the time of his death, thanks to lawsuits and bad investments. Most of this went to the lawyers when he was gone.

Although seldom remembered in Chicago today, Yerkes lives on in literary history, as he provided the basis for the character of Frank Cowperwood in Theodore Dreiser's two classic novels, *The Titan* and *The Financier*. Yerkes' style lived on in the city for years after his departure as well. His reckless and open manipulation of the system, through bribery and swindles, was a precursor to the gangsters who made Chicago their cashbox in the years that followed him.

FEAR THE "REAPER"

Cyrus Hall McCormick

Cyrus Hall McCormick was born in Virginia in 1809 and came to Chicago in 1845 with only $60 in his pocket. He established a factory to manufacture a mechanical reaper that he devised and within a few years was a millionaire many times over. It would be this same reaper that would change the face of Chicago forever and would also play a major part in the Union victory in the Civil War. The mechanical efficiency of the reaper on the flat farmlands of the Midwest easily accomplished the work of the half million men in uniform who were away from their farms during the harvest season.

McCormick was a stout man of great temper and perhaps an even greater persistence to succeed. He fought his many competitors with constant lawsuits, widespread advertising, and yearly field days when his reapers would be pitted against other models. He offered easy credit, good service and a product that was far superior to anything else on the market. Throughout the 1870s, he sold more than 10,000 reapers and binders a year. The money came pouring into his coffers in such substantial amounts that in 1879 he built a fabulous sandstone mansion on Rush Street that was rivaled in the city by only the castle of Potter Palmer. The house was so massive in size that it contained a 200-seat private theater.

McCormick's claim to being the sole inventor of the reaper was open to question, even by his own family. However, his assembly procedures, his sales methods that put thousands of reapers into fields where wheat would have rotted before, and his constant improvements on the machines did make him a pioneer in the industry. Whatever he may have lacked in actual invention, he more than made up for when it came time to put the machinery to work and to get it into the hands of those who could use it.

Even though he was generous to a number of charities and causes in Chicago, including the Presbyterian Theological Seminary (later named in McCormick's honor), he was mostly known for being tight-fisted with a dollar. Once, when charged what he felt was an unjust $8.70 fee for excessive luggage by the railroad, he sued the company and fought the suit in court after court for 18 years, finally winning it in the Supreme Court. When he took his family to dine at the elegant Palmer House, he insisted on a special rate, which Palmer gave to him because he quickly learned that it was not worth the time to argue the matter. In McCormick's later years, when he was crippled with rheumatism, he became even more difficult and fired household servants on the spot if he felt they were being impertinent. McCormick died in 1884 and had been an invalid for nearly four years before his death.

McCormick's claim to fame was the invention of the first mechanical reaper, the Plano Harvester. Although his claims of being the sole inventor of the device is open for debate, the Reaper made him a millionaire many times over.

His tight handling of a dollar did not endear McCormick to his employees. He worked them hard, including his own brother, and for low wages. Like all of the other Chicago titans during America's so-called "Gilded Age," he was puzzled when the employees were not grateful for what they were given and was enraged when they dared to ask, and organize, for more. All of the major employers, including McCormick, saw constant unrest among their workers over job conditions, wages and shorter workdays. There was no question that conditions in many plants were poor and men worked 10-12 hours, six days a week, for very little pay. Strikes and protests soon became commonplace.

During the tense summer of 1877, when there were riots in the city that were part of a nationwide strike effort by railroad workers protesting wage cuts, Marshall Field volunteered the use of his delivery wagons to transport policemen from one problem area to another. Three men were killed and eight wounded during a demonstration at a Burlington Railroad roundhouse and the next day, 10 more strike sympathizers were killed at the Halsted Street viaduct. Federal troops who came directly from fighting Indians out west were sent in to restore order. The following year, Field, McCormick and others secretly subscribed to a fund that would furnish Gatling guns and uniforms for the Illinois National Guard. This was done, according to McCormick's assistant, to prepare for "what danger if any was to be anticipated from the communistic element in the city."

Strikes and protests continued but the Haymarket Square Riot in 1886 would change the face of the labor movement forever.

THE HAYMARKET SQUARE RIOT

The events that culminated in blood at Haymarket Square had been brewing since the end of the Civil War. The years after the war saw a rise in the power of the labor unions. Many prominent capitalists had preached the moral correctness of the war --- often more interested in the profits that could be made from it than because of any just cause --- but they failed to predict what would happen afterward. Many of the veterans who came home after the war had a different mindset than when they had left. As soldiers, they had worked together amid danger, death and destruction, fighting a war that became about ending slavery. To equate the over-demanding expectations of their employers (for next-to-nothing wages) with slavery was a simple one. Warring with the "slave-drivers" was seen as necessary but the trouble was, there were a lot of "soldiers," but no real army.

Haymarket Square as it looked at the time of the Riot

Without a union, laborers were at a great disadvantage when compared with their employers. Workers were able to come together, strike and raise hell but only for limited periods of time. Unions of the day, many of which were newly organized, were long on principles but short on any real sense of power, save for disruption of work. Once they began working through the political process though, things began to change. They scored their first victory in March 1867 with the passage of a state eight-hour workday statute, but their sense of accomplishment was short-lived. The law was easily circumvented by employers who reduced pay, discharged employees or found loopholes to continue working their men for 10 hours or more a day. Such manipulation of the law angered workers and unrest and violence occurred throughout the city. Many of the workers, and union leaders, were not content to let strikes and walkouts speak for them. Many of them endorsed a more violent form of action. That action reached its peak in Haymarket Square, where rural farmers came to exchange produce for cash, in May 1886.

WHERE IS IT NOW?

Haymarket Square was near the intersection of Randolph and Des Plaines streets, just west of the loop and a short hike from the present site of Oprah Winfrey's Harpo Studios. In 2007, ground was broken for a new condo development overlooking the old square.

An illustration of the bomb exploding in the Square

The Haymarket Square Riot began as a mass meeting of workers to protest police actions against strikers at the McCormick factory. Six workers demonstrating for an eight-hour workday had been killed by factory guards and tensions were running high. The rally at Haymarket Square involved about 2,500 workers who turned out in the rain to listen to speeches by local labor leaders Albert Parsons, Samuel Fielden and August Spies. Despite the fact that all three men were considered "dangerous agitators" and "anarchists" by city business leaders, Mayor Carter Henry Harrison issued a parade permit for the gathering, believing there was no cause for concern.

Moments after the explosion, police officers began firing into the crowd.

However, police officials sent nearly 700 officers to the scene. Police Inspector John Bonfield led his superiors to believe that a citywide riot might take place. Mayor Harrison visited the scene and finding it peaceful, ordered all reserve officers to be sent home. Bonfield refused and two hours later, ordered the men to disperse the crowd.

As the policemen moved into formation, a crudely made pipe bomb was thrown into the midst of a column of 200 officers. The bomb exploded and one officer was killed and six others were mortally wounded. In retaliation, the policemen opened fire on the crowd and began shooting at the fleeing protestors. They continued to fire for more than five minutes.

Mayor Harrison pleaded for calm in the wake of the attack but police officials began a search for not only the man who threw the bomb, but were determined to track down those who had caused it to be thrown in the first place. The Chicago Police began a reign of terror among the city's working class citizens. All rights were suspended and hundreds of suspects were arrested, beaten and interrogated at all hours of the night. False confessions were violently extracted from those who were thought to be "anarchists" or sympathizers of the labor unions. Whoever the bomb thrower actually was, he faded away into history.

Eventually, eight conspirators were brought to trial for the riot and seven of them received the death sentence. The eighth was given 15 years in prison. All of them were tried and sentenced on conspiracy charges to incite violence that led to the deaths of the police officers. On November 11, 1887, August Spies, Albert Parsons, George Engel and Adolph Fischer were hanged at the Criminal Courts Building on Hubbard Street. Another of the conspirators died in an explosion and the death sentences of the others were commuted to prison terms.

It was widely believed that the defendants in the case had the deck stacked against them from the beginning. Rumor had it that the jurors in the trial had been given $100,000 by Chicago business leaders and that prior to the verdict being read, Marshall Field was already lobbying that the men be hanged. He also reportedly went to City Hall and demanded that the mayor repress free speech in the city, in the interest of public safety. The mayor refused, even after Field informed him that he "represented great interests in Chicago."

The city of Chicago erected a statue of a police officer in Haymarket Square on May 4, 1889 and it became the first such monument in the nation. For many years, the police were seen as the martyrs of the riot but with the rise of the big labor unions, that perception slowly changed. During the 1960s, the statue was defaced, blown up twice, repaired and finally removed to the Chicago Police Training Academy by Mayor Richard J. Daley. A small statue commemorates the workers today.

THE RISE AND FALL OF THE "PERFECT TOWN" OF PULLMAN

George M. Pullman

George M. Pullman never dreamed that anything like the Haymarket Square Riot would affect his company. Pullman was a self-described "humanitarian," who built a model company town for his employees, and never imagined that his workers could want for anything. He was born in New York and came to Chicago in 1855. As a cabinetmaker and construction engineer, he supervised the raising of many of Chicago's buildings and later developed the first railway sleeping car that was suitable for long distance travel. He also developed the dining car and parlor car through the Pullman Palace Car Company, which was organized in 1867. In 1880, he built a factory on the south side of Chicago and during the heyday of his company, created the model town of Pullman around it.

The small town was located 10 miles outside the city proper, next to the factory. It consisted of 1,800 brick homes, an arcade with a theater, a library, a hotel, stores, a bank, two churches and a school. However, there were no beer gardens or saloons and alcohol was strictly forbidden. The only bar in town was located in the Florence Hotel and was reserved for Pullman and his guests.

Rules in the company town were harsh. Any employee who dropped paper in the street and did not pick it up could be fired. Any tenant could be evicted from his home for any reason, with a 10-day notice. No labor organizers were permitted within the town. No improper books or plays were allowed at the library. In addition, rent was higher than in comparable homes in the city and all gas and water was purchased from the company, who made a profit on it. On payday, all debts owed to the company were automatically deducted from what the employee earned. This debt included rent, water, gas or food from the company store. Some families literally ended up with only few cents left after all of their deductions.

In 1893, Chicago was host to the World's Columbian Exposition and while the fairgrounds may have been dubbed the "White City," the actual city was plunged that year into what has been called the "black winter." One of

A Study in contrasts: (Left) Pullman's palatial mansion on Prairie Avenue in Chicago (Right) The homes of workers in his model town south of the city.

The "perfect" town of Pullman

The Pullman Sleeping Car -- the invention that made a fortune & changed the face of labor in America forever.

the nation's recurrent financial panics and depressions struck and in Chicago, people were going hungry and dying from the harsh weather. Soup kitchens were organized and City Hall was used to shelter as many as 2,000 people each night. The saloonkeepers were even doing their part to help, feeding as many as 60,000 jobless men each day. They did so at their own expense since most of the men were unable to afford even the nickel beer that was customary to earn the free lunch.

During this recession, Pullman laid off about one-third of the workforce and wages for those remaining on the job were cut by as much as 40 percent. Many men received nothing, or even went into debt on payday. That winter, some men went so hungry that they fainted on the factory floor. Finally, a delegation of workers went to see George Pullman about the disgraceful conditions. He refused to meet with them and in fact, fired all of them and evicted them from their homes.

An Indiana man named Eugene Debs later became the most successful Socialist candidate for president in American history. Debs organized a group of workers who demanded restoration of their wages from the Pullman Company. Needless to say, the demand was refused. On May 11, 1894, the workers went on strike and Pullman was shut down. Soon, members of the American Railway Union began a sympathy strike, which led to violence across the country. President Grover Cleveland intervened and ordered the strike to end, stating that the railway demonstrations interfered with delivery of the mail. Eugene Debs refused to bow to pressure and he was jailed.

By the middle of May, Pullman families were begging for food. Chicago's mayor sent thousands of dollars in groceries to the company town, spending money from his own pocket. Chicago city leaders and politicians from around the country urged Pullman to settle the strike, but he refused. The union sent him a letter that asked him to meet with the workers, but he would not even open it.

The union then voted to boycott all Pullman cars on the rail lines and refused to handle them. The United States Attorney General, Richard Olney, saw this as a way to end the strike. Thanks to the previous court ruling, the union could not interfere with the delivery of the mail, but the ruling said nothing about other trains. They could refuse to work on any train that was not carrying mail. Soon, the railroads began attaching unnecessary Pullman cars to other trains so that union members would not handle them. In this way, the companies forced the members to break the

Militia units formed at Pullman to quell the unrest among the striking workers

President Grover Cleveland sent Federal troops to Chicago to interfere in the strike, against the wishes of Illinois Governor John Altgeld

(Left) Workers clashed with Federal troops near 49th & Loomis, where bloody fighting occurred during the strike. (Right) The railroad bridge that stands at that intersection today.

law by refusing to allow the mail to go through.

With that accomplished, President Cleveland sent soldiers into Chicago on July 2. It was an act that marked the first time that federal troops had been used to intervene in a labor issue and it was done against the express wishes of Illinois governor John Altgeld, who believed the state could handle the issue. Regardless, it was something that was a long time coming. Following a strike at the McCormick factory in 1885, Marshall Field had proposed establishing a military base near the city so that federal troops would be nearby in case of problems. Business leaders had previously been using Pinkerton agents to break strikes but using the military instead appealed to all of them. With a donation of land on the north shore of Lake Michigan, Fort Highwood (later re-named Fort Sheridan by General Sheridan himself) was established in 1887.

In July 1894, troops from the fort were sent into the south side of the city to control the strikers, who, up until that point, had been peaceful. Angry that troops had been sent in, the workers began to riot. On July 5, seven buildings were burned and the following day, a mob of 6,000 set 700 railway cars on fire. On July 7, another mob attacked a military command post, located at a railroad bridge at 49th and Loomis. The soldiers fired into the crowd, killing four men and wounding another 20. Several soldiers were also killed, including some cavalrymen.

On July 8, more federal troops were sent in to control the violence and the mobs were again ordered to disperse. After more violence, including more railroad cars being overturned and set on fire, the riots finally came to an end. It was estimated that more than $685,000 in damage occurred during the riots and the death toll included 34 members of the American Railway Union.

In the end, the strikes and riots had little effect on the situation at the Pullman plant. The strikers went back to work and the plant re-opened in August. There were scores of new workers on the payroll and each of them had to sign a pledge that they would not join the Union. All of the Union workers who were hired back had to surrender their Union cards. However, many of the men were not hired back.

This prompted Illinois Governor Altgeld, who had fought against federal interference in the strike, to go to Pullman and

GHOST ALERT!

Some believe that a ghost from the railroad strike of 1894 still lingers near an old railroad bridge at 49th and Loomis streets, on the far south side. According to stories in the neighborhood, a headless cavalry rider often appears during the summer months, around the anniversary of the riots that occurred near the bridge. This site was organized as a command post for riflemen and cavalry riders, who had an encampment nearby. These men were assigned the task of guarding the railroad tracks and preventing the rioters from burning and looting any other railroad cars. Legend has it that during the July 7 attack, one of the cavalrymen was killed when his horse fell and his head was crushed against a wagon. The stories say that he has never left this site. On summer nights, neighborhood residents claim they sometimes hear the sound of a horse's hooves beating on the pavement near the bridge, while others relate seeing the apparition of the rider himself. The specter, dressed in a military uniform of the late 1800s, rides down the darkened street, a vacant space where his head should be. In a rush of smells that includes horse sweat and stark fear, the cavalryman thunders past and then disappears into the gloom.

personally ask that the men be hired back. He arrived in the company town and was taken on a tour by the Pullman Company vice-president. Pullman himself was too busy to entertain him. The idea was to show the governor what a wonderful place the town was. Instead, Altgeld found more than 6,000 people with no food, families living in poverty and women and children in unsuitable living conditions. He was appalled by the place and realized that Pullman was simply oblivious to the lives of his employees. Altgeld returned to Springfield and quickly dispatched a letter. He asked that Pullman hire back all of the replaced workers and in addition, cancel all rents from October 1 so that the workers could get back on their feet. Pullman refused to accept the letter until he was literally forced to take it by an Illinois National Guard officer. Then, of course, he did nothing.

In 1898, the Illinois Supreme Court ordered the company to sell off its housing stock in the town of Pullman, bringing an end to this twisted element of Chicago history.

As for Pullman, his victory in breaking the strike was short-lived. He succeeded in losing the love of his daughters, losing the respect of his workers, and earning the disdain of most of the national press. He died three years later in 1897 and was buried in Graceland Cemetery. His grave was fortified with railroad ties and reinforced concrete so that "radicals, anarchists and embittered workers" would not be able to violate his crypt.

The factory town of Pullman, as well as the Pullman Palace Car Company, is nothing but a distant memory today. Only faded pieces of Pullman remain as brick homes on the south side of the city, occupied by residents who know little or nothing of this infamous time from the city's distant past.

"HOG BUTCHER TO THE WORLD"

In the latter part of the 1800s, Chicago was deluged with European immigrants looking for housing and work in the growing city. Many of them ended up on the south side and went to work for an industry that earned Chicago both acclaim and scorn and was personified in a stream of putrid water. The waterway was dubbed "Bubbly Creek," because it would literally bubble as bacteria devoured the horrific products that had been dumped into it. Bubbly Creek was the derisive name given for 50 years to the Stock Yards Slip, which was actually the East Fork of the South Fork, beginning just below West 37th Street in the Stockyards area. Once located just beyond the Archer Avenue Bridge was a place that, along with the other factories that processed meat, combined to give this part of Chicago its questionable reputation.

Carl Sandburg called Chicago the "hog butcher for the world" but it was actually beef that made the city wealthy. Until the 1800s, cuts of beef were prepared only by local butchers. However, in 1872, a man named Gustavas Swift began buying cattle from the western ranges and shipping sides of beef to the East on express trains that ran in the winter months with their doors open to preserve the butchered meat. Later, Swift developed refrigerated rail cars and soon, he and his chief competitor, Phillip Armour, were shipping most of the nation's beef and pork products.

Both Armour and Swift had come to Chicago in 1875. Armour had passed through the Midwest on his way to the California gold fields in 1851 and in 1863, he moved to Milwaukee and went into business with John Plankington, a produce man. One of Armour's brothers, Joseph, was placed in charge of the Chicago branch and by 1867 Armour & Co. had been founded and was packing hogs in the city. When Joseph became ill in 1875, Armour moved to Chicago.

Armour was a "packer" in the true sense of the term, long before the word was used to describe anyone who killed stock and shipped meat. During the winter, Armour & Co. slaughtered, pickled, cured and smoked hog meat, shipping the final product all over the country. Salt pork, smoked sausage, corned beef, hams, and bacon were their specialties.

Fresh beef was not Armour's first concern. That trade was dominated by a German named Nelson Morris, who had been in Chicago since he was a boy. Morris had first worked for the old Sherman stockyards, the precursor to the great Union Stockyards, and having no money, bought hogs and steers whose legs had been broken in crowded shipments. He quickly butchered them and sold the meat to local shops, amassing funds for a larger operation.

Armour and Morris were powerful enough to frighten off most of the competition, but not all of it. One determined butcher, Gustavas A. Swift, would take his place among the greatest names in the industry.

Swift was born in 1839 and, at a young age, worked as a butcher's helper and slaughterhouse operator in Massachusetts. In 1875, he brought his family to Chicago to be closer to the cattle supply. He had come to buy steers in the Union Stockyards, but Swift (who his son Louis called the "Yankee of the Yards") saw a better way to make money than to ship live steers. Instead of paying the freight to ship a whole steer to an eastern slaughterhouse, why not just ship the edible parts? He soon began slaughtering cattle and shipping the dressed meat to New England during the winter months. He eventually became rich but it took him several years to convince the Easterners that Western beef was even better after it had been hung and cooled for a few days. In order to get his beef into Eastern homes, he slashed prices, and took his losses for the good of the company. The company nearly failed several times,

"HOG BUTCHER TO THE WORLD"

The Union Stockyards on Chicago's south side created thousands of jobs for workers, many of whom had toiled on the Illinois & Michigan Canal. For these men, mostly immigrants, the pay was abysmal and working conditions were usually horrific, at best.

The stockyards slaughtered millions of head of cattle and hogs every year. It was commonly said that they used "every part of the hog but the squeal.

The desperately poor conditions of Packingtown, home of the stockyards workers, were especially hard on the children. Many of them did not survive into adulthood.

but Swift managed to win over not only the New England butchers, but the housewives they served, as well.

In 1878 and 1879, he worked on a refrigerated railroad car, which would permit Chicago to export fresh meat all year around. Many inventors competed with designs and, as the decade came to an end, both Swift and Armour had their own fleets of these revolutionary cars, carrying meat to every part of the country, no matter what the weather was like.

Both men also remained busy trying to eliminate waste and finding uses for the parts of cows, hogs, and sheep that had never been used before. They developed glue, fertilizer, soap and dozens of other products, all of which swelled their fortunes. They had begun the record of efficiency that created the universally known joke, "The Chicago packers use very part of the hog but the squeal." That boast, according to legend, is credited to Swift, but it may not have been merely a jest.

A man walks on the crusted and frozen sewage waste of Bubbly Creek in Packingtown (Library of Congress)

Chicagoans often claimed to see him, dressed in his frock coat, prying around the outlets of the sewers that ran from his packinghouse, looking for traces of grease on the water. If he caught a sign of fat going to waste, one of his superintendents would be severely chastised before the day was out.

But the meat packing industry was not simply a tremendous achievement that would have millions of tourists coming to Chicago and asking to see the Stockyards where the packers worked their "miracles." It also had a dark side that, if they saw it, would likely have had those same sightseers vowing to never eat another piece of meat again.

The slaughterhouses were located south of the city, in an area often referred to as "Packingtown," named for the tenement housing near the stockyards. The workers lived in these rundown slums, receiving pay so poor that many of the children in this area scavenged for food from the garbage dumps. Nearby was "Whiskey Row," a district of more than 200 saloons. Here, the stockyard workers were usually given a free lunch, but only on the condition that they bought a drink.

The slaughterhouses were filthy and dangerous places to work and the workers were treated with little regard. And while the plants used "every bit of the hog but the squeal," there was still waste to be disposed of. The slaughter refuse was dumped into an open sewer that ran through Packingtown into Bubbly Creek. Filled with greasy sewage, the creek was supposed to have a scum so thick that a steer could walk on it without sinking. The water, and the entire area, smelled so disgusting that the Sanitary District eventually forced the plant owners to "abate the nuisance." Later, the Racine Avenue pumping station was used to speed the outflows through its sewers, causing Bubbly Creek to vanish into limbo.

Before that happened, though, the horrific conditions of Packingtown caught the attention of Frank Warren, the editor of a weekly Socialist newspaper. He decided to send one of his reporters, a young man named Upton Sinclair, into the district to write an exposé on the packinghouses. Sinclair was an impoverished writer and his threadbare clothing helped him to blend in with the workers in Packingtown. He found that by carrying a pail with him, he could get into anywhere that he wanted to go. He gathered his material and the article that he wrote ran as a newspaper series, starting in February 1905. He later expanded the pieces into a novel titled The Jungle.

The 1906 book, The Jungle, changed the American meat packing industry forever.

For months, Sinclair was unable to find a publisher who would even consider printing the book. No one believed that his description of the conditions in Packingtown could be accurate. Sinclair insisted that it was. He had created fictional characters in the novel, but they had been based on real people --- and the conditions of Packingtown were just as he had described them.

The Jungle was published by Doubleday in 1906. The graphic accounts shocked readers and the book sold more than 100,000 copies the first year it was in publication. Author Jack London called it "the Uncle Tom's Cabin of wage slavery." Another admirer of the book was President Theodore Roosevelt, who had long been a critic of the nation's meat packers. During the Spanish-American War, he stated that he would have rather eaten his old hat than consumed the meat that the packing companies sent to Cuba. He believed that Sinclair's book could help him do something about the problem.

Roosevelt began actively pursuing government regulations of the meat packing industry, including thorough inspections of the factories where the meat was being slaughtered and processed. The meat packers opposed the new standards, but with sales falling in the wake of Sinclair's book, they began claiming that they had cleaned up the plants on their own. Doctors began visiting the plants and their reports supported Sinclair's claims and the unsanitary conditions caused the public to turn against the industry. A popular rhyme that made the rounds in Chicago in 1906 went, 'Mary had a little lamb, and when she saw it sicken, she shipped it off to Packingtown, and now it's labeled chicken.'

President Roosevelt pushed ahead with his plans and the first meat inspection bill was passed one year later. A novel had changed an entire industry and meatpacking was never the same again.

THE WORLD CAME TO THE "WHITE CITY"

The World's Columbian Exposition, celebrating the 400th Anniversary of Christopher Columbus' landing in America, was held in Chicago in 1893, one year later than the actual anniversary. Chicago, New York, Washington and St. Louis all competed vigorously for the honor of hosting the fair and it was during this jockeying that the city of Chicago actually gained the title of the "Windy City." As Chicago was doing more boasting about its landscape and amenities than any of the other cities, Charles A. Dana, editor of the New York Sun, advised his readers to ignore the "nonsensical claims of that windy city." This was the first use of the term and had nothing to do with wind gusts along Lake Michigan. Chicago's lobbyists eventually won out and on April 25, 1890, President Benjamin Harrison signed the act that designated Chicago as the site of the exposition. It took three frantic years of preparation to produce the fair and although dedication ceremonies were held on October 21, 1892, the fairgrounds were not actually opened to the public until the following May.

By all accounts, the fair was a great success for the city of Chicago and for the city's burgeoning crime and vice elements, as well. Attendance at the gin joints and brothels of the Levee tripled and everyone seemed to be making money. The city also attracted many famous, and infamous, visitors, including Gentleman Jim Corbett, Diamond Jim Brady, John Phillip Sousa, Lillian Russell and many others. Scandal was even provided when Princess Eulalia of Spain snubbed Bertha Palmer, the queen of Chicago society, when she was invited as a guest to the Palmer Castle. The princess turned up her nose and stated that she preferred "not to meet with an innkeeper's wife." However, she

did later turn up at the castle after breakfasting with the Carter Harrisons, but there was little exchange between Bertha and the princess. Mrs. Palmer got her revenge a number of years later when she was in Paris and was invited to dine with the princess. She politely sent her regrets, saying, "I cannot meet with this bibulous representative of a degenerate monarchy."

President Grover Cleveland arrived in Chicago in May 1893 to open the fair and nearly 400,000 people turned out to cheer and enjoy the event. The fairgrounds that had been constructed were made up of 630 acres and between May and October of 1893, they attracted 25,836,073 people -- a number that equaled nearly half of the population of America at that time.

The grounds included palaces, lagoons and immense buildings of plaster. Many of them became electrically lighted fantasies at night and so gleamed in the daylight sun that the grounds were dubbed the "White City."

Cleveland arrived riding in front of 23 horse-drawn carriages that conveyed the city's most influential citizens. Thousands crushed into the area near the main reviewing stand and their cries and shouts were nearly drowned out by an orchestra that blared the "Columbian March." Crushed children wept, women screamed as their dresses were torn and some even fainted and had to be rescued from being stomped into the muddy lawns. In the midst of the chaos, President Cleveland opened the fair with the press of an electric key. The president's high silk hat had been damaged in all of the excitement but he placed it aside and made a speech that could not have been heard by the gathered throng. He pressed the key with enthusiasm and the flags of the United States and the red banner of Spain were run up their staffs. Fountains began to spurt water and throughout the fairgrounds, vast and mysterious machines began to turn. Across the lake, the thunder of guns from the warships assembled there began to sound and the fair was officially opened.

WHERE IS IT NOW?
A few footprints of the 1893 Fair remain on the grounds; bits of docks and sidewalks are visible here and there, and the Japanese temple on the wooded island still stands, though most of it is a reproduction; most of the original was destroyed shortly after the Japanese attack on Pearl Harbor. An original World's Fair bathroom stands in a nearby schoolyard, where it functions as a tool shed.

The main site of the fair was bounded by Stony Island Avenue on the west, 67th Street on the south, Lake Michigan on the east and 56th Street on the north. The Midway, which was one of the most popular attractions of the fair, was a narrow strip of land that ran between 59th and 60th Streets and extended west from Stony Island to Cottage Grove Avenue. Daniel H. Burnham and Frederick Law Olmstead, America's foremost landscape architect and creator of New York's Central Park, were responsible for the design of the fairgrounds. Jackson Park, which remains from Olmstead's efforts, is still regarded as one of the city's most beautiful gardens. A distinguished group of architects was assembled to create the buildings, including Henry Ives Cobb, Richard Morris Hunt, Charles McKim, George B. Post and Louis Sullivan. Sophie Hayden, the first woman awarded a degree in architecture from the Massachusetts Institute of Technology, designed the famous Women's Building.

Daniel Burnham was the man who assembled the architects and planners for the event and in 1891, had faced the bleak task of turning a patch of sand and wild oak that was seven miles from downtown Chicago into a glorious World's Fair. Burnham was at the mid-point of his career in those days and was already

Daniel Burnham

responsible of many of the city's most acclaimed buildings. He and his partner, John W. Root, had joined their fortunes less than two years after the Great Fire, when both men were in their early 20s. They operated out of a single room for years, slowly earning a reputation. When the era of the skyscraper arrived, Burnham and Root designed the first very tall building - the Montauk Block, a ten-story monster that was the first building in the country set upon "spread foundations" of concrete and railroad ties. They followed this with grand achievements like The Rookery and many others.

In 1891, the two men were selected to see that the World's Fair was constructed according to the vast general plan. But Root never had the chance to put his soul into it. His death in early 1891 left Burnham to bear the burden and reap the glory alone. Burnham, still grieving for his friend, went bravely ahead with the work of organizing, harmonizing and strategizing the fair. He fought and won a battle with a large and stubborn group of Chicago businessmen who were intent on telling him how to compose the building and grounds committee and persuaded them to give up on the idea of competitive designs and allow him to invite a group of selected architects to submit their work.

Meanwhile, civic patriot and nature lover James W. Ellsworth, a member of the World's Fair Board, managed to persuade Olmstead to tackle the swamp that would become Jackson Park. Ellsworth was reported to have promised him "$15 million

The magnificence of the 1893 Fair was unlike anything the people of Chicago had ever seen before, from wondrous pavilions to amazing shows of electric light that illuminated the night skies.

and a free hand" and Olmstead agreed, achieving a design that would not only serve the immediate purpose, but would be a thing of permanent beauty. Olmstead set to work to change a wasteland of sand, where little would grow and flooding was frequent, into one of the finest parks in the nation. Acres of sand were sliced from the surface and carloads of soil were brought in to replace them. He brought in thousands of beautiful plants and ferns, trees and flowering shrubs, all of which were carried for miles to beautify lagoons and a wooded island.

Burnham enlisted the reserved and eccentric sculptor Augustus Saint-Gaudens to serve on his staff and he brought into the effort such sculptors as Daniel C. French, Paul Bartlett, Karl Bitter and many others. All of them, like Chicago's Lorado Taft, were eager to work with Saint-Gaudens and provided Burnham with scores of ideas and designs for the White City.

However, not everything went smoothly. Burnham often had a battle on his hands when it came to the architects that he had chosen. The planners selected a classical architectural theme for the fair buildings, over the strenuous objections of the more innovative architects. In fact, Chicago's Louis Sullivan later predicted that "the damage wrought by the World's Fair will last for half a century from its date, if not longer." He believed the Greek and Roman style "temples" and pavilions were old-fashioned and out-dated but there was little worry that any of them would be around for long. The buildings that were created were meant to be amazing, both for their beauty and for their size, but they were constructed from temporary materials and were not supposed to be permanent. The buildings were made from a material called "staff," which was plaster and a mixture of fibers that would harden and be adaptable, like wood. By pouring the staff into glue molds, many ornamental pieces, which appeared to be

The famous "Midway" was perhaps the greatest attraction to ordinary people who came to the Fair in 1893. Visitors to the Midway could be treated to a cold beer, good food and could have their pockets picked by the best "dips" in the city.

handmade, could be achieved in a short time. The structure underneath the material was always steel or wood so that the buildings would not collapse.

Only one of the 200 buildings that were constructed for the fair, the Palace of Fine Arts, remains today. Like most of the others, this building was also a temporary structure that was made from staff, but it housed the Field Columbian Museum after the fair's closing until 1920. During the late 1920s, the building was reduced to its steel skeleton and rebuilt with stone, and then was re-opened in 1931 as the Museum of Science and Industry.

The buildings on the grounds housed 65 exhibits that followed the theme of each building. Some of the most popular exhibits were curiosities, rather than serious displays of technology or progress. These included a hygienically stuffed whale that attendees could walk through, an 11-ton piece of cheese, a 1,500-pound replica of the Venus de Milo made from chocolate, and a 70-foot tower of light bulbs in the Electricity Building.

There was always something to see on the fairgrounds and in those simpler times, the sights amazed the visitors, whether they had come from the city or the farm. There were movable sidewalks; replicas of Columbus' three ships that had actually sailed from Spain in 1892; an Irish Village; Blarney Castle, with an appropriately fake Blarney stone that was actually a Chicago paving stone; and even a Nicola Tesla high current wire that powered a long-distance telephone line to New York. Visitors could also see real Parisian fashions; Miles Standish's pipe; a full-sized replica of Washington's Mount Vernon; the Liberty Bell; and an a presentation by a woman named Susan B. Anthony, who cherished the seemingly hopeless dream of a woman's right to vote.

INNOVATIONS FROM THE WORLD'S FAIR

The 1893 Columbian Exposition introduced a number of new products to the world, including:

* A moveable sidewalk, now a staple in airports
* The Ferris wheel
*Thomas Edison's Kinetograph (which showed the first moving pictures)
*The first zipper for clothing
*Cracker Jacks
*Aunt Jemima's - a box that contained everything you needed to make pancakes
*The U.S. Mint's first commemorative coins
*Cream of Wheat
*Shredded Wheat (which some fair-goers referred to as "shredded doormat")
*Pabst Beer (which won a Blue Ribbon, hence the name change)
*Juicy Fruit gum
*The first hamburgers

The Columbian Exposition was the first world's fair to ever feature a separate amusement and entertainment area, dubbed the Midway. The noisy and distracting attractions there were concentrated in a central area so that not to disturb the park-like setting of the rest of the exposition. The Midway's features ranged from a replica of the streets of Cairo to carnival rides and it was the greatest attraction of the fair to those often referred to as the "great unwashed." It was there that the world's first Ferris wheel was exhibited, invented by George W. Ferris. The 250-feet high steel structure had 36 cars, carrying 60 persons in each one.

Visitors to the Midway could be treated to a cold beer, good food and could have their pockets picked by the best "dips" in the city.

It was along the "Streets of Cairo" exhibit that fairgoers were entertained by an attraction that became the most popular, and the most controversial, of the fair. This was the first amusement to introduce the art of exotic dancing to

America. While shocking to many, the exhibit proved to be the most successful Midway attraction and its backers realized more than double the profit on their investment. Without a doubt, the sensation of the exhibit was Fahreda Mahzar, better known as "Little Egypt." Fahreda was a belly dancer and the diamonds on her garter, her colorful brassiere, and suggestive dance fascinated everyone who saw her and easily gained her the title of sexiest dancer at the fair. Little Egypt later became the wife of a Chicago restaurant owner and while her clothing would have been tame by modern standards, she was remembered for years as the most beautiful and wondrous attraction of the entire exhibition.

But not everything was pristine and beautiful with the Columbian Exposition. Despite the public face that had been put on the event, a darker side shimmered just below the surface. The area was a prime target for confidence men, pea-shell and three-card Monte men, and thieves of every kind. Newspapers (mostly from out of town) reported muggings and robberies, country yokels who were conned by loaded dice, marked cards, the gin joints, and the prostitutes, who could easily be found within walking distance of the fairgrounds.

Among its other problems, the fair also happened to be held during a panic on Wall Street and a depression that severely affected the city of Chicago and the rest of the nation. The Chemical National Bank, with a branch at the fair, failed just eight days after the exhibition opened.

The Jewelry Exhibition, a supposedly impregnable repository, was broken into and two large diamonds were stolen, along with a riding whip that was owned by King Leopold of Belgium.

Unfortunately, at least one great tragedy marred the fair during its 183-day run. "Chicago Day" at the fair was a great success and its acceptance by the local residents was said to be a display of affection for Mayor Carter Harrison, who organized the day and welcomed all manner and class of people to the fairgrounds. Soon after the day was held, though, Harrison received a visitor in his home, Patrick Eugene Joseph Prendergast, who shot the mayor to death.

Prendergast was a newspaper distributor in Chicago and in 1893, supported Harrison's re-election campaign. Unfortunately for the mayor, he was also more than a little unhinged. Prendergast was under the delusion that if Harrison won the election he would receive an appointment as Corporation Counsel. When the appointment didn't come, Prendergast visited Harrison at his home on October 28, 1893 and shot the mayor four times. Harrison had no idea who Prendergast was. During his first trial, Prendergast's attorney tried to have him found insane, but failed. Clarence Darrow later won a hearing on Prendergast's sanity, but it also failed. Prendergast was hanged on July 13, 1894.

The fair flags were lowered to half-staff when news of the murder broke and on the Midway, minor rioting broke out and whiskey bottles were shattered on the facades of

THE WORLD'S FAIR FERRIS WHEEL

George Washington Gale Ferris, a bridge builder from Galesburg, Ill., invented the Ferris wheel specifically for the 1893 Columbian Exposition.

The wheel was 264 feet in height, 250 feet in diameter, and 825 feet in circumference. The axle was the largest piece of forged steel in the world at that time, weighing 142,031 pounds. This was heavier than anything that had ever been lifted before and it had to be mounted on top of eight towers. This was not your average carnival ride! The Ferris wheel held 36 wooden cars the size of small railroad coaches, each capable of holding 60 people.

The contraption looked very fragile and extremely dangerous and a similar project could never exist today because no company would dream of insuring it. But every day, fair-goers paid 50 cents each to climb into the cars and soar for 22 minutes above the city. Rumors spread about suicides, but the company denied these allegations. The cars had barred windows to keep people from jumping out, although some passengers discovered their fear of heights a little too late. One man panicked and hurled himself against the bars with such forced that he shattered the glass and bent the iron. He pushed away everyone who tried to hold him back until one woman (to everyone's shock), lifted her skirt and placed it over the man's head until he calmed down. Needless to say, the man was quickly subdued.

The Wheel was the Exposition's most popular attraction. It was dismantled at fair's end but then rebuilt in St. Louis for the 1904 World's Fair in that city. It was scrapped in 1906 (and portions of it buried in Forest Park, the St. Louis fairgrounds) but its design was copied all over the world.

Mayor Carter Harrison

the white buildings. Not since the arrival of Abraham Lincoln's funeral train had there been such a weeping and thronging procession of mourners as when the mayor lay in state at Chicago's City Hall. It was, some have said, a fitting climax to the soon-to-be-closing fair.

As the lights went dark on the fairground, many breathed a sigh of relief that the element that had been attracted to the city would finally be sent on its way. The Midway was scattered among the variety shows and museum circuits around the country, including the exotic dancers, whom some called one of the worst abominations ever invented. Little Egypt's imitators were now loose in America and for years afterwards, small-time carnival midways were sure to feature "the Original Little Egypt -- direct from the Chicago Exposition."

All in all, though, Chicago did well during the fair. If not for the exposition, it's likely that the local economy would have been hit even harder than it was by the depression of the day. The gate receipts brought in more than $10 million and the concession receipts at least $4 million more. This did not include the millions made from souvenir books, commemorative coins and other items that were sold or even the bank interest that was earned on the deposits that were made. It was thought that at least $3 million was left over to divide between the investors, a not insubstantial sum in those days.

But the glory of the Columbus Exposition was a transient one for Chicago. The White City was gone, except for the great buildings, which some were now calling "white elephants" for which no purchasers could be found. The problems and woes of the city had returned and the autumn and the winter brought misery. As the winds grew colder, the effects of the closed factories, stores running at reduced force, and the scores of men and women laid off from their jobs had started to show.

At City Hall, the stone corridors were filled at night with sleepers. The halls were so crowded that men were forced to sleep with their heads against the walls with a narrow path left between two rows of outstretched feet. Police stations all over the city sheltered between 60 and 100 men each night. In the Harrison Street station, cells were packed and, in a 10-foot-long corridor, in which the shrieks of prisoners could be heard, men slept elbow-to-elbow, sometimes with rats running over them. Reporters stated that the corridor was "paved with bodies." There were young boys sleeping in the station, too, and in the women's section, mothers with babies.

The winter after the fair was terrible for children. Scores were turned out on the street. Babies were given to overcrowded orphanages. Evictions ran to the hundreds per day - partly because rents had been raised so high during the World's Fair. Jane Addams, and other settlement workers, labored to keep mothers and children from the poorhouse, but there were just too many to care for.

The streets were filled with people begging for a handout, some of them stranded World's Fair vendors, who now found their Armenian rugs and glittering fake jewelry impossible to sell. On every corner, poor outcasts, who had profited during the days of plenty, now cried for help but got very little.

Even with hundreds of thousands of people out of work, Chicago was still the "city of big shoulders," as Carl Sandburg would later call it. Funds were given by wealthy men to rent vacant stores where soup kitchens could be opened. Merchants made contributions of food. In slum districts, aldermen distributed food and clothing to needy persons, who, of course, immediately became loyal constituents. Saloon operators and brothel owners sheltered and cared for hundreds and "free lunches" saved many from starvation. It was later reported that during the worst of the crisis, 60,000 men were fed each day for free by saloonkeepers.

Chicago would not be defeated by mere depression and financial setbacks. It was a city that had completely rebuilt itself after a devastating fire and a place that had created the world's most dazzling fair out of a few miles of sand and barren lakefront. The crisis of the middle 1890s passed and Chicago moved on to embrace another century. As author Lloyd Lewis wrote, "The city of those days, no less than now, abounded in comedy, alternating with eruptions of tragedy."

"SAY IT AIN'T SO, JOE": THE 1919 WHITE SOX SCANDAL

Civil War General Abner Doubleday has long been considered the inventor of baseball and while he may have popularized the pastime, he certainly did not create it. Based on the British sport of cricket, the official rules were set down in New York by Alexander Cartwright in 1845. The next year found the first game of record to be played in Hoboken, N.J., with the New York Nine defeating the Knickerbockers in four full innings with a score of 23 to 1.

The first professional team, the Cincinnati Red Stockings, appeared in 1869 and the rest, as they say, is history.

From these humble beginnings, baseball evolved into a major league sport and became big business. And when sports began to make money, the sportsmen began to brush shoulders with gangsters and gamblers. Prior to 1919, the fixing of baseball games for betting purposes was by no means unheard of, but it was in that year that it went too far and resulted in the most famous scandal in baseball history. Eight players of the Chicago White Sox (later nicknamed the "Black Sox") were accused of throwing the World Series that was being played against the Cincinnati Red Legs, 5 games to 3.

The 1919 Chicago White Sox, or the "Black Sox" as they later became known

The details of what actually happened during the series remain unclear and it's still unknown just how deeply the accused men were actually involved. It was, however, front-page news around the country and even though they were acquitted of criminal charges, the players were all banned from professional baseball for life. The eight men included the great "Shoeless" Joe Jackson; pitchers Eddie Cicotte and Claude "Lefty" Williams; infielders Buck Weaver, Arnold "Chick" Gandil, Fred McMullin and Charles "Swede" Risberg and outfielder Oscar "Happy" Felsch.

In those days, baseball was truly an American sport and almost everyone in the country watched the local games or followed some favorite team. The events that took place in Chicago, as the days of summer faded into fall, shook the country to its core. Having just weathered a great world war, and now standing on the eve of Prohibition, when lawlessness would become a way of life to even the average person, the White Sox scandal can actually be seen as the final loss of innocence for the celebrated American way of life.

The White Sox were formed in 1900 as a franchise in the American Baseball League and were owned by Charles A. Comiskey. They were originally called the White Stockings, but the name was changed in 1902. In the team's first year, they won the league championship and the following year, the American and National Leagues agreed to meet in an end of the season play-off that had been dubbed the "World Series." In 1906, the White Sox won the championship by defeating the Chicago Cubs, four games to two. This would be the last of the team's victories for a while, though, and over the course of the next eight years, they lost many more games than they won.

In 1901, however, Comiskey decided to build a new ballpark on Chicago's south side and he dedicated himself to building a strong ball club. In 1915, he purchased the contracts of three players: outfield Joe Jackson, second baseman Eddie Collins, and center fielder Happy Felsch. Comiskey was closely involved with the changing of the team and, in fact, as a former first baseman, is credited with being the first to teach his players to adjust their field positions according to the habits of the batter. In 1917, the Sox won the World Series and by 1919 had the best record in the American League. Comiskey had succeeded in building baseball's most powerful team.

But despite their success on the field, the White Sox were

White Sox owner Charles Comiskey

  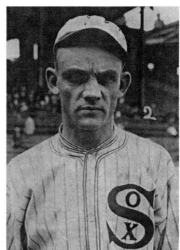

(Left to Right) "Shoeless" Joe Jackson; Eddie Collins; Chick Gandil

a troubled and unhappy team. They may have played better than every other team in 1919, but were the worst paid in both leagues. Many have stated that they believe Comiskey himself was really the one responsible for the World Series scandal. If he had not grossly underpaid his players and had not treated them so unfairly, it's likely that none of them would have agreed to throw the series. He was able to get away with paying them so poorly because of a "reverse clause" that has been put into their contracts. This clause prevented the players from changing teams without the permission of the owner and with no union, the players had no bargaining power at all.

Comiskey also made frequent promises to the players that he did not keep. For instance, he once assured them that they would receive a large bonus if they won the pennant. After their win, the "bonus" turned out to be nothing more than a case of cheap champagne. He even charged the players for laundering their uniforms, so in protest, the players wore the same dirty uniforms for several weeks. Comiskey finally had the filthy uniforms removed from their lockers and cleaned, then fined the players for their demonstration.

To make matters even more volatile, the White Sox team members did not get along well with each other. Their constant bickering was marked by jealousy and verbal abuse, dividing the team into separate factions, one led by second baseman Eddie Collins and the other by first baseman, Arnold "Chick" Gandil. Collins' group was educated, sophisticated and able to negotiate salaries as high as $15,000. Gandil's less polished faction, who earned only about $6,000, bitterly resented the disparity.

All of these things combined to make for a bad situation in 1919. The year before, with the country disrupted by World War I, interest in baseball dropped to a record low. By the time of the World Series in 1919, however, baseball and America were back on track. In fact, baseball was more popular than ever and the enthusiasm for it took everyone by surprise. Fans eagerly followed the games and national interest in the World Series was so great that baseball officials decided for the first time to make it a best of nine series, instead of the traditional best of seven.

This probably explains the marked interest with gamblers in the game, as well. Gamblers were often visibly present at the ballpark and there had been rumors of games being fixed for many years. Rumors even circulated that players were supplementing their incomes by throwing games and some of them had gained reputations for working closely with the gamblers. One smalltime Chicago gambler, Joseph Sullivan, had allegedly made money using inside information from Sox player Chick Gandil. Sullivan's bets were always safer when he knew a pitcher or hitter was sick, injured or even just having an off week. Many of the team owners attempted to curb the presence of gamblers in the ballpark. Comiskey posted signs throughout the stadium that stated "No Betting Allowed in this Park" but unfortunately, the signs were not enough. Player resentment was high and the gambler's offers, which were usually several times a player's usual salary, were often too tempting to refuse.

Over the years, the facts behind the throwing of the World Series have become cloudy but those who have researched the case believe that it was likely Gandil who was the ringleader. A few weeks before the 1919 World Series, Gandil approached gamblers Joseph "Sport" Sullivan and William "Sleepy Bill" Burns of New York about fixing the series. He allegedly told them that for $10,000, he and several of his teammates could make sure that the White Sox lost the series. Because the gamblers felt that they needed more capital to finance a huge win, they approached the country's leading gambler, Arnold "The Brain" Rothstein. It is unknown whether or not Rothstein entered into the plot, or if he turned them down and then simply went ahead and bet at least $60,000 on Cincinnati because he knew the fix was in and saw no need to pay the bribe money himself. Whatever actually happened, the main operator behind the fix became Abe Attell, a former featherweight boxing champion.

Famous gambler Arnold Rothstein, who was believed to have been involved in the World Series fix.

After Gandil gained the support of the gamblers, he went to work getting the cooperation of his teammates. Gandil was known as a rough character and had been in trouble before. At the age of 33, he was getting ready to retire but wanted to make one last shot at big money before he went. He had been linked to gamblers in the past and had been suspended temporarily earlier that same season. The White Sox had been playing the Cleveland Indians at Comiskey Park and Gandil had become annoyed with the Indians' Tris Speaker. In the eighth inning, Speaker had smacked a grounder to Gandil at first and then had come sliding into first base with his spikes flying. Gandil's shins were cut and at the end of the inning, when Speaker came out of the dugout to take his place in center field, the two men got into a brawl. They hammered at one another for several minutes before seven police officers were able to separate them. The fans were upset and began to throw soda bottles at the Indians until Sox manager, William "Kid" Gleason, walked out onto the field with a police officer. He asked them to stop before someone got hurt or the game ended up being forfeited. They settled down and the Sox won the game. Both Gandil and Speaker were temporarily suspended the next day by Bancroft B. Johnson, the president of the American League.

In order to make his World Series gamble work, Gandil needed to recruit as many of his fellow players to the scheme as possible. If the gamblers were going to put up $100,000, Gandil needed to make sure that a sufficient number of players would go along with the fix. Two of the Sox pitchers, Cicotte and Williams (some say that Williams became the go-between for the players and gamblers) had won 52 games between them in the 1919 season and Gandil needed their participation to succeed. Cicotte had his own grudge against Comiskey, too. The team owner had once promised Cicotte that if he won 30 games, he would receive a $10,000 bonus. When Cicotte won 29 games, Comiskey benched him with an excuse that he needed to rest up for the pennant games to come. Comiskey never gave him the money. That was surely on his mind when he told Gandil that if he wanted him to go along with the scheme, Cicotte would need $10,000 up front. Williams and Risberg were also interested and McMullin, who overheard Gandil talking to Risberg, also wanted in.

Jackson and Weaver are the two players whose involvement in fixing the series is most disputed. According to Jackson, when Gandil offered him $10,000 in exchange for helping to throw the games, Jackson turned him down. Gandil upped the amount to $20,000 but Jackson still refused. Gandil then supposedly told Jackson that he could take it or leave it because the fix was already going to happen as long as the gamblers came up with the money. Jackson's refusal was a problem, though, as he was the team's star player and it's likely that the gamblers would have wanted his involvement. Most believe that Gandil simply lied to them and told them that Jackson was part of the scheme, even though he actually wasn't. As for Weaver, he attended several meetings of the players who planned to fix the games, but he also apparently refused to be a part of the actual conspiracy.

When the series finally kicked off, the White Sox were matched up against the Cincinnati Reds and were favored to win. They were almost the identical team from the 1917 championship, and the 1919 World Series should have been easily won. It was said that most people came to the games not to see if the Sox won, but how they actually went about it. Early odds favored Chicago 5 to 1 but the day before the series started in Cincinnati, rumors of a fix were flying. As soon as the big money started changing hands, the odds began to shift toward the Reds.

On the night before the first game, Cicotte found $10,000 waiting for him in his hotel room.

Chicago lost the first game with a score of 9 to 1 but the players didn't receive the $20,000 in cash that Gandil had promised them for losing the game. They were willing to lose game two, they told him, but only as long as the money came in at the end of the next day. They lost that next game 4 to 2 and needless to say, Sox players not involved in the fix began to get suspicious. Catcher Ray Schalk knew that something was wrong with the pitching and he and Kid Gleason reportedly got into fights with Gandil and Williams over their pathetic performances. After the game, Gandil went searching for Abe Attell, looking for the $40,000 that he and his fellow conspirators were owed for throwing the two games. He received only $10,000 and now the players were having second thoughts about losing.

Angry at being stiffed for the initial amount they were promised, the players put an extra effort into the next game and managed to win. The gamblers who had been betting on individual games lost a bundle and feeling betrayed, Attell refused to pay any more. Sullivan however, came up with $20,000 before the fourth game and at least some of the conspirators were still willing to lose. Cicotte made several clumsy but crucial errors and the Reds won the game 2 to 0. Chicago lost game five as well, with a final score of 5 to 0.

By now, the gamblers had missed another payment and the players decided that it just wasn't worth it to lose. At least if they won the series, they would take home $5,000 each. The White Sox then managed to win game six with a score of 5 to 4 and the seventh game, 4 to 1. The team was back to playing to the best of their abilities and it seemed inevitable that the championship title would go to Chicago.

But then any chance of winning was curbed by Arnold Rothstein, who had not bet on the individual games, but on Cincinnati to win the entire series. With his investment now at risk, he sent one of his men to go and have a talk with Claude Williams, who would be pitching the eighth game. He "explained" to Williams that Rothstein wanted the series to end the following day and he got his point across by telling the pitcher that his wife would pay the price for his refusal to obey orders. Terrified, Williams pitched the worst game of his career and Chicago lost 10 to 5. Cincinnati had just won the World Series.

During the series, a sports writer for the *Chicago Herald & Examiner*, Hugh Fullerton, was paying close attention to the rumors that he heard about a fix. He had hinted about the potential problems with the series in his columns and used the rumors to encourage team owners to do something about the involvement of gamblers in baseball. His columns met with little response, though. The public never dreamed that anyone could, or would, fix the World Series. Team owners, fearing that the public would turn their backs on baseball for good if they found out players were throwing games, refused to acknowledge the problem and hoped that it would simply go away. Fullerton suspected that something shady had occurred during the 1919 World Series, but he could never put his finger on just what it was or who was actually involved.

And the whole thing might have faded from memory if the gamblers' involvement in the sport had not continued to cause problems. During the 1920 season, players on other teams began to take advantage of the offers made to them by gamblers. Widespread rumors began to surface about games being thrown by players with the New York Giants, the Yankees, the Atlanta Braves and the Cleveland Indians.

Finally, in September 1920, a Cook County grand jury convened to look into allegations that the Chicago Cubs had thrown games that were played against the Philadelphia Phillies. The investigation grew and eventually extended to the 1919 World Series and baseball gambling in general. The White Sox were enjoying a good season in 1920 when the grand jury began calling players, owners, managers, writers and gamblers to testify about what had taken place the year before. At the urging of Comiskey, who was trying to cover up his knowledge of the conspiracy, Jackson and Cicotte were the first to admit what they knew about the fix.

When the grand jury concluded its investigation, eight White Sox players were indicted, as well as Abe Attell, Joe Sullivan and several of Rothstein's men. Rothstein, who made a reported $270,000 on the series, was never indicted. He later moved on to bootlegging during Prohibition, then drug dealing and labor racketeering. Years later, he was murdered by a rival gambler who Rothstein had accused of fixing a poker game.

The trial of the accused White Sox players began in June 1921. The players had not been suspended until they were only three games left to play in the 1920 season. By that time, the confessions of three of the players forced Comiskey to act. When the trial got started, it was discovered that the grand jury records, including the confessions of Jackson, Cicotte and Williams, were missing. (Note: they turned up four years later in the possession of Comiskey's lawyer, George Hudnall, who never explained why he had them) After a month of hearing testimony, it took the jury just two hours and 47 minutes to acquit all of the defendants. The lack of any real evidence, and the missing confessions, resulted in a not-guilty verdict. The trial never answered any of the lingering questions in the case and the facts, which were never really clear in the first place, continued to be manipulated and distorted into outright lies.

After the 1920 season, club owners realized that if they were going to regain the public trust in baseball, they were going to have to clean things up. The three-man national commission was replaced by a single, independent commissioner with dictatorial power over baseball. Federal Judge Kenesaw Mountain Landis was appointed commissioner and he acted quickly to restore the public trust in the sport. Immediately after the accused White Sox players were acquitted of all criminal charges, Landis banned all eight players from the game -- for life. An outcry went up from certain quarters, but Landis refused to budge.

"Regardless of the verdict of the juries, no player who throws a ball game, no player who undertakes or promises to throw a ball game, no player who sits in confidence with a bunch of crooked players and does not promptly tell his club about it, will ever play professional baseball," he pronounced. And true to his word, Landis never allowed any of the eight men to play professional ball again.

Although banned from baseball, several of the so-called "Black Sox" were unwilling, or unable, to give up the game entirely. Not only did they love the sport but for several of them, it was the only profession that they had ever known. While some of the players distanced themselves from sports, Joe Jackson, Eddie Cicotte and Swede Risberg continued to play the game in outlaw leagues or with semi-professional teams. When Joe Jackson was unable to play ball anymore, he owned and operated a liquor store. He died in 1951, shortly after being inducted into the Cleveland Baseball Hall of Fame. Eddie Cicotte became a game warden and security guard and died in 1970. Swede Risberg worked for many years on a Minnesota dairy farm and died in California in 1975. Third Basemen Buck Weaver attended meetings where the fix was planned but refused to participate and he made a number of attempts to appeal to Judge Landis for reinstatement to the game. They were all unsuccessful and he ended up running a drugstore and died of a heart attack in 1956. Fred McMullin died in California in 1952. Lefty Williams ran a poolroom for a while and then moved to California, where he had a landscaping business. He died in 1959. Happy Felsch operated a tavern in Milwaukee until his death in 1964.

As the years passed, the story of the Black Sox scandal became a tragic part of baseball history --- and a heartbreaking piece of American folklore, as well. The story goes that when several of the accused players left the grand jury room at the start of the investigation, a small group of young boys were waiting for them. One of them spoke up to Shoeless Joe Jackson. "It ain't true, is it, Joe?" he asked.

"Yes, boys," the outfielder replied sadly. "I'm afraid it is."

"Say it ain't so, Joe," the boy cried and his words have yet to be forgotten.

THE CUBS AND THE CURSE OF THE BILLY GOAT

"You know the law of averages? They say anything will happen that can. But the last time the Cubs won the National League pennant was the year we dropped the bomb on Japan!"
Steve Goodman, 1982 (though it's still true today!)

The story is among Chicago's best-known legends. In 1945, on the cusp of winning the World Series for the first time since 1908 in a series against Detroit, Billy Sianis, of the Billy Goat Tavern, brought his pet goat to the ballpark. In some versions of the story, the goat was actually a regular at Wrigley Field, and was even known to bleat excitedly at good plays. But on the day of the final game of the World Series, the management informed Sianis that the goat was no longer allowed at the ballpark, and that he would have to leave.

Sianis flew into a rage and put the team under a curse. Not only would they lose the World Series, he shouted, but as long as the Cubs played at Wrigley Field, they would never again win the National League pennant.

The story of the curse was popularized a couple of decades later by newspaper columnist Mike Royko, who was a regular at the Billy Goat Tavern, and a good friend of Billy Sianis' son, who took over the operation of the place. Exactly how much of the story is fact, and how much is fiction, will probably never be known.

But the story does, in fact, contain at least a kernel of truth, like all good legends. According to contemporary accounts, Sianis did take a goat named Sonovia to Wrigley Field during the 1945 World Series. The goat, which had its own ticket, was paraded around the box seats bearing a sign proclaiming,

William "Billy Goat" Sianis

"We've got Detroit's goat!" Andy Frain, who was in charge of security, argued a bit with Sianis, but eventually convinced him that the goat had to leave the ballpark. If there was a curse placed, newspapers didn't mention it at the time. However, it was later reported that after the Cubs lost the series, Sianis sent a telegram to Philip Wrigley asking, "Who smells now?"

Sonovia, whom Sianis had rescued after she fell from the back of a truck, supposedly stayed at the tavern until 1963, when it moved to its famous location below Michigan Avenue. At that point, she was sent to a farm in Indiana,

Sianis and Sonovia the Goat share a drink at the Billy Goat Tavern

but came back for regular visits. During one of these visits, it was said, she got excited and ran headlong to her death in the Chicago River.

However, when years went by without another World Series on the North Side, people began to wonder if there had, in fact, been a curse. Sianis certainly claimed that there was, and told reporters that he had no intention of lifting it as long as he was alive, and that his heirs would carry it on. He himself claimed to have lifted the curse, temporarily, in 1969, but the Mets pulled ahead of them and claimed the pennant in one of the greatest come-from-behind stories in sports history. Sianis died the next year. In 1973, Sam Sianis, Billy's nephew, visited Wrigley Field with Socrates, a descendant of Sonovia, and was ejected.

However, as the years dragged by, the Cubs owners tried to make nice with the tavern and began to take steps to have the curse removed. The curse has been "removed" numerous times since then. In 1981, Wrigley Field began inviting Sam Sianis to bring a goat into Wrigley Field. In 1982, he accepted the invitation, and brought the goat to the field, where he was paraded around as the cheering fans chanted "Goat! Goat! Goat!"

But the Cubs losing streak stretched on. Other attempts were made to have the goat walk around the stadium backwards, but all to no avail. Over the years, as the Billy Goat Tavern gradually changed from being an obscure watering hole to a Chicago landmark (with its own sketch on *Saturday Night Live*), the story of the hex grew and grew. The fact that the Cubs continued to blow chances at the pennant year after year didn't help matters.

Perhaps no event brought the curse story more believers than the 2003 playoffs. The Cubs were a win away from their first World Series in over half a century when a fan inadvertently blocked a play on a foul ball, setting off a string of bad luck that led to the Cubs losing. The ball in question was purchased by Harry Carey's restaurant, which blew up the ball in a public ceremony, then mixed the remains in with spaghetti sauce, which was then sold to customers!

2. WEIRD CHICAGO PEOPLE

Satan (impatiently) to Newcomer: The trouble with you Chicago people is, that you think you are the best people down here; whereas you are merely the most numerous.
Mark Twain "Pudd'nhead Wilson's New Calendar," 1897

Here is the difference between Dante, Milton, and me. They wrote about hell and never saw the place. I wrote about Chicago after looking the town over for years and years.
Carl Sandburg

Chicago is a place of unusual people and strange characters. Whether they be colorful characters, local eccentrics, or just plain interesting folks, we wanted to include them in the pages of this book. To define something as "weird" does not necessarily mean that it's strange or bizarre; it is merely different and beyond the norm. "Weird," to our way of thinking, is a compliment and sets these people apart from the crowd. And believe us when we tell you that Chicago has a long history of people who have stood apart from the crowd.

The Chicago characters who follow have done something that makes them different, and that makes them worthy of attention. In many instances, these people may have been better known to local residents than the mayors of the city at the time! We hold these unique individuals (in most cases) in the highest regard and mean no disrespect toward them (unless they've earned it!) We appreciate their presence and the way that they manage to make Chicago a more interesting place.

WEIRD CHICAGO POLITICIANS

"Vote early … and vote often."
Famous Chicago Political Slogan

There is no city in America that has been as maligned as Chicago when it comes to politicians, corruption and questionable voting practices. Even Chicago's most famous nickname of the "Windy City" comes from the hot air that was expelled by the city's politicians, rather than for the speed of the local air currents.

This reputation dates back to the earliest days of the city when blatant voter fraud managed to gain Chicago its charter. It's no wonder that "vote early and vote often" became a phrase to ridicule Chicago voting habits in years to come. Since that time, the city has become known for its backroom politics, "smoke-filled" rooms, backhanded favors and outright bribes. Needless to say, Chicago's politicians have long been colorful characters, starting with those who served as mayor.

The mayors of the city were always men of importance. It's true that the early pioneer mayors are barely remembered today but later on, as the mayors became more entrenched in the city's political system, they became capable of causing riots and firing the entire police force. Some of them were controlled by gamblers, befriended by gangsters, or manipulated behind the scenes by merchants and businessmen. Occasionally, good men would be elected to office and each would try valiantly to clean up the town. They would start reform movements to purge the city of corrupt officials, to close down saloons on Sunday and brothels on weeknights, and to raid all of the gambling dens within spitting distance of City Hall. But in most cases, these good men were not supported by an honest administration and soon, the people of Chicago would be drawn to another man, who spoke louder and made more promises than the rest. For the most part it seems that the best Chicago mayors have been the ones who have more or less let the city run them, rather than to try and run the city. They have been men who have enforced the laws to the point that respectable citizens could walk the streets, but never caused enough trouble to scare off the tourists or irritate the local folks who wanted to drink, gamble or carouse a little.

Some authors have said that Chicago is a religious town but it's not religious in any traditional way. The town has a moral façade that it maintains to disguise its sinful activities. Chicago loves the money that its reputation for being a bloody city that is tied to gangsters and ghosts brings in but the "official" stance on the subject rejects this image. Many of the city's mayors have epitomized this attitude. They made deals with crooks and gangsters, while issuing self-righteous statements about how awful crime was.

WILLIAM OGDEN

William B. Ogden
(Chicago Historical Society)

The first mayor of Chicago was a man named William Ogden, who made an amazing impact on the early city. In addition to being the first mayor, he was also the first president of the Union Pacific Railroad, which brought the line to Chicago. He was also responsible for the first drawbridge across the Chicago River, helped to create the Illinois-Michigan Canal, was the first president of Rush Medical College, and was a heavy investor in local real estate. In addition, Ogden bankrolled International Harvester when he gave Cyrus McCormick $25,000 so that he could build his reaper works in Chicago.

Ogden didn't start out with such grand plans, however. He had to be talked into coming to Chicago at all. Some of his relatives had purchased a large amount of property during one of the city's first real estate booms and Ogden had been sent to the region to inspect it. He looked out over the muddy wasteland and wrote to his family that they had "been guilty of the grossest folly."

But he soon changed his mind. Later that summer, Ogden sold a third of the land and gained back the entire initial investment. He began to believe that Chicago had a future and soon his own investments in land and business convinced him of the fact.

He was elected mayor on May 2, 1837, defeating John Kinzie's son for the position. Even then, the local Democratic Party was accused of "large scale election fraud." Ogden weathered problems and scandals during his time, including a period when the state of Illinois went bankrupt. Ogden refused to allow the fledgling city to ignore its debts and arranged for special script to be issued that would get Chicago through this rough series of years.

Later, Ogden and his friend, Walter L. Newberry, were instrumental in the building of Holy Name Cathedral, the city's most illustrious church. But the two men did not do so for religious reasons. They actually donated the block where the church stands in exchange for the Catholic vote for a new bridge over the Chicago River. The bridge was needed so that land owned by Newberry and Ogden could be developed and sold.

THE MAYOR WHO WAS ALMOST CHARGED WITH TREASON

Only one former Chicago mayor was ever arrested for treason, although more of them perhaps deserved to be. His name was Buckner Smith Morris and he was the city's second mayor in 1838. He did nothing memorable during the time he held office; his infamy came years later.

During the Civil War, he was a member of the Sons of Liberty, a group that was loyal to the Confederacy. In 1864, he was arrested on suspicion of treason during an escape scare connected to Camp Douglas, the prison camp on the city's south side. It was widely rumored that the southern sympathizers were going to free and arm the thousands of prisoners in the camp in hopes that they would sack the city and create a second front during the war.

Morris was arrested mainly because his wife often supplied clothing to the prisoners. He had nothing else to do with the camp and, in fact, knew very little about her charitable activities. Morris was taken to Cincinnati, where he was tried by court-martial, and acquitted. To add insult to injury, his wife later left him.

THE MAYOR WHO CAUSED A RIOT OVER BEER

Dr. Levi Day Boone

In the early 1850s, a wave of sentiment that claimed to be patriotic swept the country and out of this came the "Know Nothing" political party. Its slogan was: "Put none but Americans on guard," meaning that only native-born Americans could serve on the police force and in politics. Dr. Levi Day Boone, grandnephew of famous Indian fighter Daniel Boone, was the head of the Know Nothing party in Chicago and somehow managed to get himself elected mayor, despite the fact that the city was made up of mostly Irish and German immigrants.

He implemented his new political policy and demanded that all applicants for city employment, especially those on the new police force, be able to prove that they were born on American soil. Many in Chicago were angry with this, but not as angry as they were about the enforcement of the old (but seldom used) law that forced saloons to be closed on Sunday. This might have still been acceptable except for Boone's peculiar manner of enforcing it. Only beer halls, which were mainly located on the north side with its German population, would be closed. Saloons that sold whiskey, on the south side, could remain open. Boone also recommended that annual licensing fees for beer halls be raised from $50 to $300.

The owners of the German beer halls and beer gardens refused to close and they refused to pay the higher fee. More than 200 people were arrested over this and put on trial. The hearing was scheduled for April 21, 1855 but on that morning, a mob of over 400 Germans marched on the courthouse. Their representatives entered the courtroom and announced to Judge Henry C. Rucker that if any of the defendants were found guilty, a riot would commence. The mob then left the courthouse and stopped all traffic on Randolph and Clark streets until a legion of police officers could be summoned. The officers, led by Captain of Police Luther Nichols, charged into the mob with clubs, causing the Germans to break ranks and run. Shots were fired, but no one was injured.

Meanwhile, the mob retreated to the north side to make new plans. They returned to the area around the courthouse that afternoon with over 1,000 men, who had armed themselves with shotguns, rifles, pistols, clubs, butcher knives, and hammers. Mayor Boone countered this by bringing every police officer in town to the area, plus about 150 deputies. He even ordered that cannons be brought to the courthouse.

The rioters marched on the Clark Street Bridge and as they approached it, the mayor ordered that the bridge be opened so that the group would be unable to cross. The mob shouted and yelled until (for some inexplicable reason) the bridge was put back into place. They swarmed across the river and collided with the police officers on the other side. Shots were fired and knives flashed --- and all for the right to drink beer on Sunday! The pitched battle lasted for almost an hour and a number of injuries were later reported, along with a single death. One of the Germans, Peter Martin, fired off a shotgun and Patrolman George Hunt lost his arm from the blast. Martin was then killed where he stood. Rumor persisted for some time that more than one man was killed, but this was never confirmed, as the Germans were close-mouthed about their injuries and fatalities. Hunt was later arrested for the murder, but was released and given a $3,000 reward by the city council.

Mayor Long John

In the end, 60 people were arrested for their part in the Lager Beer Riots but only 14 were tried and only two were found guilty of anything. They were later granted new trials but nothing ever came of it.

Eventually, the story faded away into memory -- just as the Know Nothing party did. Boone lost his bid for re-election and two months after the riot, the voters soundly defeated a prohibition law in Chicago.

"LONG JOHN" WENTWORTH

Long John Wentworth was undoubtedly the most colorful of all of Chicago's mayors. During his tenure in office, he fired the entire city police force, personally caught and arrested gamblers, tore down advertising signs that personally offended him, and illegally leveled an entire neighborhood. He definitely made an impression on the city of Chicago and if that impression had been any greater, the city might not have survived his term in office!

Wentworth was 21 when he arrived barefoot in Chicago. It was October 1836 and the young man had almost nothing to his name. Somehow, though, within four weeks, he was the owner of the local newspaper and by age 28, was in Congress. He soon was offered his first bribe -- by the people of Wisconsin. They badly wanted to become a state, but needed the population of Chicago to do so. They told Wentworth that if he would vote to have the boundaries of Wisconsin redrawn down to the southern tip of Lake Michigan, swallowing up Chicago, they would make him their first senator. Wentworth refused, having no interest in becoming a citizen of Wisconsin.

"Long John" certainly earned his nickname. He stood six feet, six inches tall and weighed over 300 pounds. He would usually order as many as 30 courses for a single dinner and would insist that everything be placed on the table before him when he was ready to eat, from soup to dessert. He always sat alone at a table that had been made for four or five diners and would spin the table around so that whatever dish he wanted to eat from next was always within reach.

He became mayor of Chicago in March 1857, taking office after a violent campaign that saw one man killed and several others wounded near polling places. Early in his administration, he decided that he didn't like low advertising signs since he constantly bumped his head on them. He decided that they should be removed. On June 18, 1857, he gathered all of the police officers and express drivers in the city and prepared them for their mission by personally pouring them all shots of bourbon. He then ordered them to remove "every swinging sign, awning post or box found protruding two feet or more beyond the front of buildings." All of the signs were thrown into a large pile on State Street and their owners were allowed to retrieve them if they wished -- and to hang them somewhere else.

This would not be the only time that Wentworth would create his own laws and it was certainly not the last time that he personally enforced them. One night, Wentworth went along with police officers on a raid of Burrough's Place, a notorious gambling den. When the police arrived, the owners sounded an alarm and the fleeing customers ran out the front door and into the clutches of the city's enormous mayor! Wentworth personally supervised the booking of 18 of the prisoners who were captured that night. Later, the establishment's lawyer, a man named Charlie Cameron, appeared at the jail and demanded to speak to his clients. His request was denied, so he crept around to the back of the building and whispered a conversation through the barred window. Enraged, Wentworth grabbed the attorney and locked him up, too. Police returned to the gambling parlor and stripped the place and Burrough's never re-opened.

That same year, Wentworth's plans to clean up the city went beyond just closing a gambling den and he decided to level an entire neighborhood. For years, an area known as the Sands had been a blight on downtown Chicago. This vice district was located along a stretch of lake that was just north of the Chicago River, and had originally been the site of a few lodging houses and some saloons. Gradually, it enlarged to between 20 and 30 ramshackle buildings where gambling parlors, saloons and brothels could be found. The Chicago Tribune called it "decidedly the vilest and most dangerous place in Chicago." Little could be done about this area because the ownership of the property was tied up in court battles -- or at least that was the case until Long John Wentworth decided to get involved in the matter.

Wentworth led a procession of about 30 policemen, and hundreds of well-meaning citizens, across the Clark Street Bridge one afternoon. They managed to tear down nine building with hooks and chains that afternoon and by the time that darkness was starting to fall, they had burned the rest of the district to the ground. Unfortunately, the plan to clean up vice in Chicago backfired. Once the Sands was destroyed, the gamblers, criminals and whores simply spread out all through the city.

Concerned about gambling and vice or not, this event angered many Chicagoans and they began to question Wentworth's authority, especially when it concerned the police force. The mayor was so busy making arrests, writing laws and designing uniforms and badges that many had to wonder how he was managing to run the city. Wentworth had overstepped his bounds, many believed, and so local citizens convinced the state legislature to create a board of three police commissioners to take control of the Chicago police force out of the mayor's hands.

Undaunted, Wentworth decided to fire the entire police force in protest. On March 26, 1861, the force was assembled in the courthouse and Wentworth discharged them from duty, leaving the streets unprotected and the stations empty and abandoned. Of course, it was all done for effect. Wentworth had left custodians in all of the police stations and had told the men to be ready to be called to action if the town bells were sounded. Symbolically, though, Chicago had been turned over to the criminals!

How long the city was actually unprotected is open to debate. Some say that it was for as short a time as 12 hours, while others say that 36 hours passed before the police board began to re-hire the officers. There are those who say that the old police force was so inept though that no one ever knew the difference!

One of the most famous statements that Wentworth ever made during his tenure occurred during Chicago's first royal visit. The distinguished guest was the Prince of Wales, who later became King Edward VII. When he came to Chicago in 1860, Wentworth introduced the royal guest from a hotel balcony to a crowd that was gathered on the street. He slapped the Prince on the back and said, "Boys, this is the Prince of Wales. He's come to see the city and I'm going to show him around. Prince, these are the boys!"

But Wentworth's ego knew no bounds, even when it came to the heir to the throne. When he was asked how he felt sitting next to the future king of England, he corrected the questioner by saying "I was not sitting beside the prince. He sat beside me." An author once submitted a new history of Chicago to him for his approval and Wentworth scratched out all of the entries in the book that did not pertain to him and handed it back. "There is a correct history of the city," he reportedly said.

Wentworth was even filled with himself when it came to his death. Before he died, he bought a huge burial plot at Rosehill Cemetery that took up nearly two-thirds of an acre. He died on October 16, 1888 and was buried beneath a 70-foot monument of his own design. It remains the largest in the cemetery and for years, had no inscription on it. When he was asked about this peculiarity, he replied that if nothing was placed on the stone, people would ask whose monument it was and when told, they would "ransack the libraries to find out who John Wentworth was." But few libraries were actually "ransacked" and so his name and list of accomplishments was eventually added to the stone. Cemetery inscription, or not, "Long John" Wentworth will always be remembered in Chicago.

THE TWO CARTER HARRISONS

Carter Harrison and his son, Carter Harrison II

Aside from the Daleys, there have been two other mayors in Chicago history that have had the same name. The two men, both named Carter Harrison, were father and son and between them, they held office for more than two decades. The elder Harrison was elected first in 1879 and the last time in 1893, just in time to preside over the city during the Columbian Exposition. It was believed that Harrison was elected for one final term, just in time for the fair, thanks to the criminal element in the city, which bribed him to allow gambling and prostitution to continue unmolested during the exposition. He may have done so to the city's benefit, however. The story persists that he made a deal with Mike McDonald, a long-time leader in the vice community, that agreed that no one's pocket would be picked at the entrance to the fair. The agreement specified that any pickpocket who was arrested at the gates would have to either return the money to their victim or would have to pay a fine of $10. In exchange, any pickpocket arrested in the city's central area during daylight hours would be immediately released from the Central Station House.

The fair was considered to be a great success, by all accounts, and marked the crowning achievement of the elder Carter Harrison's career. Unfortunately, though, he met with a tragic and premature end. He was at home one day during the waning days of the fair and, because he had no bodyguards of any sort, a man named Patrick Eugene Joseph Prendergast was able to walk into the house. Before visiting Harrison, Prendergast had visited Adolph Kraus, the Corporation Counsel for the city. Kraus had already received several threatening postcards from Prendergast, who wrote in red ink, "I want your job." "Do not be a fool. Resign." and "Third and final notice. You either resign or I will remove you."

When Prendergast arrived at his home, Kraus immediately humored him by telling him that the job was now his. Unsure of what to do, Prendergast became flustered and insisted that he did not want the job that day. Confused, he wandered out of the house. Obviously unbalanced, Prendergast fancied himself a religious man and a politician but a more apt description would have been "fanatic." He believed that it was his divine duty to force the elevation of streetcar tracks in the city. When he arrived at Harrison's home, he walked in and fired three bullets into the mayor's chest. Hearing the shots, Preston and Sophie Harrison ran to their father's side, while the mayor's valet, William Chalmers, rushed in pursuit of the killer.

Prendergast, firing over his shoulder, ran down the street and vanished. He paused long enough to put away his gun and to climb into a streetcar, which he rode until reaching Des Plaines Avenue. Less than 15 minutes after Harrison had been shot, Prendergast strolled into a police station, handed his weapon to the desk sergeant and surrendered. At almost the same moment, Carter Harrison died.

Prendergast was put through two exhausting trials with his sanity being called into question by his attorneys and by Clarence Darrow, who spoke for two hours at the man's sentencing hearing, begging for the killer's life. However, the assassin remained unrepentant and flippant throughout the trials, even while his lawyers were testing the insanity defense for the first time in Illinois criminal history. The jury was unconvinced that he was insane and Prendergast was sent to the gallows on July 13, 1894. He made the sign of the cross just before the trapdoor sprung open and ended his life.

By most of the accounts, the second Carter Harrison was not as easily swayed by the questionable elements of the city as his father was. During his first mayoral campaign in 1897, he was pictured with both of his hands in his pockets, leading citizens to laugh that they might actually get a mayor who could keep his hands in his own pockets for a change.

But Harrison never had a chance when it came to really cleaning up the city, and he was not adverse to admitting it. When he took office, he described the city council as being a " 'motley crew' of saloon keepers, proprietors of gambling houses and undertakers." He accused them of having no outstanding characteristics except for an "unquenchable lust for money." Those interesting characters included "Hot Stove" Jimmy Quinn, who claimed that his cronies would steal anything they could get their hands on; Johnny Powers, who bought the votes of fellow councilmen for about $10 each; "Umbrella Mike" Boyle, who collected bribes in an umbrella; and Mike McInerney, who once said that the smoke from the stockyards was good for babies.

And these were the men running the city! It is any wonder that Harrison later suggested that good citizens might want to "carry revolvers strapped outside of their clothing" for protection?

Even so, Harrison did manage to clean things up as well as could be expected. By the last year of his final administration, in 1915, Chicago was as empty of vice as it ever had been. His administration had been free from official corruption and none of his friends had gotten rich from bribes or at the expense of the public. But this state of affairs would not continue in city government for long.

THE BAR BRAWLING MAYOR

Chicago Mayor Fred "Go to Hell" Busse

Between the second Carter Harrison's first terms, and what was perhaps the most corrupt administration in Chicago history, there was really only one mayor of note, Fred A. Busse, a bar brawler, drunk, and personal friend of a well-known Chicago gangster. He was a man of few words and never took criticism with style. Once when questioned by a reporter about his close ties to business in the city, he simply smirked and snapped, "Go to Hell."

Busse did achieve some worthwhile accomplishments during his term as mayor, although suspending the closing time of his favorite saloon and raiding the Illinois Athletic Club after he was insulted during a card game there were not among them. He also took some criticism for his relationship with gangster Christian "Barney" Bertsche, who killed a detective and two police officers shortly after Busse took office in 1907. Aside from all of this, Busse did help to create the Chicago Plan Commission, which eventually saved the lakefront for the people and reluctantly supported the massive 1911 Vice Commission Report. Ironically, that report was considered "pornographic" at the time and was banned by the U.S. Postal Service. Busse also ended the infamous First Ward Ball, a genuine annual orgy that involved many Chicago politicians.

He was considered a "reform mayor" during his time, but most recalled him as a crude, overweight ice and coal merchant who had little time for anyone. He never even bothered to make speeches during his campaign and yet somehow managed to get elected. No real scandals rocked his term in office, but it should be noted that when Busse died, his safe-deposit box was opened to reveal a huge block of stock that indicated his ownership in the company that sold all of the manhole covers to the city! Any question as to how they managed to get that particular contract?

AL CAPONE'S FAVORITE MAYOR

William Hale "Big Bill" Thompson served as the mayor of Chicago during what was likely the city's most corrupt and violent period. When he finally left office after three terms, the *Chicago Tribune* wrote that Thompson's rule had meant "filth, corruption, obscenity, idiocy and bankruptcy" for Chicago. They added that he had "given the city an international reputation for moronic buffoonery, barbaric crime, triumphant hoodlumism, unchecked graft, and dejected citizenship. He nearly ruined the property and completely destroyed the pride of the city."

In Thompson's defense, he served as mayor through the most difficult era in Chicago history. In those days, Chicago seemed to be filled with gangsters - gangsters who slaughtered one another (214 dead in four years); gangsters killed by the police (160 during the same period); gangsters shooting up buildings, throwing bombs, and speeding in big automobiles; gangsters bribing city officials, ward bosses and aldermen; gangsters dining in expensive restaurants and attending plays, operas and baseball games; gangsters with shotguns, rifles and machine guns, convoying beer trucks; pretty much gangsters everywhere -- except in jail!

"That's all newspaper talk," scoffed Mayor Big Bill Thompson. Although, just for the record, according to the Illinois Crime Survey, Al Capone was one of the largest contributors to Thompson's mayoral campaign and at his headquarters in the Lexington Hotel, Capone sat under framed portraits of George Washington, Abraham Lincoln --- and Big Bill Thompson.

But how corrupt was Thompson? Did he purposely allow the criminal element of Chicago to run unchecked during his terms of office? Or was

"Big Bill" Thompson, one of Chicago's illustrious mayors. One of his friends once said : "The worst thing that you can say about him is that he's stupid."

he just so inept that he had no idea of the lawlessness around him. Who can say? But we should note that when he first started his political career, one of his supporters stated, "The worst thing that you can say about him is that he's stupid."

Thompson's early life was spent avoiding education. He went out west as a young man to become a cowboy, but returned to Chicago after the death of his father. He later achieved a small amount of fame as captain of the Chicago Athletic Club's water-polo team, which was his only qualification for office when he ran for the first time. He first ran for alderman in 1900 after making a $50 poker bet with friends who said that he was too afraid to run. His speeches were dull, his delivery was listless and he had little idea what he was talking about. In fact, he was so clueless that when it was time for him to smile or laugh, a friend would let a brick fall to the floor as a signal.

Thompson ran for mayor with the naiveté of a champion athlete on the side of truth, justice and the American way. He actually vowed in this first campaign that "I am going to clean up Chicago" but by this third campaign, his picture was hanging in Capone's office and the gangster was donating as much as $260,000 for Thompson's re-election. After winning that first election, Chicago became a wide-open town once again as far as vice and crime were concerned.

But Thompson's ability to win elections did not always come from Chicago's criminals. In 1915, he was largely elected due to his pro-German stance. In fact, he was often nicknamed "Kaiser Bill." A short time later, his stance caused a great amount of controversy when he refused to invite Marshall Joffre, hero of the Marne, and Rene Vivani, the French Minster of Justice, to Chicago as part of their national tour to drum up American support for their side in the Great War. Thompson noted that Chicago was the "sixth largest German city in the world" and added that he didn't think many of the residents would be interested in having the Frenchmen here. Joffre and Vivani were finally given the invitation, but not before Theodore Roosevelt was heard to say, "We'll hang old Thompson from a sour apple tree."

Even after the visit, though, Thompson continued to oppose the United States getting involved in the war. A bishop from Texas was quoted as saying, "I think that Mayor Thompson is guilty of treason and ought to be shot... what this country needs is a few first class hangings, then we could go one with our work without fear of being stabbed in the back."

Scandals continued to plague Thompson throughout his first two terms as mayor. He employed a henchman of Al Capone as city sealer, the person in charge of honest weights and measures, and a local court once ruled that Thompson and his associates owed the city over $2 million, an amount they had allegedly plundered. He almost had a nervous breakdown over this decision until it was thrown out on appeal.

After his first two terms (he was elected in 1915, 1919 and 1927), there were so many scandals, indictments of his friends, and signs of obvious corruption that Thompson believed that he would never be able to run again. He decided to leave town and look for headlines instead. He found them by organizing an expedition to the South Seas in search of the legendary "tree-climbing fish." Thompson set sail on a ship called the *Big Bill*, with a crew that included a theater owner who wore nothing but a jockstrap on most days. The expedition ended before the ship ever left the Mississippi River.

Fred Lundin turned on Thompson after running his campaigns for years.

Thompson decided to run again in 1927 and it was this final campaign and term in office that marked him as the most irresponsible, dangerous and corrupt mayor that ever presided over Chicago politics. The 1927 campaign was so out of control that it was only surpassed by Thompson's losing 1931 primary effort.

Thompson was so immersed in the corruption that had plagued his former terms in office by this time that he was oblivious to what was going on around him. He had lost his mentor, Fred "Poor Swede" Lundin, who ran his campaigns and bossed his patronage throughout most of his career, and had also lost Dr. John Dill Robertson, a longtime supporter. The two men began backing Thompson's rival in the Republican primary, Edward R. Litsinger, and Thompson was not above "slinging mud" in every direction. At one point, he appeared at a theater for a campaign rally and was accompanied by two caged rats that he called "Fred" and "Doc." He also noted that Litsinger "lived back of the gashouse, and when he moved to the North Side, he left his old mother behind." His opponent seemed nonplussed by his comments and simply said that Thompson had "the carcass of a rhinoceros and the brains of a baboon."

During that same campaign, Thompson also spent a lot of time maligning the King of England, who was definitely not interested in being the mayor of Chicago. He even boasted that he would punch the monarch in the nose if he ever dared set foot in Chicago. No one seems to know where this bizarre obsession with England came from, but even after he was elected, he spent a lot of time trying to get allegedly pro-British history books banned from the Chicago Public Library. A henchman named Urbine J. "Sport" Herrmann even threatened to burn all of the offensive books at the lakefront until a court order stopped him. It wouldn't have been much of a fire anyway since Thompson only found four offending volumes in the library's collection and one of them was dedicated to George Washington.

Thompson's election night victory celebration was as big a farce as his campaign had been. He and his cronies ended the night aboard his Fish Fan Club ship, drinking illegal hooch. The 1,500 followers who came so overloaded the boat that the ship actually sank in six feet of water. This was perhaps a precursor of things to come, for Thompson nearly sank the city during his terms in office and he assuredly sank his own career.

All of his terms were marked with criminal activity, especially during election time. The most stunning events occurred during the so-called "Pineapple Primary" in 1928, when "pineapples" (hand grenades) were used to convince voters of which way to cast their ballots. A series of bombings occurred in Chicago when Senator Charles S. Deneen's faction of the Republican Party opposed the faction headed by Thompson and State's Attorney Robert E. Crowe. Thompson's political machine was so powerful by this time that they controlled practically all of the jobs and patronage in the city, county and, in association with Governor Len Small, the state of Illinois, as well.

Senator Charles S. Deneen, who opposed Thompson in the so-called "Pineapple Primary"

Several bombs were exploded during the early days of the campaign, mostly directed against supporters of Thompson and Crowe. On March 21, 1928, assassins killed "Diamond Joe" Esposito, a racketeer who was behind the Genna gang of bootleggers. Esposito was also a close friend of Senator Deneen and one of his most influential supporters. On the morning of his

(Right) Big Bill & his wife, Maysie. After Thompson's death, his widow would have to right it out with his long-time mistress for control of his estate.

funeral, bombs were also set off at the homes of Senator Deneen and Judge John A. Swanson, Deneen's candidate for State's Attorney.

The bombings prompted Crowe to make a huge blunder. He issued a statement saying that he was "satisfied that the bombings were done by the leaders in the Deneen forces... and were done mainly to discredit Mayor Thompson and myself." The mayor made a similar statement a short time later, but the reaction against Crowe was tremendous. Newspapers, which had been supporting him, now turned against him, saying that, "the callous, cynical note in this led to public exasperation." Meetings were held to denounce his candidacy and the Chicago Crime Commission, which had been friendly to him, now released a letter recommending his defeat. The Deneen faction managed to carry the election and this began to spell the beginning of the end of the rampant days of crime in Chicago.

In 1931, Thompson tried to maintain his hold on the office but failed. He lost to Anton J. Cermak, his Democratic rival. This ended his political career, but it did not end the rumors and scandals that would plague him -- even after his death. Thompson passed away on March 19, 1944 and it was thought that his estate amounted to about $150,000, which would have indicated that, despite the rumors, his claims of being honest were true and that it had been the newspapers creating scandalous tales about him all along. However, when his safe-deposit boxes were opened, cash literally came tumbling out. One box held $1,466,250 in cash, plus stocks, bonds and gold certificates. Another had $112,000 in stocks and bonds and two other boxes contained nearly $250,000 in stocks and cash made up of $50 and $100 bills. In the end, his estate totaled well over $2 million. No one had any idea how the money had gotten there -- but there were plenty of theories, which have continued to this day.

To make matters worse, his death also sparked a battle between his mistress of a dozen years, Ethabelle Green, who settled for $250,000 and his wife, Maysie, who got most of the estate. By the time that she paid off all of her attorney bills, she managed to end up with just $100,000.

The *Daily News* sounded the last note on Thompson in that he "was not a great man, he was highly successful in his field. He was not a statesman; he was a consummate politician. His success was based on deception and distraction. He was the most amazingly unbelievable man in Chicago's history."

"JUST LIKE CHICAGO, EH MAYOR?"

Anton J. Cermak

On February 15, 1932, Chicago Mayor Anton J. Cermak was shot in Bayfront Park in Miami. Cermak was on the reviewing stand and, after President-elect Franklin Roosevelt made a short speech in an open car, he waved over Cermak to join him. As Roosevelt's car was about to start, shots rang out and Cermak and four others were hit. They were shot by a man named Giuseppe Zangara, whose intention had been to kill the president.

Those are the general facts of the event that ended the life and career of Anton Cermak, but many mysteries about the event still remain, including whether or not Cermak's murder was ordered by none other than Al Capone. On December 19, 1932, two police officers invaded the headquarters of Frank Nitti, Capone's "enforcer" and the man who became the public face of the Outfit after Capone was sent to prison for tax evasion. Rumor had it that the police were operating under orders from new mayor Cermak, who was determined to assist Ted Newberry (who had taken over the O'Banion and Moran mob) redistribute the territories of the Capone gang. Shots were fired and Nitti was badly wounded. He lingered near death for a time, but recovered only to end up standing trial for the shooting of one of the cops during the gun battle. The jury was convinced that the officer had actually shot himself in the finger in order to look like a hero and the trial ended in a hung jury. Nitti walked away a free man and the officer lost his job.

This was not the end of story, though. Rumors lingered for a time that Al Capone himself reached out from the walls of the penitentiary to get revenge on Cermak a few months later.

Anton Cermak was a dynamic, albeit somewhat typical, Chicago mayor of days gone by. He was the city's first foreign-born mayor, emigrating from Prague to work in the Illinois coalmines. He started a real estate company and for years spoke out against banning alcohol. He also organized the "wet vote," which would help to defeat Prohibition and it won him the appreciation of Franklin Roosevelt, whom Cermak was accompanying when the mayor was assassinated.

When Zangara shot Cermak in Miami, the mayor was rushed to the hospital but died a short time later. As he was taken away by ambulance, Cermak was supposed to have said to the president, "I am glad that it was me instead of you." They became the most famous words that Cermak ever uttered -- or they would have been, if he had really actually said them. A reporter who was there that day, Ed Gilbreth, stated that the phrase was created by the Chicago Herald-American to make a good headline and sell some papers. Cermak never said anything before he died.

Although some words uttered by another reporter who was standing nearby might have provided more of a clue in the shooting than officials would admit. Just as the shots rang out, a reporter who was nearby allegedly joked to Cermak, "Just like Chicago, eh Mayor?"

Cermak's life and career ended on this bitter note, but his achievements, after he took control of both the Democratic Party and the Mayor's office, including nominating and electing Henry Horner, Illinois' first Jewish governor, and cutting into the control the Irish had over Chicago politics - but only for a time. After his death, men of Irish descent occupied the Mayor's office for the next four decades.

In addition to helping to end Prohibition, Cermak also helped to create the modern Democratic Party in Chicago, something he is rarely given credit for. He also brought together various ethnic groups in ways that had never been done before and made sure that he didn't inconvenience the local gangsters. He sought power and got it through his vast knowledge of the city's political machine, then lost it to a bullet.

YOU DON'T HAVE TO BE A MAYOR TO RUN CHICAGO: MORE POLITICAL HI-JINKS IN THE WINDY CITY

The story goes that a Chicago politician was once asked if there was ever a good, hard-working, honest alderman on the City Council. According to the story, he admitted there had once been, but they had given him a lesser job and made him a U.S. Senator.

The person who had asked the question was dumbfounded. A U.S. Senator was less powerful than being a Chicago alderman?

The politician shrugged. "Sure," he allegedly replied. "How many jobs does a Senator control compared to an alderman?"

It's a simple fact that he who controls the jobs has the loyalty of the voters when Election Day comes around. This has been proven time and time again in Chicago history and the pages that follow will show that you don't have to be the Mayor to have good stories told about you in Chicago. In fact, it's usually more than enough to be just a little strange, or a little crooked, and to have just enough power to be remembered in the years to come.

ABRAHAM LINCOLN & CHICAGO'S "SMOKE-FILLED" ROOM

Probably the most shocking political event to occur in Chicago in the middle 1800s was on May 18, 1860, when Abraham Lincoln was nominated for the Presidency of the United States in a two-story wooden hall called the Wigwam.

It was a carefully engineered event (Chicago to the core!) and one that almost never occurred. To this day, there are still many who are pondering the mystery of how a minor contender in the presidential race managed to achieve a sweeping victory with the third nomination ballot. They key to solving the mystery is Chicago itself. Lincoln's supporters, who had fashioned the man with the image of the backwoods rail-splitter, were thrilled that the event was held in the city. Lincoln was an Illinois man and had many friends, along with newspaper support, on the prairie.

The Republicans were holding what was only their second national convention and for the first time, had a chance to usher one of their candidates into power. The dominant Democratic Party was split over the issue of extending slavery into the territories and their divided vote gave the Republicans hope. Coming into Chicago, the favorite to win the nomination was New York senator William H. Seward and his supporters and delegates were so assured of his victory that they focused more on his choice of running mate than on his actual nomination.

The convention opened on the morning of Wednesday, May 16 with over 10,000 people packed into the Wigwam, while an additional 20,000 stood outside. Four years earlier, in Philadelphia, the Republicans had drawn no more than 4,000 people to their convention. The meeting was called to order and was followed by a stirring address from David Wilmot of Pennsylvania. After that, the remainder of the day was spent electing a chairman and constructing a platform. The platform was adopted and modified on Thursday, with the first ballot scheduled for later that evening. Many expected Seward to be chosen by a landslide, so a chorus of groans greeted Chairman George Ashmun when he announced that the printers had failed to deliver the tally sheets. Since no vote could be taken, a motion was adopted to adjourn until Friday.

Abraham Lincoln was not a well-known candidate in 1860, but in Chicago -- he managed to be nominated for president.

(Left to Right): Ward Hill Lamon & William Herndon, two of Lincoln's friends and supporters who masterminded his nomination -- by all means necessary -- in Chicago.

Lincoln's campaign manager, David Davis, was thrilled. He and his compatriots, who included Lincoln's long-time friends Ward Hill Lamon, William H. Herndon, and Stephen T. Logan, saw the delay as a sign from God. Led by Lamon, a number of Lincoln's friends began scrawling the names of convention officers on admission tickets while Norman B. Judd, a railroad attorney, arranged for special trains to bring more Lincoln supporters to the city.

While Lincoln's men worked behind the scenes, Seward's followers publicly declared their man the winner and even put a brass band into the streets on Friday morning. They marched from their hotel to discover that the Wigwam was so crowded that few people other than delegates were able to find seats. The bogus tickets that had been passed out by Lincoln's men had been used in such numbers that the hall was now packed with his supporters.

The first roll call of the states gave Seward 173.5 votes, but 236 were needed to win. Lincoln followed with 102 votes, with Simon Cameron of Pennsylvania, Salmon P. Chase of Ohio and Edward Bates of Missouri each receiving about 50 votes. Recognizing that Pennsylvania would be crucial in winning the nomination, David Davis arranged

The Chicago Wigwam, where Lincoln was nominated to the presidency

WHERE IS IT NOW?
The Republican Wigwam stood around what is now the corner of Wacker and Lake avenues. A small plaque to commemorate it was eventually placed there.

for delegates of that state to be seated between Illinois and Indiana, both of which strongly backed Lincoln. He then convinced the delegates from Pennsylvania that if Seward won the nomination, the party would lose the election. As a result, Cameron withdrew.

When the second ballot was tallied, it offered a stunning surprise, especially to Seward's supporters. Their candidate had only gained 11 votes but Lincoln's total had increased by 79. That left Chase of Ohio in third place with 42.5 votes.

Workers in the Lincoln campaign had been busy contacting delegates from every state, using a deceptively simple strategy. Instead of asking for votes on the first ballot, they persuaded as many men as possible to make Lincoln their second choice. They also stressed the contrast between Lincoln and Seward. Lincoln had been guarded in his campaign so far and had been careful not to offend anyone. Seward, meanwhile, had made his position clear on most national issues. Seward was the only nationally known Republican who had allegedly praised John Brown's recent attack on Harper's Ferry and had hinted at a civil war by warning that an "irrepressible conflict" seemed to be coming because of slavery. Lincoln, on the other hand, was on record as opposing the extension of slavery into the territories, but he also underscored the conviction that slavery where it existed was lawful and that it should not be challenged. He believed that the institution would eventually die out.

It was obvious that there was a sharp contrast between the familiar candidate with controversial views and the little-known rival who was not nearly so eager to enter into war, but the contrast was not enough to allow Lincoln to win on just those merits. Lincoln's managers seemed to be willing to promise almost anything to those who would back him. Legend has it that Lincoln sent a telegram to Davis from Springfield that instructed him to make no bargains. "Make no contracts that bind me," he allegedly wrote and it has been said that Davis used that message to show to those who hesitated in backing Lincoln that the candidate was not offering positions in his administration with a free hand. Legend tells otherwise, though, and stories have since been told that Davis managed to persuade delegates to abandon their favorite candidates with promises of positions in Lincoln's cabinet.

While in Chicago, Abraham Lincoln usually stayed at the Tremont House at Wacker and Lake avenues. He even spoke from the balcony. John Wilkes Booth lived at the same hotel during periods in 1862 when he was performing in Chicago. During two long engagements during the winter and summer of that year, Booth played most of the greatest Shakespeare roles at the nearby McVicker's Theatre. He was the hit of the year and the Chicago Tribune called him a genius. Imagine how strange it must have been in 1865 for people who had been in the audience to think back on Booth's speeches plotting to murder kings and princes as Hamlet, Macbeth and Richard III!

Whatever happened in Chicago's notorious "smoke-filled rooms" remains a mystery. What we do know is that when the third ballot was taken, Seward had lost 4.5 votes and now needed 56 to win. Lincoln however had gained 53.5 votes and was within 1.5 votes of the nomination. The interior of the Wigwam became nearly deafening with the mingled shouts, cries and laughter of the assembled party. And as soon as he could be heard above the commotion, David K. Carter of Ohio jumped up and shouted that five of the delegates from the Buckeye State wanted to switch their votes over to Lincoln. When the commotion subsided again, other states began to call for Lincoln as their new nomination. After all of the 466 votes had been cast, Lincoln had 364 of them -- 128 more than the number he needed to win.

But how did Lincoln manage to pull of such a sweeping victory? Did his campaign managers really trade positions for votes? No one knows and nothing was ever documented that said for sure either way. Journalist Charles H. Ray, a member of Lincoln's inner circle, later said that the managers promised Indiana and Pennsylvania anything and everything they asked for. Carter of Ohio, who started the dramatic third-ballot uprising, was said to have been promised a high level cabinet position and while other rumors abound, nothing has ever been proven.

One thing is clear, though. Many who stepped aside for Lincoln, or who worked for him behind the scenes, were chosen for important posts. Seward was made secretary of state; Chase received the Treasury Department portfolio; Cameron became secretary of war and the fourth contender for the nomination, Edward Bates, became Lincoln's attorney general. David Davis had hoped to become a federal judge and was appointed to the U.S. Supreme Court in 1862. Ward Hill Lamon, who created all of the bogus tickets, became marshal of the District of Columbia. William P. Dole, who was credited with securing the Indiana and Pennsylvania votes, was named commissioner of Indian Affairs. And the list went on...

Abraham Lincoln is today considered one of the nation's greatest presidents, but his nomination to that office came very close to never taking place. If not for backroom politics, he might not have made it to the White House. In this case, it's a good thing that the convention was held in Chicago - where questionable politics are the accepted method of doing business.

HINKY DINK KENNA & BATHHOUSE JOHN

Michael "Hinky Dink" Kenna and "Bathhouse" John Coughlin (Chicago Historical Society)

Chicago's South Side Levee District took shape during the Columbian Exposition in 1893, when thousands of people from all over the world descended on the city. Many believe that the growth of a vice district on the south side may have been what spurred Potter Palmer to flee the region and to build his castle on North Lake Shore Drive, far from the illicit goings-on. And he was not the only one of the wealthy to flee either. Prairie Avenue soon fell into gradual ruin as the Levee began to grow and prosper in the early 1900s.

Visitors to the district could partake of just about every form of vice imaginable from drink to women and it became a seedbed of crime that would go on to spawn men like Al Capone, Johnny Torrio and the generations that followed them and who became the modern Chicago "Outfit". Three vice rings formed the criminal organization that ruled the Levee and which provided the areas various forms of entertainment. The area was filled with brothels, gambling parlors and saloons of every type. While reformers considered the Levee District a "blight" on the city of Chicago, it brought in millions of dollars every year and was one of the wealthiest "business" districts in the city.

And while criminal elements ran the district, there was no question as to the identity of the real "bosses" of the Levee. Michael "Hinky Dink" Kenna and "Bathhouse" John Coughlin, Chicago politicians, ran the notorious, gangster-infested First Ward for almost four decades, between 1897 and 1938. They made a legendary team, collecting graft and doling out favors in the area to those who paid the most. In 1911, when Mayor Harrison gave the word to Captain Patrick J. Harding to order his divisional inspector John Wheeler to close down the famed Everleigh Club brothel, the inspector did nothing until he received the okay from aldermen Kenna and Coughlin.

Coughlin was known as "Bathhouse" because he had once been a masseur in a Turkish bath. He was a large, poetry-spouting buffoon who was known for being outgoing and good-hearted and a bizarre dresser, sporting garishly colored waistcoats. His poetry often appeared in Chicago newspapers and in his public statements, many mistook him for being simple-minded. Mayor Harrison once asked his partner, Kenna, if Bathhouse was crazy or taken with drugs. Kenna replied that he was neither. "To tell you the God's truth, Mayor, they ain't found a name for it yet."

Kenna was Coughlin's mirror opposite. He was small, glum and quietly dressed and was known for being shrewd and close-mouthed. At Kenna's Workingman's Exchange on Clark Street, patrons were served what was referred to as the "Largest and Coolest Schooner of Beer in the City" and the best free lunch around, too. There were no orchestras here, no women, no music and no selling to minors. Here, for more than 20 years, the bums, the homeless and the jobless of the First Ward ate and drank for a nickel. Kenna also found jobs for the down and out and often rescued them from trouble with the police.

But he also told them how to vote and in more than 40 years, he never lost an election or primary. He and Bathhouse created this astonishing record by marshaling the ward's party workers on Election Day to get votes from railroad hands, tramps, thieves and any other warm bodies that were available. They were taken to a polling place and were given already marked ballots that were deposited in a box. When they returned with the unmarked ballots (taken from the polling place), they could turn them in for a fee of 50 cents or a dollar. Those ballots were then marked and used at another polling place, where the whole scheme was repeated.

The two men made an unlikely pair, but were a highly effective and increasingly wealthy duo. In addition to the other services they offered, such as guaranteed voting in the First Ward, they also provided protection for a variety of illicit enterprises. They exacted regular and weekly tributes that ranged from $25 per week from the small brothels, and as much as $100 from the larger ones. They received an additional fee if drinks were sold or gambling occurred there. They also offered fees for legal work as well, such as stopping indictments for charges of grand larceny, pandering, theft or kidnapping. These fees could range from $500 to $2,000.

They were able to provide such services thanks to the fact that Coughlin and Kenna had men who were beholden to them in every municipal, county, state and federal office in the city. They controlled the jobs of city workers, including inspectors and the police, and were also, as aldermen, in a position to grant favors to respectable businessmen in Chicago. They could usually count on a routine take of between $15,000 and $30,000 per year, over and above the stipend of $3 per council meeting that they received from the city. Special votes that were purchased bought them in anywhere from $8,000 to $100,000 each, depending on the importance of the matter. The two men went carefully about their business filling the requests that the financiers of Chicago were willing to pay for, such as zoning variances, permits, tax deductions, licenses and other amenities.

However, things didn't always go smoothly and the pair did sometimes manage to get attention brought to them, both personally and professionally. For instance, one of Bathhouse's pet projects was the construction of a zoo on land that he owned in Colorado Springs in 1902. The zoo featured a refugee elephant from the Lincoln Park Zoo who had managed to lose part of her trunk in a trap door. Princess Alice, as she was called, was purchased by Coughlin and shipped to Colorado, where she caught a severe cold in the winter of 1906. Coughlin suggested that she be given whiskey, which cured his own ailments, and so keepers gave the elephant an entire quart, which quickly cured her cold. After that, Princess Alice acquired a serious taste for the hard stuff and began searching the zoo, looking for visitors with flasks. She would beg for drinks from them and when whiskey was given to her, she would sip it daintily, then go off somewhere, and pass out.

As mentioned, Bathhouse was also noted for his horrible poetry. Epics that he penned included titles like "She Sleeps by the Drainage Canal," "Ode to a Bathtub," "Why Did They Build the Lovely Lake So Close to the Horrible Shore?" "They're Tearing Up Clark Street Again" and others. It was later revealed, however, that John Kelley, a reporter for the Chicago Tribune, was the actual author of many of Coughlin's poems, which he read regularly at city council meetings. But only Coughlin would have taken credit for a terrible song that he wrote called "Dear Midnight of Love," which was performed for the first and last time at the Auditorium Theater in October 1899.

Bad poetry aside, though, it was not weak prose that brought Coughlin and Kenna to the attention of the public and to every reform organization in Chicago from 1897 onward. It was constantly, and justifiably, assumed that the two of them were corrupt, although nothing was ever proven against them. Their most famous exploit was an annual party and it was such an outstanding example of public debauchery that it was eventually shut down.

The First Ward Ball, which they organized, was referred to as an "annual underworld orgy." It was required that every prostitute, pimp, pickpocket and thief buy at least one ticket, while the owners of brothels and saloons had to purchase large blocks of them. The madams usually had their own boxes, where they could rub shoulders with city officials and politicians. The ball continued a tradition that started around 1880, when there was a charity party to honor Lame Jimmy, a pianist who worked for the renowned madam, Carrie Watson. These parties continued on until 1895, when a drunken detective shot another police officer at the gathering.

After the end of the charity soirees, Coughlin and Kenna took responsibility for throwing the annual affair. It grew larger every year until the two aldermen were making as much as $50,000 from it. They held the ball at the Chicago Coliseum and after one spectacle, the Tribune wrote that, "If a great disaster had befallen the Coliseum last night, there would not have been a second story worker, a dip or pug ugly, porch climber, dope fiend or scarlet woman remaining in Chicago."

The Chicago Coliseum -- Home to the annual First Ward Ball (Chicago Historical Society)

The 1907 First Ward Ball was perhaps the most widely reported and, for this reason, seemed to raise the most ire among the various reform movements in the city. When the ball opened that year, there were 15,000 people jammed into the Coliseum. One newspaper reported that there were so many drunks inside that when one would pass out, they could not even fall to the floor. Women who fainted from the closeness of the Coliseum were passed over the heads of the crowd to the exits.

As the event opened, a procession of Levee prostitutes marched into the building, led by Bathhouse John, with a lavender cravat and a red sash across his chest. Authors Lloyd Wendt and Herman Kogan described the parade: "On they came, madams, strumpets, airily clad jockeys, harlequins, Dianas, page boys, female impersonators, tramps, panhandlers, card sharps, mountebanks, pimps, owners of dives and resorts, young bloods and 'older men careless of their reputations'..."

At this point, the party really got started as women draped themselves over railings and ordered men to pour champagne down their throats. "The girls in peek-a-boo waists, slit skirts, bathing suits and jockey costumes relaxed and tripped to the floor where they danced wildly and drunkenly ... drunken men sought to undress young women and met with few objections." A further description of the ball was the first mention of Chicago's "drag queens" of the era and reformers later described the antics of these men in women's costumes as "unbelievably appalling and nauseating."

Even though there had been 100 policemen detailed to the party, there were only eight arrests and one conviction -- that of Bernard Dooley, who was fined for entering the party without paying. Hinky Dink Kenna later called the party a "lollapalooza" and added that "Chicago ain't no sissy town!"

Reform elements had attempted every year to prevent the ball from taking place, but had never succeeded. After the 1907 affair, though, they were even more determined. In 1908, the rector, warden and vestry of the Grace Episcopal Church asked the Superior Court for an injunction against the event, but the court simply stated that the affair was not within its jurisdiction. On December 13, just two days before the ball was to be held, a bomb exploded in the Coliseum, wrecking a two-story building that was used as a warehouse and breaking windows as far as two blocks away. The police who investigated said that it had been the work of "fanatical reformers" and the ball was given as scheduled. In fact, Bathhouse John told reporters that it was the "nicest Derby we ever had."

Reverend Melbourne P. Boynton of the Lexington Avenue Baptist Church, who apparently attended, said that it was "unspeakably low, vulgar and immoral." Public opinion sided with the minister and the 1908 First Ward Ball was the last. When Coughlin announced plans for the event in 1909, such a storm of opposition arose that Mayor Fred Busse refused to issue a liquor license. On December 13, Coughlin and Kenna gave a concert in the Coliseum, but less than 3,000 people attended and police were on hand to make sure that no liquor was served and that no one got out of hand. It was the dullest affair that the Levee had ever seen and there has been no attempt to hold the First Ward Ball since.

The end came for Chicago's two most colorful aldermen not with a bang, but with a sad whimper. Bathhouse John Coughlin died on November 8, 1938, an old and fading politician and a veteran of 46 years on the city council. After all of the money that had had made over the years, he died more than $50,000 in debt, thanks to

> Harry "Prince Hal" Varnell became warden of the Cook County Insane Asylum in 1880 and made it the place to visit, spending thousands of dollars on lavish renovations, throwing parties and even opening suites of rooms for local politicians who needed a place to live. He served one year in the Joliet Penitentiary for misuse of public funds. Although much has been written of what Varnell did as the warden of the asylum, there is no record as to what became of the inmates --- or if they could be distinguished from the visiting politicians.

gambling losses.

Hinky Dink took care of his old friend's funeral arrangements, but there were few people around to do the same thing for Kenna when he passed on in 1946. After more than 50 years as boss of the First Ward, there were only three cars with flowers at the graveside and the mayor didn't even attend. Unlike Coughlin, though, Hinky Dink died a millionaire, leaving behind piles of cash (mostly in $1,000 bills), two pints of vintage 1917 bourbon, 11 suits of woolen long underwear and a 1930 Pierce Arrow Limousine. After Coughlin's death, Kenna rarely ever left his suite at the Blackstone Hotel and toward the end, he never left it all. He died mostly forgotten and if not for the blatant corruption that reigned during his tenure as an alderman, and the debauchery of the First Ward Ball, it's unlikely he would be remembered at all.

"I MUST HAVE BEEN TEMPORARILY INSANE..."

Despite a number of questionable public officials that have served in Illinois office since 1956, a state auditor from Chicago named Orville Enoch Hodge still holds the record for the most money ever blatantly stolen from the state of Illinois.

"I don't know why I did it. I must have been temporarily insane," Hodge later said.

There are varying estimates as to just how much money Hodge actually pocketed, but it was close to, or just over $2.6 million. Hodge was on his way to the Governor's mansion in 1956 when a *Chicago Daily News* reporter named George Thiem began investigation the depths of Hodge's corruption.

Most crooked politicians in Chicago merely overpay contractors and later get quiet kickbacks - all part of the secret tradition of graft in the city. Hodge, however, violated that tradition by cutting out the middleman and effectively just writing checks to himself. He figured that it saved him both time and money. This bit of nutty behavior led one Republican politician to call him "a likeable jerk."

According to Thiem's investigation, Hodge spent the money on tailor-made shirts, two custom Cadillacs, farmland, registered cattle, two airplanes, two motorboats, a pearl necklace and matching earrings, a mink cape and stole, a hi-fi stereo system, tickets to Europe and the list went on and on.

Of the money taken, about $1.5 million was recovered when Hodge was caught. He served six years, five months and 11 days in prison for helping himself to the state cookie jar and set a record for the most money ever taken by a single local public official.

CHICAGO'S MOST FAMOUS MADAMS

The famous Everleigh Sisters: Minna (Left) & Ada

The real history of the acclaimed Everleigh Sisters, Chicago's most famous madams, will likely never be known. They invented and re-invented their personal backgrounds many times over throughout the years, adhering to the old adage made famous by Harry Houdini: "If the legend is better than the truth, print the legend."

What we do know is that the two sisters, Minna and Ada Lester, were born in Virginia and created the finest brothel in the world, right on the streets of the South Side Levee District, one of Chicago's most notorious crime and vice areas. The fact that they created such a fine establishment was no accident. They traveled all over the country, doing careful, painstaking research, and became determined to open a brothel that offered the finest luxuries, the best girls, and, of course, catered to the wealthiest clients.

According to the story they passed along to biographers, the sisters had been born to a wealthy attorney in Virginia in the 1870s. He had sent them to finishing school to ensure that they became proper ladies and they were quite popular on the social scene. The two married brothers, but neither marriage lasted and the girls set off on a theatrical tour, eventually opening a brothel in Omaha with an inheritance that they received after their father died. After becoming tired of Omaha, they traveled to New York, New Orleans, and San Francisco, studying what would be required to open a world-class house. They eventually settled in Chicago.

The Lesters (who were to become known as the Everleighs) purchased a brothel on the south side, located at 2131-2133 South Dearborn Street. The double building had once belonged to a madam named Lizzie Allen. They purchased the place for $55,000 ($20,000 down, the remainder to be paid in six months, with $500 a month in rent) and received the

South Dearborn Street (The Everleigh Club is on the right)

The Everleigh Club at 2131-2133 South Dearborn Street

WHERE IS IT NOW?
The once-world-famous Everleigh Club was demolished in 1933, a number of years after the Levee itself had ceased to exist. The site of the club is now where the Hilliard Homes, a public housing project, currently stands.

lease, all of the fixtures, and all of the working girls. Minna and Ada fired the girls and threw out the furnishings, determined to redecorate the entire house.

By February 1, 1900, the house was ready to be opened. It soon became renowned as the most opulent bordello in the city. Ada and Minna Everleigh recruited refined and cultured young women and charged their wealthy patrons as much as $500 a night for their entertainment. They hired chefs, porters and servants to provide background staffing for the six parlors and 50 bedrooms located on the premises. The rooms were amazingly furnished with tapestries, oriental rugs, impressionist paintings and fine furnishings and there

"GETTING EVERLEIGHED..."

The Everleigh Club was unlike any other brothel in Chicago and there has never been anything like it since. The Everleigh sisters were determined to provide a complete experience for their customers and because of this, the club has become the stuff of legend.

The lavish main entrance of the Everleigh Club

The Japanese Throne Room

The Oriental Music Room

The alcove of the Blue Bedroom at the club

Hallway leading away from the main entrance, covered in Oriental rugs

was even a huge library for the education of the young women who worked there. There was a waterfall in one room and orchestras often appeared in the drawing rooms. The musicians would sometimes play all evening, or musical entertainment would be provided by the club's "professor," a black piano player named Davenport Davenport, who played all of the popular tunes of the era. Occasionally, visiting musicians, like Scott Joplin, would be allowed to sit in for the evening.

The house was adorned with golden silk curtains, silk damask easy chairs, mahogany tables, gold bathtubs, gold-rimmed china, Irish linen, and a gilded piano that had been purchased for $15,000. The rooms were equipped with fountains that periodically sprayed perfume into the air.

> One of the more famous anecdotes about the Everleigh Club involves a day when a painter accidentally left a handprint in the fresh paint. The next day, one of the sisters told a workman to "come upstairs, so I can show you where a man put his hand last night." The worker replied, "if it's all the same to you, I'll just have a glass of beer."

Meals at the Everleigh Club were as sumptuous as the décor. Breakfast for the girls, which was usually served at 2:00 p.m., often included iced clam juice, eggs Benedict, kidney pie, clam cakes with bacon, whitefish, breast of chicken, ham, buttered toast, and hot coffee. The girls usually had breakfast in their rooms. Dinner, which was served at 8:00 p.m., included pheasant, capon, roast turkey, duck, quail on toast, au gratin cauliflower, spinach, creamed peas, parmesan potatoes, pear salad with sweet dressing, artichokes, stuffed cucumber salad, asparagus, candied and plain carrots with fruit, and more. Dinner, like the post-midnight meal, was served in the Pullman Room of the club, which had been fashioned as a replica of a Pullman railroad car. The late night meal often consisted of fried oysters, Welsh rarebit, devilled crab, lobster, caviar with lemon juice, and scrambled eggs and bacon.

A friend of the Everleighs, Charles Washburn, later wrote a biography of the sisters called *Come into My Parlor*. In it, he described some of the inner workings of the club - but only what the Everleighs allowed him to know. He told of how, before the club actually opened or before new girls were put to work, the prostitutes were given evening gowns and proper schooling on how to conduct themselves. Minna and Ada did not want the club to be just another brothel on the Levee. Minna instructed them: "Be polite and forget what you are here for. Gentlemen are only gentlemen when properly introduced. We shall see that each girl is properly presented. No lining up. There shall be no cry 'in the parlor girls' when the visitors arrive. The Everleigh Club is not for the rough element, the clerk on holiday or a man without a checkbook."

Over the years of operation, scores of men were turned away at the door and often no one would be admitted without a letter or card of recommendation, unless he was known to the Everleighs. The only customers who got a free pass to enter were police officers, newspaper reporters, and politicians who were in positions to do favors for the Everleighs. They already received protection from Levee enforcers like Ike Bloom and Big Jim Colosimo, but knew that cops and reporters were also good to have on their side, as well.

The sisters did not allow the girls to rob their clients, use drugs, or become connected to a pimp. They had strict standards. Minna continued, "It means that your language will have to be lady-like. You have the whole night before you and one $50 client is more desirable than five $10 ones." The girls initially scoffed at the idea of earning $50 in one night, but not for long. An average client could spend several hundred dollars on the girls, and on food and drink, in a single night and many spent as much as $1,000 during an era when a working man earned about $6 a week.

The Everleigh Sisters would later retire with several million dollars in the bank. If there was one key to the success of their club, it was a certain type of client. They later said, "If it weren't for married men, we couldn't have carried on at all and if it weren't for cheating married women, we could have made another million."

The Everleigh Club was the starting place of a number of Chicago stories that are still told today. One of them involved Prince Heinrich, the brother of Kaiser Wilhelm II, King of Prussia and the German emperor, who visited the club during a trip to the city. During an elaborate show that was performed by the girls, they danced in fawn skins and tore apart a cloth bull, which thrilled the Germans.

During dinner, a historic event took place. One beautiful Everleigh

Prince Heinrich of Prussia, whose visit to the Everleigh Club started one of the world's greatest drinking traditions

girl began dancing on the table and accidentally kicked off her slipper, which struck a bottle of champagne. A gallant gentleman immediately drank from the slipper, after which each man removed a shoe of a woman sitting near him, filled it with champagne and toasted the Prince, the Kaiser and "beautiful women the world over." It was the first time that champagne was drunk from a woman's slipper and it set a new standard for cringe-inducing gallantry all over the world.

Perhaps the most dangerous story connected to the Everleigh Club involved the death of Marshall Field, Jr., son of the dry goods millionaire. The younger Field had been married since 1890, but this did not prevent him from being a frequent visitor at the Everleigh Club. He lived in a home at 1919 South Prairie Avenue and tragedy came to call there on November 22, 1905. Just before dinner that evening, Field fired a bullet into his left side while he was seated in his dressing room. The shot would eventually prove to be fatal. According to the newspapers the following

The mansion on South Prairie Avenue where Marshall Field Jr.'s body was found. Rumors swirled that he had actually been killed at the Everleigh Club.

morning, the gunshot had been a tragic accident. Field had been examining a loaded revolver in anticipation of an upcoming hunting trip to Wisconsin when the gun went off. It was said that it had accidentally discharged, reports said, and the bullet lodged in his side, piercing his liver. Field was rushed to Mercy Hospital, where he lingered at death's door for several days.

The police were summoned to the house and the servants were closely questioned but no one had witnessed the shooting and Mrs. Field had been away for the afternoon. Satisfied with the "cleaning the gun" story, the police looked no further into the incident. Marshall Field, Jr. died on November 27, 1905 and was buried in a lavish ceremony at Graceland Cemetery on the city's north side. But his death created a mystery that soon involved the Everleigh Club.

While police detectives may have accepted the "accidental discharge" story, many reporters and members of the general public were not so quick to do so. Many reporters knew of Field's frequent visits to the Levee District, and the Everleigh Club in particular, and soon rumors began to circulate that he had not really been at home when the fatal shot was fired.

Stories spread (and it was later revealed that an Everleigh prostitute was paid $25,000 by a rival madam to concoct the story) that Field had actually been shot, not in his dressing room, but at the Everleigh Club. The stories varied, stating that he had either been involved in an altercation in the brothel and was shot by one of the bouncers, or that he was shot by one of the prostitutes when he became violent with her. Regardless, his body was then smuggled home to avoid scandal for the Field family. He was later found in his dressing room "having had an accident while cleaning his gun."

The story was, of course, denied, but not with much vehemence. Minna knew that rumors of this sort were not entirely bad for business. This is likely the reason that the story still continues to be told today by those who have a hard time believing that a pistol with two safety catches could have been fired by accident.

The Everleigh Club thrived for a number of years and was finally closed thanks to the forces of the reform movement - and a publicity campaign that somehow went awry. They were eventually shut down because of a handsome, leather-bound, privately printed booklet, which the sisters hoped would make their establishment even more famous. The booklet, which offered a tasteful write-up and professional photographs of the club, were sent out all over the country. It garnered them plenty of attention, but not the kind they wanted.

Mayor Carter Harrison II was said to be embarrassed by the interest that the Everleigh Club was bringing to Chicago. When visiting associates asked about the city's greatest attractions, he mentioned the soaring mosaic ceiling at Marshall Field's, the beautiful waters of Lake Michigan, the performances by the Chicago Grand Opera Company... but he was forgetting something, they said. What about the Everleigh Club?

Even when the mayor left town, it followed him. At a banquet in 1911, a young man approached him, pumped Harrison's hand, and laughed, "Pretty snappy town yours, isn't it?" He followed that up with a wink and a joke about the Everleigh Club.

Soon, Harrison, who had always been willing to allow vice in Chicago to remain segregated as long as those who provided it kept to their place, needed to make a statement. Closing down the Everleigh Club, he knew, would do just that. The closing of the club would be the beginning of the end of the entire Levee District.

The final closing of the Club, on October 11, 1911, was delayed for 12 hours because of behind-the-scenes political maneuvering. In the end, even Bathhouse John and Hinky Dink Kenna couldn't save the place. The sisters were allowed to throw one last, grand party at the club for their best customers and long-time supporters.

At 2:45 a.m., there was a knock on the door and a police lieutenant was there to mournfully enforce the orders that he had been given. He told them, "Sorry, girls, if it was us, you know how we'd be."

Minna asked, "What do we do now?"

"Better clear out the house," he told her. "Get rid of the guests."

The crowd inside quietly gathered their coats and left. They milled around outside of the club for hours, lingering in the street and refusing to accept the idea that this night of getting "Everleigh-ed" would be their last.

But it was really over. Within 24 hours, the famous prostitutes of the Everleigh Club had received hundreds of telegrams and telephone calls, offering them work at imitation brothels all over the country. They had to accept the offers, but most agreed, working anywhere else would never be the same. The world's most extravagant brothel was no more.

After closing, and realizing that no amount of money or connections could open the club again, the Everleighs took a six-month vacation in Europe before returning to Chicago. When they came back, they lived on the west side for a time, but decided to avoid the attention they received by moving to New York. They lived there for their rest of their lives, comfortably enjoying their earnings in the brothel business. Those who knew them never suspected what they had done in their previous life. They usually explained that the nude paintings hanging on their walls and the risqué books on their shelves had been "inherited from a relative."

Before she died in 1948, Minna was quoted as saying, "We never hurt anybody, did we? We never robbed widows and we made no false representations, did we? Any crimes that were attributed to us were the outcries of jealousy. We tried to get along honestly. Our business was unholy, but everybody accepted it. What of it?"

Ada followed her sister to the grave in 1960 and both were buried, side-by-side, in Virginia.

THE LAST SURVIVOR OF THE BOSTON TEA PARTY?

One of Chicago's great early con artists, David Kennison

Plenty of bodies besides that of Ira Couch are still in Lincoln Park, which was once City Cemetery, but only one of them besides Ira Couch still has a grave marker there: David Kennison, one of Chicago's first great con artists.

Kennison was an old man living in the care of the William Mack family (or Henry Fuller, depending on which source you're reading) when he came to Chicago in 1848. At the time, he claimed to be 111 years old, and that, while he was mostly bedridden, he could still get up and walk 20 miles in a day if he felt like it. He further claimed to have been the last surviving participant of the Boston Tea Party, and bequeathed to the historical society a small vial of tea leaves that he swore were from the tea party itself - the Chicago Historical Museum still has a box of tea leaves with a signed note from Kennison today!

But his participation in the Boston Tea Party was the only the beginning of Kennison's story. He further claimed to have been present at the Boston Massacre, the Battles of Bunker Hill, Lexington, Brandywine, and just about every other major battle of the Revolution, up to and including Cornwallis's surrender at Yorktown. And, even though he was in his mid-70s when the War of 1812 broke out, he had fought in seven battles in that war, as well.

The story was awfully farfetched, but Chicagoans ate it up. When he died in February of 1852, hundreds attended the funeral at Clark Street Methodist Church, a military band (his favorite kind) accompanied the funeral procession, and he was buried with full military honors in City Cemetery. The local Daughters of the American Revolution named their chapter in his honor, and a generation of Chicagoans considered him one of the greatest heroes of the city's pioneers.

After the cemetery was moved, Kennison's body was left, but the marker disappeared. In 1880, the *Chicago Tribune*

According to documents "dug up" by Pamela Bannos of Northwestern University, an expert on City Cemetery, Kennison's actual burial site is probably a couple of city blocks south of the boulder.

launched a search for old-time residents who had attended the funeral and could remember exactly where he was buried. Those who were still present were able to pinpoint the spot within a few feet at a spot just North of the Couch tomb, and a flag was raised on the spot until a more permanent monument could be erected. Today, a large granite boulder stands on the spot within a few feet of his burial place with an aluminum plaque listing his accomplishments.

Several official city sources still speak of Kennison as a hero of the Revolution, but this only speaks to his real skill - Kennison was one of Chicago's first great con artists. At the time of his death, researchers have now learned, he was actually only in his mid 80s. His stories of being a Revolutionary War hero were entirely made up. Throughout his time in Chicago, he took several opportunities to use the fabricated story of his life to hit people up for donations.

Still, he seems to have made good use of his powers as a con man. Thinking they had a hero in their midst gave some of the earliest Chicagoans a reason to be proud of their city. And, when a group met in Chicago to debate whether or not slavery should be expanded into Illinois, Kennison is said to have attended and to have proclaimed that he had fought for the freedom of all people, not just the white ones, and urged all those present to do everything in their power to abolish slavery. Perhaps a few of the Chicagoans were thinking of his words when they volunteered for service in the Civil War a decade later!

"THERE'S A SUCKER BORN EVERY MINUTE"

Gambler Mike McDonald (Right)

Although most people today don't remember Mike McDonald, the Chicago gambler and political boss of the 1880s, he contributed three phrases to the Windy City lexicon that are still recalled today.

In 1873, McDonald built a huge, four-story gambling establishment that took up nearly a square block, which he called The Store. Just before it opened, his partner asked him if he thought the place was too large and Mike answered, "Don't worry about that. There's a sucker born every minute." Legend has it that McDonald was also the first man to utter the phrase, "Never give a sucker an even break." Both statements are still words to live by!

He was also responsible for the following quip, which became a staple of vaudeville shows of the era. McDonald loathed the police, hated them with a passion. A man came to him and asked him for $2 and Mike asked what it was for. The man replied that he and some others were burying a policeman. "Fine," Mike answered, "Here's $10. Bury five of them."

But Mike McDonald was not just a man who went about Chicago saying clever things. When he arrived in the city at the age of 15, he was already an accomplished card dealer and made his way by selling half-empty boxes of candy on trains. During the Civil War, he had another racket - enlisting in the army. There were bounties paid for enlistments and McDonald worked it out to get a commission from every one of his men that he got to join up. The men would enlist, desert, and enlist again, gaining commissions for the boss and putting money in their own pockets.

One of McDonald's gambling establishments burned in the Great Fire in 1871, but he was able to rebuild quickly. The gambling parlor went up right next to the brothels and gin joints, which legends claim were among the first structures to return after the disaster. His profits from a single gambling parlor on the west side were said to be over $100, 000 a year. In Chicago, a man with that sort of money went into politics, which was exactly what McDonald did.

Mike backed Harvey D. Colvin, a gambler who was also the general agent of the United States Express Co., for the Mayor's office. Colvin ran as a "law and order" candidate, which is ironic considering the company that he kept.

McDonald probably wasn't the first to claim that he "ran this town," but he did so enough to attract the attention of the press, who reported him stating as much half a century before Al Capone took over the city. McDonald seems to have been at least as famous in his day as Capone was in his.

During his wide-open administration, David Kalakaua, the king of the Hawaiian Islands, visited Chicago. Colvin spent most of day trying to communicate with the king in sign languages and wild gestures before learning that Kalakaua spoke fluent English.

WHERE IS IT NOW?
Mike McDonald's "Store" was at No. 176 Clark Street (665 N. Clark after the 1909 renumbering). A parking garage is on the site now, just north of the Kerryman Bar & Restaurant - and right near the spot where Weird Chicago Tours begin!

By the end of Colvin's term in office, there were two mayors of Chicago, thanks to an incredible legal blunder. The mayoral election had been changed from fall to spring and the City Council passed an ordinance calling for the election of city officers, but never mentioned the office of mayor. The Council tried to rectify the situation, but the motion for a special mayoral election was defeated. Colvin then claimed that since no election had been officially called, he could stay in office - which he did. However, this didn't stop others from holding the election. A meeting was held and Thomas Hoyne was nominated. He was "elected" on April 18, 1876, but Colvin refused to step down, despite the fact that Hoyne was in an office at City Hall, demanding to be recognized as the mayor. Eventually, the Circuit Court ruled that Colvin was Chicago's only mayor, even though the City Council had already recognized Hoyne as its presiding officer.

Meanwhile, Mike McDonald was reaping a fortune off the "suckers" who came into The Store, as well as his other establishments. In those days, he literally ran the criminal element of Chicago, taking a tariff on everything that was stolen, on all gambling proceeds and on all profits from prostitution and blackmail schemes. His control over the city was absolute. Twice each year, phony police raids were carried out on The Store (with Mike's permission, of course), so that the newspapers could have their headlines. Those who crossed McDonald, even the cops, had to answer for it. For instance, in 1880, The Store was subjected to an unscheduled raid by Police Superintendent Simon O'Donnell and, for his efforts, O'Donnell was demoted to a captain's position and was given the worst assignments for the rest of his years on the force.

The Store became a gathering place for some of the most celebrated criminals of the era. Herbert Asbury wrote that if you stayed in the boarding house that McDonald's wife ran on an upper floor, you might meet Hungry Joe Lewis, who took Oscar Wilde in a card game for several thousand dollars; Red Jimmy Fitzgerald, a swindler who made off with $7,000 that belonged to a famous diplomat; Tom O'Brien, Chicago's most celebrated bunko man; and McDonald's one-armed brother-in-law, Nick Hogan, who one policeman claimed, "if he had both arms, he'd have all of money in the world."

McDonald made a fortune with The Store but perhaps his greatest scheme was when he swindled the city of Chicago. He managed to get the city and the county to award him a contract to paint the courthouse with a "secret preserving fluid." The bill for the job was $128,250 and half of the money was paid out before the Chicago Daily News discovered that the secret fluid was only chalk and water. McDonald was never prosecuted for the scam.

Despite his decades in gambling, politics, and as an underworld boss, he died an unhappy and bitter man. In 1887, a honest mayor, John A. Roche, took over office and forced McDonald out of business. He lost The Store and decided to try and make an honest living. He purchased a newspaper, the Chicago Globe, and ran it for two years. He also helped to build the city's first elevated railway and sold stone and gravel to city contracts.

Things turned bad when his wife left him and ran away with an actor named Billy Arlington. The McDonalds reunited, however, but then Mary ran away with another man, the Reverend Joseph Moysant, assistant rector of the Catholic Church of Notre Dame. McDonald renounced Catholicism a short time later, divorced his wife, and married Dora Feldman, who was 23 years old and a former playmate of the McDonald children. Mike was 49 at the time. The marriage seemed happy at first and then Dora strayed into the arms of a teenaged boy named Webster Guerin. The violently passionate affair ended in murder when Dora stormed into Guerin's office in a fit of rage one morning in February 1907 and shot the young man in the neck. This tragic occurrence ruined McDonald's health and sent him to an early grave.

Although Mike allegedly embraced the Catholic Church again on his deathbed, and stated that Mary was his only true wife, she received nothing from McDonald's estate. Dora received a third of it, plus $40,000 for her murder defense fund. She was acquitted of the Guerin shooting in 1908.

EXTRA, EXTRA - READ ALL ABOUT IT!

For two generations, from before the time of the Great Fire until the time of World War I, there was hardly a Chicagoan who didn't know Lonny Wilson. He was hard to miss - his peg leg and bushy beard made him a tough character to miss. And for five decades, he stood at his post - first at Randolph and Dearborn streets, and then outside of the Tribune building on Michigan Avenue - selling newspapers. He was at his stand selling papers the day of the Great Chicago Fire and didn't leave until the flames got too close.

In the early days before the fire, a new newsboy named Michael came to town. When all of the newsboys went swimming one day, no one could remember the new boy's name, so Lonny began calling him "Hinky Dink." Hinky Dink Kenna kept that name for the rest of his life, and, as the best-known alderman in Chicago, retold the story for Wilson's obituary in 1918. He also said that it was Wilson who tipped him off on a luncheonette for sale - this became Kenna's first business venture.

While some of his newsie pals went on to become major players in the city, Wilson stuck with what he knew best: standing on his corner, selling papers.

THE WIZARD OF CHICAGO

Herman Billik -- the so-called "Wizard of Chicago"

One of the most mysterious killers in Chicago history is one of the least remembered today. He may not have claimed dozens of victims or carried out gruesome, bloody crimes, but he certainly aroused public interest at the time of the murders that were connected to him.

Herman Billik was a stout, handsome Bohemian with piercing black eyes and a devilish way with women. He was also a fortuneteller who read the future for a small sum and carried on a lively trade in charms and potions. In addition, he was undoubtedly an accomplished hypnotist and claimed to possess strange occult powers that he said were inherited from his mother, who was allegedly a witch. However, when Billik carried out the murders of six people -- a father, mother and their four daughters -- he did so without any sort of supernatural forces and relied on poison instead.

Billik, whose real name was Vajicek, came to Chicago in 1904 from Cleveland, where his mother had worked as a fortuneteller (not as a witch, as he often claimed) for many years. He established himself and his family, which consisted of his wife, two sons and a daughter, in a small house on West 19th Street. He immediately hung out a sign that announced that he was the "Great Billik, Card-Reader and Seer." Soon, he began to receive callers from the neighborhood, and from the surrounding area, who wanted to avail themselves of his services. As his reputation spread, he began calling himself the "Wizard of Chicago" and people began to talk about the uncanny accuracy of his predictions and the efficacy of the love charms and spells that he peddled. There were also whispers of his skills as a lover as well for a number of women went away satisfied by more than just a card reading. It's likely not a coincidence that Billik was an expert hypnotist, as well as "seer."

Located three doors away from the Billik residence was the modest home of Martin Vzral, who lived with his wife, Rose, and their seven children. Vzral was a milk dealer and one of the more prosperous inhabitants of the neighborhood in that he owned his own home, operated a successful business and had over $2,000 in the bank, a tidy sum in those days. Later, it was established that Billik had chosen the Vzrals for his victims before he moved into the neighborhood, but he made no attempt to approach them for nearly a week after moving onto the street. Not surprisingly, the Vzrals knew who he was when he finally did make contact with them because he had become the topic of gossip for blocks around.

One day, he walked into the milk depot and ordered a can of milk. As Vzral filled the container, Billik started at him intensely, muttered a few words of gibberish and then with great gravity pronounced, "You have an enemy. I see him. He is trying to destroy you."

Billik would tell him nothing else. He left the milk stand and let Vzral worry about his words for a few days. Then he called on him at his home and told him that Vzral's enemy was another milkman who lived across the street from him. But not to worry, Billik offered to use his supernatural powers in his new friend's defense. Later, at the stroke of midnight, with the entire Vzral family looking on, Billik concocted a horrible-smelling potion on the kitchen stove and then tossed the mixture onto the other milkman's front stoop. "Now you will prosper," he told them. "He cannot harm you."

And Vzral did prosper. Not because of any magic spells, but because he was a hard-working and industrious man. However, he didn't see through the illusion and credited Billik with his increase in business. He spread the word about the "wizard," even though Billik refused to accept payment for the "great service" that he had done for the milkman. The Vzrals were a strict Catholic family, but were also very superstitious and saw no reason that Billik could not be everything that he claimed to be. They listened, night after night, to the litany of supernatural wonders he had allegedly performed and within a few weeks, his domination of the family was complete.

According to reports, he seduced Mrs. Vzral and her daughters and had sex with them in the same room where

Martin Vzral stood watching. It was said that Mrs. Vzral's obsession with Billik was so intense that she refused to leave the house for days, fearing that he might come by while she was away. Billik also "borrowed" money from Vzral with every visit and by January 1905, had stripped him of his bank account, and was siphoning off the profits from the milk business. To provide more money to give to Billik, three of the Vzral girls went to work as domestic servants, turning over all of their earnings to him.

Meanwhile, Billik bought new clothing, purchased a fashionable carriage and made frequent trips to New York and California, all of which the Vzrals paid for. At his suggestion, Mrs. Vzral insured the lives of her husband and four of her daughters and made Billik the beneficiary. The only members of the family who were not insured were the oldest daughter, Emma, the son, Jerry, and an infant daughter. It's no coincidence that they were the only ones to survive Billik's evil plans.

Early in March 1905, Martin Vzral began to show signs of realizing what was happening to himself and his family. He began to worry about money and the deplorable state of his business and even asked Billik for a loan -- of money that he had given to the charlatan in the first place! Billik wondered if perhaps he had pressed the milkman too hard but to cure the man's "unsettled feelings," he gave Mrs. Vzral a white powder (which he told her was a charm) and told her to put into her husband's food. A few days later, Vzral began to complain of sharp pains in his abdomen and Billik diagnosed his ailment as mere "stomach trouble." He treated him with his own concoction, the same white powder, which was later revealed to be arsenic. Vzral slipped into a coma and died on March 27, 1905. Mrs. Vzral collected $2,000 in life insurance, which she immediately turned over to her depraved lover. Billik allowed her to keep $100 of it for burial expenses.

A few weeks passed and Emma and Mary Vzral, two of the late milkman's daughters, went to see Billik at the Riverview Amusement Park, where he was telling fortunes in a tent. He showed Emma a strangely marked card and explained to her that it was a "death omen" and that "Mary will die soon." He was correct: Mary died of "stomach trouble" on July 22, 1905. Her life had been insured for $800 and again, Billik took all of it except the money that was needed to pay for the poor girl's funeral.

By this time, Jerry Vzral had decided to speak up. He demanded that Billik be banned from their house and his anger provoked his mother to agree that she wouldn't see him anymore. Two days later, Jerry became very ill, but his sister Emma insisted on calling a doctor and he soon recovered. The police later came to believe that Billik had not intended to kill the boy but had only administered a small dose of poison to frighten him.

In December of that same year, Billik struck again. Tillie Vzral was the next to die, succumbing again to "stomach trouble" and raising $620 in life insurance for Billik. For some reason, he stayed quiet until the following August, when 14-year-old Rose died of the same ailment. She was insured for $300. Three months later, Ella died. Her tender age of 12 managed to garner Billik a mere $105. As with all of the previous deaths, Mrs. Vzral turned over all of the money to the "wizard," save for the expenses needed for the funeral.

Now, with no more insurance money in sight, and with the milk business taken over by creditors, Billik persuaded Mrs. Vzral to put her home up for sale. She received $2,900 in cash and gave every bit of it to Billik. He took a leisurely trip to Niagara Falls with the windfall and told Mrs. Vzral that he planned to stop in Cleveland on his way back to "fix" his mother. That way, he could inherit what he claimed was a sizable fortune.

When Billik did return to Chicago, he found the befuddled remains of the Vzral family with no money, no food and waiting to be thrown out of a house that was no longer theirs to live in. On the night that Billik returned, he called on Mrs. Vzral during the early morning hours. By daybreak, she was dead.

During the two-year period that Billik preyed on the Vzrals, no one in the neighborhood realized that anything out of the ordinary was going on. It seemed that the family was experiencing more than their share of misfortune but no one suspected foul play until a girl employed as a maid in a north side home was overheard by her employer to remark to another servant that, "Someone ought to look into all of the deaths in that family." The chance remark led the woman to question the maid and she learned that the girl had known Mary Vzral, who, although afraid of Billik, had been unable to resist him.

The girl's mistress repeated the conversation to her husband and he was so troubled by it that he contacted a policeman that he knew who patrolled the neighborhood. The policeman included it in his daily report and eventually this report reached Inspector George M. Shippy of the Hyde Park station. He, in turn, assigned detectives to start an inquiry.

After a few days of investigation, the detectives were curious enough to obtain an order to have Mary Vzral's body exhumed. Chemists who examined the contents of her stomach discovered a number of grains of arsenic and Billik was immediately arrested. He was placed on trial in the early summer of 1907 and was found guilty of murder in the first degree. In July, he was sentenced to death, but was reprieved by the governor. More appeals followed, even to the United States Supreme Court, and the case dragged out for another two years. During this time, Billik was held in the Cook County Jail, where he curiously became one of the most popular men, with prisoners and

Herman Billik (Center) during his trial

Jerry Vzral, one of the only surviving members of the Vzral family, at the time of Billik's trial. Strangely, Jerry would later become an outspoken supporter of Billik as groups tried to save him from the death penalty.

guards alike, to ever be incarcerated there.

While Billik's case was strange from the beginning, it became even more bizarre in the months to come. What was so unusual was the extraordinary fight that was waged to save the "wizard's" life. A Catholic priest, Father P.J. O'Callaghan of the Paulist Fathers, and a nun, Sister Rose of the Order of the Sacred Heart, led the battle. They arranged mass meetings and prayer vigils and through private solicitation, raised considerable sums of money for Billik's legal expenses.

In June 1908, just before the appeal to the Supreme Court, a prayer service was held by Father O' Callaghan at the county jail. It was reported that 400 of the prisoners attended, praying for God to save Billik from the gallows. Another service was held at the jail on June 9, at which Father O'Callaghan, Billik, Billik's wife and daughter and, unbelievably, Jerry Vzral offered prayers on his behalf. Many of the prisoners wept and moaned and Billik's cellmate, an infamous burglar, wrapped his arms around Billik, kissed him repeatedly and wept openly throughout the service. After the prayer session was over, the prisoners presented flowers to Father O'Callaghan, Sister Rose and even the jailer. On June 10, a petition signed by 20,000 people was presented to the state Board of Pardons and five rallies were held on Billik's behalf on the west side. Hundreds of women wept and screamed that he should not be hanged. They carried on to the point that many of them had to be treated for hysteria. Father O'Callaghan spoke at all of the meetings and was joined by Jerry Vzral, who tearfully claimed that he had committed perjury at Billik's trial.

Inspector Shippy was nonplussed by the rallies and weird performances. "Billik is a cold-blooded murderer of the worst type," he stated. "He is simply deceiving the people who are working in his behalf."

Guilty or not -- the mass meetings, which revolted the police officers in charge of the case -- had the desired result. Governor Charles S. Deneen commuted Billik's death sentence to life imprisonment in January 1909. He claimed to do so on the recommendation of the Board of Pardons but it's likely that the hysterical atmosphere of the rallies frightened the politicians into thinking that they would be losing votes if they failed to spare the influential "seer."

Billik was sent to the state prison at Joliet and eight years later, in 1917, the murderer of almost an entire family was pardoned by Governor Edward F. Dunne and set free. The Church, which had never let up on its crusade for him, headed a huge voting bloc in Chicago and the governor was never one to ignore any large group that threatened to vote against him or the party.

After his pardon, Billk drifted to Cleveland briefly before coming back to Chicago, where he died in the county hospital less than five months after his pardon. One has to wonder about this killer's appeal and how he managed to not only seduce and kill the greater part of a family but also how he ensnared the general public in the way that he did. How did he create a faithful following to do his bidding, beyond all reason and logic? Did he really possess some sort of strange, supernatural power or more likely, was he but one of the madmen who managed to create a "cult of personality" in modern history?

And most chilling of all -- what could Billik have accomplished if he had been of a later generation? Would he have been the leader of some terrifying cult? Another Charles Manson, Jim Jones or David Koresh? Or perhaps something even worse...

Billik shaking hands with Joliet Prison warden Michael Zimmer. He was released after just 8 years, pardoned by Illinois Governor Edward F. Dunne. Even this short sentence was hard on him and he left prison a broken man

"SLIP HIM A MICKEY..."

There are many names connected to Chicago crime that have endured throughout history but how many of them, save perhaps for Big Jim Colosimo, have been as well-known for their restaurant or drinking establishment as they have been for their ties to Windy City crime? There is only one other man, the proprietor of the Lone Star Saloon & Palm Garden, whose name has endured over the decades. In fact, his name has

been immortalized in the American lexicon and it is a name that has been spoken by literally thousands of people who have no idea that he was an actual person. This deadly little man, who stood only 5 feet, 5 inches tall and weighed less than 140 pounds, was named Mickey Finn and his name is now used everywhere as a synonym for a knockout drink.

Little is known about the life of Mickey Finn, but he was born in either Ireland or Peoria, depending on his mood when telling his life story. He first came to Chicago during the 1893 World's Fair as a "lush worker," which meant that he robbed drunks in the vice districts of South Clark Street. Not long after, he began working in a bar owned by Toronto Jim in the Custom House Levee District but only lasted here for a few months. Finn was too tough for even this notorious hangout and was constantly fighting with customers, who were mostly hoodlums and thieves. He was finally fired after knocking out a man's eyeball with a board when the customer failed to produce the money to pay for a round drinks that he had ordered.

For the next year or two, Finn operated as a pickpocket and a fence for small-time thieves and burglars. In 1896, he opened the Lone Star Saloon & Palm Garden at the southern end of Whiskey Row. This infamous area was a stretch that ran along the west side of State Street from Van Buren to Harrison streets and where for almost 30 years, every building was occupied by a saloon, wine room, gambling house, or all three combined. A police inspector named Lavin once called the place "a low dive, a hangout for colored and white people of the lowest type." Finn ran the Lone Star for about eight years and during most of this time, continued handling stolen goods. He also took in money for instructing pickpockets in the "art of the lift" and taught thievery to streetwalkers, whom he encouraged to rob the men they picked up at the Lone Star.

Finn's wife, Kate Roses, also handled "house girls" for the place. They were supposed to induce the customers to drink and to entertain them in any other manner for which they were willing to pay. Two of the in-house prostitutes, Isabelle "Dummy" Fyffe and "Gold Tooth" Mary Thornton, would later be Finn's downfall when they testified against him during a 1903 vice investigation.

But the saloon's claim to fame came from Finn's novel approach to fleecing his customers. From the beginning, the Lone Star Saloon & Palm Garden (the garden was a back room that was decorated with a sickly palm tree in a pot) was a robbers' den. For the first year or two, Finn and his associates contented themselves with picking pockets and rolling drunks, but they soon moved on to bigger things. In 1898, Finn met a black "voodoo doctor" named Hall, who sold love potions and charms to girls in bawdy houses and peddled cocaine and morphine to dope addicts. From the voodoo man, Finn purchased a bottle that contained "some sort of white stuff." The police never identified the substance but it was probably chloral hydrate.

With the "white stuff" as the prime ingredient, Mickey Finn invented two knockout drinks that would become his trademark. One of them, the "Mickey Finn Special," was made from raw alcohol, water, snuff and a liberal amount of the voodoo powder. The other drink, which he dubbed "Number Two," was beer mixed with the powder and fortified with snuff water. Finn brazenly put up a sign behind the bar that invited customers to, "Try the Mickey Finn Special." The house girls and whores who worked for him were instructed to push the concoction on every man with whom they drank. Finn was so proud of the drink that he named in his own honor that even the luckless customers who insisted on drinking beer only were given the "Number Two" in retaliation.

A customer who might be given one of the paralyzing potions usually quietly slumped over in his chair and slept until he could be given the proper attention by the proprietor. The bartender, or one of the house girls, would then drag the man into one of the rear rooms behind the

WHERE IS IT NOW?
Mickey Finn's pub would have been on the 1100 block of South State Street.

Palm Garden, which Finn called his "operating room." Finn and Kate Roses would do the actual robbing. Finn would always put on a derby hat and a clean white apron and would go to work on the man, first stripping him to the skin and searching for a money belt or anything in his pockets. If his victim's clothing was of good quality, Finn would take it and substitute rags in its place. After that, the man would be tossed into the alley out back or left on the floor of the "operating room" until the next morning. The victims were not hard to handle when awakened and were usually befuddled for a day or two afterwards as well. Few of them ever remembered where or when they were robbed.

Occasionally, though, a few of the men gave Finn problems and he always kept a club at hand in case one started to show signs of stirring. Dummy Fyffe stated that Finn was "terribly brutal" with the men that he doped but Gold Tooth Mary later testified that things sometimes took a darker turn. "I saw Finn take a gold watch and $35 from Billy Miller, a trainman," she told the vice commission. "Finn gave him a dope and he lay in stupor in the saloon for 12 hours. When he recovered he demanded his money, but Finn had gone... Miller was found afterward along the railroad tracks with his head cut off." Mary also talked of many other men that she had seen drugged and robbed in the Lone Star and explained that she had quit working in the bar in the fall of 1903 because of Finn's increasing violence.

She also reported to the commission that Finn told her that he would never be arrested because he paid the police for protection and possessed influence with corrupt aldermen Hinky Dink McKenna and Bathhouse John Coughlin. Strangely, neither one was ever asked by the graft commission to explain or deny these boastings by Finn. Not long after the prostitutes appeared before the commission, the police raided the Lone Star, but found nothing but a few bottles of liniment and some cough medicine. With no real evidence, they said, they were unable to arrest Finn. The only action the commission could take was to revoke Finn's saloon license and on December 16, 1903, the doors of the Lone Star were closed.

Mickey Finn left Chicago for a few months but returned in the summer of 1904. He tended bar in a place on South Dearborn Street and while he refrained from administering it himself, he sold the formula for his "Special" to a number of ambitious saloonkeepers throughout the city. To the underworld, the potion was known simply as a "Mickey Finn". To this day, it's a name that's applied to knockout drinks of every type --- earning one of Chicago's own a rather dubious place in history.

CAP STREETER: CHICAGO'S LAST PIONEER

Cap Streeter (Chicago Daily News)

Captain George Wellington Streeter was considered by many to have been the last Chicago pioneer. Whether he deserves this title or not is another question, but he was certainly a colorful character and one that remains surrounded by lore that is uniquely a part of Chicago. During his years in the city, he defied the laws of Chicago and the state of Illinois, fought the courts and the police to a standstill and managed to keep the residents of the region in alternating states of anger and amusement for more than 30 years.

Streeter's greatest Chicago legacy was created by nature rather than by man. The waves had been beating unchallenged against the shoreline of Lake Michigan for centuries before the settlers came to Chicago. Along the open area north of the river, the lake deposited generation after generation of silt and sand and as it did so, the shore crept ever eastward. The wealthy residents who owned land to the west, across what was Sand Street in those days and now the streets of St. Clair and Pine, claimed rights to the water's edge, no matter where it might extend to. There was never any dispute about this until one summer day in 1886 when a strange and eccentric creature laid claim to the vast Chicago shoreline.

George Wellington Streeter was the great-grandson of an American Revolution veteran and the grandson of a drum major from the War of 1812. He was an avid showman and before he arrived in Chicago, he had roamed the West, had served in the Civil War (seeing action at Missionary Ridge and Lookout Mountain), had watched his first wife run off to become a vaudeville star, had worked as a freight hauler, had been a hotel owner and for a time, was a business associate of two unsavory brothers from Missouri named Frank and Jesse James.

After his service in the war, Streeter had brought together a menagerie composed of animals no more exciting than deer, otter, porcupines, and beavers, but he still managed to exhibit them at county fairs with some success. His prize exhibit was a white Normandy hog, which he insisted was 10 feet long and weighed over 1,500 pounds. He usually billed the beast as a "white elephant," to the delight of the crowds who came to see it.

Streeter's dubious business prospered for a while but when ticket sales slumped, he traded in his animals and became a ship navigator on the waters of Lake Michigan and the nearby rivers. He landed in Chicago in the 1870s and became part owner of the Wood's Museum, a famous showplace of the time. He soon sold out and became a salesman at county fairs, then left that business and served as a short-term owner of the Apollo Theater.

Not long after this, Streeter returned to the lake, lured by the hope of striking it rich in Honduras. His second wife, Maria, was a raging drunk and would often disappear for a week at a time on a bender. Cap Streeter, as he was often called, never worried about her when she went missing. "It don't matter where she is," he would often say. "She's having a good time and will come home when she's ready." During one of her disappearances, Maria made a friend, a Captain Bowen, who convinced her that there was money to be made in Honduras. There was a revolution taking place there at the time and all a seaman had to do was to arrive in the country with a boatload of guns and he would find himself with a steamship concession on the Honduras rivers.

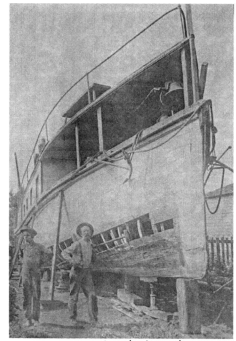

Cap Streeter at work on his boat, the Reutan. (Library of Congress)

Soon after, Streeter began to borrow money and to build his own steamship, which he called the *Reutan*. He wanted to test her for seaworthiness and decided the best place to do so was on Lake Michigan. Streeter, Maria, an engineer and four passengers set out on July 10, 1886. A sudden storm blew in off the lake and the steamboat was nearly lost. The boat managed to make it to a point near the Chicago harbor, missed the breakwater, drifted northward and finally washed up onto a sandbar along the beach. Streeter had lashed himself to the wheel to keep from being washed overboard in the storm. Despite the grounding of his boat, he was not defeated. In fact, he took a look around and decided that the spot where the boat had washed ashore would make a fine place to live.

The boat remained at the site throughout the fall and into the winter. The sandbar began to grow up around it and Streeter offered local contractors the privilege of dumping sand, dirt, garbage or anything else they wanted near his new home. The lake continued to contribute sand as well and soon, the boat was no longer in the water but resting on dry land. In this way, Cap Streeter "created" 186 acres of his very own land. He had managed to find an older map of Chicago that indicated that the shoreline was actually west of his property and now claimed that he was beyond the shore of Chicago and Illinois. He dubbed this new property the "District of Lake Michigan" and while he recognized the laws of America, he declared that he was subject to no other rules or regulations.

The local property owners, the most noted of whom were Potter Palmer and N.K. Fairbanks, made it their common cause to get Streeter removed from the land along the lake. In their eyes, he was nothing more than a crude, obnoxious squatter and a blasphemous, drunken thief who had to be ousted. Streeter was throwing loud parties for other riff-raff in the region and worse, was selling liquor on Sunday. This was against the law in Chicago, but Cap had decided that it was perfectly legal in his district. Palmer and Fairbanks soon learned that threats did not work with Streeter, so they began to pursue legal options. Had they gone to the civil courts at once, things might have turned out differently but they went to the police instead, which started a guerilla struggle that lasted for years. The battle involved the city police, the park police, special constables and dozens of lawyers. The courts were appealed to over and over again and Cap was arrested several times but always managed to go free.

Eventually, the Chicago gentry, with their now-obstructed view of the lake, thanks to Cap's boat, outhouses and ramshackle buildings, chose less subtle methods of moving Streeter off his land. In the summer of 1894, five men from Chicago Title and Trust served Cap with orders to remove himself from the property. They received shotgun pellets in their backsides for their trouble. When three policemen came to arrest Cap for the shooting, Maria doused them with boiling water, forcing them to retreat. Cap was later arrested but no charges were pressed because there was still a dispute as to whether Streeter owned the property and whether or not the men were trespassing.

Later that fall, Cap's house was attacked by 25 police officers, working on an official payroll for Potter Palmer

A houseboat that had been turned into an actual house in the new district of Streeterville (Library of Congress)

A Streeterville shack (Chicago Daily News)

Cap Streeter (holding a dog) and some of the other supporters and residents of Streeterville. Note the man to the right of Cap Streeter holding a rifle over his shoulder.
(Chicago Daily News)

and his compatriots. Streeter opened fire on the men and Maria managed to nearly sever the arm of one of them. After they were arrested, all charges against them were dismissed after they claimed "self defense." Around this same time, Cap discovered the old Chicago map that indicated that his district was outside of the city limits. He named William H. Niles as his military governor and set about creating a separate state from Illinois. In 1899, he turned one of the outhouses on his property into a courthouse, raised an American flag and issued his own "declaration of independence." Streeter and a number of his friends were arrested on charges of illegal assembly but were later released.

On May 25, 1899 (just a few weeks after Streeter declared his district independent of Chicago and Illinois), more than 500 handpicked police officers charged into Streeter's district because Cap allegedly shot at a police captain's carriage. Military governor Niles had already entrenched Cap's men around the property and he armed his troops with a cannon that had been stolen from a nearby park. The city soon had Streeter's district surrounded with officers in the front and a tugboat that was armed with a Gatling gun in the rear. The police charged but were repulsed by buckshot and rocks. Around nightfall, the police officers charged again and managed to overwhelm the ragtail "army." Streeter was captured but was soon released and the police officers involved in the fiasco were reprimanded for their roles in the affair. In those days, it was not illegal to shoot at a police captain's carriage! But no one was willing to let the matter go away quietly. One night while Streeter and his wife were out of the house, several officers broke into their house and confiscated a number of Cap's guns. Enraged, Streeter marched down to the Chicago Avenue police station and took all of the officers and staff hostage. He demanded the return of his guns and when they were given back, he left the station peaceably. Cap was soon arrested and charges were filed against him. His defense turned out to be so eloquent that he was acquitted.

Another bizarre incident occurred in the spring of 1900. A group of men, posing as land buyers (Cap had been selling off lots of real estate from an office in the Tremont Hotel) took over the district while Streeter was away and burned down his house. Cap quickly responded and after raising an army, marched into the

District and took it back. Police officers were again raised in response. Three-inch guns were mounted onto two of the city's fire tugs, 16 patrol wagons were lined up outside of the district and over 400 officers were called in to serve as troops. The volatile standoff ended when a lone policeman convinced Streeter that he should surrender himself. He did so and was acquitted again of all charges against him.

In 1902, Streeter and several of his cronies were indicted for forging the name of President Grover Cleveland on a land grant that "proved" that his district was outside of the jurisdiction of Chicago. It was later reported that the document Streeter used was actually a paper signed by President Martin Van Buren that gave certain lands to John Kinzie and his heirs. The heirs then immediately sued to have the land returned to them, which meant that the wealthy citizens who were trying to get rid of Cap Streeter for being a squatter were now being accused of being squatters themselves! The case eventually went away and Palmer and the others were able to again focus their attentions on the Streeter problem.

And it was in this same year that things took another turn and for the first time, Streeter actually ended up in jail over the matter - only this time for something

GHOST ALERT:
THE "STREETERVILLE CURSE"

The original Streeterville District extended from the Chicago River to Oak Street Beach, east of Michigan Avenue. Cap's claims to this area were little more than a nuisance to the wealthy and privileged in his day but now, the land is worth billions. Today, old Cap Streeter is barely remembered by most, except for the name Streeterville, which still persists in Chicago. For this reason, it would likely come as a surprise to many to learn that the presence of Streeter still lingers today -- in the form of a curse that allegedly "haunts" this part of the city.

Legend has it that Cap Streeter's final words were a curse on the politicians and on the city of Chicago for the real and imagined wrongs that had plagued the last several decades of his life. This story was often told, but nothing much was thought of it until the 1970s. Just a few years before, Streeterville had been changed forever by the construction of the massive John Hancock building. Erected between 1965 and 1969, the giant structure loomed high over the city around it. Despite the stories, though, no one died during the dangerous work that was done to create the building. However, that quickly changed after the tenants began moving in. A series of strange deaths began to plague the building, including the murder of a man on the sixth floor and a number of unusual fires.

The strangest, and most widely reported death, occurred during the early morning hours of August 12, 1971. The victim was one Lorraine Kowalski, the girlfriend of affluent Marshall Berlin, vice president of I.S. Berlin Press, a Chicago printing company. After spending the evening separately, they returned home and became involved in a volatile argument,. In the midst of the argument, Berlin retreated into the bathroom. When he came back out a few minutes later, he stated that the bedroom window had been shattered and that Lorraine's clothing was scattered about the room. Apparently, while he was in the bathroom, a naked Kowalski plunged out the window of the apartment and fell to the pavement many floors below. The fact that she broke the window remains one of the most puzzling parts to this mysterious incident. The double pane of glass in the apartment window was capable of withstanding 280 pounds of pressure per square foot and yet somehow, the slight 130-pound woman managed to break through it.

Berlin refused to take a polygraph test and told the investigators that Kowalski had threatened to commit suicide just moments before he went into the bathroom. No charges were ever brought in the case and it remains unsolved to this day. This death joined numerous others that occurred in the area. Was it merely a coincidence? Or is the area shadowed by Cap Streeter's legendary curse?

Staff members of a Chicago radio station that has its studios inside of the Hancock Building have reported some odd happenings at late hours of the night. It is not uncommon for overnight employees to tell of cold spots, strange whispers, knocking sounds and the presence of apparitions. On one occasion, a security officer noticed a person in the building after hours. Knowing that no one was supposed to be there, he called for the person to stop. The shadowy character began to run and the security guard gave chase. As the man began to outrun the officer, the guard called his partner in the video control room for help. His partner quickly looked up to the security monitors and saw the other officer running down an empty hallway! Even though the other man clearly saw the person he was chasing, there was no one on the video screen. The first guard pursued the figure around several corners and then it disappeared completely. A thorough search of the building discovered that no one else was present.

Cap married Alma Lockwood in 1906
(Chicago Daily News)

Cap & Alma lived in his houseboat, the Vamoose, until his death in 1921

that he didn't do! The wealthy "behind-the-scenes" men hired a gunman from Missouri named John Kirk to go in and clear Cap out, no matter what it took. Days later, Kirk's body was discovered in a Chicago alleyway, riddled with bullet holes. Streeter was shortly arrested and railroaded through the courts with a guilty charge for murder. He was sent to Joliet prison and while he was there, Maria died from exposure and hunger. Streeter cursed Chicago for her death and when he was released after nine months, with a full and unconditional pardon from the governor, he was never the same again.

In 1906, he re-married, though, this time to Alma Lockwood, who was 33 years his junior. Streeter had managed to hang on to his district, now dubbed Streeterville, for years but his days were numbered. By 1915, the land actually controlled by Cap had dwindled to nothing more than a fenced enclosure that surrounded the remains of his home. Streeter still held parties there, though, and sold liquor, even on Sundays, which was still illegal. The city informed him that he had to obtain a liquor license and sent several police officers to enforce the order. Streeter stabbed the sergeant who carried the papers in the behind with a bayonet as a reply. He was arrested but was quickly bailed out.

The following day, eight policemen charged into the district and attempted to arrest Cap again. Two of them grabbed Alma's ax but she managed to disarm six of the officers anyway. Another officer was wounded by birdshot from one of Cap's guns. Alma was arrested after the incident for "assault with intent to kill" but she was acquitted when it came out in court that none of the policemen ever identified themselves as officers.

After years of defending himself against attackers, the city of Chicago and the court system, Cap Streeter was finally defeated on December 11, 1918. On that day, the courts finally decided that Streeter had no real claim to the land that he called Streeterville. He was finally evicted and his home was burned to the ground, marking an end to one of the city's most unusual eras.

Streeter remained an eccentric Chicago character until the day he died. He began selling hot dogs and coffee at Navy Pier and lived comfortably in a new houseboat that he had purchased called the *Vamoose*. His final days came after he lost an eye while chopping wood. A sliver of kindling flew upward and put out his eye, which led to an infection. He contracted pneumonia in his weakened state and died on January 22, 1921 at the age of 84. The mayor, and half of the city, attended his funeral.

The *Vamoose* became a menace to navigation and was destroyed by city order in 1928. Alma, who saved only Cap's musket as a memento of their life together, ended her days making and selling aprons and she died in 1936. She never gave up on her husband's claims to the ownership of Streeterville, though, and she and his heirs continued their lawsuits until 1940, when a federal court finally dismissed the claims.

PETER NISSEN'S FANTASTIC VOYAGE

Perhaps every accountant dreams of a more exciting life, but few have ever pursued their dreams as eagerly - or as recklessly - as Peter Nissen.

Nissen, who lived on Francisco Street near Division, was an accountant by day and a daredevil inventor by night. All but forgotten today, his quest for adventure made him famous for a brief period at the beginning of the twentieth century. Nissen invented three boats, each named, a tad clairvoyantly, the *Fool Killer*. The first two helped him survive a deadly trip through the Niagara River rapids and whirlpool, and a third was an all-terrain rolling craft designed to bring him first across Lake Michigan and then to the North Pole. Some thought was he a visionary. Others thought he was a kook. Most likely, he was a bit of both.

Nissen's first *Fool Killer* was built over a 13-month period starting in 1899. It was described as an unsinkable vessel, containing around 300 pounds of cork. After a trial run in Lake Michigan, it was shipped to Niagara Falls in June of 1900. Nissen met up with it there and survived the trip through the rapids inside it. The boat was twenty feet long by four feet wide - it was open, so Nissen could wave to spectators. It was only at the last minute that Nissen thought to add shoulder straps, a move that certainly saved his life.

Nissen described the trip as "awful...it seemed that a hundred hammers where pounding my head." He further lamented that he had lost his hat and said at the time that if he had realized just how wild the rapids were, he never would have attempted the voyage. But he was back for more the next year in a refined craft, The *Fool Killer* No. 2. This ship was even more ambitious, featuring a steam engine and holding the record for the smallest steam vessel ever launched. It sank, and Nissen barely escaped with his life.

Still seeking escape from the drudgery of accounting, Nissen decided that he just hadn't quite pushed his luck hard enough and decided to invent an all-terrain craft that he could use to discover the North Pole.

The craft he invented, The *Fool Killer* No. 3, was likened to a giant balloon - 38 feet long and 22 feet in diameter - made of canvas stretched over wooden ribs. Inside were a wooden axle and a swinging basket hammock where Nissen would relax as the ball floated and rolled across sea and land, letting the wind propel it forward. Steering would be accomplished by moving the hammock across the axle, from which it was suspended, shifting the weight of the craft. Nissen planned for the model to be a mere prototype;

Eccentric inventor & adventurer Peter Nissen

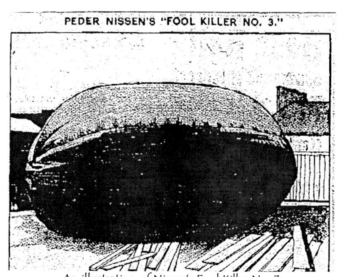

An illustration of Nissen's Fool Killer No. 3

the one he would take to the arctic would be three times as large. Rolling over glaciers and seas where no man had gone before in a giant balloon must have seemed terribly enchanting to a dreamer such as Nissen.

In a land test, the prototype rolled about 50 feet before running into a telegraph pole. Satisfied that it worked on land, Nissen then tested it on the water in Grant Park. It barely moved, and he came out of the craft looking a bit green due to trouble with air regulation. Nissen was widely mocked by people who thought that Fool Killer was an awfully appropriate name for the bizarre thingamajig, but Nissen was determined to prove them wrong and went to work fixing his craft, declaring it ready for action in the late fall of 1904.

Before making a trip to the Great White North, Nissen shocked the city by announcing that he was going to test his craft by sailing from Chicago across Lake Michigan to Michigan City, Ind.

The trip made national news, and was even covered in great detail by the *New York Times*. Lots of people thought Nissen was nuts - sailing on Lake Michigan in late November, with snowstorms blowing in, couldn't have been the brightest idea in the world. Waiting until spring probably would have been wiser, but Nissen apparently couldn't wait that long to try out his machine and prove the naysayers wrong.

Nissen packed three days worth of provisions and set out on November 29th. Onlookers cheered as the giant canvas balloon rolled over the horizon, away from the city lights. He was pursued by a tug boat, the Protection, which tried to throw him a line and reel him away from the high winds and storms (and perhaps back to reality), but Nissen refused to turn back and sailed on.

A day or so passed with no word or sign from Nissen, and people began to fear the worst. Soon, the *New York Times* was reporting that he was lost at sea, presumably either frozen to death or suffocated. A group of his friends and relatives set out in a tugboat to search for the remains of the strange ship.

On December 1, a woman found poor Nissen's body lying on the shore in Stevensville, Mich., with the craft, a total wreck, about 200 feet away. But Nissen had not frozen to death - he hadn't even needed his overcoat. According to some reports, which were later discredited, a note was found pinned to his body that read, "Cannot use the hose - N." Nissen and his craft had made it to the shore, but the ship was a wreck. Apparently still struggling with air regulation, Nissen tried to cut his way out and died of neuroparalysis the moment he hit the cold air. It was considered certain that if the hose had not broken, the trip would have been a complete success and Nissen would have arrived safely in Michigan City.

He had given his life to do so, but Nissen had proven the naysayers wrong. He may have known it, too. Some reports stated that the face of the corpse was fixed in a satisfied smile.

TOKYO ROSE

Iva Toguri -- Tokyo Rose?

Who knew that the nice old lady who ran Toguri Mercantile Co. on Belmont Avenue was one of the most notorious enemies of the United States during World War II? Well, if it makes you feel any better, she may not have been. Iva Ikuko Toguri D'Aquino was alleged to have been no other than a "Tokyo Rose," a generic name that was given by Allied Forces in the South Pacific to a dozen or so English-speaking radio announcers who spent countless hours playing music and spouting Japanese propaganda. But was Iva really one of the silky-voiced announcers or was she convicted of treason on trumped-up charges?

She was born Ikuko Toguri in Los Angeles, the daughter of Japanese immigrants Jun and Fumi Toguri. Her father had come to America in 1899 and her mother in 1913. Ikuko, who went by the name Iva, was raised a Methodist and spent time as a Girl Scout when she was a child. She attended schools in Mexico and San Diego before returning with her family to Los Angeles. There, she attended high school, and graduated from UCLA with a degree in zoology. She then went on to work in her parents' store, living the ordinary life of a young woman in the late 1930s and early 1940s.

It was a dark twist of fate that took her out of the country on the eve of World War II. On July 5, 1941, Iva sailed for Japan to visit an ailing relative and possibly, to study medicine. The U.S. State Department issued her a Certificate of Identification but she did not have a passport. In September of that same year, Iva applied to the U.S. Vice Consul in Japan for a passport, stating that she wished to return home to the United States. Her request was forwarded to the State Department, but her papers had not arrived by the time of the attack on Pearl Harbor (December 7, 1941) and she was stranded in Japan.

From the start of the American involvement in the Pacific War, Iva, like many other Americans in Japanese territory, was pressured by the Japanese government to renounce her U.S. citizenship. She refused to do so and was then declared an enemy alien and was denied a war ration card. To support herself, she found work as a typist at a Japanese news agency and eventually worked in a similar capacity for Radio Tokyo.

In November 1943, allied prisoners of war, who were forced to broadcast propaganda, chose her to host portions of the one-hour radio show called The Zero Hour. Her producer was an Australian Army officer, Major Charles Cousens, who had broadcast experience before the war. Cousens, who had been captured during the fall of Singapore, had been tortured and coerced to work on the radio broadcast, as had his assistants, U.S. Army Captain

Wallace Ince and a Philippine Army Lieutenant, Normando Ildefonso "Norman" Reyes.

The men knew and trusted Iva because she had previously risked her life to smuggle food into the POW camp where Cousens and Ince were held. After she told them that she would not broadcast any anti-American propaganda, the two men assured her that they would write scripts that prevented her from having to say anything against the United States. Iva then went on to host a total of 340 broadcasts of The Zero Hour.

Iva used the stage names of "Ann" (for "Announcer") and later "Orphan Anne," reportedly in reference to the comic strip character of Little Orphan Annie. She performed in comedy sketches and introduced news broadcasts, spending about 20 minutes at a time on the air. True to their word, the two prisoners of war never forced

Iva Toguri broadcasting from somewhere in Japan during World War II. The photo was obviously a Japanese propaganda image.

her to take part in anti-American propaganda. Iva earned only about 150 yen (roughly $7) per month, and spent part of her earnings buying food to smuggle to the Allied POWs.

Iva Toguri made most of her on-air comments to her fellow Americans, using American slang and playing American music. In one of the surviving recordings of her show, she referred to herself to herself as "your Number One enemy." In contemporary American slang, especially that used by U.S. Marines and naval forces in the Pacific, she was telling them that she was their "best enemy" (in other words, their friend), while her Japanese masters thought that it meant she was their greatest enemy.

Iva never actually called herself "Tokyo Rose" during the war, and in fact there is no evidence that any other broadcaster did, either. The name was simply a catchall used by the Allied soldiers for the women who were heard on Japanese propaganda radio.

On August 19, 1945, Iva married Felipe D'Aquino, a Portuguese citizen of Japanese-Portuguese descent. She also became a Catholic, a faith that would carry her through her prison years. The marriage was registered with the Portuguese Consulate in Tokyo, with Iva declining to take her husband's citizenship.

After Japan's unconditional surrender at the end of the war, reporters Henry Brundidge and Clark Lee offered $250, which is considered unethical "checkbook journalism" by press associations and journalism professionals today, for the identity of "Tokyo Rose."

In need of money, and still trying to get home, Iva stepped forward to claim the reward, but instead found herself arrested, on September 5, 1945, in Yokohama. She was released after a year in jail when neither the FBI nor General Douglas MacArthur's staff had found any evidence that she had aided the Japanese Axis forces. In her defense, the American and Australian POWs also stepped forward and assured the Allied headquarters that she had done nothing wrong.

The FBI's extensive investigation of her activities, which "unearthed forgotten Japanese documents, and turned up recordings of D'Aquino's broadcasts," led the authorities to decide that the evidence against her did not merit prosecution. Pregnant and expecting to be released, she asked to be allowed to return to the United States to give birth to her child on American soil. The request was never granted and

Iva was tried and found guilt of treason after the war, despite flimsy evidence against her.

circumstances turned against her.

Thanks to lobbying by influential gossip columnist and radio host Walter Winchell, Iva was not released as she hoped to be. Her baby was born in Japan, but died soon after. She was forcibly separated from her husband (whom she never saw again) and was brought to San Francisco on September 25, 1948. There, federal prosecutors charged her with treason.

Her trial on eight "overt acts" of treason began on July 5, 1949. During what was at the time the most expensive trial in U.S. history, costing more than half a million dollars, the prosecution presented 46 witnesses, including two of Iva's former supervisors at Radio Tokyo, and soldiers who testified that they could not distinguish between what they had heard on radio broadcasts and what they heard by way of rumor. Although prosecutors brought boxes of tapes of radio broadcasts to the courthouse, none were entered into evidence or played for the jury. Iva continued to claim that she and her associates subtly sabotaged the Japanese war effort.

On September 29, 1949, the jury found Iva guilty of one count of treason, which stated, "That on a day during October, 1944, the exact date being to the Grand Jurors unknown, said defendant, at Tokyo, Japan, in a broadcasting studio of The Broadcasting Corporation of Japan, did speak into a microphone concerning the loss of ships." Iva was fined $10,000 and given a 10-year prison sentence. Her attorney, Wayne Collins, citing the ridiculousness of the trial, called the verdict "guilty without evidence." Iva was sent to the Federal Reformatory for Women at Alderson, W.V., and was paroled after serving six years and two months. She was released on January 28, 1956. Iva was never reunited with her husband, who had been deported to Japan after her trial. She divorced him in 1980 and he died in 1996.

After her parole, Iva moved to Chicago. She was pardoned by President Gerald Ford in 1977. She passed away in 2006.

After her parole, resisting efforts at deportation, Iva moved to Chicago, where her father had opened the Japanese import retail store, J. Toguri Mercantile, after being released from the Gila River Relocation Center in 1943. Iva lived and worked at the store for many years, her former notoriety all but forgotten. At that time, the store was located on North Clark Street, but later moved to Belmont Avenue. It still operates today, owned by the Toguri family, and sells Asian books, artwork, foodstuffs, and art and party supplies.

In 1976, an investigation by *Chicago Tribune* reporter Ron Yates discovered that two officials from Radio Tokyo, Kenkichi Oki and George Mitsushio, who delivered the most damaging testimony at Iva's trial, lied under oath. The pair stated they had been threatened by the FBI and U.S. occupation police and told what to say and what not to say just hours before the trial. Yates' investigation led to a report on the television news program, *60 Minutes*.

Thanks to these revelations, President Gerald Ford pardoned Iva on January 19, 1977, his last day in office, after she had appealed to him in a letter. The decision was supported by a unanimous vote in both houses of the California state legislature, the national Japanese-American Citizens League, and by S.I. Hayakawa, then a United States Senator from California. The pardon restored her citizenship.

On January 15, 2006, the World War II Veterans Committee, citing "her indomitable spirit, love of country, and the example of courage she has given her fellow Americans," awarded Iva its annual Edward J Herlihy Citizenship Award. She reportedly said that this was the most memorable day of her life.

On September 26, 2006, at the age of 90, Iva died of natural causes in Chicago, bringing an end to a heroic, and often tragic life.

THE DEVIL MADE ME DO IT!

One of our weirdest Chicagoans was born in the city but gained his fame (or perhaps his infamy) elsewhere. His name was Anton Szandor LaVey and he was the founder and High Priest of the Church of Satan, as well as a writer, occultist, musician, actor, and bona fide showman. He was brilliant, always controversial, and, in the end, more than a bit of a mystery since his autobiography was so mixed with legend that it's almost impossible to separate fantasy from the truth.

Anton LaVey was born in Chicago on April 11, 1930. In the 1970s, he claimed to be born on the exact site where the Hancock building now stands in Streeterville, creating a mythology that the shape of the building was crucial to occultism and, of course, that he was somehow connected to the ominous "curse."

He was born Howard Stanton Levey and his father, Michael Levey, was a liquor distributor from Omaha. His mother, Gertrude, was a housewife. The family later relocated to the San Francisco Bay area and he spent most of his early life in California and Arizona. According to his biography, he began developing his musical skills at an early age and tried his hand at various instruments, including the pipe organ and the calliope.

He also claimed that he dropped out of high school to join up with a traveling carnival, working first as a roustabout and as a cage boy in an act with big cats. He

Weird native Chicagoan Anton LaVey

later played the calliope for the "grind shows" that were a standard part of sideshows in the 1940s. LaVey later noted that seeing many of the same men attending both the strip shows on Saturday night and the tent revival meetings on Sunday mornings reinforced his cynical view of religion. He later played as an organist in dozens of bars, lounges, and nightclubs. While playing the organ in Los Angeles, he reportedly had a brief affair with the then-unknown Marilyn Monroe as she was dancing at the Mayan Theater. This claim has been challenged by those who knew Monroe at the time, as well as the manager of the Mayan, Paul Valentine, who stated that she had never been one of his dancers.

After that, LaVey moved back to San Francisco, where he claimed to have worked as a photographer for the police department. He also dabbled as a psychic investigator, looking into weird calls about strange phenomena that were referred to him by the police department.

According to some stories, when LaVey shaved his head, it wasn't because of a ritual - he had simply lost a bet. However, he found that the new look was more "marketable" than the old one.

A short time later, LaVey met and married Carole Lansing, with whom he had his first daughter, Karla LaVey, in 1952. They divorced in 1960 after LaVey began seeing Diane Hegarty. They never married, but she was his companion for many years, and bore his second daughter, Zeena Galatea LaVey in 1963.

LaVey soon became known as a San Francisco celebrity. Thanks to his paranormal research and his live performances as an organist (including playing the Wurlitzer at the Lost Weekend cocktail lounge), he attracted many California notables to his parties. Guests included Michael Harner, Chester A. Arthur III, Forrest J. Ackerman, Fritz Leiber, Dr. Cecil E. Nixon, and Kenneth Anger. He began presenting lectures on the occult to what he called his "Magic Circle," which was made up of friends who shared his interests. A member of the circle suggested, perhaps jokingly, that he could start his own religion based on the ideas that he was coming up with.

LaVey took this seriously and on April 30, 1966, he ritualistically shaved his head, declared the founding of the Church of Satan and proclaimed 1966 as "the Year One," Anno Satanas - the first year of

LaVey on the cover of Look Magazine

the Age of Satan.

To create his version of Satanism, LaVey mixed together writings of Ayn Rand, Friedrich Nietzsche, Aleister Crowley, H.L. Mencken, and Jack London with the ideology and ritual practices that he cooked up for the Church of Satan. He wrote essays that re-worked books on philosophy and "Satanized" versions of John Dee's Enochian Keys, and turned them into books like *The Satanic Bible*, *The Compleat Witch* (re-released in 1989 as *The Satanic Witch*), and *The Satanic Rituals*.

Media attention soon followed, leading to coverage in newspapers all over the country and the cover of *Look* magazine. The Los Angeles Times and the San Francisco Chronicle were among those that dubbed him the "Black Pope." LaVey performed Satanic weddings, Satanic baptisms (including one for his daughter Zeena) and Satanic funerals, and released a record album entitled The Satanic Mass. He appeared on talk shows with Joe Pyne, Phil Donahue, and Johnny Carson, and in a feature length documentary called Satanis in 1968.

The Church of Satan was based at LaVey's home in San Francisco's Richmond District, where its purple and black façade stood out on the residential street. The interior was painted in glossy black and red and was fitted with secret passages and rooms. Grotesque paintings, created by LaVey, were on display throughout the house, as were huge murals that depicted the Devil in action. The fireplace had a trapdoor that led to the "Den of Iniquity," where Satanic rituals allegedly took place.

Hegarty and LaVey separated in the middle 1980s, and she sued for palimony. The claim was settled out of court. LaVey's next and final companion was Blanche Barton. Barton and LaVey are the parents of Satan Xerxes Carnacki LaVey, born November 1, 1993. Barton became the head of the Church of Satan after LaVey's death, but has since stepped down from that position.

Anton LaVey died on October 29, 1997, in St. Mary's Hospital, San Francisco of pulmonary edema. For reasons open to speculation, the time and date of his death was listed incorrectly on his death certificate - stating that he died on Halloween. His estranged daughter, Zeena, took credit for his death, claiming that she had put a "death curse" on him. LaVey's funeral was a secret, by invitation only Satanic service that was held in Colma, Calif. His body was cremated, with his ashes eventually divided among his heirs as part of a settlement. The ashes allegedly possess occult powers and can be used for Satanic ritual magic.

So, was Anton LaVey really the spokesman for Satan, or was he merely a master showman who managed to turn America's fascination with the occult in the 1960s and 1970s to his own advantage? Perhaps he was a little of both.

THE CHICKEN MAN

Generations of Chicagoans knew the Chicken Man. He was an old black man who would appear all over the city, on street cars, the El, buses, and on corners, with a trained chicken, which rode around on his head. The chicken would do all sorts of tricks -- it would dance, talk into a toy phone, walk across a tightrope, play dead...everything but talk! Generations of Chicagoans knew him as the godfather of all Chicago street performers. Some saw him so often, in so many places, that they believed that there was a whole network of Chicken Men operating around Chicago.

In fact, there was a whole network of chickens - but only one Chicken Man.

Born under the name Anderson Punch (or so he claimed), the Chicken Man was born in Shreveport, La., in 1870 and came to Chicago around 1910. He worked as a cook for a while before becoming a street musician. When his accordion broke in 1914, he didn't shed any tears; by that time, he had discovered the secret of training chickens.

Taking the name Casey Jones, after the title of the song he sang most often, he trained a few chickens and took his act to the street. Soon, he was familiar sight around the city. He was hauled into court early in his career on vagrancy charges and was ordered to prove that he could earn a living. Pulling out a banjo, Jones reportedly said, "Judge, give me a dime and I'll sing you the blues!"

In 1938, arrested for obstructing traffic, his chicken, Mae West Pistol Packin' Mama Caledonia, danced the Big Apple in court. In 1946, arrested again for obstructing traffic at Clark Street and Belmont Avenue, Casey spent a night in jail -- with his chicken -- as the Powers That Be suggested that the chicken be taken away from him and given to the anti-cruelty society.

"Your honor," Casey said to the judge the next day. "I love that fowl, and I'd rather die than lose her."

"I've seen you and Mae (West Pistol Packin' Mama) around for 30 years," said the judge. "I'd hate to spoil that friendship. You've got to stay south of Madison Street if I let you go, though."

Casey happily agreed, and confined himself (somewhat) to the South Side for the rest of his career -- which no one at the time would have guessed was barely half over! The next year, when Mae West Pistol Packin' Mama died, she was given a public funeral in a vacant lot on the south side.

Mae was hardly Casey's only chicken, though. At most times, he had about four "performers," which, he claimed, took only a couple of hours to train, though he refused to let anyone on to his secret for training chickens. Over the years, he was said to have owned 213 of them. "I've had some lean times," he said in 1971, "but I've never eaten one of my chickens. They die of natural causes."

Casey remained a familiar face all over the south side, estimating that he hit every single corner at one point or another (though his favorite spot, for financial reasons, was the corner of 63rd Street and Halsted Avenue), for decades to come. In 1971, he was still performing on his 101st birthday. The next year, he moved to a south side nursing home where he died in 1974. He left his chickens with a friend, though he visited them often. In 1982, the *Chicago Tribune* held him up as an example of a "true Chicagoan."

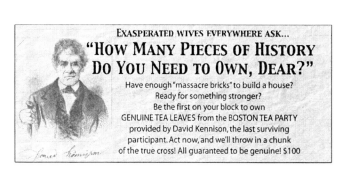

3. WEIRD CHICAGO DISASTERS

Hell has been described as a pocket edition of Chicago.
Ashley Montagu

The city of Chicago has long been a place of horror, tragedy, and death, dating back to the earliest days of the Fort Dearborn Massacre and continuing with the Great Chicago Fire in 1871. Unfortunately, those horrific events were not the only times that Chicago was marked by disaster and over the decades, the city has seen more than her share.

Fires have taken many lives in Chicago and have left a vivid mark on the city. While the Great Chicago Fire was the most famous blaze in the city's history, it was certainly not the only time that the city was scorched with flames.

THE HOTEL LASALLE FIRE

The Hotel LaSalle opened in 1909 at the northwest corner of Madison and LaSalle streets. The spacious and comfortable hotel was advertised as "the largest, safest, and most modern hotel in America, outside of New York City." It was built and owned by the Stevens family, who later built the Stevens Hotel at Michigan Avenue and Balbo Drive. The owners and the architects claimed that the hotel was fireproof, which turned out to be an exaggerated boast.

In 1936, new owners modernized the building and, unfortunately, chose profits over safety. Fire concerns were ignored, which would have dire consequences on June 5, 1946, when a carelessly tossed cigarette ignited a fire in the pit of the Number Five elevator shaft.

Within minutes, the 22-story building, which was essentially a firetrap, was burning out of control. The flames shot upwards through the elevator shaft and sent fire along the ceiling from the north elevator to the mezzanine. The flames then spread farther, up to the seventh floor, where they stopped. Deadly smoke filled the hallways, reaching the top floor. Many of the guests, thinking that cries of "fire" were a prank, remained in their rooms where they ended up suffocating from the thick smoke.

As the fire spread, escape routes were cut off. Terrified guests tossed hastily written notes down to the street, begging for rescue that never came. In those days, fire ladders only extended to the eighth floor, making rescue impossible. Many of the guests hurled luggage from their windows and into the streets below, while others took the fatal plunge themselves. Firefighters later recalled guests in their nightclothes, teetering on window ledges, as they pleaded with them to remain patient. Spectators and curiosity-seekers pushed past police barricades for a better look at the blaze and were injured by falling suitcases and other items that had been thrown from upper windows.

Air Force Lieutenant Chandler Royal went into the hotel after the fire was put out, assisting in the rescue efforts. He later remembered the charred and blackened hotel rooms and corridors as worse than some of the things that he had seen in war-torn Germany. "So many blackened corpses in the halls and rooms... it was ghastly," he told reporters.

In the end, the fire, which claimed 61 lives, could be blamed on the owners, who had shown a shocking lack of interest in safety. As early as 1927, they had been advised against the number of combustible draperies in the building, but failed to heed the warnings. Even worse, there were no instructions in the rooms as to where guests should go in the event of a fire.

The Hotel LaSalle Banquet Room

Amazingly, the hotel later re-opened, although it was demolished in 1976 and an office building now stands in its place.

THE HABER FACTORY FIRE

The Haber Corporation, located on West Avenue, just one block west of Halsted Avenue, was just like so many other grimy, industrial factories on the north side of the city in the early 1950s. The factory built machine parts for food mixers and other small appliances made by Dormeyer, a parent company that was located just down the street. The plant employed 800 unskilled assembly-line workers, most of them Eastern European war refugees who barely spoke English but were happy to have the monotonous jobs that they were given in their new country.

Fortunately for most of the employees, a reduced work force was in the plant on the morning of April 16, 1953, when at around 8:50 a.m. a tremendous explosion rocked the building, sending a wave of fire upward from the northwest corner of the first floor. A polishing machine operated by Joseph Loverde threw off a spark. It ignited a mixture of dust particles, lint, and aluminum shards, creating the enormous blast.

Within minutes, the factory was turned into an inferno. Workers who tried to escape from the upper floors found themselves trapped because someone had ordered the removal of an emergency stairway and a fire escape. The Ragnar Benson construction company had been hired to renovate the façade of the aging building, but the rusted fire escape stood in the way of the carpenters and stonemasons. The fire escape had been taken down on the orders of Harry Brady, the plant's director of safety, who, rather ironically, perished in the blaze.

A shipping room ladder was haphazardly placed against a third-floor ledge to try and help workers down from the upper floors, but it turned out to be tragically inadequate. Screaming women, with their hair on fire, plunged to their deaths from the ledge and were piled on the floor below. Stairwells blocked with Haber machine parts further impeded escape routes from the building. The positioning of some bodies indicated to Deputy Coroner Harry Glos that the intensity of the flames had simply roasted to death many of the victims where they stood.

Assistant Fire Commissioner Anthony J. Mullaney was shaken to the core when he arrived at the scene. "Everywhere I looked, there were human torches around me with their clothes and hair and bodies on fire! I still don't know what happened," he told reporters. "This is horrible. This proves that management should know more about their employees' safety. They should be more responsible."

Coroner Walter McCarron indignantly spoke out against company president Kalman Tanko at the inquest that followed the fire. "Violations were running wild," he said, "such as violations of the no-smoking rule. If the fire escape had been there, lives would have been saved!"

When it was all over, 35 victims perished in the fire and the Haber Corporation was cited with 10 violations of the fire safety code. Most Haber Corporation executives failed to show up for the inquest. The families of the dead and injured demanded that someone be held accountable, but both Tanko and the owner of the property refused to accept responsibility.

The ownership of the property was eventually traced to Titus Haffa, a notorious politician and professional bail bondsman who had served time in Leavenworth in 1929 for liquor violations during Prohibition. Haffa was the Republican alderman for the 43rd Ward, a north side bastion for crime and vice. Years before, Haffa had worked with gangsters from the Moran gang to protect his liquor business and had financed everything through the Haber Company, which he had bought for almost nothing in 1921.

Although branded as a "betrayer of the public trust" by Judge Walter C. Lindley, Alderman Haffa served only 17 months of his two-year prison sentence. He recouped his fortune during World War II, buying up old factories and handling war contracts. Haffa had transferred the title of the Haber plant to his two sisters, Doris and Pauline, who lived off their brother's generosity in an old mansion that once belonged to Robert Lincoln on Lake Shore Drive.

By the time of the Haber fire, Haffa's shady past was a distant memory. He had become an admired business leader, but then the fire brought all of it back into the public eye. The former alderman spoke of the suffering of the Haber victims in a somber tone, but dodged questions about potential liability. He told reporters, "No man's grief is greater than mine in all of this. Those who lost their lives were not just employees but friends whom I knew by their first names."

Haffa vowed that the dead would never be forgotten. Once the debris of the burned-out factory was cleared away, Haffa advised community leaders to build a park on the site to memorialize the victims for future generations. He even offered to bear the expense of it. The money meant nothing to him, he said, and he would give away his fortune if he could bring back one of the dead.

The community awaited further action from Haffa, but nothing happened. Months, then years went by, and they eventually realized there would be no park and no monument of any kind. The land was sold off and later developed into a Crate and Barrel store, the only memorial ever raised to the victims of the 1953 fire.

THE OUR LADY OF ANGELS FIRE

One of the most soul-crushing fires in Chicago's history took place on December 1, 1958 when 92 children and three nuns died at the Our Lady of Angels School on the west side. The horrible event shattered scores of lives on that day and the neighborhood where the school once stood has never fully recovered.

The Our Lady of Angels School was located at 3820 West Iowa Street. It was surrounded by a quiet Catholic parish of about 4,500 families from mostly Irish and Italian backgrounds. They lived modestly in apartments and brick bungalows until after the fire, when many of these hardworking families abandoned the neighborhood, never to return.

The fire began at around 2:40 p.m., about 20 minutes before school was to be let out for the day. Like many other

schools of that era, Our Lady of Angels was tragically without many of the safety measures that exist today. There were no smoke detectors, no sprinkler systems, no outside fire alarm and the entire building had only one fire escape. Unbelievably, the school had passed a fire inspection two months before. By 1958 standards, the building was legally safe.

It is believed that the fire started in a trash can at the bottom of the basement stairwell. There, it smoldered all day and then spread to the stairs, thanks to air from an open window. Once it was ignited, the fire quickly spread and burned up to the second floor, devouring the building as it went. By the time the first fire trucks arrived, the upper floor of the north wing was engulfed in flames. The fire had already been burning for a number of minutes before the alarm went off and more precious time was lost when the fire department trucks pulled up to the church rectory, and not the school. The dispatchers had been given the wrong address by the person who phoned in the report. Then, when the first trucks arrived at the school, they had to break through a locked gate to get inside.

Inside the classrooms, which were rapidly filling with smoke, the students heard the sound of the fire trucks approaching, but then nothing, as the trucks went to the rectory instead. At that desperate moment, the nuns asked the children to bow their heads in prayer. When the trucks finally arrived, and the extent of the blaze was realized, another alarm was sent out, ordering all available vehicles to the scene. Before it was over, 43 pieces of fire equipment were at the school.

The fire escape had now become unreachable through the burning hallways. The only way out was through the windows and soon, screaming children were plunging to the frozen ground below. The desperate firemen behaved heroically and managed to save 160 children by pulling them out the windows, passing them down ladders, catching them in nets, and breaking their falls with their own bodies. One rescuer who climbed a ladder up to the building's second floor was Lieutenant Charles Kamin. When he reached the window of Room 211, he found a number of 8th graders were crammed together and trying to squeeze out. He reached inside and, one a time, began grabbing them, swinging them around his back and dropping them onto the ladder. He saved nine children, mostly boys, because he could grab hold of their belts. He was only stopped when the room exploded and the students fell back out of his reach.

More confusion was added to the scene as terrified parents began to arrive. They hampered the efforts of the firefighters as they rushed the police lines, hysterically trying to reach their children who were trapped in the building. It took the crews a little more than an hour to put out the fire and when they entered the second-story classrooms, they discovered that flames had consumed everything and had claimed the lives of dozens of children and nuns.

For the hundreds of parents and relatives who stood outside, the huge loss of life was soon apparent as cloth-covered stretchers began to emerge from the smoldering building. A long line of ambulances and police squadrons slowly collected the bodies and took them to the Cook County Morgue, where family members could identify them. For many parents standing outside, the tragedy was made worse because many of them did not know if their children were dead or alive. Although a number of parents located children in the streets outside the school, or in homes nearby, others were left to search the seven hospitals were the injured were taken --- or worse yet, the morgue.

Chicago was stunned by the appalling loss of life and word of the disaster spread around the world. In Rome, Pope John XXIII sent a personal message to the archbishop of Chicago, the Most Reverend Albert Gregory Meyer. Four days later, Meyer conducted a mass for the victims and their families before an altar set up at the Northwest Armory. He called the fire "a great and inescapable sorrow."

Nearly as tragic as the fire itself was the fact that no blame was ever placed for the disaster. In those days, there was no thought of suing those responsible for the conditions that allowed the fire to happen. Outwardly, the families accepted the idea that the fire had been simply "God's will," but it cannot be denied that a number of those involved left the church, their faith as shattered as their lives. No one dared to challenge the church over what happened and life moved quietly on.

But in January 1962, the fire was news again when police in Cicero questioned a 13-year-old boy about a series of fires that had been set in the city. When they learned that he had been a troubled student at Our Lady of Angels at the time of the fire, their interrogations took another direction. The boy's mother and stepfather hired an attorney, who recommended that the boy submit to a polygraph test.

In the interview, polygraph expert John Reid learned that the boy began starting fires at the age of 5, when he set his family's garage alight. He had also set as many as 11 fires in buildings in Chicago and Cicero, usually by tossing burning matches on papers at the bottom of staircases. This was exactly how most believed the Our Lady of Angels fire started and so Reid pressed him harder. The boy denied starting the fire at first, but test results indicated that he was lying. Later, the boy admitted that he had set the blaze, hoping for a few extra days out of school. He said he hated his teachers and his principal because they "always wanted to expel me from school." His attendance record had been poor and his behavior was descried as "deplorable."

In his confession, he said that he had started the fire in the basement after leaving his classroom to go to the bathroom. He threw three matches into a trashcan and then ran upstairs to his second-floor classroom, which was soon evacuated. When Reid asked him why he had never told anyone about setting fire to the school, the boy replied, "I was afraid my dad was going to give me a beating and I'd get in trouble with the police and I'd get the electric chair or something."

The Our Lady of Angels Monument in Queen of Heaven Cemetery in Hillside

Reid turned the confession over to the police and the boy was placed in the Audy Juvenile Home. Charges were filed against him, but after a series of hearings that ended in March 1962, Judge Alfred Cilella tossed out the boy's confessions, ruling that Reid had obtained it illegally. Also, since the boy was under the age of 13 at the time of the fire, he could not be tried for a felony in Illinois. He did charge the boy with starting the fires in Cicero, though, and he was sent away to a home for troubled boys in Michigan. The boy's identity has never been released, but there are those who know it. Despite pleas from surviving family members of the Our Lady of Angels victims, it has never been publicly released.

Despite the passage of time, the fire has never been forgotten. A new parish school was constructed on the site in 1960, but it was closed in 1999 because of declining enrollments. The only memorial to the victims of the fire is located in Queen of Heaven Cemetery in Hillside, where 25 of the victims were buried. It was constructed from private donations in 1960 and to this date, no official memorial to the fire has been erected.

In addition to destroyed lives and lingering resentments, the fire has another legacy that has endured. Thanks to the horror at the Our Lady of Angels, the lives of future children may have been saved. Even though this is small comfort to the families of those who perished, the new safety regulations that went into effect because of the fire, including alarm boxes and sprinkler systems, have most likely saved the lives of thousands of children over the years.

THE IROQUOIS THEATER FIRE

This is the most flammable goddamn mess of scenery I ever saw…
Will J. Davis, co-owner of the Iroquois Theater

Dancing! Yes, the pillars of flame danced! To the multitude swept into eternity before the hurricane of flame and the few who were dragged out hideously disfigured and burned almost beyond all semblance of human beings it seemed indeed a dance of death.
Marshall Everett

Perhaps the most heartbreakingly tragic Chicago fire occurred at the famed Iroquois Theater on December 30, 1903 as a blaze broke out in the crowded venue during a performance of a vaudeville show. The fire claimed the lives of hundreds of people, including children, who were packed in for an afternoon show during the holidays. It remains one of the deadliest theater fires in American history.

The Iroquois Theater, the newest and most beautiful showplace in Chicago in 1903, was believed to be "absolutely fireproof," according to newspaper reports. The Chicago Tribune called it a "virtual temple of beauty," but just five weeks after it opened, it became a blazing death trap.

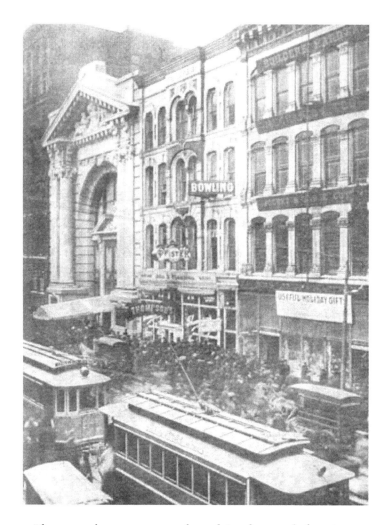

Views of the Iroquois Theater

(Left) The grand theater in 1903

(Below) A poster for "Mr. Bluebeard", the show that was being performed at the time of the disaster.

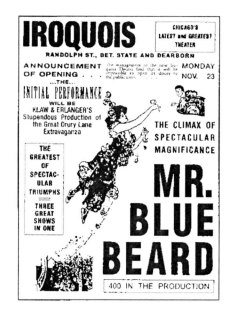

The new theater was much acclaimed, even before it was unveiled to the public. It was patterned after the Opera-Cominque in Paris and was located downtown on the north side of Randolph Street, between State and Dearborn streets. The interior of the four-story building was magnificent, with stained glass and polished wood throughout. The lobby had an ornate 60-foot ceiling and featured white marble walls fitted with large mirrors that were framed in gold leaf and stone. Two grand staircases led away from either side of the lobby to the balcony areas. Outside, the building's façade resembled a Greek temple with a towering stone archway that was supported by massive columns.

Thanks to the dozens of fires that had occurred over the years in theaters, architect Benjamin H. Marshall wanted to assure the public that the Iroquois was safe. He studied a number of fires that had occurred in the past and made every effort to make sure that no tragedy would occur in the new theater. The Iroquois had 25 exits that, it was claimed, could empty the building in less than five minutes. The stage had also been fitted with an asbestos curtain that could be quickly lowered to protect the audience.

While all of this was impressive, it was not enough to battle the real problems that existed with the Iroquois. Seats in the theater were wooden with cushions stuffed with hemp and much of the precautionary fire equipment that was to been installed never actually made it into the building. The theater had no fire alarms and in a rush to open on time, other safety factors had been forgotten or simply ignored.

The horrific event occurred on the bitterly cold afternoon of December 30, 1903. A holiday crowd had packed into the theater on that Wednesday afternoon to see a matinee performance of the hit comedy Mr. Bluebeard. Officially, the Iroquois seated 1,602 people, with approximately 700 in the expensive "parquet," the seats down in

EDDIE FOY

Eddie Foy was born on March 9, 1856, in Greenwich Village, New York City, and was, for a time, one of America's favorite actors, comedians, dancers, and vaudevillians. He has been permanently connected with the horrific fire at the Iroquois Theater in 1903.

After Foy's father died in 1862, the six-year-old began performing in local saloons first in New York and later in Chicago to support his family. He was in the city during the Great Fire of 1871. He first became famous in the 1870s as a performer in mining camps and cow towns in the West. During this period he apparently became friendly with Doc Holliday in Dodge City. One night in Dodge City, he became involved in an altercation over a girl with fellow actor Charlie Chaplin, who was drunkenly taking pot shots at Foy. The gunfire awakened Wyatt Earp, who disarmed Chaplin and sent both the players home to sleep it off. Foy is also reported to have been in Tombstone, Ariz., in October 1881, appearing at the local theatre when the Gunfight at the OK Corral occurred on that month.

In 1886 Foy married Lola Selfton, who died ten years later, and in 1888, he returned to Chicago. By this time, he was a star comedian on the vaudeville circuit. He played the variety shows for years, doing song and dance acts, eventually rising to musical comedy stardom in such Broadway hits as The Strollers (1901), and Mr. Bluebeard (1903). Foy specialized in eccentric routines and costumes, often appearing in women's clothing to hilarious effect. His upper lip extended well below his teeth, giving him an unusual V-shaped grin, and he spoke in a slurred lisp that audiences loved. In 1896, Foy married Madeline Morando and they had 11 children together, seven of whom survived into adulthood. Several of them went into show business after playing for years in a vaudeville act that their father created called "Eddie Foy and The Seven Little Foys." They toured successfully for years and appeared in one motion picture. When Foy remarried in 1923 - to Mary Reilly Coombs - the children went their separate ways. A dedicated trouper, the elder Foy continued to appear in vaudeville and starred in the hit Broadway comedy "The Fallen Star" in 1927. He died of a heart attack at 73 while headlining on the Orpheum circuit in Kansas City, Mo.

front that overlooked the orchestra pit; more than 400 in the first balcony and probably just under 500 in the steep, upper balcony. There were four lower boxes, each seating six people, and two upper boxes designed to hold four people in each, but the owners had managed to crowd eight chairs into those boxes.

Added to those who had purchased tickets to the show in advance were the usual late arrivals. Some came to buy tickets for available standing room; others had guest passes from connections they had with the management, contractors, actors, and theater employees. Others had been given tickets by city inspectors who had done favors for the owners of the theater. Estimates varied, but because the managers wanted to make up for earlier, smaller shows, that there may have been considerably more than 200 standees that afternoon. By curtain time, an estimated 1,840 people, most of them women and children, were packed into the house. This was far beyond capacity. The overflow had people filling the seats and standing four-deep in the aisles. Another crowd filled the backstage area with 400 actors, dancers and stagehands.

As the show was about to begin, actor Eddie Foy was delighted at the size of the crowd. "That Wednesday afternoon, the house was packed and many were standing," he later said. "I was struck by the fact that I had never seen so many women and children. Even the gallery was full."

What Foy did not see beyond the bright stage lights was that the Iroquois auditorium was not merely full, it was dangerously overcrowded. Not only was the standing room only crowd packed into the designated area behind the last row of seats, they were also sitting in the aisles and standing along both side walls. One usher would later claim there were at least 500 people standing in the auditorium.

Anticipation mounted as the lights dimmed for act one of the show. In accordance with the owner's standard operating procedures, most of the doors leading from the balcony and gallery had been locked or bolted by the ushers to keep out gate crashers and prevent those sitting or standing in the upper tiers from sneaking down in the darkness to the more expensive seats. This was done regardless of the fact that it was obvious that there were no empty seats anywhere.

The audience was thrilled with the show's first act. During the intermission, those in the expensive sections and boxes retired to the smoking room, or went to freshen up, relax on the plush couches and mingle on the promenade. Those in the balcony and gallery, behind the locked and bolted gates, flowed through the upper promenade and used the restrooms.

By 3:20 p.m., the second act of Mr. Bluebeard was well under way. During one of the early scenes, possibly while Foy was riding a baby elephant, Nellie Reed of the aerial ballet was hooked to a thin trolley wire that would send her high above the audience during a musical number. The sequence was made spectacular through the use of hundreds of colored lights. Some of the bulbs were concealed inside two narrow concave metal reflectors that were located on each side of the stage. Called "front lighting," each reflector was mounted on vertical hinges and, when not needed, was supposed to be pivoted by stagehands so that they disappeared into niches in the wall. The lights were not needed for the number that was about to start, but a member of the stage crew, for some reason, had not retracted the right stage reflector. It was left slightly extended, an edge of it in the path of the curtains. In the usual business of moving scenery, adjusting lights, moving backdrops, and the hundreds of other things that needed to be done, no one noticed the error.

In the scene that followed, all of the house lights were extinguished, bathing the stage in a soft blue glow from one of the backstage carbon arc lamps, a powerful spotlight that was created by an electric current arcing between two carbon rods. The spotlight was positioned on a narrow metal bridge that was about 15 feet above the stage and within a foot or so of the theater's drop curtains and the fixed curtain that prevented the audience from seeing into the wings. The spotlight was a bulky piece of machinery, with a large metal hood and reflector, and could generate temperatures as high as 4,000 degrees Fahrenheit.

As the action continued on the stage, bringing beautiful chorus girls and young men in uniform into the softly lit gardens, the carbon arc lamp suddenly began to sputter and spark. A cracking sound was heard and then a few inches of orange flame appeared and began to spread out, dancing along the edge of the fixed curtain. On the stage below, the cast went into an up-tempo song as stage hands tried to slap at the small flame with their bare hands. Within seconds, though, the tiny blaze had grown, consuming the material above their heads and beyond their reach. It was soon spreading into the heavier curtains and they shouted to a man on a catwalk above to try and put the fire out. He also began slapping at the fire with his hands.

The audience was engrossed in the romantic musical number onstage as on either side of the garden set, stagehands, grips, and those on the catwalks frantically tried to get to the fire and put it out. But the flames had grown larger and were now out of reach. Black smoke was starting to rise.

William Sallers, the house fireman, was on his usual rounds to make sure that no one was smoking and as he made his way up the stairs from the dressing rooms in the basement, he spotted the flames. He immediately grabbed some tubes of Kilfyre (a powdery flame retardant) and ran up the vertical stairs of the light bridge and began frantically tossing powder onto the still-growing fire. The platform was only 18 inches wide, so he had to hold onto a metal rail with one hand as he threw the powder with the other. But it was too late. The flames had spread to the point that the small amount of powder was almost comically ineffectual.

At first, the actors on stage had no idea what was happening, but after a few sparks began to rain down, they knew something was seriously wrong. They continued to sing and dance, waiting for something to happen. Later, some of the actors would recall hearing shouts and bells that signaled for the curtain to come down, but they were muffled by the music.

In the orchestra pit, the musicians spotted the fire and an order was given for them to play as fast as they could. The tempo picked up, but soon faltered as more of the musicians spotted the flames and began to get rattled. Several of them calmly put down their instruments and exited through the orchestra pit door beneath the stage.

Depending on where they were sitting or standing, some members of the audience saw the fire by simply following the gaze of the actors, who were now looking up. At first, many of them were merely puzzled, but others were becoming alarmed. Most of the children in the front main floor rows remained in their seats, believing that the glow that was spreading across the upper reaches of the theater was another of the show's magical effects.

Those in the upper gallery who saw the eerie flickering of the

Over a decade before the Iroquois fire, there was a fire at Turner Hall on 12th Street (now Roosevelt) just east of Halsted. The theatre, which was presenting The Greenhorn in Yiddish, had induced children to attend the show by including tickets with a drawing for a doll. In the panic of the fire, as in the Iroquois, several people were injured - and a handful killed - because of doors that opened inward. And, like at the Iroquois, members f the company stood onstage begging people not to panic. There was one major difference, though - there was no actual fire! The panic was simply caused by someone shouting "fire" after seeing a puff of smoke onstage.

flames had no idea at first about what was happening, until bits of burning fabric began falling down around members of the cast who were still trying to go on with their number. But it was becoming obvious that some of them had fallen out of step with the music and others seemed to have lost their voices. Most were terribly frightened but survivors of the fire would later say that seeing those girls remaining there, still dancing in an effort to quiet the audience, was one of the bravest acts they had ever witnessed.

Backstage, things became more frightening and chaotic. The stage manager, William Carelton, could not be found (he had gone to the hardware store) and one of the stagehands, Joe Dougherty, was trying to handle the curtains from near the switchboard. But Dougherty was filling in for the regular curtain man, who was in the hospital, and could not remember which drop should be lowered. The asbestos curtain ran on an endless loop of wire-enforced rope but he was not sure which rope controlled which curtain.

High above him, Charles Sweeney, who had been assigned to the first fly gallery, seized a canvas tarpaulin and, with some of the other men, was slapping at the flames. The fire was out of their reach, however, and it continued to spread. Sweeney dashed down six flights of stairs to a room filled with chorus girls and led them down to a small stage exit. In the rush to escape, most of the girls dropped everything and left the building wearing only flimsy costumes or tights. Other men raced downstairs to rescue girls who were in the dressing rooms under the stage.

High up in the theater's gridiron, The Grigolatis, a group of 16 young German aerialists (12 women and four men), had a horrifying view of the scene. Clouds of thick, black smoke was rising toward them and blazing pieces of canvas the size of bed sheets were falling down on the stage and the footlights. William Sallers, still above the stage, saw the same thing and knew the theater was doomed.

The Grigolatis had only seconds to act. One of them, Floraline, who was perched some distance away from the others, was suddenly engulfed in flames from a burning piece of scenery. Before the others could reach her, she panicked, lost her grip on the trapeze, and plunged to the stage, 60 feet below. By the time her companions were able to unhook themselves from their harnesses and scramble down some metal scaffolding to the stage, Floraline had vanished. They could only hope that she had been carried to safety.

In all of the confusion, no one remembered Nellie Reed, who was still attached to her wire.

In one of the dressing rooms, five young female dancers were sitting and talking when they heard the cries of "fire!" In the rush to get out, one of them, Violet Sidney, twisted her ankle and fell. The other girls ran, but Lola Quinlan stopped to help her. She managed to drag Violet down five flights of stairs and across the back of the burning stage to safety. She was badly burned in the process, but she refused to leave her friend behind.

Voices screamed for the asbestos curtain to come down, but nothing happened. Joe Dougherty and others were still confused about which curtains should be lowered and more time was lost. A stagehand who had been ordered to sound the fire alarm found that no alarm box had ever been installed. He burst out of the theater and ran as fast as he could through the streets to notify Engine Company 13 of the blaze.

Inside his dressing room, Eddie Foy, in tights, misshapen shoes, short smock, and red pigtailed wig, was preparing for his novelty act as the Old Woman Who Lived in a Shoe. Foy heard the commotion outside and rushed out onto the stage to see what was going on. As soon as he opened the door, he knew something was deadly wrong. He immediately searched for his young son, who had accompanied him to the theater that day, and quickly found him in the darkness. As he stumbled with the boy in his arms, he heard terrified voices raising a cry of "fire!" At that moment, the nearly 2,000 people packed into the "absolutely fireproof" Iroquois Theater began to panic.

Some of the audience had risen to their feet, others were running and climbing over the seats to get to the back of the house and to the side exits. Many of the standees were blocking the aisles and, since the new theater was unfamiliar to them, were unsure about which way to turn. The initial runners soon turned into a mob that was trying to get out the same way they had come in. Their screams and cries were muffled by the music and by the show's cast, which was still singing as the burning scenery fell around them. Terrified families were quickly torn apart from one another.

Eddie Foy grabbed his son and rushed to the stage exit, but felt compelled to go back and try and help. He pressed the boy into the arms of a fleeing stagehand and went back to try and help calm down the audience and finally bring the curtain down. By the time he arrived, the cast had abandoned the stage and he stood there alone, the blazing backdrop behind him and burning bits of scenery raining down around him. Smoke billowed around him as he stepped to the edge of the footlights, still partially clothed in his ridiculous costume. He urged everyone who could hear him to remain calm and remarkably, some of the people in the front rows took their seats again. Even some of the people in the gallery sat back down. From the edge of the stage, Foy urged musical director Herbert Gillea to get some of the remaining musicians to play an overture, which had a temporary soothing effect on the crowd.

A few moments later, a flaming set crashed down onto the stage and Foy asked everyone to get up and calmly leave the theater. He told them to take their time, to not be frightened, and to walk slowly as they exited. The, he dropped his voice to stagehand who was on the brink of fleeing from the theater himself. He ordered him, "Lower that iron curtain! Drop the fire curtain! For God's sake, does anyone know how this iron curtain is worked?"

Foy heard timbers cracking above his head and he made one last entreaty that everyone proceed slowly from the theater, but by now, no one was listening. As he looked out into the auditorium, he later recalled seeing many of the people on the main floor leaving in an orderly fashion, but what he saw in the balcony and the gallery terrified him. In the upper tiers, he said, people were in a "mad, animal-like stampede."

Lester Linvonston, a young survivor who vividly recalled seeing Foy standing at the edge of the stage, pleading for calm, was only distracted from the comedian by a macabre sight that appeared above Foy's head. "Almost alone and in the center of the house," he later said, he watched "a ballet dancer in a gauzy dress suspended by a steel belt from a wire. Her dress had caught fire and it burned like paper." The gruesome vision was Nellie Reed, the British star of the aerial ballet.

Finally, the asbestos curtain began to come down. Most of the stage crew had fled the theater but someone had figured out a way to lower what was

Crowds gathered when it was realized that the Iroquois Theater was on fire. Hundreds were trapped inside.

thought would be a fireproof shield between the stage and the audience. It began inching its way down a steel cable between two wooden guide tracks. As if in slow motion, it descended and then, less than 20 feet above the stage, it suddenly stopped. One end was jammed on the light reflector that had not been properly closed and the other end sagged down to about five feet above the stage. The wooden guide tracks tore apart and the curtain, which was supposed to have been reinforced and made stiff by steel rods and wires, began to billow out over the orchestra pit and the front rows of seats, pushed by the draft coming from an open stage exit that had been mobbed by the cast and crew.

Some stagehands tried to yank down the curtain, but it was no use. The rest of the crew ran for their lives. The theater's engineer, Robert Murray, ran down to the basement and told his crew to shut off the steam in the boilers heating the building, bank all of the fires to prevent an explosion, then get out as fast as they could. Then he helped a group of chorus girls escape from a basement dressing room by pushing them one at a time through a coal chute than led to an alley. One or two of them were wearing street clothes, but the others were clad in their thin costumes or worse, in nothing but undergarments.

Murray rushed back up to the stage level and found a young woman whose costume and tights were shredded and burned and whose skin was charred and blistered. Nellie Reed had somehow unhooked herself from her wire, but was seriously injured and in great pain. He managed to get her out into the street, where he handed her to some rescuers.

The entire stage had been turned into a blazing inferno and if one of the stagehands had not opened one of the big double scenery doors, the entire cast might have perished. Opening the doors undoubtedly saved the lives of the cast and crew, but it sealed the fate of the audience in the upper

Beautiful Nellie Reed of the Flying Ballet died from injuries sustained in the fire.

tiers. The contractors who had built the theater not only failed to connect the controls for the roof's ventilating systems, but had nailed shut the vents over the stage and left open vents above the auditorium, creating a chimney effect. The blast of cold air that rushed in the scenery doors, which caused the curtain to billow out from the stage, instantly mixed with the heated air fueled by the flames and the result was a huge deadly blowtorch that one fire official later described as a "back draft."

A churning column of smoke and flames burst out of the opening under the curtain, whirled above the orchestra pit and floor seats, and swept into the balcony and gallery under the open roof vents like a fiery cyclone. The fireball sucked the oxygen from the air, burning and asphyxiating anyone in the upper tiers who remained in their seats or were trapped in the aisles.

Moments later, the last of the ropes holding up the scenery flats on stage gave away and with a roar that literally shook the building, tons of wood, ropes, sandbags, pipes, pulleys, lights, rigging, and more than 280 pieces of scenery crashed to the stage. The force of the fall instantly knocked out the electrical switchboard and the auditorium was plunged into complete and utter darkness.

The aisles had become impassable and as the lights went out, the crowd milled about in blind terror. The auditorium began to fill with heat and smoke and screams echoed off the walls and ceilings. Many of those who died not only burned but suffocated from the smoke and the crush of bodies. Later, as the police removed the charred remains from the theater, they discovered that a number of victims had been trampled in the panic. One dead woman's face even bore the mark of a shoe heel. Mothers and children were wrenched away from one another and trampled by those behind them. Dresses, jackets, trousers and other articles of clothing were ripped to shreds as people tried to get through to the exits and escape the flames and smoke. When the crowd reached the doors, they could not open them as they had been designed to swing inward rather than outward. The crush of people prevented those in the front from opening the doors. To make matters worse, some of the side doors to the auditorium were reportedly locked.

In desperation, some of those whose clothing had caught fire jumped from the first balcony to the floor below. Many of them died instantly. Others suffered agonizing deaths from broken backs that were caused by landing on armrests and seat backs.

A brief burst of light illuminated the hellish scene as the safety curtain burst into flames. The curtain, it turned out, was not made completely from asbestos, but from some cheaper material that had been chosen by the theater's co-owner, Will Davis.

At that moment, Eddie Foy made a fateful decision. He needed to get out of the theater as quickly as possible and first considered following the crowd through the Randolph Street doors. But, wanting to find his son, he changed his mind and made his way through the burning backstage and out of the scenery doors. He would only realize how lucky his decision had been after he learned of the hundreds of victims found crushed inside those doors.

Inside the theater, the badly burned house fireman William Sallers was shoving members of the cast and crew out of the scenery doors and into the alley. By now, he believed that Engine 13 should have arrived and he stepped outside and began shouting for the commander, Captain Jennings. Sallers believed that if he could get the fire crew through the scenery doors and onto the stage, they could prevent the blaze from reaching the audience. But when he looked behind him, he saw flames roaring out of the doors. He later recalled, "I knew that anybody who was in there was gone. I knew there was no chance to get out."

In the time that had been lost because the Iroquois had no alarm system, before Engine 13 and other units began arriving, the theater had turned into an oven. When collecting valuables after the fire, the police found at least a dozen watches that had been stopped at about the same time, 3:50 p.m. This meant that nearly 20 minutes had elapsed from the time that the first alarm had been raised. This certainly accounted for the jamming at the exits and the relatively few people that eyewitnesses saw leaving the theater. Some of the witnesses later stated that nearly seven minutes passed from the time they saw fire coming from the roof of the theater and the front doors on Randolph Street being opened.

Strangely, when Engine 13 arrived at the Randolph Street doors, the scene outside of the theater was completely normal. If not for the smoke billowing from the roof, the firefighters would have assumed that it was a false alarm. This changed when they tried to open the auditorium doors and found they could not --- there were too many bodies stacked up against them. They were only able to gain access by actually pulling the bodies out of the way with pike poles, peeling them off one another and then climbing over the stacks of corpses. It took only 10 minutes to put out the remaining blaze, as the intense heat inside had already eaten up anything that would still burn. The gallery and upper balcony sustained the greatest loss of life because

For doors to open to the outside in theatres had been the law in Chicago for over 20 years, but the laws were seldom enforced. It was the Iroquois fire that led to changes in the way these laws were enforced around the country.

the patrons who had been seated there were trapped by locked doors and gates at the top of the stairways. The firefighters found 200 bodies stacked there, as many as 10 deep.

A few who made it to the fire escape door behind the top balcony found that the iron staircase was missing. In its place was a platform that plunged about 50 feet into Couch Place, a cobblestone alley below. Across the alley, behind the theater, painters were working on a building occupied by Northwestern University's dental school. When they realized what was happening at the theater, they quickly erected a makeshift bridge using a ladder, which they extended across the alley to the fire escape platform. Several people made it to safety, but then as another man was edging his way across, the ladder slipped off the icy ledge of the university building and the man plummeted to his death.

After the ladder was lost, three wide boards were pushed across to the theater and the painters anchored them with their knees. The plank bridge worked for a time, but it could not handle the crush of people spilling out of the theater exit. The painters helped as many people as they could but when what sounded like a bomb went off in the theater (the sound of the rigging and scenery falling to the stage), they watched helplessly as the people trapped inside tried in vain to escape.

Those who swarmed from the fire escape exit were pushed to the edge of the railings with nowhere to go. It was impossible for them to turn back because of the crowd behind them and they

The Couch Place alleyway after the fire. The makeshift bridge that was created to get people out of the upper balcony can still be seen in the smoke and haze..

were pushed over the side. Some of people tried to crawl across the planks but in the confusion and smoke, slipped and fell to the alley. Others, whose clothing was on fire, simply gave up and jumped from the railings.

The boards began falling away and as the fire grew, flames shot out the doors and out of the windows along the theater's wall, many of those hoping for rescue were burned alive in full view of the painters and the students at the dental school. From some of Northwestern University's windows, onlookers could see directly into the theater, which was a solid mass of flames. In the middle of the inferno, they could see men, women, and children running about and students later said that they did not even look human.

In the aftermath of the fire, Couch Place was dubbed "Death Alley" by reporters who arrived on the scene and counted nearly 150 victims lying on the slush-covered cobblestones. The bodies had been stacked there by firemen, or had fallen to their death from above.

For nearly five hours, police officers, firemen and even newspaper reporters, carried out the dead. Anxious relatives sifted through the ruins, searching for loved ones. As the news spread, public response was immediate and overwhelming. A nearby medical school sent 100 students to help the doctors who had been dispatched to the Iroquois. A hardware company down the street emptied its stock of 200 lanterns. Marshall Field's, Mandel Brothers, Carson, Pirie, Scott and other department stores sent piles of blankets, sheets, rolls of linen, packages of cotton and large delivery wagons, and converted their ground floor restrooms and lounges into emergency medical stations. Montgomery Ward sent one of its new, large motorized delivery wagons, but even with its bell ringing, it could not get through the crowds that were jammed into the streets and had to turn back. Other bodies were taken away by police wagons and ambulances and transported to a temporary morgue at Marshall Field's on State Street. Medical examiners and investigators worked through the night.

Within a short time, small restaurants, saloons, and stores in the vicinity of the Iroquois had been turned into improvised aid stations as medical workers and volunteers began arriving in large numbers. Chicago's central telephone exchange was overwhelmed by emergency calls.

AFTER THE IROQUOIS THEATER FIRE...

The gutted auditorium of the theater

Firemen survey the ghastly damage & the score of bodies scattered throughout the theater.

Fire-blasted seats in the balcony

Interior Hallways of the Theater

A lounge area that was scorched by the fire. The new paint was literally melted off the walls.

Because the hardware store lanterns were not powerful enough to illuminate the blackened auditorium, the Edison Company rushed over 40 arc lamps and, when they were turned on, fire and rescue workers were stunned by what they saw. Some of the audience had died sitting up in their seats, facing the stage, staring straight ahead. Others had no burn marks or bruises on them because they had suffocated quickly from the smoke. Many women were found with their heads resting on the back of the seat in front of them. A young boy's head was missing. One woman was bent back over the seat she had been sitting in, her spine severed. Hundreds had been trampled. Clothing, shoes, pocketbooks, and other personal belongings were strewn about. Some of the bodies were burned beyond recognition.

The lobby of the theater was almost untouched by the fire, but many died as they tried to force themselves out of the Randolph Street doors.

Scores of victims had been wedged into doorways. A husband and wife were locked so tightly in one another's arms that they had to be removed from the theater together. A mother had thrown her arms around her daughter in a hopeless effort to save her and both had been burned beyond recognition. The number of dead children was heartbreaking. Many were found burned, others trampled. Two dead children were found with the kneeling body of their mother, who had tried to shield them from the flames.

At the edge of the auditorium, a fireman emerged from the ashes with the body of a little girl in his arms. He groped his way forward, stumbling toward Fire Marshall William Henry Musham, who ordered him to give the child to someone else and get back into the auditorium. Another senior officer also ordered him to hand the child off to someone else. As the fireman came closer, the marshal and the other officers could see the streaks of tears on the man's soot-covered face. "I'm sorry, chief," the man said, "but I've got a little one like this at home. I want to carry this one out."

Musham told him to go ahead and the other officers stepped aside. The weeping fireman carried the little body down the steps of what only an hour before had been the glittering promenade of the grandest theater in Chicago.

With the aid of the Edison arc lights, Deputy Fire Chief John Campion searched the theater's interior while his men continuing to douse hot spots that occasionally still burst into flames. Campion called out for survivors, looking around at the burned seats, the blackened walls, and the twisted piles of debris that littered the stage.

The devastated Iroquois Theater was silent.

In possibly less than a quarter of an hour, 572 lives had ended in the Iroquois Theater. More died later, bringing the eventual death toll up to 602, including 212 children. Hundreds more had been injured in what was supposed to be the safest theater in the city. The number of dead was greater than those who had perished in the Great Fire of 1871. A few hours before, the Iroquois had been a luxurious palace but, as newspapers reported that evening, "From the galleries, it looked like a burned-out volcano crater."

The next day, the newspapers devoted full pages to lists of the known dead and injured. News wires carried reports of the tragedy around the country and it soon became a national disaster. Chicago mayor Carter Harrison, Jr. issued an order that banned public celebration on New Year's Eve, closing the night clubs and making forbidden any fireworks or sounding of horns. Every church and factory bell in the city was silenced and on January 2, 1904, the city observed an official day of mourning.

Someone, the public cried, had to answer for the fire and an investigation of the blaze brought to light a number of troubling facts, including the faulty vents and that one of them was nailed shut. Another finding showed that the supposedly "fireproof" asbestos curtain was really made from cotton and other combustible materials. It would have never saved anyone at all. In addition to not having any fire alarms in the building, the owners had decided that sprinklers were too unsightly and too costly and had never had them installed.

A line of victims was laid out after the fire

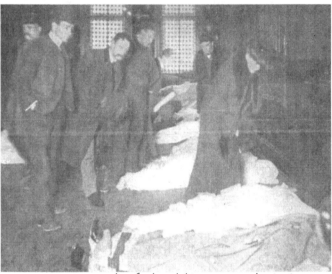
A woman searches for her children among the dead

To make matters worse, the management also established a policy to keep non-paying customers from slipping into the theater during a performance --- they quietly bolted nine pair of iron panels over the rear doors and installed padlocked, accordion-style gates at the top of the interior second and third floor stairway landings. And just as tragic was the idea they came up with to keep the audience from being distracted during a show -- they ordered all of the exit lights to be turned off! One exit sign that was left on led only to ladies restroom and another to a locked door for a private stairway. And as mentioned already, the doors of the outside exits, which were supposed to make it possible for the theater to empty in five minutes, opened to the inside, not to the outside.

The investigation led to a cover-up by officials from the city and the fire department, which denied all knowledge of fire code violations. They blamed the inspectors, who had overlooked the problems in exchange for free theater passes. A grand jury indicted a number of individuals, including the theater owners, fire officials and even the mayor. No one was ever charged with a criminal act, though. Families of the dead filed nearly 275 civil lawsuits against the theater but no money was ever collected. The Iroquois Theater Company filed for bankruptcy soon after the disaster.

Nevertheless, the building was repaired and re-opened briefly in 1904 as Hyde and Behmann's Music Hall and then in 1905 as the Colonial Theater. In 1924, the building was razed to make room for a new theater, the Oriental, but the façade of the Iroquois was used in its construction. The Oriental operated at what is now 24 West Randolph Street until the middle part of 1981, when it fell into disrepair and was closed down. It opened again as the home to a wholesale electronics dealer for a time and then went dark again. The restored theater is now part of the Civic Tower Building and is next door to the restored Delaware Building. It reopened as the Ford Center for the Performing Arts in 1998.

There are a number of oddities and mysteries about the 1903 Iroquois Theater fire that still linger today. It seems that official Chicago police and fire department records on the fire do not exist, nor does the Chicago Historical Society possess such records. According to the Cook County Courts, the records of the legal proceedings that followed the disaster were thrown out

GHOST ALERT!

The Iroquois Theatre is long gone. In its place stands the even more majestic Oriental Theatre, which was erected on the spot in the 1920s. But there has never been anything but a theatre on the site, and ghosts began to be reported early on. In fact, they've stuck around to this day. According to employees, the curtain has a tendency to get stuck at about five feet down - just as the fire curtain did. Others claim that one spotlight - right near the location of the light that started the fire - tends to break off from the now-computerized circuits and behave as through it had a mind of its own.

Many employees claim to have seen people in the balcony, particularly during rehearsals, and found no one there - and the doors locked - when they go to shoo them off.

Still others have reported backstage encounters with the ghost of a woman wearing a tutu. Traditionally, this has been attributed to Nellie Reed, the aerialist who was killed in the fire. However, details of Reed's death are sketchy - the *Chicago Tribune* alone has reported several different stories, some claiming that she was stuck on a high platform and unable to get down during the fire, and others saying she was in a high dressing room and, afraid of elevators, took the burning staircase instead. Still other reports claim that she didn't die in the theatre, but in the hospital shortly afterward.

But the woman in the tutu is not the only specter seen around the theatre. Recently, several employees have reported the apparition of a man in a red shoulder cape. Several others have reported a ghost in the balcony ventilation system. The identity of the man in the cape would be is anyone's guess - there were, however, over a thousand costumes in use in Mr. Bluebeard, and the idea that one might have been wearing a red shoulder cape is certainly possible. The phantoms could also be ghosts of the other employees killed - one other actor, a bit-part player named Burr Scott, was killed, along with an usher and two female attendants.

It's also possible that some of these ghosts may not be the ghosts of the victims of the Iroquois fire. The theaters that have occupied the spot since 1904 have their share of horror stories, too. In 1943, a patron attending a movie at the Oriental put a note to his wife, mentioning the song "You'll Never Know How Much I Miss You," a song from the movie, in his pocket. As the song played in the movie, he shot himself to death. There have also been at least two suicides in the alley behind the theatre - Death Alley - in which people have jumped from high buildings to their doom in the alley.

Death Alley, in fact, is often said to be more haunted than the theatre itself. Cold spots - localized areas that are about ten degrees cooler than they ought to be - are common in haunted sites, and some say that the whole of Death Alley is a cold spot. Poltergeist activity has been reported around the Dearborn Street entrance to the alley, particularly by mothers of small children.

Farther back, around the area where the bodies fell, more strange things are reported. Pictures have been taken in which the very bricks in the wall seem to show a woman's screaming face. The woman in a tutu appears here, too, in the form of a silhouette that is seen from time to time. Digital camera batteries frequently drain mysteriously in the alley, only to be charged up again a short time later.

Many who pass through Couch Place often find themselves very uncomfortable and unsettled there. They say that faint cries are sometimes heard in the shadows and that some have reported being touched by unseen hands and by eerie cold spots that seem to come from nowhere and vanish just as quickly. A number of women claim that they have been touched as they walked though the alleyway, often experiencing something like a small hand holding onto their own as they walk along. Others claim to have heard the sounds of singing, shouting, and, perhaps most eerie of all, a group of children laughing and playing.

One night, on a Weird Chicago Tour, a woman came forward who told us of a night that she had been attending a play at the Oriental and actually called over an usher and asked him to go out and quiet down the group of children that were being noisy outside of the theater's exit doors --- doors that led directly out into Death Alley. She saw the same usher again later and asked him what had been going on. He shook his head, she told us, and explained that the alley had been empty. There had been no children playing there. The woman claimed that she had no idea that the alleyway was alleged to be haunted and knew nothing of the 1903 fire.

Is this alleyway actually haunted? And do the spirits of those who met their tragic end inside the burning theater still linger here? Perhaps, or perhaps the strange sensations experienced here are "ghosts of the past" of another kind --- a chilling remembrance of a terrifying event that will never be completely forgotten.

decades ago to make room for new documents.

The building next to the Iroquois still stands at Randolph and State streets, looking just as it did back in 1903, except there is a McDonald's where a cigar store was once located. The Delaware Building, as it is known, has a small lobby with a collection of framed photos of the some of the prominent hotels and theaters in the vicinity. However, there is no photograph of the Iroquois and no mention of the horrible events that occurred next door. Instead, there is a later photograph of the theater building after it was refurbished, renamed, and turned into a vaudeville house.

Worst of all, there is not a single marker or plaque that is dedicated to the hundreds of victims who perished in the blaze. There was a plaque unveiled by politicians and city leaders in 2003, the 100th anniversary of the fire, but it has never been installed at the theater, in Couch Place, or anywhere else.

There is also much mystery and confusion that remains about the fire, partly because of the haste with which city newspapers were forced to meet their deadlines at the time. On the day after the fire, for instance, the Chicago Tribune reported that a woman had been revived by doctors at Thompson's Restaurant, but in the same edition, a woman with the same name is listed among the dead. The fate of many of the victims also reflects confusion. For example, what happened to Floraline, the German aerialist who plunged to the stage? She simply disappeared from the newspaper coverage of the disaster. And even the famed Nellie Reed disappeared. Her body was returned to New York, but British newspapers, aside from mentioning that she was from London, never reported whether or not her remains were returned home.

The controversy over the fire may have faded away many years ago, but the lessons learned from it should never be forgotten. The Iroquois Theater Fire ranks as the nation's fourth deadliest blaze and the deadliest single building fire in American history. It remains as one of Chicago's worst tragedies and a chilling reminder of how the past continues to reverberate into the present.

THE ST. PATRICK'S DAY DANCEHALL DISASTER

Lake View Hall, located at 3233-3239 North Clark Street, was just like so many other private lodges and ballrooms scattered about the north side of the city. For many years, generations of Chicagoans gathered at fraternal lodges and dancehalls to drink, dance, and socialize with friends and family. There used to be dozens of buildings of like this, brick buildings that spanned the length of a city block, housing dance floors, bowling alleys, meeting rooms, and street-level retail stores. There aren't many such places like this today, but years ago, a landlord could make good money renting public space to immigrant groups like Swedes, Germans, and notably to the Irish. All of them gathered in such places to celebrate their ethnic heritage and the ties they shared with the old country. Special events, especially around the holidays, were highly anticipated in these days before television and St. Patrick's Day was considered by many Irish Chicagoans to be the biggest day of the year.

March 17, 1948 was the night of the annual St. Patrick's Day party at Lake View Hall. The Connaughtmen's Social Club rented the building's third-floor ballroom and the Yankee Division Club of Chicago, a smaller space. Two Irish bands were hired to play dance music in the adjacent rooms, thrilling the revelers and packing the house. Patrons of the bowling alley on the second floor could hear the sounds of Irish folk music and the stamping of dancing feet from above - but none of them could even imagine that the entire third floor was about to come crashing down on their heads.

The first warning of the calamity to come occurred at 10:10 p.m., just moments after one of the bands returned from a brief intermission. A loud, ominous cracking sound was heard and then seconds later, a section of the flooring at the north end of the ballroom collapsed, bringing with it sections of the roof. The floor collapsed at a steep angle, sending men and women tumbling down onto the lunch counter of the Lakeview Bowling Alleys below.

In the collapse, 106 people were injured, but only one person fatally. The bloody survivors were taken to Illinois Masonic Hospital while rescuers used electric saws to try and pry loose a woman named Ann Hunt, who was pinned to the fallen floor by a section of the roof. They worked for two hours as they tried to remove the debris, using chairs to try and prop up the collapsed ceiling. Unfortunately, by the time they were able to free her, Mrs. Hunt had died.

The *Chicago Sun-Times* started an investigation into the disaster and uncovered evidence of a massive city licensing scandal. At least 298 public places were operating without a license and had not been cleared by the zoning board or the police, fire, and health departments. Many of the places had even been denied a license because they were unsafe. In most cases, they were operating on city-issued receipts for payment of the fee, even though a license was never actually issued. In other words, corrupt city inspectors were pocketing bribes and looking the other way while dangerous and unstable buildings all over the city remained open for business.

John R. Jenkins, the manager and one of the owners of the Lake View Hall, never even bothered to apply for a license. Money in the right hands insured that his place stayed open.

The investigation forced well-meaning Mayor Martin Kennelly to issue orders preventing the city from taking money and issuing licenses until the violations were corrected. However, his new rule was completely ignored. The licenses were an important source of graft for the men who oiled and maintained the Chicago political machine.

No one was ever named as the responsible party in the St. Patrick's Day Dancehall Disaster. John Jenkins tried to explain that he simply didn't know what the capacity of his building was supposed to be, but he guessed it was "around 500 people, give or take." City records showed that his second-floor bowling alley had been refused a license one year earlier for failing to meet the minimum city safety requirements.

Lake View Hall is now long gone. It was demolished years ago and only an empty lot remains today as a reminder of the horrific event that occurred on the site in 1948.

THE TROLLEY OF DEATH

The fates of 33 people were tragically changed in 1950 because of a rainstorm. On the night of May 24, a sudden and torrential downpour flooded the 63rd Street underpass at State Street, making the road impassable for the electric CTA trolley cars. No one knew what horrific events would follow this rainstorm or how simply missing a signal would send the occupants of a Green Hornet trolley along a path of no return.

During the first half of the twentieth century, electric streetcars were a familiar sight on Chicago streets. Trolleys had first appeared in the Windy

A brand new Pullman-built Green Hornet trolley in 1947

City, pulled by horses, back in 1859. By the 1890s, electricity had replaced the horses and the cars began to travel along steel rails that had been fitted into the city streets. Trolleys were so popular that during World War I, Chicago operated the largest streetcar system in the country.

And while many riders relied on the trolleys to get them to and from work each day and to allow them to travel throughout the city, the vehicles did have their drawbacks. The most obvious problem was that they lacked the ability to maneuver around accidents and flooded areas, causing the cars to have to be diverted to alternate routes. For this reason, among others, trolleys were eventually replaced by buses. The fact that the trolleys were unable to change routes with ease would later lead to the worst loss of life involving a motor vehicle in America.

On the morning of Thursday, May 25, the low-lying underpass at State Street remained flooded with rain water from the storm and so, throughout that day, a flagman detoured southbound cars to a turnaround track on the east side of State Street, making 63rd Street the temporary end of the line. By rush hour, the area remained closed, but this fact was apparently missed by the driver of the Green Hornet, Paul Manning. The trolley that he was driving was known for being one of the newest and sleekest vehicles on the CTA line and it was in perfect working order. Only a terrible mistake could be blamed for what happened that night.

Manning was driving the Green Hornet at a speed that was estimated to be about 35 m.p.h., which some believe was too fast for the wet conditions. The CTA flagman was still in place at 62nd Street, one block north of the turnaround, and when he saw Manning's trolley come into view, he frantically began signaling the driver to slow down. Instead of slowing, the vehicle continued along the street. The flagman continued to wave frantically, attempting to warn the driver that a switch in the track was open for a turn that would put the Green Hornet directly into the path of oncoming northbound traffic.

In the opposite lane, heading north, a semi-trailer truck that was driven by Mel Wilson was also quickly approaching the viaduct. The semi-truck was hauling 8,000 gallons of gasoline destined for south side filling stations.

How Manning failed to see the flagman's signal is unknown, but we do know that he was unaware of the closed underpass and also unaware of the open switch that was being used to bypass the trolleys. It's likely that he simply

thought that the car would clip right along on the route that he normally took. However, when the trolley hit the open switch track, it violently swung to the left, throwing the passengers aboard to the floor. Manning was last seen throwing up his hands and screaming in terror as the streetcar hurled through the intersection and rammed into the tanker truck. The impact ripped open the tanker's steel skin, creating a shower of sparks that immediately ignited the gasoline that was flooding onto the street. The two vehicles erupted into a single fireball that incinerated the trolley.

At the time of the accident, every seat on the Green Hornet had been filled. Those on board had been thrown to the floor by the sudden turn and they suddenly felt the tremendous heat as the fire swept through the car. In the terror and confusion that followed, the trapped and burning victims pushed against the side doors, but they refused to open. The windows were covered with steel bars, making them useless as an escape route. Somehow, 30 people managed to crawl away from the scene, leaving 33 others behind to die. The fortunate few who survived were treated for severe burns at Provident Hospital.

Meanwhile, the explosion shook the entire neighborhood as the flames soared two and three stories into the sky. The burning gasoline managed to engulf seven buildings on State Street and the fire was so hot that it twisted metal, fused windows and melted sections of asphalt on the street. The walls of several of the buildings collapsed, although the occupants managed to escape. Drivers who had been lined up in traffic were able to leave unharmed, as well.

More than 30 fire companies were called to the scene and it took more than two hours to get the worst of the fire under control. It would be a long time before a sense of calm could be restored to the area, though, and the smell of scorched flesh hung in the air long after the debris was cleared away. According to newspaper reports, as many as 20,000 people lined the streets hoping to catch a glimpse of the fire, the destroyed vehicles, and the blackened bodies that were taken away to the morgue.

It's likely that some of the emergency workers who had to deal with the carnage would have gladly traded places with the curiosity-seekers. When they forced open the rear doors of the trolley, they were met with a ghastly scene. "In some cases we found only the skulls and parts of limbs," Fire Marshall Albert Peterson later recalled. "We had to remove all of them and make a temporary morgue on the sidewalk."

A number of the passengers escaped the trolley thanks to a 14-year-old girl who had thought quickly enough to pull down a red safety knob that opened the center doors. However, the rear doors had no such device and were in fact designed to be entry doors only, not opening from the inside. This created a opened the doors, they found a mass of bodies that had been literally fused together by the heat.

In the investigation that followed, it was found that the Green Hornet had been in perfect working order, as had the gasoline truck. Mel Wilson, the driver of the truck, had been burned to death in the accident. Most pointed fingers of blame at Paul Manning, who had been involved in 10 minor accidents during his career, but the real problems were the design flaws in the trolley itself. These included the lack of safety pulls (now standard equipment on buses and elevated lines), the steel bars that blocked an emergency escape through the windows, and doors that would not open from either side. It took the senseless deaths of 33 innocent victims to learn what should have been a simple lesson from the start.

In the years that followed the Green Hornet crash, trolleys slowly began to disappear from Chicago streets and were replaced by buses. The final run of a Green Hornet trolley took place on June 21, 1958 and another chapter closed in Chicago's history of disasters.

THE WRECK OF THE ROUSE SIMMONS

This is the tale of the Christmas Ship
That sailed o'er the sullen lake;
And of the sixteen souls who made the trip,
And of death in the foaming wake.
Vincent Starrett

For many years, one of the great traditions of Chicago was the arrival of the famous "Christmas Tree Ship." Starting in 1887, Captain Herman Schuenemann and his brother, August, began returning with bundles of their fragrant cargo. Schuenemann sold Christmas trees and hand-made wreaths from his mooring on the Chicago River near the Clark Street Bridge.

The tallest trees drawn from the shipment were presented to the grateful owners of downtown theaters and in return, the brothers received complimentary season passes. The rest were sold to celebrating citizens, many of whom spoke of their fond memories of the Schuenemanns and the *Rouse Simmons*, their "Christmas Tree Ship" for generations. By 1912, Chicagoans anxiously looked forward to the ship's arrival and anticipated searching for the perfect tree among the wares, which ranged in price from seventy-five cents to a dollar. Herman affixed a hand-painted sign to the dock each year, reminding his customers that he had ventured into the deep snows of the Upper Peninsula to hand-pick just the right trees for his fine friends back in Chicago.

Herman Schuenemann, the master of the *Rouse Simmons*, his wife, and three young daughters lived in a small apartment at 1638 North Clark Street, just a little over a mile north of the river. His oldest daughter, Elsie, was devoted to her father and had recently become active in the family's seasonal business.

It was a business that was not without risk. The month of November, when the shipment of trees had to be sailed across the Great Lakes, was a particularly treacherous one for Lake Michigan. High winds and deadly gales had sent many ships to the bottom of Lake Michigan and in 1898, Captain Schuenemann's brother, August, went down with all hands while manning the schooner *S. Thal* in the waters off north suburban Glencoe.

But his brother's death, and the threat of more dangerous weather, failed to deter Herman Schuenemann. He knew the *Rouse Simmons* was a sturdy ship. Built in 1868, the wooden schooner was fitted with three masts and had been intended for use in the lumber industry. Its large hold made it perfect for storing hundreds of Christmas trees each season.

On November 22, 1912, Captain Schuenemann, with a crew and passenger list of 16 and between 27,000 and 50,000 trees tied and bundled below decks, set sail from Manistique, Mich., bound for Chicago. The skies were

(Left) The "Christmas Tree Ship" is moored in Chicago

(Below) Captain Herman Steinmann (center) standing aboard the Rouse Simmons as the crew prepares for the holiday season.
(Chicago Daily News)

Elsie Schuenemann kept the family business going
after the disappearance of her father
(Chicago Daily News)

overcast and high winds were predicted but the *Rouse Simmons* headed straight into the open waters of the lake. When a storm broke, the wooden ship was hopelessly trapped, far from shore. The ship foundered in the rough water and eventually, the sails blew out and the ice-covered masts collapsed. A short time later, the *Rouse Simmons* disappeared.

Captain Herman Schuenemann was never heard from again, although many of his trees were found washed ashore in Wisconsin a few days after the ship vanished. The people of Chicago, and the family of Captain Schuenemann, were grief-stricken and stunned. Newspaper reporters found Elsie Schuenemann and her mother weaving Christmas garlands that came from the splintered trees recovered by Wisconsin residents on the lake's shoreline. Facing destitution, they sold the garlands to the public. Every dollar the family possessed had been tied up in the Rouse Simmons and its ill-fated cargo. The *Chicago Inter-Ocean* newspaper, with help from the Lake Seaman's Union, organized an emergency relief fund for the family.

Elsie told the newspaper reporters, "I am going to attempt to carry on father's Christmas tree business. I will get friends to help me and send trees by rail to Chicago and sell them from the foot of Clark Street. Ever since I was a little girl, Papa has sold them there, and lots and lots of people never think of going anywhere else for their trees."

As a sales location for the trees, W.C. Holmes Shipping, for whom Schuenemann had operated a vessel in his younger days, offered the family the use of a schooner, the *Oneida*. It was moored at the Clark Street Bridge where the *Rouse Simmons* had rested for years and after the *Rouse Simmons* disaster, the new ship was filled with trees each year and the cherished Christmas tradition was unbroken.

Meanwhile, in 1912, the search for clues and survivors from the *Rouse Simmons* continued. The U.S. Treasury Department offered the use of one of their cutters to search the small islands of Lake Michigan for any sign of the small ship. The hopes and prayers of the families of the crew and passengers went with the cutter, but those hopes quickly faded.

No sign of the men were found, but two bottle messages were reportedly recovered. The first was found on a beach at Sheboygan, Wisc., on December 13, 1912. It read, "Friday. Everybody goodbye. I guess we are all through. Sea washed over our deck load Tuesday. During the night, the small boat washed over. Ingvald and Steve fell overboard on Thursday. God help us. Herman Schuenemann."

A weird story surfaced in newspapers while Chicago was anxiously awaiting news about the missing "Christmas Tree Ship" in 1912. Hogan Hoganson, a superstitious Swede who lived at 413 North Milwaukee Avenue, had signed on with the *Rouse Simmons* to make her final voyage. However, at the last minute, he decided not to go aboard the ship after seeing several rats flee from the schooner and scurry for cover on the docks. It was a tradition of the sea that when rats abandon ship, disaster is coming soon.
"The boys laughed at me for they were mostly not old sailors. To them, the rats leaving meant nothing - but to me, who had heard of this strange thing for years - well, I'm glad that I got the hunch and came back by rail," Hoganson said.

Ingvald Newhouse was a deck hand taken on board just before sailing and Stephen Nelson was the first mate and son of Captain Charles Nelson, who was also lost.

The second bottle note, this one written by Captain Nelson, was found years later, in 1927. It read, "These lines were written at 10:30 p.m. Schooner R.S. ready to go down about 20 miles southeast of Two Rivers Point, between 15 and 20 miles off shore. All hands lashed to one line. Goodbye."

From time to time, other curious artifacts, including a human skull believed to have come from the "Christmas Tree Ship," were washed up along beaches or snagged in fishermen's nets. On April 23,

1924, Captain Schuenemann's wallet, containing business cards and newspapers clippings, was recovered at Two Rivers Point. But the final location of the Rouse Simmons remained a mystery until October 1971. A diver named G. Kent Bellrichard of Milwaukee found the remarkably preserved wreck under 180 feet of water off the coast of Two Rivers.

As to the fate of the rest of the Schuenemann family, Elsie made good on her promise to continue the tradition of the "Christmas Tree Ship." They maintained the tree lot at the Clark Street Bridge every holiday season until 1933, bringing happiness to thousands of Chicago families every year.

THE EASTLAND DISASTER

The afternoon of July 24, 1915 was a special day for thousands of Chicagoans. It was the afternoon that had been reserved for the annual summer picnic for employees of the Western Electric Company. Officials at the utility company had encouraged the workers to bring along as many friends and relatives as possible to the event, which was held across the lake at Michigan City, Ind. In spite of this open invitation, they were surprised to find that more than 7,000 showed up to be ferried across Lake Michigan on the three excursion boats that had been chartered for the day. The steamers were docked on the Chicago River, between Clark and LaSalle streets, and included the *Theodore Roosevelt*, the *Petoskey* and the *Eastland*.

The *Eastland* was a rusting Lake Michigan steamer that was owned by the St. Joseph-Chicago Steamship Company. It was supposed to hold a capacity crowd of 2,500 people but it is believed

The Eastland was a rusting steamer that had been used on the Great Lakes for years -- but no one could have foreseen what occurred in Chicago in 1915.

that on the morning of July 24, more than 3,200 climbed on board. In addition to being overcrowded, the vessel had a reputation for being unstable. Years before, it was realized that design flaws in the ship made it top-heavy. In July 1903, a case of overcrowding had caused the *Eastland* to list and water to flow up one of its gangplanks. The situation was quickly rectified, but it was only the first of many such incidents. To make matters worse, the new federal Seaman's Act had been passed in 1915 because of the *RMS Titanic* disaster. This required the retrofitting of a complete set of lifeboats on the *Eastland*, as well as on other passenger vessels. The Eastland was so top-heavy that it already had special restrictions about how many passengers it could carry. The additional weight of the mandated lifeboats made the ship more unstable than it already was.

The huge crowd, the lifeboats and the negligence of the crew created a recipe for disaster.

The *Eastland* was moored on the south side of the river and after the passengers were loaded on board, the dock lines were loosed and the ship prepared to depart. The massive crowd, dressed in their best summer clothes, jammed onto the decks, calling out and waving handkerchiefs to those who were still on shore. Many of the passengers went below decks, hoping to warm up on this cool, cloudy morning. As the steamer eased away from the dock, it started to list to the port side. Unknown to the passengers, the crew had emptied the ballast compartments of the ship, which were designed to provide stability, so that more passengers could be loaded on board. They didn't count on a sudden shift in weight that would cause the vessel to lean even farther toward the port side. That sudden shift was caused by a passing fireboat, which fired off its water cannons to the delight of the crowd. The passengers hurried over to the port side for a closer look and moments later, the *Eastland* simply rolled over. It came to rest on the river bottom, which was only 18 feet below the surface.

The passengers who had been on the deck were thrown in the river, thrashing about in a moving mass of bodies. Crews on the other steamers, and on passing vessels, threw life preservers into the water, while those on shore began tossing lines, boxes, and anything that would float to the panicked and drowning passengers. The overturned

Two views of the Eastland after she rolled over in the water of the Chicago River. Rescuers were immediately on the scene but they were too late to prevent the deaths of hundreds of people who had been on board.

The body of a woman is pulled from the ship
(Chicago Daily News)

Divers were used to search for bodies along the bottom of the Chicago River. The men faced the grim task of pulling dozens of corpses to the surface. (Chicago Historical Society)

ship created a current that pulled many of the floundering swimmers to their doom, while many of the women's long dresses were snagged on the ship, tugging them down to the bottom.

The unluckiest passengers were those who had been inside the ship when it turned over. These ill-fated victims were thrown to one side of the vessel when it capsized and many were crushed by the heavy furniture below decks, which included tables, bookcases and a piano. As the river water rushed inside, those who were not immediately killed drowned a few moments later. A few of them managed to escape to the upturned side of the ship, but most of them didn't. Their bodies were later found trapped in a tangled heap on the lowest side of the *Eastland*.

Firefighters, rescue workers, and volunteers soon began to arrive and started cutting holes in the ship's hull that was above the water line. The few who had scrambled to safety inside the ship emerged from the holes but, for most of them, it was simply too late. Those on shore eagerly watched for more survivors, but there just weren't any more. The men who had come to rescue the trapped and the injured had to resign themselves to pulling waterlogged corpses from the river instead. The bodies were wrapped in sheets and placed on the *Roosevelt*, or lined up along the docks. The large stores downtown, like Marshall Field's, sent wagons to carry the dead to the hospitals, funeral homes and the makeshift morgues.

Corpses were fished out of the river using large grappling hooks, but those who had been trapped beneath the ship had to be pulled out by police divers and volunteers. According to newspaper accounts, one of these divers, who had been

> Contrary to popular belief, none of the bodies from the *Eastland* were taken to the Chicago Historical Society, the current site of the Excalibur Club. Most likely, this story came from confusion about photos from the armory that were labeled "Chicago Historical Society." The labels referred to the owner of the picture, not the location.

bringing up bodies from the bottom of the river for hours, went insane. He had to be subdued by friends and police officers. City workers dragged the river where the *Eastland* had capsized, using large nets to prevent the bodies from being pulled out into the lake. By the time it was all over, 841 passengers and four crewmembers perished in the disaster. Many of them were women and children and 22 families were completely wiped out.

The hundreds of bodies that were recovered on the morning of the disaster were taken to the nearby Reid-Murdoch Building and to local funeral homes and mortuaries. The only public building that was large enough to be used as a morgue was the Second Regiment National Guard Armory, which was located on Carpenter Street, between Randolph Street and Washington Boulevard. The dead were laid out on the floor of the armory in rows of 85 and assigned identifying numbers. Any personal possessions that were found with the corpses were placed in envelopes bearing the same number as the body.

Chicagoans with loved ones who had perished in the disaster filed through the rows of bodies, searching for familiar faces, but in 22 cases, there was no one left to identify them. The families were completely wiped out, including grandparents, parents, children, aunts, uncles and cousins. The names of these victims were learned through the efforts of neighbors who came searching for their friends. The weeping, crying and moaning of the bereaved echoed off the walls of the armory for days. The American Red Cross

While in use as a training vessel, the former *Eastland* was actually used to sink a submarine after World War I. The German U-boat (not to be confused with U-505, the U-boat on display at the Museum of Science and Industry) had been brought to the United States as a war trophy. Under the Treaty of Versailles, all such trophies had to be sunk by July 1, 1921. The *Eastland*, by then known as the *U.S.S. Wilmette*, sunk the ship in Lake Michigan with less than a month to go before the deadline. The wrecked U-boat is still beneath the water of the lake today. Interestingly, the newspapers reported that the shot that sank it was fired by one J.O. Sabin, who, it was said, fired the first shot of the war onboard the *S.S. Jupiter* in 1917. He had, papers said, fired both the first and last shots of the war.

The 2nd Regimental Armory building, which is now the site of Oprah Winfrey's Harpo Studios (Chicago Historical Society)

The line of people that formed at the Armory to identify the dead (Chicago Daily News)

The Eastland dead were arranged in long lines so that they would be easier to identify (Chicago Historical Society)

treated 30 women for hysteria and exhaustion in the days following the disaster.

The last body was identified on Friday, July 30. A 7-year-old boy named Willie Novotny of Cicero, #396, was the last. His parents and older sister had also died on the *Eastland* and his identification came from extended family members, who arrived nearly a week after the disaster took place. After Willie's name was learned, a chapter was closed on one of Chicago's most horrific events.

Officially, the mystery of what happened to the *Eastland* that day was never solved. No clear accounting was ever made to explain the capsizing of the vessel. Several hundreds lawsuits were filed but almost all of them were dismissed by the Circuit Court of Appeals, which held the owners of the steamer blameless in the disaster. After the ship was raised from the river, it was sold at auction. The title was later transferred to the government and the vessel was pressed into duty as the gunboat *U.S.S. Wilmette*. The ship never saw action but was used as a training ship during World War II. After the war, it was decommissioned and put up for sale in 1945. Finding no takers, it was scrapped in 1947.

The *Eastland* was gone, but its story has continued to linger for years.

GHOST ALERT!

On the morning of the *Eastland* disaster, many of the bodies of the victims were taken to the Second Regiment National Guard Armory. As the years passed, there was no longer a need for a National Guard armory to be located so close to downtown Chicago. It was closed down by the military and the building was sold off. It went through several incarnations over the decades, including uses as a stable and a bowling alley, before being purchased by Harpo Studios, the production company owned by Oprah Winfrey. Winfrey is one of Chicago's greatest success stories and is the host of one of the most popular talk shows in television history, a film star, producer, publisher and well-known personality.

Unfortunately, though, the success of the show that is filmed in the former armory has done nothing to put to rest the spirits that linger from the *Eastland* disaster. A number of staff members, security guards and maintenance workers claim that the ghosts of those who perished in 1915 restlessly wander this building. Many employees have had encounters with things that cannot easily be explained away, including the sighting of a woman in a long, gray dress who walks the corridors and then mysteriously vanishes into the wall. There have been many occasions when this woman has been spotted but, each time she is approached, she always disappears. Some have surmised that she is the spirit of a mourner who came here looking for her family and left a bit of herself behind at the spot where she felt her greatest pain.

> Oprah's reaction to the supposed haunting of the building seems to vary depending on whom you ask. Some sources say that she talks freely about the ghosts and isn't scared of them at all. Others say that she refuses to talk about them or to be in the building alone at night. Winfrey herself was unavailable for comment.

The woman in gray may not be alone in her spectral travels throughout the old armory. Staff members have also claimed to hear whispers, the sounds of people sobbing, moaning noises, and phantom footsteps. These footsteps, which sound as though they belong to a group of several people, are usually heard on a staircase in the lobby. Doors that are located nearby often open and close under their own power. Those who experience these strange events have come to believe that the tragedy of yesterday is still visiting itself on the former armory as it exists today.

The site of what became the Second Regiment Armory morgue is not the only location in Chicago that still resonates with chilling stories of the *Eastland* disaster ghosts. Reports of the ship being haunted date back to the time just after the disaster and prior to its sale to the Navy. During that period, it was docked near the Halsted Street Bridge and regarded with much superstition by passers-by.

The recovery efforts of the Eastland's dead continued into the night, creating an "unearthly glow" on the river. Eerie lights are also reported today that have no explanation -- could history be repeating itself as a haunting?

One lonely caretaker, Captain M.L. Edwards, lived aboard it and said he was awakened by moaning noises nightly, though he attributed them simply to the sound of the ship falling apart. Amused though he was to see people hurry across the bridge, terrified, when they saw a light in his cabin, he was very glad to move off the ship after its sale to the Navy in December 1915.

The site on the river where the disaster occurred has its strange stories, as well. For many years, people who have passed on the Clark Street Bridge have claimed to hear moaning and crying sounds coming from the river, along with bloodcurdling screams and pleas for help. In addition, some witnesses state that the cries are accompanied by the sounds of someone splashing in the river and even the apparitions of people helplessly flailing about in the water. Strange Glowing lights are also sometimes seen in the river, but their source remains a mystery.

During several incidents, witnesses have actually called for help from emergency services, believing that someone was actually drowning in the river. At least one man jumped into the water to try and save what he thought was a person who was unable to swim. When he returned to the surface, he discovered that he was in the river alone. He had no explanation for what he had seen, other than to admit that it might have been a ghost!

In the same way that the former armory seems to have been impressed with a ghostly recording of past events, the Chicago River seems haunted, too. It seems that the horror of the Eastland disaster has left a memory behind at this spot and it continues to replay itself over and over again - ensuring that the luckless victims from the Eastland will never truly be forgotten.

THE FLIGHT 191 DISASTER

Before the horrific events of September 11, 2001, the worst airline-related disaster in American history occurred on Memorial Day weekend of 1979 in Chicago. On Friday, May 25, American Airlines Flight 191 literally fell from the sky, killing all of the 271 passengers and crew on board. The flight was meant to be a non-stop journey from Chicago to Los Angeles but as fate would have it, the plane would never leave the Windy City.

It was a beautiful holiday weekend in Chicago and throngs of people filled into O'Hare International, the world's busiest airport. The passengers of Flight 191, including a number of Chicago literary figures bound for Los Angeles and the annual American Booksellers Association conference, boarded the McDonnell-Douglas DC-10 shortly before 3:00 p.m. There seemed to be nothing out of the ordinary about the flight. The DC-10 was a top-of-the-line aircraft and this particular model had logged more than 20,000 trouble-free hours since it left the assembly line. The crew was top-notch as well, including Captain Walter Lux, a 22,000-hour pilot who had been flying DC-10s since their introduction into service eight years before, and First Officer James Dillard and Flight Engineer Alfred Udovich, who had nearly 25,000 flight hours between them.

At 2:59 p.m., the plane was cleared to begin its taxi to the runway's holding point. Then, at 3:02 pm, Flight 191 started down the runway. All went smoothly until a point about 6,000 feet down the runway, just prior to rotation. The tower controller saw parts of the port engine pylon falling away from the aircraft and a "white vapor" coming from the area. A moment later, the plane pitched into rotation and lifted off. As it did so, the entire engine and pylon tore loose from their mounting, flipped up and over the wing and crashed down onto the runway.

Moments after take-off, Flight 191 plummeted to the earth and exploded, killing everyone on board.

GHOST ALERT!

Ghostly tales soon began to spring up about the site of the Flight 191 crash. According to Des Plaines police officers, motorists began reporting odd sights within a few months of the crash. They called in about seeing odd, bobbing white lights in the field where the aircraft had gone down. First thought to be flashlights carried by ghoulish souvenir hunters, officers responded to the reports to find the field was silent and deserted. No one was ever found, despite patrols arriving on the scene almost moments after receiving a report.

More unnerving, though, were the accounts that came from the residents of the nearby mobile home park, which was adjacent to the crash site. Many of these reports came within hours of the crash, when residents claimed to hear knocking and rapping sounds at their doors and windows. Those who responded, including a number of retirees and off-duty police and firefighters, opened their doors to find no one was there. Dogs in the trailer park would bark endlessly at the empty field where the plane had gone down. Their masters could find no reason for their erratic behavior. This continued for weeks and months and even escalated to the point that doorknobs were being turned and rattled, footsteps were heard approaching the trailers, clanging on the metal stairs, and on some occasions, actual figures were confronted. According to some reports, a few residents opened their doors to find a worried figure who stated that he "had to get his luggage" or "had to make a connection" standing on their porch. The figure then turned and vanished into the darkness.

The tragedy, and the strange events that followed, caused many of the residents to move out of the park but when new arrivals took their place, they too began to report the weird happenings. One sighting was described by a man out walking his dog one night near the area where Flight 191 went down. He was approached by a young man who explained that he needed to make an emergency telephone call. The man with the dog looked at this person curiously for he seemed to reek of gasoline and also appeared to be smoldering. At first, he just assumed the man had been running on this chilly night and steam was coming from his clothing, but when he turned away to point out a nearby phone and then turned back again --- the man had vanished! The man with the dog had heard stories from other local residents about moans and weird cries emanating from the 1979 crash site, but he never believed them until now. He was now convinced that he had encountered one of the restless passengers from Flight 191 for himself!

Flight 191 went down in a mobile home park near O'Hare Airport

Immediately, the tower controller tried to raise the plane on the radio: "American 191, do you want to come back? If so, what runway do you want?"

There was no reply from the aircraft but it proceeded to climb out normally, only dipping the left wing for a moment. It quickly stabilized and the plane continued its descent. About 10 seconds later, at a height of around 300 feet, the aircraft began to bank to the left, first slightly, then sharply. The nose of the plane dipped and as the aircraft began to lose height, the bank to left increased until the wings were past vertical --- then it fell to the earth!

The left wingtip hit the ground first and the sound of tearing metal was followed by a massive explosion. The fireball went down about a half mile northwest of O'Hare and slammed into an abandoned hangar on the site of the old Ravenswood Airport on Touhy Avenue, just east of a mobile home park. It was mostly vacant ground, although the plane narrowly missed some fuel storage tanks on Elmhurst Road and the busy I-90 Expressway. However, two people were killed on the ground and several homes were damaged in the trailer park. As for the crew and passengers aboard the aircraft --- all 271 of them had been killed instantly.

The enormity of the tragedy was felt throughout the country and people everywhere demanded answers from the airline, the airport and the National Transportation Safety Board (NTSB). How could something like this have happened? It is a standard in the industry for planes to be able to finish a flight with only one engine, so how did the loss of one engine seal the fate of Flight 191? The findings of the long and grueling investigation by the NTSB were released on December 21, 1979. It attributed the probable cause of the crash to damage to the left wing engine pylon that occurred during an earlier engine change at American Airlines' aircraft maintenance facility in Tulsa, Okla., on March 29 and 30, 1979. Evidence came from the flange, a critical part of the pylon assembly. Investigators found it was damaged before the crash, and a check of the plane's maintenance history found it was serviced eight weeks before the crash. The pylon was damaged due to the engine removal procedure itself. The original procedure called for the engine to be taken off, prior to the removal of an engine pylon. To save time and costs, American Airlines, without the approval of McDonnell Douglas, started doing this by a faster method. They instructed their mechanics to remove the engine with the pylon together as one unit. A large forklift was used to support the engine while it was being detached from the wing. This procedure was extremely difficult to execute successfully, because the engine assembly had to be held perfectly straight while it was being removed. This was almost impossible to do without causing a crack. After the accident, cracks were found in the bulkheads of many other DC-10s.

The fracture in this particular plane went unnoticed for several flights, getting worse with each flight that the plane had taken. During Flight 191's takeoff, enough force was generated to finally cause the pylon to fail. At the point of rotation, the engine detached and was flipped over the top of the wing.

A tiny crack had caused the flight to end in disaster.

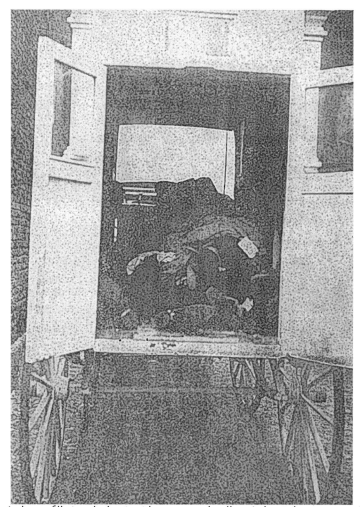

An ambulance filled with the dead leaves "Death Alley" behind the Iroquois Theater

4. WEIRD CHICAGO PLACES & ROADSIDE ODDITIES

We struck the home trail now, and in a few hours were in that astonishing Chicago--a city where they are always rubbing a lamp, and fetching up the genii, and contriving and achieving new impossibilities. It is hopeless for the occasional visitor to try to keep up with Chicago -- she outgrows her prophecies faster than she can make them. She is always a novelty; for she is never the Chicago you saw when you passed through the last time.

Mark Twain

Chicago is a city of amazing architectural achievements, from the White City of the Columbian Exposition to the Hancock Building, the Sears Tower, and beyond. But we at Weird Chicago find ourselves looking for other places on the Chicago skyscape, which are perhaps not as well known and are definitely far to the left of center. The locations that follow are spots that you will rarely find mentioned on tourist maps of the city and are places that are generally overlooked by those who consider themselves Chicago historians. However, we feel they are a part of what makes Chicago so great and believe they are an integral part of our unique and eccentric Windy City history.

House of Crosses in 2004

TRIBUTE TO THE HOUSE OF CROSSES

In January 2007, the Weird Chicago crew paid tribute to a vanishing icon of Chicago's West Side, the fabled House of Crosses. By then, the old and rotting staircase was gone and the tree that once stood proudly in front of this unusual house had been removed. Many of the brightly colored crosses that were once scattered over the face of the house had vanished, erased by time and the elements. The neighborhood too, which was once predominantly Polish, then Hispanic, had changed too. It had become another victim of Chicago "gentrification," as old houses and forgotten businesses were destroyed to make way for yet another condominium complex. Such was the fate of what many called "the weirdest house in Illinois."

LAST DAYS OF THE HOUSE OF CROSSES

(Left) The House of Crosses from across Chestnut Street in January 2007.
(Right) A close-up view of some of the many crosses that decorated the house.

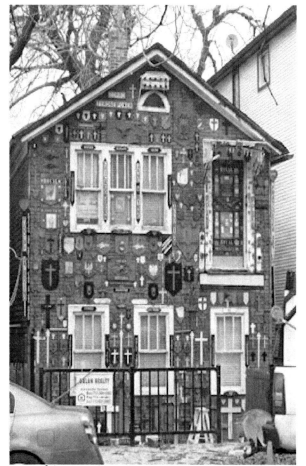

Some of the rarely seen (and never photographed) crosses that were attached to the coach house at the back of the property. Mitch's nephew was kind enough to give us unprecedented access to the property.

Some of the demolition work on the house begins with the removal of the original staircase.

Workmen tear out the remains of the tree that was located in front of the house

Until the early days of 2007, there was no way that a traveler with a penchant for the weird could miss this house as he turned onto West Chestnut Street, a narrow thoroughfare in the West Town neighborhood of Chicago. It had been called many things ---- the "House of Crosses," the "Cross House," the "It's What I Do House" by the American Institute of Architects and, by others, well, it had been called downright weird. Whatever you wanted to call it, though, you had to see it to believe it. Because for almost 25 years, the owner of the house covered it with hundreds of wooden crosses, plaques and shields that were colored red, black and silver. Dozens and dozens of the crosses were marked with famous names. But why did he do it? What drove a man named Mitch Szewczyk to create such a weird and unusual place?

What came to be called the House of Crosses started out as a modest West Side home when it was built in 1879. It was constructed by a Polish immigrant who used it to woo his prospective bride to Chicago from Poland with the promise that she would have a home of her own to live in when she came to America. The family was happy here for decades. Children were born and one of them, Mitchell, took up residence in the coach house located in the rear of the property. He later moved into the upstairs apartment in the back so that he could take care of his elderly mother in her later years.

After Mitch moved into the apartment, he began decorating it with crosses. In addition to being a devout Catholic, he was also fascinated with the Crusades and by medieval history. Many of the wooden crosses and shields that he made, mostly using material that he found in the streets, were of a Templar and medieval design. He never intended to do anything with them (his mother forbade him to decorate the outside of the house with them) but he kept busy making them in his spare time.

In 1977, Mitch's mother passed away and by this time, the West Town neighborhood had taken a turn for the worse. Mitch started having problems with gang members and crime in the area and for some reason, decided to hang a single red cross on the outside of the house. He did it in hopes that it might deter troublemakers from causing problems on this property. Strangely enough, it worked. Mitch never had problems with neighborhood crime again but just to make sure of this, he decided to hang a couple of other crosses on the house and around the yard. And, so it began....

Starting in 1979 and continuing for almost 25 years, Mitch made more and more of the wooden crosses and nailed them all over the house. The pattern changed from being merely protection from crime to an artistic tribute to saints, the Pope, local politicians, and even to the movie stars of his youth. It was not an attempt to be morbid because many of the names of the people that appeared on the crosses had not died and many of them, like Tarzan and Zorro, had never really lived at all.

As time passed, Mitch added more movie stars, movie characters and even movie titles to what was rapidly becoming a strange and colorful place. Just some of the dozens of names included Mickey Rooney, Sammy Davis, Jr., Sir Lancelot, Bing Crosby, Bette Davis, Zsa Zsa Gabor, Buckwheat, the Cisco Kid, and even former Chicago Mayor Jane Byrne, who had a prominent spot. Mitch also planted crosses all over the yard and constructed a shrine to Pope John Paul II. In fact, when the pope visited Chicago, he came to this largely Polish area and his caravan even made a stop at the Houses of Crosses to view the shrine that had been created in his honor.

Mitch never stopped adding to the house, right up until the time that he became bedridden in the early 1990s. His biggest regret was that he was not able to complete his King Kong cross. He claimed that it would be the biggest and best that he had ever made. Mitch passed away a few years later and the fate of the House of Crosses went into limbo.

Family members remained at the House of Crosses for a number of years after Mitch died, but the deteriorating condition of the house made it more and more treacherous for Mitch's elderly sister. As the neighborhood began to turn into condos, there seemed to be little else to do but sell the place --- bringing an era of Weird Chicago history to an end.

In 2007, the house was put up for sale and was presumed to be a teardown property. We featured the place on our Weird Chicago Tours for as long as we could (it was one of our guests' favorite spots), but the crosses were eventually removed, leaving only the old house beneath. We hope that our readers will, along with us, remember with fondness this unusual house and, most importantly, the unusual and beloved man who created it.

BUGHOUSE SQUARE

Washington Square Park, between Clark and Dearborn streets and a couple of blocks above Chicago Avenue, is the oldest park still in existence in Chicago. Washington Square has always been the official name, though for many years it was known by the much more colorful nickname of "Bughouse Square."

The history of Bughouse Square began in the 1840s, when a developer named Erasmus Bushnell left a cow pasture to the city to be used as a park. Supposedly, his will contained a provision that a wall be built around the park. The city got around this in the 1870s by putting up a limestone wall less than a foot tall that is still present today.

The will is also said to have contained a provision that anyone who wanted to must be allowed to make a speech at the park at any time, and from roughly the 1890s through the 1960s, speeches could be heard there any night when the weather was good. It quickly gained a reputation as a popular spot for wackos -- hence the nickname of Bughouse Square ("bughouse" was a slang term for a mental institution.)

Some of the great speakers of the day were regulars - including Clarence Darrow, Eugene Debs (socialist candidate for President), Lucy Parsons (anarchist labor organizer), her lover Ben Reitman (a controversial physician), Emma Goldman (an anarchist who was eventually deported to Russia), Studs Terkel (who plans to have his ashes scattered in the park when he dies) and poets Carl Sandburg and Kenneth Rexroth. The widows of the executed Haymarket Square anarchists made occasional appearances at the park for decades.

Of course, there were plenty of lesser-known characters who hung around, including Slim Brundage (founder and janitor of the College of Complexes, the "indoor bughouse square"), "One-Armed" Charlie Wendorf (who had the constitution memorized), Herbert William Shaw, alias "the Cosmic Kid" (described as "the first soapboxer to take his audience on philosophic flights into empyrean realms of thought"), "Weird Mary," (a religious fanatic) and William Lloyd Smith (the Beatnik Party's anti-candidate for President in 1960.) Another regular was The Bird Woman, a psychotic woman who sold crumbs to be fed to birds and believed that she had been charged by God himself to feed His birds. She was known to chase people who declined to buy a bag of crumbs, screaming that they would burn in hell

"One-Armed Charlie" is especially remembered today for his ability to deal with the ever-present hecklers. When one of them shouted at him, he would reply, "If your brains were bug juice, you couldn't drown a gnat!" He is thought to have been the first "mayor" of Bughouse Square.

The Cosmic Kid was no less respected. When

Bughouse Square in 1905

Bughouse Square today.

he died at age 76 in 1949, Bughouse regulars pitched in to give him a Druidic funeral, complete with torches, under the streetlights in the park.

Very few details of the debates in the park seem to have survived, but at least one detailed report of a debate between One-Armed Charlie and the Cosmic Kid survives to give us an idea of what Bughouse Square was like at its

height. It was July of 1947, and newspapers were carrying reports of flying saucers being spotted in the sky. In particular, they were reporting a saucer that was said to have crashed in Roswell, N.M.

One-Armed Charlie attributed the flying discs to nothing more than mass hysteria, and stated that the visions could be erased by healthy living, but noted that, to eat healthy, "you got to eat living things." He further noted that he himself ate 50 dandelions every day.

The Cosmic Kid disagreed, stating that the discs were evidence of life on other planets. The people of Mars, he said, "have an understanding of the cosmic process in advance of ours and have a theory that the interpenetration of radiation of energy into interstellar space holds the solar systems together." Reporters were especially impressed that he got all this out in one breath. No wonder they called the guy The Cosmic Kid!

"Porkchops Charlie," a hobo, had his own theory: he claimed that he had seen "flying discs" many times while riding in boxcars, but that the visions were caused by moving shadows between the sun and the Earth which deceived the eye via "electric vibration."

Still another man claimed that the flying discs were inventions of the government used to cook t-bone steaks in the sky. Whether he was serious or just a joker is not known.

At its height, some said that going down to Bughouse Square to heckle a wacko was the best entertainment -- and education -- in the city. It even became a great spot for tourists who wanted to, in Mike Royko's words, "go home and say they heard a dirty man talk about free love right there in a public place."

But the history of the place is not all pleasant; for many years, it was a notorious gathering place for pickpockets, dope addicts, and other underworld types. In 1930, three men in the park were shot by a group of Al Capone's henchmen during a flare-up in gang warfare. One of them, a gangster known as Joe Ferrari, was killed.

In the 1970s, by which time the park was mostly abandoned by the orators, it became a notorious after-house cruising ground for male prostitutes and their clientele, including John Wayne Gacy, Jr., who allegedly picked up victims there while dressed as a police officer.

As the Gold Coast neighborhood got nicer, things in the park got a lot quieter. Today, the park has come full circle to what it was in the 1840s, it's now simply a very pleasant place to stroll on a warm day. Dog walkers and senior citizens wander peacefully about, and there's seldom a single wacko to be seen, except for one day every July when the adjacent Newberry Library sponsors the annual Bughouse Square Debates, an event that still brings the city's great speakers -- and great eccentrics -- to the square year after year.

THE DIL PICKLE CLUB

In the early 20th century, the area around the old Water Tower near Chicago and Michigan avenues became known as "Towertown" - Chicago's own version of New York's Greenwich Village. Bughouse Square was right in the heart of Towertown. Near that was Turner Hall, a meeting place for unionists (August Spies, one of the Haymarket anarchists, spoke there regularly) and home to the renowned Radical Bookstore. In the 1930s, there were a number of "pansy parlors," forerunners to the transvestite hangouts that would flourish there in the 1970s. Towertown attracted radicals of all stripes, but anarchists, Marxists, and religious reformers were present in especially high numbers. Bughouse Square gave them all a place to talk, but it was hard to draw a crowd in the snow. To cure this problem, the Dil Pickle Club, "the indoor Bughouse Square," was formed.

The Dil Pickle (spelled with one L to avoid potential copyright issues) was founded in 1917 by Jack Jones, a prominent member of the Industrial Workers of the World, better known as the Wobblies, a radical labor group. Sherwood Anderson once called him "the P.T. Barnum of the revolution."

The actual location of the place was in the back of an old barn (eventually expanded to three of them) at 858 North State Street, but to get there, one had to squeeze through a hole in the wall (literally) into narrow Tooker Alley to come to a green light over a four-foot high orange door, on which were the words "Step high, stoop low, and leave your dignity outside." One had to practically crawl to get inside the place, and it was not known for smelling pleasant. But the conversation was always stimulating.

The usual program for the evening would be a speech lasting anywhere from five minutes to an hour on a variety of topics, many of which weren't discussed in polite company, followed by heckling and discussions. Some nights the entertainment included jazz music, dancing, sing-a-longs (with Carl Sandburg, a regular, playing guitar and singing folk songs), plays, or demonstrations. Alcohol was not served (it was Prohibition, and, while alcohol was still readily available, it was far too expensive for my Dil Pickle patrons, and it's unlikely that Jones could have afforded the necessary bribes), but soft drinks and sandwiches were available.

The tiny hole in the wall quickly landed itself as a place on the map as a coffee shop, forum, theatre, art gallery, and meetinghouse for hoboes, intellectuals, and nuts. Jane Addams and Clarence Darrow both spoke there, as did Edgar Masters, Emma Goldman, and boxer Jack Johnson. Jones had a real talent for getting very serious speakers to speak for the not-always-serious crowd. Indeed, the list of regulars is almost a who's who of Jazz Age literati. One patron said, quite seriously, that more

Entrance to the Dil Pickle Club

famous people had been in the Dil Pickle than had passed through the doors of any 50 universities. But being serious, or even smart, was no requirement. Jack would let anyone speak, "as long as he was a nut about something."

On one memorable occasion in 1919, the club was addressed by none other than Captain George Wellington Streeter, who, the year before, had finally been forced off of his "deestrict." He arrived an hour late and claimed not to have made up his mind about what to say, but ended up covering "every topic but...the ethical code of the dinosaurs," according to the *Chicago Tribune*. He rambled on class conflict, money, Ireland, George Washington, Riparian rights, and, with great gusto, his 30-year war against the city. The Pickle was surely Streeter's sort of place. "People oughtn't be dragged off to prison for arguin'," he said that night. "That's what they done in Ireland, and what's the result? The Irish is just as bad as ever."

Tax problems forced the Dil Pickle Club out of existence in 1932, but by then it was only one of dozens of such forums. Five years later, there were more than 60 of them downtown.

> **WHERE IS IT NOW?**
> The Dil Pickle Club is gone, but Tooker Alley is still there, functioning as an unnamed alley used mainly for parking. It is accessible off Dearborn just south of Bughouse Square.

BEWARE OF SNUGGLEPUPPIES: THE WIND BLEW INN

In 1922, 10 years after the Everleigh Club was shut down, the most notoriously racy spot in town wasn't a brothel at all (although there were still plenty around) - it was a bohemian tearoom, The Wind Blew Inn, on the corner of Ohio and Michigan avenues.

The proprietress, a young woman named Lillian Collier, had come from New York's Greenwich Village to "preach the gospel of real life." Her poetry made her a darling of the Dil Picklers before she opened the Wind Blew Inn in 1921."There aren't many real people here," she said. "Those who see the light. But I'll try to struggle on and teach these people the value of aesthetic effectiveness."

The Wind Blew Inn was hardly a rowdy place, but it was apparently a rather shocking place for its time. Owners of neighboring taverns complained that their customers were frightened away by the sound of syncopated blues

GIRLS SENTENCED TO READ FAIRY TALES TO END BOHEMIAN FANCIES

MISS LILLIAN COLLIER

Lillian Collier and the "Flappers" who frequented the Wind Blew Inn were widely covered in the newspapers

FLAPPER SLANG: HELP US BRING THESE TERMS BACK!

"Snugglepupping" ended up listed in a couple of "flapper slang" dictionaries printed in newspapers in the 1920s. Other terms included:

"lollygagger" - one who spoons in hallways
"snugglepuppy" - a girl who enjoys snugglepupping (the male version was "snugglepup.")
"applesauce" - nonsense
"cake-eater" - lounge lizard
"cuddle cootie" - one whose idea of a good date is to take a girl for a ride on the bus
"barney mugging" - sex

music emanating from the inn's piano. Rumors went around that the inn -- like so many thousands of other places in town -- was serving things a little stronger than tea (which it almost certainly was). And, worst of all, rumor had it that young people were meeting there for "petting parties."

In early 1922, police raided the supposed den of depravity and forced Lillian to cover up the statues of Greek nudes that served as decorations. She complied, covering them with overalls, but wasn't happy about it. "Oh art, where art thou?" she moaned.

In court, Lillian denied the stories of booze and petting. She stated that they served nothing stronger than chocolate eclairs, and that "there is no snugglepupping at the Wind Blew Inn." One wonders how, if the petting parties didn't go on, she had ever thought of such a fantastic word as "snugglepupping." The term briefly caught on; parents worried that their daughters were becoming "snugglepuppies."

In the trial after the raid, Collier was not convicted, but, in what must be one of the most bizarre rulings of the 20th century, the judge ordered Collier and a co-defendant to read a book of fairy tales to cure them of bohemianism. "All that's the matter with you," declared the judge, "is that you have a false value of the things of life in general. Start on the fairy tales right away."

As ordered, Collier checked out a copy of a book of fairy tales at the library on her way home from the courthouse.

Mere weeks later, the Wind Blew Inn came to end after succumbing to a fire which Collier blamed on puritan arsonists. She moved to a new location on LaSalle Street next to a police station to save the detectives the trip for the next time, but the new location wasn't a success - it was too clean. "People," wrote Alfreda Gordon, "wanted some dirt with their 75-cent drink."

Unfazed, Collier went on to become a leading advocate of the flapper movement before vanishing from public life in 1924. Several people named Lillian Collier appear in the records after that including a woman who married an Olympic fencer and a poetess in Canada, but none have been determined to be the same Lillian Collier who ran the Wind Blew Inn. Whatever happened to her has become one of the greatest mysteries the Weird Chicago crew has come across!

WHERE IS IT NOW?
The site of the Wind Blew Inn is now occupied by an Eddie Bauer store at Ohio Street and Michigan Avenue.

THE COLLEGE OF COMPLEXES

There were those who said that the College of Complexes was little more than The Dil Pickle with a bar attached. There were others who said, "So what?"

The College of Complexes was one of Chicago's - and the world's - most unusual taverns, known as "The playground for people who think." Slim Brundage, the founder and janitor of the college, put it this way in 1955: "We cater to artists, writers, intellectuals and assorted screwballs. And every now and then, we get somebody with the price of a drink." A sign above the entrance proclaimed "Through these doors pass the most obnoxious people in the world: Our customers." Other signs advertised some of the drinks on offer "Fallout Cocktail - prevents having mutants for heirs" and "Castro Cocktail - puts hair on your chin!" The college was one of few places in the city at the time where minors were never served. In fact, a sign on the door indicated that minors were admitted only if accompanied by their grandchildren.

The club, having a tendency to be shut down every now and then, occupied several locations, first at 1561 North Wells St., then near the old Dil Pickle and Bughouse Square at 862 North State St., and then near the corner of Clark Street and Grand Avenue.

A patron never knew what he'd find on entering the College of Complexes, but an interesting time was guaranteed for all. The walls of at least one location were composed entirely of blackboards, which would be covered with such phrases as "World War III - where all men will be cremated equal," or "I don't care whose last supper it is - no ID, no wine!" Eventually, writing on the walls came to be a sort of contest in which collegians would try to outdo each other for sheer wit - a couple of the most popular phrases were "learn to complain without suffering" and "one more genius and I'll cut my goddamned throat!" "The place," Brundage explained, "was full of geniuses. Or so they told me, one after another, every day."

Courses on a given evening might include a review of a popular novel, a debate about jazz, a re-enactment of the death scene from Julius Caesar, folk singing, or a "Miss Beatnik of Chicago" pageant. On the occasional slow nights, one might even see fencers dueling in the corner.

The tavern considered itself to be, first and foremost, a college. To qualify for admission, one had to be found to be lacking in sanity by the college's psychiatrist, who was a cab driver with an IQ of 190.

The usual format of the curriculum would be the "speech of the evening," followed by an open discussion. Speakers on a given night might include a nudist with a speech entitled "is anti-nudism a racket?" or "Yellow Kid" Weil, a noted con artist, who presented a demonstration of his methods (and usually ended up taking the crowd for a few bucks as part of the speech). One notable debate was between Jo Fowler and Guy Bush on the subject of whether sex would ever replace nighttime baseball as the national pastime.

Like the nearby Bughouse Square, not all of the college's denizens were flat-out weirdos. Some of them were notable, even legendary weirdos. Some speakers included mayoral candidates, congressmen, United Nations delegates, Duke Ellington, Kenneth Rexroth, Nelson Algren, Ken Nordine (who invented "word jazz" and recorded voiceovers for thousands of commercials a year), Major League baseball players, Big Bill Broonzy (a blues legend who sang at the college on Wednesday nights for a while), Studs Terkel, and just about every other Chicago notable of the 1950s. Almost unbelievably, the courses were actually quite organized. A publication called The Official Neurosis would publish a schedule of events four months in advance. Eventually, the schedule fell into a routine. (Right)

The IRS forced the college out of operation in the early

A publication called The Official Neurosis would publish a schedule of events for the College of Complexes four months in advance. Eventually, the schedule fell into a routine:

Monday: radical night
Tuesday: drama and improvisations
Wednesday: beatnik night
Thursday: poetry night
Friday: intellectual night
Saturday - discussions followed by a sing-along with "Clark Street Mary." Mary, a septuagenarian, had been singing on Clark Street for decades. Her most popular song was called "Don't Clark Street Me."

1960s, after about 10 years in business. Though it lacks a building of its own, the college still holds courses today on Saturday nights at the Lincoln Restaurant at 4008 North Lincoln Ave.

MAURY'S BEATNIK BOOKSTORE & THE PRESIDENTIAL CAMPAIGN OF 1960

By the 1950s, as television began to take over as the popular way to spend an evening, the bohemian near north side was starting to quiet down, though Bughouse Square and the College of Complexes still drew crowds. In the late 1950s, the popularity of the "beat generation" gave the area a bit of a revival. Ground zero for Chicago's beats was, for a time, Maury's Beatnik Bookshop, at the corner of State Street and Tooker Alley, two doors down from the College of Complexes and sharing a rear wall with what had once been the Dil Pickle Club.

Owner William Lloyd "Bill" Smith proudly claimed that Maury's was the only 24-hour bookstore in the world (although he was probably not quite correct). Late at night, the place would be crowded with young, disaffected youths who rolled their eyes at being called beatniks, but were exactly that. Oddly, very few books were available. A few volumes were scattered across a table, but Smith claimed that they hardly ever actually sold a book. Such a business model didn't make for great success; the store didn't last long, and Smith ended up running a bookstore in the College of Complexes.

In 1960, as Republicans met in Chicago to nominate Richard Nixon as their presidential candidate, Slim Brundage led a delegation of local beatniks to New York, where they convened at the short-lived Greenwich Village branch of the College to hold their first annual Beatnik Party convention.

The beats set about forming a platform, which set them up as opposed to atomic warfare, sex laws, and squares. One plank called for a $10 billion dollar subsidy for artists, another called to abolish the working class. The press took particular notice of their foreign policy, which called to "make peace with all nations, because all beatniks are cowards."

When it came time to nominate a candidate, Slim Brundage expected to run away with it, but the beats, angry that he had only arranged for one-way tickets to New York, passed him by. It may have been the only convention that year that wasn't rigged!

One candidate, Joffre Stewart, raised his hand and asked, "is there a bastard in the house?" Stewart, another Chicagoan, felt that a bastard was a perfect candidate (or anti-candidate) for a party that was, in essence, an anarchist party. Stewart claimed to have been arrested more times than anyone else in Chicago, and was notable among beatniks for having been mentioned in Allen Ginsberg's seminal poem "Howl," which described as him as "investigating the FBI...passing out incomprehensible leaflets."

About four hands went up, including that of one Jimmy the Greek, who Stewart proceeded to nominate.

In the end, though, the nomination went to none other than Bill Smith. Smith was considered a "responsible beatnik," though he was, in fact, an anarchist. In order to "balance the ticket," the vice presidential slot went to Joffre Stewart, an "irresponsible beatnik."

Smith's main plan was remarkable. His first act as president would be to dissolve the federal government. His next would be to resign. The main goal of the party was not to win -- it was to keep people from voting at all. They proudly announced that, "A vote for Bill Smith is no vote at all" and traveled the country to promote their anti-candidacy by hopping freight trains.

Naturally, they lost the election. But in 2007, Stewart proudly claimed that they had been a "blip in the history of electoral politics."

Joffre Stewart, who in 1960 claimed to have been arrested more times than any man in Chicago.

OZ PARK

In 2005, the hit musical *Wicked* opened at the Oriental Theatre (on the old site of the ill-fated Iroquois Theatre) for an open-ended run that would last until January 2009. The musical told the story of Glinda and Elphaba, the witches of Oz. Chicago was a natural home for the show; after all, the first musical adaptation of *The Wizard of Oz* had premiered in there in 1902!

Statues of Dorothy, the Tin Man, Cowardly Lion & the Scarecrow can be found in Chicago's Oz Park

The original book, *The Wonderful Wizard of Oz*, was written by L. Frank Baum, who came to Chicago in 1891. Baum took a job as a reporter for the *Chicago Evening Post*. It was in his home near Humboldt Park on the West Side that he wrote *The Wonderful Wizard of Oz*, which was published to great acclaim in 1900.

Although most people don't know it, the beloved character of Dorothy was actually based on a real girl named Dorothy Louise Gage. She was born on June 11, 1898 to Sophie Jewel and Thomas Clarkson Gage, the brother of Maud Gage Baum, who was the wife of novelist L. Frank Baum.

Maud and her husband had four sons and had always longed for a little girl. For this reason, she was thrilled when Dorothy was born and spent as much time as a doting aunt as she possibly could. She often traveled back and forth to see the little girl, especially after Dorothy became ill later that same year. Tragically, on November 11, five months to the day from when she was born, Dorothy died. The cemetery records give the cause of her death was "congestion of the brain." When Maud heard the news, she was overcome with grief to the point that she required medical attention. "Dorothy was a beautiful baby," Maud wrote to her sister. "I could have taken her for my very own and loved her devotedly."

At the time of the little girl's death, L. Frank Baum was putting the finishing touches on the story that his wife had been urging him to put to paper for a long time, a tale called *The Wonderful Wizard of Oz*. The story, as legend has it, evolved as Baum wove it together for his children and their friends. It was a fantasy story about a magical land and a little girl who accidentally found herself there and wanted to go home. Seeing his wife so distraught after the funeral of her niece, and not knowing how to comfort her, he decided to name the heroine of his story after little Dorothy, forever immortalizing the child as "Dorothy Gale," rather than "Gage."

Chicagoans (like the rest of America) embraced the story and the first musical adaptation opened in Chicago at the Grand Opera House (which was on Clark Street between Randolph and Washington) two years later. It was a very loose interpretation of the book and resembled a vaudeville show more than an actual adaptation. Some of the songs included "It Happens Every Day" and "The Different Ways of Making Love." Baum wrote the script himself.

In 1976, the park on North Burling Street in Lincoln Park was named Oz Park in Baum's honor. In 1995, the statue of the Tin Woodsman was added in a prime location on Lincoln Avenue. Statues of Dorothy, the Scarecrow and the Cowardly Lion were added by the end of 2007, making it a magical place for children of every age who loved the story of a girl named Dorothy and her fabulous adventures in Oz.

REEBIE STORAGE & MOVING

The 1920s were an era when Egyptian design and motifs were all the rage in America. After the discovery of King Tut's tomb in 1922, people began creating apartment houses, theaters, businesses and even cemetery tombs in what was called the Egyptian Revival style. The Reebie Storage & Moving building, which is located at 2325-2333 North Clark St., is an excellent example of this unusual style.

Designed by architect George Kingsley and sculptor Fritz Albert in 1922, the building has been added to the National Historic Register and has been praised for its accurate use of ancient Egyptian imagery and even hieroglyphics, regardless of the fact that the message they spell out is a little untraditional. The building was

The very cool Reebie Storage & Moving Building on North Clark Street

commissioned by twin brothers John and William Reebie, who planned to use it for their moving and storage business.

The interior lobby has decorative metalwork, art glass windows, lotus-leaf columns and plaster casts of Ancient Egyptians moving grain on barges. The front doors, which open onto Clark Street, are guarded by two large pharaohs in full Egyptian attire. According to local legend, the faces of the pharaohs are those of the Reebie brothers, pretending to be Ramses II. The exterior is covered with brightly colored terra cotta sculptures that were crafted by Fritz Albert. It is unknown who did the work on the hieroglyphics above the door but they translate as "I give protection to your furniture" and "Forever I work for all your regions in daylight and darkness." That's the kind of service that everyone would like to get!

TED'S AUTO BODY MUFFLER MAN

In years past, during the real heyday of automobile vacations and highway travel, motorists passed hundreds of signs, murals, and other forms of roadside advertising, each hoping to grab its share of attention. Among the most famous of these were the fiberglass giants that were created during the 1960s by International Fiberglass of Venice, Calif.. Roughly 150 of these giants were produced before the molds were broken and the concept discontinued.

Many of the giants, known as "Muffler Men," were designed to hold automobile mufflers and were originally placed in front of service stations as retail attention-getters. As these businesses closed and the giants were sold off, they soon became everything from lumberjacks to cowboys, to spacemen and more.

Chicago has its very own Muffler Man, standing proudly atop Ted's Auto Body on Grand Avenue, just east of Pulaski Road. For some reason, his muffler is gone but he now holds a bent bar of iron in his hands. Is this to show off his mighty strength? Or perhaps to intimidate those who might consider getting their car worked on anywhere else?

THE 63RD STREET INDIAN

The tobacco store Indian that looms above 63rd and Pulaski has been a landmark for decades - and to some, it's a bit of a naughty one! The Indian stands atop a tobacco shop that has several other stores connected to it. Years ago, the banner on his chest advertised White Owl' cigars but over the years, it's been changed to advertise for the eye vision store next door instead. The Eye Care Center is on Pulaski Street, next to the tobacco shop.

For those who grew up in the area (and for juvenile people like the Weird Chicago crew), the Indian's thumb offered a dirty, inside joke. If you look at the Indian from a northwestern view (approximately in front of the flower shop on 63rd Street), hits thumb appears to be an entirely different appendage, protruding from his pants.

CARS ON A SPIKE: FINAL TRIBUTE TO "THE SPINDLE"

One of the most eccentric pieces of artwork in suburban Chicago was undoubtedly "The Spindle," a strange sculpture that defied not only the traditional standards of art but where artwork could be displayed. In 1989, the Cermak Plaza shopping center in Berwyn commissioned artists to decorate the plaza, but what they created managed to upset the locals for almost two decades. And to be honest, curious visitors usually went away scratching their heads in confusion as well.

Along the sidewalk were 20 visual and sound-related sculptures that were in various stages of disrepair. One of the weirdest was the "Pinto Pelt," a smashed and flattened version of one of the flammable Fords. Another appeared to be some sort of flying machine with what looked to be a robot at the controls. Over time, the pieces lost some of the flair of their original installation, but they were always entertained.

Eye Care Indian asks "How many fingers am I holding up?"

The largest artwork, which attracted the most attention, both negative and positive, was called "The Spindle." Creator Dustin Shuler skewered eight automobiles on a giant nail in the center of the parking lot. It looked like a metal-eating giant's idea of a shish kabob! Critics howled in complaint when the sculpture appeared, objecting that it attracted pigeons. Things did quiet down, though, after the "artwork" appeared in the movie *Wayne's World* and since that time, local residents just got used to it and then sort of became attached to their notoriety as the home of this eccentric work of art. Stories even had it that the Berwyn police used the shopping mall as a way to haze new recruits, sending the rookies out to the plaza to investigate an "eight-car pileup!"

But time was not kind to The Spindle, leaving it battered and rusted by Chicagoland weather and caked with years of pigeon poop, and neither were the developers. The shopping center's owners, who had commissioned the artwork in the first place, began calling for it to be removed so that they could construct a new Walgreens store with a drive-thru pharmacy.

Defenders of the sculpture howled and activists fought to have it preserved. The city of Berwyn, which saw The Spindle as a tourist attraction, wanted to save it, but their hands were tied since it was on private property. Then, under the cover of darkness, on May 2, 2008, Berwyn's most famous pop icon was demolished after a failed attempt to sell it on eBay. The top two cars -- a VW Beetle and a BMW -- were lifted off the spike (for possible future display) then the rest of the sculpture was toppled with a backhoe.

The Spindle is now gone for good, banished only to memories, photographs and the movies.

THE LEANING TOWER OF NILES

The suburban city of Niles was so generous to the people of Chicagoland that you no longer have to go to Europe to see the Tower of Pisa - you can see it right here in Niles! In 1933, the city constructed a half-scale replica of the famous leaning tower as a reservoir to supply water for the three swimming pools of industrialist Robert Ilg.

Architect Albert Farr was criticized for what was considered a silly building --- it was commonly called "Farr's Folly" ---- but it has become a popular attraction in Niles and a novelty that just might outlast its namesake, which leans a little more every year. Farr's smaller version remains steadfastly at the angle at which it was purposely placed. It remains an attention-getter for the local YMCA, but it's no longer filled with water. A park has been built around its base, complete with reflecting pools and a European-style telephone booth.

THE GOLD PYRAMID HOUSE

One of the world's great un-solved mysteries has long been just how the ancient Egyptians were able to create their spectacular pyramids without the aid of modern technology. We may never know the answer to that --- but equally as mysterious is why someone would build a 100th scale reproduction of the Great Pyramid at Giza north of Chicago?

The word "eccentric" doesn't quite cover this weird home, but it is the actual residence of the Onan family, complete with a replica of King

Tut's tomb and a 64-foot statue of the pharaoh Ramses standing on the front lawn. The place is known as the largest gold-plated object in the world and has inspired many stories and legends about its construction and the mystical energy that is said to pervade the property.

According to the stories, strange occurrences began at the Gold Pyramid House during construction when a bulldozer uncovered a large rock that turned out to be rich with high-grade gold ore. It was recorded as the only actual gold strike in the state of Illinois. Owner James Onan saw this as an omen that he should continue the building. As work progressed, an underground spring was uncovered and began to bubble out of the center of the pyramid site. The water from the spring formed a natural moat around the structure and was so pure that the owners were able to bottle and sell it.

The Onan family continues to live in the house and to operate an Egyptian emporium from their website. At one time, the place was open to the public for tours, but then it was closed to all but private groups. A schedule of such gatherings remains erratic but should you get the chance to go inside this fantastical place, don't miss out.

One of our favorite doors in Chicago! The Big Monster Toy Co. door is a huge oversized, cartoon door with a monster peering out of the window. Awesome!

5. FORGOTTEN & LOST CHICAGO

Chicago is a city of contradictions, of private visions haphazardly overlaid and linked together. If the city was unhappy with itself yesterday -- and invariably it was -- it will reinvent itself today.
Pat Colander

As many writers have stated, Chicago is a city that constantly re-invents itself. Like a young woman who can't decide on what dress to wear for a dance, Chicago constantly "changes her clothes, discarding one bit of architecture for another. Many of us lament these changes, worrying over the history that has been lost. Others don't care and see the vanishing warehouses and old neighborhoods, inevitably replaced by condominiums, as "progress" for the future. Whether we love these changes or hate them, we cannot deny that re-invention is an integral part of Chicago.

It's been that way from the beginning, when the first frame houses replaced the log cabins that were constructed along the river. It happened again when the rough town of frame tenements and wooden homes were destroyed by the Great Fire and replaced by a new Chicago of brick and mortar. In the years that followed, we lost most of Prairie Avenue, the Coliseum, the White City of the Columbian Exposition, and sites almost too numerous to even mention.

In the chapter ahead, we'll take a look at some of our favorite "Lost & Forgotten" places, from the notorious to the entertaining, and explore what all of these places once meant to the people of Chicago. It's been a long, strange journey so far and this chapter may serve as a warning about getting too attached to your favorite neighborhood bar - it just may be "re-invented" in the near future!

"WHERE GOOD MEN FEARED TO WALK..."
CHICAGO'S VICE DISTRICTS

By the late 1850s, Chicago was able to boast almost 1,500 businesses within its borders, dozens of banks, railroad lines, millions of dollars worth of imports and exports, 40 newspapers and periodicals, a half-dozen theaters, 80 ballrooms "where bands played from morning to night" and a still-growing population of more than 93,000 people. But not all of Chicago's accomplishments were ones to be proud of. Crime of every description had increased dramatically in just two decades and a national bank panic was spreading throughout the country, causing businesses to fail and widespread unemployment in the Windy City. This led to burglaries, shootings and holdups by bands of young men who had once been respectable laborers. They were driven, according to one lurid newspaper account "from sheer want and by the sufferings of their families to try their fortunes as garrotters, highwaymen, burglars and thieves."

But such incidents of thievery and murder were not the real scourge of Chicago crime -- and certainly not where questionable fortunes were being made. The real problems came from the vice and red-light districts, many of which have become legendary in Chicago history.

One of the earliest vice districts was called "The Sands." It was described as the "vilest and most dangerous place in Chicago" by the Chicago Tribune and by 1857, consisted of a few dozen ramshackle buildings, each housing gambling parlors, saloons and brothels, in which a charge for services ranged between 25 and 50 cents. Originally, the area, which was located on a stretch of lakeshore just north of the Chicago River, catered mostly to sailors and canal men but expanded into a resort area and a hiding place for all manner of criminals. The leaders of this unsavory community were Dutch Frank, who ran dog fights; Freddy Webster; Mike O'Brien; a burglar and former fighter; his son Mike, a pickpocket and a pimp for his four sisters and John Hill and his wife, Mary.

The Hills were said to be the first couple in Chicago to work the "badger game," an old-time sex swindle in which a woman picks up a man and brings him home. Her husband then "accidentally" comes in and catches them in the act, demanding satisfaction from the man, which comes in the form of the sucker's money. Unfortunately, John Hill had a wide jealous streak and after every con, he always tried to kill his wife for encouraging the victim in the racket to get into bed with her!

Freddy Webster owned a brothel that was incredibly vicious, even for The Sands. One of his girls, Margaret McGinness, was said to have been neither sober, nor out of the house, for five years, and not to have had her clothes on for three. She customarily entertained between 10 and 40 men each night. She died in March 1857 from alcoholism and, at the time, was the seventh unnatural death in The Sands that week.

The Sands came to an end during a period of violence that marked the tenure of Mayor "Long John" Wentworth. Long before Wentworth was elected mayor, there had already been talk of demolishing the haphazard shacks of The Sands, but the land on which they stood was tied up in litigation with the courts. As the Tribune explained it: "In view of the uncertainty of the law, the litigants were disinclined to take violent measures to eject the occupants." In other words, the landowners were too scared, or were being too well paid, to run the brothel and saloon keepers off the property. Finally, though, in April 1857, William B. Ogden bought out several of the landowners, notified the denizens of The Sands to vacate the buildings, and also told those who owned their own buildings that he would gladly purchase their shacks. A few sold out but most of the squatters vowed that they would never leave. This was reported to the mayor and he promised to take action as soon as he could without risking bloodshed.

The opportunity came during a dogfight between one of Dutch Frank's dogs and an animal owned by Bill Gallagher, a Market Street butcher. The event was to be held at the Brighton racetrack and on April 20, every able-bodied man in The Sands accompanied Dutch Frank to the scene. Chicago legend has it that Mayor Wentworth may have arranged this fight and caused it to be advertised, but no one really knows for sure. Regardless, he took advantage of it. Dutch Frank and his cohorts had barely left The Sands before Wentworth led a procession of about 100 well-meaning citizens, a deputy sheriff bearing orders of eviction, 30 or so police officers, and a team of horses drawing a wagon that was loaded with hooks and chains. They managed to tear nine buildings down by evening and by the time darkness was starting to fall they burned the rest of the district to the ground. When the inhabitants of The Sands returned from the dogfight later that night, the district was in ashes.

Unfortunately, Wentworth's plan to clean up vice in Chicago backfired. Once The Sands was destroyed, the gamblers, criminals and whores who called the place home simply crossed the Chicago River and, instead of being mostly confined to one small area, spread out throughout the city.

During the 1860s, largely due to the helplessness of the Chicago police force, the city acquired a reputation for being "the wickedest city in the United States." Human refuse from all over the United States swarmed into the city. They were drawn to Chicago by the easy money of those boomtown days, as well as by the thousands of soldiers on the loose with Army payrolls, and by the knowledge that there was little to fear from the police.

The newcomers took over and enlarged the resorts that had been formed by the refugees from The Sands and within a year after the start of the Civil War, there was hardly a downtown street that didn't have a row of brothels, saloons, gambling dens and cheap boarding houses. The criminal class almost wholly occupied the South Side below Madison Street, from the lake to the river, until the Great Fire finally burned them out.

One journalist of the period stated that the "very core of this corruption" was Roger Plant's resort on the northeast corner of Wells and Monroe streets. Originally, the dive was situated in a single, two-story house but after one adjoining establishment after another was added onto it, the resort was extended about halfway down the block on both streets by the middle 1860s. The police called the place "Roger's Barracks" but Plant referred to it as "Under the Willow," thanks to a lone willow tree that drooped at one corner of the main building and the name stuck. The appearance of the place was further enhanced by a bright blue shade at each of the windows that bore the words "Why Not?" in gold lettering. This became a catch phrase all over the city.

Under the Willow was described by author Fredrick Francis Cook as "one of the most talked about, if not actually one of the wickedest places on the continent." It was believed that a tunnel ran from the resort under Wells

Street to a number of underground dens that were located along Wells Street and along the south branch of the river. There were at least 60 rooms in the sprawling place and it offered just about every vice imaginable. The place included a saloon; two or three brothels where customers were often stripped, robbed and dumped into alleys; rooms for men to meet the ladies of the night; cubicles that were rented to streetwalkers; and hideaways that were used by various species of crooks.

WHERE IS IT NOW?
No trace remains of any vice district on the corner of Wells and Monroe today. Like most of the vice districts, the traces were carefully removed by one reform effort after another.

The landlord of the place was Roger Plant, a diminutive Englishman who only stood an inch above five feet and never weighed more than 100 pounds. In spite of this, he came to be regarded as a deadly fighter, adept with all kinds of weapons, especially his teeth. Ordinarily, he carried a knife and a gun secreted on his person but when he got drunk, he would put aside his weapons and ceremonially drench the willow tree outside with a mixture of whiskey and water. He managed to keep his customers in line, but he was, in turn, dominated by his wife, a huge woman who tipped the scales at nearly 300 pounds. She was said to frequently tuck her spouse under one arm and spank him with her free hand. Mrs. Plant organized the affairs of the prostitutes in the resort and when she was not busy with this, she was producing children. No one knows the exact number of children the Plants raised, but it was generally believed to be about 15. Each of them learned to pick pockets not long after learning to walk!

Under the Willow operated for about 10 years with no interference. In 1868, having made more money that he ever expected, Plant closed the resort, bought a house in the country and began living a respectable life.

The Great Fire in 1871 destroyed the worst of the city's vice areas, burning the dangerous saloons and the disease-ridden brothels but within half a decade after the rebuilding of Chicago had begun, a dozen vice districts that were even more vicious had been established. To the inhabitants and to the police, they were known by colorful nicknames like the Black Hole, the Bad Lands, Satan's Mile, Hell's Half Acre, and many others. Most of these areas were on the west and south sides and became places of renown in the annals of Chicago's criminal history.

THE BLACK HOLE

The infamous Black Hole district was a group of saloons, cribs and bordellos that were reserved for African-American customers only. They were located near Washington and Halsted streets in the heart of a vice district that was bounded by Sangamon, Halsted, Lake and Monroe streets. The "pride" of the Black Hole in the 1870s and 1880s was a placed called Noah's Ark, on Washington near Halsted. The place was described as a "queer old three story mansion" that was owned by Chicago alderman Jacob Beidler, a wealthy lumber dealer from a rich and devoutly religious family. The place was said to be a seething hive of corruption with two saloons and a half dozen brothels. A former drawing room of the old mansion had been curtained off into cubicles that were just large enough to hold single cots. These cribs were rented out to streetwalkers, who charged from 25 to 35 cents to a customer for a tumble -- depending on whether he removed his shoes or not. Noah's Ark became quite famous for robberies during its time in

WHERE IS IT NOW?
The area eventually became industrialized and filled mainly with restaurant suppliers. Loft condos and fancy restaurants have moved in to Washington Street today, but several warehouses are still there. Very little is there today to remind one of the Black Hole district.

operation, thanks to the methods devised by two of the denizens of the place. One of the girls, seizing on a moment when she knew the man was completely distracted, would hold him by the arms while her partner cracked him over the head. Once relieved of the contents of his pockets, he was hurriedly deposited in the alley outside.

The largest whorehouse in the Black Hole was Ham's Place, a second floor dive that was famous for its company of uniformed women who were always clad only in white tights and green blouses. No one knew who really owned the place, but it was believed to be an establishment under the control of Diddie Biggs, who ran another brothel on Halsted, in which the most popular girl was a midget named Julie Johnson. The place also boasted a 300-pound piano player named Del Mason.

LITTLE HELL AND "DEATH CORNER"

In the early 20th century, the Italian/Sicilian section just north of the Loop was commonly known as Little Hell. To say that it was the worst neighborhood in town would be a bold statement, but it was certainly a dangerous neighborhood, mostly due to the notorious Black Hand, a loose-knit extortionist organization that preyed on Italians. Many Black Handers went on to form Chicago's organized crime families.

The legendary spot known as "Death Corner", the prime location for murders carried out by the "Shotgun Man" of the Black Hand.

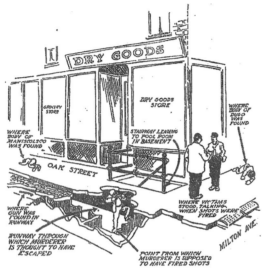

Early 1900s newspaper illustration of how murders were carried out at "Death Corner".

WILLY SAYS:

I grew up in Cabrini Green, but I never heard the Candyman story until I started driving on ghost tours!

THE BAD LANDS & LITTLE CHEYENNE

There were few who could tell the difference between where the Bad Lands ended and Little Cheyenne began. They were both located on Clark Street between Van Buren and Twelfth but the police considered the section south of Taylor Street to be the worst, so they dubbed the area the "Bad Lands." Police detectives described the whole stretch of Clark Street as being "about as tough and vicious a place as there was on the face of the earth."

The area was filled with saloons, dance halls and

WHERE IS IT NOW?

The area once known as Little Hell is now occupied by the Cabrini Green housing projects. Milton had a name-change; the corner of Oak and Milton is now the corner of Oak and Cleveland.

Perhaps the most dangerous spot was the corner of Oak Street and Milton Avenue, which came to be known as "Death Corner." Between 1910 and 1915, that single corner averaged close to a murder per week! Even the police feared "Death Corner." They refused to investigate murders that took place there. Stories of blackmail and extortion, as well as tales of deadly revenge carried out with ruthless precision, were common in the neighborhood. Most of the shootings were carried out with revolvers or sawed-off shotguns, and were probably attributable to the Black Hand. As recently as 1914, the *Chicago Tribune*, which was never shy about ethnic stereotypes in those days, was asserting that the Black Hand gang was a myth, and that the violence in Little Hell was just an "inborn trait of (the) natives." While the 1910s were probably the worst period, murders continued to occur at Oak and Milton with alarming regularity until Little Hell was finally razed in the early 1940s.

GHOST ALERT! OKAY, NOT REALLY!

Some people claim that Cabrini Green is home to "Candyman," a bloodthirsty ghost who appears in mirrors and murders those foolish enough to say his name five times. According to the story, it's the ghost of a young black man who was covered in honey, stung to death by bees, and burned, causing the honey to caramelize into candy. Some say the story is true and have even gone as far as to say that the 1992 film *Candyman*, which was filmed in Chicago at Cabrini Green, was based on this true tale of hometown horror.

However, this is not the case and in fact, is an outright fabrication. The film *Candyman*, which starred Virginia Madsen and Tony Todd, was based on an earlier Clive Barker story called *The Forbidden*. The story, which set in England, not Chicago, focuses almost solely on the character of Helen Lyle and Candyman only appears in the final few pages. For the film, the producers set the story in Chicago and did not base it on any contemporary legends of the city. Any ghost stories about "Candyman" were spawned by the film, not the other way around!

brothels and one of the most famous characters of the Bad Lands was Black Susan Winslow, who ran a brothel in a broken-down, two-story shack on Clark Street, under the approach to the Twelfth Street viaduct. The roof of the place was level with the sidewalk, so entrance had to be gained by way of a rickety staircase. Black Susan had from two to five girls living with her and they employed all manner of methods of attracting the attention of men passing along the sidewalk. For a long time, they would ring a sheep bell and then started setting off an alarm clock at regular intervals. Then, (for some reason) began tapping on the windows and hissing like snakes. Finally, they rigged up an electric battery and attached it to the figure of a woman with a hinged arm. The figure would strike the window and then swing back again, making a motion to theoretically invite customers inside.

There were so many complaints made about robberies at Black Susan's that scores of arrest warrants were issued for her over the years. But every officer who attempted to actually arrest her returned to the station house with no idea as to how he was actually going to do so. The problem was that Susan weighed over 450 pounds and was wider than any door or entrance of her brothel. Officers often wondered how she could have gotten inside in the first place! Clifton R. Woolridge, the famous police detective of the 1890s who billed himself as the "Sherlock Holmes of Chicago," finally solved the problem. He made it a mission to take Susan into custody and so he journeyed to her bordello in a patrol wagon, passing through an alley to the back door. After reading the arrest warrant to Winslow, who laughed at him the entire time, he removed the back door from its hinges and using a handsaw, cut out the frame and about two feet of the wall. Then he placed two oak planks, each about 16 feet long and a foot wide, on the doorsill and on the rear end of the wagon. One of the horses was unhitched, a heavy rope was attached to the animal's collar, and the other end was looped around Black Susan's waist. At Woolridge's command, the horse lurched forward and pulled the enormous woman from her chair. She was dragged about three feet up the planks before she began to scream. Woolridge had used rough timber and Black Susan was now pierced with splinters. Finally, she agreed to enter the wagon on her own and thundered gloomily up the planks. As they rode to the police station, Susan lay prone on the floor of the police wagon while one of her girls carefully removed the splinters from her large behind.

"After this," Woolridge later wrote, "the police had no more trouble with Susan Winslow."

Little Cheyenne was named in honor of Cheyenne, Wyo., which was considered to be the toughest of the "railroad end towns" that sprang up during the building of the Union Pacific line. Just north of the Bad Lands was a gin mill owned by Larry Gavin and next to that was a place called the Alhambra. They were typical of the establishments in this area. The Alhambra was a place that was then called a "goosing slum," meaning that it was a small room with a low ceiling and sawdust on the floor. The liquor was of the cheapest sort and was staffed by the lowest of the area's streetwalkers. They would sit at the tables and wait for someone to buy them a drink or to make a proposal for anything else.

> The residents of Cheyenne, Wyo., were not amused by the name of the area, and, in response, they began calling their own worst neighborhood Little Chicago.

Gavin's place was just as bad and was called "about as tough a place as you would want to visit" by a contemporary newspaperman. He stated that the "rickety old chairs are occupied by females even more dilapidated.... it was one of the vilest of places." The reporter took samples of liquor from Gavin's and from the Alhambra and had them analyzed. He reported that Gavin's whiskey was full of "pepper and acids" and that the Alhambra's brandy actually contained rat poison!

As bad as these places were, they were no worse than the other joints in the district, like the Pacific Garden Saloon, Concert Hall & Oyster Parlor at Van Buren Street. This place was not as classy as it sounded and was nothing more than a typical vice district dive. Later on, the place closed down and became, of all things, a religious mission. It is worth noting that it was in this mission that famous evangelist Billy Sunday was converted, decided to quit professional baseball and become a preacher. Other establishments included the 50-cent brothels of Nellie St. Clair and Candy Molly Jones, who gave a stick of candy to every customer as a souvenir of her place. One clever newspaper writer commented that it was "probably not the only thing a patron took home from her place but those souvenirs usually lasted a bit longer."

> ### WHERE ARE THEY NOW?
> The area from Taylor to Twelfth (now Roosevelt Road) bears little or no resemblance to the notorious Bad Lands - efforts to clean it up were entirely successful.

WHISKEY ROW

The vice district known as "Whiskey Row" was located on the west side of State Street from Van Buren to Harrison and for more than 30 years, every building on this stretch was occupied by a saloon, a wine-room with girls, a gambling parlor, or all three combined. Most of the places were simply thieving dens, where safe-blowers, pickpockets, burglars, con men and gamblers socialized. Since just about every man on both sides of the gambling table was a cheat, there must have been some very interesting card games played here!

One of the most important operators here was an African-American gambler named Mushmouth Johnson, who possessed considerable political influence in the city because he could deliver large blocks of black votes. He dominated the policy business in Chicago and ran a number of poker, faro, and craps establishments. Johnson came to Chicago from St. Louis in the mid-1870s and for several years worked as a waiter at the Palmer House. In 1882, he took a job as a floor man in a gambling house on South Clark Street and after a few years, the owner gave him an interest in the place. For years, it was known as one of the best cheap resorts in the city. It catered to players of all races, offered all games, and bets as low as a nickel could be made at its wheels and tables. Johnson later sold out his interest and opened a new house at 464 South State St. and it remained open around the clock for the next 17 years. Unlike most gamblers, Johnson never bet on anything himself. Probably for this very reason, he accumulated a fortune of more than $250,000 in the saloon business. He died in 1907 with most of his money intact.

Another Whiskey Row dive-keeper was Tom McGinness, who went from peddling potatoes from a pushcart to running a saloon and gambling den called the Berlin Café. Al Connolly, who was a Democratic Committeeman from the First Ward for many years, also operated a saloon on Whiskey Row. During the Columbian Exposition, he served as a bail bondsman from the back room of the place for pickpockets who got nabbed on the fairgrounds.

> ### WHERE IS IT NOW?
> A few traces of Whiskey Row, such as a bar at 666 S. State St., survived for decades, but none seem to remain visible from the street today.

Whiskey Row was also home to the famous Lone Star Saloon and Palm Garden, which was owned and operated by Mickey Finn, who appeared in an earlier chapter.

Johnny Rafferty established himself on Whiskey Row in the 1890s and earned considerable newspaper notoriety for his frequent use of the expression: "I love a good thief!" In 1903, when the Chicago Journal called him a crook, Rafferty indignantly offered to prove that he had "never gouged out an eye, cut off a goat's tail, beaten a policeman, held up a train, or bitten off a bulldog's nose."

Andy Craig, who was a bail bondsman, politician, saloonkeeper, fence, pickpocket and burglar, was one of the more notorious denizens of Whiskey Row. In 1891, he served a four-year prison sentence for burglary and in 1898, opened a saloon called The Tivoli, which he boasted, contained $8,000 worth of mirrors. The Tivoli became a meeting place for all sorts of lowlifes and Craig served as a fence and a banker for thieves. He also became a bondsman for First Ward alderman Kenna and Coughlin. Thanks to his political connections, he was able to get his picture and record expunged from the city's rogue's g allery, but this didn't exempt him from investigations. During a 1903 examination of graft in the police department, Craig's liquor license was revoked for flagrant violations of the law. He sold The Tivoli to Howard McPherson, a cigar-maker, the following year. Craig said, "There is no use trying to do business when a lot of reformers are after you. They'll get you sooner or later." But nobody ever got Andy Craig; he died 25 years later, managing brothels for a new boss, Al Capone.

HELL'S HALF ACRE

The fabled Hell's Half Acre was comprised of an entire block that was bounded by Polk, State and Taylor streets and Plymouth Place. It was said that every building there was occupied by a saloon, bordello or gambling den and that the area was so dangerous that police officers never entered except in pairs ---- and seldom even then. The center of Hell's Half Acre's social activity was the Apollo Theater and Dance Hall, on Plymouth Place, which was noted in the 1870s and 1880s for the masquerade balls that were sponsored by the brothel musicians, or "professors," as they were called at the time. The balls became so famous because at midnight the dancers would remove not only their masks, but all of their clothing, as well. The Apollo was in existence as late as 1910, but by the late 1890s was frequented by mostly low-class prostitutes and their pimps.

In the middle of Hell's Half Acre was Dead Man's Alley, a narrow passage that ran from Polk to Taylor Street between State and Plymouth Place. The dark and forbidding passage was always filled with trash and scattered debris and on one side of it were a number of abandoned carriages that were used by prostitutes. Thieves and cutthroats frequented the alley and anyone who dared to walk through it, having no business there, was almost inevitably robbed. For more than a decade, the leader of the gang that operated in this area was a man named Henry Foster, who was better known as Black Bear. His usual method of robbery was to sneak up on a passerby from behind, wrap his massive arms around him, fling him to the ground, and then rifle through his pockets.

> ### WHERE IS IT NOW?
> Plymouth Court still stretches between Taylor and Pierce, but no trace of Hell's Half Acre or Dead Man's Alley remains visible today.

This type of strongarm work was done by Foster and male members of the gang, but the "brains" behind the operation was a skinny woman named Minnie Shouse, who lured men to the mouth of the alley and then divided the loot of those foolish enough to follow her into the shadows. She was arrested more than 300 times in a half dozen years but usually escaped punishment by returning a portion of the stolen money or by paying a policemen to threaten her victim with arrest for consorting with a prostitute. She managed to elude capture until early 1895, when she was finally sent to prison for robbing a farmer. Black Bear got into serious trouble not long after Minnie was locked up. He was hanged on July 1, 1895 for the murder of a saloonkeeper.

CUSTOM HOUSE PLACE

Adjacent to Hell's Half Acre, and almost a part of it, was Custom House Place. During the Civil War, there had been perhaps eight or nine brothels in the northern part of this district but after the Great Fire, this portion of the area was mostly taken over by businesses and the vice moved south of Harrison Street. The Custom House vice district that became renowned as one of the most famous red-light districts in America sprang from the ashes of the Great Fire. For nearly 30 years, the area would be regarded as a blight on the downtown. Like most segregated vice areas, where gambling, liquor and prostitution were indulged, the Custom House thrived on not only its proximity to the railroads but to an alliance with the police. The closest police could be found at the nearby armory station and they turned a blind eye to questionable activity in the district --- for a price, of course.

The Dearborn Street station was once essential to vice operations in the Custom House Place district.

The Custom House district existed between Harrison Street on the north and Polk Street and the Dearborn train station to the south. It is an area more popularly known as "Printer's Row" today. The boundaries of the area tended to change and expand with the opening of each new saloon or house of ill repute. It also tended to shrink when any of the owners neglected to make their protection payments. A police raid usually followed such absent-minded behavior.

The Dearborn Station became essential to operations in the area as it made a perfect recruiting spot for prostitutes during the gaslight era. Naive young women who stepped off the train were often greeted by one of the army of pimps who waited in the station. From that point, they were introduced to immoral acts and lured into the "scarlet patch" of the Custom House district.

The most infamous bordello here was Carrie Watson's place on South Clark Street. Despite the seediness of the area, the beautiful Miss Watson's "house" enjoyed a wide reputation for being a charming place, with Carrie having 60 women in her employ. Over the years, she has become a character of legend in the annals of Chicago vice and her beginnings in the city have long been the subject of fascination.

Caroline Victoria Watson was the daughter of an upper middle-class family in Buffalo, N.Y., where she was born in 1850. According to the lore, she grew up and saw her older sisters and their friends doing little more than eking out a living working in stores or slaving away as domestic help. Knowing that such a life was not for her, Carrie was said to have taken stock of her capabilities and decided that her greatest opportunity lay in the field of prostitution. So, in 1866, 16 and still a virgin, she came to Chicago and became an inmate of a brothel called the Mansion in order to learn the business and to prepare herself for her future career as a madam. She remained in the house for two years, hoarding her money and learning the ways of the customers.

When a madam named Annie Stewart left Chicago in 1868 after the killing of a police officer, Carrie Watson took over the lease of her bordello on South Clark Street, between Polk and Taylor. She immediately installed new beds and furnishings and hired new girls, as well. She later bought the building with the help of her security man, Al Smith, who ran a saloon and gambling house up the street. Annie Stewart had run her brothel as a wide-open operation, admitting any customer who came calling, but from the beginning, Carrie catered exclusively to the carriage trade and was just beginning to build up a wealthy clientele when the Great Fire disrupted businesses of

WHERE IS IT NOW?
After Custom House Place was closed down in 1910, the deserted area was slowly taken over by commercial printing houses and bookbinderies, creating the name the district bears today, "Printer's Row." Eventually, the printing houses joined the bordellos and they too faded away. Around 1979, it was converted into the condominium and rental community that exists today. The railroad freight yards have also disappeared, although Dearborn Station still stands at 47 W. Polk St. Today, it's essentially a mini-mall, housing a few retail establishments and bunch of law offices. The venerable Jazz Showcase, formerly on Grand, recently acquired new premises there. The Custom House vice district is now only a memory.

every type. According to legend, the fire destroyed the house but in fact, it was almost two blocks south of the burned area and was not damaged. It hurt her business badly, though, and it took nearly two years for Carrie to recover.

Early in 1873, Carrie made extensive alterations to the property and when they were completed, re-opened what must have been the finest resort of its kind in America. The three-story brownstone mansion had five parlors, more than 20 bedrooms, a billiard room and reportedly, a bowling alley in the basement. The furniture was expensively upholstered, imported rugs covered the floors and the walls were hung with rare artwork and European tapestries. A three-piece orchestra played music and wine was brought into the parlors in silver buckets and served in gold goblets for $10 per bottle. The girls, who numbered 10 to 20 ordinarily, but twice that number during the World's Fair, received callers in silk gowns and performed on linen sheets. The business of the house was conducted with great subtlety and there was no red light over the door, no red curtains and no hawkers hustling men in off the street.

Carrie's brothel operated for nearly 25 years and enjoyed worldwide fame, thanks to its high prices, the loveliness of the ladies who worked there and the luxurious surroundings of the building. Carrie Watson herself, who was extremely rich by the time she retired, was renowned for her silks and diamonds, her two white carriages with bright yellow wheels, her charities and the fact that she paid a larger personal property tax than most Chicago millionaires. Shang Andrews' Sporting Life stated with enthusiasm that, "In all the world, there is not another Carrie Watson!"

Most other resorts in Custom House Place were not so elegant or refined. Of all of the brothels in the red-light districts, the ones that gave the police the most trouble were the "panel houses," which were more robbers' dens than brothels. Often an unsophisticated visitor would stumble into one of these places, where he might be drugged and tied up while an accomplice slipped through a hidden panel in the wall and liberated him of his valuables. More often, the secret panels hid thieves with long hooks who could lift a customer's wallet from pants hanging on the bedpost, placed there while he was otherwise engaged. Few of these victims would report the robbery to the police, lest they suffer the humiliation of having their names printed in the newspaper. As much as $10,000 was often reported being taken from panel houses at the Harrison Street police station in a single night, as the officers logged from 50 to 100 complaints. One can only wonder how many robberies were never reported at all.

In 1896, the police managed to shut down 52 panel houses and they closed about 45 more in 1898. During that same year, the keepers of 28 of these places were arrested and while there is no record to say that any of them were ever punished, by centering the attack on such establishments, the police soon put an end to the business.

By the time of the Columbian Exposition in 1893, Chicago had become known as the "Paris of America" for its many illicit attractions. Reformist W.T. Stead, in his book If Christ Came to Chicago, counted 37 bordellos, 46 saloons, 11 pawnbrokers, an opium den and numerous gambling parlors in the Custom House district while writing his exposé on Chicago vice.

The official stance on such districts was to leave them alone, as long as the operators, thieves and undesirables stayed in the district and kept to themselves. However, this was rarely the case. Granted a wide berth by city officers, the dealers in vice exploited the situation with prostitutes being arrested in the theater district and posing as salesgirls in reputable stores. By 1903, conditions had become intolerable and reformers would no longer stand for it. A wave of criminal indictments, pushed through by church groups and the mayor himself, sent the vice operators reeling. Most of them moved to the South Side Levee District where they were welcomed with open arms. The

Custom House Place Levee had vanished completely by 1910.

THE SOUTH SIDE LEVEE

Home to the Everleigh Sisters, the notorious First Ward Ball of Hinky Dink Kenna and Bathhouse John, and Big Jim Colosimo, the South Side Levee district remains as Chicago's most infamous region for vice. The Levee took shape during the Columbian Exposition in 1893, when thousands of people from all over the world descended on the city.

Visitors to the district could partake of just about every form of vice imaginable from alcohol to women and it became a hotbed of crime that would go on to spawn men like Al Capone, Johnny Torrio and the generations that followed them. Three vice rings formed the criminal organization that ruled the Levee and which provided the areas various forms of "entertainment."

James Colosimo, an old-world Italian brothel keeper, controlled the street sweeper's union and was linked to the legendary Black Hand. After striking it rich selling the services of young women in two of his bordellos (one of which was named in honor of his wife!), he opened a famous café on South Wabash Avenue that attracted both society patrons and gangsters to its doors. Italian opera stars often dropped in to sample Colosimo's famous pasta, and to rub shoulders with dangerous Levee characters, as well. The café was closed only twice during Prohibition and remained in business long after the proprietor was dead. Colosimo himself was shot to death inside the vestibule of his restaurant on May 11, 1920 and his garish funeral procession included three judges and nine aldermen as pallbearers. The café was taken over by Mike "The Greek" Potson, a former Indiana saloonkeeper.

Maurice Van Bever and his wife Julia, who operated an interstate white slavery ring that extended from St. Louis to Chicago, controlled another Levee vice ring. The ring inspired the passage of the Mann Act in 1910. Representative James Robert Mann of Illinois introduced the act that made it illegal to transport women across state lines for immoral purposes. It was believed that operators in the Levee had imported more than 20,000 young women into the United States to work in their brothels.

Charley Maibum, who ran a pay-by-the-hour hotel where the local streetwalkers could take their clients for a quick rendezvous, operated the third vice ring. He often served as "muscle" and protection for other brothels that ran into trouble with competitors or law enforcement officials.

In addition to these, there were scores of independent operators in the district. The Levee arcade featured a number of "dollar a girl" joints, where the women provided services on a volume basis. Many of these unfortunate young ladies ended up on the Levee thanks to the smooth charm of oily con men, who lured them away from small-town life with promises of romance and marriage in the big city. Instead of a love and excitement, they ended up robbed, beaten and "broken in" at the hellish dives of the Levee. In those days, most could see the need for organized prostitution but saw the methods used to induce women to become prostitutes as far more unwholesome. In Chicago (and in every other major city of the day), vice operators had no problem paying off police officers and politicians for permission to run houses of prostitution. However, the officials were less tolerant of what was called the "procuring" of the girls, although the right amount of money could always get them to look the other way. Chicago's vice trade required so many women that procurers operated here with or without approval, and the city became a supply point for other cities in the

Big Jim Colosimo (Above) & Vic Shaw (Below) were two of the leading brothel-keepers in the South Side Levee

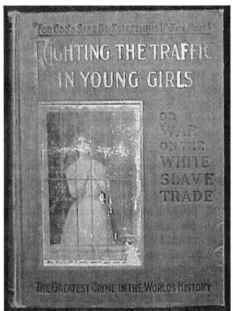

(Left) Vic Shaw's resort in the Levee district.
(Right) Ernest A. Bell's 1910 book, "Fighting the Traffic in Young Girls, or the War on the White Slave Trade", a hysterical (&largely fictional) account of the modern white slave trade, centering on Chicago. It was one of the catalysts for the reform movement that eventually closed down the Levee.

Midwest.

But not all of the bordellos in this part of town were cheap dives that were filled with "white slavery" victims and broken-down old whores. It was also home to the Everleigh Club (detailed in an earlier chapter) and a number of other brothels that, while certainly not the Everleigh Club, were not exactly flophouses either. Those other houses were operated by Vic Shaw, Zoe Millard, and Georgie Spencer, a trio of madams who were in constant competition with the Everleighs. Shaw was a prominent red light district fixture for almost 40 years and even after the Levee was shut down, she continued to operate brothels and call-out operations until she was well into her 70s. Millard was inclined to blame anything bad that happened in the Levee on the Everleighs and once inflicted a terrible beating on one of her girls for defending the sisters. Spencer, whose brothel was on South Dearborn Street in the same block as the Everleighs, flaunted her operation and was eventually driven out of business by the police, who usually turned a blind eye to anything that was going on. Spencer was so abrasive, however, that they refused to look the other way.

Despite the almost frantic efforts of these three madams, the Everleighs always maintained that their biggest problems came from Ed Weiss, who with his wife ran a brothel next door to the Everleigh Club. Weiss had married a former harlot who had worked for the Everleighs, Aimee Leslie, and the pair of them bought out the brothel next door, which had belonged to Julia Hartrauft. They remodeled the place, creating sort of a scaled-down Everleigh Club, which irritated the sisters. The success of the place was due to in some part to its luxury and the beauty of the girls Weiss hired, but most of it came from Weiss' shrewdness in putting most of the Levee cab drivers on his payroll. When a drunken spender got into a cab and asked to be driven to the famed Everleigh Club, he would be taken to Weiss' place instead. Most of them never knew the difference.

The brothel on the other side of the Everleigh Club was called the Sappho, and was owned and operated by Weiss' brother, Louis. It was also a better class of resort but it was never as popular as Ed's. A number of other cheaper brothels, like the Casino, which was run by Vic Shaw's husband, Roy Jones, the Old Ninety-Two, French Charlie's, and the California, which was run by Blubber Bob Gray and his wife, Theresa McCafey. The California was one of the toughest parlor houses in the district. There were about 30 to 40 girls who worked the place at one time, wearing shoes, flimsy chemises and nothing else. They stood naked in the windows and doorways whenever a policeman was not in sight and two men worked the sidewalk outside, inviting in those who passed by. When customers appeared, the girls were brought into a large room that was empty except for a couple of benches along one wall. The girls were paraded in and the customers were allowed to choose. The going rate for a tumble was $1, but 50 cents would do if the man turned out his pockets and proved that he didn't have a dollar to his name. The

California remained one of the seediest dives in the district until 1909, when it was raided by federal immigration agents who were searching for immigrant women who had been brought to the United States for "immoral purposes." They found six "white slaves" at the California. Blubber Bob, who weighed over 300 pounds, tried to escape when the authorities burst in, but he got stuck in a window and it took three men to pull him out.

WHERE IS IT NOW?
The Bucket of Blood stood on the southwest corner of 19t and Federal streets (between Clark and Dearborn). Bed Bug Row was on the Southeast corner. The area is now filled mainly by pleasant-looking South Loop townhouses.

There were several other celebrated houses in the Levee during its heyday, including that of Frankie Wright, who called her brothel the Library. It got its name for the single case of well-worn books that graced its parlor. Big Jim Colosimo owned two large brothels in the district, the Victoria and the Saratoga. The Victoria was named in honor of Colosimo's wife, Victoria Moresco. The Saratoga was managed by a New York gangster named Johnny Torrio, who Colosimo had brought to Chicago as a bodyguard in 1908. Colosimo himself spent most of his time at his restaurant on Wabash Avenue, near Twenty-Second.

At one end of the district was a notorious saloon called the Bucket of Blood, which stood across the street from Bed Bug Row. Nearby was a brothel called Black May's, which offered light-skinned African-American girls for white customers and allegedly presented "animal acts" for those with a taste for such things, and the acclaimed House of All Nations, which had prostitutes from foreign countries. The place boasted a $2 entrance and a $5 entrance, although the same girls worked both sides of the house.

The Levee was a wide-open place for years, under the protection of its vice leaders, well-paid Chicago cops and, of course, aldermen Kenna and Coughlin, who made sure that the necessary money made it into the right hands. But things did not always go smoothly in this area for segregated vice. Reformers, especially religious ones, constantly hampered operations in the Levee and eventually, the crusade (and propaganda) against "white slavery" would get the better of the district.

One of the most dramatic of the many attacks against the district was the invasion of the Levee by the famous English evangelist Gipsy Smith during a series of revival meetings held in the fall of 1909. On October 15, Smith announced that he planned to lead "an army of Christians" into the red light district. He went ahead with the plan despite the protests of police officers and religious leaders, who felt that he would only bring attention to the Levee. The evangelist replied that he wanted to advertise the place; that sin had to be exposed before it could be destroyed.

After his revival meeting on the night of October 18, Smith led a congregation of men, women and children, many of them wearing long black gowns and carrying unlighted torches. Smith and his followers walked for blocks in silence, accompanied only by the sound of trudging feet, a booming drum, and the occasional jeering laugh from idlers and scoffers who stood on the street. The reformers made no effort to march in formation and by the time they reached the Levee, reporters on hand estimated that Smith's crowd had grown to nearly 20,000 people.

As they reached the Levee, their torches were light and the assembly began to sing. They shuffled through the Levee in a funeral march, traversing every street and passing each brothel and bar several times. In front of the Everleigh Club, the House of All Nations, and other notorious houses, the evangelist and his followers knelt in prayer. After an hour, they marched out of the district and followed Smith to the Alhambra Theater at State Street and Archer Avenue, where the evangelist led them in a prayer service for those who had fallen in sin.

The Levee received this strange visitation in utter silence - some say an effort coordinated by the police and politicians. Brothels and saloons were closed and darkened and the streets were nearly deserted. Even the hoodlums who formed a large procession of sightseers were strangely quiet, voicing no threats and few jeers. But within 10 minutes of Smith's departure, the Levee came to life. Red lights were turned back on, doors swung open, and music began to blare once more. While Gipsy Smith prayed at the Alhambra Theater, the Levee enjoyed the biggest night in its history - and hundreds of young men who had only heard about vice in passing now knew exactly where to come to have a good time. One madam, who was interviewed by a newspaper reporter, smugly said, "We were certainly glad to get all of this business, but I was sorry to see so many

Gipsy Smith

nice young men down here for the first time."

The newspapers widely reported the crusade march the following day and, for the most part, their editorials dismissed it as the futile gesture of a crank. Politicians laughed and city officials refused to comment, while ministers quickly disavowed any connection to the invasion. Vice was better controlled if it could be segregated in one place, most believed, and that way, it would not overrun the city. In the end though, Smith's crusade had little short time effect, but it did mark the first time that anyone had dared to launch an attack against segregated vice. Nothing that had happened in Chicago, not even the publication of W. T. Stead's shocking *If Christ Came to Chicago*, had so focused public attention on what was considered "the evil within its borders."

Inspired by Smith, new reform groups began public challenges against segregated vice in the city. Between the formation of the Chicago Vice Commission and the crusade against "white slavery," the days of the Levee were numbered. Embarrassment over an advertising campaign gone wrong closed down the famous Everleigh Club in 1911 and the rest of the South Side Levee only survived for another year.

A massive civil welfare parade that was organized on September 29, 1912 spurred grand jury indictments and complaints to be filed against property owners in the district. This resulted in the end of "segregated vice" in Chicago, but the Levee did not completely disappear. Many of the famous resorts from this area were bulldozed, as they stood in the way of an important east-west railroad corridor, but others remained and became the jazz clubs of the 1920s. A number of deadly occurrences still plagued the district in the years to come, but when Colosimo's was finally closed in 1945 (Mike "The Greek" was convicted for income tax evasion) and demolished in 1957, an era in Chicago's sordid history finally came to a close.

THE COLISEUM

An old postcard photograph of the Coliseum. The stones of Libby Prison were incorporated into the front of the structure after the Civil War museum was closed down.

Although it gained notoriety as the home of the infamous First Ward Ball, the Coliseum played host to almost every large event in Chicago for many years. Located on the southwest corner of 14th and South Wabash, the history of the place stretched back to the time of the Great Fire. Around that time, a German immigrant named Charles Gunther opened a candy factory at 21 South State St. Along with making chocolate, Gunther was also a collector of Civil War artifacts. As his collection grew, he began looking for a place where it could be displayed as a tourist attraction. As he searched for a place to house the artifacts, he found the scandalous Libby Prison in Richmond, Va. It was ranked as one of the most inhumane prisons during the war and it was estimated that thousands of Union soldiers died while confined there.

Gunther purchased the old prison and it was taken apart, one stone at a time, and shipped to Chicago on 132 railroad cars. In 1888, it was reconstructed on Wabash Avenue and the building was an imposing, Gothic-like castle, complete with colonnades and spires. Inside the walls of the structure, Gunther added a small building he called "Uncle Tom's Cabin," which became one of the first museum gift shops in Chicago. Commemorative spoons, Libby Prison cigars, and Gunther's chocolate were a few of the items offered for sale. Across Wabash, Gunther added a hotel and a restaurant.

The Civil War was still fresh in the public's memory when Gunther's attraction opened for business. While it was in questionable taste, it was tremendously popular. Hundreds of thousands of visitors, including scores of people who came for the Columbian Exposition, poured through the gates of Libby Prison to see the bed Abraham Lincoln died in and the table where Lee signed the surrender at Appomattox Court House. Many of these items are in the possession of the Chicago Historical Society today.

Eventually, interest in the museum faded and Gunther closed the place down and formed the Chicago Coliseum Company. Realizing that the growing city was in need of a large venue to hold grand events, he built the massive Coliseum to be a political hall. He used the outer walls of Libby Prison and built the Coliseum around them. The site was first put into use in 1896 for the Democratic Convention. Beginning in 1907, the Coliseum became the site of the annual First Ward Ball, the sordid fundraiser used by Hinky Dink Kenna and Bathhouse John to grease the wheels of city government and the palms of crooked police officers and politicians.

The powerful Chicago political machine brought a record 25 Presidential Nominating Conventions to the Coliseum. In 1896, 20,000 people were whipped into a frenzy by William Jennings Bryan when he delivered his famous "Cross of Gold" speech, turning him into a national figure. He would run for president in 1900, 1906, and 1912, always without success. In 1912, violent floor fights erupted over the inclusion of Progressive ideas in the party platform and forced the Republicans to add two days to their convention. The party eventually nominated William Howard Taft to run for a second term. Although Theodore Roosevelt had handpicked Taft four years earlier, he opposed his second term. The Republicans split on the issue of Progressivism and the splinter group walked out. They returned to the Coliseum on August 5 to nominate Roosevelt as the candidate of the Progressive Party, which was popularly known as The Bull Moose Party.

After 1920, there was little political activity at the Coliseum and it began to be used increasingly as an entertainment venue. The Coliseum was also used for religious meetings and gatherings and evangelists like the controversial Aimee Semple McPherson

(Above) The interior of the Coliseum
(Below) The Coliseum at the time of the 1907 Republican National Convention

Roosevelt ended up coming in second in 1912, losing to Woodrow Wilson, but most of the Bull Moose platform eventually became law. Today, the platform almost reads like a template for later Democratic Party goals. Roosevelt spent a full week in a Chicago hospital during the campaign recuperating after being shot in the chest during a campaign stop in Milwaukee. Before leaving Milwaukee for Chicago, though, he made a 90-minute speech in a bloody shirt with the bullet in his chest, roaring, "It takes more than that to kill a bull moose!"

drew huge audiences. Athletic and music events also packed in crowds. The Chicago Blackhawks hockey team played at the Coliseum from 1926 to 1929 and the Bulls made the venue their home for one season in 1967. In 1930, the Coliseum became the first site of roller derby. In its initial incarnation, roller derby did not allow any physical contact. The first race called for the participants to skate 3,000 miles (roughly the distance from New York to California) around the Coliseum's circular track. In 1937, sports writer Damon Runyon suggested adding contact to the sport and it likely would not have

WHERE IS IT NOW?
The site of the Coliseum on Wabash between 14th and 16th streets is now marked by Coliseum Park, which covers a very small portion of the grounds.

survived without it.

Although long used as a venue for sports and music, the Coliseum saw one more important political moment in 1968. Anti-war demonstrators who had gathered to protest the Democratic National Convention used the Coliseum as a gathering place before marching to Grant Park. The protests that followed turned into violent riots that stunned the nation, shocked the city of Chicago, and became a turning point in the debate over the Vietnam War.

By 1982, the Coliseum's usefulness had been exhausted and most of the events that had once filled it had moved to the Chicago Stadium (which was torn down in 1995). The aging building was demolished. Although the walls of Libby Prison were preserved for a time, they were also eventually lost. Today, there is not much to see at the location that was once the famous Coliseum. Only memories still linger here.

THE FOUR DEUCES

Just at the edge of the South Side Levee District, and steps away from Big Jim Colosimo's restaurant, was a four-story red brick building that once housed a saloon and whorehouse called the Four Deuces. The place was opened by Johnny Torrio during World War I, just a couple of years before his uncle, Jim Colosimo, was murdered in the vestibule of his café.

The Four Deuces was a hive of illegal activity and a throwback to the "wide-open" days of the Levee. In later years, it was supervised by Charlie Carr, who bought and sold Thompson machine guns for his employers, the Capone gang. A saloon occupied the first floor. The bookkeeping offices, along with Torrio's private office, occupied the second floor. A gambling den where poker, roulette, and blackjack were played was hidden behind a steel door on the third floor, and the fourth floor was a cheap brothel that housed about 30 girls.

The Four Deuces

Torrio earned his fearsome reputation at the Four Deuces. Working to expand his uncle's operations, he was often brutal with those who crossed him. He preferred to negotiate with his enemies, but he knew when to use violence to get his point across. Rumor had it that a number of people were tortured and killed in the basement of the Four Deuces, after which their bodies were taken out through a secret tunnel and dumped.

In 1919, Torrio put Al Capone to work at the Four Deuces. He was a $35-a-week saloon bouncer and sidewalk "capper," whose main responsibility was to draw men into the action inside the club. In those days, Capone adopted the alias of "Al Brown" and he was still a few years away from the notoriety that would come to him as

WHERE IS IT NOW?
Once Capone abandoned the place, the former club fell on hard times and by the 1960s, was nothing more than slum housing. It was torn down around 1966. Today, the site at 2222 South Wabash shows no sign of the club ever being there at all and in fact, the address no longer exists, erasing the days of one of the Roaring '20s most famous crime spots. Some concrete remaining on the site may be the Four Deuce's original foundation.

Chicago's most famous criminal.

That notoriety was achieved on May 8, 1924, when Capone murdered "Ragtime" Joe Howard, a con man who dared to slap Four Deuces business manager Jake Guzik in the face. The shooting occurred at Henry Jacob's saloon, a few doors down from the Four Deuces.

As his stature in the gangland community continued to rise, Capone outfitted an empty storefront adjoining the Four Deuces with a sign outside that read, "A. Brown Antiques Dealer," but there was little in the way of buying and selling old stuff going on there. But to keep up appearances, Capone's men put a piano, three tables, a planter, rugs, and an aquarium in the front window.

The Four Deuces maintained its violent reputation during the early years of Prohibition and it became the target of several raids by reform Mayor William Dever. During these years, Capone moved his operations to Cicero, abandoning the famous place that launched his career in crime.

LEXINGTON HOTEL

In 1986, television reporter and talk show host Geraldo Rivera took a national television audience into what was then one of the last remaining landmarks of the Chicago crime era and the reign of Al Capone ---- the old Lexington Hotel at the corner of Michigan Avenue and 22nd Street. Rivera was in search of lost treasure, a fortune that Capone had allegedly left behind in secret vaults in the hotel. Earlier in the 1980s, a local women's construction company had investigated the possibility of restoring the hotel, which was by then merely a shadow of its former self. As the construction workers searched the building, they discovered a shooting gallery that had been used by Capone's cronies for target practice and dozens of secret passages and stairways, including one behind Capone's medicine chest. The passages led to hidden tunnels that connected taverns and whorehouses on the Levee and to the immediate west. The tunnels had been designed to provide elaborate escape routes from police raids and attacks by rivals.

This led to more interest in the hotel and soon researcher Harold Rubin came to the crumbling old building and began a search of the premises. In addition to recovering many priceless artifacts from the days of the hotel's glory, Rubin also stumbled across one of the great secrets of the place when exploring the escape tunnels. It was said that Capone also had vaults in the lower levels of the Lexington where he had stashed some of his loot. These vaults were so well hidden that even Capone's closest accomplices were not aware of them. Rubin's discoveries led to a newspaper article in the *Chicago Tribune* but his excellent research would be overshadowed by Geraldo Rivera, who stated that if the secret money vaults could be found, he would discover them -- and would do so on national television.

The Lexington Hotel had opened in 1892 and had been designed by Clinton Warren, the architect of the famed Congress Plaza Hotel. The brick and terra cotta building had been hurriedly opened to serve the masses of visitors who came to Chicago for the 1893 World's Fair. These were boom years on the city's South Side and the fine hotel attracted scores of wealthy and famous visitors, including President Benjamin Harrison, who once addressed an audience

One of the last photographs taken of the Lexington Hotel before it was torn down.

GHOST ALERT!

After the St. Valentine's Day Massacre, Al Capone began claiming that he was being haunted by the ghost of James Clark, one of the massacre victims and the brother-in-law of Bugs Moran. While living at the Lexington Hotel, there were many times when his men would hear from begging for the ghost to leave him in peace. On several occasions, bodyguards broke into his rooms, fearing that someone had gotten to their boss. Capone would then tell them of Clark's ghost. Did Capone imagine the whole thing, or was he already showing signs of the psychosis that would haunt him after his release from Alcatraz prison?

Whether the ghost was real or not, Capone certainly believed that it was. The crime boss even went so far as to contact a psychic named Alice Britt to get rid of Clark's angry spirit. Not long after a séance was conducted to try and rid Capone of the vengeful spirit, Hymie Cornish, Capone's valet also believed that he saw the ghost. He entered the lounge of Capone's apartment in the Lexington and spotted a tall man standing near the window. Whoever the man was, he simply vanished.

Years later, Capone would say that Clark followed him to the grave.

from the balcony.

Al Capone, who became the Lexington's most famous resident, abandoned the Metropole Hotel (one block to the south) in July 1928 and moved into a luxurious fifth-floor suite of rooms at the Lexington. He registered under the innocuous name of "George Phillips" and ran his operations from the hotel until he was escorted off to prison in October 1931. Capone held court in an office that overlooked Michigan Avenue while in the Lexington's lobby, armed gunman kept a careful eye on the front doors. Additional guards with machine guns patrolled the upper floors or were hidden away in closets.

Capone was ensconced at the Lexington at the time of his downfall, following the infamous St. Valentine's Day Massacre. While this bloody event marked the end of any significant gang opposition to Capone, it was also the act that marked the decline of Capone's criminal empire. He had just gone too far and the authorities, and even Capone's adoring public, were ready to put an end to the bootleg wars. The massacre started a wave of reform that would send Capone out of power.

Capone's days at the Lexington were numbered by this time because in 1930, the United States government got involved in Chicago's dilemma over how to get rid of Al Capone. Washington dispatched a group of treasury agents to harass Capone and try to find a way to bring down his operation. In the end, though, it would not be murder or illegal liquor that would get Capone, it would be income tax evasion. He was sentenced to 11 years in federal prison, was first sent to Leavenworth, and in 1934 was transferred to the brutal, "escape proof" prison known as Alcatraz.

The remnants of Capone's gang abandoned the Lexington in 1932 and after that, the ownership of the hotel changed several times as the state of the place declined with the surrounding neighborhood. It was re-named the New Michigan Hotel in the 1950s but soon after became a bordello, a transient hotel and finally, a crumbling eyesore. By the 1980s -- and the arrival of Geraldo Rivera -- it was scheduled for demolition. But the Lexington had one last act still left in its old bones.

On that night in 1986, Rivera and his camera crew went out live to America from the deserted and empty hotel. The place had already been picked clean by vandals and souvenir hunters, but Rivera was sure that secrets from the past still remained. In a basement chamber, the crew blasted away a 7,000-pound concrete wall that was believed to be hiding a secret compartment that contained thousands, perhaps millions, of dollars. The Internal Revenue Service had agents on hand to claim their share of the loot. When the smoke cleared, however, only a few empty bottles and an old sign were found. The fortune, if it had ever been there at all, had long since been spirited away.

After Geraldo managed to try and upstage everyone in Chicago who had researched Capone for years, the person who actually discovered the location of the vault, Harold Rubin, got the last laugh. He worked for the production company that produced one of the most-watched television specials ever and was interviewed on CBS television on the night of Geraldo's blunder. To this day, no one has ever done as much research into the history of the Lexington and Rubin stands as the man who discovered the old place's greatest secrets -- whether the vaults were empty or not.

The Lexington Hotel finally "gave up the ghost" in November 1995. By that time, the ten-story structure had fallen into ruin after years of neglect and it was torn down. Another chapter in the history of Chicago crime had been closed for good.

THE LAST DAYS OF MAXWELL STREET

The neighborhood around the old Maxwell Street market has never been short on history. A booming marketplace came into existence in this area south of Roosevelt Road as early as 1910. The immigrants that crowded the West Side in those days included scores of pushcart vendors that provided a variety of goods to the working class families. Gradually, the vendors began to congregate on Maxwell Street, providing a central shopping area for just about every kind of ethnic group. In 1912, a city ordinance created the market on Maxwell Street, transforming one of the earliest residential streets in Chicago into a shopping area that would endure for almost a century. The tradition of bartering and discount shopping created in the early 1900s would remain an integral part of the market for almost 90 years.

But this was not the only thing that the area was known for. Around this same time, the nickname of "Bloody Maxwell" was given to this police district, thanks to the escalating murder rate. One of the most famous spots in

Maxwell Street in the early 1900s

the district was "Deadman's Corner" -- a moniker whose meaning should be obvious to the reader. The community was a thriving one, though, consisting of row after row of tenement houses that were filled with Greeks, Jews and Italians. The Maxwell Street neighborhood was always one of the most integrated in Chicago, attracting people of all races and countries of origin.

The Maxwell Street police station was always a central fixture in the neighborhood. By the time the station became familiar to people all over America, it had already garnered a nearly century old reputation in Chicago. In the early 1980s, television viewers saw the station house appear as the fictional *Hill Street Blues* precinct house on NBC, but people in Chicago had long been aware of its stories and lore.

The station had been constructed in 1889 to replace the old Second Precinct station, which had been located in the heart of the "Terror District" and was abandoned that same year. This new building cost more than $50,000 to build from red and gray stone and it was meant to be a refuge in the "wickedest police district to be found within the confines of civilization."

Captain William Ward, who commanded the column of police officers who were blown up by the Haymarket Square bomb in 1886, was placed in command of Maxwell Street that first year. It had been because of the unrest at Haymarket Square that the police force had greatly expanded its numbers and had built two new stations, including the one at Maxwell Street. The station was meant to serve as a threat to worker unrest and also as a buffer between the central business district and the heavily populated immigrant areas that encroached on the district from the south and west.

At that time, thousands of Jews, Italians, Greeks, Poles, Irish, Germans and other refugees from Europe came to the frenzied neighborhoods along Roosevelt Road, Taylor Street and Halsted. This was during the great wave of immigration that occurred between 1880 and 1920 and with the new arrivals came poverty, violence and crime. The Chicago Tribune said that the all around the neighborhood "are corners, saloons and houses that have seen the rise, the operations, and even the deaths of some of the worst criminals the land has ever known."

At the southern end of the area was the Walsh School, a public institution and the scene of one of the bloodiest feuds in American history -- a war between rival gangs of schoolboys that started in 1881 and continued for almost 30 years. During this time, several were killed and numerous others were shot, stabbed and beaten. The gangs called themselves the "Irishers" and the "Bohemians." The allegiance was not determined, as one might think, by nationality, but rather by place of residence. The Irishers lived east of Johnson Street and those who lived west of Johnson were the Bohemians. For years, the boys carried knives and revolvers to school and occasionally slashed one another, or shot it out, in the classrooms, the streets and the playground. The last of the gun battles was fought in

The old Maxwell Street Police Station

GHOST ALERT!

Although the cops and robbers of yesterday are now gone, the stories of the infamous dungeon of the Maxwell Street police station still linger -- in more ways than one. Accounts persist in saying that the prisoners who were beaten and so hideously abused in the station's basement still linger here. As the years have gone by, police officers and passersby claim to have heard the sound of bloodcurdling screams coming from this part of the building. Moaning and crying sounds are commonplace, although when anyone checks to see who might be wandering about this darkened space, the rooms are always found to be abandoned. Whether or not they are actually empty, however, is another matter entirely!

December 1905, when some 25 Irishers, led by Mike and George McGinnis, marched against an almost equal number of Bohemians, commanded by Joe Fischer. Between 40 and 50 shots were fired before the police arrived, but no one was hit. The ages of the gangsters ranged between 10 and 15 and many of them were so small that they had to use both hands to raise their revolvers to fire them. For many years after this last climatic battle, every boy who attended Walsh School had to be searched before he was allowed to enter.

Just north of the Maxwell Street Station was the liquor warehouse of the six "Terrible" Genna brothers, Angelo, Pete, Tony, Jim, Sam and Mike. On the eve of Prohibition, they had been granted a special dispensation from the government to sell industrial alcohol from this location on Taylor Street. Their brother-in-law, Harry Spignola, had invented the formula for the alcohol and the Gennas paid neighborhood residents $15 a week to cook up a home brew, which contained rotgut whiskey with caramel or coal tar added for color. The result was so vile that it actually killed the warehouse rats that were curious enough to sample it. From the filthy warehouse, the Gennas paid off the cops of the neighboring districts to leave them alone after it became apparent that the alcohol was not for "industrial" purposes. The Gennas sold the mixture for $3 a barrel, which was half the going rate that was being charged by Irish bootlegger, Dion O'Banion, who hated the Gennas. However, the brothers managed to maintain neutrality with not only O'Banion, but with Al Capone, as well. That ended when they began selling their brew to North Side barkeeps. The Gennas had stumbled too far into O'Banion's territory and war erupted. The Gennas were all but wiped out in a few short years and the warehouse was closed down in 1926.

Around 1905, the term "Bloody Maxwell" was coined. Thanks to the horrific murder rate and the threats of the Black Hand, a crime organization that terrorized the Italian immigrants in the neighborhood, the West Side was starting to gain an even more fearsome reputation. Things were especially frightening for the immigrants there, who feared not only the criminals but the police, as well. Thanks to the rumors that were circulating about the station, the immigrants were terrified of being arrested on some pretense and tossed into the rat-infested dungeon of the Maxwell Street station.

Prisoners who lacked the resources to buy their way out of this "hole" were often savagely beaten and this brutal treatment spawned many other shocking stories. For years, the prisoners in the dungeon urinated and bled into troughs that had been dug into the floors and which flowed beneath the cells of the other convicts. There were also stories of prisoners who "accidentally" fell down the two flights of stairs to the front desk, were beaten with telephone books (so as not to leave marks) and who suddenly turned up dead in their cells, even though nothing had been wrong with them when arrested. In 1921, Health Commissioner Herman Bundsen declared the Maxwell

Street dungeon to be unfit for human habitation and a few years later, the basement was closed down. However, rumors that the dungeon continued to be used as a punishment for the worst offenders were still being whispered in the 1970s. The city of Chicago and station officials denied the charges.

Stories about the Maxwell Street police station circulated for years but by this time, the term "Bloody Maxwell" had become a thing of the past and what most people knew about Maxwell Street was the thriving market that was located there. The market provided convenient, inexpensive goods for shoppers, along with a livelihood for the many vendors on the street. The concentration of people also drew black musicians who could not find employment in the whites-only music clubs. In particular, blues players from the South began to gather on Maxwell Street and play in the market. In the 1920s, guitar manufacturers had responded to the growth in recorded music and attempted to make louder instruments. By the 1930s, amplified guitars began to become available. Faced with a need to be heard in the loud Maxwell Street market, blues players plugged amplifiers into the outlets that had been installed to provide electricity for the street vendors. The fusion of a jazz band style amplified guitar with Mississippi blues created Chicago Blues - a loud, raw style of music that became a major influence on bands and performers like The Rolling Stones and Eric Clapton. The pioneers of the movement could be found playing outside of the market even after they achieved a measure of success. A visitor to Maxwell Street might hear Muddy Waters, Howling Wolf, Little Walter Jacobs, Jimmy Lee Robinson, and many others.

Maxwell Street in 1939

Blues musicians (like "Blind Jim" Brewer, pictured here) became a staple for Maxwell Street and the area has come to be considered as the birthplace of Chicago Blues.

The influence of Jewish immigrants on Maxwell Street helped to create one of the area's most famous traditions, the Sunday Market. Closed on Saturday for the Sabbath, Jewish merchants opened their shops and stalls on Sunday morning to do business. The area was adjacent to a large number of churches and many parishioners came directly to the market after mass to do their shopping. The Sunday shopping became a tourist attraction, drawing people from all over Chicago. Many of them came to shop and many visitors came to see the birthplace of the Chicago Blues.

No matter how popular the area, Chicago always feels the need to re-invent itself. As "urban renewal" became the policy of the city in the 1950s, Maxwell Street was seen as a blight that needed to be removed. The street itself had been neglected for years and construction of the Dan Ryan Expressway cut off part of the eastern border of Maxwell Street. Mayor Richard J. Daley selected Halsted and Harrison to be the site of the University of Illinois Chicago, which displaced over 14,000 residents and 800 businesses. Although the end would not arrive for a few more decades, the site selected for the university would mean the death of Maxwell Street.

In 1990, the University announced plans to acquire land south of Roosevelt Road to expand its campus, an expansion that the city government strongly supported. City sanitation in the area was cut off and the police staff was decreased. Many residents and businesses felt that the city was intentionally trying to turn the neighborhood into a slum by its neglect. If that was the goal, it worked and the area quickly declined. Buildings were abandoned and alleys were filled with trash. Homeless people moved into the area and the last of the residents fled. The Maxwell Street police station was closed down because, by this point, there was no longer a neighborhood to protect. The university had reduced it to empty lots, tennis courts and campus housing. The station house was saved and is now being used by the UIC campus police as their headquarters.

Despite attempts to preserve the area, the Maxwell Street market was relocated and the final destruction of the old street went forward. Business that had been in existence for 70 or 80 years left the area or closed down and the buildings that held them were reduced to rubble. While a reminder of the market still continues near Roosevelt Road on Sunday mornings, the authentic Maxwell Street had become a forgotten novelty of the past.

PRAIRIE AVENUE

Prairie Avenue in the days when it was home to Chicago's wealthiest families and was widely known as "Millionaire's Row"

There is no street in Chicago quite like Prairie Avenue. It boasts a rich history, which includes the last three decades of the 19th century, when a six-block section of the street served as the residence of many of Chicago's elite families and an additional section that was also known for its grand homes. Many of the city's most important historical figures lived on Prairie Avenue. This was especially true during the years after the Great Fire in 1871, when the area drew city leaders and businessmen, who found refuge among their own kind. This was the most exclusive and fashionable neighborhood in the city. Here lived the Fields, Armours, Pullmans, Hubbards, Blackstones, and other great families of the late Victorian era. In those days, it was a quiet, elegant street that was shaded by trees, bordered by wonderful homes and admired by those visitors who were lucky enough to be invited to call there. As the years went by, though, the millionaires fled the area to the North Side, fearing that the crime of the Levee was encroaching on their fabulous domain. The millionaire's flight to the Gold Coast on the North Side brought an end to the elegance of Prairie Street, leading to decay, and ultimately, destruction.

In its early days, Prairie Avenue was simply an Indian trail that linked Fort Dearborn to Fort Wayne in Indiana. It was in this future neighborhood of Chicago city leaders where the horrific massacre of 1812 took place. Potter Palmer once erected a monument to the massacre victims in his yard, which was very near to the where the incident took place.

Development in the area began as early as 1853, when only one grand home existed there. In 1870, Daniel Thompson erected the first large upper-Prairie Avenue home. By 1877, the eleven-block area of Prairie Avenue was home to Chicago's elite. In the years that followed, the most illustrious members of the city's society were building mansions on the street, each equipped with carriage houses, beautiful gardens, and a staff of

Prairie Avenue today is a mix of new homes that have been built to resemble the mansions of the past and a few original homes (like the Keith House on the right) that have been thankfully restored.

GHOST ALERT!

According to reports from a former caretaker of the Glessner house, he often spotted "something...in the shadows" of the house and in the courtyard area. He heard the sound of heavy footsteps walking through empty rooms and often those on tours of the house would complain of an "unsettling presence," especially in the chamber where the large portrait of Henry Richardson was placed. There were also accounts of lights turning on and off in the house, even though no one was there at the time.

There also started to be consistent (and current) reports of the ghostly figure of a man that was seen walking along the cobblestone path on the west side of the house and in the open area just south of the building. We have spoken to two different individuals who claim to have seen this shadowy figure. Neither of them knew the other but both gave nearly identical descriptions of a large, bulky man who walked slowly, as if admiring the lines of the house. Each time, the man simply turned and vanished. Both witnesses stated that they had no idea the man was not a real person until he disappeared.

The resident ghost at the Glessner house is believed to be that of the architect, Henry Richardson, who never lived in the house, but loved the place. He saw it as the pinnacle of his career, a career that was cut short by his death just three weeks after the house was completed. Richardson was very enthusiastic about the project and often stated that he wouldn't mind living in the place himself. Could his love of the house and his tragically severed life have been enough to cause his spirit to return to the place? Perhaps so, for it should be noted that Richardson was a large man, weighing in at around 350 pounds at the time of his death, which matches the description of the ghostly figure that has been seen admiring the house from the walkway outside.

The Glessner House in the Prairie Avenue Historical District

servants. In the 1880s and 1890s, the homes of George Pullman, Marshall Field (and Marshall Field, Jr.), John B. Sherman, and Phillip Armour anchored a neighborhood of over 50 mansions known as "Millionaire's Row."

Commercial activity from the city began to draw close to Prairie Avenue and in 1905, the Kodak Company built a factory on 18th and Indiana Streets and in 1915, the Hump Hair Pin Company erected a building on Prairie Avenue itself. The close proximity of the Levee District, combined with the industrial buildings coming to the South Side, caused many of the neighborhood's wealthiest residents to start looking for a new place to live. After Palmer Potter built his castle, anchoring the Gold Coast along Lake Shore Drive, the elite residents began to move north.

By 1911, warehouses and factories cramped the Prairie Avenue District. Within a few years, many of the grand homes had become high-class rooming houses and only a few of Prairie Avenue's prominent residents remained in their Victorian neighborhood. Soon, they too abandoned hope of the area's revival. Throughout most of the 20th century, Prairie Avenue was a ghost of its former self. Most of the big, mansard-roofed and turreted mansions were deserted and only dust and cobwebs filled windows were lace curtains and draperies once hung. The once-proud facades of the houses were now only pictures of decay and ruin. A few of the stone mansions were still in use, serving as offices and businesses but most of the houses fell vacant and most of them were town down.

It would be the salvation of one house, though, the John Glessner House, by a group of architects in 1966 that would provide the impetus for the creation of the

Prairie Avenue Historic District ten years later.

Although it was regarded as something of an oddity when it was constructed on Prairie Avenue in 1886, the Glessner House has achieved worldwide fame for is strange design. The house was built in what was referred to as a Romanesque design, although this designation was later changed to "Richardson Romanesque" to reflect the special touches that the architect had achieved with this place. The architect who had been retained to design the home for John and France Glessner was Henry Hobson Richardson of Boston, one of the America's foremost architects of the day. Glessner had likely been intrigued by the design that Richardson created for another Chicago building, the Marshall Field wholesale house (torn down many years ago), and hired him to create another magnificent design for this home along "Millionaire's Row." As it turned out, the Glessner House was Richardson's final design. He died, at 48, just three weeks after the house was completed.

Richardson decided to break with the style of the time and create something truly outstanding for Glessner. He wanted a building that was simple, direct, solid and tastefully designed. The Glessner House was built of rough-hewn granite blocks, resembling a medieval fortress. Richardson designed no bay windows or other unnecessary ornaments on the house, but it was bright and comfortable on the inside and instead of looking out beyond the plain and solid walls, it opened to and open, interior courtyard. And while it appears cold on the exterior, the interior of the house was meant to be warm with oak wainscoting, marble fireplaces, great wooden beams, a large kitchen and a glassed-in conservatory.

After the house was completed, the Glessners lived here with their children and quietly entertained some of the leading members of Chicago society until the 1930s. They were important patrons of the arts in the city and principal contributors to the Chicago Symphony Orchestra. In 1932, France Glessner passed away and her husband's death followed in 1936. John Glessner, one of the founders and for years a director of the International Harvester Company, deeded his home to the Chicago chapter of the American Institute of Architects with the stipulation that they take possession of it. The architects were to maintain the house as a museum, library, gallery and education institution, including a school of design. Unfortunately, though, such an undertaking was beyond the means of the group at that time and they turned it back over to the Glessner heirs.

By 1965, the Glessner House, like the rest of the Prairie Avenue homes, had fallen into ruin and was scheduled for demolition. Realizing the historic importance of the building, a group of concerned architects and colleagues banded together and incorporated as the Chicago School of Architecture Foundation. In 1966, they purchased the Glessner mansion and saved it from the wrecking ball. Ten years later, the house was designated a National Historic Landmark and it became the centerpiece and catalyst for the restoration of the Prairie Avenue District. The foundation, which changed its name to the Chicago Architecture Foundation in 1977, began tours of the Glessner House and the Loop and also helped to development a four-acre park (which had been empty lots) and improvements for the streets along Prairie Avenue.

Eventually, the foundation voted to spin off its historic property operations and the Prairie Avenue House Museums incorporated to own and operate the Glessner House on behalf of the City of Chicago. It is open to the public as a historical museum today.

Chicago, trying to undo some of the damage that was done by the destruction of Prairie Avenue, designated it a historical site in the middle 1970s, nearly a century after the neighborhood had been created. While only a small number of the original houses remain on the street, the area (even with new development) still manages to stand as a time capsule to the city of yesterday. The recent arrivals to the neighborhood have given the place a vitality that it has not enjoyed for many years.

Perhaps we should not be surprised by the fact that the ghostly sounds of carriages have been heard traveling along the stone streets in the district in recent years. It seems that with the new awakening of Prairie Avenue the spirits of the past have awakened, as well.

TRACES OF FORGOTTEN CHICAGO

Make no mistake about it, the city has changed a lot over the years, inventing and re-inventing itself. But the ghosts and the old stories aren't always the only reminders sticking around. If you know where to look, traces of the past are everywhere.

OLD ADDRESSES

In the late 19th century, there was quite a vogue for having the address of a building in ornately stained glass above the door. Thousands of Chicago buildings both public and private jumped on the bandwagon. Others buildings had the address carved into the façades.

However, in 1909, the city's system for numbering buildings changed. Prior to that time, address numbers were

Traces of old Chicago area everywhere, especially in old buildings that bear their original address. (Left) A building lists Damen Avenue by its original name -- Robey. Two other photos show both the old and new addresses of the sites.

vaguely based on the building's proximity to the river. The new, easy-to-navigate grid based the numbers on the distance to State Street (for east-west streets) or Madison Street (for North-South streets), with every 800 or so representing a mile (with numerous exceptions, of course). Nearly every building was re-numbered, and the city became a whole lot easier to get around.

But what about the buildings that had the numbers carved in stone, or lovingly formed in stained glass? Quite a few people knocked out the old stained glass - some replaced it with a new stained-glass window bearing the new number, and others, not wanting to mess with the expense, put up something much plainer.

But others didn't want to destroy the beautiful window, or bother to break up the part of the building where the old number was. Hence, they simply left the old number up. It didn't create too much confusion after all, since most of the new numbers were far different from the old ones.

Some of these original addresses are still visible today. You can find them all over the city, but if you want a see a few, your best bet is probably the Ukrainian Village/Wicker Park area.

STREETCAR LINES

Chicago was once full of streetcars in addition to the El. The last of them stopped running in the late 1950s, but you can still occasionally see the tracks peeking up through the potholes, especially in the spring, when potholes are most pronounced. There are some that are visible near Racine and Grand. These tracks are from the Racine-Aberdeen line, which has no equivalent in the bus routes today.

Old streetcar line tracks are still visible in the street near Racine & Grand

The Y Logo can be found hidden on many buildings throughout the city

THE MUNICIPAL DEVICE

The "Y" logo functions as a municipal logo for the city of Chicago - the shape is based, at least roughly, on the shape of the rivers in the city. It's largely forgotten today, as the municipal flag has pretty much taken over, but you can still find the Y carved into buildings and structures all over town. Finding the hidden Ys in town isn't unlike looking for the "hidden Mickeys" at Disneyland!

GHOST SIGNS

"Ghost Signs," the old painted ads of long ago, are visible all over the city, along the side of old buildings and in narrow alleys. Some have faded away, others are in very narrow alleys or were painted with lead paint, which is still easy to read, if you can find them. Here are some of our favorites:

Kaplan's Department Store stood near Chicago and Ashland

Coaches and Delivery Wagons: near the corner of 11th and Wabash

The Viceroy Hotel near Union Park was only recently abandoned

The old Gossard Corset buidling on Michigan still shows an old sign

THE DOWNTOWN COW PATH

In 1833, before the city was even incorporated, a farmer named William Jones purchased a large plot of land on the northwest corner of Clark and Monroe for $200. In 1844, when he began selling off strips of the land, he continued to reserve the right to use the cow path on the property to lead his cows to a pasture, which then stood

The once open cowpath is now closed off today (Left) & inside, looks like just about any other alleyway in the city.

where the Board of Trade building stands today.

Transporting livestock in the Loop was outlawed in the 1870s, but, according to the contract, one small patch of Jones' purchase was still reserved as a cow path. In 1928, when the building now standing at 100 West Monroe was erected, they left the cow path in the middle of the building!

WHERE IS IT NOW?

The cow path today doesn't look much different from any other alley, except that it goes through the middle of a building. While generally kept locked up these days, you can still clearly see the entrance just to the left of the building's front door at 100 W. Monroe St.!

Whether this was actually the location of the cow path, and whether Jones or his descendants would have possibly had any claim to it by 1922, it a bit of a question mark. A historical marker placed there by the Chicago Historical Society was eventually removed when the society decided that the authenticity of the thing was questionable -- but by the 1930s, it was functioning as a cow path again!

In 1932, a cow named Northwood Susan VI was led down the path with her three-week-old calf, Buttercup, as part of a publicity stunt to convince city slickers to attend the International Livestock Expo at the Union Stockyards. This made Northwood Susan VI and Buttercup the first cows to use the path in at least half a century, but, thereafter, cows would be led down the path whenever doing so seemed like a worthwhile publicity stunt!

THE OLSON RUG CO. WATERFALL

Perhaps the most lamented loss for nostalgic Chicagoans was the park and waterfall once located next to the carpet factory of the Olson Rug Co. at Diversey Parkway and Pulaski Road. The family-owned business was started in 1874 and it became a Chicago tradition and "the place" to buy rugs in the city. Walter E. Olson built the renowned 22-acre Olson Memorial Park next to the factory in 1935. The project took an army of 200 workers almost six months to complete, using about 800 tons of stone and 800 yards of soil. More than 3,500 perennials were planted, along with numerous species of junipers, spruces, pines, and annuals. The park consisted of a stunning rock garden, a duck pond, and, of course, the waterfall,

which was a replica of a real waterfall near Olson's Wisconsin summer home. The park was noted in contemporary newspaper accounts as "the most pretentious undertaking of its kind in the country."

Olson Park became a popular spot for family outings since, in the midst of the Great Depression, it was as close to the wonders of nature as most Chicagoans could get. During the first Sunday after its dedication, Olson Park attracted as many as 600 visitors per hour. Thousands of families picnicked on the grounds over the years, watching visiting American Indians do war dances in full regalia. The park's opening had corresponded with the 100th anniversary of the expulsion of Native American tribes from the Chicago area and so, as a small measure of making amends, the Olson waterfall was symbolically deeded back to the Indians.

In 1965, Olson Rug sold its building to Marshall Field's and in 1971, the waterfall was turned off and the park was dismantled to make room for a parking lot. Olson Rug still remains today (as anyone who grew up on Chicago radio can tell you, their commercials were heard almost as frequently as those by perennial favorite - Empire!) and is a 17-store Chicago-based chain that sells a wide variety of carpet, area rugs, wood and laminate floors, ceramic tile, and vinyl.

The Olson Park and Waterfall, however, exists today only in memories.

ESSANAY STUDIOS

Before there was Hollywood, there was Chicago. During the early days of the American film industry, Chicago was home to several movie studios, but the biggest of them was Essanay, which existed for just 10 years between 1907 and 1917. The Essanay Film Manufacturing Company was founded in Chicago's Uptown neighborhood by George K. Spoor and "Bronco Billy" Anderson, the S and A of Ess-an-ay.

Essanay was originally located at what is now 1300 North Wells St. The studio's first film, "An Awful Skate, or The Hobo on Rollers," starred Ben Turpin, who was then the studio's janitor. It was produced for only $200, but managed to gross several thousand dollars when it was released. Essanay soon prospered and eventually moved to its more famous address at 1333-45 West Argyle St.

Movie performers soon began flocking to Chicago. At that time, filmmakers were abandoning the East Coast, hoping to stay one ahead of the stringent copyright rules that had been imposed on the fledgling industry by Thomas Edison. Chicago was just far enough West to stay under the radar, at least for a while. Essanay produced silent films with up-and-coming and future stars like Wallace Beery, Francis X. Bushman, Gloria Swanson, cowboy star Tom Mix, Edward Arnold, and of course, former janitor Ben Turpin. The Uptown neighborhood became home to the stars and the site of many location shots. The nearby Chicago & Western railroad tracks along Ravenswood were often featured in the "Perils of Pauline" cliffhangers and Castlewood Terrace became a one-block forerunner to Beverly Hills. Gloria Swanson and Wallace Beery were married on the Essanay lot in 1916.

Essanay's films took the public by storm. The mainstays of the company, however, were the popular "Bronco Bill" westerns and comedies by Charlie Chaplin. Allan Dwan was hired by Essanay Studios as a screenwriter and went on to be a famous Hollywood director. Louella Parsons was also hired as a screenwriter and went on to become Hollywood's best-known gossip columnist. Both George K. Spoor and Bronco Bill Anderson received honorary Academy Awards in 1958 for their

"Bronco Billy" Anderson

pioneering efforts with the Chicago studio.

The popularity of Essanay's westerns, along with Chicago's seasonal weather patterns, eventually led the company to open the Essanay-West studio in Niles, Calif. Until that point, the Chicago studio had produced over 450 movies --- at a time when four out of every five American movies were produced in Chicago.

Working at Essanay Studios

The Chicago studio, as well as the California branch, continued to produce films for another five years, churning out a total of more than 1,400 titles. The Chicago studio produced many of Essanay's most famous movies, including the very first American "Sherlock Holmes" (1916), the first "A Christmas Carol" (1908) and the first Jesse James movie, "The James Boys of Missouri" (1908). Essanay also produced some of the world's very first cartoons, in which "Dreamy Dud" became the most popular character.

In 1914, Essanay succeeded in hiring Charlie Chaplin away from Mack Sennett's Keystone Studio, offering Chaplin a higher salary and his own production unit. Chaplin made 14 short comedies for Essanay in 1915, plus he made a cameo appearance in one of the "Bronco Billy" westerns. The landmark film of Chaplin's Essanay movies was "The Tramp" (1915), in which his famous character finds work on a farm and is smitten with the farmer's daughter.

Chaplin left Essanay after only one year for more money and more creative control elsewhere. His departure caused a rift between founders Spoor and Anderson and the company resorted to making "new" Chaplin comedies using old footage and outtakes. Once Chaplin was gone for good, Essanay hired French comedian Max Linder, who had often been compared to Chaplin in Europe. Audiences didn't respond and in a last-ditch effort to save the company, Essanay joined in a four-way merger arranged by Chicago distributor George Kleine in 1918. Kleine's new combine, V-L-S-E, was an amalgam of the Vitagraph, Lubin, Selig, and Essanay companies. Only the Vitagraph brand name continued into the 1920s, and was absorbed by Warner Brothers in 1925. Essanay was closed down for good.

George K. Spoor continued to work in the motion picture industry, introducing an unsuccessful 3-D system in 1925, and Spoor-Berggren Natural Vision, a 65mm widescreen

format, in 1930. He died in Chicago in 1953. "Bronco Billy" Anderson became an independent producer, sponsoring Stan Laurel in a series of silent comedies. Anderson died in Los Angeles in 1971.

The Essanay building in Chicago was later taken over by independent producer Norman Wilding, who made industrial films. He actually stayed at the location longer than Essanay did, but eventually, he left, as well. Today, the Essanay lot is the home of St. Augustine's College, and its main meeting hall has been named the Charlie Chaplin Auditorium. The studio's logo, along with the Indian head insignia, can still be seen over the doorway to the old studio building on at 1345 West Argyle.

"RUMOR HAS IT IT'S THE END OF PARADISE"

Although it gained immortality on the cover, and as the title, of a Styx album in the 1980s, the lavish Paradise Theater was actually a pretty unsuccessful addition to the West Side's amusement scene. The impressive theater opened in 1928, designed by famous theater architect John Eberson. The 3,500-seat movie palace was one of the most elaborate theaters in the city, but its poor acoustic quality damaged its popularity once talking films came on the scene. It started out as a grand dream, though, and one that could only be found in Chicago.

Paradise Theater

Theater impresario Louis Guyon first envisioned an enormous movie theater near the busy intersection of West Madison and Crawford (now Pulaski) in the early 1920s. Guyon was a leading West Side entrepreneur and owned a number of properties in the immediate area. His Paradise Ballroom, which catered to a middle-class dance crowd, had earned him a reputation as a great showman. Looking to build on the success of the ballroom, he launched two new ventures. The first was a lavish apartment hotel next to the ballroom and in 1925 he laid plans for the second - a grand movie theater to be built directly across the street from the ballroom and hotel.

Poor financial planning on Guyon's part soon undermined the theater project. Forced to cut his losses, he sold the partially completed theater to the Cooney Brothers, two South Side movie men, who in turn were forced by their own money problems to abandon the expensive project. When the Cooneys bowed out, the Balaban & Katz Company, operators of the city's largest circuit of theaters, purchased the unfinished structure. The place fit well into their ambitious plans. At the time, the Marks Brothers were building a new theater on Madison Street, just around the corner from the future Paradise. The theater, later named the Marbro, was scheduled to open in 1927 and it threatened to shut Balaban & Katz out of the West Side market if they could not match its number of seats. By taking over the Paradise project, Balaban & Katz hoped to put themselves into a competitive position with the Marbro.

Balaban & Katz spared no expense in an effort to make the Paradise one of the greatest showplaces in the city. They had vast sums of money to invest, thanks to the profits from their other nine theaters, and shortly after taking over the project, they instructed architect John Eberson to add hundreds of new features and fantastic embellishments to the original design. Eberson incorporated a wide array of religious and mythological imagery into his updated design for the Paradise. The theater's marquee, one of the largest in Chicago, featured a sunburst design and it was outfitted with electric lights in ten different colors. The lobby was just as spectacular. Marble statuary adorned the huge area and murals depicting the zodiac were arrayed on the ceiling. This was nothing compared to the main auditorium, though, where audiences were met with a simulated night sky, complete with twinkling stars, at the moment of daybreak. The huge proscenium arch was decorated with Apollo, the sun god, riding behind a team of marble-carved horses as they raced across the sky.

The Paradise Theater opened on September 14, 1928 with the film 'The Fleet's In,' starring Clara Bow. Balaban & Katz prepared for the event by launching one of the largest advertising campaigns in the company's history. Gigantic ads celebrating the theater's extravagant design and stunning amenities appeared in Chicago newspapers weeks ahead of the opening and continued well into October.

But the lavish décor and the slick advertising campaign were not enough to ensure the Paradise's success as a movie theater. Once the novelty wore off, only quality entertainment could keep the patrons coming back and as it turned out, the Paradise was no match for the Marbro, its biggest rival on the West Side. This became even more apparent when silent films were replaced by taking pictures. Audiences found the Marbro to be much more acoustically pleasing than the dome-like Paradise. When the Depression caused Chicago moviegoers to cut back on trips to watch films, business at the Paradise slumped to devastating new lows. In 1931, Balaban & Katz decided to close the theater until the economy improved. Although the Paradise re-opened in 1934, it never lived up to the expectations that its owners had for it.

The Paradise struggled along for two decades and by the 1950s, it was clear that the theater was obsolete when it came to the meeting the needs of the changing movie industry. In 1956, Balaban & Katz agreed to demolish the theater and sell the vacant parcel of land to a developer who planned to open a grocery store on the site. Ironically, though, John Eberson had designed the building so well that it took a demolition contractor nearly two years to complete what should have been an easy six-month job.

Old memories, as they say, die hard.

"HARK, HARK, THE CLARK!"

Sometimes I feel that my whole purpose in life is to tell people who might not have seen it that such a place as the Clark existed.
Daniel Pinkwater

He took in the 4 a.m. show at the Clark /
Excitable boy, they all said
Warren Zevon

Another long gone, but fondly remembered, Chicago institution was the Clark Theatre, a 23-hour-per-day movie

Adelphi Theater: The Adelphi, located at 7074 North Clark St., was built in 1917 for the Ascher Brothers circuit. The theater stood on Clark Street at Estes Avenue in Chicago's Rogers Park neighborhood. In the 1930s, the Adelphi was remodeled into an Art Deco theater and then "modernized" again in the 1940s and 1950s. It began to show second-run features starting in the late 1960s, and closed briefly in the early 1980s, after several years screening Spanish movies. In the middle 1980s, the Adelphi reopened as the North Shore Theater, but was again known as the Adelphi when it began to show East Indian films and became the premiere venue for "Bollywood" features in the Chicagoland area. The Adelphi closed in January 2002 and was demolished in 2006.

Belmont Theater: Located at 1635 West Belmont Ave., the Belmont was one of the more popular North Side movie houses, as it was surrounded by a bustling retail area and located close to public transportation in the Lakeview neighborhood. The theater opened in 1925 and was taken over by the Balaban & Katz chain in May 1930. This 3200-plus-seat palace was originally a venue for both live entertainment and movies, but later turned to films only. In the middle 1960s, the Belmont was converted into a bowling alley, which it remained until its closing in the mid-'80s. In 1996, with the revival of the Lakeview neighborhood, a mixed condominium and retail complex was built on the site of the Belmont, which was demolished except for its Spanish Baroque style terra-cotta façade, which still remains today.

Brighton Theatre: The Brighton Theater, located at 4223 South Archer Ave., achieved notoriety in 1956 when it became the last place that the Grimes Sisters were ever seen alive. (More about this unsolved case in a later chapter). The theater opened as the Brighton Park in 1919, and it was named for the neighborhood in which it was located and stood on Archer Avenue near Sacramento Avenue. The Brighton Park Theatre, which did not have a stage and was built specifically for movies, also contained a grand Kimball organ. After a long life as a popular neighborhood house, it closed its doors in 1991, and in September 2003, was torn down.

Colony Theater: Located at 3208 West 59th St., the Colony Theater opened in the Marquette Park neighborhood in 1926. The Colony featured movies in its early years, along with live entertainment. However, it later moved to a film-only format, and remained so through the 1970s. During the late 1970s and into the 1980s, the Colony was used for rock concerts and later, for religious stage shows. In the early 1990s, the theater housed a flea market for a short time, and by the latter part of that decade, the Colony was used for storage. Since then, the theater has been vacant. It did very briefly come to life for a few days in the late 1990s when the defunct CBS series, "Early Edition," which was filmed on location in Chicago, used the Colony's lobby and exterior for a scene.

Devon Theatre: Located at 6225 North Broadway, the Devon opened in 1915 in Chicago's Edgewater neighborhood. It was originally named the Knickerbocker, and oddly, was more than two blocks away from Devon Avenue. It mostly served as a second-run house, and was quite plain. It continued to operate through the 1970s, and later housed a church for a time. The Devon was razed in 1996 after the block was acquired by Loyola University's expansion into Edgewater. The Devon was owned by Herschell Gordon Lewis, of exploitation movie fame, from 1967 to 1972.

Garrick Theatre: Originally named the Schiller Theater after Frederick Schiller, German playwright, poet and philosopher, and the Dearborn Theater, it became the Garrick in 1903 as a legitimate theater. It was located at 64 West Randolph St. in a building designed by Adler & Sullivan. In March 1934, it became a movie theater when it was acquired by Balaban & Katz. From the late 1940s and into the middle 1950s, the Garrick stage was used for live local (and later national) television broadcasts. In 1957, Balaban & Katz resumed showing movies. The theater closed in 1960 and was torn down and replaced by a monstrous parking garage, which in turn was razed in the late 1990s.

Loop Theater: Located at 165 North State St., the Loop Theater was located next to the Chicago Theater. Originally known as the Telenews, this small venue was once the place where moviegoers could see a couple of cartoons, a newsreel, a comical short, and the famous "March of Time" news reports, all in a single hour. Keeping with its newsy theme, a United Press telecdatype machine clacked away in the lobby where an usher would spike the copy on the wall behind the machine. The Telenews operated from 1939 into the 1950s. As the Loop, the house exhibited a mix of first-run features and a lot of Russ Meyer-type, B-movie and exploitation films. The theater thrived during this second life but by the late 1970s, was closed down. For years, the former Loop Theater housed a retail store. The building was demolished to make way for new developments in December 2005.

McVicker's Theatre: At 25 W. Madison, the McVicker's was built in 1857. In the late 1860s, bizarre rumors went around that John Wilkes Booth had not been killed at all, but was in fact alive and hiding out in the McVicker's! It would have been a natural place for him; Booth had been the theatrical sensation of Chicago when he played there for a total of five weeks in 1862. The theatre was destroyed by the Great Fire in 1871 then rebuilt several times. It became a movie house in the early 1960s, and, by the 1970s, was, like most theatres in the area, showing mostly b-movies. It was demolished for good in the mid-1980s.

Roosevelt Theater: Located directly across the street from the main entrance of Marshall Field's at 110 North State St., the Roosevelt opened in 1921.With its Greek Revival façade and faux columns, many complained that it looked more like a bank than a theater. Unlike some of its larger, more extravagant neighbors (the Chicago, Oriental and State Lake, which were all within a block or two of the Roosevelt), it did not feature live entertainment, but was designed specifically to show movies only. It was acquired by Balaban & Katz a few years after it opened and was a popular movie house in the Loop until the early 1970s, when it was reduced to showing "blaxploitation" and kung-fu films. The theater was closed in 1979 and a decade later, was razed to make room for new development.

Southtown Theatre: The Southtown, located at 610 West 63rd St., was the last of the massive movie palaces to be built in Chicago in 1931. The theater had 2,200 seats on the main floor and another 1,000 in the balcony. The most incredible feature was the Flamingo Pool and fountain in the Grand Lobby, which boasted a waterfall and live fish. The floor plan of the theater had box offices, a grand lobby, a grand inner lobby (where the Flamingo Pool was located), a children's playroom, a women's lounge, a men's lounge, an exit lobby, a huge auditorium and a balcony. The mezzanine featured dioramas of famous Chicago events, like the Great Fire. The theater finally closed in 1958 and was demolished in 1991 after serving for many years as Carr's department store and after that, a flea market.

WHERE IS IT NOW?
The Clark stood next to the Blue Note Jazz Club on Clark Street (of course) just below Washington, across from the Chicago Temple building. The building is now long-gone.

theatre at 11 North Clark St. that specialized in showing a different double feature -- often a bizarre pairing -- every day. In an age before home video took hold in the early 1980s, revival houses such as the Clark were the only chance people had to see older films that weren't shown on television.

The Clark opened in 1933 and went to a "revival" format in 1951. Over time, it became a haven for nighthawks, bohemians, and lonely weirdos. The manager, Bruce Trinz, sent out fliers reading "Hark, hark, the Clark" and describing each film with a couplet, such as "Sled is the bane / of Citizen Kane," or, for the Marx Brothers' "Horse Feathers," "Marx Brothers at College / Make a farce out of knowledge." The theater even took requests. Customers could write the name of a film they wanted to see on a card, put it in the suggestion box, and the management would almost always be able to find the movie in question.

Without question, the Clark was a bargain. For just a few cents, patrons got two movies and parking in the Loop (and, according to some stories, a seven-course meal at the Chinese restaurant next door.) It's even rumored that people lived there, hiding out in the bathroom during the hour between 6:30 and 7:30, when the Clark was closed for cleaning, and managing to get a month's rent for the price of one admission. Others simply made stops there a regular routine. After getting off work in the middle of the night, they'd wander over to the Clark and see whatever happened to be showing that night.

For many, however, the Clark wasn't just a place to sleep, make out, or get a night of cheap entertainment; it was an education. A generation of college students, including such notables as Roger Ebert, was introduced to the concept of film as art in the Clark. Ebert describes being "educated" by Bruce

Trinz, crime writer Jay Robert Nash, and various obscure film directors who would tell him he "had" to see certain films.

Alas, the Clark didn't survive the growth of the city or the spread of television and video. By the early 1970s, it was showing mostly adult films and kung-fu movies before being razed, along with most of the block on which it sat.

Old Chicago's Grand Opening (Bolingbrook Historical Society)

GHOST ALERT!

One not-exactly-lost theatre in Chicago is the Admiral, at 3940 W. Lawrence. Built as a vaudeville house in the 1920s, it closed down in the '50s, then re-opened in the late '60s for a brief stint as a movie theatre that showed nothing but cartoons. Today, it serves as a gentleman's club, and is said by the staff to be haunted by a mysterious male apparition. Some speculate that it could be the ghost of Patsy Ricardi, a former owner who was involved in mafia pornography distribution and was found dead in the trunk of a car in 1985.

OLD CHICAGO

Anyone who grew up listening to WLS in Chicago (back when it was the best rock-n-roll station in the city) was barraged with ads for Old Chicago in the late 1970s. Old Chicago, the world's first totally enclosed theme park, opened in 1975 in the suburb of Bolingbrook. At the time, it was something completely new: an amusement park with a huge roof over it so that patrons could ride the rides all year around, no matter what the weather was like outside. If you believed the radio deejays of the day, there was nowhere else in Chicagoland where you could have as much fun as at Old Chicago. But guests soon discovered that it was not all that it was cracked up to be and disappointment, along with troubles at the park, closed the place down just five years later.

Plans began to be made for Old Chicago in June 1973, when developer Robert Brindle appeared before the Bolingbrook planning commission with the idea for a 345,000 square-foot complex with indoor amusement park rides and retail stores. It would, he promised, "put Bolingbrook on the map." The city heard the plan with great enthusiasm - and so did Romeoville, who felt that the location of the proposed site, south of Interstate 55, put it into their domain.

The victory eventually went to Bolingbrook, who seemed to lose enthusiasm with the plan. Without city approval, Robert Brindle laid the foundation of his building in late 1973, only to be told that it exceeded setback requirements in the Bolingbrook city code. This was the first of many legal troubles that would be encountered by Old Chicago. Soon after, the city refused to issue any building permits. Brindle begged for approval of his plans, unable to get more financing for the project without approval. A new series of hearings were called but Brindle went ahead and had the 15-foot-wide, 40-ton wall sections of the structure lifted into place - still without the city's approval.

Old Chicago was eventually constructed and in June 1975, a pre-opening party was scheduled - even though not all of the construction had been

Old Chicago (Bolingbrook Historical Society)

Two views of Old Chicago's heart and soul -- the
indoor amusement park
(Bolingbrook Historical Society)

finished. Again, without approval from the city, Brindle went ahead with the party and between 10,000 and 16,000 invited guests created a mammoth traffic jam on Route 53. Soon after, word reached Old Chicago from the city that it was not allowed to open because of threats from exposed wiring and half-completed storefronts. The threats from the city were answered with threats from Old Chicago, placing Bolingbrook officials in a no-win situation: they either allowed "civilians to enter the building still under construction" or they turned away thousands of guests who filled the parking lot and jammed up Route 53. The pre-opening party took place as planned.

The official opening for Old Chicago was on June 26. Prior to that, construction crews worked around the clock to pass a last-minute inspection by the city. When the doors opened, an estimated 15,000 people attended the celebration at the large square building with the domed roof. Part of the event included a tap dancer performing atop the dome. Guests found the rides and attractions (the "Old Chicago Fairgrounds") in the center of the structure, under the dome. The shopping area was located around the perimeter of the building.

The "shopping mall" had a cobblestone floor, and was designed to resemble a Chicago street from the early 1900s. At various points, windows opened up to look out into the amusement park. There were no anchor stores or major retailers in the mall, only gift shops, specialty stores, and snack bars.

For most, the "Fairgrounds" were the main attraction of the park, offering "31 great rides and attractions," crammed into the domed center of the building. At the time it opened, Old Chicago charged a $1 admission fee to the park and then a flat fee for unlimited rides. In addition to all of the standard fairground rides like the Scrambler, the Octopus, Merry-Go-Round, Tilt-a-Whirl, Bumper Cars, and a Ferris wheel, there were also two roller coasters: the Zyclon and the Chicago Loop. There was also a water ride called the Chicago Log Race, a small circus, a vaudeville theater, a haunted house, a few kiddie rides, and a number of carnival games.

Various events took place at Old Chicago from time to time. Chicago radio stations held "back-to-school bashes," and did dozens of remote broadcasts from there during their Chicago segments. The first Chicagoland "Pepsi Challenge" was held at Old Chicago. Director Brian DePalma filmed scenes for his movie "The Fury" at Old Chicago but accidentally sent part of a ride crashing through the window of the Biergarten, one of the park's two restaurants. Extras in the movie included a number of Bolingbrook residents who are seen during the two-minute sequence that immortalizes Old Chicago in the film.

Here are some of the other highlights (good and bad) from Old Chicago's short history:

* Just days after opening, the village of Bolingbrook shut down the park for six hours because of sprinkler malfunctions. Heated discussions between Brindle and the city lead to Brindle believing he is being persecuted. He claims that an average of 50,000 people visit Old Chicago every weekend, which is believable considering that traffic is snarled on Route 53 all the way to Lisle.

* In October, 500 people are evacuated from the park after a fire breaks out in a trash compactor. Old Chicago management complains that the fire department overreacted to a small fire.

* Also in October, Miss Teen Chicago is crowned at the park.

* In November 1975, the "Comedy King of Air," Jimmy Troy, falls 20 feet to his death from the trapeze at the Old Chicago circus.

* In January 1976, Old Chicago files for bankruptcy, mostly due to overruns in construction costs. Management refers to the bankruptcy as "only a technical readjustment" and announces new attractions that will put Old Chicago on the right track. Soon after, the Marriott Corporation opens its new "amusement extravaganza" of Six Flags in Gurnee.

* By February 1976, founder Robert Brindle, who conceived and built Old Chicago, is completely out of the park and control now rests with IC Industries. The conglomerate meets with retail merchants at the park and unveils plans to revamp the amusement park area.

* In the summer of 1976, features are added to the park to attract more people, including psychic fairs, drum competitions, graduation nights, family nights, antique and car shows, the Acapulco High Dining Team, and a 'Human Torch," who literally sets himself on fire. In July, the Bolingbrook Jaycees stage their annual fireworks display at Old Chicago, accompanied by parachute teams and midget racers.

* Billed under the headlines of "Public Executions at Old Chicago" a desperate public relations gimmick promotes the celebration of Bastille Day at the park with fun shows featuring "the rack," cat-o-nine-tails and other antique torture devices. Obviously, this was not "family night."

* In November, some of the promised updates to the park are opened. The Fun Factory, a multi-level play area for younger kids, is unveiled with a separate admission fee and entrance. New rides include the Screamer and the Barnstormer, an airplane thrill ride. Also included in the improvements are a new laser light show (very big in the late 1970s) and colorful sound baffles that are hung under the dome to tone down the deafening noise of amusement park rides being run indoors.

* Despite the changes and updates, Old Chicago only limps along through the winter and following summer. In August 1978, the first of the shutdowns begin when the "open-365-days-a-year" park is closed to the general public on Mondays and Tuesdays.

* In February 1979, a fire in the Old Chicago Tobacco Company is quickly put out, destroying tobacco that is being dried with electric heaters. There were no sprinklers in this area.

* In March, (another) new management team begins re-thinking the shopping mall idea and shifts all of the stores to the front area near the entrance. A management spokesman admits for the first time that amusement rides and shopping might not be compatible. He suggests adding movie theaters and a bowling alley.

* In July 1979, the professional fireworks display that Old Chicago hires instead of the Jaycees literally blows up in their faces when a spark ignites all of the fireworks prematurely. One technician suffers first- and second-degree burns, in addition to minor injuries to a 6-year-old, but most of the crowd is safe behind barricades. The Jaycees had finally backed out of the annual fireworks show because of numerous complaints from Bolingbrook residents who didn't want to do anything to help Old Chicago.

* In January 1980, Old Chicago announces plans to construct new concert stage with a new three-way sound system for its "Live at Old Chicago" concert series - a series that never happened.

In March 1980, Old Chicago finally closed down. Work began almost immediately to dismantle and sell off the amusement rides, but some of the shops stayed open. Lawsuits filed on behalf of some of these businesses kept the stores lingering in the defunct amusement park until August 1981, even after plans to turn the place into a giant outlet mall fell apart. Old Chicago was legally, officially, and literally boarded up.

Rumors floated around for several years about turning the building into a retail outlet, a gambling casino, and some sort of indoor entertainment facility. "An indoor Poplar Creek" was one suggestion. Problems with vandals continually plagued the boarded-up park, but not for long. In March 1986, many of the board members and residents of Bolingbrook got their way and Old Chicago was no more. The walls were demolished and a few weeks later, all traces of it were gone.

Financially, Old Chicago was a disaster. Without major retail chains, there was not enough of a mall to attract customers and there was simply not enough of an amusement park to bring people back after their initial visit to "just see what it's like." But to those who still remember the place with fondness, there was just enough novelty to Old Chicago to make it unique - and to make them look back on the park with nostalgia.

There are no traces of Old Chicago left today save for memories and a few faded souvenirs. After it was torn down, a car lot purchased the site and these days, a few hotels and restaurants occupy the spot where the park once stood. All that's left as a reminder is a street sign for Old Chicago Drive.

OTHER LOST AMUSEMENT PARKS: WHITE CITY

Old Chicago is certainly not the only lost amusement park remembered by Chicagoans. Opened in 1905, White City was one of the South Side's most popular entertainment venues. The amusement park was located at 63rd

White City's Shoot-the-Chutes Ride & the famous Electric Tower

Street and South Parkway (now Martin Luther King Drive). White City's front gate sat just a few steps from the South Side Elevated, which attracted visitors from all over the city. Brightly lit at night by thousands of lights, the attractions at the park included several roller coasters, a shoot-the-chutes, two ballrooms, inexpensive food, and its landmark Electric Tower. Though parts of the park remained in operation into the 1950s, most of White City was shut down in 1934, when financial difficulties sent the park into bankruptcy. The park's name -- White City -- was a reminder of 1893 World's Columbian Exposition in Jackson Park.

From its first day of operation, White City was jam-packed with thrilling rides and entertaining attractions, including the Electric Tower, which was nearly 300 feet tall and illuminated by 20,000 light bulbs. The park also offered a "Fighting the Flames" attraction, which offered visitors a look at how fires were battled. The outdoor set was a life-sized city block that required the use of two trolley cars, five cabs, two automobiles, several fight-fighting wagons, as well as 14 horses and 250 actors. Other real-life attractions included the Johnstown Flood Show, which was a walk-through diorama that depicted the famous Pennsylvania disaster; baby incubators were premature babies were placed on display; and a Midget City, which was a "model miniature village of twenty-five tiny buildings peopled by a host of midgets of world-wide renown." This early sideshow was one of the park's most popular attractions.

The rides at White City were bragged about by anyone who experienced them. They included the Canals of Venice, which was a favorite with young lovers, and offered a "romantic gondola ride through the moonlit water streets of Venice" where patrons could view "correct reproductions" of the city's "famous buildings and statuary groups"; the Scenic Railway, the park's first roller coaster; the Speed Toboggan, another roller coaster; the Bumps the Bumps ride, in which park-goers slid down a padded mat; the Shoot-the-Chutes water ride, said to be the "longest in America" at 500 feet; a huge Ferris wheel; and a large midway area that was filled with games of skill and chance.

The College Inn was a moderately priced restaurant on the grounds that featured both indoor and outdoor seating. The restaurant served primarily German fare, but, in deference to the advocates of temperance, initially did not serve alcoholic beverages. Nearby was the White City Ballroom, the first of two ballrooms to be built at the park. It could accommodate up to 1,000 dancers and was often filled to capacity. Floorwalkers roamed the dance floor to ensure that couples did not dance too closely.

Among White City's more unusual attractions of the time was its two boardwalks. The parallel boardwalks ran the length of the park and were designed to send guests from one end of White City to the other. There was only one way into White City and that was through its colossal front gate at the corner of 63rd Street and South Parkway. Once inside the park, visitors proceeded down either the east or the west boardwalk to the south end of the park. From there, they generally returned to the north end via the opposite boardwalk, pausing along the way to enjoy rides and attractions that caught their interest. The boardwalks turned out to be more than just a method of transportation, though, they also helped deal with the unending problem of litter disposal. Raised four feet above the ground and laid out with one-half-inch crevasses between planks, much of the daily accumulations of popcorn, peanut shells, candy wrappers, soda straws, and ticket stubs produced by visitors simply fell through the cracks in the boardwalk, never to be seen again. The owners were thrilled with this under-appreciated feature of the boardwalks and apparently had few concerns about the health risks - and rats - this practice attracted.

OTHER LOST AMUSEMENT PARKS: RIVERVIEW

Riverview Amusement Park operated in Chicago from 1904 to 1967 and was located on 74 acres around Belmont and Western avenues on the city's North Side. During that time, it offered a world of inexpensive amusements to Chicagoans and every summer, thousands flocked to the park to enjoy its combination of thrilling rides, fascinating exhibits, cheap eats, and interesting people.

Riverview Amusement Park's Carousel & Aerostat Swing, 1910

Riverview was the creation of William and George Schmidt. In 1900, they purchased what was then known as Sharpshooter's Park at Belmont and Western avenues. The park was the home of a German gun club where guests shot at targets set up on an island in the middle of the river and hunted for game in the woods nearby. The Schmidts decided to expand the variety of amusements in the park and increase its appeal to families. In 1903, George Schmidt visited Copenhagen's famous Tivoli Gardens while on a tour of Europe. Apparently inspired by the park's beauty and variety of amusements, Schmidt returned to Chicago determined to turn Sharpshooter's Park into a similar pleasure spot.

Riverview's first season of operation as an amusement park was the summer of 1904. The main attractions during the park's early years included a toboggan slide, a giant swing, the Old Mill tunnel-of-love ride, water chutes, a carousel, a miniature railway, and a traditional midway featuring a variety of shows,

A Riverview Refreshment stand, 1910

games, and eateries. Daily performances by German bands were very popular as well, especially among the North Side's sizable German population.

As time passed, Riverview's owners updated and improved the park's attractions to lure guests back every summer. This was especially true with the park's most popular rides, the roller coasters. Starting out with the rather tame Scenic Railway in 1907, other coasters included the Comet, the Blue Streak, the Pippen, the Jack Rabbit, the Flying Turns (which came from the Century of Progress Exposition) and perhaps the most famous, the Bobs. Built in 1926 at a cost of $80,000, this coaster jostled its riders from beginning to end on sharp curves and shortened dips in low-riding cars that clanked loudly to intensify the ride's dangers and seemingly life-threatening speeds.

Riverview Amusement Park was wildly popular, but everything was not always "shiny and bright" at the entertainment center. The park became known for the large number of deaths and mishaps that occurred on the grounds. In 1908, a man was killed when he fell out of his seat on the Royal Gorge ride. In 1910, 26 people were hurt in two separate incidents involving the collision of two cars at the loading platform of the Derby roller coaster and the derailment of a car on the Royal Gorge ride. In 1911, the operator of a shooting gallery was killed when an 11-year-old boy shot him when he turned his back to clean a target. In 1914, four cars on the Jack Rabbit coaster collided at the bottom of the ride's highest incline and injured 40 people, most of them children. In 1916, a nine-year-old boy died when he fell 40 feet to the ground after reaching for a hat that had blown off on the Greyhound roller coaster. In 1924, a young man fell from a roller coaster and died. A second man died in the same way the following season. In 1937, two trains in the Pippen coaster collided, injuring 22 park-goers. And the list went on...

It was not the fear of injury or death that caused some people concern about Riverview Park. While the place was promoted as a family amusement center, some social reformers worried about the potentially demoralizing effects that the park might have on young people, especially young women. They were worried about Riverview's ballroom, where unchaperoned girls, if left to their own judgment, might be lured into a life of prostitution.

And during the early years of Prohibition, federal agents regularly raided the park and its picnic grove in search of home-brewed beer. Park-goers, however, grew accustomed to the raids, sacrificing a token keg or two to the agents and then sounding an "all clear" for local residents and bootleggers to deliver the rest of the day's illicit beer supply.

Riverview continued to attract large crowds during the 1950s and 1960s. Chicagoans, as they had for most of the century, continued to enjoy the park's exciting combination of wild rides, upbeat music, lively crowds, and tasty food. Eventually, rising taxes and costs brought about Riverview's closing after the 1967 season. The site was redeveloped for industry and retail stores and no trace of the place that brought so many generations of Chicagoans a summer of happiness remains today.

LOST CHICAGO AMUSEMENTS: THE MONKEY SPEEDWAY

Although not technically a fixture on the Chicago amusement scene, Monkey Speedways were a staple of sideshows and carnivals that came to the city for years. While researching some other aspects of the forgotten in the city, we ran across this fascinating piece of lost Americana.

The monkey speedway was a large circular speedway that measured about 40 feet in diameter. It was made of wood with metal runners. The track was slightly slanted, allowing the public to see the racing cars at every angle. A monkey was strapped into each car, appearing to the carnival-goers (there was a reason the carnies called them 'marks') that the monkey was the driver and could control the speed of the car. The cars would line up at the starting line and they would begin their race around and around the track. Of course, the actual operation of the cars were under the control of the attendant, who controlled the electric motors with foot pedals. The races

usually lasted about 20 minutes, offering all sorts of entertainment for those who came to the carnival to see how much cotton candy they could eat and forget about the real world for awhile.

6. WEIRD (AND HAUNTED!) CHICAGO EATERIES & WATERING HOLES

Then stand to your glasses steady
And drink to your comrade's eyes
Here's a toast to the dead already
And hurrah for the next who dies.
Drinking song popularized by Chicago reporters at the Whitechapel Club

Everybody knows about the food in Chicago - just like everybody knows about the gangsters. "Al Capone and pizza," it was once said, were two things that made Chicago great, or at least memorable. It doesn't matter if you have never been to the city, outside of Chicago's bloody history of beer wars, there is perhaps no greater legendary connection for people who have never traveled to the Windy City (except perhaps the ghosts!) than the food. There also seems to be no greater culinary contribution to American culture that Chicago's deep-dish pizza and hotdogs. Both are dishes that are best served as a "hands-on" experience and many visitors never fail to experience them when they come to the city. It doesn't matter if you go somewhere else and they call their pizza or hot dogs "Chicago style;" there is no fooling the real connoisseur of Windy City delicacies. Nobody else has the real thing!

With that said, the reader should probably know that the history of food and drink in the city is closely linked to the history of Chicago itself, which likely explains the number of unusual restaurants, taverns and pubs that can be found in the region. Chicago has gained national attention for its food and drinks over the years and in the pages ahead, we'll be exploring some of the reasons why our eateries and watering holes are just so darn weird!

THE WHITECHAPEL CLUB

One of the weirdest drinking establishments in Chicago's history was not so much a tavern as it was a private club. Although located in the basement of Henry Koster's saloon at the southwest corner of Calhoun Place and LaSalle Street, the Whitechapel Club operated in a world all its own. In fact, author John Drury once said that he had never found anything to equal it. "It was the weirdest, most fantastic organization I ever heard of," he said. "It even went to the extent of becoming gruesome."

The club was founded by an eccentric and good-humored band of Chicago authors, newsmen, artists and essayists in 1889, the year after Jack the Ripper began his murderous crime spree in London's Whitechapel District. The serial killer does not seem to figure too prominently into the name of the club, though. It seems the name really came from the murder of Dr. Patrick Henry Cronin in Chicago in May 1889. Charles Goodyear Seymour, a noted *Chicago Herald* writer, and his colleagues on the crime beat were looking for an out-of-the-way place to compare notes on the murder, and the public stir around it, over beer and sandwiches. It was a jeer at the hated English that these Irishmen named the place "Whitechapel."

Thus the "blood and guts" drinking club was born and 94 men were welcomed into membership. These men included poet and novelist Wallace Rice; Chicago Tribune artist John T. McCutcheon; Frederick Upham Adams; Eugene Field; humorist George Ade; Opie Read; Alfred Henry Lewis; Hobart Chatfield-Taylor and many others. The

The Whitechapel Club

only entrance to the club was through a heavy wooden door that led into the basement of Koster's Saloon. The saloon was located on a corner of Calhoun Place, the western exposure of which was then known as "Newsboys Alley" in honor of the reporters, editors and illustrators from the nearby Herald and Times offices. Above the door of Koster's, a stained-glass window was inscribed with the words: "Abandon hope, all ye who enter here!"

The interior of the club was decorated with all sorts of odd and bizarre artifacts from various collections and from Chicago crime history. Crime reporter John Kelley started this decorating theme by donating a rare, 12-foot snakeskin that was hung on the wall. After that, members worked to outdo one another with their ghoulishness, bringing in guns, knives, swords, hangman's ropes, exotic weapons, weird photos and illustrations and even a bullet that was removed from the corpse of "Doc" Haggerty, who had been killed in a duel with criminal "Bad" Jimmy Connerton.

Dr. John C. Spray of the Elgin State Mental Hospital gave a collection of skulls to Whitechapel member Chrysostom "Tombstone" Thompson and he immediately incorporated them into the décor of the club. Dr. Spray had used the skulls to compare the differences in size and shape between insane and "normal" people and Thompson converted the skulls into globes for gas jets by drilling holes into the top of them. Another skull, which became known as the most famous piece in the club, was that of "Waterford Jack," a Civil War-era madam named Frances Warren, who supervised a stable of girls working the back alleys near the Chicago River.

The members of the club gathered around a large table that had been fashioned in the shape of a coffin to smoke and drink. During the years it was in its heyday, the club welcomed two future presidents, William McKinley and Theodore Roosevelt, and a number of celebrity guests like bare-knuckle fighter John L. Sullivan, author Rudyard Kipling, and others. The club's glory days began to wind down in 1892 when Koster moved down the alley to a larger location. When Chicago Herald publisher James Wilmot Scott died in 1895, the club went dark. Scott had paid the rent on the location each month since Whitechapel Club members maintained a policy of "No gas. No water. No police. No Rent. No Taxes." Scott never minded this and considered the rent a small price to pay for the entertainment that he enjoyed meeting with his friends and colleagues in such an unusual setting. With his death, the club died too and in 1902, its corporate charter was canceled. Seven years later, Koster's original saloon was torn down to make way for the LaSalle Hotel.

In 1921, the superior court of Cook County formally dissolved the Whitechapel Club but years later, what was left of the grisly artifacts, the beer glasses and photographs were set up again in the lobby of the LaSalle, where a "Whitechapel Pub" was established as a tribute to the old days.

The LaSalle has since gone the way of the Whitechapel Club and it was demolished in 1976.

> **WHERE IS IT NOW?**
> The Whitechapel Club was located at LaSalle Street and Calhoun Place in the Loop - in those days, Calhoun Place was known as Newsboys Alley. No trace remains of it today.

THE CHICAGO HOT DOG TOUR

As noted already, Chicago has plenty of local cuisine that's admired worldwide, from chicken vesuvio to Italian beef sandwiches to the oft-misunderstood deep-dish pizza ("deep-dish" does NOT mean "thick crust.") But nothing turns heads like a proper Chicago-style hot dog. When done correctly, a Chicago-style hot dog is a flavorful, bright red dog on a poppy seed bun, topped with yellow mustard, neon green relish, onions, tomato slices, sport peppers (which are traditionally not eaten, but saved for throwing at cars later), a pickle spear, and celery salt. Notably absent from this list is ketchup, which is generally regarded as being a topping for kids, not adults, when it comes to hot dogs. Some of the best hot dog places in town refuse to put ketchup on dogs themselves, keeping a bottle off to the side so that customers who insist can add it themselves.

The hot dog itself may have been introduced in Chicago at the 1893 Columbian Exposition (though this is hotly debated), but this particular style, sometimes known as the "depression sandwich," is usually said to have originated at Flukey's on Michigan Avenue in the late 1920s. By the 1950s, it was a Chicago staple. Today, there are more independently-owned hot dog places in Chicago than McDonald's, Wendy's, and Burger King's combined!

Unfortunately, today, many Chicago hot dog merchants are resting on their laurels. The dogs at Wrigley Field and the new Comiskey Park are a disgrace, and many places that purport to sell Chicago-style dogs are offering wimpy dogs in limp, stale buns that fall apart. These places tend to leave out the poppy seeds and the celery salt, and the pickles and tomatoes aren't so much spears and slices as slivers.

However, in the midst of all of this, there are plenty of fantastic places where a great hot dog can be had. A few places to try include:

HOT DOUG'S --
3324 N. CALIFORNIA - WWW.HOTDOUGS.COM

Doug Sohn is the greatest hot dog genius in Chicago, and, therefore, the world. Open only for lunch, the line to get in snakes around the block on even the coldest days. Inside, the decor is cheerful. Doug cracks corny jokes with every customer, and a properly-done Chicago-style dog can be had for less than two bucks, making it the cheapest gourmet eatery in Chicago.

But in addition to the Chicago-style dogs, Doug, a culinary school graduate, has made a name for himself offering some of the most wildly inventive hot dogs the world has ever known. The menu of specials changes weekly, but has included such delicacies as: Sweet and tart rabbit sausage dogs with goat cheese, pomegranate crème fraise and vodka-soaked dried blueberries; Cranberry-cognac-infused chicken sausage dogs with citrus mustard and Morbier cheese; and Kangaroo sausage with anchovy aioli and smoked Gouda cheese. Other sausages served over the years have included ostrich, pheasant, rattlesnake and alligator.

Doug's made national news in 2007. Shortly after the city banned the use of foie gras in restaurants, Doug became the first restaurateur to be fined -- for putting it on hot dogs! Doug, who told Weird Chicago that he a bit of a problem with food rules, will put just about anything on a dog -- even ketchup. But the snobs of the world forgive him. After all, Hot Doug's is the most legendary hot dog establishment in Chicago in at least a generation.

ROCK STAR DOGS
801 N. ASHLAND
WWW.ROCKSTAR-DOGS.COM

Rockstar Dogs, on Chicago and Ashland, deserves to be in the Weird Chicago book for two reasons right off the bat: for one thing, it's thought to be the narrowest-eat-in restaurant in the city. Years ago, when Ashland Street was widened, the already-narrow building was chopped in half. For another, it's probably the only hot dog place in town that boasts its own stripper pole. If not, it's certainly the only one where you'd want to eat.

Rockstar Dogs are new to the Chicago scene, but deserve to take their place among the new generation of Chicago dog icons. While the all-hot-dog menu isn't as wildly original as Hot Doug's, one doesn't get the sense

that these guys are trying to be quite like Doug -- this is a hot dog joint with attitude. A sign on the menu specifies that ketchup is not allowed unless you're under 13 (the fastest way to a Chicago dog connoisseur's heart), the decor is mainly rock photos by Philin Phlash, whose work also adorns much of The Liar's Club, and the place is open until the wee small hours of the night. The logo features a woman in a bikini holding a hot dog in one hand and a bottle marked "XXX" in the other.

Given the style of the place, the food almost seems like an afterthought, but it turns out to be fantastic. The Chicago-style dogs are perfectly executed, well constructed, and wonderfully tasty. The fries, which come with every dog, are well above average, too. To top it all off, each one comes with a guitar pick. Another true Chicago original!

RELISH THE THOUGHT
3207 N. HALSTED

Some Chicago restaurants have retro vibes, and some wonderful places take you truly back in time. Step into the Green Mill, Margie's Candies or the 11 City Diner, and you find yourself transported back several decades into history. Some hot dog joints do this, too, but most of them don't take you to the 1930s, '40s or '50s -- they take you back to the concession stand of a little league ball field or waterslide park from the 1980s with their faded Bears posters, outdated Pepsi ads, old video games, and pinball machines. It's hard to tell if this is intentional or if they've just never gotten around to redecorating, but the effect is true.

The food at these places varies wildly, but Relish the Thought, a short walk from Wrigley Field, has never, ever let me down. The hot dogs and fries are great, the service and conversation are friendly, and the pinball is totally awesome.

THE WIENER CIRCLE
2622 N. CLARK

There are a few places in the city, such as Ed Debevik's and its noisier, less cheerful neighbor, Dick's Last Resort, where the somewhat sarcastic staff is all part of the show. But nothing can really prepare you for The Wiener Circle after dark.

At no time is the Wiener Circle a place for the faint of heart; the portions are so huge that carrying a hot dog, a drink and fries is a three-hand job, and places to sit down are at a real premium. The dogs, topped with thicker-than-average tomato slices and TWO pickle spears, are massive, and liable to fall apart in your hands. The fries come in a pile the size of your head, and are excellent.

But it's a brave soul who ventures into this all-night joint after dark, when the drunks from the nearby bars come in to get harassed. The staff shouts any insult or swear word at you that comes into their heads, without a single hint that it's all part of an act. On a good night, the swearing gets remarkably creative, and the obscene staff usually runs circles around the obscene drunks, at least verbally. It's an experience like no other!

SUPERDAWG
6363 N. MILWAUKEE

In addition to hot dog places that take you back to the 1980s, there is one that will bring you cheerfully into the 1950s: Superdawg, the northwest-side drive-in that doesn't appear to have changed since 1955. Drive up and feel like you're on your way to a drag race.

The hot dogs are good, and they pair well with the fries and the milk shakes, but the place is probably best known for its style. The Big Weenies atop the Superdawg Drive-in are definitely Chicago's best-known roadside food attractions. The uninitiated, however, are often a bit surprised traveling along Milwaukee Avenue when they look over and see two giant wieners perched on top of a drive-in restaurant. They will soon shake off the surprise, though, especially if they are curious enough to stop and sample some of the establishment's offerings. Superdawg has been owned by Maurie Berman since 1948 and it's one of Illinois' last great drive-ins. Just like the old days, you never even need to leave your car to eat since you place your order through the call boxes and the car hops deliver your food.

And as they say, the burgers here are great but the weenies are enormous! The two trademark figures of Superdawg are best appreciated after dark, when their eyes glow a bright red that is a bit unsettling, but during the daylight hours one can get a full view of them. The Tarzan Weenie is clad in a leopard skin and strikes a muscleman pose that is obviously meant to impress his topless Jane Weenie companion, who looks on adoringly in her mini-skirt.

If these eccentric figures aren't enough to convince you to stop here for a dog and an order of fries, then nothing would be!

GETTING A CHICAGO HOT DOG?

If you find yourself in a downtown hot dog place, it's best to be a bit skeptical. See if anyone else orders a Chicago-style dog, and see if what he gets looks right. If the dog isn't in a poppy seed bun, you should probably get something else. If the place advertises gyros more than hot dogs, get the gyros. Another safe bet at these places is another Chicago street-food confection: the pizza puff. The pizza puff is similar to frozen pizza rolls, except that some guy with a real bone to pick with America's arteries said, "I know! Instead of ten little ones, let's just make one big one!" Order one, and scowl at the owner of the place for not doing Chicago hot dogs properly.

CHICAGO'S BRITISH PUB

While most visitors to Chicago would never believe it, there just happens to be an authentic British pub located on the North Side, just across North Lincoln Avenue from the famed Biograph Theater. For many years, it had a reputation for being one of the most "spirited" dining and drinking establishments in the city.

The Red Lion Pub opened in 1984 in a two-story building that dated back to 1882. Over the years, it reportedly saw many uses, including a grocery store, apartments, a country and western bar called "Dirty Dan's," and an illegal gambling parlor.

John Cordwell bought the building in the middle 1980s with plans to refurbish it into a pub. Cordwell passed away before the remodeling could be completed, but the project was finished by his son, Colin, and

The Red Lion Pub on North Lincoln Avenue

his son-in-law, Joe Heinen. The place soon opened for business and began serving what most consider some of the most authentic pub fare in the city.

The ghost stories of the place are an integral part of the business and date back to long before John Cordwell purchased the property. Former residents of the apartments on the top floor told stories about the proprietor of Dirty Dan's, the bar that once occupied the space, and how he often talked to what he called his "invisible friends" in the building.

During the renovations to turn the place into the Red Lion, workers often found their tools missing, or scattered about. There was never any indication of anyone being in the building during their absence but these strange events continued throughout the renovations and continue to occur in other ways today.

Customers in the pub experienced the strange manifestations as soon as the place opened for business. One of the happenings most often noticed were heavy footsteps that trudged across the upper floor, moving from west to east. Customers and staff members often heard the sound, even though everyone present was aware that no one is upstairs. When anyone went to check on the sounds, they found the second floor abandoned. The phantom footsteps were most active during the cold weather months, but they occurred at other times of the year, as well. The footsteps were sometimes joined by what sounded like tables and chairs being overturned in the small bar area on the second floor. Alarmed, staff members often ran upstairs to see what was going on only to find the second floor empty and quiet and the chairs and tables untouched.

One night, Colin Cordwell, and several others on the first floor heard a terrific crash from upstairs. Colin put down what he was doing and dashed up the stairs to see what was going on. However, the second floor was darkened and silent. As he searched the room, though, he discovered a cricket bat lying on the floor. It had somehow been thrown from where it had been hanging on the wall to a location about 20 feet away. There was no explanation for how this could have happened.

Who the ghosts are in this building is unknown for certain, but there suspects. There were a couple confirmed deaths in the building, including those of an elderly couple who once lived in one of the second floor apartments. Years earlier, their daughter had also died in the building. Her name was reportedly "Sharon" and, according to the remembrances of those who lived in the neighborhood for years, she was mentally disabled. They remembered her often sitting on the front stoop of the building, chatting with passersby. How Sharon died is a mystery, but many believe that she haunts the building today and manifests herself through the strong, sweet smell of lavender perfume. The scent has been encountered all over the pub, although mainly on the second floor.

Another manifestation that might have also been attributed to Sharon was an icy cold spot that appeared in the small bar area upstairs. There were no air ducts nearby and the cold spot came and went without warning. According to legend, the spot marked the location of Sharon's bedroom before the upper floor was remodeled.

Although it was a rare occasion, ghosts were sometimes seen in the pub. Reports from customers and employees told of a blond-haired man who mysterious vanished, a bearded man in a black hat, and a man in cowboy clothing, who might have been the specter of "Dirty Dan" himself. Dan Danforth was a reputed troublemaker who cursed the day that he was evicted from the building. Before his death, John Cordwell believed that he encountered this nasty spirit. As he was going up the stairs one day, he felt a hard push on his chest, which knocked him back down the steps. Since this was so out of character with the rest of the hauntings in the place, Cordwell was convinced that it was the hard-drinking Danforth who was looking to carry out on his threats of revenge. Since that time, no other events that have reportedly occurred at the Red Lion have been particularly threatening or dangerous.

If you get the chance, stop in some time for an order of fish and chips, some Irish stew, or perhaps just a cold glass of beer. The spirits in your glass may not be the only spirits that you find at the Red Lion!

THE OLE ST. ANDREW'S INN

Although it's known today as the Ole St. Andrew's Inn, this Scottish -themed pub first gained notoriety as the "Edinburgh Castle Pub." The place has operated as a Scottish bar since 1961, but before that, the place was simply a neighborhood bar owned by a colorful character named Frank Giff. Frank had a taste for playing pool, joking and chatting with the customers and for vodka (although not necessarily in that order.) He loved to sample the wares of the tavern and dipped into the stock every evening, drinking with the customers until he would become even more loaded than they were. Sadly, one night in 1959, Frank drank himself to death. The lovable prankster was found slumped onto the floor behind the bar one morning by his wife. Frank Giff had died -- but his spirit never left his beloved bar!

Frank's wife, Edna, operated Giff's for a time but it was never the same without Frank and she eventually put the bar up for sale. In 1961, it was purchased by Jane McDougall, a native of Glasgow, Scotland, who converted the bar into a Scottish pub. McDougall brought in tartan carpet, Scottish memorabilia, a line of ales and whiskeys from the old country, and dubbed the place the Edinburgh Castle Pub. But even with all of the changes, one thing about the place remained the same -- Frank Giff!

As time passed, Jane began to notice large quantities of vodka were disappearing from the stock. As first, she suspected that the bartenders were stealing from her and thinking that she would catch them in the act, she started covertly marking the level in the bottles with a wax pencil. She was shocked to find that the levels were still dropping and even more shocked when she realized that this was occurring at night, when the bar was empty and no one was in the building! She was not a believer in ghosts, but this weird happening was quickly starting to convince her that the pub was haunted. And she began to believe that it was haunted by a man she knew -- Frank Giff -- for she recalled his tragic death and his love for vodka.

The Ole St. Andrews Inn -- home to Chicago's girl-watching ghost

Soon, other events began to lead her to believe that she was right. Glasses started flying across the room and mysteriously breaking. Several times, the glasses were actually taped down to the rack where they hung above the bar. These glasses were hurled with such force that their bases were snapped off and left in place, while the rest of the glass was tossed away. At other times, drinks were disappearing almost in front of startled customers. The drinks, which had been left unattended, would suddenly be drained dry. Ashtrays slid down the bar without assistance. Cash registers and other electronic devices would often stop working, or at least behave erratically, when they were first brought into the bar. Later, they would be left alone -- as if Frank had gotten used to them being there.

The pub was remodeled a number of times after 1961 and each time, Frank seemed to make his objections to the changes widely known. Perhaps the most actively haunted spot in the bar was right around the area where Frank died. As things have been changed around quite a bit since Frank's day, the spot can now be found in the dining area of the pub. There is a booth that marks the location and many people who have eaten there complain of a shifting cold spot that sometimes occurs, as well as a numbness that seems to spread through their legs and feet.

Sometimes, attractive young women who sit in this area (or who just generally visit the bar) encounter the "friendly" spirit of the place. Some of these ladies have reported feeling a cold hand that grabs hold of their shoulder, knee or even a more sensitive part of the anatomy. They describe it as being like fingers that lightly grasp or brush against their skin or clothing, as if they are being gently caressed. The majority of the women who have reported this sensation have been blonds or redheads. Jane McDougall believed that Frank might be mistaking these women for his wife, Edna, who was a strawberry blond.

The haunting has continued here over the years, despite the changes in ownership and the name of the place. Jane McDougall retired from the bar business and died in 1996 but Frank still remains -- greeting customers from the other side. In his time and place, perhaps little has changed here at all or perhaps the afterlife offers an endless party for Frank and his spectral drinking buddies. So, if you make it down to the Ole St. Andrew's Inn one evening, be sure to lift a glass in honor of Frank Giff. And have one for us, too!

THE BUCKTOWN PUB

One of the most unique bars in Chicago is the Bucktown Pub, an eclectic neighborhood place that is not only a nice place to come for a drink, but a pop art museum, as well. The décor includes original poster art, both musical and political, from the 1960s and 1970s, autographed photos of celebrities and rare pieces of underground comic book art that you'll find nowhere else.

Today's trendy Bucktown neighborhood has changed much since the early days of Chicago. There are a couple of different versions as to how the region gained its name, but most believe that it was coined in the 1830s. Many of the Polish settlers who lived here raised goats (the male is called a buck) and the number of animals in the vicinity inspired the name. The area known as Bucktown is bounded roughly by Fullerton on the north, on the east by the Kennedy Expressway, the Milwaukee Road railroad tracks on the south, and on the west by Milwaukee Avenue to Western, and Western north to Fullerton.

Bucktown's history predates that of the city of Chicago. One of the earliest settlements outside of Fort Dearborn was located here. Many Polish immigrants fled their war-torn homeland in 1831 and migrated to America, some to Chicago. They settled in an area that later came to be known as Holstein. It was ideally situated near the river and not far from Fort Dearborn, which was easily accessible by an Indian trail that later became Milwaukee Avenue.

By the 1840s, the area had its own post office and hotel, the Powell House, at Milwaukee and Armitage. The fact that Milwaukee Avenue, then the Northwestern Plank Road, ran in front of the Powell House was no accident. Mr. Powell, after erecting a flagpole in front of the hotel, announced to the road-building crew that if they aimed in the direction of the pole, he would provide whiskey for the entire group of workers. Both parties upheld their respective ends of the bargain.

The Bucktown Pub has been located on a corner along Cortland Street for many years and there have been records of a bar operating there since 1933. Prior to this, most believe the location was a speakeasy during Prohibition. Before the current owner, the Pub was owned by a cantankerous old man named Wally. He was described as being opinionated and loud and would sit on a bar stool and direct the operations of the bar, bellowing orders at his employees as they hustled to keep up with the customers and his shouts. Wally and his wife, Annie, lived in an apartment above the barroom and it was there that Wally committed suicide one day in 1986. In a second floor bedroom, over the bar, he placed a gun to his head and pulled the trigger. After that, the place stood empty for a few years until 1991, when it was purchased by Krystine Palmer. She transformed the plub into its current incarnation and it continues to operate today as one of the coolest places to stop in Bucktown.

It's also said to be one of the most haunted.

Most believe the ghost that haunts this place is Wally, the disapproving former owner. Strange events began to occur in the place almost as soon as it opened. The morning after it became the new Bucktown Pub, bottles were found to be rearranged, as if Wally wanted them to be put back the way they were when he owned the place. Similar things began to occur during the nights that followed when napkins, coasters, and glasses began to move about without assistance. Bottles were found in different positions each morning. Occasionally, customers and staff members would catch a glimpse of a person on a nearby bar stool, but when they turned their heads to look closer, the person would always be gone. At other times, the jukebox would behave strangely and songs would be rejected for no reason - except for the fact that maybe Wally didn't like them? The entire jukebox often shut off or would suddenly come to life, even though no one had been near it.

The bartenders and the staff members seemed to be the main targets of the ghostly activity. One new employee who came to work at the Bucktown Pub several years ago was a complete skeptic when it came to ghosts. Not only did she state loudly that she did not believe the place was haunted, but she even went so far as to dare Wally (as if he really existed, she laughed) to do something to prove that he was there. Wally was quick to oblige. There came a loud noise from above the bar and a beer statuette vaulted off its shelf and came crashing down, narrowly missing the young woman's head. He certainly got her attention and she never talked critically about Wally again.

LOTTIE'S PUB

Most people in the Bucktown neighborhood are told that Lottie's, located at 1925 West Cortland, was a speakeasy when it first opened. This isn't quite true; by the time it opened in 1934, Prohibition was over. But drinking was the least of what went on in the place.

The original Lottie, Lottie Zagorski, was a real Chicago character. She opened the place as a grocery store named Zagorski's in the 1930s, and gradually expanded it into a bar. A hermaphrodite (meaning that she had both male and female sex organs), Zagorski served as both the bouncer for the bar and the madam for the prostitution ring that was run in the basement, which was also the main spot for gambling in the neighborhood at the time. She was eventually trusted by both the underworld and public officials, making Lottie's an ideal place for making pay-offs. However, she was best known around the neighborhood for driving around and randomly passing out dollar bills to children.

By the 1960s, the bar, then known as Lottie's Rathskellar, was a part of the vast Northwest side gambling ring run by Andy The Greek. Lottie was first arrested in 1966 when gambling gear was found in her purse. She was rounded up again the following year with dozens of others in a massive sting on city gambling operations. She died in 1973 of natural causes.

There is some indication that even the gambling and prostitution were not the worst of what went on in Lottie's basement. In 2004, workers renovating the basement found a handful of bones, one of which appeared to be a human femur. The city ruled the bones were "most likely animal bones," an explanation that satisfied practically no one. Could the bones have been those of a murder victim from years before?

GHOST ALERT!

Some believe that the bones found buried in Lottie's basement belonged to a murder victim whose ghost still haunts the bar today. Many strange happenings have been reported there over the years, from doors opening and closing to lights turning on and off to things moving about without explanation. The discovery of the bones seemed to provide an explanation for the weird events that had been occurring for the last few decades.

GHOSTS OF THE LIAR'S CLUB

The Liar's Club is one of the most interesting stops on our Weird Chicago Tour. We were first contacted by Herb Rosen, the owner of the bar located at 1665 Fullerton Ave. in Chicago around October of 2005. The bar has a plain look about it from the outside; in fact when driving past, most people think it's a social club and not a bar at all. Inside, it has an older, darker swinger's lounge feel to both floors of the bar. Then you get to see Herb's two favorite things: the place seems to be a mecca for Shriners (a fez appears everywhere there should be a lamp shade) and there is paraphernalia from the band KISS scattered throughout the bar. The upper level has walls that look like giant Legos. A fireplace, pool table, two pinball machines and a giant Shriner's fez dominates the center.

Herb is not only the owner of the bar, he is also a Chicago bar scene icon and the lead singer of a punk band called the Beer Nuts. He is also known to tell a tall tale now and again, so when he named his bar the Liar's Club it seemed appropriate. Because of this reputation I tended to have some doubts about actual hauntings when he approached us to do a ghost investigation. We gave him the benefit of the doubt, though, and started doing our background research.

We started our interview with Herb, who let us know that he did not believe in ghosts, but had experienced a number of strange occurrences in the club involving electrical malfunctions, severe temperature changes, and a little poltergeist activity. He said that the oddities "freaked him out a bit" when he was alone during the day there, but they were explainable. He passed along tales of a pair of dancing specters on the main dance floor and a ghostly torso of an old man on the second floor of the bar near the pinball machines. We interviewed 17 people about the hauntings at the bar and many attributed the spectral activity to an axe murder that happened there in the 1950s. When we asked Herb about the murder, he was unsure of the details but that was more than enough to get us interested in an investigation.

We started our research by looking for newspaper files that had the address of the building mentioned in them and we found one right away. It was a story about a murder, but not an axe murder -- it was a soda bottle murder. In 1968, the building was being used as a homeless shelter. Two men, John Parlea, 70, and Samuel Castell, Jr., 27, got

The awesome giant fez on the second floor of the Liar's Club

into an argument over a pair of used pants. Castell was so enraged that Parlea would claim ownership of said smelly pants that he took a Coca-Cola bottle and beat the old man to death, then shoved him out of a second floor window. In most cases, when we do these investigations, that would be the end of it. Sometimes an alleged axe murder was actually a Coca Cola bottle murder that had been exaggerated through the years to "become" an axe murder. When we have a murder that occurs at a site where we are doing an investigation, we call upon a specialist (a former FBI agent) whom we know who has contacts with both the FBI and the local police. When we asked about the murder, we discovered there was not just one murder at the site of the future Liar's Club, there were four! And two of those murders were committed with an axe.

The first murder was a fatal shooting after a heated and drunken argument between two men outside the address when it was an apartment. The second murder inside the building occurred in 1958 when it was one of the first lesbian bars in Chicago. The owner was a man who was physically, emotionally and sexually abusive to his wife. She got fed up and took an axe and hit him in the head with it 17 times. This happened in the same corner of the second floor where the next three murders also occurred.

The previously described Coca-Cola bottle murder of 1968 was the third of the four murders.

The last slaying was another axe murder. Frank Hansen, 29, was the tavern owner. His wife Julia, 24 was the aggressor. She was a large woman who had a short, skinny husband. She called him names and abused him emotionally and generally made fun of the little guy. He took it for years and then one crisp, April morning in 1986, he picked up an axe and dismembered her in the northeast corner of the second floor.

If all of this wasn't weird enough, the place that was to be the Liar's Club was also the studio and apartment of Joe Walsh of The Eagles for five years.

Today the place is still a mecca for celebs in the movie and music industry looking to get away and have a drink (or many) without being bothered. It's not uncommon to see some of the hottest celebrities around having a drink, playing pinball -- or even throwing up on the sidewalk outside. The Liar's Club is a great place for scenesters, punk rockers, and weirdoes like us. If you have a chance stop in, sample the libations and listen to the great music they spin there... and watch out for the ghosts!

KEN SAYS:
I'm often asked what scares me the most on my tours. My response almost every time is taxes and/or student loans. The man who gets me through these frightening times is the best bartender in the known universe and front man for punk band the Beer Nuts, Mike O'Connell. Stop in at the Liar's Club, the Holiday or any other libation station where he might be bartending for a fast drink just the way you like it, a keen ear and good times.

EXCALIBUR

One of the most haunted clubs in downtown Chicago is the Excalibur. Built in 1892 as the home of the Chicago Historical Society, the building now houses the popular nightspot and it has seen more than its share of history, and some would say hauntings, over the years. The building was designed by the famous architect Henry Ives Cobb for the historical society, which occupied it until 1931.

After the Historical Society moved to its new location near Lincoln Park, the castle-like structure saw a number of occupants, including the Loyal Order of the Moose, the prestigious Institute of Design, recording studios for blues performers in the 1950s and 1960s, the WPA, the Illinois Institute of Technology, and even swanky Gallery magazine. Most recently, though, it has been used as a nightclub. The place began operating as the Limelight in 1985, but the name was changed to the Excalibur after new owners purchased the building in 1989.

Shortly after the Limelight opened, it started to be widely reported that the place was haunted. At first, they were just little events that were experienced by the staff after hours but soon customers began to notice odd things, too. Items often fell over under their own power, or moved about, glasses shattered or rolled off tables and onto the floor. Tom Doody was the special events and public events coordinator for the club for several years and he quickly came to believe that the building was infested with ghosts. He witnessed much of the reported poltergeist phenomena for himself, as well as many of the mysterious late night happenings. One of the most active spots that Doody recalled was the VIP lounge, where there were several pool tables. One evening, a pool table had been set up and was left racked and ready to play on. Then suddenly, the balls began rolling all over the table, as if someone had just broken -- even though no one was in the room.

The Excalibur nightclub was once the building used by the Chicago Historical Society. Despite rumors (& outright lies) the building was never used as a morgue during the Eastland Disaster. So, why is it so haunted?

Sometimes during the early morning hours, after all of the customers were gone, staff members who were closing the place down would hear their names being called. When they would search to see where the voices were coming from, they would find no one. They also told of hearing what appeared to be large crates or boxes being dragged around in a downstairs storage room, but when the room was opened, nothing was found disturbed. The room only had one way in or out and the sounds were often heard when the door was in full view of the employees outside.

The Limelight closed down in 1989 and the new owners opened the Excalibur in its place. They spent several million dollars to renovate and update the building, adding nearly 17,000 square feet to its design. The name of the club obviously came from King Arthur's magical blade, but the owners also opened an offshoot from the rest of the club called "Aura" in the historical society's former lecture hall. This area is often called the "Dome Room" because of the lofty ceiling dome here. Inside the dome is a breathtaking mural of the mythical god Zeus, angrily glaring down at the customers below him. If that's not unsettling enough - there are also the ghosts!

There have been many strange happenings in the Dome Room over the years and many legends have been associated with this part of the building, including that a number of the bodies that went down with the Eastland steamship were brought to the historical society when it served as a temporary morgue. There is absolutely no truth to this story, although several victims were taken to a funeral parlor that was located next door.

No matter who the ghosts are, though, they remain very active at the club. Staff members have complained that even though motion detectors and alarms systems have been left on in the building at night, beer glasses are still found scattered about, bottles are opened, and alcohol is missing. There have also been sightings of apparitions, including a small girl, a glowing blue figure who was seen floating up the stairs on two occasions, and a man in a tuxedo standing behind a bar. Cold spots have been reported in the upstairs women's restroom, which has also been plagued by the sound of crying and water faucets that turn on and off. On several occasions, women have found themselves locked in the bathroom and are unable to get out. They swear that the door is being held shut on the other side - even though staff members can clearly see that no pranksters are around.

The building that holds Excalibur remains a fascinating place, no matter what business is located there, and it's obvious that the ghosts are engrained in the history of the place. While music and dance are the primary functions of the building today, ghost hunters who come here are usually not disappointed.

ADAM SAYS:
The task involved with separating myth from reality regarding the history of the building (namely that it was a temporary morgue for the Eastland disaster) has made it a very frustrating location for ghost hunters today. Some have given up on it altogether, but more and more stories keep coming from the staff.

TALES OF THE TONIC ROOM

Nothing about the swanky decor of The Tonic Room in Lincoln Park, located at 2447 North Halsted St,, makes it look haunted (or even weird) today -- unless you go into the basement.

The staff knew when they moved in that the place had formerly been the site of an occult supply shop in the 1970s known as El Sabarum. What they didn't realize was that former owner Frederic de Arechaga, was also known by the name of Ordun, and was the leader of a group known as the Sabeans. The Sabeans practiced a religion that was a blend of ancient Egyptian religion and modern occult practices based, in part, on the teachings of Aleister Crowley. Weird enough for you?

When the Tonic Room took over, the basement was full of Egyptian hieroglyphs and stars of Babylon. In the summer of 2007, during renovations, a rusty, skull-headed dagger was found buried upright in the ground beneath the basement. However, these occult remnants may or may not have anything to do with the ghosts reported on the site. Staff members have witnessed a good deal of poltergeist activity, and several people have seen the apparition of a man who appears to be from the 1930s.

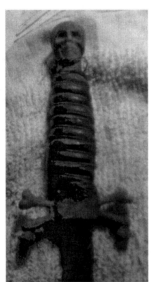

The dagger found buried in the Tonic Room's Basement

According to the owner, the man has been seen walking up and down the stairs from the basement and seems oblivious to the fact that anyone else is around. If you visit the Tonic Room some evening and hear someone knocking on the door of your bathroom stall, don't worry. It's likely not someone trying to come inside with you, it's probably just one of the prank-playing specters. They also like to steal drinks and, in one case, tie people's shoelaces together while they are enjoying a drink.

HAUNTINGS AT FADO

Walking down lower North Clark Street today, there are only a few reminders of the old days. These days, lower North Clark is a bastion of nice restaurants that cater mainly to tourists. But, in the midst of it, one still comes upon the odd adult book store and dive bar -- a lasting reminder that "Clark Street" was synonymous with squalor not too long ago. In fact, lower North Clark has always bounced back and forth between respectability and a distinct lack thereof. Nowhere is this more evident than at the corner of Clark and Grand, which has been the home of grand hotels, scummy rooming houses, The College of Complexes, and countless cabarets and strip clubs -- often at the same time! On the northwest corner sits an 1876 Italianate building, currently the home of Fado, an Irish pub featuring furnishings that have been painstakingly imported from several venerable pubs around Ireland. But the decor isn't the only part of the building that serves as a reminder of the old days -- there are ghosts there, too.

Several staff members have reported seeing the ghost of a woman in a nightgown. She is described as being fairly young, but dressed and made up in such a way as to make witnesses assume that she comes from the late 19th or early 20th century. Especially active around the holidays, she is sometimes blamed for the many electrical disturbances, cold spots, slamming doors, and the sensation of a hand on employees' shoulders. When Fado first purchased the building, the burglar alarm would go off nightly, indicating that someone had broken into the office on the third floor. No such intruder was ever found, and for someone to break into the office without setting off any of the other alarms along the way would have been impossible.

The woman in the nightgown may not be responsible for all of the ghostly activity in the building, though; other ghosts have been seen as well, including the ghosts of two men in suits on the first floor. These men, according to witnesses, appear to come from the 1950s.

So, who could these ghosts be? Attempts to identify them have been frustrating, mostly because several previous owners quite purposely covered up the tracks of the building's history.

The building was first constructed in 1876, and has served many purposes over the years. It has been a shoe store, the St. Lawrence Hotel, and several restaurants, saloons, cabarets and strip clubs at various times in its more than 130-year history. Finding actual data on them is rather frustrating, as the owners seem to have been often confused about what number to use as an address. Prior to 1909, it would have been 105 North Clark, on the corner of Clark and Indiana streets. Since the change of Indiana Street east of the river to Grand Avenue, and the 1909 renumbering, the address has been listed in a number of different ways. When the law firm of Conklin and Adler moved into the building, they began to use the side street as the main entrance, and the listing became 100 W. Grand, which Fado still uses today.

Several strange things have happened that may have led to hauntings in the building. In 1953, a waitress working (and possibly living) in the building set a couple of fires there to impress her boyfriend. Apparently, she intended to save his life from the fire she had set herself! She was sentenced to three to ten years in prison, and then escaped after three years. The footsteps found in the mud leading from the prison to the highway are the last traces she appeared to have left behind!

Perhaps the most notorious use of the building came a few years later, when it became the site of the Shore Club, a strip club owned by Mike Glitta, who was described by the police as a crime syndicate hoodlum and the number two man in the Chicago numbers racket. The strip club, it was said, was a front for a syndicate-owned prostitution ring. Mayor Daley himself revoked the club's liquor license in 1959. Shortly thereafter, the place was described as "a strip club where they don't take their clothes off anymore" by Slim Brundage, who ran the College of Complexes across the corner. It's easy enough to imagine that there was murder and suicide in the building at the time, and that the tracks would have been completely erased. The apparitions of the two men in suits may date to this period.

Tracing the woman in the nightgown has proven even more difficult, as covering up traces of crime and death in the building goes back a long time. In 1898, during a meeting of Clark Street businessmen to discuss the decline of Clark Street, it was mentioned that there had recently been a murder and suicide that was so well hushed up that few of the neighbors had even heard about it. Apparently, late one night, a "jealous railroad brakeman" had "a few beers" (blaming all crimes on "a few beers" was a sort of running joke in the area at the time) and used a revolver to murder a woman in a rear apartment before turning the gun on himself. This rear apartment would have probably been on the third floor, where the ghostly woman in a nightgown is most frequently reported. Given the lateness of the hour, it's certainly not unreasonable to assume that the murdered woman would have been wearing a nightgown.

However, the story was told only in passing, as evidence of how crime was commonplace in the area at the time. Who knows what else may have happened that never made the papers at all? At the same meeting, it was mentioned that at around the same time, two female saloonkeepers had fought in the street, and one, Tillie Wolf, was stabbed through the skull with a sharpened umbrella.

Clark Street began to turn itself around in the early 1980s. Today, the sheer notion of a woman being stabbed in the brain with an umbrella in that area is practically unthinkable. A few reminders still stand: the upscale Clark Street Ale House still displays the neon sign from a previous saloon, the elegantly named Stop and Drink. And, if reports from Fado are accurate, a few ghosts remain, as well!

THE GREEN MILL

In a city where almost every remnant of the gangland wars of the 1920s has been erased, there is one reminder of the days of Al Capone that is still in operation: the legendary jazz club known as the Green Mill on North Broadway. As the city's oldest nightclub, it's been offering continuous entertainment since 1907 and remains today as an authentic link to not only Al Capone but to the club's former manager, and Capone henchman, "Machine Gun" Jack McGurn.

The Green Mill opened in 1907 as Pop Morse's Roadhouse and from the very beginning, was a favorite hangout for show business people in Chicago. In those days, actors from the North Side's Essanay Studios made the roadhouse a second home. One of the most popular stars to frequent the place was "Bronco Billy" Anderson, the star of dozens of silent Westerns from Essanay. Anderson often rode his horse to Pop Morse's and the proprietor even installed a hitching post that Anderson's horse shared with those of other stars like Wallace Beery and William S. Hart. Back then, even screen greats like Charlie Chaplin stopped in occasionally for a drink.

Around 1910, the Chamales Brothers purchased the club from the original owners. They installed a huge, green windmill on the roof and re-named the place the Green Mill Gardens. The choice of the name "Green Mill" was inspired by the infamous Moulin Rouge in Paris (Moulin Rouge is French for "Red Mill") but green was chosen so that it would not be confused with any of the red light districts in Chicago. The new owners added outdoor dancing and live entertainment in the enlarged sunken gardens and also added a rhumba room next door. The Green Mill Gardens was more of a roadhouse that spanned an entire block than a cocktail lounge in those days. Tom Chamales later went on to construct the Riviera Theater, around the corner from the Green Mill. He and his brother leased the Green Mill to Henry Van Horne and it soon began to attract the best --- and worst --- of the late-night denizens of Chicago.

By the time that Prohibition arrived, the Green Mill had become known as the most jumping spot on the North Side. Jazz fans flocked to the club to savor this new and evolving musical art form, which had been born in the south but had been re-created in Chicago after World War I. The jazz crowd ignored the laws against alcohol and hid their bootleg whiskey away in hip flasks, which they eagerly sipped at the Green Mill. The club helped to launch the careers of singers who went on to become legends like Helen Morgan, Anita O'Day, and Billie Holliday. It also offered an endless procession of swinging jazz combos and vaudevillians who dropped in to jam or just to relax between sets at other, lesser clubs.

Vintage postcard of the Green Mill Gardens

In the middle 1920s, Van Horne gave up his interest in the place and the Chamales Brothers leased the club to Al Capone's South Side mob. Capone himself, although straying into the enemy's territory on the North Side, often enjoyed hanging out at the club, listening to the music and drinking with friends. His favorite booth, which offered a clear view of both the front and side doors, is still our favorite place to sit when visiting the club. Capone also had a trap door installed behind the bar that offered access to tunnels under the building (which still exist today), in case the place was raided by the police or attacked by rival gangsters.

At the Green Mill, though, it's not the remnants of Al Capone that attracts crime buffs, it's the legend of Jack McGurn, who managed the club for Capone in the 1920s.

James Vincenzo De Mora, or Jack McGurn as he later became known, was born in Chicago's Little Italy in 1904. He grew up as a clean-cut kid from the slums who excelled in school and was an excellent boxer. A fight promoter managed to get him into the ranks of professional fighters and at the man's suggestion James adopted the ring name of "Jack McGurn." He seemed to have a great career ahead, until his father, Angelo De Mora, a grocer with a store on Halsted Street, ran into trouble with the terrible Genna brothers and McGurn stepped over the line into the world of crime.

At the start of Prohibition, the Gennas had transformed all of Little Italy into a vast commercial area of alcohol cookers. Stills were set up in almost every home, franchised by the Gennas, making homemade rotgut whiskey that was popular in neighborhood speakeasies. Angelo De Mora sold sugar to the Gennas for their operations, a relatively safe enterprise until some competitors for the position appeared on January 8, 1923 and Angelo was found shot to death in front of his store.

McGurn rushed home when he heard about his father's death. He was only 19 but he immediately took the role of head of the household, shielding his mother and five brothers from the police. When a police officer asked him if he was afraid for his life now that he was the man of the house, McGurn ominously answered, "No. I'm big enough to take care of this case myself."

McGurn never got back into the ring. He picked up a gun and started working for Al Capone, who regarded him as his most trustworthy gunman and the man to carry out the most dangerous and grisly assignments. Within a few years, "Machine Gun" Jack McGurn was the most feared of Capone's killers.

McGurn relished his work, especially when six of his targets were part of the Genna mob, which he believed were responsible for his father' death. In just over a month's time, he wiped out the Gennas' top men. He learned that one of these men had referred to his father as a "nickel and dimer." So, after each of them had been machine-gunned to death, McGurn pressed a nickel into each of their palms, his sign of contempt and a trademark that would be forever linked to his murders.

Jack McGurn and his regular squeeze & favorite alibi, Louise Rolfe

McGurn continued to earn his pay --- and his reputation. Joe Aiello's feud with Capone over West Side beer territories reached its peak when Aiello offered a $50,000 reward for Capone's murder. He imported four out-of-town killers to do the job when no one in Chicago took him up on his offer. Days after their arrival, the four men met with the wrath of Jack McGurn. All of them were found riddled with machine gun bullets --- and with nickels pressed into their palms.

When not working for Capone, McGurn frequented Chicago's hottest jazz spots and managed to become part owner of several of them through intimidation and violence. By the time he was 23, McGurn owned pieces of at least five nightclubs and managed a number of other lucrative properties. He also managed the Green Mill for Capone and was later given 25 percent of its ownership in exchange for his loyalty. This became his usual hangout and he could often be found sipping liquor in one of the green-plush upholstered booths.

McGurn was fiercely loyal to the Green Mill and so, in 1927, became enraged when the club's star attraction, singer and comedian Joe E. Lewis, refused to renew his contract, stating that he was going to work for a rival club. Lewis opened to a packed house at the New Rendezvous the next night. Days later, McGurn took Lewis aside as he was about to enter his hotel, the New Commonwealth. McGurn had two friends with him and all three of them had their hands shoved in their pockets. McGurn told Lewis that they missed him at the club and that "the old Mill's a morgue without you."

Lewis assured him that he would find another headliner and when McGurn told him that he had made his point and needed to come back, Lewis refused. He bravely turned his back on the killer and walked away.

On November 27, three of McGurn's men stormed into Lewis' hotel suite, beat him and then cut his throat almost from ear to ear. The comedian survived the attack, managed to recover his singing voice and continued with his career. Capone, unhappy with McGurn's actions, but unable to rebuke one of his best men, was said to have advanced Lewis $10,000 so that the performer could get back on his feet.

WHERE IS IT NOW?

Both the North and South Side gangs went after "The Terrible Gennas." Tony Genna was shot outside of a grocery store on Grand Avenue. The building it was in still stands at the corner of Grand and Aberdeen (which was formerly called Curtis Street.) The surprisingly modest funeral was held at the De Cola funeral home, which is now a Mexican restaurant a couple of blocks west on the north side of Grand Avenue. Tony was the third Genna brother to be shot in a very short time frame. The remaining three brothers wisely left Chicago.

A short time later, McGurn's own career was almost cut short. Two machine gunners for George Moran, Pete and Frank Gusenberg (both killed during the St. Valentine's Day Massacre), caught up with McGurn in a phone booth inside the McCormick Inn. Several bursts from their Tommy guns almost finished McGurn for good but major surgery, and a long period of secluded convalescence, saved the killer.

In early February 1929, McGurn visited Capone at his Palm Island, Fla., home for a discussion about the North Side gang run by George Moran. Ten days later, the St. Valentine's Day Massacre took place. This hardly seems to be a coincidence!

CHICAGO TUNNELS

Television specials about The Lexington Hotel and the Green Mill never fail to mention the underground tunnels that were utilized by bootleggers during prohibition. Such tunnels are all over the city, and almost all of them, in the grand Chicago tradition, are said to have been used by Al Capone - but very few of them were. The tunnels weren't created by the bootleggers, who were rarely quite that industrious. Most often, they were built years before Prohibition for drainage, coal delivery and waste management. In mansions and hotels, the tunnels and passageways were usually built so servants - particularly black servants - could move about more or less invisibly. However, when Prohibition came around, some of the tunnels became awfully convenient to the bootleggers.

Most tunnels in the city, such as the one connecting the Congress Hotel to the Auditorium Theatre, are long-since bricked off, but many old buildings still have entrances to various networks of tunnels - the May Street Market on Grand and May, for instance, was once connected via tunnel to several other nearby buildings, and rumor has it that the tunnels originally went all the way to the Loop.

Perhaps the most extensive network of tunnels remaining in Chicago is that of the freight tunnels below the Loop. Construction of these six-feet-wide by seven-feet-high tunnels began in 1899, and, by the time they were abandoned in 1950, there were nearly 60 miles of them - all beneath the Loop! The tunnels were used for a variety of reasons - electric cable cars rolled around in them delivering mail, picking up waste, and managing coal delivery. Nearly every major building in the city had an entrance to them.

Today, almost all of these entrances have been bricked off for safety reasons- but the tunnels are still there, used primarily by electric companies who use them for cables. In 1992, a flood in the tunnels resulting from a worker driving a stake into them while working in the river caused the Loop to be shut down for days!

Though the freight tunnels are still there today, and said to be remarkably free of unpleasant things such as rats and debris, they are not open to the public, and obtaining permission to get into them is nearly impossible. No one we know has successfully cut through the red tape necessary to get inside legally!

McGurn has always been connected to the massacre, as has Fred R. "Killer" Burke. A teenager named George Brichet was walking past the garage when five men entered on February 14. Bricket overheard one of the men call another "Mac". Bricket picked out McGurn's photograph from police mug shots. Armed with an arrest warrant, police broke into McGurn's suite at the Stevens Hotel on February 27. As they hauled the gangster away, they were cussed out by McGurn's sweetheart, showgirl Louise Rolfe. The press dubbed her "the blonde alibi" and she swore that McGurn was with her at the time of the murders. McGurn was later indicted but he married Louise soon after and thanks to this, she was not required to testify against him.

McGurn's defense attorneys insisted four times that their client be brought to trial, so that he could prove his innocence, of course. Each time, the prosecution stated that it was not ready to proceed. Under Illinois law, the prosecution was only allowed four legal delays of this kind. After that, they had to drop the case. McGurn was set free on December 2, 1929.

McGurn's likely role in the St. Valentine's Day Massacre led to Capone putting him "on ice." He began to be seen less and less with the boss and was not seen at all during Capone's tax trial, when the job of bodyguard was given over to Phil D'Andrea.

Once Capone went to prison, McGurn's prestige started to slip. He busied himself with his nightclubs, most of which went under during the Depression and Louise left him when his money ran out. Alone and flat broke; McGurn met his end on February 13, 1936, the eve of the anniversary of the St. Valentine's Day Massacre.

McGurn was in the middle of his third frame at the Avenue Recreation Parlor, a bowling alley located at 805 North Milwaukee Ave., when remnants from the old Moran gang finally caught up with him. Five men burst into the bowling alley and while three of them pretended to rob the place, the other two machine-gunned McGurn to death on the hardwood lanes.

In his left hand, the killers placed a comic valentine, which read:

You've lost your job.
You've lost your dough,
Your jewels and handsome houses.
But things could be worse, you know.
You haven't lost your trousers.

In the palm of "Machine Gun" Jack McGurn's right hand, the killers placed a solitary nickel.

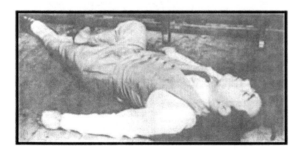

WHERE IS IT NOW?
The Avenue Recreation Parlor is now the site of an H&R block. The building has recently been totally renovated, but a couple of original walls are still visible on the outside

MARIE'S RIP TIDE LOUNGE

"Marie didn't come to Bucktown - Bucktown came to Marie"
Shecky's Bar, Club & Lounge Guide

Chicago is a city that, on occasions when you just don't want to pack it in and head for home at 2:00 a.m. on a Friday night, offers a myriad of options. There are a number of bars, some scary and some not so much, that have 4:00 a.m. liquor licenses, allowing patrons to drink until it's almost dawn. Out of all of these places, there are few as unique as Marie's Rip Ride Lounge, located at Armitage and Hermitage avenues. Sure, the décor may not have been updated since the 1960s and the jukebox may be stocked with creaky oldies, but there is just something about the place and its retro-cool feel that makes it unique. Is it the bar - or is it the owner and namesake of the place, Marie Wuczynski, who makes the Rip Tide Lounge a required stop when making the late-night rounds in Bucktown?

Marie has been holding court at the Rip Tide Lounge since the day the place opened for business in 1961 and not much has changed about the place since then. The diner-like interior, the aging décor, and even the electronic skeet shooting game have all been there since day one. When Marie bought the place, she planned to give it a Hawaiian theme (hence the name). She planned to buy flowered shirts, pass out leis, and serve drinks with umbrellas. But there ended up being nothing tropical about the bar so "I went Polish instead," Marie laughed.

In the early days, polka bands played several times a week for regulars from the neighborhood, but a beer cooler now occupies the spot there the stage once stood. Little Richard (the one known as Chicago's Polka King, not the one of "Good Golly Miss Molly" fame) used to perform regularly on that stage in the 1960s, sometimes even with Marie singing along. Today, the jukebox belts out tunes from Sinatra, Petula Clark, Englebert Humperdinck, Bobby Darin, Wayne Newton, Patsy Cline, and Elvis Presley, which just adds to the sometimes surreal nature of the bar.

Music is not the only entertainment at the Rip Tide Lounge, though. Marie has often entertained her customers by singing, telling bawdy jokes, and occasionally, doing magic tricks. Even without trying, though, Marie is entertaining just by being around. She gabs with the regulars until the wee hours of the morning and the place is so beloved by Chicago night owls that it's even inspired songs. A country-rock band called The Juleps dubbed Marie the "Mistress of Mixology" in a tune they wrote named for the bar and singer Michael McDermott titled an album "Last Chance Lounge" in honor of Marie's place. Marie said she was flattered by the attention, but she was really just doing a job that she loved.

Marie Wuczynski was born in 1922 and grew up in Chicago with her parents and four sisters. She believes that she inherited her strong work ethic from her father, a Polish immigrant who spoke little English. After two years of high school, Marie began working at a candy factory, at the Schwinn Bicycle Co., and later, in her uncle's bar on Division Street. She met her husband, Mike, soon after and Marie described him as several things that

THE MIDGET CLUB:
Definitely one of the most unusual bars in Chicago was the famous Midget Club, owned and operated by Parnell St. Aubin. The proprietor had a short career (ha!) in Hollywood playing a Munchkin soldier in the 1939 classic The Wizard of Oz. After the filming, he moved back to Chicago and opened a tavern on the southeast side. Since he only stood three feet, seven inches tall, he had to climb onto a barstool to reach the register but he never let this bother him.

One Christmas season, St. Aubin went downtown to see the toy display at Goldblatt's department store, which featured little people as Santa's elves. Among them was a young woman named Mary Ellen Bacon and the two of them fell in love. Mary Ellen had also had a show business career. Standing just one inch taller than her future husband, she had toured with vaudeville companies as a member of Rose's Royal Midgets.

The two of them married, moved the tavern to the southwest side and scaled down their operation to create the Midget Club, first at 6356 South Kedzie, then at 4016 W. 63rd St. The bar was an immediate hit and St. Aubin made the place work for him this time, installing a walkway behind the bar to lift him up so that he could comfortably serve the customers.

The Midget Club ran from 1948 to 1982, when Parnell retired. He died five years later and closed a unique chapter in Chicagoland history.

GHOST ALERT!
METAL SHACK, A.K.A. THE PEACOCK LOUNGE

In 1962, Andrew Zelek, owner of the Peacock Lounge, was closing the place up for the night when a knock came at the door. Apparently recognizing the callers, he let them in. Once inside, though, they shot him six times - three times in the chest, three times in the head. They then robbed the register, pouring booze over it in attempt to wash away the fingerprints.

The killers were never caught. A coroner could only rule that that the cause of death was murder.

The Peacock Lounge, at 3394 North Milwaukee, stayed in business for years, changed hands a couple of times, and recently became The Metal Shack. The owner and employees claimed to have felt the presence of - and even seen - the ghost of an unidentified man. A few people have even taken photographs that appear to show a vague human form, which they believe to be the ghost of Andrew Zelek.

GHOST ALERT!
COUNTRY HOUSE RESTAURANT

The Country House Restaurant in Clarendon Hills has become known for two things over the years - great burgers and ghosts! The haunting began in the late 1950s after a young woman was killed nearby in an auto accident. She had been a regular customer who was dating one of the bartenders, although their relationship was on the rocks. One afternoon, she showed up in the tavern visibly distraught and asked if she could leave her baby there and return for him later in the day. When the owner refused her request, she left the bar visibly upset. A short time later, news reached the tavern that she had driven her car into a telephone pole on 55th Street. It was thought that she had killed herself, along with the baby.

Since that time, her ghost has been seen looking out an upstairs window and the disembodied voice of a crying infant has been heard around table 13. This seems to be an especially active corner of the restaurant. In addition, electronic devices often behave erratically and things have been known to move around on their own.

If you are looking for a place where good food and ghostly chills go hand in hand, consider dropping in at the Country House Restaurant some evening. Whether you are a believer or not, it's unlikely that you'll go away disappointed!

she was not: tall, quiet, and serious. She always loved to make him laugh, she said.

Marie, who has three daughters, was a stay-at-home mother for years, but eventually, she went to work at the bar that pre-dated the Rip Tide Lounge. When it went up for sale in 1961, she bought the bar and transformed it into the place that it remains today. What Marie continues to love the most about the Rip Tide are the customers - from the college kids, the night owls, the weirdos, the musicians, bartenders, waitresses, and actors who stop in during the early morning hours on their way home from work. Over the years, Marie had entertained more than her share of celebrities, too, including Davy Jones and allegedly, John F. Kennedy. Bill Murray and John Belushi were regulars in the 1970s and Andy Richter showed off the Rip Tide Lounge on "Late Night with Conan O'Brien" in 1997.

Finding the Rip Tide Lounge is easy. It's at the corner of Armitage and Hermitage, almost under the Kennedy Expressway. There are no flashy lights to mark the place, however, just a black and white sign in retro script over a wall of stone slabs, with a quadrangular window set into it, at the base of a three-story, brick building. When you walk through the door, you step back in time and follow a worn rug that stretches down a narrow aisle between a row of padded booths and a long, linoleum-topped wooden bar. The bartenders here, whether it be Marie or one of the other long-time gals who work for her, dispense a selection of bottled beer and bags of chips amongst shelves of booze, coolers, and a back bar

Marie's Rip Tide Lounge -- Open 'til 4

filled with porcelain dolls, plates, an empty aquarium and appliances and fixtures from when Eisenhower was still in office.

If you get a chance, stop in around any of the major holidays because Marie and Shirley, her long-time manager, are well known for their decorations, especially around Christmas, when the place features its famous "snow-covered bar." But holidays or not, be sure to stop in at some point and experience this little bit of "real Chicago" while it's still around!

ONE LAST BITE ....THAT STEAK JOYNT

Of all of the haunted drinking and dining spots in Chicago, there was none so haunted as That Steak Joynt, which was formerly located at 1610 North Wells St. Before the restaurant was closed down, customers and staff members reported bizarre, supernatural experiences there for years. Owner Billy Siegel, who allowed dozens of séances and paranormal investigations to be held in the place, always believed that the haunting was the result of two unsolved murders that took place around the turn of the last century. Both of the victims were found in what was called Piper's Alley, an open corridor that passed just outside of the restaurant. Siegel speculated that the ghosts of these past crimes had somehow found their way into his establishment. Regardless of the identities of the ghosts, there was little question that while it was in operation, That Steak Joynt enjoyed a reputation for being one of the most haunted places in Chicago!

That Steak Joynt in the late 1980s
(Dale Kaczmarek)

In the late 1860s, the future location of That Steak Joynt, was Piper's Bakery. This large factory employed more than 500 workers and even housed a school for their children. It was one of the busiest bakeries in the region and shipped bread and baked goods all over the country. The Great Chicago Fire of 1871 should have brought all of that to an end but Henry Piper refused to give up. He rebuilt on the same site, making the new bakery even bigger and more magnificent than the original. He continued baking for 60 years before finally retiring and closing Piper's for good.

The building was never shuttered, though and was constantly in operation with a variety of businesses from a laundry to a hardware store and in 1962, it became That Steak Joynt. It soon gained a reputation for being haunted and in the 1980s, séances were regularly held at the restaurant. Managers reported that they had a difficult time getting employees to work at night, especially janitors and cleaning crews. No one wanted to be in the building after hours, thanks to reports of singing sounds and the numerous claims of apparitions that had been seen. On one occasion, a server was actually grabbed by the wrist and dragged to a flight of stairs by an unseen assailant. She quit working there soon after!

After That Steak Joynt closed, the building on North Wells remained empty for a number of years. It is currently open again as the Adobo Grill, serving upscale Mexican food. If there have been any strange happenings in the old bakery since it re-opened, we have not heard about them. Did the years of silence serve to quiet the haunting for good? No one knows, or at least no one is talking, so only the future will reveal if the spirits are still restless there.

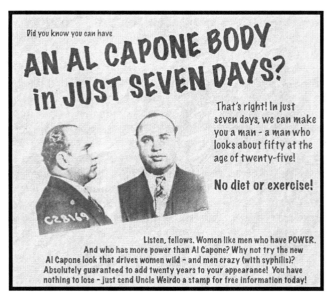

7. WEIRD CHICAGO CRIME & MURDER

You can get much further with a smile, a kind word and a gun than you can get with just a smile and a kind word.
Al Capone

I hope when my time comes, that I die decently in bed. I don't want to be murdered in beside the garbage cans in some Chicago alley.
George "Bugs" Moran

Chicago was a town where nobody could forget how the money was made. It was picked up from floors still slippery with blood.
Norman Mailer

GUNS, ROSES & VALENTINES
CHICAGO & THE BEER WARS OF THE 1920S

The rise of organized crime in Chicago really began with the start of Prohibition, the ill-fated law that made it illegal to buy, sell, or manufacture alcohol in America. Its decline began almost a decade later in February 1929. It was on St. Valentine's Day of that year that the general public no longer saw the mob as "public benefactors," offering alcohol to a thirsty city, but as the collection of killers and thugs that it truly was.

Of course, the St. Valentine's Day Massacre (along with the destruction of the North Side mob and the conviction of Al Capone for income tax evasion) was not the death knell for the mob in Chicago. Organized crime will always be with us but it was this bloody event that changed the face of crime in the city forever. In the years that followed, empires crumbled and lives were destroyed, bringing an end to the "glory days" of the mob in Chicago.

The story of organized crime in the Windy City begins with two of the most prominent criminals in pre-Prohibition Chicago, John Torrio and Big Jim Colosimo. Torrio was born in Orsara, Italy, and came to New York with his family two years later, in 1884. The family settled on the Lower East Side and while still in his early teens, Torrio led his own gang and gained a reputation for viciousness. More importantly, he gained a reputation for being intelligent and quick-thinking. He never carried a gun -- a fact that speaks volumes about him during a time when even the lowliest street thug carried at least one weapon -- because he always surrounded himself with men who carried out his dirty work. Torrio went on to own his own bar and whorehouse by the age of 22 and he also got involved in local politics. In 1904, he and his gang were instrumental in the election of New York's mayor, George Brinton McClellan, stuffing ballot boxes and violently preventing people from voting for McClellan's rival.

Torrio had a cousin in Chicago named Vittoria (Victoria) Moresco, who was one of the city's leading brothel-keepers. In 1902, Vittoria married the flamboyant Jim Colosimo, an Italian who had worked his way up from cleaning streets to head the Street Laborer's Union and the City Streets Repairer's Union. At this point in his career,

Colosimo was befriended by the two most powerful political bosses in Chicago: First War committeeman Michael Kenna and alderman John Coughlin. Within the First Ward lay the notorious Levee District, an area filled with whorehouses, saloons and gambling parlors. Kenna and Coughlin employed Colosimo as their collector in return for the votes of all of the members of his unions. This ensured his political clout and maintained his ability to operate his criminal enterprises without opposition.

(Left) Colosimo's Restaurant in the South Side Levee District
(Right) Big Jim Colosimo

Colosimo's marriage to Torrio's cousin, Vittoria, made him even more prosperous. By 1912, he and his wife owned dozens of brothels, catering to all income levels. His base of operations, Colosimo's Café, decorated in the most lavish style, was one of the most popular restaurants in Chicago. He entertained wealthy residents, city officials and even show business types like Enrico Caruso, the famous Italian tenor. Colosimo liked to wear white linen suits that were sewn with diamonds, earning him the nickname of "Diamond Jim." He also liked to keep a handful of diamonds in his pockets and while he stood talking to his customers, he would pour the stones from hand to hand and watch them glitter in the light.

As one of Chicago's wealthiest Italians, Colosimo was a natural target for Black Hand extortionists. There were three different attempts made on his life and each time, Colosimo succeeded in killing his attacker. In 1909, however, he received a demand for $50,000 and this time, Vittoria convinced her husband to call John Torrio, her cousin in New York. Torrio took the train to Chicago, starting what came to be called the "New York-Chicago Pipeline" by which gangsters shuttled between the two biggest mob cities in the United States. Torrio dealt with the Black Hand extortionists who were threatening the Colosimos by subcontracting two gunmen who shot them dead at the money drop.

Colosimo asked Torrio to stay in Chicago and in gratitude for what Torrio had done, he put him in charge of his empire of saloons, whorehouses and gambling dens. In 1915, he also gave Torrio permission to set up his own criminal organization. He purchased a building at 2222 South Wabash Ave., which would be known from then on by the number of its address, the Four Deuces. The Four Deuces soon became the headquarters for a criminal enterprise far beyond anything that Big Jim Colosimo could have imagined. Within a short time, Torrio was controlling over 1,000 enterprises that were all devoted to drinking, gambling or sex. His stable of gunmen eliminated anyone who opposed him.

The age of the automobile had begun and Torrio had the foresight to see that the future of vice lay not in its traditional center, places like the Levee, but in the suburbs. The vice-ridden city had seen many reform movements over the years, but as the Prohibition era drew near, they became more effective. There were protest marches against everything from prostitution to gambling. However, it was alcohol that the protestors saw as the basis for all of this corruption, and men like Johnny Torrio knew that it was only a matter of time before the Prohibition movement managed to ban alcohol entirely.

When Prohibition finally arrived in 1920, Torrio was determined to profit from the opportunities that it presented. He soon realized that the only way for his organization to operate was by sitting down with rival gangs and marking out territory, otherwise the

Colosimo is show dead in his own restaurant, paving the way for Johnny Torrio and Al Capone

battle to supply illegal liquor to the thousands of speakeasies that sprang up would lead to chaos and ongoing war. His went to his mentor, Colosimo, and presented his plans to him.

Colosimo was disinterested in Torrio's plans. At that time, he had become distracted by his romantic interest in a woman named Dale Winters, a young musical-comedy actress who had been stranded in Chicago after an unsuccessful theatrical tour. She accepted an invitation to perform in one of Colosimo's establishments and the two fell in love. In 1920, he divorced his wife and married Dale three weeks later. Torrio was astonished to find that Colosimo couldn't be bothered to protect his operations from major rivals like Roger Touhy and Dion O'Banion. This left only one solution for the problem in Torrio's mind: Colosimo had to be eliminated.

On the afternoon of May 11, 1920, Colosimo left for his restaurant with plans to meet his new wife later that night for dinner. When he arrived, he went to his office and spoke with his secretary, Frank Camilla, who had been meeting with the chef about that evening's dinner. Colosimo spoke with them for a few minutes and then, about 4:30 p.m., he allegedly took a telephone call from Johnny Torrio that explained that a shipment of whiskey was being delivered to the restaurant and Colosimo had to sign for it personally. Colosimo left the office and walked out in the lobby, likely preparing to step outside. A moment later, two shots were fired and Frank Camilla went to investigate the sounds. He found Colosimo's dead body lying on the floor of the lobby with a bullet wound in the back of the head. The second bullet was lodged in the plaster wall. From the angle of the shots, the killer, the police concluded, must have been hiding in the cloakroom.

The funeral of Big Jim Colosimo was held on May 15 and was the first of the gaudy burial displays that were the fashion in Chicago's underworld throughout the 1920s. Thousands attended, including both gangsters and politicians, further underscoring the alliances between the two.

After Colosimo's death, Torrio immediately took over Colosimo's entire operation. He had an army of between 700 and 800 men working for him but he always had room for more. One of the soldiers that he recruited was a young man from Brooklyn whom he had known since age 14. In 1921, Torrio invited this man to come to Chicago and work for him. His name was Alphonse Capone.

THE RISE OF AL CAPONE

Al Capone

Capone was born in Brooklyn in 1899 and made a name for himself as a slugger and a gunman with the famous Five Pointers gang in New York, of which several of his cousins were members. Capone was only 22 when he came to Chicago and he started out on the bottom rung of the ladder, working as a promoter outside of one of Torrio's whorehouses. At this time, Capone met Jake Guzik, a member of a large Jewish family involved in prostitution. They became friends and Guzik went on to become the treasurer for the Torrio-Capone organization.

In 1922, Capone became Torrio's first lieutenant and the chief of his gunmen. As far as the general public was concerned, he remained an obscure member of Torrio's organization for the first two years he was in Chicago. In those days, he was rough and brutal but there was little to indicate that he was destined for criminal greatness in the years to come. In the underworld, he was generally known as "Scarface Al Brown," a nickname that was due to the two parallel scars on his left cheek that had been sustained during a knife fight. Soon though, all of Chicago would be familiar with his name.

Torrio and Capone moved up quickly following the death of Colosimo. They took over a number of breweries and then began to organize the major Chicago gangs, assigning each their own territory. In return, the gangs forced saloons to stock Torrio's alcohol and also protected shipments and assisted distribution. The North Side of the city fell to Dion O'Banion. The West Side was divided between Terry Druggan and Frankie Lake, leaders of the Valley Gang. Torrio controlled the south side, and the rest was divided between mobsters Ralph Sheldon, Danny Stanton, Frank McErlane and Joe Saltis.

Two gangs left out of Torrio's syndicate were the Klondike O'Donnell Gang, based in Cicero, and the unrelated O'Donnell brothers, led by Spike O'Donnell, who at the time was in prison for bank robbery. When he got out,

Spike began hijacking Torrio's trucks and moving in on the territory of Frank McErlane and Joe Saltis. Spike O'Donnell and his men were massacred or driven out of the city between 1923 and 1925.

In 1923, Torrio and Capone, motivated by the election of a reform mayor, William E. Dever, who closed down 7,000 speakeasies, decided to move their headquarters from the Four Deuces in downtown Chicago to the Hawthorne Inn, located in the suburb of Cicero. This independent township was outside the jurisdiction of the mayor of Chicago. The area was dominated by the Western Electric plant, which paid its 40,000 employees well, meaning that the local populace had plenty of money to spend in the gambling parlors and saloons. Cicero also had a large number of Czech immigrants, who were accustomed to thick, Bohemian beer. This was supplied by the West Side O'Donnells, who had not joined the Torrio-Capone syndicate, and who regarded Cicero as their territory.

Torrio decided to probe the extent of the O'Donnells' power in Cicero by setting up a whorehouse on Roosevelt Road. The Cicero police, acting for the O'Donnells, shut it down. The O'Donnells disapproved of prostitution but they did allow gambling, but only at slot machines. The slot machines in Cicero were all controlled by Eddie Vogel, a local politician. Torrio, in retaliation for the brothel closing, sent out the Cook County Sheriff to confiscate Vogel's slot machines. Torrio then sat down with the O'Donnells and Vogel and negotiated a truce. The slot machines were returned and Torrio agreed not to open any more whorehouses in Cicero. In addition, Torrio allowed them to continue to supply beer to some areas of the city. In exchange, the Torrio syndicate was granted the right to sell beer everywhere else in Cicero, and to run gambling parlors and dance halls wherever it wanted.

Torrio, having gained entry into Cicero, left everything in Capone's hands and left for Italy with his mother and several million dollars. He bought his mother a villa and deposited the money in an Italian bank. He then returned to Chicago.

The first challenge that awaited Capone in Cicero was taking over the city government. His chance came with the mayoral election of 1924 between Democrat Rudolph Hurt and Republican Joseph Z. Klenha. The election took place on April 1 and Capone threw the weight of the syndicate behind Klenha. By this time, Capone had brought his entire family to Chicago, and his brothers Ralph and Frank and his cousin Charley Fischetti helped bring out the vote for Klenha and other syndicate candidates. They were assisted in this task by more than 200 gunmen, who stationed themselves at polling booths and made sure that voters only cast ballots for the candidates of choice. Those who opposed them were violently beaten and those who went along were allowed to vote as many times as they wished.

News of the violence and voter fraud reached Judge Edmund K. Jarecki, who ordered 70 policemen to go into Cicero and stop it. They wore plain clothes and arrived in unmarked cars. As they drove past the Western Electric plant, the first mobster they spotted was Frank Capone. The officers stopped and jumped out of their cars. Frank, thinking that they had come to kill him, reached for his gun and was cut down by shotgun blasts before he could get to it. The police then emptied their revolvers into his body as he lay bleeding on the street.

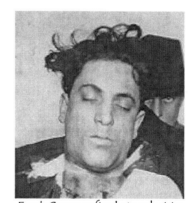

Frank Capone after being shot to death by police officers in Cicero

Frank was 29 and was given a magnificent gangland funeral. He was placed in a sliver-plated casket and the modest Capone home on South Prairie Avenue was filled with more than $20,000 worth of flowers. A procession of 100 cars took the casket to Mount Carmel Cemetery. Capone had lost a brother but he had won the election. The mob was now in charge of Cicero.

O'BANION'S NORTH SIDE GANG

Not long after Capone made inroads into Cicero politics, trouble began to brew in Chicago. Problems had started to develop between Torrio-Capone ally Dion O'Banion, leader of an eccentric legion of mostly Irish gunmen, and the Gennas, a family of Sicilian brothers from Taylor Street who supplied Torrio with poorly made liquor that

Dean O'Banion

was manufactured in neighborhood stills. The Gennas had started selling their cheap whiskey on the North Side of Chicago, O'Banion's territory, in a clear infringement of the syndicate agreement. O'Banion complained to Torrio, who was reluctant to intervene. The Gennas were extremely violent and politically well connected, so Torrio did not want to provoke them. Impatient, O'Banion hijacked a Genna delivery truck with a cargo of liquor worth more than $30,000. Torrio had to use all of his diplomatic skills to restrain the Gennas so, in retaliation, they began flooding other territories with their liquor. O'Banion was fed up and it was clear that the Torrio truce was breaking down.

Dean Charles O'Banion was born in 1892 in the small Central Illinois town of Maroa. His father, Charles, was a barber by trade who hailed from Lincoln, Ill., and his mother, the former Emma Brophy, was the Chicago-born daughter of an Irish immigrant father and American mother. She had been just eight months old when the Great Chicago Fire leveled the city in 1871. Charles and Emma married in 1886 and moved to Maroa the following year, where Charles' parents lived.

Dean spent the early years of his life in Maroa but soon after the birth of his sister, Ruth, his mother contracted tuberculosis and died in 1901. Dean was only nine years old at the time and the loss was a devastating one. The remaining family members packed up and moved to Chicago, where Emma's parents had a place for them. Dean (soon to be known as Dion) saw the end of his innocent years. The hard times, and the legend, were about to begin.

Upon moving to Chicago, O'Banion found himself turning to the streets for a playground. He became involved with a street gang known as the Little Hellions and began picking pockets and rolling drunks. At the same time, he sang in the choir at the Holy Name Cathedral and, on Sundays, he served as an altar boy. Some of the priests at the church believed that perhaps his devotion might lead to the priesthood but O'Banion soon learned to ration his religion to Sundays and to devote his remaining time to robbery and, as he reached young adulthood, to burglary: "a man's profession."

On the streets, O'Banion met, and befriended, notorious safecrackers and thieves like George "Bugs" Moran, Earl "Hymie" Weiss, Vincent "The Schemer" Drucci and Samuel "Nails" Morton. With these men at his side, O'Banion put together one of the most devastating gangs in Chicago. They centered their activities on the North Side, around Lincoln Park and the Gold Coast.

When Prohibition came along, O'Banion purchased several of the best breweries and distilleries on the North Side. Capone and Torrio on the South Side were forced to import beer and whiskey at high prices or rely on rotgut produced by the Gennas to supply their outlets, but O'Banion had the finest beer and booze available. All over the city, society people and the owners of better restaurants bought from O'Banion. The quality of his product was better and he was thought to be more trustworthy than Capone, who was also running brothels and floating gambling operations. O'Banion publicly agreed to keep his operations north of the "dividing line," or Madison Street, but he still serviced his special customers on the South Side, as well.

As the Torrio truce began to fall apart, O'Banion went on the offensive, selling his beer and liquor all over the South Side. At first, this encroachment on Capone-Torrio territory was tolerated. Capone attempted to negotiate with him, stating that if O'Banion was going to run booze on the South Side, then Capone should be allowed to have liquor warehouses in Lincoln Park. O'Banion refused --- not because he couldn't deal with Capone, but because he was morally offended by Capone's dealings in prostitution. During the tenure of the O'Banion operation (and later the Weiss and Moran gangs), not one professional brothel operated in the opulent northeast section of Chicago. However, O'Banion's religious compunctions did not apply to hijacking Capone's trucks, robberies, gambling casinos, and killing anyone who got in his way.

Torrio constantly tried to negotiate with O'Banion, rather than use the violence that Capone began to urge. Dozens of meetings were held between Torrio, Capone and O'Banion, and each ended with the same results. O'Banion always promised to recognize the territory of the South Siders and then turned right around and began encroaching upon it again. Capone wanted to hit O'Banion, but Torrio asked him to wait. Torrio knew that if he killed O'Banion, it would mean all-out war in Chicago.

But Torrio's hesitation backfired on him in May 1924 when O'Banion came to him and told him that he planned to retire and wanted to sell Torrio his largest gambling den and his favorite brewery, Sieben's. He had a good excuse for doing so, stating that he planned to retire from bootlegging and work in his flower shop. As everyone knew, despite the fact that he had one of the largest liquor operations in the city, O'Banion hated liquor and beer. He did love flowers, though, so he purchased a half interest in the Schofield Flower Shop at 738 North State St., directly across the street from Holy Name Cathedral. O'Banion easily convinced Torrio that he planned to get out of the liquor business because of this.

Torrio agreed to buy up O'Banion's concerns and reportedly paid him a half-million dollars in cash two days later. The gang leaders agreed to meet at Sieben's on May 19, as Torrio wanted to inspect his new property. But he had not been there for more than 10 minutes before Police Chief Collins, leading 20 officers, raided the place and arrested O'Banion, Earl "Hymie" Weiss and Torrio. This was Torrio's second arrest for violating Prohibition. He had been arrested once and fined in June 1923 but a second arrest could mean jail time -- a fact of which O'Banion had been very much aware. Torrio also realized that O'Banion had no intention of retiring. He had conned Torrio into buying a brewery that he knew the police were about to shut down.

O'Banion was very amused by the "joke" he had pulled on Torrio but Hymie Weiss pleaded with his boss to "take it easy with those guys." O'Banion laughed, "When are you gonna learn? Those people are gutter rats, dumb bastards all of 'em: Torrio, Capone, them Gennas. To hell with them Sicilians!"

It was time, Torrio decided, to get rid of O'Banion. He and Capone informed Mike Merlo, the founder and president of the powerful Unione Sicilian, that they planned to kill O'Banion but Merlo urged restraint, knowing that it would cause a gang war. Out of respect for Merlo, who was dying of cancer, Torrio waited. When Merlo died in November 1924, O'Banion's fate was sealed.

On November 10, James Genna and Carmen Vacco entered O'Banion's flower shop and ordered a wreath for Merlo's funeral. They gave O'Banion $750 to pay for the arrangement. They told him that they would send some boys back to pick it up later. Then they left the shop.

Five minutes later, the telephone rang and an unknown caller wanted to know if O'Banion had the flowers ready. He promised that they would be ready at noon and at five minutes past the hour, a blue Jewett touring car pulled up in front of the shop.

One of the shop's employees, a black man named William Crutchfield, who was sweeping up flower petals in the back room, looked up to see three men get out of the car and walk into the shop. Another man remained at the wheel of the car outside. O'Banion, dressed in a long white smock and holding a pair of florist's shears in his left hand, came out from behind the counter and extended his hand in greeting. He said to them: "Hello, boys, you from Mike Merlo's?"

The three men walked abreast and approached O'Banion with smiles on their faces. The man in the center was tall, clean-shaven and wearing an expensive overcoat and fedora. It was determined years later that this man was Frankie Yale. The other two, believed to be John Scalise and Albert Anselmi, were shorter and stockier, with dark complexions.

Crutchfield heard the man thought to be Frankie Yale reply, "Yes, for Merlo's flowers." He then stepped closer to O'Banion. Yale grabbed the other man's hand in greeting and pulled O'Banion toward him. The two men at his sides moved around him and drew pistols. Then, at close range, Yale rammed his own

The scene outside of Schofield's Flower Shop on the day that O'Banion received what would become the first "Chicago Handshake"

pistol into O'Banion's stomach and, holding his arm in a vice-like grip, opened fire. The other two men also fired their weapons and the bullets ripped into O'Banion. Two slugs struck him in the right breast, two hit him in the throat and one passed through each side of his face. The shots were fired at such close range that powder burns were found at the opening of each wound. From that point on, this method of murder became known as the "Chicago Handshake."

O'Banion fell, dead on his feet, into a display of geraniums. The three men fled from the store and climbed into the car outside, which drove slowly away from the scene.

The Genna brothers, Capone and Torrio were all arrested on suspicion of homicide but were all soon released after supplying airtight alibis. Frankie Yale was arrested at the La Salle train station, departing for points unknown, but he was also released. The investigation, headed by ace Detective Captain William "Shoes" Shoemaker, went nowhere.

At an elaborate funeral service, O'Banion's friends filed past his body, tough gangsters weeping as they walked into Sbarbaro's Funeral Home. He was placed inside a $10,000 bronze casket that had been fitted with bronze and silver double walls. A heavy plate glass window had been installed over O'Banion's patched-up face and his men could peer down and see his head where it reclined on a white satin pillow.

O'Banion's funeral was the most lavish in Chicago gangland history. The hearse was led to Mount Carmel Cemetery by 26 trucks filled with flowers worth more than $50,000. The scene at the cemetery was even more bizarre. On one side of the grave, lowering the body to rest, were O'Banion's friends, Hymie Weiss, George Moran, and Vincent Drucci; on the other, Al Capone, Johnny Torrio and Angelo Genna. The North Siders glared at the South Siders but no one made a move toward their guns ----- not yet, anyway.

Torrio was right about one thing: O'Banion's death ignited an all-out war in Chicago. It would be Torrio who got the first taste of the wrath of the North Side gang.

A few days after O'Banion's funeral, in November 1924, Torrio and his wife got out of a chauffer-driven limousine in front of their house at 7011 Clyde Ave. (Torrio lived there under the name Frank Langley) and Anna Torrio began to walk inside. As Torrio reached in the car to pick up some packages from their shopping trip, a black Cadillac screeched to a stop across the street. Inside, four men with pistols and shotguns watched for a moment and then two of them, George "Bugs" Moran and Hymie Weiss, jumped from the car and ran towards Torrio with their guns blazing.

Torrio fell immediately with a bullet in his chest and one in his neck. The other two men in the Cadillac, Vincent Drucci and Frank Gusenberg, jumped out and opened fire on the limousine with their shotguns. Meanwhile, Moran and Weiss ran to the fallen Torrio and, standing above him, fired bullets into his right arm and another into his groin. Moran leaned over to put the next one into Torrio's head but his gun was empty. As he reached for another clip, Drucci began honking the horn of the Cadillac, signaling frantically that they needed to leave. Moran and Weiss ran to the car and they sped away.

Newspaper photographers captured Torrio wearing a scarf to hide the bandages on his throat when he appeared in court.

Somehow, Torrio managed to start crawling to the house and his wife, who was screaming, came out and pulled him inside. A neighbor, who witnessed the shooting, called an ambulance and Torrio was raced to the hospital. Unbelievably, he survived with a permanent scar on his neck. Reporters soon surrounded his hospital bed, demanding more information. Torrio stated that he knew all four of the assailants involved but "I'll never tell their names," he said.

In February, Torrio (still bandaged) was sent to federal court for the Sieben's brewery fiasco and he received a nine-month jail sentence to be served in the Waukegan County Jail, which had medical services for the still-ailing mobster. Earl Weiss, who had taken over the leadership of the North Side gang, was fined for his first offense on violation of Prohibition charges and when the clerk called the name of Dion O'Banion and the prosecutor announced that he was "deceased," Weiss shot Torrio an evil look. Torrio got the hint ---- the North Siders may have botched their first attempt to kill him but they wouldn't miss the second time. He left for Waukegan filled with fear.

However, the treatment that Torrio received in prison was equal to the status of the gangland boss. The windows of his cell were covered with bulletproof glass and extra deputies guarded him day and night. Easy chairs, throw rugs, books and other luxuries were added as well. Torrio also received the special privilege of taking his evening meals in the sheriff's home and was allowed to relax on the sheriff's front porch for a while each night, visiting with his wife and his associates, such as Al Capone.

As he finished serving his time, Torrio had a lot of time to think. When he got out, he announced that he was tired of the rackets and that he was turning his entire operation over to Capone. All that he needed, he told his younger friend, was to get out of Chicago alive. Capone promised that he would, and he made good on his assurances. Torrio and Anna left the city in an armor-plated limousine and were escorted by two roadsters filled with gunmen. When they reached a train station, just over the Indiana state line, Capone's men patrolled the station with shotguns and machine guns until the train, which held the Torrios, departed for Florida. After that, they went on to Italy, living in Naples for three years.

Torrio got bored in Italy but knowing that he couldn't return to Chicago, he went to New York instead, where he went into the real estate business with the blessing of Meyer Lansky and Charles "Lucky" Luciano. He also helped to establish a liquor cartel along the Atlantic Seaboard and established himself as an elder statesman of the underworld. He lived a sedate and quiet life after Prohibition was repealed but, in 1936, was arrested for income tax evasion. After a series of trials and appeals, he served two years in Leavenworth and was paroled in 1941. He died in a barber's chair (of natural causes) in 1957.

THE BEER WARS & THE "PINEAPPLE PRIMARY"

Torrio's departure from Chicago shoved Al Capone into the violent spotlight of the Chicago underworld and it also made him the top man in the city at only 25. He now had an annual income that would actually land him a place in the Guinness Book of World Records. And he also had a bloody gang war on his hands. Hymie Weiss offered to stem further violence by having Capone hand John Scalise and Albert Anselmi over to him. It was a poorly kept secret that they had been in the flower shop when O'Banion had been murdered. Capone refused and made plans to knock off Hymie Weiss instead. He was too slow though ---- Weiss and Bugs Moran had already planned their next move.

On May 26, 1925, they murdered Angelo Genna, one of Capone's supporters. A month later, Mike Genna was

The Hawthorne Hotel, Capone's headquarters in Cicero

killed by the police as he, John Scalise and Albert Anselmi were about to ambush George Moran. Scalise and Anselmi killed two police officers before escaping. Tony Genna was murdered soon after by the Gennas' own gunman, Giuseppe Nerone, who may have been paid to assassinate him by Capone. The surviving Gennas soon left for Italy.

Hymie Weiss struck again a short time later. Capone was sitting with his most trusted bodyguard, Frank Rio, in the restaurant of the Hawthorne Hotel in Cicero on September 20, 1926. The street outside was filled with shoppers and automobiles and, at first, no one noticed as nine cars filled with North Side gangsters slowly cruised down Twenty-Second Street. One of the cars accelerated away from the others and as it passed the windows of the restaurant, black barrels of machine guns appeared from the windows and opened fire. Glass shattered and wood splintered as bullets riddled the restaurant. The car sped off and Rio jumped to his feet, gun in hand. But as Capone started to get up from the floor, his bodyguard pushed him back down again because he spotted the other cars in the procession.

The other eight touring cars were filled with men and machine guns. They opened fire on Capone's Cicero stronghold, emptying clip after clip into the hotel, spraying everything in sight. Hymie Weiss boldly climbed from his car with Moran close behind him. Capone had over 100 men inside the heavily armed fortress and yet none of them faced the withering fire from outside. Weiss ran up to the door of the hotel and opened fire with his machine gun, waving the weapon back and forth across the width of the passageway beyond the doors. When he finished firing, he walked coolly back to the car and with honking and shouts, the North Siders drove away. Over 1,000 rounds had been fired into the building and every window in the place was shattered. Amazingly, no one had been killed.

That violent incident was Hymie's one moment of glory and revenge for O'Banion's murder. And while he continued to live a fearless life (to the point of stupidity) and to goad Capone at every opportunity, his days were numbered.

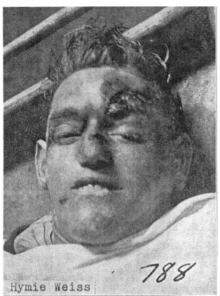
Hymie Weiss death photo

On October 11, Weiss was attending the murder trial of "Polack Joe" Saltis and his driver Frank "Lefty" Koncil, and decided to take a break and return to his office above O'Banion's old flower shop. As Weiss and gunman Patrick Murray drove toward the office, they had no idea that four machine gunners were waiting for them. These men, believed to be John Scalise, Albert Anselmi, Frank Diamond and Frank Nitti, were hiding on the third floor of a nearby building. Weiss was a marked man as soon as he left his car on Superior Street, just south of the Holy Name Cathedral. He approached the flower shop with Murray by his side and at the deafening sound of Tommy guns, the pedestrians on the street scattered.

Murray died instantly but Weiss took 10 bullets and survived long enough to be pronounced dead at Henrotin Hospital without regaining consciousness. The bullets that killed Weiss tore away portions of the inscription on the church's cornerstone and left bullet holes as a graphic reminder of the event. Church officials tried to obliterate them years later but the chips and marks have managed to stay. They can still be seen on the corner of the cathedral today.

Meanwhile, the assassins fled their third-floor lair, exited the rear of the building and disappeared into the crowds along Dearborn Street. A discarded machine gun was found in an alley off Dearborn but it couldn't be traced back to the killers.

And one has to wonder how hard the police looked for them. Chief Morgan Collins issued a gruff statement: "I don't want to encourage the business, but if somebody has to be killed, it's a good thing the gangsters are murdering themselves off. It saves trouble for the police."

In December 1926, Capone went to New York to negotiate with Frankie Yale over the purchase of Canadian whiskey. Soon after he returned to Chicago, he moved his operation into another area, the largely Italian suburb of Chicago Heights. At the time, it was controlled by a group of Sicilians who ran a protection racket on home distillers. Capone's men killed off the Sicilians and he took over their operation.

Capone was now running Chicago Heights, but this was not the best news that he would receive in the spring of 1927. In April, reform Mayor William E. Dever lost the election to gangland's favorite candidate, William Hale Thompson. Capone had sponsored "Big Bill" with over $250,000 of his own money because he knew that with Thompson in office, he could literally rule the city. According to legend, Capone had three framed portraits over the desk in his office: George Washington, Abraham Lincoln and "Big Bill" Thompson.

A month later, in May 1927, as a result of a court case U.S. vs. Sullivan, the United States Supreme Court passed an unusual law. The law stated that profits from the illegal sale of alcohol could be taxed like any other income.

Capone gunman, "Machine Gun" Jack McGurn

Although the law seemed ridiculous, it became a powerful law enforcement tool against bootleggers. No one was going to readily admit that they were engaged in illegal activity, and making money from it, but if the police could prove that someone was a bootlegger by raiding their operation, the bootlegger could be sent to jail for not filing income tax returns. And if he filed an income tax return, he implicated himself in an illegal act. The U.S. Attorney's office in Chicago estimated that Al Capone had grossed over $105 million from bootlegging, vice and gambling but he had never filed a single tax return.

Soon after Mayor Thompson took office, four unsolved murders took place, all linked to Capone. Each of the dead men had been shot to death and was found with a nickel clenched in his hand. Rumor had it that the dead men were out of town mobsters who had come to Chicago to kill Al Capone. Before they could, each was taken out by Capone's favorite gunman, "Machine Gun" Jack McGurn.

The 1927 murder victims were believed to be gangsters hoping to collect a $50,000 bounty that was placed on Capone's head by Joseph Aiello, a Sicilian from Castellamare. Aiello and his brothers, Antonio, Dominick and Andrew, ran a numbers racket and levied a tax on California grapes unloaded in Chicago railroad sidings. After sending hitmen against Capone, Aiello next tried to bribe one of his cooks with $10,000 to poison him. The cook wasted no time in informing Capone. When Capone discovered that Aiello had set up a machine gun position across the street from the store where Capone made payoffs, Capone informed friends on the police force, who arrested Aiello and suggested that he leave town. Capone later had Aiello gunned down in New Jersey.

In early 1928, Capone and his family left Chicago for Miami. Toward the end of 1927, Capone had repeatedly stated in public that he planned to retire from bootlegging, even calling a press conference to announce his intentions to a skeptical group of reporters. In Florida, he purchased a house in the name of his wife, Mae, on Palm Island, near Miami. The purchase attracted the attention of the Internal Revenue Service, which was determined to go after Capone for non-payment of income tax. A relentless IRS agent named Elmer Irey investigated the sale, but, because the house was in Mae's name, he was unable to use it to indict Capone. Irey was stunned to discover that, given Capone's lavish lifestyle, an income of greater than the allowable exemption of $5,000 could not be traced. Capone did all of his business through front men and it was difficult to link him to the operations that were generating the colossal sums of money.

"Big Bill" Thompson's first year back in office had been a disaster and discontent about his incompetence and corruption was spreading, especially with the city of Chicago almost $300 million in debt. Primary elections for city offices were scheduled for April 8, 1928 but election violence began in January with a bomb attack on the home of a city controller. In February, Judge John Sbarbaro's home was also bombed. Sbarbaro had strong connections to Capone because, in addition to his position as a judge, he was also involved in bootlegging and he owned gangland's preferred funeral home. The funeral home had a way of dealing with inconvenient corpses by burying them in "double-decker" coffins, placing the bodies of murdered mobsters in the same graves with legitimate burials.

There were 62 bomb attacks that took place over a short period of time, most taking place against politicians and city officials who were opposed to Thompson. Hysteria gripped the city, mostly caused by not knowing who was responsible. Of course, Capone, although he was in far-off Miami, was inevitably blamed. The election came to be known as Chicago's "Pineapple Primary" since "pineapple" was a slang term for a hand grenade. When the election finally came, Thompson remained as mayor but lost control of the city government.

On July 1, 1928, Capone was responsible for one of the most significant gangland assassinations of the year: the murder of Frankie Yale. Yale had started out as a member of a gang in Manhattan's Five Points neighborhood with Johnny Torrio in 1908. In 1918, after having proven his mob credentials, he took over the Unione Siciliana, which had evolved from a fraternal order to a criminal organization. Based out of the Harvard Inn at Coney Island, Yale started in the bootlegging business when Prohibition went into effect in 1920. Yale supplied Capone's liquor needs in Chicago and was also on call to perform assassinations for him if needed. Eventually, the two men had a falling out for several reasons. Against Capone, Yale was trying to take over the Chicago branch of the Unione Siciliana, which controlled the home distilleries in the Italian community. Not only that, but Yale's whiskey shipments to Capone were being hijacked and Capone suspected that Yale himself was responsible.

Capone sent four gunmen, three of whom were likely McGurn, Scalise and Anselmi, to Brooklyn. On July 1, 1928, they followed Yale's bulletproof car and shotgunned him through the window. Then they finished the job with a Thompson submachine gun, marking the first time that a "Tommy gun" was used in New York. Yale's speeding car crashed into the front of a house and his bloody and bullet-ridden body was thrown out onto the sidewalk.

Yale's killers had thrown their guns away after the murder, as was the custom, but they were later recovered by the police. Investigators traced the guns back to Capone, who denied any knowledge of the crime. Since this was the only evidence that they had against the killers, no indictments against Capone, or his gunmen, were ever returned.

A few weeks after Yale's murder, Capone left his wife and son in Florida and returned to Chicago, He set up new headquarters on the south side at the Lexington Hotel, at first renting 10 rooms and eventually taking over most of the hotel.

Around this time, he saw the first repercussions for the killing of Frankie Yale. Capone's candidate for the presidency of the Unione Siciliana, Antonio Lombardo, was believed to have been involved with Capone in Yale's killing. Lombardo was shot in the head while out for an evening stroll on September 8. Lombardo's successor, Pasqualino Lolardo, also a friend of Capone's, was killed in January 1929. His murder was also thought to be in retaliation for the death of Frankie Yale.

January 1929 also saw the first successful federal raid against a Capone operation. In December 1928, the police chief of Chicago Heights had been shot down by two men as he sat reading in his front parlor. He had been scheduled to testify against two local bootleggers. U.S. Attorney George Johnson (whose house had been bombed

(Left) George "Bugs" Moran, who took over the North Side mob after the assassination of Dean O'Banion. By 1929, he was the only remaining opposition to Capone's (Right) Chicago empire.

during the "Pineapple Primary"), in cooperation with the Chicago Police Department, raided Chicago Heights. Before breaking up stills and closing down breweries, though, they took the unprecedented step of arresting the entire Chicago Heights police force, which was thought to be on Capone's payroll. During a raid on the home of the manager of one of Capone's gambling parlors, they found ledgers recording profits from slot machines. After carefully scrutinizing the entries in the ledger, an indictment was filed against Capone's brother, Ralph, for income tax evasion.

THE ST. VALENTINE'S DAY MASSACRE

In the midst of all this, the problems with the North Side gangsters had never gone away. Most of the leaders of the gang were wiped out or forced to flee from Chicago, leaving only George Moran.

George "Bugs" Moran was born in Minnesota in 1893 but moved to Chicago with his parents around 1900. Here, he joined up with one of the North Side Irish gangs and was befriended by a young tough named Dion O'Banion. The two began working together, robbing warehouses, but after one fouled-up job, Moran was captured. He kept his silence and served two years in Joliet prison without implicating O'Banion in the crime. He was released at age 19 and went back to work with his friend. He was soon captured again and, once more, he kept silent about whom he worked with. He stayed in jail this time until 1923.

When Moran, known as "Bugs" because of his quick temper, got out of prison, he joined up with O'Banion's now

The S-M-C Cartage Co. as it looked in the 1920s. The site is an open lot today but the apartment building on the left still stands. The distinctive pillars in front are still recognizable on Clark Street today.

formidable north side mob. They had become a powerful organization, supplying liquor to Chicago's wealthy Gold Coast. Moran became a valuable asset, hijacking Capone's liquor trucks at will. He became known as O'Banion's right hand man, always impeccably dressed, right down to the two guns that he always wore. When O'Banion was killed in his flower shop in 1924, Moran swore revenge. The war that followed claimed many lives and almost got Moran killed in 1925 when he was wounded in an ambush on Congress Street.

By 1929, Moran stood alone against the Capone mob, most of his allies having succumbed in the fighting. He continued to taunt his powerful enemy, always looking for ways to destroy him. Two of his gunmen, Pete and Frank Gusenberg, caught up with Capone's right-hand man Jack McGurn in a phone booth inside the McCormick Inn. Several bursts from their Tommy guns almost finished McGurn for good but major surgery, and a long period of secluded convalescence, saved the killer.

In early February 1929, McGurn was summoned to visit Capone at his Palm Island, Florida, home for a discussion

A crowd gathers in the alley behind the S-M-C Cartage Co. as the bodies of the massacre victims are removed from the garage.

This view of the massacre victims was printed by Chicago newspapers so that readers would not have to turn their papers to identify the victims

about the North Side gang run by George Moran. Ten days later, the St. Valentine's Day Massacre took place.

The plan for one of the most insidious assassinations in gangland history was deceptively simple. Through a contact in Detroit, Capone arranged for someone to call Moran and tell him that a special shipment of hijacked whiskey was going to be delivered to one of Moran's garages on the North Side. Adam Heyer, a friend of Moran, owned the garage and it was used as a distribution point for North Side liquor. A sign out front read "S-M-C Cartage Co. Shipping - Packing - Long Distance Hauling." The whiskey was to be delivered the following day, February 14, and Moran was asked to accept the delivery personally.

On the morning of February 14, a group of Moran's men gathered at the Clark Street garage. One of the men was Johnny May, an ex-safecracker who had been hired by Moran as an auto mechanic. He was working on a truck that morning with his dog, a German shepherd named Highball, tied to the bumper. In addition, six other men waited for the truck of hijacked whiskey to arrive. The men were Frank and Pete Gusenberg, who were supposed to meet Moran and pick up two empty trucks to drive to Detroit and pick up smuggled Canadian whiskey; James Clark, Moran's brother-in-law; Adam Heyer; Al Weinshank; and Reinhardt Schwimmer, a young optometrist who had befriended Moran and hung around the liquor warehouse just for the thrill of rubbing shoulders with gangsters.

Moran was already late for the morning meeting. He was due to arrive at 10:30 a.m. but didn't even leave for the rendezvous, in the company of Willie Marks and Ted Newberry, until several minutes after that. He later stated that he had overslept that day.

While the seven men waited inside the warehouse, they had no idea that a police car had pulled up outside, or that Moran had spotted the car as he was driving south on Clark Street and rather than deal with what he believed was a shakedown, he stopped at the next corner for a

Highball, Johnny May's German Shepherd,
who alerted local residents to the murders

cup of coffee.

Five men got out of the police car, two of them were in civilian clothing and the other three were in Chicago Police Department uniforms. All three of these men carried Thompson submachine guns. The men entered the building but the gangsters inside were not alarmed. Like George Moran, they figured that this was another police shakedown. They were ordered to line up facing the wall. Then, a few moments later, the clatter of machine gun fire broke the stillness of the snowy morning. Soon after, five figures emerged from the building and drove away. May's dog, inside the warehouse, began barking and howling.

The landlady in the next building, Mrs. Jeanette Landesman, was bothered by the noise of the dog and she sent one of her boarders, C.L. McAllister, to the garage to see what was going on. McAllister came outside two minutes later, his face white. He ran frantically up the stairs to beg Landesman to call the The police were quickly summoned and, upon entering the garage, they were stunned by the carnage. Moran's men had been lined up against the rear wall of the garage and sprayed with machine gun fire. Pete Gusenberg had died kneeling, slumped over a chair. James Clark had fallen on his face with half his head blown away and Heyer, Schwimmer, Weinshank and May were thrown lifeless onto their backs. Only one of the men survived the slaughter but only for a few hours. Frank Gusenberg had crawled from the blood-sprayed wall where he had fallen and ended up out in the middle of the dirty floor. He was rushed to the Alexian Brothers Hospital, barely hanging on. Police sergeant Clarence Sweeney leaned down close to him and asked who had shot him.

Gusenberg groaned a reply, "No one. Nobody shot me." He died later that night.

Police canvassed Clark Street between Webster and Garfield (now Dickens) avenues. In 1929, this was a district of mostly rooming houses and there were dozens of landlords and tenants to interview. Transients came and went, the detectives were told, but a couple of women did remember that teams of suspicious men had recently rented rooms with street views, for $8 per day.

The car that the murderers had been driving, turned into a smoldering wreck, was found in a rented garage on Wood Street. It had been set on fire with acetylene torches and chopped up with a hacksaw. Ownership of the car was traced to Cook County Commissioner Frank J. Wilson, who had sold it to an auto dealership on Irving Park Road a short time before.

The death toll of the massacre stood at seven, but the killers had missed Moran. When the police contacted him later and asked who had sent the men to the garage, he "raved like a madman." To the newspapers, Moran pointed to Capone as ordering the hit. He told them, "Only Capone kills guys like that."

And Moran was undoubtedly right. The murders broke the power of the North Side gang and while there have been many claims as to who the actual shooters were that day, most likely they included Scalise, Anselmi and "Machine Gun" Jack McGurn, all of whom were among Capone's most trusted men. All three men, along with Joseph Guinta, were arrested but McGurn had an alibi and Scalise and Guinta were killed before they could be tried.

The St. Valentine's Day Massacre marked the end of any significant gang opposition to Capone, but it was also the act that finally began the decline of Capone's criminal empire. He had gone too far and the authorities, and even Capone's adoring public, were ready to put an end to the bootleg wars. The massacre started a wave of reform that would send Capone out of power for good.

Chicago, in its own way, memorialized the warehouse on Clark Street where the massacre took place. It became a tourist attraction and the newspapers even printed the photos of the corpses upside-down so that readers would not have to turn their papers around to identify the bodies.

In 1949, the front portion of the S-M-C Garage was turned into an antique furniture storage business by a couple that had no idea of the building's bloody past. They soon found that tourists, curiosity-seekers and crime buffs visited the place much more often than antiques customers and they eventually closed the business.

In 1967, the building was demolished. However, the bricks from the bullet-marked rear wall were purchased and saved by a Canadian businessman named George Patey. In 1972, he opened a nightclub with a Roaring '20s theme called the Banjo Palace and rebuilt the wall, for some strange reason, in the men's restroom. Three nights each week, women were allowed to peek inside at this macabre attraction.

The club continued to operate for a few years and when it closed, the owner placed the 417 bricks into storage. He then offered them for sale with a written account of the massacre but had trouble selling the entire wall in one large piece. Patey, along with a friend named Guy Whitford, who contacted me about the wall in 2002, tried to sell the single piece for some time. The original lot came with a diagram that explained how to restore the wall to its original form. The bricks were even numbered for reassembly. They remained on the market for nearly three decades, but there were no buyers. Eventually, Patey broke up the set and began selling them one brick at a time for $1,000 each. Patey died in December 2004 and had sold most of the bricks by that time.

GHOSTS OF THE ST. VALENTINE'S DAY MASSACRE?

Stories say that the site on Clark Street where the St. Valentine's Day Massacre occurred is one of the most haunted spots in the city. People walking along the street at night have reported the sounds of screams and machine guns as they pass the site. The building is long gone now, demolished in a

misguided attempt by city officials to erase all vestiges of Chicago's gangster past. A portion of the block was taken over by the Chicago Housing Authority and a fenced-in lawn that belongs to a senior citizen's development now marks the area where the garage once stood. Five trees are scattered about the site and the one in the center actually marks the point where the rear wall once stood, where Moran's men were lined up and gunned down. The apartment building, where Mrs. Landesman lived and heard the sound of Highball barking in the garage, still stands but all remnants of the S-M-C Cartage Co. have vanished.

Or have they?

According to reports, residents of the senior housing complex built on one end of the lot have had strange encounters in the building, especially those who live on the side that faces the former massacre site. A television reporter from Canada interviewed a woman who once lived in an apartment that overlooked the small park area and she often complained that, at night, she would hear strange voices, sounds and knocking on her door and her window. She complained to the management, who dismissed her claims as imagination but assigned her another apartment. A new tenant moved into the rooms and she also complained of odd happenings, including knocking sounds that would come at her door at night. When she opened the door to see who was there, she never found anyone nearby. One night, she stated that she saw a dark figure that was wearing an old-style hat. He remained in place for a few moments and then faded away. Most of the strange phenomena experienced by the new tenant also faded away and soon eerie events either stopped completely or she got so used to them that they no longer bothered her anymore.

Outside, along Clark Street, passersby and the curious have sometimes reported strange sounds, like weeping and moaning, and the indescribable feeling of fear as they walk past the former site of the garage. Skeptics have tried to laugh this off, saying that the sounds are nothing more than

KEN SAYS:
There have been a number of alleged ghosts at the sight of the St. Valentine's Day Massacre including mysterious misty rings, a number of orbs and screams heard in the alley. Although there is psychically a general feeling of anger and despair, I have never sensed any ghosts at the location. The mist was, in fact humidity banks captured by digital cameras, the orbs here are dust, and the screams probably just people. The other oddity that is clamed is that the only survivor to the massacre, a dog named Highball left his psychic impression on the area causing other pooches to bite and attack the fence. I saw several dogs lift their leg on the fence and one that barked at a man that passed by, but that's about it.

the overactive imaginations of those who know what once occurred on the site but based on the reports of those who had no idea of the history of the place, something strange was apparently occurring.

And those who were accompanied by their dogs also reported their share of weirdness, too. The animals seemed to be especially bothered by this piece of lawn, sometimes barking and howling, sometimes whining in fear. Their sense of what happened here many years ago seems to be much greater than our own.

However, many believe that what dogs are sensing here is not the human trauma experienced at the massacre site, but rather the trauma that must have been experienced by Johnny May's German Shepherd, Highball. The poor animal must have been terrified by what occurred that morning, from the deafening sounds of the Tommy guns to the bloody slaying of his beloved owner. Tied to the front bumper of the truck, Highball had nowhere to run. It should be noted again that it was not the sound of machine-gun fire that alerted Landesman to the horror inside the garage: it was the howling and barking of the terrified dog.

Could the animals that passed by this empty lot have been sensing the trauma suffered by Highball so many years ago? As any ghost buff can tell you, it's the events of yesterday that create the hauntings of today and sometimes those who lived in the past can leave a little piece of themselves behind to be experienced in the present over and over again.

Even after all of these years, the violent events of the city's gangster era still reverberate over time. Men like Al Capone, whether city officials want to admit it or not, left an indelible mark on Chicago. It seems that the events of St. Valentine's Day 1929 may have left one, too.

PUBLIC ENEMY NUMBER ONE

John Scalise (Left) & Albert Anselmi were murdered in May 1929. The two men may have been involved in the St. Valentine's Day Massacre & were rumored to have been killed by Capone himself.

Capone returned to Chicago in May 1929. On May 8, the bodies of John Scalise, Albert Anselmi and Unione Siciliana President Joseph "Hop Toad" Guinta, were found near a gangland dumping group called Wolf Lake, located southeast of the city. They had apparently been taken on one of the mob's infamous "one-way rides." The beaten and bullet-riddled bodies of the three men were discovered inside a car that had been dumped into a ditch on an undeveloped part of Wolf Lake property, just across the Indiana border. Who actually killed these three men remains a mystery to this day.

Some believe that rival gangsters did them in. They had been accused of being involved in the St. Valentine's Day Massacre and had been brought in for questioning by detectives and by the Cook County state's attorney. They were released on bond and it's thought that perhaps gangsters working for George Moran's North Side mob may have caught up with them.

Others hold to the theory that the men were taken out by Al Capone himself. Informants allegedly told him that Scalise, Anselmi and Guinta had allied themselves with Capone's old enemy, Joseph Aiello. Capone, after corroborating the rumor, invited the three men, along with about 100 other guests, to a gangland banquet that was thrown to celebrate the victory over the Moran gang. After dinner was over, Capone is said to have savagely beaten the three men to death with a baseball bat and then his gunmen shot them to pieces. The story cannot be verified but, if it happened, the likely location was a nightclub that was located in Hammond, Ind. The car was then driven off the road near Wolf Lake, a place where countless other Prohibition murder victims were also deposited.

A few days later, on May 10, Capone went to Atlantic City, accompanied by a young man named Anthony "Joe Batters" Accardo, who would later run the Chicago Outfit. In Atlantic City, they met with crime leaders from all over the country, concerned about the publicity and heat that had been generated by what newspapers were calling the "St. Valentine's Day Massacre." The guests at this gathering included "Boo-Hoo" Hoff and Nig Rosen from

Philadelphia; Abe Bernstein from the Purple Gang in Detroit; Leo Berkowitz and Moe Dalitz from Cleveland; John Lazia from Kansas City; Longy Zwillman from New Jersey; and Daniel Walsh from Rhode Island. The New York contingent was the most formidable and the angriest at Capone. It was made up of Meyer Lansky, Dutch Schultz, Charles "Lucky" Luciano, Albert Anastasia, Louis Buchalter, Ben Siegel, Joe Adonis and Frank Costello. They also brought with them Johnny Torrio. All of them were upset with Capone for killing Frankie Yale without permission - and for having the gall to do it on their home territory.

The delegates talked for three days, often walking on the beach, where they could be far away from prying ears. They adopted a series of resolutions, some designed to cut Capone down to size and others to lay a groundwork for organized crime after Prohibition. The delegates also formed a commission, with retired Torrio as the head, which would deal with all disagreements between members. Capone's organization was to be disbanded immediately and his gambling joints taken over by the commission. There would be no more killing and the new head of the Chicago Unione Siciliana would be Capone's enemy, Joseph Aiello.

Other resolutions were to have serious consequences for organized crime in the future. There were two men who were conspicuously absent from the Atlantic City conference: Joe Masseria and Salvatore Maranzano, rival Mafia leaders in New York, who were at war over which of them would be the leader. For Luciano, Lansky and the others, such Mafia battles were a thing of the past, a holdover from the days of the ethnic gangs. They wanted a Syndicate in which each member controlled his own territory and no one person was in charge. Thanks to the bloodshed and the publicity that the war was generating, they decided that Masseria and Maranzano had to be removed. The old Sicilian Mafia would be replaced by a new American version.

It was also agreed that it would be good public relations if Al Capone went to jail for a time. It was arranged for him to be arrested in Philadelphia on a charge of carrying a concealed weapon. Two detectives were paid $10,000 each to arrest him in the lobby of a movie theater, charge him and get him sentenced as quickly as possible. It all happened in just 16 hours and he was sentenced to spend a term of one year at the Eastern State Penitentiary.

When Capone returned to Chicago in March 1930, he found the climate of the city had changed considerably during the time he had been away. His popularity had waned and the police were adamant about putting his operations out of business. Police Captain John Stege even posted a guard of 25 policemen in front of the Capone home on South Prairie Avenue with orders to arrest him as soon as he arrived from Pennsylvania. Capone slipped quietly into the city, though, and took up residence at the Hawthorne Inn in Cicero, where he spent four days answering mail and getting caught up on the state of operations. Then, he and his attorneys blatantly called on Captain Stege, and the United States District Attorney, and found that neither of them had an actual warrant for his arrest. With that settled, he returned to Chicago and moved into the Lexington Hotel.

Capone's modest home on South Prairie Avenue

While no charges had actually been filed against Capone, there was nothing to prevent the police from keeping him under surveillance. Two uniformed policemen were assigned to follow Capone everywhere he went, day and night. Capone's empire was starting to crumble and he began losing some of his men.

Fred "Killer" Burke was one of the most deadly of Capone's gunmen and was allegedly one of the machine gunners at the St. Valentine's Day Massacre. He was a known murderer and he and his partner, James Ray, had robbed several banks in Ohio dressed as policemen, the same M.O. used by the St. Valentine's Day killers. In December 1929, St. Joseph, Michigan police officer Charles Skelly spotted Burke fleeing the scene of a traffic accident. Skelly curbed Burke's car and jumped on the running board. Burke shot him in the stomach three times and drove away. Skelly died three hours later.

The gunman was badly unnerved by the policeman's murder and he crashed his car into a telephone pole, where it was later found and traced to his address. In the house, they found a machine gun that was later found to be one of the guns used during the St. Valentine's Day Massacre. Burke was captured in April 1930 but was never convicted for the massacre. He was convicted of Officer Skelly's murder instead and was sent to the Michigan State Penitentiary for life.

Michael "Mike da Pike" Heitler was another Capone henchman, although Heitler turned on Capone after he was ignored and demoted in 1931. Angry, he wrote a letter to State's Attorney John A. Swanson and disclosed all he knew about Capone's prostitution organization. A few days later, Capone had Heitler brought to his headquarters at the Lexington Hotel and threw the unsigned letter in the gunman's face. He told Heitler that he knew that only "Mike da Pike" could have sent the letter but Capone never explained how he had gotten his hands on it. On April 29, 1931, Heitler's corpse was found in a burned-out house in Barrington. Investigators reported that Heitler had been burned alive.

Capone also found that his brother, Ralph, who had been left in charge of Capone's operations while he was in prison, had been indicted for income tax evasion. However, Capone discounted the problems that his brother was having. It seemed unlikely that anyone would be convicted of a crime as small as not paying taxes. But the government's strategy was a sound one. Juries that would never convict a gangster of murder, fearing retaliation, were much more likely to send them to prison over what was seen as little more than a bookkeeping error. Capone was stunned when Ralph was convicted and faced 22 years in prison.

Capone also found that a young Prohibition agent named Eliot Ness was making a nuisance of himself, as well. Ness has been born in Chicago in 1903 and was raised in the city. He graduated from the University of Chicago and in 1928, joined the Bureau of Prohibition, working under the District Attorney, George E.Q. Johnson. Ness began working undercover, posing as a corrupt official, an investigation that resulted in 81 indictments and the destruction of a bootlegging operation that was bringing in almost $36 million a year.

Ness was then promoted and began trying to dismantle the Capone operation in Cicero. He soon found that the Prohibition Bureau was so riddled with corruption that little progress had been made against the bootleggers. Ness was determined to change that. He selected and led a small team of honest agents whose resistance to the Capone organization's efforts to buy them off led to them being dubbed the "Untouchables" by the newspapers. The destruction that Ness managed to do was carried out by just nine agents.

At the time that Capone was serving his sentence at Eastern State Penitentiary on a concealed weapon charge, and his brother Ralph was in charge of operations, Ness managed to tap Ralph's telephone and learn the locations of some of the secret breweries that supplied the Capone organization. He raided a large brewery on South Wabash Avenue, ramming through the front door with a snowplow, and shut the place down, seizing hundreds of cases of beer. The team also managed to trace beer barrels on their journey from speakeasies back to the brewery and was able to locate and raid six Capone breweries and five distribution plants. They seized 25 delivery trucks and confiscated beer worth about $9 million. To humiliate Capone, Ness drove the trucks down Michigan Avenue past Capone's headquarters at the Lexington Hotel after calling the mob boss and telling him to look out the window.

Ness managed to arrest 69 Capone bootleggers and his raids caused substantial damage to the organization. He survived several attempts on his life, once discovering a bomb in his car. In the end, it was not Ness' efforts that caused Capone's downfall, but they certainly contributed to it.

Despite the changes that had taken place in his organization, and the efforts of the "Untouchables," Capone was still at the height of his power when he returned to Chicago in 1930. The Atlantic City Commission never enforced its sanctions against him and when Capone returned from prison, he was able to take back control of the organization and continue things just as they had been before. Capone even went to the trouble of rubbing the Commission's nose in the fact that they could do nothing to stop him by killing their appointed head of the Unione Siciliana, Joe Aiello. He was shot and killed on Capone's orders and the Commission took no action against him. At 31, Al Capone was now the most powerful man in Chicago but it was not going to last.

During this time, a citizens' group called the Chicago Crime Commission published a list of the most prominent criminals in the city. The first name on the list was, of course, Al Capone. The idea of "public enemies" was picked up across the country and J. Edgar Hoover, head of the FBI, created a "Most Wanted" list that still adorns the walls of U.S. Post Offices today.

Capone was bothered by the list, since it seemed to show how far his popularity had slipped in the eyes of the general public. He began making efforts to try and undo some of the damage that had been done by the St. Valentine's Day Massacre. The U.S. Stock Market had crashed on October 29, 1929, and by 1931, as the Great Depression worsened, hordes of the unemployed appeared on the streets of Chicago. Capone tried to shrug off his "Public Enemy" image by opening a soup kitchen on South State Street during the winter months. On Thanksgiving, he fed more than 5,000 people. The goodwill that this generated did a great deal to soften Capone in the eyes of the ordinary Chicagoan, but it did nothing to help his image with the federal government; they wanted to know where he got the money to pay for all of that generosity.

THE FALL OF AL CAPONE

For years, investigators (joined by federal agents) toiled endlessly to find proof of murder, bootlegging and racketeering against Al Capone. Nothing that they uncovered would stand up in court, so authorities instead began concentrating on his expenditures compared to his declared income. Internal Revenue Service agents blanketed stores in Chicago and Miami, calculating the cost of Capone's furniture, automobiles, tableware and clothing: right down to his underwear. After interviewing hundreds of people and looking over thousands of receipts, it was clear that his income was vastly different than what he stated. Government agents were able to prove that Capone owed $215,080.48 in taxes. Capone offered to pay off the tax but his offer was rejected. On June 5, 1931, he was indicted for income tax evasion. He was brought to trial on October 7 and convicted on five counts, three of evading taxes from 1925 to 1928 and two of failing to file tax returns in 1928 and 1929. He was sentenced to 11 years in prison and fined $80,000.

Legal problems began to plague Capone starting in 1931

Capone was incarcerated at the Cook County Jail while he appealed his sentence. Needless to say, this was still Chicago and many public officials were now capable of repaying favors for past kindnesses that had been shown to them by Capone. Warden David Moneypenny installed him in a one-man cell on the fifth floor with a private shower. He was allowed to make telephone calls and send telegrams and continue running his operation from behind bars. However, anonymous telegrams that were sent to the Department of Justice, describing

Capone in U.S. District Court in 1931

Capone's privileged life in jail, put an end to it. After an investigation, Moneypenny was ordered to ban all visitors except the prisoner's wife, mother, son and lawyers. Capone was transferred to the hospital ward with a detail of deputy U.S. marshals assigned to 24-hour guard duty. On February 27, Capone learned that the District Court had rejected his appeal.

Capone's next appeal attempt was made with the U.S. Supreme Court, which rejected his application on May 2. On May 4, he was taken from the Cook County Jail. His original destination had been Leavenworth but since so many of Capone's men were already incarcerated there, officials decided that he should go to the Atlanta Penitentiary instead.

When Capone arrived at Atlanta, he was stripped to the skin and his clothing was replaced with a blue denim uniform. Fingerprinted and photographed, his hair was shaved close to the skull and then he was transferred to the hospital ward for a three-week stay to determine if he carried any communicable diseases. Tests that were taken here determined that Capone had syphilis, although Capone believed that he had been cured of it three years before. More tests were ordered, which included a spinal tap, but Capone refused them. It would later turn out that Capone did have the disease and, in fact, it was eating away at his brain. Toward the end of his life, it would utterly destroy him.

The overcrowded Atlanta Penitentiary had no single cells, only two-man and eight-man cells. Capone was assigned to an eight-man cell, whose occupants included an oil-well promoter, a former judge who had been convicted of mail fraud, a criminal from Ohio, and four mail robbers serving 25-year sentences. One of the mail

Capone's booking photograph when he arrived at the
Atlanta Federal Penitentiary

robbers turned out to be Red Rudensky, a mechanic whom Capone knew from his early bootleg days. Rudensky thought highly of Capone and the two of them sat up talking during Capone's first night, as the gangland boss was unable to sleep.

The other prisoners mostly admired Capone and when Rudensky, who stage-managed most of the entertainment at the theater, introduced him, Capone received a standing ovation. Rudensky remained close with Capone. He arranged the smuggling of cash to him from the gang by way of a trusty who drove a supply truck. With this money, Capone bought privileges from certain guards and loyalty and protection from other prisoners. He usually had a band of bodyguards who surrounded him at work and during recreation times in the yard.

Over the course of the next several months, Capone's family continued his legal battles on the outside, attempting to appeal his case. His attorney, William E. Leahy, was one of the most prominent lawyers in the country and he attempted to re-open Capone's case, stating that the statute of limitations run out. He based this on a similar case that had been decided in Boston, maintaining that Capone's case was parallel and that his client was being imprisoned illegally. Capone appeared before federal Judge E. Marvin Underwood, who took the petition under advisement.

Capone was still waiting for the judge's decision when an announcement came that President Franklin D. Roosevelt had ratified the repeal of the Eighteenth Amendment. Prohibition had come to an end. This was, perhaps, a bad omen for Capone. Prohibition had allowed him to make all of the money that he had gone to prison for and now it was over, just like Capone's final court case. The judge dismissed the petition and Capone remained in jail. And to make matters worse, word had just come from the Justice Department that he was going to be transferred to the new, brutal "escape-proof" prison, Alcatraz.

Al Capone arrived at the prison in August 1934. Upon his arrival, he quickly learned that while he may have once been famous, on Alcatraz, he was only a number. He made attempts to flaunt the power that he had enjoyed at the federal prison in Atlanta, where he was used to the special benefits that he was awarded by guards and wardens alike. He was arrogant and unlike most of the other prisoners, was not a veteran of the penal system. He had only spent a short time in prison and his stay had been much different than that of most other cons. Capone had possessed the ability to control his environment through wealth and power, but he was soon to learn that things were much different at Alcatraz.

After Capone and the prisoners who arrived with him were unloaded from the train, they were taken to a low barge that brought them across the water to Alcatraz. The guards who had transferred him from Atlanta took off his leg irons, but not his handcuffs. Capone hobbled along with the rest of the men onto the boat, across the bay and then up the steep, spiraling roadway to the top of the island.

Warden James Johnston had a custom of meeting new prisoners when they arrived to give them a brief orientation. When Capone entered the rear of the cell house, Johnston sat at a desk. When he called out the names of the prisoners, a guard removed their handcuffs and brought them to the desk. Johnston later wrote in his memoirs that he had little trouble recognizing Capone when he saw him. Capone was grinning and making comments to other prisoners as he stood in the lineup. When it became his turn to approach the warden, Johnston ignored him and simply gave him a standard prison number, just like all of the other men. Johnston wrote: "It was apparent that he wanted to impress other prisoners by asking me questions as if he were their leader. I wanted to make sure that he didn't get any such idea. I handed him a ticket with his number, gave him the instructions I had given every other man, and told him to move along."

The guards led Capone to the bathhouse to be stripped, medically examined, and his ears, nose, mouth and rectum probed for contraband. For weekday wear, he was issued pants and a shirt made of gray denim and for Sunday, a blue denim uniform. For cold weather, he was given a wool-lined pea coat. The fronts and backs of his clothing were stamped with Capone's number, 85, that could be seen from 20 yards away. He was then given sheets, a pillowcase, towel, comb, and a toothbrush and taken to his cell, where he would spend about 14 hours out of every 24, seven days a week. Capone drew the fifth cell from the right, third tier, block B. The entire process must have been quite a shock to the crime boss, from the clothing to the accommodations. Even in Atlanta, he had been used to special treatment, his own clothing, special food and drink and even silk underwear. He quickly discovered that

Alcatraz was not the same sort of prison.

Warden Johnston had a policy to listen to any prisoner who wanted to speak with him and when, on the day after he arrived, Capone requested an interview, Johnston had him brought to his office. He asked what the interview was about and Capone explained, "Well, I don't know how to begin but you're my warden now and I just thought I better tell you that I have a lot of friends and expect to have lots of visitors and I want to arrange to see my wife and mother and my son and brothers."

Capone spent his last days incarcerated at Alcatraz, the most feared penitentiary in America

Johnston explained to him that, like all of the other inmates, Capone had very limited visiting privileges, extending to blood relatives only, except for his brother, Ralph, who had a prison record. None of his "friends and business associates" were allowed to visit. No rules were going to be bent for any of the inmates, no matter who they were.

Capone smiled feebly as he said, "It looks like Alcatraz has got me licked."

Johnston granted another interview request from Capone the following week, where Capone again tried to plead his case for special visitors. He explained that among his important friends were big businessmen who depended on him for help and advice. Johnston again sent him on his way.

Capone's cell at Alcatraz is at the center of the photo

Capone may have struck out with the warden but he was determined to try and gain the kind of leadership within the prison that he had enjoyed at Atlanta. Capone tried to dispense favors to his fellow prisoners, offering to have money sent to their relatives and to buy musical instruments for those who, like himself, wanted to play in the prison band. Johnston thwarted all of his efforts. When it became apparent that Capone could not obtain even the smallest consideration, he lost respect, as Johnston intended, among the inmates, especially among the minor criminals who made up the majority of the prison population. He soon found that his safety was in danger.

It was deprivation of news from the outside world that led to Capone's first punishment. He spent a full 19 days in the hole for attempting to bribe a guard to bring him a newspaper. He also did two 10-day stretches in the hole for talking to other inmates when the rule of silence was in effect. Each time that Capone was sent to the hole, he emerged a little the worse for wear.

Capone was assigned to work in the prison's basement laundry room, to which the Army posts around the bay area sent their wash. The laundry room was damp and badly ventilated and when an Army transport ship anchored in the bay with an accumulation of wash, the workload became backbreaking. In January 1935, Capone was at his usual station when 36 of his co-workers walked off the job in protest. The strikers were quickly surrounded, separated and sent to the hole. Because Capone took no part in it, her aroused a great deal of hostility from the other workers. A month later, one of the strikers, Bill Collier, was catching laundry as Capone fed it into the machine. He complained that it was coming to him too fast but Capone ignored him. Finally, Collier picked up a sopping bundle and flung it into his face. Before the guards could stop the fight, Capone blacked both of his attacker's eyes. Both men spent eight days in the hole for the altercation.

Another strike, this time a general one, took place without Capone in January of the following year. The immediate provocation was the death of a prisoner with a stomach ulcer, whom Johnston had refused medical treatment because he thought he was pretending to be sick. Capone stuck to his post again, once more incurring the wrath of the strikers. But it was not cowardice that kept him from striking; he knew the odds and knew there was nothing to be gained by going up against the guards. He asked to be excused from work and allowed to remain in his cell until the strike ended. Capone was not alone in his idea. Nearly all of the prison's high-profile inmates - felons like Doc Barker, George "Machine Gun" Kelly, kidnappers Albert Bates and Harvey Bailey, and train robber

GHOST ALERT!

Alcatraz is considered to be one of the most haunted places in America and ghostly happenings are widely reported at the abandoned prison. Weird noises and eerie apparitions continue to be encountered and one of the most prominent ghosts still lingering on the island may be one of the most famous men to have served time there: Al Capone. It's not uncommon for rangers and guides to sometimes hear the sound of banjo strings being plucked on the cell block or in the bath house, where Capone once cleaned and became known by the derogatory nickname of the "wop with the mop." Many who have experienced these strange sounds have no idea that Capone once played the banjo and one ranger even surmised that perhaps it was a ghostly echo from the time when Alcatraz was a military fort. Others have come to believe that the sound of the banjo is the only lingering part of a man who left his sanity behind on the island. Is it merely an imprint from the past, or is Al Capone still here on Alcatraz, a lonely and broken spirit still plucking the strings of a spectral banjo that vanished decades ago?

and escape artist Roy Gardner - shared Capone's prudence and likewise incurred the dislike and hatred of the strikers.

Capone's request was granted. On his first day back at work, the strikers having been starved into submission, an unknown person hurled a sash weight at his head. Roy Gardner saw it coming and threw himself at Capone, shoving the other man aside. The weight still managed to strike Capone's arm, inflicting a deep cut. After that, he was transferred to the bathhouse cleaning crew. The bathhouse adjoined the barbershop. On the morning of June 23, five months after the second strike, Jim Lucas, a Texas bank robber, reported for his monthly haircut. When he left, he grabbed a pair of scissors, slipped up behind Capone, who was mopping the bathhouse floor, and drove the blades into his back. Capone recovered after a week in the hospital and Lucas went to the hole.

After this incident, a San Francisco lawyer, representing Mae Capone, appealed to the Attorney General to have Capone incarcerated somewhere else, but all of his requests were refused. Other attempts followed to kill or maim the "wop with the mop," as his enemies now referred to him. His friends exposed a plan to doctor his coffee with lye one morning and on his way to the dentist, he was jumped and almost strangled before he broke his attacker's hold and knocked the man down.

The attempts on Capone's life, the trips to the hole, the grinding daily routine and likely what was, by now, an advanced case of syphilis began to take their toll on Capone. Eventually, he stopped going into the recreation yard and practiced his banjo instead. Once practice was over, he returned immediately to his cell, avoiding all of the inmates except for a few of his closest friends. Occasionally, guards reported that he would refuse to leave his cell to go to the mess hall and eat. They would often find him crouched down in the corner of his cell like an animal. On other occasions, he would mumble to himself or babble in baby talk or simply sit on his bed and strum little tunes on the banjo. Years later, another inmate recalled that Capone would sometimes stay in his cell and make his bunk over and over again.

When the guards decided that the weather was cold enough for the inmates to wear their pea coats, they indicated the decision with three blasts of a whistle. The morning of February 5, 1938, started off unseasonably warm and no whistle blew, signaling that the men needed their winter coats. Capone nevertheless put on his pea coat. For a year, he had been on library duty, delivering and collecting books and magazines. Alvin Karpis, the bank robber who struck up an acquaintance with Capone and who occupied the second cell to the left of Capone and always followed him in the line to the mess hall, had a magazine to return and he tossed it into Capone's cell as he passed it. Seeing Capone standing there in his winter coat, including a cap and gloves, he called to him that he didn't need his jacket that day. Capone seemed to neither hear nor recognize him. He simply stood there, staring vacantly into space.

He failed to fall into line when ordered to do so, a breach of discipline ordinarily punished by a trip to the hole, but the guards sensed something was seriously wrong and watched without disturbing him. He finally left his cell and entered the mess hall last in line. A thread of drool dripped down his chin. As he moved mechanically toward the steam table, a deputy warden, Ernest Miller, spoke to him quietly and patted his arm. Capone grinned strangely and for some reason, pointed out the window. Then, suddenly, he started to choke and retch. Miller led him to a locked gate across the hall and called to the guard on the other side to unlock it. They helped Capone up a flight of stairs to the hospital ward.

To the prison physician, and a consulting psychiatrist that he sent for, Capone's symptoms suggested damage to the central nervous system characteristic of advanced syphilis. When Capone, after a return to lucidity, understood this, he finally agreed to the spinal puncture and the other tests that he had refused in Atlanta. The fluid was rushed to the Marine Hospital in San Francisco for analysis. Warden Johnston later stopped by his bed to ask him what had happened to him that morning. Capone replied, "I dunno, they tell me that I acted like I was a little whacky."

The report from the Marine Hospital confirmed the doctor's diagnosis. Word of it reached the press and newspapers from coast to coast painted a picture of Capone as a man driven insane by the horrors of Alcatraz. Mae Capone pleaded with Warden Johnston by telephone, imploring him to free her husband, an act that was far beyond his power. The hardened warden must have taken some pity on the former "King of Chicago." Capone was never returned to the cellblock and spent the remainder of his sentence in the hospital ward, subjected to injections of arsphenamine, shock treatments and induced fever. His disease was slowed down but not stopped. He alternated between lucidity and confusion, coming to the brink of total insanity. He spent most of his time sitting by himself, plucking at the strings of his banjo, unaware of his surroundings.

His last day on Alcatraz was January 6, 1939 but he still owed another year's sentence for the misdemeanor offense of failing to file a tax return. Due to his deteriorated state, officials decided not to ship him to Chicago to serve out the sentence at the Cook County Jail. Instead, they sent him to the newly opened federal prison at Terminal Island, just outside Los Angeles. He was taken there by three armed guards with extra weights added to his leg chains, which was rather pointless since he was partially paralyzed.

The following November, after the last of his fines were paid through a Chicago gang lawyer, Capone was transferred to the U.S. Penitentiary at Lewisburg, Pennsylvania. He arrived on November 16 and was met by Ralph and Mae Capone, who drove him to Baltimore's Union Hospital. Until spring, he lived with Mae in Baltimore as an outpatient of the hospital under the care of Dr. Joseph Moore, a syphilis specialist.

In Chicago, reporters asked Jake Guzik if Capone was now going to return to Chicago and take command of the mob again. Jake, despite being one of Al's closest and most loyal friends replied, "Al is nuttier than a fruitcake."

Capone's final years were lived out on his estate near Miami. He cried at night and the sight of an automobile, especially one carrying men, would throw him into a panic. No outsiders were ever allowed into the compound or near Al because, Ralph cautioned, in his foggy mental state, he might talk about the organization.

At least four times each week, Mae attended mass at St. Patrick's Cathedral in Miami Beach. Capone never accompanied her because he claimed that he would embarrass the pastor, Monsignor William Barry. Capone's boy, Sonny, had gone to the private preparatory school run by the monsignor, who took a special interest in the shy, semi-deaf boy, helping him to rise above the problems caused by his name. In 1937, Sonny had entered Notre Dame under his father's alias, Al Brown. He withdrew after his freshmen year, when his identity became known. He eventually earned a business degree from the University of Miami.

Probably because Capone slept so badly, haunted by his dreams of slain gunmen, the household kept strange hours. They often retired around 10 p.m. and were up again by 3 a.m. Most of the day was spent next to the pool. Capone, wearing pajamas and a dressing gown, would spend hours on the dock, smoking cigars and holding a fishing rod. Occasionally, he would hit a tennis ball over the net that had been strung across the yard. He hated to be alone and always wanted people around him, provided that he recognized them as trusted friends. He had grown obese and looked much order than his years. He also enjoyed playing gin rummy and pinochle; but the mental effort was usually too much for him and his friends let him win.

On December 30, 1941, Capone overcame his reluctance and went to church to witness his son's marriage to Diana Ruth Casey, a girl that Sonny had first met in high school. After the honeymoon, the newlyweds remained in Miami, where Sonny had opened a florist shop a few months earlier. His wife bore him four children, all girls, on whom their grandfather doted, constantly buying them expensive gifts and playing with them in the Palm Island swimming pool.

The course of Capone's syphilis was unpredictable. At times, he seemed normal but at other times, his speech was slurred, he was disoriented and he suffered from tremors and seizures. Even at the best of times, Capone lacked mental and physical coordination and he skipped abruptly from subject to subject, humming, whistling and singing as he chatted about nothing. By 1942, penicillin had become available, but in an extremely limited supply due to the war. Capone's doctor was able to procure dosages for Capone, who became one of the first syphilitics to be treated with antibiotics. His condition did stabilize somewhat after that, but no therapy could reverse the extensive damage that had been done to his brain.

On January 19, 1947, at just after 4 a.m., Capone collapsed from a brain hemorrhage. Dr. Kenneth Phillips arrived, followed by Monsignor Barry, who administered the last rites. The newspapers announced that Capone was dead, but he rallied and Dr. Phillips pronounced him out of danger. The following week, though, he developed bronchial pneumonia and reporters began to gather outside the compound's locked gates. As the hot day wore on, Ralph let them inside and offered them iced beer. On Saturday evening, January 25, Capone died at the age of 48.

Capone's body was returned to Chicago for burial. He was buried on a cold, winter's day in Mount Olivet Cemetery, sharing a black granite marker with this father, Gabriel, and his brother, Frank, who had been killed by police in Cicero. This was no typical "gangland funeral." It was a simple affair with only family and Al's closest remaining friends in attendance. When Capone's mother, Teresa, died in 1952, Capone's body was moved to Mount Carmel Cemetery, where he now lies in the same burial ground with Dion O'Banion, Hymie Weiss, the Genna brothers, Jack McGurn and Sam Giancana.

It was a quiet end to the life of the man who once ruled Chicago.

The leaders of the Chicago Outfit after Capone: (Left to Right) Jake "Greasy Thumb" Guzik; Paul "The Waiter" Ricca; and Tony "Joe Batters" Accardo

THE CHICAGO OUTFIT AFTER CAPONE

When Al Capone arrived in Chicago in 1921, the city was a confusion of ethnic gangs, battling one another for control of the vice and prostitution rackets. Ten years later, when Capone was in prison, the city had completely changed. After Prohibition was repealed in 1933, the old ethnic gangs vanished, the members absorbed into either the Capone organization, the civilian world, the penitentiary, or the graveyard.

Many expected that with Capone behind bars at Alcatraz, his organization would fall apart. The press had created the impression that Capone was the sole criminal mastermind behind the organization, single-handedly responsible for corruption in politics and the police force and for the violence and mayhem on Chicago's streets. His prosecutors also thought that, once he was imprisoned, organized crime in the city would fade away. It was not long before they realized that things were not going to be so simple.

Capone had inherited an efficient operation from John Torrio and had transformed it into a modern corporation that would outlive its creator. Prohibition had provided the organization with the money to diversify and to create a network that linked the Chicago mob to other crime groups across the country and into Canada and the Caribbean. All of the cities involved had been part of a network of illegal liquor production, smuggling, and shipping operations. Groups that would have had no contact otherwise were now in almost daily communication. Capone had created a system that rivaled nearly any legitimate businesses of the time.

In Chicago, with Capone gone, the mob was taken over by a "board of directors" made up of Jake Guzik, Johnny Roselli, Paul "The Waiter" Ricca and Murray Llewellyn Humphreys, with Antonio "Joe Batters" Accardo as the head. These men were insulated from the operational end of the business by layers of "managers," each with an area of authority, from bootlegging to prostitution. At the street level were the collectors, enforcers and gunmen. The organization was dubbed the "Outfit" and remains a viable entity in Chicago today, although downsized and changed greatly from what it was in the 1930s.

The Outfit had a number of rules. It tried to discourage flamboyant dress (so-called "gangster chic") and urged its members, from the managers on down to the gunmen to avoid drawing attention to themselves. The members were asked to dress well, but in somber business suits, and to not create a spectacle when dining out or socializing. Mild social drinking was allowed but anything more was frowned upon. Most of the members worked 12-hour days and no drug dealing was allowed. Anyone who broke that rule was killed. Wives and families were sacrosanct and, if possible, had no knowledge of Outfit operations. Widows of Outfit members were paid pensions. Mae Capone, for example, received monthly payments of $25,000 until her death in 1986.

The Chicago organization was no longer creating mayhem on the streets of the city. Massacres and gang assassinations were, for the most part, a thing of the past. But there would be more trouble to come in the Windy City.

CAPONE'S "ENFORCER": FRANK NITTI

During the Great Depression, one of the only thriving industries in America was the movie business. This was enough to attract the attention of the Chicago Outfit. The Outfit had begun to control the entertainment industry in Chicago, where many films were shot beginning in 1910 and throughout the 1920s, by taking over trade unions like the Motion Picture Operator's Union. They also set up a protection racket on movie theater chains, often demanding up to 50 percent of their take. A former pimp named Willie Bioff, who became the Outfit's bagman in Hollywood, ran the racket. Another Chicago gangster, Johnny Roselli, broke into Hollywood as a result of the 1933 strike by the International Alliance of Stage Employees (IATSE). The studios went to Roselli to break the strike, which he did by hiring thugs to intimidate the strikers.

Frank Nitti

Meanwhile, in Chicago, the board of the Outfit had summoned George Browne to a meeting. Browne was a candidate for next president of the IATSE and the Outfit guaranteed his election in return for control of the union. Browne, already in trouble with the Outfit for running a protection racket in their territory, quickly agreed. He was quickly elected president and, in fact, not other candidate was even nominated to run.

Browne and Bioff were sent to New York. Soon afterward, Browne was able to demonstrate his power by calling for a strike against the RKO and Loews theater chains. He then went to the chairman of RKO and offered to call it off for the sum of $87,000. It was quickly handed over. The president of Loews, Nick Schenk, then paid Browne and Bioff $250,000 for a no-strike deal that would last for a period of seven years. In exchange, Browne agreed to reduce worker wage increase demands by two-thirds.

Bioff was put in charge of the Hollywood branch of the IATSE in 1936. He and Browne then levied a two percent surcharge on paychecks as "strike insurance." This levy generated more than $6 million, a hefty percentage of which went directly to the Outfit.

With the major unions under control, the mob then moved against the film studios. By controlling the unions, they could cripple any studio that refused to pay protection against strikes. They could close down all of the theaters in the country with a single telephone call. They went to Nick Schenk first and demanded $2 million, finally settling for $1 million before they started making the rounds to other studios.

The Outfit was soon in control of Hollywood but it was not meant to last. Unfortunately for them, Bioff was the weak link in the organization. He made a down payment on a piece of property using a $100,000 check from Twentieth Century Fox, run by Nick Schenk's brother, Joe. The check proved to be Bioff's undoing. A breakaway organization from the IATSE, the International Alliance Progressives, was determined to remove the underworld control of the union. They began to convince workers to defy Bioff. At the same time, Bioff tried to take over the Screen Actor's Guild, which started to investigate Bioff's activities. The California State Legislature became interested in him, as well. The $100,000 check and Bioff's past history as a Chicago pimp came to light. The case against Bioff was put on hold but Joe Schenk was prosecuted, and his explosive testimony began to unravel the mob's Hollywood operation. Even worse was to come. The press discovered from Chicago police files that, in 1922, Bioff had been convicted of beating a prostitute. He was still wanted on that charge and a warrant was issued for his arrest. He ended up serving five months in jail.

In New York, Joe Schenk was indicted for fraud. In returned for a suspended sentence, he agreed to tell everything that he knew about Bioff and Browne. There were indicted in 1941 for tax evasion and racketeering. Desperate to keep their names out of the case, the Outfit sent their lawyer, Sidney Korshak, to Hollywood. He told Bioff to confess to being Schenk's bagman but to admit nothing else. To Korshak's dismay, Bioff entered a "not guilty" plea, which meant that he could be questioned - the last thing the Outfit wanted. Bioff was sentenced to 10 years in prison and Browne to eight.

During the trial, Bioff had let slip a reference to Chicago. This was the lead that the government had been waiting for. Terrified of being murdered for this error, Bioff decided to cooperate with the authorities. In March 1943, several members of the Outfit were indicted on extortion and conspiracy charges.

It was a charge that led to the downfall of the man who had been known for years as "Capone's Enforcer."

Frank Nitti (or Nitto, which was the preferred family spelling) was a man of mystery. Intensely private and quiet, he is only scarcely remembered today as being part of the legendary Capone gang. If not for the television series based on the exploits of Eliot Ness and his "Untouchables," it's possible that he would only be known to the most dedicated gangster buffs and researchers and not to the general public at all. Nitti was a small man but one with incredible will. He maintained discipline in the ranks and acted as Capone's enforcer and troubleshooter. He was also one of the only gangsters in the organization who never used an assumed name, which got him into trouble when investigators discovered a check he had endorsed. This put him into prison for 18 months in the early 1930s, an experience that had a lasting effect on him.

Nitti was born in 1888 and started out in crime as a barber who also fenced stolen goods. His methods of peddling stolen whiskey put him in touch with Capone and Johnny Torrio at the start of Prohibition and he was a high-ranking member of Capone's organization by the middle 1920s.

After Capone went to prison, the newspapers looked for a new leader for the mob and Nitti was hailed as that man. It's possible that he may have even believed this himself but insiders knew that the remaining men in Capone's gang would not take orders from Nitti. While an efficient organizer under Capone, it had been his job to make sure that Capone's orders had been carried out, not to give orders himself. When Luciano and Lansky established the Syndicate, they dealt with Paul "The Waiter" Ricca as the leader of the Chicago mob and not with Nitti.

However, Ricca and the others did use Nitti's high profile with the press to keep the heat off the real inner workings of the Outfit. He became a valuable man to take the heat. Chicago mayor Anton Cermak even dispatched his own police "hit men" to try and take out Nitti so that he could replace him with other gangsters that kept him on the payroll. On December 19, 1932, two police officers invaded Nitti's headquarters, allegedly under orders from new mayor Cermak, who was determined to assist Ted Newberry (who had taken over the O'Banion and Moran mob) redistribute the territories of the Capone gang. Shots were fired and Nitti was badly wounded. He lingered near death for a time but recovered only to end up standing trial for the shooting of one of the cops during the gun battle. However, the jury was convinced that the officer had actually shot himself in the finger in order to look like a hero and the trial ended in a hung jury. Nitti walked away a free man and the officer lost his job.

Nitti served prison time for an income tax charge related to the check that was discovered bearing his name, but he stayed out of the newspapers until November 1940, when he was indicted for influencing the Chicago Bartenders and Beverage Dispensers Union of the AFL. Nitti was accused of putting mob members into positions of power in the union and then forcing the sale of beer from mob-owned breweries. The trial rested on the testimony of one man, George McLane, the president of the union. He allegedly was forced to follow Nitti's orders but the pressure got to him and he went to the authorities and explained what the mob was doing. McLane was all set to testify until two mob soldiers showed up at his door and told him that if he talked in court, his wife would be mailed to him in small pieces. When the day came, McLane pleaded for his rights under the Fifth Amendment and the case was dropped.

Nitti's body was discovered alongside the railroad tracks. He had been killed by an apparent self-inflicted gunshot wound.

The heat was on Nitti again in 1943 during what came to be called the "Hollywood Extortion case." After Bioff and Browne decided to talk, indictments were brought against Nitti, Paul Ricca and several others. A meeting was called at Nitti's home in Riverside and Ricca decided that now was the perfect time to take advantage of Nitti's perceived top position in the mob. He ordered Nitti to plead guilty in the extortion case and to take the rap for everyone. He would be taken care of when he got out, as long as he kept his mouth shut while he was inside.

But there would be no "inside" for Nitti. He refused to go back to prison. His earlier jail time had so traumatized the gangster that he now had a terrible fear of small, confined spaces. He urged Ricca to come up with another plan or to allow some of the others to share the responsibility with him. Ricca was enraged and demanded that Nitti be a "standup guy." When Nitti still refused, Ricca told him "he was asking for it."

Nitti took these words to mean his death sentence but he simply couldn't face another stretch in prison. He made a last-ditch effort to try and bribe the prosecutor in the case, M.F. Correa, but his attempt was coldly rebuffed.

So, on March 19, the day after the meeting, Frank Nitti placed a gun in his pocket and went for one last walk through his neighborhood. When he made it as far as the Illinois Central Railroad tracks, he shot himself in the head and died next to a nearby fence.

Nitti was laid to rest in Mount Carmel Cemetery, not far from where the body of Al Capone also lies. His simple stone is marked with his family name of "Nitto" and bears a direct and ominous inscription: "There is no life except by death," marking an end to his role in Chicago's gangland history.

DILLINGER: DEAD OR ALIVE!

On the evening of July 22, 1934, a dapper-looking man wearing a straw hat and a pin-striped suit stepped out of the Biograph Theater, where he and two girlfriends had gone to see a film called "Manhattan Melodrama" starring Clark Gable. No sooner had they reached the sidewalk than a man appeared and identified himself as Melvin Purvis of the FBI. Purvis ordered the man in the straw hat to surrender, but he decided to run instead. Several shots rang out and the fleeing man fell dead to the pavement, his left eye shredded by shots fired by the other agents who lay in wait.

And so ended the life of John Herbert Dillinger, the most prolific bank robber in modern American history and the general public's favorite Public Enemy No. 1 - or did it?

John Herbert Dillinger was born in Indianapolis, Ind., in 1903. He came from humble rural beginnings and work dominated his early life. His mother died in 1907 and Dillinger was raised by his older sister, Audrey, and his father, John Wilson Dillinger, who ran a grocery store and maintained several houses that he rented out.

GHOST ALERT:

Even though Frank Nitti committed suicide and was buried at Mount Carmel Cemetery, it has never been believed that Nitti rests here in peace. For many years, it has been a local legend in the North Riverside and Forest Park areas that the ghost of Frank Nitti still walks along the railroad tracks where he committed suicide in 1943. There are many who claim to have not only sensed his last anguished moments but who also state that they have seen the eerie figure of a man here, as well. The figure often appears along the railroad tracks at Cermak Avenue and begins walking west, plainly visible under the harsh lights of a nearby shopping center. The tracks, which are seldom used these days, can be found next to a toy store, a restaurant and a large shopping mall. The area that marks Nitti's suicide is almost remote and isolated from the activity of the retail area - and it is here where his ghost is said to walk.

John Dillinger

Dillinger's father was strict but never had much trouble with his son, who was a quiet child with good grades and who was popular with friends and teachers. When he was quite young, he proved to be an excellent athlete, especially excelling at baseball.

Dillinger's first brush with the authorities took place when he was in sixth grade. He was charged with stealing coal from the Pennsylvania Railroad yards and selling it to neighbors. He was released into the custody of his father and soon after, the elder Dillinger packed up his family and moved them to a modest farm outside Mooresville, Ind., about 20 miles south of Indianapolis. He reportedly wanted to get his son away from the corrupting influences of the city. It didn't seem to do much good, though. Dillinger refused to help his father on the farm and to return to school. Instead, he took a job back in Indianapolis as an apprentice machinist, driving back and forth to the farm each day on his prized motorbike.

Eventually, just to please his father, he decided to go back to school but dropped out during his first semester at Mooresville High School. However, Dillinger did join the Martinsville baseball team and became known as a remarkable second basemen. He also started dating a young woman named

Frances Thornton, his Uncle Everett's stepdaughter. The two of them fell in love and Dillinger asked his uncle for her hand in marriage. His uncle refused, telling John that they were both too young. In truth, he wanted the girl to marry a wealthy boy from Greencastle, Ind.

Angry, Dillinger returned home and on the night of July 21, 1923, he impulsively stole a car from the parking lot of the Friends Church in Mooresville. Hours later, he abandoned it in Indianapolis. Fearing arrest, he enlisted in the Navy. Unknown to Dillinger, the owner of the car, Oliver P. Macy, knew John and refused to press charges. Regardless, Dillinger enlisted under his real name but gave a false St. Louis address when he filled out his paperwork. After basic training at Great Lakes, he was assigned to the U.S.S. Utah. He went AWOL several times and was thrown in the brig and when the ship was anchored off Boston in December, Dillinger jumped ship permanently. The Navy listed him as a deserter and posted a reward for his capture but Dillinger made it back to Indiana.

At home, Dillinger met and began courting Beryl Ethel Hovius, 16, and the two of them married in the spring of 1924. They moved in with Beryl's parents but Dillinger spent more time playing baseball and shooting pool than paying attention to his wife and the marriage didn't amount to much.

On the night of September 6, 1924, Dillinger finally stepped completely over the line of the law. Cooking up a plan with a former convict and umpire for the Martinsville baseball team, Edgar Singleton, the two men decided to rob Frank Morgan, a Mooresville grocer who carried his week's receipts home on Saturday nights. They jumped him and hit him over the head, but the 65-year-old man refused to go down. One of the would-be robbers brandished a gun but Morgan knocked it away and a shot was accidentally fired. Dillinger and Singleton, both frightened, took off running.

Morgan's head required 11 stitches but he told Deputy Sheriff John Hayworth that he couldn't identify his attackers. Hayworth looked into the case and came to believe that Dillinger was involved. He took Morgan out to the Dillinger farm and the grocer confronted John. He recalled how the boy had purchased candy from his store and insisted that he wouldn't have hurt him. It couldn't be John, Morgan told the lawman. Hayworth took Dillinger in for questioning, anyway and, when his father came to collect him from the county jail, the tearful young man confessed to the hold-up attempt. The prosecutor promised the elder Dillinger that his son would receive a lenient sentence if he threw himself on the mercy of the court. The farmer convinced his son to do so and Dillinger, just 20 years old, entered a guilty plea. To his surprise, he was fined $100 and sentenced to concurrent sentences of 10-20 years in prison. His accomplice, through his attorney, received a change of venue and a much lighter sentence that resulted in his parole in just two years.

Betrayed and angry, Dillinger was sent to the Indiana State Reformatory with no plans to cause trouble, he said, "except to escape." Over the course of the next several years, he tried to break out over and over again, always getting caught. One night, he was found to be missing from his cell and was discovered under a pile of clothing in the laundry. Another time, he made a saw and cut his way out of his cell. He was captured in the corridor. He tried again in 1925 and was captured once more.

About this time, Dillinger met a man who would influence his future career: a bank robber named Harry Pierpont. The soft-spoken ladies' man had been captured after single-handedly robbing a bank in Kokomo, Ind. Pierpont and Dillinger became close friends and were soon joined by another young bank robber, Homer Van Meter. The two earned Dillinger's respect by being the toughest criminals in the prison. They spent more time in solitary confinement than in their cells. Eventually, officials gave up trying to control them and they were both shipped off to the state prison in Michigan City.

In 1929, the same year his wife filed for divorce, Dillinger came up before the parole board. He was turned down but, luckily for him, Indiana governor Harry Leslie was sitting in on the hearing. Dillinger had once been playing baseball in the prison yard and had overheard the governor remark that he ought to be playing professional ball. When he knew that he would not be getting out of jail, he asked the board to send him to the state prison in Michigan City because it had a real baseball team. Governor Leslie convinced the board that a move was in order, because it might help Dillinger to find work when he finally got out. Dillinger was sent to the state prison on July 15 and happily hooked up with Pierpont and Van Meter again.

His friends introduced him to another bank robber, John Hamilton, who began instructing Dillinger on the art of robbing banks. He also met Charles "Fat Charley" Makley and Russell Lee Clark. Both men had been arrested on robbery charges and Clark, especially, was known as a dangerous and brutal man. He had attempted to escape several times and had even tried to kill guards on several occasions. He and the others would figure into Indiana's largest prison break (masterminded by Dillinger) four years later and would form a gang of bank robbers who would make headlines around the country.

Since Dillinger would be out of prison before any of the others, he was cultivated as the contact man on the outside. It would be his job to hit a number of small town banks, targeted by Pierpont and Hamilton, and use the

The original "Dillinger Gang: met in prison (Top Row, Left to Right): Prison mug shots of Dillinger, Harry Pierpont, Russell Lee Clark

(Bottom Row, Left to Right): John Hamilton & Charles Makley

funds to finance the prison break. During his last four years inside, Dillinger was a model prisoner, which was all part of the plan. On top of his good behavior, Governor Paul McNutt received a petition from Dillinger's Mooresville neighbors, asking that he be released to help his father on the farm. Even the judge who had sentenced him, perhaps regretting his harsh decision, signed the petition. Dillinger was set free on May 22, 1933 and he immediately rushed to Mooresville, where his stepmother was seriously ill. She died just an hour before Dillinger arrived.

The following Sunday, Dillinger attended church with his father and sat weeping as he listened to the pastor give a pointed sermon on the return of the prodigal son. When the service ended, he told the minister how much good it had done him. Two weeks, later Dillinger began robbing small banks and isolated stores.

Dillinger recruited a small-time hoodlum named William Shaw and using the list that his friends devised, robbed a bank at New Carlisle, Ind., netting $10,600. Unfortunately, Dillinger would find that many of Pierpont's targets had gone under during the Depression and he was often met with empty buildings instead of banks that were ripe for the picking. Shaw was arrested a short time later (luckily, he only knew Dillinger as "Dan") and Dillinger recruited Harry Copeland, another bank robber and former convict from Michigan City.

They struck the Commercial Bank at Daleville, Ind., on July 17. Dillinger strolled into the bank, wearing what became his trademark straw boater, and walked up to cashier Margaret Good, who was the only person in the bank at the time. He pulled out a gun and reportedly said, "This is a stick-up, honey."

He then jumped over the railing and entered the vault. Harry Copeland left the getaway car parked in front of the building and also came inside, lining customers up at gunpoint as they entered the bank. Dillinger packed up $3,500 and ordered everyone inside the vault. Then, he and Copeland casually walked out and drove away. Margaret opened the door from the inside and a short time later, she told police that Dillinger was "the most courteous of bank robbers." His identity as a polite, but daring, bank robber was verified by the other witnesses and now police throughout Indiana were looking for him.

But Dillinger was already in Ohio seeing his new girlfriend, Mary Longnaker, who lived in Dayton. Dillinger took Mary to the World's Fair in Chicago and he chuckled as he photographed a policeman and then asked the cop to snap a picture of himself

Dillinger & Mary Longmaker at the Chicago World's Fair. The snapshot was taken by an unsuspecting police officer.

and Mary.

On August 4, Dillinger and Copeland robbed the National Bank of Montpelier, Ind. He was thrilled to find $10,100 in the small bank's vault. His next haul would not go so well. Dillinger, Copeland, Sam Goldstine and two other, unknown men hit the Citizens National Bank in Bluffton. Dillinger and Copeland entered the bank and announced that it was a robbery. After going through the teller drawers though, Dillinger demanded to know where the rest of the money was. Bookkeeper Oliver Locher pointed to the bank's vault at about the same time that the alarm went off. One of the lookouts came in and called out that the police were coming but Dillinger ignored him and began filling a sack with small bills. When Dillinger and Copeland didn't come out, the men outside began firing wild shots into the air to discourage the curious. Finally, after collecting only $2,100, they joined the men out on the street. They piled into a sedan and quickly sped away.

Dillinger was discouraged by the small take, still needing much more to finance the Michigan City prison break. He and Copeland decided to try a larger city bank the next time, settling on the Massachusetts Avenue State Bank in downtown Indianapolis. Using Hilton Crouch, a professional racetrack driver as a wheelman, Dillinger and Copeland entered the bank and immediately began cleaning out the teller drawers. Dillinger stole everything in sight and netted $24,800.

With a major share of this, Dillinger moved to Chicago and bribed the foreman of a thread-making company to secretly place several guns inside a barrel of thread being sent to the shirt shop at the Michigan City prison. It was sealed and marked with a red "X" on the top. Dillinger had earlier attempted to free Pierpont and the others by tossing handguns wrapped in newspaper over the prison walls under the cover of darkness. The guns were supposed to be found, by Pierpont, in the athletic field but were found by other inmates instead and they turned them over to the guards.

While the barrel was being shipped, Dillinger went to Dayton to see Mary Longnaker. Unknown to him, the police had received a tip from the Pinkerton Detective Agency that Dillinger was seeing a Dayton woman and the authorities had tracked Mary down because she was the sister of one of Dillinger's prison friends. Mary's rooming house was staked out and her landlady phoned in a tip to the police when Dillinger arrived. Two detectives, carrying shotguns, broke into Mary's apartment and Dillinger was arrested on the spot.

As things would turn out, Dillinger was in the Lima, Ohio jail four days later, waiting to be indicted for the Bluffton bank robbery, when his friends escaped from the Michigan City prison using the guns that Dillinger had smuggled in to them. Ten men went out the front gates of the penitentiary, driving cars that were stolen from in front of the administration building. The escapees included Harry Pierpont, Charles Makley, Russell Clark, John Hamilton, Edward Shouse, Joseph Fox, Joseph Burns, Jim "Oklahoma Jack" Clark, Mary Longnaker's brother, James Jenkins, and Walter Dietrich.

Pierpont, Makley, Clark, Hamilton, Shouse and Jenkins took one auto and headed for Leipsic, Ohio, where Pierpont's family lived. Somewhere near Bean Blossom, Ind., a bizarre accident took place. Rounding a corner, the door of the car flew open and Jenkins fell out. Since the police were everywhere, searching for the convicts, Jenkins was left to fend for himself. He walked up the road about a mile and ran into three farmers who were part of a posse searching for the escapees. When Jenkins pulled out a pistol, the farmers blasted him with their shotguns and he was killed.

Before Dillinger had been captured, he left money with Mary Kinder, a contact for the gang. Pierpont used this money to equip his men with new clothes, a new automobile and an arsenal of weapons. He also decided to put together some traveling money by robbing the First National Bank in St. Mary's, Ohio, the hometown of Charles Makley. Inside the bank, Makley ran into an old friend, W.O. Smith, who was the bank president. He chatted with Smith while Pierpont cleaned out the till. The gang left the bank with $14,000 without ever firing a shot.

On October 12, Pierpont, Makley, Clark, Hamilton and Shouse went looking for Dillinger. They arrived at the jail around 6:20 p.m. that evening, armed with pistols, and walked into the jail office. Sheriff Jess Sarber, his wife, Lucy, and Deputy Wilbur Sharp were reading newspapers after a dinner of pork chops and mashed potatoes. Sarber looked up when the men came in and asked if he could help them. Pierpont replied that they were officials from Michigan City and needed to speak with prisoner Dillinger. Sarber agreed but asked for the credentials. Pierpont pulled out a pistol instead and pointed it at the sheriff's face. "Here's our credentials," he said.

Sarber gasped and put out a hand to wave away the gun. Pierpont fired two shots and hit the sheriff, once in the stomach and once in the hip. He fell to the floor, leaving his wife and deputy to gape in astonishment. Pierpont demanded the keys as Sarber tried to get up. Makley smacked him on the head and he fell back to the floor.

Lucy Sarber screamed, "I'll get the keys! Don't hurt him anymore!"

At the sound of the first shots, Dillinger knew that his gang had arrived. Pierpont, grinning, unlocked his door and the two men hurried out. As they reached the office, Dillinger knelt down to inspect the damage that had been done to Sheriff Sarber, who had been kind to Dillinger while he had been housed in his jail. Regretfully, Dillinger left the man on the floor. Sarber called out to him and asked why he had to do this, but the bank robber was gone. According to the story, he then looked over to his wife and said, "Mother, I believe I'm going to have to leave you." Sheriff Sarber died moments later.

"The Terror Gang," as the press dubbed them, headed for Indianapolis, where Mary Kinder, who had taken up with Pierpont, and Evelyn "Billie" Frechette, who Dillinger had met in Chicago, waited for them. The gang made plans for a string of new bank robberies but first they had to arm themselves. They raided the police arsenal in Peru, Ind., and walked away with machine guns, bulletproof vests, shotguns, handguns, rifles and bags filled with ammunition. To pull off such a daring robbery, Dillinger and Pierpont devised a new approach. Posing as tourists, they came up to a policeman and asked him what preparations the local lawmen had taken in the event that the Dillinger gang came to town. The officer and a desk sergeant proudly gave the men a tour of the arsenal, only to be restrained as the two men began carrying armloads of weapons out to their car.

Chicago became the base of operations for the gang, of which Dillinger and Pierpont shared the leadership. Pierpont was the more experienced of the two, but he encouraged his friend to take the role of leader. Most of the decisions made by the group were made by these two or by Hamilton, who was the "old pro" among them. The idea that there was an actual "Dillinger gang" was a product of the newspapers of the day. It was really more of a criminal community that included several robbers who Dillinger worked with when possible and when the law and luck allowed. The group lived in twos and threes in several apartments on Chicago's north side. None of them drank hard liquor, sticking only to an occasional beer, so as not to draw any unwanted attention.

On October 23, 1933, the gang traveled to the Central National Bank in Greencastle, Ind.. Clark stayed behind the wheel of a Studebaker touring car while Pierpont, Dillinger and Makley went inside. Hamilton stayed near the door to watch for suspicious activity on the street. Dillinger and Pierpont had cased the bank several days in advance, pretending to be newsmen, and knew where all of the important areas of the bank were. Dillinger quickly jumped over the counter and began walking through the teller cages, scooping money into a sack while his confederates kept guns pointed at the employees. Makley watched everything with a stopwatch in his hand. At the five-minute mark, Makley called time and Dillinger abruptly stopped filling the sack. He turned, hopped back over the counter and started to walk out. He looked over and saw an old farmer standing at one of the teller's windows. In front of him on the counter was a small stack of bills. Dillinger asked him if the money belonged to him or to the bank.

Even though he had other girlfriends, Dillinger called Evelyn "Billie" Frechette the "love of his life" and often dreamed of escaping to South American with her so they could live in peace.

The farmer nervously replied, "It's mine."

Dillinger had a quick reply, "Keep it; we only want the bank's."

The men walked out without firing a shot and drove away. They traveled along back roads, following pre-marked maps, and drove leisurely out of the county. They avoided every roadblock put up by the state and local police. In the car, Dillinger opened the bag from the bank and found $75,346, their biggest haul yet.

About a month later, Dillinger was almost captured in Chicago. He was suffering from barber's itch, a skin disorder, and went to see Dr. Charles Eye for treatment. Edward Shouse, who had been kicked out of the gang for drinking and for making advances toward some of the other men's girlfriends, informed the Chicago police that Dr. Eye was treating Dillinger and told them where the bank robber could be captured. Dillinger managed to stay one step ahead of them.

On the night of November 15, he and his girlfriend, Billie Frechette, were on the way to Dr. Eye's office but Dillinger became suspicious when he saw several cars parked next to the building on Irving Park Road. The cops had been dumb enough to park facing the wrong direction. Dillinger quickly shifted gears and raced off down the street with the police cars in pursuit. Flooring the accelerator of his favorite car, a Hudson Terraplane, Dillinger lost all but one of the police vehicles, which was driven by Sergeant John Artery. With his partner, Art Keller, leaning out the window with a shotgun, Artery pulled up alongside Dillinger's car. They were traveling at a speed of almost 80 miles an hour along Irving Park Road. Keller opened fire on Dillinger but the bank robber did a high-speed turn onto a narrow side street, causing Artery to speed on past. By the time that they had turned around, Dillinger had vanished.

The gang moved on to Milwaukee and made plans for another robbery. On November 20, Harry Pierpont walked into the American Bank and Trust Company just before closing time. Staff members watched in bewilderment as Pierpont unrolled a huge Red Cross poster in the lobby and pasted it over the middle of the bank's large picture window. Moments later, Makley, Dillinger and Hamilton walked in. Makley pulled out a gun and pointed it at head teller Harold Graham - who proceeded to ask Makley to step to the next window!

Oblivious, Graham didn't realize what was going on until Makley told him to put up his hands; they were robbing the bank. Graham moved suddenly and Makley shot him through the elbow. When he fell, he triggered the alarm button, which did not ring in the bank but in the Racine Police Department headquarters. Two local policemen were slowly dispatched to the bank but they were in no hurry to get there. The alarm had sounded several times previously when careless tellers had accidentally set it off. When they finally did arrive, Pierpont disarmed them, but one of them was slow to hand over his gun. Makley shot him, attracting the attention of a large crowd outside.

Once the gang had gotten the money together, they needed to get out of the building. By this time though, more people had gathered, including more police officers. Dillinger and the others pushed several women out the front door, using them as shields from the shots that were being fired from across the street. The police, when they saw what was happening, fired high to avoid hitting the women and the other bystanders. The gang left the human shields standing in place and ducked back into the bank.

While the cops were distracted, thinking that the bank robbers were still crouched behind the shields, Dillinger and the others ducked out the back entrance, where Clark was waiting for them with the car. They piled into it, dragging along the bank president and the bookkeeper as hostages. They drove frantically along back roads for about 20 minutes and then let out the hostages before continuing on. The haul from the bank was $27,789.

After that, the gang decided to avoid the harsh Chicago weather and winter in Florida. Packing up, they headed for Daytona Beach, where they rented cottages along the ocean. They played cards, fished, and listened to the radio before becoming bored and heading out to Arizona. Between the time the gang left Dayton Beach and arrived in Tucson, the First National Bank of East Chicago, Ind., was robbed by two unknown men and a policeman named Patrick O'Malley was machine-gunned to death. Dillinger and Hamilton were accused of the crime and Dillinger was said to have been the policeman's killer -- but he always denied it. Billie Frechette, who was interviewed by legendary crime writer Jay Robert Nash before her death in 1969, always maintained that Dillinger never left the gang during this period and could not have committed the robbery that was blamed on him.

Regardless of that, Tucson turned out to be a disaster. Clark and Makley were arrested after a fire broke out in their hotel. They paid a fireman hundreds of dollars to rescue their suitcases but he became suspicious when he noticed one of the suitcases was extremely heavy. He opened it and found a machine gun and several pistols. Pierpont, Dillinger, Billie and Mary Kinder were soon identified, arrested, and then sent back East. Dillinger was extradited to Indiana to stand trial for the East Chicago robbery (the one robbery that he probably didn't commit), while Clark, Makley and Pierpont were sent to Ohio to stand trial for the killing of Sheriff Sarber.

Dillinger was locked up in the Crown Point, Ind., jail, which was said to be "escape proof." Armed citizens patrolled the grounds, ready and waiting in case any of Dillinger's friends decided to break him out. But all of them were also in jail, so he decided to break out on his own. A month after he was locked up, Dillinger escaped using a fake gun that he had carved and blackened with shoe polish. The "gun," which looks extremely crude in old photographs, looked real enough to

One of the chummy-looking photos with Dillinger that managed to ruin prosecutor Robert Estill's career.

Officer Sam Cahoon and Deputy Sheriff Ernest Blunk when Dillinger waved it at them on the morning of March 3, 1934.

In minutes, he rounded up a dozen guards and made his way down a flight of stairs with a couple of the officers along as hostages. He drove along back roads until he made it into rural Illinois. He let the officers out along the side of the road and gave them $4 for food and carfare. Dillinger apologized and told them that he would have given them more if he had it.

The wooden revolver that Dillinger allegedly blackened with shoe polish and used to escape from the Crown Point, Indiana jail.

Dillinger avoided Chicago and moved on to St. Paul, Minn. Billie Frechette, who had been freed with Mary Kinder after the Tucson arrests, joined him there. Dillinger started putting together a new gang, including Michigan City parolee Homer Van Meter. He also recruited Eddie Green, Tommy Carroll and John Hamilton, who had gone to Chicago instead of Tucson after leaving Daytona Beach. One more man was needed so Dillinger recruited a former Capone gunman named Lester Gillis, who became better known as "Baby Face Nelson," an unhinged killer who had robbed banks all over the Midwest. He was known to be quick on the trigger and he killed without mercy and without conscience.

Homer Van Meter had become Dillinger's right-hand man, and he and Nelson argued constantly. Dillinger often had to step between them to keep them from killing one another. Dillinger needed to raise a large amount of cash and needed Nelson to do so, whether he liked the man or not. By this time, Dillinger was planning a permanent escape from the law and he also wanted to help Pierpont, Clark and Makley, who were still in jail awaiting trial.

On March 6, the gang struck the Security National Bank in Sioux Falls, S.D. The robbery went off without incident until Nelson spotted an off-duty policeman getting out of a car. He jumped onto a desk and fired several shots though the bank window, wounding the officer. According to accounts, he began to laugh manically and to shout that he "got one of them!"

Meanwhile, Tommy Carroll was outside, standing in the middle of the street with a machine gun. Without firing a shot, he had lined up and disarmed the city's entire police force, including the chief. Thousands of spectators watched the scene, chuckling and laughing. Unbelievably, were under the impression that a Hollywood movie was being shot in their town -- and that the bank robbery was just part of the action! Just the day before, a movie producer had been in town spreading the word that he would be filming in Sioux Falls the following day. The "movie producer" had been Homer Van Meter.

The bank robbers piled into a Packard with a sack that was stuffed with $49,000. They raced out of town and after traveling for several miles, Dillinger ordered the driver to stop the car. He and Hamilton got out and sprinkled roofing nails all over the road, which would slow down any pursuit.

Then, Eddie Green was sent out to search for the next target. He found it at the First National Bank in Mason City, Iowa, when he learned that the vault contained more than $240,000. The gang arrived at the bank on March 13. Nelson stayed with the getaway car but the gang inside ran into one problem after another. When the bank president, Willis Bagley, saw Van Meter walk in carrying a machine gun, he thought that a "crazy man was on the loose." He ran into his office and bolted the door. Van Meter, knowing that Bagley had the keys to the vault, fired a number of shots through the door, but gave up trying to break in and helped his associates clean out the teller drawers.

Moments later, a guard in a special steel cage above the lobby fired a tear gas shell at Eddie Green. It hit him in the back and almost knocked him down. As he swung around, he fired off his machine gun and several bullets clipped the guard.

At the same time, a female customer, who was missing a shoe, ran out of the bank and down the alley outside, where she ran directly into a short man wearing a cap. She begged him to call for help -- the bank was being robbed. The short man was Baby Face Nelson and he sent her back into the bank.

Meanwhile, John Hamilton was having his own problems. Cashier Harry Fisher had barricaded himself in the locked room with the vault. Since Hamilton could not open the door, he ordered Fisher to start passing money to him through a slot in the door. Fisher began handing him stacks of one-dollar bills.

Dillinger was outside, guarding prisoners on the street. An elderly policeman named John Shipley spotted him from his third-floor office and took a shot at him. He winged Dillinger in the arm and the bank robber whirled around and fired a burst from his machine gun. The bullets bounced off the front of the building and Shipley ducked away unhurt. With that, Dillinger decided that it was time to leave. He sent Van Meter inside to get the others.

Hamilton was still having problems with Cashier Fisher. He could see the stacks of bills on the shelves inside of the vault where Fisher stood. He demanded that the man open the door but Fisher told him that he couldn't do it without the key. Hamilton continued to threaten him with his gun and Fisher continued to load stacks of one-dollar bills into the bandit's bag. He was enraged when Van Meter came inside and told him that they were leaving as he had only about $20,000 in his bag and there was over $200,000 still sitting in the vault! Gritting his teeth in frustration, he turned and ran out of the bank, leaving the crafty Fisher to count his blessings. Hamilton later groaned that he should have shot the man -- just out of spite.

At the same moment that Hamilton ran out of the bank to join the others, Officer Shipley returned to the overhead window and started shooting again. He wounded Hamilton in the shoulder but the bank robber managed to get to where Dillinger and the others were waiting. They had forced 20 hostages to stand on the running boards, fenders and hood of the getaway car, serving as human shields. The bank robbers piled inside and drove slowly away, the car groaning and creaking under all of the extra weight. The police were unable to shoot or try and stop them with all of the hostages on the vehicle so they were forced to follow at a distance. A few miles out of town, Baby Face Nelson climbed out of the car and fired his machine gun in their direction, finally forcing the police to turn back. After following back roads at slow speeds for more than two hours, Dillinger dropped off the reluctant passengers and headed for St. Paul. What should have been a prosperous raid had netted the outlaws a disappointing $52,000.

When the gang reached St. Paul, Dillinger and Hamilton sought medical treatment for their wounds and then decided to lay low for a while. They had no idea that trouble was brewing in town. Local FBI agents had received information that a man named "Carl Hellman" was living in a rooming house somewhere in St. Paul with a woman that was believed to be Billie Frechette. "Hellman" fit the description the agents had of Dillinger and they began working to find the rooming house.

All of this was unknown to Dillinger as he tried to recuperate from his wound. He wrote letters to his sister in Indiana and bemoaned the fact that he was unable to visit. He was worried about his father and could do nothing more than send funds to the family through intermediaries. He also worried about his friends in Ohio -- Pierpont, Clark and Makley -- who were standing trial for the murder of Jess Sarber. Each was tried and Pierpont and Makley both received the death penalty, while Clark was sentenced to life in prison. Dillinger knew there was no way that he could get to them, and this sent him into a depression.

The guards around the Lima, Ohio, jail were made up of regular officers, armed citizens, local and state policemen and even Ohio National Guardsmen who had been called up for duty. Heavy machine guns had been mounted on rooftops around the jail and gigantic searchlights were used to illuminate all approaches to the building. The authorities insisted that Dillinger was coming to free his friends with an army of outlaws.

However, Dillinger was far from Ohio and in enough trouble of his own. On the night of March 31, 1934, FBI agents learned that "Carl Hellman" was living at the Lincoln Court Apartments in St. Paul. They arrived at the door and Billie answered the knock. She explained that her husband, Hellman, was asleep and that she was not dressed. If they could wait a moment, she would get him up. She then locked the door and ran into the bedroom to tell Dillinger that FBI agents were at the door. He got dressed and grabbed a machine gun.

Waiting on the other side of the door, the agents were surprised to see a young man come walking up the stairs to the same door. When they asked who he was, Homer Van Meter stated that he was a soap salesman. The agents asked to see his samples and Van Meter said that he had them out in the car and asked the agents to come downstairs with him. One of them followed him down and when they reached the first floor, Van Meter produced a handgun and shoved it in the agent's face. He allegedly said, "You asked for it, so I'll give it to you!"

With that, the FBI agent ran for the door but Van Meter was laughing so hard that he didn't even fire at him. Instead, he ran outside and jumped on a horse-drawn delivery wagon that was parked at the curb. He donned the driver's cap and whipped the horses down the street.

Wondering what had become of his partner, the second agent also went downstairs to investigate, leaving the door to Dillinger's apartment unguarded. Dillinger, dragging Billie behind him, escaped down a flight of back stairs, firing a burst of bullets down the stairwell just in case. As the pair ran out the back, the second agent hurried after them and opened fire from the back door. Just as Dillinger was getting into the car, a bullet clipped him in the back of the leg and he stumbled into the driver's seat. He slammed the Hudson into gear and backed out of the alley at high speed.

Eddie Green tracked down a doctor to treat Dillinger's leg wound but, by this time, the gang had decided to leave St. Paul. Pat Reilly, a fringe member of the group, told Dillinger about a quiet Wisconsin resort that he knew of called Little Bohemia. It was a remote fishing camp that was not due to open until May and would make the perfect place to lay low for a time. Over the next day or two, they drove into the Wisconsin woods and checked into the Little Bohemia lodge to plan their next robbery.

Little Bohemia seemed to be just the answer for the gang but somebody talked and soon, Melvin Purvis, the head of the FBI office in Chicago, received a tip from a rival resort owner in Rhinelander, Wisc., that Dillinger was at Little Bohemia. Within hours, Purvis moved dozens of agents from Chicago and St. Paul to the forests of Wisconsin. They planned a raid on the lodge for April 22, 1934.

On the night of the assault, Purvis moved his agents into position at the front of the lodge just as three men were emerging from the building and getting into a parked car. As the engine started, Purvis shouted for the men to stop but they never heard his warning. Seconds later, the FBI agents unleashed a hail of gunfire and ripped the car apart. Eugene Boiseneau, a Civilian Conservation Corps worker, was killed instantly and his two fishing buddies were both wounded.

Little Bohemia Lodge in Wisconsin, where the FBI missed Dillinger again -- and shot three fishermen instead.

Hearing the gunfire outside, Dillinger, Van Meter, Carroll and Hamilton ran out the back of the lodge and disappeared into the woods along the lake. Baby Face Nelson, who was staying in a nearby cabin with his wife, ran outside, fired some random shots at the agents and also vanished into the trees. Purvis, believing that Dillinger was still inside the lodge, ordered the assembled agents to continue firing into the building. They pounded the lodge all night long, shattering windows and splintering the walls, floors and ceilings with bullets. When morning came, and there was no resistance, they entered the building to capture the gang's girls, who had been hiding in the basement all night.

Dillinger, Hamilton and Van Meter had stolen a car and had driven to St. Paul. Nelson, after killing an FBI agent while making his escape, had also stolen a car and headed for Chicago. And Tommy Carroll had stolen yet another vehicle and had taken off for Michigan.

The Little Bohemia fiasco put Purvis and J. Edgar Hoover under the harsh glare of public criticism. They became even more determined to get Dillinger, and Hoover placed a shoot-to-kill order on the bandit's head, along with a $10,000 reward. Another $10,000 was offered by five states in which Dillinger had planned bank robberies. The newspapers screamed Dillinger every day and, over the course of the next couple of months, half a dozen men who resembled the bank robber were arrested or almost shot. The FBI and local authorities in Chicago, all over Illinois, Wisconsin, Minnesota, and Indiana were looking everywhere for the elusive outlaw.

But Dillinger was nowhere to be found.

In May, Dillinger appeared briefly at his father's farm for a Sunday chicken dinner and reportedly told the elderly Dillinger that he was soon going to be leaving on a long trip and his Dad wouldn't have to "worry about him" anymore. Then, he disappeared again.

Melvin Purvis (Left), the man that J. Edgar Hoover (Right) gave the task of getting Dillinger, dead or alive -- preferably dead.

Dillinger was next reported in Chicago. In preparation for whatever trip he was planning, or perhaps because he knew that his luck would only hold out for so long, he allegedly contacted a washed-up doctor, Wilhelm Loeser, who had done time for drug charges. Dillinger was said to have paid him $5,000 to perform some plastic surgery on his recognizable face, changing the bridge of his nose, getting rid of three moles and removing a scar and the cleft of his chin. The doctor agreed to the surgery and left Dillinger in the care of his assistant, Dr. Harold Bernard Cassidy, to administer the general anesthetic. An ether-soaked towel was placed over Dillinger's face and Cassidy told him to breathe deeply. Suddenly, Dillinger's face turned blue, he swallowed his tongue and died! Cassidy had just succeeded where FBI agents and hundreds of law enforcement officials had failed - he had killed John Dillinger.

Loeser immediately revived the gangster and proceeded to do

(Left) The Biograph Theater on the night that Dillinger came to see "Manhattan Melodrama".
(Right) Chicago madam Anna Sage, who became known as the "Lady in Red" (even though her dress was actually bright orange). Sage operated a brothel just south of Wrigley Field and often provided a hideout for Dillinger.

the surgery. Dillinger supposedly had no idea how close he had come to death, according to the later testimony of Loeser and Cassidy. Many believe this story to be pure fiction because, while the FBI would later contend that Dillinger had received recent plastic surgery, the medical examiner was unable to detect any signs of it on the body that was taken to the morgue, which the FBI claimed to be Dillinger's.

Which story was true? Did Dillinger have plastic surgery or not? Loeser and Cassidy maintained that he did. In fact, Cassidy was paid $500 for assisting with the surgery and this payment came from Dillinger himself. Two months after the nearly botched operation, Dillinger met up with Cassidy at the corner of Kedzie and North Avenue. Slouched down in a car with Polly Hamilton, Dillinger handed over five crisp $100 bills and thanked him for his help. Cassidy quickly spent the cash, celebrating a few moments of a bleak and otherwise lonely existence. Loeser and Cassidy were later indicted on charges of harboring a fugitive, but both were given suspended sentences in exchange for their testimony. Cassidy never really recovered from his brush with Dillinger, though. With his medical career in shambles, Cassidy was later reduced to practicing on an Indian reservation during World War II. After the war ended, he returned to Chicago and moved in with his sister. Deeply depressed over his station in life, he committed suicide in July 1946.

But if Dillinger did have plastic surgery, then why didn't the coroner see any sign of it on the body that was brought to the morgue after the shootout at the Biograph Theater? Could the corpse have belonged to someone else?

It certainly could have happened that way. On June 30, 1934, word spread that Dillinger came out of hiding again, this time in South Bend, Ind. Once again, though, this seems to be a case of Dillinger getting credit for someone else's bank robbery. The Merchant's National Bank in South Bend was robbed and the local police claimed that Dillinger was the culprit. Eyewitnesses claimed to recognize him and, not only that, they also said that his companions were Baby Face Nelson and Pretty Boy Floyd. This seems impossible, though, as Nelson was on his way to California, unnerved by the Little Bohemia raid, Floyd was in Ohio and Dillinger was in Minnesota at the time of the robbery.

So, if Dillinger was mistakenly identified in South Bend, could the same thing have happened three weeks later in Chicago?

In early July 1934, Detective Sergeant Martin Zarkovich, of the notoriously corrupt East Chicago, Ind., police department, approached Chicago police Captain John Stege with an interesting deal. Zarkovich claimed that he could, with assistance from a long-time friend and whorehouse madame, deliver Dillinger to the Chicago police. There was only one catch, though - Dillinger had to be killed, not taken alive. Stege kicked Zarkovich out of his office, refusing to go along with it. He told him, "I'd even give John Dillinger a chance to surrender."

Melvin Purvis had no such qualms, however. When Zarkovich presented his offer to the FBI official, he quickly agreed. Zarkovich's friend, Anna Sage, would agree to set up Dillinger but the FBI had to agree to stop deportation proceedings against her. Purvis agreed, as long as she delivered Dillinger. Ultimately though, Sage would end up being shipped back to Europe as an "undesirable" in 1936.

When Dillinger walked into the Biograph Theater on the night of July 22, 1934, Anna Sage promised her FBI contacts that she would be wearing a red dress (actually, it turned out to be bright orange) for identification purposes. She would be accompanying Dillinger, along with his newest girlfriend, Polly Hamilton Keele. At about 8:30 p.m., Dillinger appeared at the Biograph's box office in the company of two women. He was outfitted in a white summer shirt, gray trousers, white canvas shoes and his usual straw boater hat. He seemed to be completely at ease.

WILLIE SAYS:
This place is hard to park at, unless you actually drive into the alley or park by the fire hydrant. They sure have some big rats in there, though!

Sixteen FBI agents, cops from East Chicago and Detective Martin Zarkovich waited outside the theater with Purvis for more than two hours, watching for the unknowing Dillinger to exit. Purvis paced nervously, chain-smoked cigarettes and, several times, even entered the darkened theater to be sure that Dillinger was still in his seat. Just before 10:30 p.m., the lights came up, the doors opened and the crowd filed out into the street. Finally, Dillinger left the theater and was spotted by Melvin Purvis, who was standing in front of the Goetz Country Club, a tavern just south of the theater. Dillinger looked Purvis right in the face as he walked past but, for some reason, despite Purvis being featured in numerous newspaper articles, he did not recognize him.

As the man walked past, Purvis struck a match to light his cigar, a signal for the FBI agents and the East Chicago police assassins to move on their target. Glancing up the street, Purvis was shocked to see that two of the East Chicago cops did not see the signal. They had been distracted by several Chicago plainclothes detectives who showed up on the scene to make sure that the man who was killed really was Dillinger. According to reports, these men had some doubts about the man's identity. Detective Zarkovich, who saw what was happening, hurried across the street to his men. Meanwhile, two FBI agents were just finishing showing their credentials to the Chicago officers when they spotted the action outside the Biograph. They immediately started toward Dillinger.

As all of this was taking place, Dillinger allegedly sensed that something was wrong. Polly later reported that she felt his arm tense. He scanned the area around him and slipped a hand into his pocket, where a gun had been hidden. He knew the alley up ahead was his best chance for escape so he picked up his pace.

If Dillinger had any doubts about what was about to happen, they disappeared when he reached the mouth of the alley. Several men had fallen into step behind him and he saw two men up ahead with guns in their hands. Moving forward, he turned his head to try and look behind him and then turning the girls loose, he tried to run. As he clawed for the gun in his pocket, he collided with a woman outside the alley and was spun halfway around. He grabbed at the woman and then shoved her away, realizing that she was a civilian. The assassins didn't hesitate over the woman's presence and they immediately opened fire.

One slug burned through Dillinger's chest at a sideways, downward angle and punched out beneath his left rib. The second slammed into the base of his neck, ripped through his brain and exited beneath his right eye. The impact of the bullets, following his collision with the woman on the street, caused him to spin around like a top. FBI agents continued to fire five more times as Dillinger went down in the alley. None of the last bullets struck him but they splintered a telephone pole that was a short distance behind him.

Dillinger stumbled a bit and then collapsed, falling hard onto his face and elbow. A lens in his eyeglasses shattered and the brim of his straw hat snapped in two. His Colt revolver, its safety still on, remained in his hand. Melvin Purvis reached down and took it from his hand. One of his agents leaned down and heard the man on the ground try to speak. He later reported, "He mumbled some words I couldn't understand. That was the end."

It was later recalled that a long moment of silence seemed to follow the shooting and then chaos broke out. As Dillinger's blood spilled out onto the pavement, automobiles and streetcars came to a halt on North Lincoln Avenue. Passengers, followed by nearby pedestrians, poured into the street, all pushing for a closer look. Within moments, people were shouting the name,

The alley near the Biograph, looking out toward Lincoln Avenue

MYTHS AFTER DILLINGER

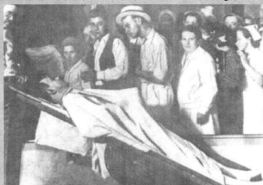

There is no denying that John Dillinger remains an iconic figure in Chicago, and Midwestern, history. For Americans of the time, he was the last great anti-hero and he literally became a legend in his own time. In addition to the stories --- and possibility ---- of his survival after being gunned down by the feds, there have been a number of other myths and legends created around this charismatic bank robber. One has shades of the truth, while the other is merely the product of faulty information and wishful thinking. So, based on the fact that the man shot down outside of the Biograph really was John Dillinger, here are some of the myths surrounding his death....

One story holds that Dillinger's brain was "stolen" during his autopsy. This story does contain elements of the truth. On the night that Dillinger was shot down, an autopsy was performed and Dillinger's brain was removed and sent to the pathology department. Some in the medical community still expected to find obvious abnormalities in the brains of criminals. That was the last time that the doctors ever saw it. A short time later, an undertaker reported that the brain was missing. As no one seemed to have it, the word "stolen" began finding its way into newspaper stories.

Cook County authorities scrambled to try and solve the mystery of the missing brain but never managed to communicate with each other well enough to keep their stories straight. Coroner Frank Walsh first tried to deny that the brain was missing at all, only to then learn that the Medical Examiner had already acknowledged the removal of "an ounce or two" of the gray matter for scientific testing. Unaware of this announcement, a coroner's toxicologist contradicted both of them by reporting that he had half of the brain in a jar of preservative and that he thought the other half had been placed inside of the corpse's stomach, to avoid re-opening the skull. Before that information reached the Medical Examiner, he suddenly remembered having sent the toxicologist two-thirds of the brain and keeping one-third of it in his lab. On August 3, a wry reporter for the *Chicago Daily News* added up the fractions of brain supposed to be located in all of the different departments and complimented the coroner's office on finding more of Dillinger's brain than he had to start with! It was later announced that whatever portions of the brain had been removed had been destroyed during the tests. None of the tests revealed any abnormalities.

Unfortunately, this does not end the story. Years later, someone connected to Northwestern University's Medical School was supposed to have discovered Dillinger's brain, mostly intact, hidden in a laboratory that was remodeled during World War II. One of the professors supposedly kept it for a time as a souvenir, then gave it to a physician friend in another state, who eventually sold it to a Chicago optometrist named ---- or so the story has it --- Dr. Brayne.

This leaves only the story of Dillinger's most private body part --- his allegedly massive penis. The fact that Dillinger was able to easily charm women with his roguish smile, rugged good looks and swaggering self confidence has never been questioned, but how this translated into his having a penis of gigantic proportions will always be a mystery.

Since none of his friends, and certainly none of the many women that he romanced, ever mentioned that his penis was anything other than average-sized, it can only be assumed that this legend was created after a photograph appeared on the front page of the *Chicago Daily News*. The photo, taken while Dillinger's body was on display at the morgue, appears to give his sheet-covered body a very impressive erection. Most other papers that published the photograph had it retouched to flatten the sheet, an effect that was actually caused by the position of the dead man's arm, but enough people saw the original photo that a rumor soon started about the massive size of Dillinger's organ. Before long, the story took on mythic proportions and soon it was considered general knowledge that the size of the penis had qualified it for display at the Smithsonian Institution, or even at the National Medical Museum, which was located on the Institution's grounds for many years. The story became so widespread that, for decades, both organizations had to print form letters that politely denied that they possessed, much less displayed, any part of Dillinger's anatomy ---- especially his penis.

"Dillinger!"

Above the clamor, the screams of two women could be heard. The first, Etta Natalsky, was the woman whom Dillinger had bumped into. A stray bullet, from the gun of either an FBI agent or an East Chicago cop, had passed through the fleshy part of her thigh. The second injured woman was Theresa Paulus, who had been leaving the Biograph with a friend when a bullet from the other direction had clipped her in the hip. Neither one was seriously hurt but, once again, the FBI had claimed civilian casualties while hunting Dillinger.

Two of the agents crossed the alley and ducked into a Chinese restaurant to place a telephone call and announce that Dillinger was dead. They officially informed the local cops that the Department of Justice had "made an arrest" outside the Biograph Theater.

Back outside, several of the agents hovered over the body as others tried to keep back the surging crowd. Agent Grier Woltz, who had been stationed next to Dillinger, later reported that Dillinger was "still kicking and moving around" on the pavement. He estimated that he lived about three minutes after the shooting and he took one last shuttering breath before he died. No one did anything to try and help him. Agent Woltz also made one odd observation about the dying man. He later stated that his eyebrows were "discolored and seemed to be painted a heavy, dark brown." No explanation has ever been provided for this.

Polly Hamilton and Anna Sage, curiously, melted into the crowd.

As the two women vanished down the alley, a police van appeared on North Lincoln Avenue. Agent Woltz assisted as Dillinger's bloody body was lifted onto a stretcher, carried to the van and placed on the floor in back. Five FBI agents climbed in with three Chicago cops and the body was taken to the Alexian Brothers Hospital at 1200 Belden Ave. Dr. Walter Prusaig turned them away at the door. He placed a stethoscope to Dillinger's chest and announced, "This man is dead."

Finally, a Chicago police detective ordered the body to be taken to the Cook County Morgue on Polk Street. Mobs greeted the body of the man believed to be Dillinger at the morgue, but the scene at the Biograph Theater remained chaotic. Spectators mobbed Lincoln Avenue outside the theater. The "extra" additions of the newspapers were already on the streets. One of them reported, "John Dillinger died tonight as he lived, in a hail of lead and swelter of blood. He died with a smile on his lips and a woman on each arm."

Tradition tells that passersby ran to the scene and dipped their handkerchiefs in the blood of the fallen man, hoping for a macabre souvenir of this terrible event. Others pried bullet fragments from a wooden light pole in the alley until the pole became so unsteady that it had to be removed by city workers. The theater would go on to become a famous, and infamous, location in the days, weeks and even years to come.

Ever since the night of the shoot-out at the Biograph, eyewitness accounts, and the official autopsy itself, have given support to the theory that the dead man may not have been Dillinger at all. Rumors have persisted that the man killed by the FBI was actually a small-time hood from Wisconsin who had been set up by Martin Zarkovich and Anna Sage to take the hit. Many historians have called this theory "revisionist nonsense," but it's hard to ignore some of the strange facts that have come to light.

To start with, even would-be debunkers have admitted that Zarkovich was a corrupt cop and that he was tied into the mob through Sonny Sheetz, crime boss of Lake County, Ind. Until Anna Sage had been run out of Lake County in 1927, Zarkovich had been protecting her operation for a percentage of the take and privileges with Sage or one of her girls. Many have pondered the question of why he would have gone out of his way to set up Dillinger unless he had been asked to for some reason. And why had he insisted that the bank robber be killed instead of captured? Did he owe someone a favor so that he would make sure that "Dillinger" was murdered - perhaps so the real bank robber could permanently escape?

Some believers in the idea that Dillinger may have escaped have pointed to the odd behavior of the man thought to be the bank robber that night at the Biograph. During the film, FBI agents, including Melvin

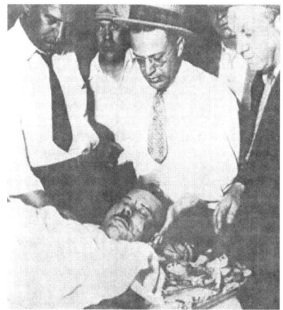

The body alleged to be Dillinger at the Cook County Morgue

Purvis, repeatedly entered the theater and walked down the aisles of the auditorium, making sure that Dillinger was still in his seat. It seems hard to believe that Dillinger (if it was him) would not have noticed this careless surveillance. This was a man who had managed to elude capture for years, escaping from what should have been iron-clad traps, and yet he did not notice these obvious and clumsy attempts to check up on him. It's difficult to believe the movie could have been that riveting.

In addition, many also find it odd that Dillinger did not recognize Melvin Purvis when he looked directly in his face as he was leaving the Biograph. Purvis' face had been plastered on almost as many newspaper stories as Dillinger's own. It seems likely that the clever bank robber would have familiarized himself with the men who were after him, especially Purvis, who had been praised as a "dogged pursuer" and had been well publicized as the G-man in charge of the hunt. But, for some reason, Dillinger looked right at him without a flicker of recognition and kept on walking. Could it have been because the man in the straw hat didn't know who Melvin Purvis was? John Dillinger undoubtedly would have, but this man never recognized the federal agent.

Most interesting, though, are the many striking errors in the autopsy report - which, conveniently, went missing for almost 30 years. The dead man had brown eyes while Dillinger's were blue. The corpse had a rheumatic heart condition since childhood while Dillinger's naval service records said that his heart was in perfect condition. He could not have played baseball, joined the Navy or carried out many of his athletic bank robberies with the sort of heart condition that his corpse allegedly had. It's also been said that the man who was killed was much shorter and heavier than Dillinger and had none of his distinguishing marks. The corpse also had a top right incisor - a tooth that Dillinger is clearly missing in photographs taken of him around this time.

Police agencies claimed that Dillinger had plastic surgery to get rid of his scars and moles, but also missing were at least two scars on Dillinger's body. The dead man had not received any plastic surgery, although the FBI stated that Dillinger had undergone surgery to compensate for the obvious facial differences between the dead man and Dillinger. So, which version of the "plastic surgery story" was the truth?

Newspaper reports almost immediately stated that the body was matched to Dillinger by way of a fingerprint card, but there are those who insist that the card was planted in the Cook County Morgue days before the murder. Strangely, the FBI never released the name of the man who allegedly took the dead man's prints and matched them to Dillinger. The signature at the bottom of the fingerprint card was illegible. Of course, there is no proof that the card was actually "planted," and it's this small doubt that debunkers use to dismiss the entire possibility that the FBI got the wrong man, ignoring the color of the eyes, the scars and the heart condition.

But if the FBI killed the wrong man, who was he?

The most likely suspect for the man killed in Dillinger's

GHOST ALERT:

The alleyway near the Biograph is reportedly haunted. It is here, in what was for many years a dark and dingy passageway that many people claimed to encounter a ghost - a ghost created by the lingering remnants of the life that was cut short on the dirty stones of the alleyway.

But, who is this ghost? Is this phantom that of John Dillinger, playing out the last few seconds of his life over and over again? Or could this be the specter of Jimmy Lawrence, doomed to repeatedly run for his life after being betrayed by two women whom he trusted?

Whoever the man killed outside of the Biograph Theater may have been, his final moments have left a lasting impression behind. It would be many years after his death before people passing by the Biograph on North Lincoln Avenue would begin to spot a blue, hazy figure running down the alley next to the theater, falling down and then vanishing. Along with the sighting of this strange apparition were reports of cold spots, icy chills, unexplainable cool breezes, and odd feelings of fear and uneasiness. The odd encounters continue to this day.

place was a North Side man named Jimmy Lawrence. On the night of the shooting, Lawrence disappeared. He was a small-time criminal who had moved to Chicago from Wisconsin in 1930. He had lived in the neighborhood around Lincoln Avenue during the same time that Dillinger had been in prison in Michigan City, Ind., and often came to the Biograph Theater. He also bore an uncanny resemblance to John Dillinger, which leads many to believe that he may have been killed in Dillinger's place.

A piece of possible evidence to this is a photograph that was taken from the purse of Dillinger's girlfriend, Billie Frechette, after an arrest, which showed her in the company of a man who looked like the person killed at the Biograph. It is a photo that was taken before Dillinger ever allegedly had plastic surgery. Could Jimmy Lawrence have gone on a date to the Biograph, not knowing (thanks to Anna Sage) that the FBI was waiting for him there?

Some writers have suggested this is exactly what happened. As respected crime writer, Jay Robert Nash, an expert on Dillinger, reported in his book *Dillinger: Dead or Alive?* Dillinger's attorney, Louis Piquett, along with Martin Zarkovich and Anna Sage, rigged the whole affair. According to Nash, Sage was a bordello madame who was in danger of being deported. To prevent this, she went to the police and told them that she knew Dillinger. In exchange for not being deported, she would arrange to have him at the Biograph, where they could nab him. She agreed to wear a bright, red dress so she would be easily recognized. While FBI agents waited, "Dillinger" and his girlfriends watched the movie and enjoyed popcorn and soda. When the film ended, the Feds made their move. Nash believes, however, that they shot Jimmy Lawrence instead of Dillinger. He also believes that when they learned of their mistake, the FBI covered it up, either because they feared the wrath of J. Edgar Hoover, who told them to "get Dillinger or else," or because Hoover himself was too embarrassed to admit the mistake.

So, what happened to the real John Dillinger?

According to testimony from a bank robber named James "Blackie" Audett, a friend of Dillinger's, the two of them escaped from Illinois (Dillinger was hiding in Aurora at the time) just hours after the shooting at the Biograph. He claimed that they drove up into Wisconsin and Minnesota then went straight west. Dillinger's only

A photograph found in the possession of Billie Frechette shows her standing next to a man that is not Dillinger, although he looks like him. The man also bears an uncanny resemblance to the man shot outside the Biograph Theater and wears a ring just like the one photographed with the body. More evidence that Dillinger did not die that night?

regret, Audett said, was that he had to leave Billie Frechette behind. She was in jail at the time for harboring Dillinger. Audett claimed that he left Dillinger at an Indian Reservation out West, where he later settled down and married a local woman.

Before the shooting, Dillinger had visited his father and left a sum of money with him with which to pay for his funeral. He told his father that he planned to get away so that he would "not have to worry about his son anymore." Dillinger's sister, Audrey, was well aware of the fact that her brother was alive (as were other members of the family) and she corresponded with Audett up until the time of Audett's death.

After leaving Dillinger at the Indian Reservation, Audett was apprehended for his own crimes and sent to serve time on Alcatraz. He was the last prisoner to leave "The Rock" in 1962. Audett claimed that he saw Dillinger on the West Coast several times before he was arrested again for a Seattle bank robbery and sent to prison in 1974. He was later paroled into the custody of Jay Robert Nash, who interviewed him extensively about the "posthumous" activities of Dillinger. Audett died of a stroke in 1979 and until the day he died, he claimed that Dillinger was still alive. No amount of persuasion from Nash could get Blackie to tell him where Dillinger was living.

Was Blackie Audett just an old man who was spinning tales to get attention in his sunset years? Or could he have been telling the truth? Did John Dillinger survive his last run-ins with the FBI and escape to the West to live out his last years in peace? Jay Robert Nash became convinced that Dillinger had gotten away - and he wasn't the only one to think so.

In the late 1930s, a federal agent who was passing through Mooresville, Ind., reported that a substantial number of citizens remained convinced that Dillinger had somehow slipped out of the hands of the FBI and had escaped. He also learned that the bank robber's family had received a letter from someone claiming to be Dillinger and that it contained enough private information that they were convinced it was genuine.

The agent was unable to learn any details about the letter but it seemed to be common knowledge around town that the Dillingers believed "Johnnie" was alive. Those who had doubts were asked the simple question of how John Dillinger, Sr., a farmer with little money, had managed to pay for his son's elaborate burial, which involved encasing his casket in concrete. Wouldn't this have been very expensive? And well beyond his means?

Some claimed that Dillinger had been killed with thousands of dollars in his pocket and that the money went to his father. This was not the case. The man shot down at the Biograph Theater had the clothing on his back; a pair of white buckskin Nunn-Bush shoes, size 9D; one ruby ring; a yellow-gold Hamilton pocket watch with a gold chain and tiny knife attached; a white handkerchief with a thin brown border; two keys tied with string (one fit Anna Sage's apartment); and a fully loaded, spare magazine for his Colt pistol. The official record stated that Dillinger was carrying $7.70 in his pocket - hardly enough to pay for a funeral.

Could Dillinger have actually gotten away? It certainly seems possible, despite official denials and the derision afforded to these "conspiracy theories" by many writers in the crime field. Believe it or not, though, many still unanswered questions remain about the Dillinger assassination - but the answers to those questions will likely never be known.

DR. THOMAS NEILL CREAM

Dr. Thomas Neill Cream

Dr. Thomas Neill Cream came to Chicago around 1879. He may have been on the run from the law; his first wife had died under strange circumstances, and another of his patients had been found chloroformed and killed in Scotland. Once in Chicago, he opened an office at No. 434 Madison St. and began to practice medicine. Dr. Cream used his position as a doctor not to heal, but to kill. He became known as one of the most vicious poisoners in history.

Cream was associated with a doctor named Greer. When a girl wishing to procure an abortion came to Greer, he would say that he didn't do that himself, but offered to sell them Cream's address for $5. Not all of these girls survived, and Cream narrowly avoided hanging.

Cream soon began to market a strange potion that he claimed cured epilepsy. It was through this that he met Julia Stott, the wife of an epileptic named Daniel Stott. She complained that his disease (compounded by the fact that he was awfully old) had wrecked her sex life. Dr. Cream took, shall we say, a "hands-on approach" to solving her sex problems, and Julia began to visit the office frequently. When her husband became suspicious, Cream added a large quantity of strychnine to his medicine. It seemed like the perfect crime - no one would suspect that the "elderly epileptic" had died of anything more than natural causes!

He would have gotten away with it, except that Cream himself, trying to collect on the insurance money, suggested that the body be exhumed and examined! After Stott was found to be poisoned, Julia swore in court that she'd seen Cream add poison to her husband's medicine. In 1881, he was sent to Joliet Prison, where he spent the next 10 years.

After his release, Cream returned to England, where he embarked upon a career in killing prostitutes in addition to his regular poisonings. What got him caught this time was an attempt to blame the murders on a neighbor and blackmail him - once again not content to get away with deaths that would not have otherwise been thought of as murder! After barely a year back in England, Cream was convicted of murder and sentenced to be hanged in November 1892.

Bizarrely, Cream's last words as the trap on the gallows was sprung were said to be, "I am Jack The..." Apparently, Cream was claiming to be Jack the Ripper, the notorious killer who had been active in London in 1888. While Jack the Ripper was active, Cream was actually in prison in Joliet, half a world away from London. Was his bizarre claim evidence, as some have suggested, that he bribed his way out of prison or was replaced there by a double? Or is

WHERE IS IT NOW?
The building at No. 434 Madison would have been at 1255 West Madison after the 1909 renumbering. Newer buildings and parking areas mark the spot today.

it just evidence that, as one of his accountants said, he was "completely insane?"

The mystery will linger forever - but the latter is certainly more likely!

THE CITY COURTHOUSE & GALLOWS

The old Criminal Court building on Hubbard Street still stands today, converted into offices and condos. It was first built around the time of the great fire, then was torn down and rebuilt in 1892. At the time, the county jail was right behind the courthouse (where the fire station stands today). There were two prisons, the "old jail" and the "new jail," which opened onto Dearborn Street and blocked the old jail from the sight of passers-by. They were connected to the courthouse by means of an enclosed archway that passed over the alley. It was in this alley behind the courthouse (now a parking lot) where condemned criminals were hanged -- at least when the weather was good. More often, particularly in colder weather, the gallows would be erected in the jail yard and moved inside the old jail for the hanging itself. Some 95 men were hanged in the vicinity until 1927, when the state changed the method of execution to the electric chair. Only a few people were electrocuted in the precincts before the jail was moved to a new location on the Southwest side. The jail buildings were torn down a few years later, leaving only a small two-story structure behind the courthouse. Known as "the morgue," it was here that new prisoners were deloused and executed prisoner's bodies were stored until they could be claimed. The morgue remained standing on the site for years.

Police officers outside the Cook County Jail & Courthouse

After the business of the criminal courts was moved elsewhere, the building changed hands a few times, first becoming a shelter for Depression-era derelicts who could sleep on the floor for free or on a cot for a dime. Local hoboes nicknamed the place "The Hotel Hoover." After that, it was taken over by the Chicago Board of Health.

The city's permanent gallows used on the site was built in 1885 for the execution of three men convicted of a "trunk murder." Two years later, after the Haymarket Riot, they were expanded to be large enough to hang five people at once.

Next door to the courthouse was a small

Preparations being made for a hanging

restaurant from which the condemned prisoners would usually be brought a last meal. At times, the restaurant even offered a "hangman's special," apparently based on the most recent "last meal" served! Steak, veal cutlets, and french-fried potatoes seem to have been the most popular requests.

A good hangman can do his work very quickly. Condemned prisoners are to be carefully weighed and measured, allowing the hangman to calculate exactly how long the drop needs to be to break the neck instantly. If the drop is too short, the condemned prisoner will die a slow, agonizing death by strangulation. If the drop is too long, it can result in decapitation. The best hangmen could have a prisoner dead within 30 seconds of being led from their cell.

However, Chicago's hangmen don't seem to have been very good at what they did (in fact, the Tribune insisted that there was no hangman at all, and that "Monsieur de Chicago" was only an urban myth) and the people who attended the hangings didn't help matters. Few people seem to have died quickly on the Chicago gallows -- most were reported to have slowly strangled to death. And the operation was seldom done quickly. While Chicago

GHOST ALERT:

Most ghosts seem to be associated with sudden, traumatic, or unexpected deaths. This may be the reason that few ghosts have been reported in the old gallows alley: none of the executions on the gallows were unexpected, and most were anything but sudden, since it took the prisoners so long to die.

Still, plenty of ghosts have been reported. The first ghost to be sighted was that of Louis Lingg, one of the anarchists sentenced to be hanged on the gallows for the Haymarket Riot. Of the five condemned to die, Lingg was the only one not to be hanged -- he died the night before by biting into a dynamite cap. The next day, reporters attending the execution said that they could still hear the sound of Lingg screaming. Some papers attributed the sounds to a black cat that lived in the jail yard.

The other ghost is of Carl Wanderer - or his voice, anyway. Rumor has it that on certain nights, at just the right time, people passing through the alley where the gallows once stood can still hear his voice, singing the last words to ever pass his lips: "if you can hear my prayer away up there, old pal, why don't you answer me?" When people say they've heard this, we're inclined to believe them for the simple reason that they actually know how the song goes to begin with!

The old jail building was thought by many of the prisoners and guards to be haunted, particularly on nights before a hanging. The prisoners would swear they could hear the sounds of the scaffold being erected overnight -- even though the workers wouldn't actually be arriving until the next morning! Other nights, when the scaffold had already been assembled indoors, the noise from the trap door, dropping apparently of its own accord, would wake every prisoner in the place. Other guards reported lights turning themselves off and on, papers flying around, and objects mysteriously disappearing. When reporters asked one guard if he felt that the building was haunted, he replied, "I wouldn't say that; it would make me look foolish. But I want to tell you that I wouldn't stay in this place alone!"

In particular, the ghost most often thought to be on the premises was that of Peter Neidermeir, one of the three Car Barn Bandits, who were among the first American criminals to use automatic pistols to murder their more than 20 victims. As he was dragged down the hallway of the old jail to be executed, he loudly cursed the place and everyone in it. As he was placed on the trap door in the scaffold, he reportedly shouted, "You can't kill me, you scoundrels! I will come back, and when I do, you will be sorry for what you've done!" He squirmed so violently that he had to be tied to a chair to be hanged, and was described as swinging grotesquely.

Niedermeir wasn't the only man to be hanged seated -- or the only one to vow revenge from beyond the grave. Others, such as Johann Hoch, the "Chicago Bluebeard," (see later in this chapter) also hinted that they'd be back for revenge, if not quite so loudly. But it was Neidermeir's ghost that was blamed for most of the disturbances in the jail -- and there were many. Many prisoners told of waking up to hear the sound of pounding above their head, or to see a white light shining in their face. Guards said that men would wake up frightened nightly, and, though they'd initially try to laugh it off, they'd often admit that they'd been awakened by ghosts. One swore that he'd seen the ghosts of men who were executed, including the Car Barn Bandits, re-enacting their hangings.

Though the old jail is gone -- and the site doesn't seem to report any further disturbances -- the courthouse remains intact today, and is a Chicago landmark. Many of the original furnishings, including the old vaults, are still there. Many of those who work there say the building is haunted. People report the heavy oak doors opening and closing of their own accord, and at least one employee often hears the sound of typewriters clacking away. Workers on the fifth floor claim to have seen the ghost of a woman in white on several occasions!

banned public executions very early on, there were often as many as 300 spectators invited to attend the proceedings. Crowds numbering in the thousands were known to gather outside of the courthouse, trying to get a view. And the attendees, usually composed mainly of reporters, tended to try to drag things out in order to make sure they got a good story. In fact, it's been said that Chicago papers genuinely enjoyed reporting hangings -- even if they weren't taking place in Chicago. One of the Chicago Times' more memorable hanging-related headlines -- "Jerked To Jesus" -- actually referred to a hanging in Nevada.

Condemned criminals were expected to put on a good show on the gallows. Reporters would encourage them to make a final speech, or even sing a song. Carl Wanderer, the murderer of the "Ragged Stranger" (more later in this chapter) sang a few bars of "Old Pal," a maudlin parlor song popular at the time, in such a clear voice that one reporter stated, "He should have been a song plugger!" (although another supposedly said that he should have been hanged for his voice alone.) Another man, known as "the Chanticleer of Murderers Row," did an excellent impression of a rooster while standing on the gallows.

When the courthouse building was abandoned, movers found the basement to be filled with roulette wheels and other objects that had been confiscated as evidence, including a whole box of dynamite! But among this rubble was something else -- the gallows itself, which had never been destroyed. In fact, they remained in storage in the basement of the courthouse building for 50 years after their use was abandoned!

The reason they were kept so long was that authorities thought -- hoped, even -- that they might be needed one last time, for "Terrible Tommy" O'Connor, a robber and murderer who had been sentenced to hang in 1921. Four days before his scheduled execution, O'Connor stole a guard's gun, scaled the prison walls, and ran north up the alley to Illinois Street. There he jumped onto the running board of a car, waved his revolver at the driver and ordered him to "drive like hell." Thus, he disappeared into the night. Some say that he fled to Ireland and fought in the Black and Tan wars. Others maintain that he hid out the rest of his life on the South Side of Chicago. But the police never quit searching for him and, if they ever found him, his sentence made it clear that they were going to have to hang him within the precincts of the courthouse on Dearborn and Hubbard, even years the after the gallows location became a parking lot!

Finally, in 1977, a judge declared that O'Connor, who would have been 87, was probably already dead, and, in any case, would never be found, and ordered that the gallows be sold at auction. They were purchased by a Wild West museum in Union, Ill., which kept them on display until 2006, when they were sold at auction to the Ripley's Believe it Or Not Museum for just over $68,000.

THE TRUNK MURDER OF 1885

There were plenty of murders in Chicago in 1885, but none captured the national interest as much as "The Trunk Murder." Newspapers described the murder as the most atrocious deed in years -- this may have been an exaggeration, but it was certainly one of the more bizarre murders in the city's recent history.

In April of 1885, three Italian immigrants, Giovanni Azarro, Augustino Gilardo, and Agnozzio Sylvestri, decided to murder a 20-year-old fruit peddler named Fillipo Caruso. Caruso, of 75 Tilden Ave., was an industrious young man with $300 to $400 in savings. Not trusting the bank, he was in the habit of carrying his money around with him at all times.

Azarro was the mastermind of the group. After learning just how much money Caruso was carrying, he enlisted Gilardo and Sylvestri to help him with the robbery.

On April 30th, Caruso walked up the block up visit with Azarro and have a shave. In those days, it was a custom among Italian businessmen to take turns shaving each other. Caruso shaved Azarro first, handed off the razor, and took his place in the chair. Azarro prepared a thick lather, which he spread over Caruso's throat. A second later, a makeshift noose was slipped over Caruso's neck, and, as Gilardo held Caruso down, Sylvestri tugged on the noose. Caruso was dead within a minute.

This sort of murder was not terribly uncommon in Chicago in those days. What differentiated the case from others is what happened next: having murdered Caruso, the three assailants decided to stuff the body in a trunk and mail it to Pittsburgh.

Two days later, the trunk arrived in Pennsylvania, emitting so foul an odor that authorities felt it necessary to crack the trunk open. Inside was the horribly discolored body of Caruso, still dressed in a suit. A money order giving his name was found in the pocket.

The trunk was quickly traced back to its point of origin, and the three murderers soon confessed to the deed. Six months later, they were led to the brand new gallows that had been built just to hang the three of them.

Over time, they would be expanded, repainted and modified, but, according to later newspaper reports, these were the gallows that would remain the city's official instrument of execution for decades to come.

THE DEVIL CAME TO CHICAGO
H.H. HOLMES & THE WHITE CITY

I was born with the devil in me. I could not help the fact that I was a murderer, no more than the poet can help the inspiration to sing. I was born with the "evil one" standing as my sponsor beside the bed where I was ushered into the world, and he has been with me ever since.

H.H. Holmes

In 1893, Chicago was host to a spectacular World's Fair - The Columbian Exposition - that celebrated the anniversary of Columbus' discovery of America. It was a boom time for the city and thousands of people came from all over the country to attend. Unfortunately, the list of those "gone missing" at the end of the fair was extensive and as the police later tried to track down where these people had vanished to - the trail often turned cold on the South Side of Chicago. Everything was not as shiny and beautiful as the advertising for the Exposition's "White City" would have everyone believe, for a devil who became known as America's first real serial killer was alive and well on the city's South Side, luring visitors to his "hotel," where scores of them vanished without a trace - never to be seen again.

Today, the neighborhood of Englewood is a part of Chicago but in the late 1800s, it was a quiet, independent community on the southern outskirts of the Windy City. It was a tranquil place and the abode of housewives and shopkeepers. Among these decent folk was a "Mrs. Dr. Holden," as the newspapers mysteriously referred to her, who ran a drugstore at 63rd and Wallace. There was almost too much trade for the woman to handle, as Englewood was rapidly growing, like so many of Chicago's suburbs were in those days. She was delighted, therefore, to find a capable assistant who said that his name was Dr. Henry H. Holmes. He turned out to be a remarkable addition to the place.

In 1887, being a druggist meant also being a chemist and most drugstores were rather crowded places stocked with all manner of elixirs and potions. When Dr. Holmes compounded even the simplest prescription, he did so with a flourish, as if he were an alchemist in the midst of some arcane ritual. His long, pale fingers moved with a surgeon's skill, his handsome face grew intense and his blue eyes grew bright. But he was by no means a socially inept scientist; he was a gentleman of fashion and charming of manner. His politeness and humorous remarks brought many new customers into the drug store, especially the ladies in the neighborhood. In addition, he kept a sharp eye on the account books and was concerned with the profit the store was making. He was, in short, the perfect assistant to the proprietress.

Evil came to Chicago as dashing H.H. Holmes, the city's most prolific killer

It was not long before Holmes seemed to be more the manager of the store and less the prescription clerk. He began to spend more and more time working with the ledgers and chatting pleasantly with the ladies who came into the place, some of whom took a very long time to make a very small purchase. Dr. Holmes became a familiar figure as he strolled down 63rd Street, the main thoroughfare of Englewood. He appeared to be heading for a leading position in the local business community.

Trade at the drug store continued to improve, making Mrs. Dr. Holden exceedingly happy. But as for Holmes, he was still not satisfied with his lot and he had many plans and visions that drove him onward. Strangely, in 1887, Mrs. Dr. Holden vanished without a trace. A short time later, Holmes announced that he had purchased the store from the widow just prior to her "moving out West." The unfortunate lady had (not surprisingly) left no forwarding address.

Two years later, he acquired a large lot across the street from the drug store and began construction on an enormous edifice that he planned to operate as a hotel for the upcoming Columbian Exposition in 1893. There are no records to say what Holmes decided to call this building but for generations of police officers, crime enthusiasts and unnerved residents of

Englewood, it was known simply by one name - "The Murder Castle."

Henry H. Holmes, whose real name was Herman W. Mudgett, was born in 1860 in Gilmanton, N.H., where his father was a wealthy and respected citizen and the local postmaster for nearly 25 years. Early in life, Mudgett dropped his given name and became known as H.H. Holmes, a name under which he attended medical school and began his career in crime. He was constantly in trouble as a boy and, in later years, was remembered for his cruelty to animals and smaller children. His only redeeming trait was that he was always an excellent student and did well in school. In 1878, Holmes married Clara Lovering, the daughter of a prosperous farmer in Loudon, N.H., and, that same year, he began studying medicine at a small college in Burlington, Vt. He paid his tuition with a tidy legacy that had been inherited by his wife. Even as a student, though, Holmes began to dabble in debauchery.

In 1879, he transferred to the medical school of the University of Michigan in Ann Arbor and, while there he devised a method of stealing cadavers from the laboratory. He would then disfigure the corpses and plant them in places where it would look as though they had been killed in accidents. Conveniently, Holmes had already taken out insurance policies on these "family members" and he would collect on them as soon as the bodies were discovered.

A few months after he completed his most daring swindle, insuring a corpse for $12,500 and carrying out the plan with an accomplice who would later become a prominent doctor in New York. He left Ann Arbor and abandoned his wife and infant son. Clara returned to New Hampshire and never saw her husband again.

After that, Holmes dropped out of sight for six years. What became of him during most of this period is unknown and later on, even Pinkerton detectives were unable to learn much about his activities during this time, although they did come across traces of his trail in several cities and states. For a year or so, he was engaged in a legitimate business in St. Paul and he gained so much respect from the community that he was appointed the receiver of a bankrupt store. He immediately stocked the place with goods, sold them at low prices and then vanished with the proceeds. From St. Paul, he went to New York and taught school for a time in Clinton County, boarding at the home of a farmer near the village of Moore's Forks. He seduced the farmer's wife and then disappeared one night, leaving an unpaid bill and a pregnant landlady.

In 1885, Holmes turned up in Chicago and opened an office (he was posing as an inventor) in the North Shore suburb of Wilmette. Upon his re-appearance, Holmes filed for divorce from Clara Lovering but the proceedings were unsuccessful and the case dragged on until 1891. However, this did not stop him from marrying another woman, Myrtle Z. Belknap, whose father, John Belknap, was a wealthy businessman in Wilmette. Although the marriage produced a daughter, it was nevertheless a strange one. Myrtle remained living in Wilmette while Holmes began living in Chicago. John Belknap would later discover that Holmes had tried to cheat him out of property by forging his name on deeds. He would also claim that Holmes had tried to poison him when he was confronted about the fraudulent papers. Myrtle ended the marriage in 1889.

Stories claim that the house in Wilmette where Myrtle lived is haunted today. One has to wonder if the spirit who walks here is that of John Belknap or Myrtle herself. It's possible that her unhappy marriage, and horror as the later crimes of her husband were revealed, has caused her to linger behind.

Shortly after Holmes married Myrtle, he opened another office, this time in downtown Chicago, selling the A.B.C. Copier, a machine for copying documents, which was about the only honest business that he was ever connected with. He operated from an office on South Dearborn but the copier was a failure and he vanished again, leaving his creditors with $9,000 in worthless notes.

The Wilmette resident of H.H. Holmes
(Chicago Daily News)

A few months later, he began working in the Englewood drugstore owned by Mrs. Dr. Holden, who vanished in 1887. Apparently, no one had any reason to doubt Holmes about his "purchase" of her store and she was never found when the police finally began to investigate his activities a few years later.

In 1889, Holmes began a new era in his criminal life. After a short trip to Indiana, he returned to Chicago and purchased an empty lot across the street from the drugstore. He had plans to build a huge building on the property

The ill-fated Connor family. (Left to Right) L.L. "Ned" Connor; Julia Connor; and little Pearl Connor (*Chicago Daily Tribune* & *Chicago Times-Herald* illustrations)

and work was started in 1890. His trip to Indiana had been profitable and, with the help of an accomplice named Benjamin Pietzel, he had used the journey to pull off an insurance scheme. Pietzel later went to jail as a result of the swindle, but Holmes came away unscathed.

He continued to operate the drugstore, to which he also added a jewelry counter. In 1890, he hired L.L. "Ned" Connor of Davenport, Iowa, as a watchmaker and jeweler. The young man arrived in the city in the company of his wife, Julia, and their daughter, Pearl. The family moved into a small apartment above the store and soon, Julia managed to capture the interest of Holmes. He fired his bookkeeper and hired Julia to take the man's place. Not long after, Connor began to suspect that Holmes was carrying on an affair with his wife, and he was right. Luckily for him, he decided to cut his losses, abandoned his family and went to work for another shop downtown.

Now that Holmes had Julia to himself, he took out large insurance policies on the woman and her daughter, naming himself as a beneficiary. Years later, it came to be suspected that Julia became a willing participant in many of Holmes' schemes and swindles. When he incorporated the jewelry business in August 1890, he listed Julia, along with her friend, Kate Durkee, as directors.

By this time, much of Holmes' interest was going into the construction of the building across the street. It was an imposing structure of three stories and a basement, with false battlements and wooden bay windows that were covered with sheet iron. Holmes acted as his own architect for the site and he personally supervised the numerous construction crews, all of whom he quickly hired and fired, discharging them with great fury and refusing to pay their wages. As far as the police were able to learn, he never paid a cent for any of the materials that went into the building

The castle was completed in 1892 and, soon after, Holmes announced that he planned to rent out some of the rooms to tourists who would be arriving en mass for the upcoming Columbian Exposition. It is surmised that many of these tourists never returned home after the fair, but no one knows for sure. The list of the "missing" when the fair closed was a long one and, for most, foul play was suspected. How many of them fell prey to Holmes is a mystery, but no fewer than 50 people who were reported to the police as missing were traced to the place. Here, their trails ended.

An advertisement for lodging during the fair was not the only method that Holmes used for procuring victims. A large number of his female victims came through false classified ads that he placed in small town newspapers, offering jobs to young ladies. When the ads were answered, he would describe several jobs in detail and explained that the woman would have her choice of positions at the time of the interview. When accepted, she would then be instructed to pack her things and withdraw all of her money from the bank because she would need funds to get started. The applicants were also instructed to keep the location and the name of his company a closely guarded secret. He told them that he had devious competitors who would use any information possible to steal his clients. When the applicant arrived, and Holmes was convinced that she had told no one of her destination, she would become his prisoner.

Holmes placed newspaper ads for marriage as well, describing himself as a wealthy businessman who was searching for a suitable wife. Those who answered this ad would get a similar story to the job offer. He would then torture the women to learn the whereabouts of any valuables they might have. The young ladies would then remain his prisoners until he decided to dispose of them.

Amazingly, Holmes was able to keep his murder operation a secret for four years. He slaughtered an unknown

A contemporary view of the "Murder Castle"

number of people, mostly women, in the castle. He would later confess to 28 murders, although the actual number of victims is believed to be much higher. To examine the details of the story, the reader cannot help but be horrified by the amount of planning and devious detail that went into the murders. There is no question that Holmes was one of the most prolific and depraved killers in American history.

In 1893, Homes met a young woman named Minnie Williams. He told her that his name was Harry Gordon and that he was a wealthy inventor. Holmes' interest in her had been piqued when he learned that she was the heir to a Texas real estate fortune. She was in Chicago working as an instructor for a private school. It wasn't long before she and Holmes were engaged to be married. This was a turn of events that did not make Julia Connor happy. She was still involved with Holmes and still working at the store. Not long after the engagement became official, both Julia and Pearl disappeared. When Ned Connor later inquired after them, Holmes explained that they had moved to Michigan. In his later confession, he admitted that Julia had died during a bungled abortion that he had performed on her. He had poisoned Pearl. He later admitted that he murdered the woman and her child because of her jealous feelings toward Minnie Williams. "But I would have gotten rid of her

The Williams Sisters: Minnie (Left) lived at Holmes' castle for more than a year and likely knew more about his crimes that anyone else. Some believe she murdered her sister, Nannie (Right), as a rival for Holmes' affections.

Emmeline Cigrand

anyway. I was tired of her," he said.

Minnie Williams lived at the Castle for more than a year and knew more about Holmes' crimes than any other person. Police investigators would state that there was no way that she could not have had knowledge about many of the murders. Besides being ultimately responsible for the deaths of Julia and Pearl Connor, Minnie was also believed to have instigated the murder of Emily Van Tassel, a young lady who lived on Robey Street. She was only 17 and worked at a candy store on the first floor of the Castle. There is no indication of what caused her to catch the eye of Holmes but she vanished just one month after his offer of employment.

Minnie also knew about the murder of Emmeline Cigrand, a beautiful young woman who worked as a stenographer at the Keely Institute in Dwight, Ill. Ben Pietzel went there to take an alcoholism cure and told Holmes of the girl's beauty when he returned to Chicago. Holmes then contacted her and offered her a large salary to work for him in Chicago. She accepted the job and came to the Castle - but never left it.

Emmeline became homesick after a few weeks in Chicago. She had planned to marry an Indiana man named Robert E. Phelps and she missed him and her family. Holmes later confessed that he locked the girl in one of his soundproof rooms and raped her. He stated that he killed her because Minnie Williams objected to his lusting after the attractive young woman. Some time later, Robert Phelps made the mistake of dropping by the Castle to inquire after her and that was the last time that he was ever reported alive. Holmes described a "stretching experiment" with which he used to kill Phelps. Always curious about the amount of punishment the human body could withstand (Holmes often used the dissecting table on live victims), he invented a "rack-like" device that would literally stretch a person to the breaking point.

In April 1893, Minnie's property in Texas was deeded to a man named Benton T. Lyman, who was, in reality, Ben Pietzel, Holmes' accomplice. Later that same year, Minnie's brother was killed in a mining accident in Colorado, an "accident" that was said to have been arranged by Holmes.

A visit to Chicago by Minnie's sister, Nannie, may provide more evidence of Minnie's murderous ways and her willingness to go along with Holmes' schemes. In June 1893, Holmes seduced Nannie while she was staying at the Castle and had no trouble persuading her to sign over her share of some property in Fort Worth. She disappeared a month later with an explanation that she had gone back to Texas but, according to Holmes, it had been Minnie who killed her. When Minnie found out that Nannie had been consorting with Holmes, the two of them got into a heated argument. Minnie hit her sister over the head with a chair, killing her. Then she and Holmes dropped the body into Lake Michigan.

A short time later, Holmes and Minnie traveled to Denver in the company of another young woman, Georgianna

Bank robber Marion Hedgepeth

Yoke, who had come to Chicago from Indiana with a "tarnished reputation." She applied for a job at the Castle and Holmes told her that his name was Henry Howard and that Minnie was his cousin. On January 17, 1894, Holmes and Georgianna were married at the Vendome Hotel in Denver with Minnie as their witness. After that, the wedding party (which apparently consisted of the three of them) traveled to Texas, where they claimed Minnie's property and arranged a horse swindle. Holmes purchased several railroad cars of horses with counterfeit banknotes and signed the papers as "O.C. Pratt." The horses were then shipped to St. Louis and sold. Holmes made off with a fortune, but it would be this swindle that would later destroy him.

The threesome returned to Chicago and their return marked the last time that Minnie was ever seen alive. Holmes explained that Minnie had killed her sister in a fit of passion and then had fled to Europe. The police believed him, as he was known for being an upstanding citizen and it was not until much later that he confessed to killing her, too. Although her body was never found, it is believed to have joined those of other victims in the acid vat in the basement.

In July 1894, Holmes was arrested for the first time. It was not for murder but for one of his schemes: the earlier horse swindle that ended in St. Louis. Georgianna promptly bailed him out but, while in jail, he struck up a conversation with a convicted train robber named Marion Hedgepeth, who was serving a 25-year sentence. Holmes had concocted a plan to bilk an insurance company out of $20,000 by taking out a policy on himself and then faking his death. Holmes promised Hedgepeth a $500 commission in exchange for the name of a lawyer who could be trusted. He was directed to Colonel Jeptha Howe, the brother of a public defender, and Howe found Holmes' plan to be brilliant.

Holmes then took a cadaver to a seaside resort in Rhode Island and burned it, disfiguring the head and dumping it on the beach. He then shaved his beard, altered his appearance and returned to the hotel, registering under another name and inquiring about his friend, Holmes. When the body was discovered on the beach, he identified it as "H.H. Holmes" and presented an insurance policy for $20,000. However, the insurance company suspected fraud and refused to pay. Holmes returned to Chicago without pressing the claim and began concocting a new version of the same scheme.

A month later, Holmes held a conference with Ben Pietzel and Jeptha Howe and put his new plan into action. Pietzel went to Philadelphia with his wife, Carrie, and opened a shop for buying and selling patents under the name of B.F. Perry. Holmes then took out an insurance policy on his life. The plan was for Pietzel to drink a potion that would knock him unconscious. Then, Holmes would apply make-up to his face to make it look as though he had been severely burned. A witness would then summon an ambulance and while he was gone, Holmes would put a corpse in place of the "shopkeeper." The insurance company would be told that he had died. Pietzel would then receive a portion of the money in exchange for his role in the swindle but he would soon learn, as so many others already had, that Holmes could not be trusted. Unfortunately, this education would come too late to be of any use.

The "accident" took place on the morning of September 4, when neighbors heard a loud explosion from the patent office. A carpenter named Eugene Smith came to the office a short time later and found the door locked and the building dark. For some reason, he became concerned and summoned a police officer to the scene. They broke open the door and found a badly burned man on the floor. The death was quickly ruled an accident and the body was taken to the morgue. After 11 days, no one showed up to claim it so the corpse was buried in the local potter's field. Days later, the police learned that the dead man (Pietzel) had come to Philadelphia from St. Louis and the police of that city were asked to search for relatives. Within days, attorney Jeptha Howe filed a claim with the insurance company, on behalf of Carrie Pietzel, and collected the money. He kept $2,500 and Holmes took the remainder. He later gave $500 to Mrs. Pietzel but then took it back, explaining that he would invest it for her.

The claim was paid without hesitation and everyone got their share of the money, except for Ben Pietzel and Marion Hedgepeth. Holmes never bothered to contact the train robber again, a slight that Hedgepeth did not appreciate. He brooded over this awhile and then decided to turn Holmes in to the authorities. He explained the scheme to a St. Louis policeman named Major Lawrence Harrigan who, in turn, notified an insurance investigator, W.E. Gary. He then passed along the information to Frank P. Geyer, a Pinkerton agent, who immediately began an investigation.

Ben Pietzel never received his share of the money either, but even if he had, he would not have been able to spend it. What Holmes had not told anyone was that the body discovered in the patent office was not a cleverly disguised corpse, but Ben Pietzel himself. Rather than split the money again, Holmes had killed his accomplice and then burned him so that he would be difficult to recognize. Holmes kept this part of the plan a secret because he and Georgianna were now traveling with Carrie Pietzel and her three children. Carrie believed that her husband was hiding out in New York. The group was seen in Cincinnati and then in Indianapolis on October 1. Carrie was then sent east and the children were left in the care of Holmes and Georgianna. Holmes made arrangements for Carrie to meet him in Detroit, where he assured her that her husband was now hiding. He arrived in Detroit several days before the appointed time and put the three children into a boarding house. Then he went to Indiana, returned with Georgianna, and installed her in a second boarding house. When Carrie arrived, she was lodged in yet another establishment. Then, Holmes began moving about the country, apparently aware that the Pinkerton detective, Frank Geyer, was on his trail. The journey lasted for almost two months but on November 17, 1894, Holmes turned up in Boston alone and was arrested and sent to Philadelphia.

As fate would have it, he was not arrested for insurance fraud

Holmes' accomplice, & unlucky victim,
Benjamin F. Pietzel

The Pietzel children: (Left to Right) Alice, Nellie & Howard -- They were perhaps the most tragic victims of H.H. Holmes and were the children of slain accomplice Benjamin Pietzel. Their remains were eventually discovered through the dogged detective work of Pinkerton agent Frank Geyer.

but for the horse swindle that he, Minnie and Georgianna had pulled off in Texas. He was given the choice of being returned to Texas and being hanged as a horse thief, or he could confess to the insurance scheme that had led to the death of Ben Pietzel. He chose insurance fraud and was sent to Philadelphia. On the way there, Holmes offered his guard $500 if the man would allow himself to be hypnotized. Wisely, the guard refused.

The entire insurance scheme was now completely unraveling. A week later, Georgianna was found at her parent's home in Indiana and Carrie Pietzel was discovered in Burlington, Vt., where Holmes had rented a small house for her to live in while she awaited the arrival of her family. Holmes had lived at the house with her for several days but had left angry when she questioned him about a hole that he was digging in the back yard. The police came to believe that he was digging her grave but for some unknown reason, he chose not to kill her. Mrs. Pietzel was arrested and was taken to Philadelphia but was soon released. No charges were ever brought against her.

Detective Geyer was slowly starting to uncover the dark secrets of Henry Howard Holmes, he realized, but even the seasoned Pinkerton man was unprepared for what lay ahead. He was beginning to sift through the many lies and identities of Holmes, hoping to find clues as to the fates of the Pietzel children. At this point, he had no idea about all of the other victims. Holmes swore that Minnie Williams had taken the children with her to London, where she planned to open a massage parlor, but Geyer was sure that he was lying. In June 1895, Holmes entered a guilty plea for a single count of insurance fraud but Geyer expanded his investigation.

Throughout his questioning, Holmes refused to reveal any explanation about what had become of Carrie Pietzel's three children, Howard, Nellie and Alice. Fearing the worst, Detective Geyer set out to try and discover their fate - and his worst fears soon came to realization. In Chicago, Geyer learned that all of Holmes' mail had been forwarded every day to Gilmanton, N.Y. From Gilmanton, it had been sent to Detroit; from Detroit to Toronto; from Toronto to Cincinnati; from Cincinnati to Indianapolis; and then on from there. He followed Holmes' trail for eight months through the Midwest and Canada, stopping in each city to investigate the house that Holmes had been renting there. In Detroit, a house that Holmes had rented was still vacant and a large hole had been dug in the cellar floor. Geyer was relieved to discover that it was empty.

In Toronto, the Pinkerton detective searched for eight days before he found the cottage at No. 16 Vincent St. that had been rented to a man fitting Holmes' description. The man had been traveling with two little girls. Holmes borrowed a shovel from a neighbor, which he claimed he wanted to use to dig a hole to store potatoes in. Geyer borrowed the same spade and, when digging in the same location, found the bodies of Nellie and Alice Pietzel secreted several feet under the earth. In an upstairs bedroom, he found a large trunk that had a piece of rubber tubing leading into it; the other end was attached to a gas pipe. Holmes had told the girls that he wanted to play hide and seek with them, tricked them into climbing into the trunk and then had asphyxiated them.

This shocking discovery made Geyer work even harder to find what had become of Howard Pietzel. While questioning the neighbors, he learned that the Pietzel girls had told them that they had a brother who was living in Indianapolis. With this small clue, Geyer went to Indiana and painstakingly searched 900 houses for any trace of

Holmes. Finally, in the suburb of Irvington, he found a house that Holmes had rented for a week. The place had been empty since Holmes' occupancy and in the kitchen stove, Geyer found the charred remains of Howard.

Now the door was open for Chicago detectives to search Holmes' residence in the Windy City. They would never forget what they found in the "Murder Castle" and it became a sensation in Chicago that stretched on throughout the entire summer, but there was even more to this story than most people knew!

(Left) Pinkerton detective Frank P. Geyer
(Right) No. 16 St. Vincent Street in Toronto, Canada, where Holmes murdered Alice & Nellie Pietzel.

PAT QUINLAN
THE DEVIL'S APPRENTICE?

In 1914, the news of a man's suicide in the small town of Portland, Mich., was barely noticed by the newspapers of the day. The man's name was Patrick Quinlan, a poor Irishman who mostly kept to himself. Even the strange circumstances of his death failed to attract any real attention. Quinlan had taken a fatal dose of poison and left a note lying on the floor next to his body. On the scrap of paper, he had scrawled just four words: "I could not sleep."

The cottage in Irvington, Indiana, where Holmes murdered Howard Pietzel

Few remembered Quinlan's claim to infamy as the accused accomplice of a man named H.H. Holmes, one of the most prolific murderers in American history. Shortly after Holmes' arrest in 1895, Patrick Quinlan, who had worked as a janitor at Holmes' "Murder Castle," was also taken into police custody. He was soon released and forgotten, mentioned mostly as an afterthought in the myriad of writings that have appeared about the murderous life of Holmes.

But was Patrick Quinlan really as innocent as the police said that he was? There were many who didn't believe so, including a man who claimed that he was almost murdered by him, neighbors who believed that he disposed of damning evidence --- and perhaps even Quinlan himself. What really led to his suicide? Guilt over what he had done while in the employ of Holmes or was he, as some would later claim, hounded to his death by the ghosts of his victims?

Holmes was arrested on November 17, 1894 but his links to Chicago, and the "Murder Castle," would not be explored until the following summer. Holmes' various confessions led authorities to look into his Chicago properties, which Holmes had abandoned the previous year. Rumors had been circulating that the bodies of people who had gone missing after being connected to Holmes were buried in the cellar of the Englewood building. The police had planned to investigate the "Castle" for some time but had been put off by the shopkeepers who were still operating on the first floor. They were reluctant to have the police digging up the basement, likely because it would be bad for business. When the bodies of two of the Pietzel children were found in Toronto, however, Inspector Fitzpatrick of Chicago's Central Detective division became determined to go ahead with the search.

Detectives and police officers entered the structure and the news of what they found inside shocked the people of Chicago. It would be during this time that the public perception of H.H. Holmes underwent a dramatic shift. Suddenly, he was seen as something infinitely more diabolical than just a cold-blooded schemer who killed an accomplice for the money. After news emerged about what was found inside the "Murder Castle," Holmes began to

Patrick Quinlan

be seen as a monster of mythic proportions, a creature on the order of the Devil himself.

Investigators first entered the "castle" on Friday night, July 19, 1895. They descended to the cellar first and its size, measuring more than 50 by 165 feet, made a complete excavation a daunting task. After poking around by lantern light for a few hours, the men left for the night.

They returned early on Saturday morning, accompanied by a crew of city construction workers. Using picks and shovels, the men set about their work, searching for any likely spot where Holmes might have disposed of his victims.

While all of this was going on, Detective Sergeants Fitzpatrick and John Norton, accompanied by several newspaper reporters and a Pinkerton agent, ascended to the second story of the building, where Holmes kept his private chambers. They were dumbfounded by what they encountered: a labyrinth of narrow, winding passages with doors that opened to brick walls, hidden stairways, cleverly concealed doors, blind hallways, secret panels, hidden passages, and dangerous trap doors.

The second floor also held 35 guest rooms for the hotel that Holmes operated during the Columbian Exposition. Half of them were fitted as ordinary sleeping chambers, and there were indications that they had been occupied by the various women who had worked for Holmes, by tenants during the fair and perhaps by the luckless females Holmes had seduced while waiting for an opportunity to kill them. Several of the rooms were without windows and could be made airtight by closing the doors. It was later discovered that some of them were lined with sheet iron and asbestos, fitted with trap doors that led to smaller rooms beneath, or were equipped with lethal gas jets that could be used to suffocate the unsuspecting occupants.

Stunned and bewildered, the investigators struggled to make sense of what they had found. It would be several more weeks before the second floor of the "Castle" was fully surveyed and charted and, even then, many of its bizarre features would continue to defy explanation.

However, one thing was clear: in the middle of one of the most thriving cities in America, H.H. Holmes had managed to construct a dwelling place that rivaled any castle of horrors that could be found in works of lurid fiction.

On the top floor of the building, they found other grim surprises, including a clandestine vault that was only big enough for one person to stand in. The room was alleged to be a homemade "gas chamber," equipped with a chute that would carry a body directly into the basement. The investigators suddenly realized the implications of the iron-plated chamber when they found the single, scuffed mark on the inside of the door. It was a small, bare footprint that had been made by a woman who had attempted to escape the grim fate of the tiny room.

This floor also contained Holmes' private apartment, consisting of a bedroom, a bath and two small chambers that were used as offices. The apartment was located at the front of the building, looking out over 63rd Street. In the floor of the bathroom, concealed under a heavy rug, the police found a trap door and a stairway that descended to a room about eight feet square. Two doors led off this chamber, one to a stairway that exited out onto the street and the other giving access to the chute that led down to the basement.

Inside Holmes' office was an immense iron stove, standing eight feet tall and measuring more than three feet in circumference. Opening its door, which, as one reporter noted, was "sufficiently large to admit a human body", Sergeant Fitzpatrick began poking through the debris with his cane. Suddenly, he gasped, reached inside and pulled out a charred object that bore a striking resemblance to a human rib bone. Pulling off his coat and rolling up his shirtsleeves, he scooped out the ashes from the stove onto the floor. Among them, they found more bone fragments, buttons from a woman's dress, and the remains of a lady's watch chain that was later determined to belong to one of Holmes' victims, Minnie Williams.

As Fitzpatrick carefully wrapped the evidence in a handkerchief, one of the newspaper reporters took down the

THE HORRORS OF THE MURDER CASTLE REVEALED

Contemporary newspaper illustrations revealed the strange & terrible things that were hidden inside of the Murder Castle. (Left to Right) Bones were found in basement quicklime pits; trap doors were discovered in secret rooms; strange chambers were discovered secreted in the walls

stovepipe and peered into the chimney. He let out a cry of disgust and then reached into the opening and pulled out a large clump of charred hair.

By that time, the men working in the basement had made some gruesome discoveries of their own, including what was theorized to be a dissecting table that was covered with blood, surgical instruments, homemade torture devices, jars of what were believed to be poison, and a slipper and pieces of a dress that were sifted from an ash heap in a dark corner of the cellar. They also found a large pit of quicklime, which would have been capable dissolving an

A mysterious tank was found in the basement, extending out into the street. A strange odor was discovered coming from inside of it but no use has ever been revealed for this container.

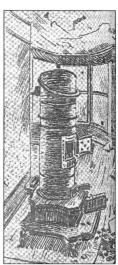

The remains of some of Holmes' victims were found inside of a furnace. Investigators found bones, buttons, jewelry & bits of human teeth.

entire body in a matter of hours. The men searched through the pit and uncovered a portion of a skeleton. Examining the bones by lantern light, Dr. C. P. Stringfield pronounced they were almost certainly the rib cage and pelvis of a human being which, based on their size, could only have come from a child between four and eight years old. Investigator believed them to be the remains of Pearl Connor, the daughter of another of Holmes' many victims.

As the search continued, detectives were convinced that a mass grave would be found in the basement. They made their way along the south wall, tapping on it at regular intervals with their tools, until they discovered a hollow spot about 25 feet from the Wallace Street side. Using their picks, construction workers quickly broke through the wall. Peering into the darkness, they were able to see a mysterious wooden tank, fitted with metal pipes. One of the men squeezed into the opening and tapped on the tank with his pick. The point of it pierced the side of the tank, releasing an odor so foul that the men threw down their tools and fled from the basement.

A plumber was summoned but, before he could arrive, three of the men went down into the cellar to see if the fumes had dispersed. As they made their way across the dark chamber, one of the men struck a match against the wall.

The strange wooden tank exploded.

The blast shook the building, sending the terrified first-floor shopkeepers running out into the street. An alarm was raised and, within minutes, Fire Chief Joseph Kenyon was on the scene with Engine No. 51 and Truck No. 20. By then, several of the workmen had gone down into the basement to search for their comrades. The men were buried in piles of debris but no one was seriously injured.

Before the firefighters could set up their equipment, the fire had burned itself out. Chief Kenyon decided to open the tank and let the noxious fumes dissipate. He and several of his men made their way into the basement but were so overcome by the vapors that they barely managed to stagger back up to the street. Kenyon was most affected by the gas, and, according to the *New York World* newspaper, "He was dragged out and carried upstairs, and for two hours acted like one demented." He remained delirious for nearly two hours and, at one point, even seemed close to death. He finally recovered later in the afternoon. What the gas might have been, or what the mysterious tank might have been used for, remains unknown.

By Sunday morning, the air in the basement was breathable again and investigators and crewmembers went back to work. However, their efforts were hampered by the throng of curiosity-seekers who had swarmed the building, drawn by the lurid newspaper headlines about Holmes' "Murder Castle." The police eventually managed to clear everyone out, but not before many of them had helped themselves to souvenirs, including personal letters and files from Holmes' private office. It will never be known if one of these intruders made off with a vital clue that might have identified one of the people who vanished during the Columbian Exposition, feared to be a victim of Holmes - but never proven.

The only new discovery made in the basement on Sunday was that of a bloodstained dress that Sergeant Fitzpatrick found in an ash heap in the northeast corner. The crew doubled their efforts on Monday and turned up a woman's shoe, the broken lid of an opera-glass case and some skeletal fragments. Then, at the west end of the cellar, they came upon a padlocked storage room, which they promptly broke open. The floor of the small room was littered with rubbish and underneath, the police found a length of stout rope that had been tied at one end into a loop. The opposite end, which was darkly stained with what appeared to be blood, had been tied into a hangman's noose. A reporter for the Philadelphia Inquirer wrote, "The length of rope is such that were the plaited loop attached to the upstairs wall of the secret dumb-waiter shaft, a body hanging from the noose would just clear the bottom of the shaft. This coincidence convinced some of the detectives that Holmes' alleged victims had been pushed through the upstairs door in the dumb-waiter and strangled to death in the shaft below."

As news of the "Castle's" grisly discoveries continued to spread, the authorities slowly realized that they were dealing with a frightening new phenomenon: a killer who was so unique in their experience that they were unable to give him a name. A Chicago journalist came up with the term "multimurderer" but it would be nearly 100 years before criminologists coined the term "serial killer" to describe a monster like H.H. Holmes.

With each day that passed, more horror was realized by the people of Chicago. And with each passing day, the list of Holmes' possible victims grew. The list included Emmeline Cigrand, a lovely young stenographer who had gone to work for Holmes in 1892 and disappeared a short time later and Emily Van Tassel, a pretty grocery store cashier who had vanished soon after striking up an acquaintance with Holmes in 1893. There was also Wilfred Cole, a wealthy lumberman from Baltimore who had traveled to Chicago on unspecified business with Holmes and was never seen again. A physician named Russler, who was allegedly a close friend of Holmes, had vanished in 1892. Harry Walker, a young man who had gone to work as a private secretary for Holmes had disappeared in 1893, a few months after a $15,000 life insurance had been taken out on him with Holmes as the beneficiary. The police also wondered about the whereabouts of a wealthy and attractive widow named Mrs. Lee, who had kept company with Holmes and then vanished. The list also included three missing members of the Gorky family: a middle-aged widow named Kate, who ran a restaurant on the first floor of Holmes' building during the time of the Columbian Exposition; her lovely sister, Liz, and her pretty teen-aged daughter, Anna. There were also an indeterminate number of female clerical workers who had allegedly vanished after taking jobs at the "Castle," including a beautiful Boston girl named Mabel Barrett, a 16-year-old stenographer named Kelly and perhaps dozens of others. One report stated that Holmes had "employed more than 100 young women during his years in Englewood." How many of these young women were never heard from again remains a mystery to this day.

Among the many crimes attributed to Holmes during the first frenzied days of the exposure for the "Murder Castle" was the murder of Mrs. Patrick Quinlan, the wife of the building's janitor. The front-page story of the July 25 edition of the Chicago Inter Ocean asked, "Are more murders to be added to the list of Holmes' atrocities? Is the wife of Pat Quinlan alive? Did Holmes the arch-fiend make away with her, and are her bones rotting in some cellar buried in quick lime?"

Less than 24 hours after the newspaper posed these chilling questions, Mrs. Quinlan showed up at Chicago police headquarters and was taken into custody, along with her husband. They were arrested on charges of conspiring with Holmes and both were subjected to relentless questioning. After countless hours of interrogation, Mrs. Quinlan finally broke down and confessed to her knowledge of at least some of Holmes' insurance scams.

Her husband, however, refused to admit to anything. Patrick Quinlan sobbed to reporters after one brutal interrogation, "I am innocent. I knew Holmes and worked for him. All these people you say were murdered, I knew, and when they went away, as Holmes claimed, I thought it was funny. You say I helped him to commit murder, but I did not. I am innocent and I cannot tell you what you claim I know. Let me alone. I am innocent!"

Police Chief Badenoch, however, scoffed at Quinlan's protestations. He stated flatly that the man was a murderer. At the time of his arrest, the janitor had been carrying a big iron ring that contained 37 keys to various locks throughout the "Castle," even to doors that hid Holmes' secret rooms and "asphyxiation chambers." No one with that sort of access to the innermost passages of the building could have been ignorant of deadly secrets like acid vats, quicklime pits, dissecting tables, private crematorium and scattered piles of human bones. Quinlan was either a willing accomplice or was one of the stupidest human beings on earth.

The same evening that Quinlan was arrested, on July 26, the police searched his apartment and found a letter that had been sent to him by Holmes, who was in prison in Philadelphia at the time. The letter was written on two scraps of common Manila paper and looked remarkably as if it were meant to be found and read by the police. Holmes apparently tried to establish alibis for himself and Quinlan with the letter. It was written on June 18 --- before Pinkerton agent Frank Geyer discovered the body of Howard Pietzel at a small cottage near Indianapolis. It read:

> *Dear Pat:*
>
> *Among their other fool theories they think you took the Pietzel boy to Michigan and either left him there or put him out of the way. I have always told them that I never asked you to do anything illegal, but they are bull-headed. October 19, I saw you at the factory, I think. Can you show where you were all the rest of the month? If they question you, or threaten to arrest you, tell them everything there is to tell about this or any other matter. They may want to know if you were in Cincinnati or Indianapolis about October 12. It is well for you to know where you were working. I am awfully sorry, Pat, for I have always tried to make things easy for you. When Minnie killed her sister, I needed you in the worst way, but would not drag you into it.*
>
> *If the detectives go to New York, as I want them to, they would find where Minnie took them by boat. I have done no killing, Pat. One by one, they are finding them alive. Minnie will not come here as long as there is any danger of her being arrested. A Boston man knows where she is, and her guardian (Messie H. Watt) will, at the safe and proper time, go to her. Let your wife write me anything you wish, not oftener than twice a month, directing H.H. Holmes, County Prison, Tenth and Reed Streets, Philadelphia. I cannot write many letters to you. I am doing all I can for all. Expect to hear shortly from you. Give my love to your wife and Cora. Tell her I have her picture in my room and thank her for it. I have a tame mouse and spider to keep me company. My feed is the worst part here. Clarence Phillips' restaurant at its worst would be fine compared with it. I only eat once a day. Shall be out of it sooner than you expect. They kept Mrs. P. shut up here for six months when we would have let her out on bail. Made a fool of her. Write soon and free. Ask any questions you want to. Georgiana is visiting her mother. Went about two weeks ago.*
>
> *With regards to all,*
> *H.H. Holmes*

The discovery of the letter, despite its claim that Quinlan was not involved in anything illegal, made the police even more convinced that the janitor was involved in Holmes' operations. Chief Badenoch told reporters on July 27, "I think I will be able to wrest a confession from Quinlan before long. I do not intend to let him turn state's evidence, if I can help it, although I believe he is weakening to such an extent that should such a suggestion be made to him, he would grasp it eagerly and at once."

On July 28, astounding new evidence came from another witness that seemed to firmly cement Quinlan's role as an accomplice in Holmes' crimes. This testimony convinced the police of the man's guilt but in the end it was also what ultimately freed him from custody.

According to newspaper reports that appeared that afternoon, Sergeant Fitzpatrick was allegedly able to track down four skeletons that had been removed from the "Castle" under the direction of Holmes and Quinlan. The skeletons were said to have been prepared by a man named Charles M. Chappell, who had first met Holmes in the summer of 1892. Chappell had seen a newspaper advertisement that Holmes had posted, looking for a machinist, and had applied for the job. Chappell was soon hired and had worked for several months when Holmes asked him if he could mount a skeleton. Chappell told him that he could and so Holmes led him to a dark room in the center of the second floor of the "Castle." They walked into the chamber and, using a lantern, Holmes pointed out the body of a man on the floor. Chappell stated, "There was considerable flesh on the lower limbs, but the arms were practically denuded of flesh." Chappell took the arm bones and skull away with him that night and Holmes delivered the rest of the skeleton to the machinist's house the following day, which was October 1, 1892.

On January 2, 1893, Chappell claimed that Holmes asked him to articulate another skeleton for him. Another trip to the dark room revealed another skeleton, this time that of a female. This body had much more flesh on it than the other and when he described its condition to the police, Chappell said, "The body looked like that of a jackrabbit when had been skinned by splitting the skin down the face and rolling it back off the entire body. In some places, considerable amounts of the flesh had been taken off with it."

Even though the newspapers reported that Chappell had turned over an entire skeleton (possibly that of Julia Connor) to the police, he actually provided only a skull. The reports also erroneously claimed that detectives recovered the skeletons of two adult women - one from the home of a West Side physician and the other from the LaSalle Medical School - plus a trunk containing an assortment of "human relics," including an arm bone, a hand and a skull. Not surprisingly, the sensational press published these wild rumors as fact. In truth, the bodies and "human relics" never turned up.

Charles Chappell did exist, however, and he did tell the police about the skeletons that he allegedly articulated for Holmes. Perhaps most damning in his allegations was the testimony that he gave against Patrick Quinlan, whom Chappell claimed knew all about Holmes' illegal activities. Chappell stated that while he was working on the remains for Holmes, Quinlan was on the premises and appeared, in the machinist's mind, to be Holmes' "trusted man."

Chappell also led the police to another witness who could vouch for Quinlan's intimacy with Holmes' crimes. This second witness was a black man named Cephas Humphrey, who drove an express wagon. Humphrey told detectives that one day in June 1893, Holmes summoned him to the "Castle" and asked him to take a trunk and a box to Union Station. Holmes told him, "I want you after the stuff about dark as I do not care to have the neighbors see it go away."

Humphrey returned later that evening. He claimed that he was taken to the dark room in the center of the second floor by none other than Patrick Quinlan. Humphrey described the room as "an awful-looking place. There were no windows in it at all and only a heavy door opening into it. It made my flesh creep to go in there. I felt as if something was wrong ..."

Humphrey then went on to tell of how he found a large box that looked like a casing ordinarily used for a coffin. He carried it downstairs and started to stand it on end on the sidewalk but as he did so, he heard a sharp tapping noise on coming from above and behind him. He looked up and saw Holmes peering out of a second floor window. He told Humphrey not to stand the box on end but rather to lay it down flat. After loading the box into his wagon, Humphrey retrieved the trunk and then was instructed to take them both to Union Station and leave them on a certain platform. He was told not to say anything to anyone, but simply leave the packages. A man there was expecting them and knew what to do with them. The express driver vaguely remembered that the box was supposed to go to Philadelphia, but he could not remember where the trunk was sent.

According to the newspapers, the police were excited to hear of these new developments and felt they now had Quinlan securely in their grasp. More and more evidence seemed to be piling up against him, including the fact that he was a bricklayer by trade, which seemed to suggest that he might have been the one who built the secret vaults for Holmes in the cellar of the "Murder Castle."

Chief Badenoch publicly stated that he believed Holmes had corrupted Quinlan, who was known as an honest man before he met Holmes. He had worked for Holmes for $2 per day but rarely did any real labor, acting more as a confidential agent. This was the reason, detectives believed, that he was well aware of what Holmes was doing. Badenoch felt that with the new information that they had received, Quinlan would soon confess to his role in the many murders of H.H. Holmes.

Chief Badenoch had no idea at the time that he made these statements that he would be forced to release Pat Quinlan from custody a few days later.

At this same time, the police were finally wrapping up their search of the "Murder Castle." Convinced that the building had yielded its darkest secrets, they halted their search on Monday, August 5. The only question that now remained was what to do with the place. Some called for its immediate demolition. The building was a "death trap" - and not just for the unlucky victims who never left the place. E.F. Laughlin, an inspector for the Chicago Department of Buildings, made a tour of the "Castle" and was appalled by its shoddy construction. He wrote in a report, "The structural parts of the inside are all weak and dangerous. Built of the poorest and cheapest kind of material... All dividing partitions between flats are combustible... The sanitary condition of the building is horrible." His final recommendation was that the building should be condemned.

To others, the destruction of the "Castle" seemed a terrible waste. The place might not be fit for habitation, but there were other uses to which it might be put. On July 28, nearly 5,000 people had flocked to Englewood, hoping for a glimpse of the "Castle's" ghastly interior and its "torture chamber," "suffocation vault" and "burial cellar." The following week, the *New York Times* published a story headlined "Knows How it Feels to Smother," about a Chicago man named William Barnes who locked himself inside a jeweler's vault because he wanted to "learn the sensations of some of Holmes' victims."

It was clear that the "Devil" had a firm grip on Chicago's imagination and that there was good money to be made from such a morbid fascination, as an enterprising former policeman named A.M. Clark was quick to realize. Even before the police had called a halt to the investigation, Clark had arranged to lease the building from its court-appointed receiver. On Sunday, August 11, he made his announcement to the press. Beginning that week, the "Castle" would be opened as a tourist attraction - a "murder museum" with an admission charge of 15 cents per person and guided tours conducted by Detective John Norton, who had first-hand knowledge of the case.

As Clark was preparing his new "murder museum" for its grand opening, the police received unfortunate news in the Pat Quinlan investigation. Quinlan and his wife were still in custody and no matter how the police questioned them, both refused to admit to any part in the murders that Holmes committed. Mrs. Quinlan had confessed to knowing about Holmes' insurance schemes, but her husband was adamant about the fact that he had done nothing illegal. Detectives were sure that the witness statements from the machinist, Charles Chappell, and the express driver, Cephas Humphrey, would be enough to push Quinlan into a full confession - but they couldn't have been more wrong.

It would be the family of Charles Chappell who would first call his testimony into question. Aside from the fact that the police had never recovered the skeletons that Chappell claimed he had articulated for Holmes, his own family dismissed his statement as the ramblings of a delusional drunk. They claimed that his story was nothing more than a fantasy that he made up in hopes of cadging free drinks for a recitation of the tale he told the police. Chappell had done some work for Holmes, but whether or not he actually constructed any skeletons for him seemed more and more unlikely every day. Needless to say, this also caused authorities to question his identification of Pat Quinlan as Holmes' "trusted man," as well. With nothing more than suspicion, the police were forced to let Quinlan go. He never confessed to any wrongdoing and no hard evidence ever emerged against him. Two years later, Quinlan attempted to sue the police department for false arrest, but the case was thrown out of court.

Could this have been because the courts felt just as the police authorities did: that Patrick Quinlan knew much more than he was saying, even though no one could prove it? It seems possible and, in fact, questions have continued to be raised about the role that Quinlan had in Holmes' crimes, especially in light of what happened next.

Less than two weeks after it was vacated by the police, H.H. Holmes' "Murder Castle," which had been newly remodeled as a tourist attraction under the management of A.M. Clark, was ready to admit its first paying customers. However, around midnight on Monday, August 19 - just days after Pat Quinlan was released from custody - Clark's get-rich-quick scheme literally went up in smoke.

No one ever found out how the fire got started and its cause remains a mystery to this day. Some saw it as an act of divine retribution as God purged Chicago of Holmes' "chamber of horrors." Others suggested that perhaps it had been a resident of Englewood, ashamed of the blemish that the "Castle" had created on the city's reputation. The police, on the other hand, took another view. They suspected that a confederate of Holmes' had torched the place to conceal incriminating evidence that the investigators had overlooked.

Whatever the source of the fire, it made short work of the building. At precisely 12:13 a.m., a night watchman at the Western Indiana railroad crossing named George J. Myler, spotted flames coming through the building's roof. Before he could turn in the alarm, a series of explosions rocked the building, blowing out the windows of the candy shop on the first floor. By the time the first fire engines arrived, the blaze was nearly out of control. A half-hour later, the roof collapsed, taking down part of the "Castle's" rear wall. Under the direction of Chief Kenyon, the firefighters managed to keep

The last photograph of the Murder Castle, taken before it was razed to make room for a post office in 1938.

GHOST ALERT:

While reports of strange occurrences in the post office that now occupies the site may or may not have any merit, the Castle was said to be haunted when it still stood.

In 1902, it was said in one paper that, "the history of the Holmes castle since its originator was hanged reads like a work of fiction." Spaces for new stores were leased on the lower level. The upper two floors became apartments and, for a time, a hotel. Tenants were said not to last very long, and stories were told of people hearing unearthly noises and seeing ghostly apparitions.

One of the few tenants ever to discuss their experiences in the building was Mrs. Charles Hines, who lived in an apartment in which her bedroom connected to a shaft that descended into the basement that Holmes was thought to have used to lower bodies into an incinerator. Mrs. Hines claimed that, while she felt perfectly at ease in her living room by day, whenever she went into the bedroom she would be overtaken by an irresistible urge to look down the open window into the chute. Whenever she gave into the urge and had a peek, she would be overtaken by the fear that she was about to fall into the shaft to her death. Dreams of falling down the shaft plagued her night after night.

The destruction of the building may not have ended the hauntings, either. Passersby who walked their dogs past the new building claimed the animals would often pull away from it, barking and whining at something only they could see or sense. It was something that remained invisible to their human masters, but which was terrifyingly real to the animals. In addition, postal workers in the building had their own encounters, often telling of strange sounds and feelings that they could not easily explain. The location was certainly ripe for a haunting and if the stories can be believed, it was, and still is, taking place.

the fire from spreading to the frame houses at the rear. Regardless, by the time the blaze was extinguished, about an hour and a half after it was first reported, much of the structure had been consumed.

Contrary to popular belief, though, the H.H. Holmes Murder Castle did not burn down that night in 1895. In fact, the building remained on the site, and was occupied, for more than 40 years. The 1895 fire would not be the only fire in the building, either - there were at least two more in 1903 and 1907! The 1903 fire was caused by a lamp exploding in the second floor apartment of the McPherson family, causing damage to a cigar shop on the second floor and a tailor shop on the first. One man, remembering that he had left his hat inside, ran back to his third floor apartment. By the time he'd retrieved the item, the smoke was too thick for him to return to the stairs. Firemen stretched a net below, but, when he jumped, he missed the net and landed on the sidewalk. The firemen declared him dead on the spot and loaded him into an ambulance to be taken to Englewood Hospital. To their great surprise, they were almost at the hospital when the dead man sat up and declared that he wasn't hurt much at all!

Several tenants and business came and went. By the 1930s, the building was home to a sign shop and a used book and magazine store, behind the counter of which was a staircase into the basement. The sign shop still had the original tiles from Holmes' drug store on the floor. In January of 1938, the city of Chicago purchased the building for about $61,000 with the intention of tearing it down to put up a post office on the site. It was razed in May of that year.

An immediate suspect in the arson fire at the "Castle" was Patrick Quinlan, who had just been released from custody, but the police could not make the charges stick. But they did manage to track Quinlan to another building that was owned by Holmes, this one located on the Northwest side of Chicago.

On August 21, several newspapers reported that another Holmes site had been discovered about 10 miles from the "Murder Castle." It was described as a small glass-bending factory that was one-story high, 20 feet wide and 150 feet long, located near a two-and-a-half story house. The location of the structure was given as "where 65 Sobieski St. ought to be, near the tracks of the Northwestern Railroad, a little northwest of the North Robey Street crossing." Sobieski was a very small road - only about a quarter-mile long - between Robey (now Damen) and Hoyne, near Fullerton Avenue.

Neighbors identified Holmes as the owner of the building, which was closed and boarded up by 1895. They had not seen Holmes in some time but they did recognize a photograph of Pat Quinlan, who they said had come to the building a few days before and had removed a number of boxes and bundles from the place. Inside, the police found nothing but scrap metal, a wall of furnaces and a handful of papers, all bearing Quinlan's signature. The police suspected that Holmes had used the building for some of his cremations but they couldn't prove anything. They had discovered the building by tracing a Brink's express company order that had directed them to pick up a box at No. 65 Sobieski St. on December 6, 1894. Directions were given to stop at the glass company building to await further instructions. The order was signed by P.B. Quinlan. The express driver who called that day remembered being taken to the frame house at the rear of the factory. From there, a large box and several bundles were taken to the general depot of the express company, where they were shipped out two days later. What may have been in the boxes, or where they were finally taken, remains a mystery.

Once again, more suspicion was directed towards Pat Quinlan, but again, no evidence of anything illegal could be obtained. Had Quinlan been involved in the fire that destroyed most of the "Murder Castle?" Had he disposed of evidence from the Sobieski Street location? Or was he simply an unknowing and clueless accomplice?

There were those, in addition to the police, who believed that Patrick Quinlan was anything but innocent. One of those people was Jonathan Belknap, the granduncle of Myrta Belknap, a wife of Holmes who lived in Wilmette. He later stated that he believed that Quinlan had once tried to kill him,

acting under orders from Holmes. He recalled, "I knew [Holmes] was a scoundrel and I had been warned not to be alone with him. I did not want to stay in his house overnight, but he urged it, and I could not well get out of it. During the day, Holmes showed me the house, and tried to get me to go up on the roof with him, but I would not. He went away that night, and I went to bed and carefully locked the door. I did not sleep well, and late in the night, I was awakened by cautious footsteps in the hall and heard someone try to open the door. I lay quiet and presently, there came a rap. I asked what was up and Pat Quinlan answered that he wanted to come in and sleep with me. I have no doubt that if I had gone on the roof with Holmes, or had let Quinlan into my room, I would not be here now."

Jonathan Belknap believed that Quinlan was a killer, and so did many members of the Chicago Police Department, but Quinlan always publicly maintained his innocence. Yes, he had been the janitor and caretaker of the "Murder Castle" and yes, he had even helped construct some of the secret trap doors and lined rooms with asbestos, but he had no idea what they were to be used for. He was innocent of murder, he stated many times - but was he

The general conclusion we've come to about Quinlan is that he probably was an accomplice - but not a willing one. Quinlan knew that he if stepped out of line, he'd surely be next.

really?

After his unsuccessful lawsuit against the police department, Quinlan left Chicago and returned to his home in Portland, Michigan. There, he settled into a quiet life but one that was continually plagued by other people's curiosity. He often told his wife and his friends that he was constantly being stared at on the streets. People watched him, and wondered about what dark deeds he had committed. Quinlan said that while the rest of the world forgot about H.H. Holmes, the curiosity-seekers of Portland, Mich., never forgot about Pat Quinlan.

For 19 years, Quinlan was unable to sleep. At night, he would awake with a start and find himself covered in sweat, his friends later said. He would call for help and when a light would be turned on, he would recount how he was attacked in his sleep by strange hallucinations - ghosts of the many victims of H.H. Holmes.

Finally, when he could stand it no more, Quinlan wrote a note declaring: "I could not sleep," swallowed a bottle of poison and died on the floor of his Michigan home, his hastily scrawled note by his side. Was he an innocent man, driven to suicide because of guilt over what he should have known - or was he a guilty man, hounded to his death by the spirits of those whom he helped to send to an early grave?

The truth will likely never be known.

THE END OF H.H. HOLMES
The trial of Herman Mudgett, a.k.a. H.H. Holmes, began in Philadelphia just before Halloween 1895. It only lasted for six days but was one of the most sensational of the century. The newspapers reported it in a lurid and dramatic manner and Holmes created many exciting scenes in the courtroom. He broke down and wept when

H.H. HOLMES ON THE NORTH SIDE

Tracing the footsteps of H.H. Holmes is a notoriously tricky business - his use of aliases and tendency to buy buildings that were falling apart (and, hence, are long-gone) makes it especially hard. But we do know that his business wasn't relegated only to Englewood - he did a great deal of business on the North Side, as well.

FRANK WILDE'S FRUIT AND CANDY STORE

It was at this Milwaukee Avenue shop that Holmes first met Emily Van Tassel, a victim of his who lived just South of the nearby Wicker Park on Damen. When the stories of Holmes' castle came to light, it was rumored that her body was in the basement of the candy shop. Wilde disappeared at about the same time Holmes left Chicago, and police reasoned that Frank Wilde was simply one of Holmes' many aliases. The address was variously given as 1152 or 1151 Milwaukee Ave. in the papers, making it difficult to ascertain the location. However, 1152 does not seem to have existed; it probably would have been in the middle of where Honore Street now dead-ends at Milwaukee. After the 1909 renumbering, 1151 would have been 1513 N. Milwaukee. The shop is long gone; a newer building now stands on the site. The Van Tassel residence, at what would now be 1356 North Damen, is also long gone, probably on the grounds where the Pritzker School now stands.

THE SOBIESKI STREET CASTLE

In this one-story building, which was said to measure about 20 by 150 feet, Holmes carried on, or claimed to carry on, one of his glass bending businesses. Shortly after Patrick Quinlan was released from custody, he was seen at the location removing a couple of carts of garbage. Police found a whole wall lined with kilns that may have been used for cremations. The exact location of the place is hard to determine; Sobieski Street was a very short stretch of road between Damen and Hoyne near Fullerton, not far from the spot where, at the time, the Luetgert Sausage Works was thriving. The address was given as "where 65 Sobieski Street ought to be" just northwest of where the Northwestern Railroad Crosses Robey Street (which is now Damen). The building appears to be gone, though a single wall or two may have been incorporated into one of the current buildings on the tiny street, which was renamed Seeley Ave around 1896. Oddly, when we investigated this site in 2008, there was a billboard in place for Sobieski Vodka. What are the odds of that?

The building was also connected to an unidentified two-story house in the vicinity - it may have been there that Holmes murdered Emily Van Tassel. Strange occurrences with the floodlights on one nearby house have been reported during ghost tours that Weird Chicago has conducted near the site. Could this site - not far from the candy shop - be where Van Tassel was murdered?

THE PLAZA HOTEL

Upon returning, briefly, to Chicago in 1894, Holmes and his wives took up residence at the Plaza Hotel near Lincoln Park. The building was on the southeast corner of North and Clark, across from the present site of the Chicago Historical Society. It's long gone now.

THE WRIGHTWOOD RESIDENCE

Among the last places Holmes lived with Minnie Williams was a flat in a house at 1220 Wrightwood in what would now be Lakeview or North Lincoln Park (depending on what the realtor wants to charge). After the renumbering, this would be at 1140 Wrightwood. A new residential building stands on the site today.

Georgianna took the stand as a witness for the state and, eventually, he discharged his attorneys and attempted to conduct his own defense. It was said that Holmes was actually outstanding, clever and as shrewd as an attorney, but it was to no avail. The jury deliberated for just two-and-a-half hours before returning a guilty verdict. Afterward, they reported that they had agreed on the outcome in just one minute but had remained out longer "for the sake of appearances."

On November 30, the judge passed a sentence of death. His case was appealed to the Pennsylvania Supreme Court, who affirmed the verdict, and the governor refused to intervene. Holmes was scheduled to die on May 7, 1896, just nine days before his 36th birthday.

By now, the details of the case had been made public and people were angry, horrified and fascinated, especially in Chicago, where most of the evil had occurred. Holmes had provided a lurid confession of torture and murder that appeared in newspapers and magazines, providing a litany of depravity that compares with the most insane killers of all time. Even if his story was embellished, the actual evidence of Holmes' crimes ranks him as one of the country's most active murderers.

He remained unrepentant, even at the end. Just before his execution, he visited with two Catholic priests in his cell and even took communion with them, although he refused to ask forgiveness for his crimes. He was led from his cell to the gallows and a black hood was placed over his head. The trap door opened beneath him and Holmes quickly dropped. His head snapped to the side, but his fingers clenched and his feet danced for several minutes afterward, causing many spectators to look away. Although the force of the fall had broken his neck, and the rope had pulled so tight that it had literally imbedded itself in his flesh, his heart continued to beat for nearly 15 minutes. He was finally declared dead at 10:25 a.m.

There were a couple of macabre legends associated with Holmes' execution. One story claimed that a lightning bolt had ripped through the sky at the precise moment the rope had snapped his neck - but this was not the strangest one. The most enduring supernatural legend of H.H. Holmes is that of the "Holmes Curse." The story began shortly after his execution, leading to speculation that his spirit did not rest in peace. Some believed that he was still carrying on his gruesome work from beyond the grave. And, even to the skeptical, some of the events that took place after his death are a bit disconcerting.

A short time after Holmes' body was buried beneath two tons of concrete, the first strange death occurred. The first to die was Dr. William K. Matten, a coroner's physician who had been a major witness in the trial. He suddenly dropped dead from blood poisoning.

More deaths followed in rapid order, including that of the head coroner, Dr. Ashbridge, and the trial judge who had sentenced Holmes to death. Both men were diagnosed with sudden, and previously unknown, deadly illnesses. Next, the superintendent of the prison where Holmes had been incarcerated committed suicide. The reason for his taking his own life was never discovered. Then, the father of one of Holmes' victims was horribly burned in a gas explosion and the remarkably healthy Pinkerton agent, Frank Geyer, suddenly became ill. Thankfully, though, the diligent detective pulled through.

Not long after this, however, the office of the claims manager for the insurance company that Holmes had cheated caught fire and burned. Everything in the office was destroyed except for a framed copy of Holmes' arrest warrant and two portraits of the killer. Many of those who were already convinced of a curse saw this as an ominous warning.

Several weeks after the hanging, one of the priests who prayed with Holmes before his execution was found dead in the yard behind his church. The coroner ruled the death as uremic poisoning but according to reports, he had been badly beaten and robbed. A few days later, Linford Biles, who had been jury foreman in the Holmes trial, was electrocuted in a bizarre accident involving the electrical wires above his house.

In the years that followed, others involved with Holmes also met with violent deaths, including the train robber, Marion Hedgepeth. He remained in prison after informing on Holmes, although he had expected a pardon that never came. On the very day of Holmes' execution, he was transferred to the Missouri State Prison to finish out his sentence. As time passed, Hedgepeth gained many supporters to his cause, including several newspapers that wrote of his role in getting Holmes prosecuted. In 1906, he finally got his pardon and was released.

Despite the claims that he had made about his rehabilitation, including that he spent each day in prison reading his Bible, Hedgepeth was arrested in September 1907 for blowing up a safe in Omaha, Neb. He was tried, found guilty and sentenced to 10 more years in prison. However, he was released when it was discovered that he was dying from tuberculosis. In spite of his medical condition, he assembled a new gang and at midnight on New Year's Eve 1910, he attempted to rob a saloon in (of all places) Chicago. As he was taking the money from the till and placing it into a burlap bag, a policeman wandered into the place, realized that a robbery was taking place and opened fire on the thief. Hedgepeth was dead before he hit the floor.

Perhaps Holmes got his revenge after all.

CHICAGO (& AMERICA'S) MOST FAMOUS FEMALE SERIAL KILLER

While H.H. Holmes' murderous career was getting underway in Chicago, a lesser known, but equally bloodthirsty, serial killer was beginning a career of her own. Her name was Belle Gunness and she may have been the most prolific female killer in history. As with Holmes, the number of her victims will never be known, but some have speculated that it could be well over 100. Unlike Holmes, though, she didn't kill simply for the thrill of it -- she killed mostly for money. She is thought to have killed both of her husbands, all of her children, and quite a number of suitors and boyfriends, among others, over a period of more than 20 years, usually for the insurance money.

Unlike Holmes, Belle does not appear to have been born "with the devil in her." Born in Norway in 1859, her early years are shrouded in mystery, but most believe that there was nothing particularly unusual about her. However, recent evidence suggests that, while a young woman, she attended a barn dance while pregnant. When a man at the dance kicked her in the stomach, she lost the baby. After this, her personality changed remarkably. Shortly thereafter, her attacker died -- supposedly of stomach cancer -- and Belle began a three-year stint working on a farm, during which time she saved the money to cross the Atlantic to America, which she did in 1881.

In 1884, she met and married Max Albert Sorenson in Chicago, and together they opened a confectionery and stationery store on Elizabeth Street, just north of Grand Avenue. Within a year, the shop burned down under mysterious circumstances. Gunness claimed it was the result of a kerosene lamp, but no such lamp was ever found. Gunness and Sorenson used the insurance money to buy a home in the suburbs, which also burned, resulting in

Belle Gunness with her three children. No one expected the sturdy hog farmer to be a lethal seductress -- and serial killer. (La Porte County Historical Society)

more insurance money.

Sorenson may have been Gunness' first victim. In 1900, he died on the one day that two insurance policies on him happened to overlap. The first doctor on the scene suspected poisoning, but another ruled that it was heart failure. Belle took the insurance money and moved with her three daughters to a farm in La Porte, Ind.

Belle's husbands, babies and acquaintances seemed to die around her in rapid succession, and fires seemed to break out everywhere she went. In 1906, having been cleared of the murder of another husband (despite the fact that her daughter said she had murdered him with a cleaver), Belle began to place ads in Chicago newspapers advertising herself as a wealthy widow in search of an equally wealthy husband. Several men applied and came to visit her in Indiana, but only one was ever known to have left. At this time, Belle began the habit of having large trunks delivered to her house from town, and neighbors saw her digging in the fields overnight.

In 1908, the farm burned to the ground, killing Gunness and her children. But doubts as to what really happened circulated at once. Autopsies found that the children hadn't merely burned to death, they had also been poisoned. And the body identified as Belle's was found decapitated -- the head was never found. The body was identified as hers, though, and a caretaker was convicted of the arson and murder of Gunness and her children. He died in prison the next year.

Days after the fire, workers began digging around the property and found the remains of at least 40 people. With its own lime pit and dissecting table, the house seemed like a country-retreat version of the Holmes Murder Castle. On his deathbed in prison, the caretaker confessed that, while he had not committed any of the murders himself, he had helped bury dozens of bodies around the property in shallow graves. According to his testimony, Belle would make the men comfortable, drug them, and then hack them to death with a cleaver, butchering them the same way she butchered hogs on the farm. On occasions when she was too tired to bury the victims, the remains would be fed to the pigs. Furthermore, according to his story, the headless body found was not that of Gunness, but that of a Chicago woman who had recently been hired as a housekeeper.

Many people doubted that the headless corpse was really Gunness, though some of her false teeth had been found. Many assumed that she'd simply taken out the teeth herself and caught a train to Chicago, where she was, in fact, spotted many times in the years that followed. In 1931, a woman named Elizabeth Carlson was arrested for poisoning a man, and many claimed that she bore a remarkable resemblance to Belle. However, Carlson died awaiting trial.

Suspicions of Gunness' faked death were widespread enough that, in late 2007, her body was exhumed from a suburban Chicago cemetery for testing - and, immediately, more mysteries were discovered, as the casket was found to contain the bones of at least two children in addition to the remains of the woman supposed to be Gunness! If it proves not to be Gunness, Carlson's body will be exhumed next! Who knows how many more men she may have killed in the 23 years following her own alleged death?

The ill-fated candy and stationery store that Gunness and Sorenson ran on Elizabeth Street isn't the only River West candy shop connected to a tale of murder. In 2005, a candy store moved into the former location of Rose's Sandwich Shop, where one of the mafia's most public hits was carried out in 1973. And neither of these sites is far from Frank Wild's Fruit and Candy store, which was owned and

WHERE IS IT NOW?

The approximate spot where the confectionery stood is now the site of a car repair shop on Elizabeth Street, just north of Grand Avenue. But the shop may not have been built over the site -- it may have been built into it. The second story of an old brick building - thought by some to be the location of the candy shop - is still a part of the shop, and the original north and west walls remain.

operated by none other than H.H. Holmes!

CHICAGO'S "BLUEBEARD"

In order to try and adequately understand the life and crimes of a man who was known by various names, including that of Johann Otto Hoch, we have to begin by looking at the end of his criminal career, rather than the beginning. It would not be until the investigation that was started by Chicago police inspector George Shippy that the extent of Hoch's crimes would be discovered. Thanks to his tedious and detailed investigation into the murky past of the killer, Shippy would come to believe that scores of false names and identities concealed the presence of a single murderer: a man who had taken the lives of at least a dozen women. It would be after an arrest for swindling that Shippy would be able to reveal a devious criminal who was then unequaled in the annals of American homicide.

Johann Otto Hoch, who married and murdered for 19 years before his capture, was born John Schmidt in Horweiler, Germany, in 1862. He was married for the first time to a woman named Christine Ramb before deserting her and their three children in 1887. While investigating a charge of bigamy and another charge of swindling a furniture dealer, Inspector Shippy first came into contact with Hoch in 1898. At that time, he was using the alias of Martin Dotz.

Johann Otto Hoch hardly looked the part of a seductive lothario and yet he married as many as 50 women --- and murdered an unknown number of them (Chicago Historical Society)

The inspector had no way of knowing that Hoch/Dotz had murdered a dozen women all over the country but he became suspicious of him when he received a letter from Reverend Herman Haas of Wheeling, W.V. Haas had recognized Hoch's photograph in a Chicago newspaper and he sent the police a photograph of a man who was suspected of killing a Mrs. Caroline Hoch in the summer of 1895. There was no mistaking the fact that the man in the photo and the man in the police station holding cell were the same person. The problem was that the man in the photograph was supposed to have committed suicide by drowning himself in the Ohio River three years before!

"BLUEBEARD & "THE DEVIL":

Because Hoch's notoriety in Chicago came so closely on the heels of the infamy achieved by H.H. Holmes (and likely because his prey was also young women), newspaper reporters desperately tried to connect the two of them, naming Hoch as both Holmes' apprentice and his janitor. These were both charges that had been pinned on Pat Quinlan, as well. Evidence linking Johann Hoch to H.H. Holmes is dubious, but there were witnesses who came forward to link the two men, including Charles Chappel, the skeleton articulator. They claimed that Hoch had been a frequent visitor to the "Castle" on 63rd Street, using the name "Jacob Schmitt," which was one of his many aliases. There, reporters theorized, Hoch may have been trained by Holmes in the art of swindling and making poisons. Mr. Davis, who ran a jewelry store in the Murder Castle (and was always distinctly bemused by he whole affair), however, said that there was never any Jacob Schmitt and that he'd never seen Hoch around the Castle at all. Detectives eventually brushed off the claims, though they did believe that, shortly before his arrest, Hoch had a haircut in a barbershop located in Holmes' old Castle!

Shippy attempted to pursue this lead but realized that it was going to take a lot of time. He needed to keep Hoch in jail so he turned his efforts to the swindling charge. He soon had enough for a conviction and Hoch was sentenced to a year in the Cook County jail. Shippy then turned his attention back to Hoch's other illegal activities and acting on a tip, began to search for what became a dozen missing wives. He started in West Virginia.

Hoch first appeared in Wheeling in February 1895, going by the name Jacob Huff. He opened a saloon in a German neighborhood and became a popular man in the community. He began to seek out marriageable widows or at least divorced women with money. One of those he found was Caroline Hoch, a middle-aged widow. The couple married in April and the service was performed by Reverend Haas, who later alerted Inspector Shippy to the identity of the man he had in custody. It was the minister who had discovered Caroline dying in agony after he had spotted her husband giving her some sort of white powder. He did not act, however, believing that it was merely medicine and the woman died a few days later in great pain. Huff (as he was known) insisted that his wife be buried right away. He then collected Caroline's life insurance, sold her house, cleaned out her bank accounts and disappeared.

Haas later explained to Inspector Shippy what he believed happened next. Huff strolled to the nearby Ohio River on the night of his disappearance, stripped off his

6 WAYS TO WIN A WOMAN

Inspector Shippy came to believe that Hoch married at least 44 women (and perhaps more) in his career as a bigamist and a swindler. He murdered an unknown number of his unwitting wives. Oddly, Hoch was a middle-aged, balding and burly man with light-blue eyes and a handlebar mustache. There was nothing about him to suggest that he would be so attractive to the fairer sex that they would agree to marry him within days of an introduction and yet many of them did so. Hoch did have a set of rules that he lived by in which to make women fall in love with him. He imparted them on the *Chicago Sun* newspaper just a short time before he was executed:

6 WAYS TO WIN A WOMAN TOLD BY "BLUEBEARD" HOCH

- Nine out of every ten women can be won by flattery
- Never let a woman know her own shortcomings
- Always appear to a woman to be the anxious one
- Women like to be told pleasant things about themselves
- When you make love, be ardent and earnest
- The average man can fool the average woman if he will only let her have her own way at the start

Good advice or bad -- it certainly makes you wonder what Hoch had that made him so irresistible. And it was not always just women who felt that way. Remember that The Reverend Haas failed to act against the man, even when he suspected him of poisoning his wife. It was not until Hoch was long gone that he decided to act on his suspicions. Others were not so easily won over, namely Inspector Shippy, who sensed something about Hoch was wrong from the start. And it's lucky for the scores of other women who might have followed his previous wives to the grave that he did.

clothes, and walked into the water. He placed his good watch, with his photo in the locket, and a suicide note on the pile of clothing and then, holding a heavy sack over his head, walked into the river to a rowboat. He climbed into a boat, which he had earlier anchored, and dressed in the clothing that had been hidden there. Afterwards, he rowed up the river, only pausing in the deep water to drop the bag that he had carefully carried with him. He continued on to the Ohio side of the river, set the boat adrift and then resumed his journey. He was no longer Jacob Huff but Johann Otto Hoch, taking the last name of his victim. To investigators, it appeared that "Huff" had committed suicide.

For almost a year, Shippy followed Hoch's strange trail across the country and he found scores of dead and deserted women, from New York to San Francisco, with most of the victims being in the Midwest. Years later, he would unearth even more - perhaps as many as 50 --- in St. Louis, Minneapolis, Kansas City, Philadelphia and beyond. Incredibly, though, Shippy could not produce enough hard evidence to convict Hoch of anything and the man was soon due to be released from jail. Desperately, he contacted the authorities in Wheeling and begged them to exhume the body of Caroline Hoch and to look for signs of arsenic poisoning.

The request was carried out and the coffin was exhumed from the cemetery. However, officials were stunned when the lid was opened and it was discovered that all of the cadaver's vital organs had been surgically removed. It was later decided that this must have been what was in the weighted bag that Hoch carried with him and then dumped in the middle of the river. The body could not be examined, which meant there was no real case to be made against Hoch for Caroline's murder. At the end of his term for swindling, Hoch was released, much to the dismay of Inspector Shippy. He was convinced the man would murder again.

From 1900 to 1904, Hoch, using various aliases, married and murdered as many as 15 more women. Prior to his prison term in Chicago for swindling, Hoch married women and then slowly poisoned them to death, calling in doctors whom he knew would innocently diagnose his wife's ailment as a disease of the kidneys, for which there was no treatment. He took his time, spending months and murdering his wives very carefully. After his release from the Cook County jail, however, Hoch's careful method fell to pieces. He began killing in record time, marrying rich widows and within days of the wedding, heavily dosing them with arsenic. He murdered some of his wives within a week of their nuptials. He married his last victim, Marie Walcker, in Chicago on December 5, 1904, and he poisoned her days later.

On the night of her death, the victim's estranged sister, Amelia, appeared at her home. As his wife lay dying, Hoch embraced and kissed Amelia and asked her to marry him after the death of her sister. Amazingly, she agreed. Marie was buried a day later without being embalmed and Hoch married Amelia six days after the service. The killer had received $500 from Marie's life insurance policy and Amelia gave him another $750. He disappeared immediately afterward and Amelia went to the Chicago police. Inspector Shippy had Marie Walcker's body exhumed and the poison was found in her organs. The search was now on for the killer.

Shippy sent photographs of Hoch to every major newspaper in the country and a short time later, a widowed landlady in New York, Mrs. Katherine Kimmerle, recognized the likeness as being that of her new boarder, Henry Bartels. She recalled him so vividly because the strange man had proposed marriage to her only 20 minutes after he had taken the room. The authorities soon had Hoch in custody.

When he was arrested, Hoch claimed that he was being framed and the "truth" about him was misrepresented. Discovered in his room was $625, several wedding rings with the inscriptions filed off, a loaded revolver and a fountain pen that contained 58 grams of arsenic. Hoch claimed that he had planned to commit suicide with the poison. He was soon on his way back to Chicago. Inspector Shippy was waiting for him when the train arrived in the station.

During his trial, the killer hummed, whistled and twirled his thumbs in court. Until the very end, he insisted that he was innocent. When he was finally convicted of murdering Marie Walcker, Hoch only whispered, "It's all over with Johann. It serves me right." He clung to the hope that he would be released until the very hour of his death. He remained awake all night before the day of the execution, eating huge meals and demanding more and more food. Every now and then he was smile at his guards and say, "Look at me, boys. Look at poor old Johann. I don't look like a monster now, do I?" The guards did not reply.

Hoch finally went to the gallows on February 23, 1906. He once more declared his innocence and then nodded for the sheriff to place the noose around his neck. He declared, "I am done with this world. I have done with everybody." Moments later, the trap was sprung and Johann Hoch went to his death.

THE SAUSAGE VAT MURDER

The story of Adolph Luetgert has its beginnings in the heart of Chicago's Northwest Side, a place once filled with factories, middle-class homes, and with a large immigrant population. The murder of Luetgert's wife, Louisa, has an unusual place in the history of Chicago crime in that it was one of the only murders to ever drastically affect the sale of food for the better part of the summer of 1897.

Adolph Luetgert was born in Germany and came to America after the Civil War. He lived for a time in Quincy, Ill., and then came to Chicago in 1872, where he pursued several trades, including farming and leather tanning. Eventually, he started a wholesale liquor business near Dominick Street. He later turned to sausage making, where he found his greatest success. After finding out that his German-style sausages were quite popular in Chicago, he built a sausage plant in 1894 at the southwest corner of Hermitage and Diversey. It would be here where the massive German would achieve his greatest success - and his shocking infamy.

Illustration of the Luetgert Sausage Factory in 1897 from the *Chicago Daily News*

Although the hard-working Luetgert soon began to put together a considerable fortune, he was an unhappy and restless man. Luetgert had married his first wife, Caroline Rabaker, in 1872. She gave birth to two boys, only one of whom survived childhood. Caroline died five years later, in November 1877. Luetgert sold his liquor business in 1879 and moved to the corner of North and Clybourn avenues, where he started his first sausage-packing plant in the same building where he lived. Two months after Caroline's death, Luetgert married an attractive younger woman. This did little to ease his restlessness, however, and he was rumored to be engaged in several extramarital affairs during the time when he built a three-story frame house next door to the sausage factory. He resided there with his son and new wife.

His wife, Louisa Bicknese Luetgert, was a beautiful young woman 10 years younger than her husband. She was a former servant from the Fox River Valley who met her new husband by chance. He was immediately taken with her, entranced by her diminutive stature and tiny frame. She was less than five feet tall and looked almost child-like next to her burly husband. As a wedding gift, he gave her a unique, heavy gold ring with her initials inscribed inside. He had no idea at the time that this ring would later be his undoing.

After less than three years of business, Luetgert's finances began to fail. Even though his factory turned out large quantities of sausages, Luetgert found that he could not meet his supplier's costs. Instead of trying to reorganize his finances, though, he and his business advisor, William Charles, made plans to expand. They attempted to secure more capital to enlarge the factory but, by April 1897, it had all fallen apart. Luetgert, deep in depression, sought solace with his various mistresses and his excesses, and business losses began taking a terrible toll on his marriage.

(Left) "Sausage King" Adolph Luetgert & (Right) a drawing of the unfortunate Louisa Luetgert that appeared in the *Chicago Daily News* in 1897

Neighbors frequently heard him and Louisa arguing and their disagreements became so heated that Luetgert eventually moved his bedroom from the house to a small chamber inside the factory. Soon after, Louisa found out that her husband was having an affair with the family's maid, Mary Simerling, who also happened to be Louisa's niece. She was enraged at this news and this new scandal got the attention of the people in the neighborhood, who were already gossiping about the couple's marital woes. Luetgert soon gave the neighbors even more to gossip about. One night, during another shouting match with Louisa, he responded to her indignation over his affair with Mary by taking his wife by the throat and choking her. Before she collapsed, Luetgert saw neighbors peering in at him from the parlor window of their home, and he released her. A few days later, Luetgert was seen chasing his wife down the street. He was shouting at her and waving a revolver. After a couple of blocks, Luetgert broke off the chase and walked silently back to the factory.

Then, on May 1, 1897, Louisa disappeared. When questioned about it, Luetgert stated that Louisa had gone out the previous evening to visit her sister. After several days, though, she did not come back. Soon after, Diedrich Bicknese, Louisa's brother, came to Chicago and called on his sister. He was informed that she was not at home. He came back later and, finding Luetgert at home, he demanded to know where Louisa was. Luetgert calmly told him that Louisa had disappeared on May 1 and had never returned. When Diedrich demanded to know why Luetgert had not informed the police about Louisa's disappearance, the sausage-maker simply told him that he was trying to "avoid a scandal" but that he had paid two detectives $5 to try and find her.

Diedrich immediately began searching for his sister. He went to Kankakee, thinking that perhaps she might be visiting friends there, but found no one who had seen her. He returned to Chicago and when he found that Louisa still had not come home, now having abandoned her children for days. Worried and suspicious, Diedrich went to the police and spoke with Captain Herman Schuettler.

The detective and his men joined in the search for Louisa. They questioned neighbors and relatives and heard many recitations about the couple's violent arguments. Captain Schuettler was familiar with Luetger; he had

THE LUETGERT RESIDENCE.
(No. 1521 North Hermitage avenue, back of the sausage factory.)

The Luetgert home, across the street from the sausage factory

dealings with him in the past. He summoned the sausage-maker to the precinct house on two occasions and each time, pressed him about his wife. Schuettler recalled a time when the Luetgerts had lost a family dog, an event that prompted several calls from Luetgert, but when his wife had gone missing, he noted that Luetgert had never contacted him. Luetgert again used the excuse that as a "prominent businessman," he could not afford the disgrace and scandal.

The police began searching the alleyways and dragging the rivers. They also went to the sausage factory and began questioning the employees. One of them, Wilhelm Fulpeck, recalled seeing Louisa around the factory at about 10:30 p.m. on May 1. A young German girl named Emma Schiemicke, passed by the factory with her sister at about the same time on that evening and remembered seeing Luetgert leading his wife up the alleyway behind the factory.

Frank Bialk, a night watchman at the plant, confirmed both stories. He had also seen Luetgert and Louisa at the sausage factory that night. He only got a glimpse of Louisa, but saw his

GHOST ALERT!

During the investigation, Luetgert accused the police department of "hiring" ghosts. Apparently, he had seen Louisa's specter around the neighborhood, and believed that the police had hired one of his neighbors to dress up like a ghost and wander around to frighten the superstitious and excite his neighbors' suspicions of him. The police found this to be terribly amusing, but one of his neighbors, Agatha Tosch, was forced to testify that she had never dressed up as a ghost during the trial! She did say, though, that rumors that Louise's ghost was haunting the area were already being taken as fact in the neighborhood.

employer several times. Shortly after the couple entered the factory, Luetgert had come back outside, gave Bialk a dollar and asked him to get him a bottle of celery compound from a nearby drugstore. When the watchman returned with the medicine, he was surprised to find the door leading into the main factory was locked. Luetgert appeared and took the medicine. He made no comment about the locked door and sent Bialk back to the engine room.

A little while later, Luetgert again approached the watchman and sent him back to the drugstore to buy a bottle of medicinal spring water. While the watchman had been away running errands, Luetgert had apparently been working alone in the factory basement. He had turned on the steam under the middle vat a little before 9:00 p.m. and it was still running when Bialk returned. The watchman reported that Luetgert had remained in the basement until about 2: 00 a.m.

Bialk found him fully dressed in his office the next day. He asked whether or not the fires under the vat should be put out and Luetgert told him to leave them burning, which was odd since the factory had been closed several weeks during Luetgert's financial re-organization. Bialk did as he was told, though, and went down to the basement. There, he saw a hose sending water into the middle vat and on the floor in front of it was a sticky, glue-like substance. Bialk noticed that it seemed to contain bits of bone, but he thought nothing of it. Luetgert used all sorts of waste meats to make his sausage and he assumed that this was all it was.

On May 3, another employee, Frank Odorowsky, known as "Smokehouse Frank," also noticed the slimy substance on the factory floor. He feared that someone had boiled something in the factory without Luetgert's knowledge, so he went to his employer to report it. Luetgert told him not to mention the brown slime. As long as he kept silent, Luetgert said, he would have a good job for the rest of his life. Frank went to work scraping the slime off the floor and poured it into a nearby drain that led to the sewer. The larger chunks of waste were placed in a barrel and Luetgert told him to take the barrel out to the railroad tracks and scatter the contents there.

Following these interviews, Schuettler made another disturbing and suspicious discovery. A short time before Louisa's disappearance, even though the factory had been closed during the re-organization, Luetgert had ordered 325 pounds of crude potash and 50 pounds of arsenic from Lor Owen & Company, a wholesale drug firm. It was delivered to the factory the next day. Another interview with Frank Odorowsky revealed what had happened to the chemicals. On April 24, Luetgert had asked Smokehouse Frank to move the barrel of potash to the factory basement, where there were three huge vats that were used to boil down sausage material. The corrosive chemicals were all dumped into the middle vat and Luetgert turned on the steam beneath it, dissolving the material into liquid.

Combining this information with the eyewitness accounts, Captain Schuettler began to theorize about the crime. Circumstantial evidence seemed to show that Luetgert killed his wife and boiled her in the sausage vats to dispose of the body. The more that the policeman considered this scenario, the more convinced that he became that this is what had happened. Hoping to prove his theory, he and his men started another search of the sausage factory and he soon made a discovery that became one of the most gruesome in the annals of Chicago crime.

On May 15, a search was conducted of the 12-foot-long, five-foot-deep middle vat that was two-thirds filled with a brownish, brackish liquid. The officers drained the greasy paste from the vat, using gunnysacks as filters, and began poking through the residue with sticks. It wasn't long before Officer Walter Dean found several pieces of bone and two

The infamous vats in the factory basement. An Illustration from the *Chicago Daily News* in 1897.

GHOST ALERT:

According to legend, Louisa Luetgert's ghost returned not only to haunt the old neighborhood where she died, but also to exact her revenge on the man who killed her. Stories claim that toward the end of Adolph Luetgert's life, he told stories about Louisa visiting his cell at night. His dead wife had returned to haunt him, intent on having revenge for her murder. Was she really haunting him or was the "ghost" really just the figment of a rapidly deteriorating mind? Based on the fact that residents of the neighborhood also began reporting seeing Louisa's ghost, one has to wonder if Luetgert was seeing her ghost because he was mentally ill --- - or if the ghost had driven him insane. Luetgert died under what the coroner called "great mental strain," so perhaps Louisa did manage to get her revenge after all.

And Louisa, whether she was murdered by her husband or not, reportedly did not rest in peace. Not long after her husband was sent to prison, her ghost began to be seen inside the Luetgert house. Neighbors claimed to see a woman in a white dress leaning against the fireplace mantel. Eventually, the house was rented out but none of the tenants stayed there long. The place became an object of fear, the yard overgrown with ragweed, and largely deserted.

Oddly, the fire that broke out in the former sausage factory in 1904 started in the basement -- at exactly the spot where Luetgert's middle vat was once located. Fire officials stated, "The source of the fire is a mystery and none has been able to offer any better explanation than the superstitious folk who have an idea that some supernatural intervention against any commercial enterprise operating at the scene of the murder has been invoked." No cause was ever determined for the fire, leading many to believe that perhaps Louisa's specter had returned once more.

Legend has it on the Northwest Side today that Louisa Luetgert still walks. If she does, she probably no longer recognizes the neighborhood where she once lived. They say though, that if you happened to be in this area on May 1, the anniversary of Louisa's death, there is a chance that you might see her lonely specter still roaming the area where she lived and died.

gold rings. One of them was a badly tarnished friendship ring and the other was a heavy gold band that had been engraved with the initials "L.L.".

Louisa Luetgert had worn both of the rings.

After they were analyzed, the bones were found to be definitely human - a third rib; part of a humerus, or great bone in the arm; a bone from the palm of a human hand; a bone from the fourth toe of a right foot; fragments of bone from a human ear and a larger bone from a foot.

Adolph Luetgert, proclaiming his innocence, was arrested for the murder of his wife. Louisa's body was never found and there were no witnesses to the crime, but police officers and prosecutors believed the evidence was overwhelming. Luetgert was indicted for the crime a month later and details of the murder shocked the city's residents, especially those on the Northwest Side. Even though Luetgert was charged with boiling his wife's body, local rumor had it that she had been ground into sausage instead! Needless to say, sausage sales declined substantially in 1897.

Luetgert's first trial ended with a hung jury on October 21 after the jurors failed to agree on a suitable punishment. Some argued for the death penalty, while others voted for life in prison. Only one of the jurors thought that Luetgert might be innocent. A second trial was held and, on February 9, 1898, Luetgert was convicted and sentenced to a life term at Joliet Prison. He was taken away, still maintaining his innocence and claiming that he would receive another trial. He was placed in charge of meats in the prison's cold-storage warehouse and officials described him as a model inmate.

By 1899, though, Luetgert began to speak less and less and often quarreled with the other convicts. He soon became a shadow of his former, blustering persona, fighting for no reason and often babbling incoherently in his cell at night. His mind had been broken, either from guilt over his heinous crime, or from the brutal conditions of his imprisonment.

Luetgert died in 1900, likely from heart trouble. The coroner who conducted the autopsy also reported that his liver was greatly enlarged and in such a condition of degeneration that "mental strain would have caused his death at any time."

The sausage factory stood empty for years, looming over the neighborhood as a grim reminder of the horrors that had visited there. The windows of the place became a target for rocks thrown from the nearby railroad embankment and it often invited forays by the curious and the homeless.

In the months that followed his death, Luetgert's business affairs were entangled in litigation. The courts finally sorted everything out in August 1900 and a public auction was held for the factory and its grounds. Portions of the property were divided between several buyers but the Library Bureau Company, which was founded by Dewey Decimal System creator Melvil Dewey, leased the factory itself. The company used it as a workshop and storehouse for its line of library furniture and office supplies. During the renovations, the infamous vats in the basement were discarded.

In June 1904, a devastating fire swept through the old sausage factory. It took more than three hours to put out the blaze and when it was over, the building was still standing, but everything inside had been destroyed. However, contrary to what many stories have reported, the building was still there. In fact, it's still there today!

WHERE IS IT NOW?
The factory is easily recognized on Diversey near Hermitage. The deep red bricks on the east side of the building façade facing the street are a newer addition; the older, yellowish-bricks on the West side are the original factory.

Despite the damage done to the building's interior, the Library Bureau re-opened its facilities in the former sausage factory. It would go on to change owners many times in the decades that followed. In 1907, a contracting mason purchased the old Luetgert house and moved it from behind the factory to another lot in the neighborhood, hoping to dispel the grim memories attached to it. The part of Hermitage Avenue that intersected with Diversey was closed. By the 1990s, the factory stood empty and crumbling, facing a collection of empty lots that were only broken by the occasional ramshackle frame house. In 1999, though, around the 100th anniversary of the death of Adolph Luetgert, the former sausage factory was converted into loft condominiums and a brand new neighborhood sprang up to replace the aging homes that remained from the days of the Luetgerts. Fashionable brick homes and apartments appeared around the old factory, and rundown taverns were replaced with coffee shops.

The old neighborhood was gone, but the stories of this infamous crime still lingered, providing a unique place in history as the only Chicago murder that ever kept people from eating sausages!

THE CASE OF THE "RAGGED STRANGER"

There has likely been no other murder case in the country that was as colorfully solved as the Chicago case of the "Ragged Stranger." It has been recounted many times over the years; in books, in detective magazines and even in a Hollywood movie. There have been a number of different writers who have taken credit for solving the case and it's likely that this was one time when the press and the police department pooled their resources and brought a killer, a former war hero named Carl Wanderer, to justice.

Carl Wanderer

Carl Otto Wanderer was born and raised in Chicago. His parents, German immigrants, taught him the value of a dollar at a young age and by the time he was 27, he had saved enough to open a successful butcher shop with his father. His strict upbringing and frugal ways left Wanderer an unhappy and restless young man and in 1916, adventure began to call to him.

The newspapers recounted the raids by Pancho Villa into the Southwestern United States and called for volunteers to help pursue the Mexican bandit and his men. Wanderer enlisted in the military and was sent to New Mexico to serve under Black Jack Pershing as a cavalry officer. His experience with the First Illinois Cavalry gave him enough military stature to earn him a promotion to lieutenant with the first units sent to France when the United States entered World War I. He saw action on the Western front and returned home, with medals for bravery, in the spring of 1919.

On October 1 of that same year, Wanderer married his sweetheart, a chubby but attractive 20-year-old named Ruth Johnson. The couple moved into an apartment shared by Ruth's parents and it was there that any affection that he had for her died. The claustrophobic flat became unbearable, thanks to Ruth's neediness and his nagging mother-in-law, who berated Wanderer about the fact that he didn't have enough money for the couple to get a place of their own. Carl's restlessness once more got the better of him and he began dating a 16-year-old typist named Julia Schmitt. He often met her at the Riverview Amusement Park while his wife was otherwise engaged.

And then, shortly before Christmas, Ruth happily announced to her husband that she was pregnant. Wanderer would become a father the following summer. Carl accepted the news with dismay and fell into somber, sullen moods. He rarely spoke and avoided coming home. He pondered his options and as it turned out, bided his time, until a plan to rid himself of his problems slowly came to mind.

On June 21, 1920, Ruth and Carl attended an evening performance of a movie called the "Sea Wolf", a rousing Jack London adventure story, at the Pershing Theater (now the Davis) at Lincoln and Western. As they strolled home afterward, Wanderer later reported seeing a sinister-looking man lurking near Zindt's Drug Store on Lawrence Avenue. According to his story, the man crushed out a cigarette as they passed by and then he followed behind them at a distance.

"Ruth went up ahead of me when we reached the house. She opened the outer door and I heard her fumbling with her keys to the inner door of the hall," Wanderer later told the police. Ruth reached up for the ribbon dangling from the overhead light so that she could find the right key. Carl asked her if she was having trouble and she laughed.

Neither of them noticed the man who followed them into the dark vestibule. The "Ragged Stranger," as this man would come to be known, stepped forward with a gun trained on Ruth. "Don't turn on the light," the man said. "Throw up your hands!"

Before Ruth and Carl could comply with his order, the stranger fired two bullets into Ruth. Wanderer claimed that he heard the man shout out a string of obscenities as he continued to fire. Carl jerked out his own Colt .45 service revolver, which h habitually carried with him, and emptied his clip in the direction of the dark figure. It was later discovered that 14 bullets had been fired in the small vestibule in just several seconds time.

When the smoke cleared, the stranger ---- and Ruth Wanderer ---- were lying on the floor of the vestibule, sprawled out in pools of blood.

Ruth's mother rushed down to the door to find her daughter had fallen with two bullets in her. Wanderer had gone berserk with rage, smashing his gun and his fists against a man who was lying on the floor. Ruth lived just long enough to utter a few tragic words: "My baby.... My baby is dead."

Detective Sergeant John Norton arrived on the scene just minutes later. By this time, neighbors and onlookers had started to gather around Wanderer, who was covered in the stranger's blood, and Ruth's mother, who cradled her daughter's lifeless body in her arms. Norton pushed his way through. The hulking detective was well known in the neighborhood, having been shot four times during his celebrated career, and everyone knew that he would get answers quickly in the case. He started off with just one question: why was Carl Wanderer carrying a gun?

Wanderer had a quick answer: There had been a robbery attempt at his father's butcher shop a short time before and Carl was carrying his service revolver in case it happened again. He suggested to Norton that perhaps this man could have been involved. A search of the stranger's body turned up just $3.80 and a business card from a traveling circus. There was nothing else on the body, which was taken to Ravenswood Hospital for a check of fingerprints and the inquest. During questioning, Carl decided to embellish his connections with the stranger a little further. He looked familiar to him, Wanderer said. He believed the man had flirted with Ruth a few nights earlier. She had come home and reported the news to Carl in a near panic, terrified that "the stranger was laying a trap."

The morning editions of the Chicago newspapers jumped all over the story. They told of Wanderer's heroics and exemplary military record, touting his service in New Mexico and during the war. He was a Great War hero who had fought to protect America from her enemies, they said, and now this same man had been forced to endure the cold-blooded murder of his wife and unborn child. It was a heartless and horrible crime and the public reacted with shock and outrage.

Carl Wanderer was awarded the status of a hero who had defended the honor of his wife, even though the end result had been tragic. The public expected to see him charged with nothing more than justifiable homicide in the murder of the "Ragged Stranger." He deserved to be left alone to grieve for his family, they believed, and this should be the end of the story.

But little did they know --- the story of the "Ragged Stranger" was just getting started.

Detective John Norton, along with help from legendary crime reporter Harry Romanoff and his editor at the Chicago Herald-Examiner, Walter Howey, began to ask some hard questions about Wanderer's version of the murders.

To start with, there was the matter of the two guns that had been used. Both of them were big .45 caliber automatics. Carl Wanderer's gun was explained in that it was his service pistol --- but what about the matching weapon owned by the stranger? Howey and Norton could not understand how he could afford such an expensive sidearm. A man who was down on his luck could have easily hocked the weapon and made a decent amount of money. This should have been preferable to risking a street robbery. It didn't make sense so Romanoff sent a telegram to the Colt firearms company that contained the serial number of the stranger's gun. A reply soon came back. The gun had first been sold in 1913 to Von Lengerke & Antoine Sporting Goods Store in Chicago. The reporter checked with the store and found that Peter Hoffman, a telephone repairman who lived on Crawford Avenue, had purchased the gun.

The next day, Romanoff went to see Hoffman and discovered that he had sold the gun to his brother-in-law several years before. The brother-in-law's name was Fred Wanderer --- he was Carl's cousin. Stunned, the reporter confronted Fred Wanderer with the information about where his gun had ended up. Fred admitted that he had gotten a gun from Peter Hoffman but he had loaned it to his cousin, Carl, on June 21 and didn't have it anymore. Suddenly, Fred realized that this had been the day when Ruth had been killed. When this occurred to him, he was so shocked that he fainted.

Romanoff reported the problems with the gun to Detective Norton and Summerdale Police Lieutenant Mike Loftus. Carl Wanderer was brought in for questioning and was confronted with what had been discovered about the gun. Wanderer shrugged it off. Sure, he had been carrying Fred's gun, he told detectives, the other one, which had been used by the "Ragged Stranger," was mistakenly identified as his. As it turned out, this was a possibility. A check with the Colt Company revealed that the other gun had been part of a massive shipment of weapons sent to military training camps during the war. The whole thing, Carl assured them, was all an innocent mistake.

Loftus and Romanoff were not convinced.

While Carl was delayed at the police station, the two men went to the Wanderer's house to speak with Ruth's mother. While Loftus engaged the woman in conversation, Romanoff searched through Wanderer's bedroom and found incriminating photos of Carl and portions of love letters that had been written to Julia Schmitt, the young woman he had been seeing without Ruth's knowledge. When Julia was tracked down, she unraveled Carl's story and the motive for the murder became clear. Carl Wanderer had wanted to get rid of his wife and arranged to have someone carry out the crime.

When confronted with this new information, Wanderer finally confessed.

Carl had grown to hate his wife, he told detectives, and longed to be free of her so that he could marry Julia. He needless to take blame away from himself, so he began hanging around seedy saloons until he met Al Watson (whose real name may have been Bernard T. Ryan), a Canadian ex-soldier who was living in a flophouse on Madison Street, Chicago's skid row. Wanderer told Watson that he was trying to win back his wife's affections and wanted to seem like a hero to her. He would pay would pay him $5 down and $5 on completion to carry out a robbery. Carl would hand Watson a gun when the couple went into the dark vestibule and then he would

GHOST ALERT!

The last, broken sentence on the gallows was the last that was ever heard from Carl Otto Wanderer but the same cannot be said for his wife, Ruth. The legends of the Lincoln Square neighborhood have it that the house where the ill-fated couple once lived, and where Ruth died, remains haunted by her spirit to this day.

This former residence, located at 4732 North Campbell Ave., is just a half block from Lawrence and two blocks west of Western Avenue. The place has changed much since 1920. It's been remodeled several times and the number on the house is no longer visible, an oversight that was likely intentional. These days, a wooden gate protects the vestibule leading to the house. It was here where Ruth was heartlessly gunned down.

For many years, the murders that occurred here were widely discussed and few could pass this house without pointing out, often with trembling hands, the place where the murders occurred. As time passed, and the crime slipped from the public consciousness and took its place among the many other murders in the city, the story of Ruth Wanderer began to fade.

Soon after, reports of the haunting began. Sources state that in the years after World War II, in the late 1940s, regular accounts began to be heard about the sounds of a woman's screams that came from the vestibule of the North Campbell Avenue house. The screams, neighbors claimed, were those of Ruth Wanderer, perhaps re-living her final moments --- perhaps just as she realized that her husband intended to kill her. These same sources relate that the screams still come occasionally even today.

But why does Ruth Wanderer still haunt this place? And why did the spirit wait so long to make her presence known? Most believe the answer to this is that she simply wants people to remember her story, to remember that she once lived and, most heartbreaking of all, to remember the life of her child, who was never allowed to live at all.

slug Carl with it. Wanderer would seem to fight the man off and Watson would run away, restoring Ruth's faith in his hero status.

Watson saw it as a harmless way to make a few bucks and so, he agreed. That night when Watson came into the vestibule, though, Carl did not hand him a gun. Instead, he cocked both weapons and fired at both Ruth and Watson at the same time. After they had fallen, he fired several more shots to make sure they were dead and then went into his "avenging husband act" for Ruth's mother, whom he knew would rush to the scene.

Carl Wanderer was twice indicted and twice convicted, once for the murder of Ruth Johnson Wanderer and once for the death of Al Watson. After his first trial, Wanderer was sentenced to serve 20 years, which so outraged editor Walter Howey that he used the editorial might of his widely read newspaper to keep the story alive and to demand a new trial. Public outrage resulted in a second trial and a death sentence for Wanderer.

While Carl was in jail, awaiting the hangman, he became a favorite subject for doctors, who tried to discover whether or not he was insane when he planned his wife's death, and for reporters, who kept milking a good story. Two of Wanderer's favorite visitors were Ben Hecht and Charley MacArthur, Chicago's most famous writers from the colorful and sensational journalism era of the early 1900s. They were covering Carl's story for their respective newspapers and visited him often, playing poker with him and becoming quite chummy. They even convinced Carl to read two letters that they had written, hilariously attacking their bosses, from the gallows. The newsmen didn't remember until the last minute that Carl's hands and feet would be bound when he was executed so he couldn't read the letters. They asked him to croon a rendition of "Old Pal, Why Don't You Answer Me?" moments before the drop instead.

On the day of his hanging, Carl was brought to the gallows and to the surprise of everyone, save for Hecht and MacArthur, Wanderer began to sing. The hangman came forward after the first chorus but Wanderer warned him away with a shake of his head. After the second chorus, even though Carl was still singing, the black shroud was placed over his head. When the song finally finished, he was asked if he had anything to say.

"Christ have mercy on my....", Carl Wanderer began but never finished his plea. The trap sprung open and Carl shot downwards until the rope snapped tight and instantly killed him.

Charley MacArthur had the last word. He turned to his friend Ben Hecht and said with a sigh, "You know, Ben, that son-of-a-bitch would have been a hell of a song plugger."

CHICAGO'S "THRILL KILLERS" & THEIR "PERFECT CRIME"

On an afternoon in May 1924, the sons of two of Chicago's wealthiest and most illustrious families drove to the Harvard School on the city's South Side and kidnapped a young boy named Bobby Franks. Their plan was to carry out the "perfect murder." It was a scheme so devious that only two men of superior intellect, such as their own, could accomplish. These two were Richard Loeb and Nathan Leopold. They were the privileged heirs of well-known Chicago families who had embarked on a life of crime for fun and for the pure thrill of it. They were also a pair of sexual deviants who considered themselves to be "brilliant" --- a claim that would later lead to their downfall.

Nathan Leopold, or "Babe" as his friends knew him, had been born in 1906 and from an early age had a number of sexual encounters, starting with the advances of a governess and culminating in a relationship with Richard Loeb. He was an excellent student with a genius IQ and was only 18 when he graduated from the University of Chicago. He was an expert ornithologist and botanist and spoke nine languages fluently. Like many future killers, his family life was totally empty and devoid of control. His mother had died when he was young and his father gave him little personal attention. He compensated for his lack of fatherly direction with expensive presents and huge sums of money. Leopold was given $3,000 to tour Europe before entering Harvard Law School, a car of his own and a $125-a-week allowance.

Chicago's Infamous "Thrill Killers

(Left) Richard Loeb
(Right) Nathan Leopold

These two wealthy young men believed that they were above the law and could murder without consequences. They carried out their bloody crime, never believing they could be caught.

Richard Loeb was the son of the Vice President of Sears & Roebuck and while he was as wealthy as his friend was, Loeb was merely a clever young man and far from brilliant. He was, however, quite handsome and charming and what he lacked in intelligence, he more than made up for in arrogance. Both of the young men were obsessed with perfection. To them, perfection meant being above all others, which their station in life endorsed. They felt they were immune to laws and criticism, which meant they were perfect.

Loeb fancied himself a master criminal detective, but his dream was to commit the perfect crime. With his more docile companion in tow, Loeb began developing what he believed to be the perfect scheme. He also constantly searched for ways to control others. Not long after the two became friends, Leopold attempted to initiate a sexual relationship with Loeb. At first, Loeb spurned the other's advances but then offered a compromise. He would engage in sex with Leopold, but only under the condition that the other boy begin a career in crime with him. Leopold agreed and they signed a formal pact to that affect.

Over the course of the next four years, they committed robbery, vandalism, arson and petty theft, but this was not enough for Loeb. He dreamed of something bigger. A murder, he convinced his friend, would be their greatest intellectual challenge.

They worked out a plan during the next seven months. The plan was to kidnap someone and they would make it appear as though that person was being held for ransom. They would write the ransom note on a typewriter that had been stolen from Loeb's old fraternity house at the University of Michigan and make the family of the victim believe that he would be returned to them. Leopold and Loeb had no such plans though ---- they intended to kill their captive.

In May 1924, they rented a car and drove to a hardware store at 43rd and Cottage Avenue, where they purchased some rope, a chisel and a bottle of hydrochloric acid. They would garrote their victim, stab him with the chisel if necessary, and then destroy his identity with the acid.

The next day, they met at Leopold's home and wrapped the handle of the chisel with adhesive tape so that it offered a better grip. They also gathered together a blanket and strips of cloth that could be used to wrap up and bind their victim. Leopold also placed a pair of wading boots in the car because the boys planned to deposit the body in the swamps near Wolf Lake, located south of the city. They packed loaded pistols for each of them and looked over the already typed ransom note that demanded $10,000 in cash. Neither of them needed the money but they felt the note would convince the authorities that the kidnappers were lowly, money-hungry criminals and deflect attention from people like Leopold and Loeb.

Armand "Ardie" Deutsch claimed that he was saved from being Leopold and Loeb's victim only because, on the day he was to be murdered, he had a dental appointment and was driven to the dentist instead of walking home. He grew up to be, among other things, a film producer in Hollywood.

They had only overlooked one thing ---- a victim.

They first considered killing Loeb's younger brother, Tommy, but they discarded that idea. It was not because Tommy was a family member but only because it would have been hard for Loeb to collect the ransom money without arousing suspicion. They also considering killing Armand Deutsch, grandson of millionaire philanthropist Julius Rosenwald, but also dismissed this idea because Rosenwald was the president of Sears & Roebuck and Loeb's father's immediate boss. They also came close to agreeing to kill their friend, Richard Rubel, who regularly had lunch with them. Rubel was ruled out, not because he was a good friend to them, but because they knew his father was cheap and would never agree to pay the ransom.

They could not agree on anyone but did feel that their victim should be small, so that he could be easily subdued. With that in mind, they decided to check out the Harvard Preparatory School, which was located across the street from Leopold's home. They climbed into their rental car and began to drive. As they drove, Leopold noticed some boys near Ellis Avenue and Loeb pointed out one of them that he recognized --- 14-year-old Bobby Franks. He was the son of the millionaire Jacob Franks, and a distant cousin of Loeb.

Chosen by chance, he would make the perfect victim for the perfect crime.

Bobby was already acquainted with his killers. He had played tennis with Loeb several times and he happily climbed into the car. Although at their trial, both denied being the actual killer, Leopold was at the wheel and Loeb was in

Bobby Franks, the young victim of Leopold & Loeb

Police officers search the culvert at Wolf Lake where Bobby Franks body was found. It was here that they Leopold lost his eyeglasses.

the back, gripping the murder weapon tightly in his hands. They drove Bobby to within a few blocks of the Franks residence in Hyde Park and then Loeb suddenly grabbed the boy, stuffed a gag in his mouth and smashed his skull four times with a chisel. The rope had been forgotten. Bobby collapsed onto the floor of the car, unconscious and bleeding badly.

When Leopold saw the blood spurting from Bobby's head, he cried out, "Oh God, I didn't know it would be like this!"

Loeb ignored him, intent on his horrific task. Even though Bobby was unconscious, he stuffed his mouth with rags and wrapped him up in the heavy blanket. The boy continued to bleed for a time and then died.

With the excitement of the actual murder concluded, Leopold and Loeb casually drove south, stopped for lunch, and then drove for a little while longer. They had supper as they waited for the sun to go down. Eventually, they ended up near a culvert along the Pennsylvania Railroad tracks. It emptied into a swamp along Wolf Lake.

Leopold put on his hip boots and carried Bobby's body to the culvert. They had stripped all of the clothes from the boy's body and then after dunking his head underwater to make sure that he was dead, they poured acid on his face in hopes that he would be harder to identify. Leopold then struggled to shove the naked boy into the pipe and took his coat off to make the work easier. Unknown to the killers, a pair of eyeglasses were in the pocket of Leopold's coat and they fell out into the water when he removed it. This would be the undoing of the "perfect crime."

After pushing the body as far into the pipe as he could, Leopold sloshed out of the mud toward the car, where Loeb waited for him. The killers believed that the body would not be found until long after the ransom money had been received. With darkness falling, though, Leopold failed to notice that Bobby's foot was dangling from the end of the culvert.

They drove back to the city and parked the rental car next to a large apartment building. Bobby's blood had soaked through the blanket that he had been wrapped in and had stained the automobile's upholstery. The blanket was hidden in a nearby yard and the boys burned Bobby's clothing at Leopold's house. They typed out the Franks' address on the already prepared ransom note. After this, they hurried back to the car and drove to Indiana, where they buried the shoes that Bobby had worn and everything that he had on him that was made from metal, including his belt buckle and class pin from the prep school.

Finally, their "perfect crime" carried out, they drove back to Leopold's home and spent the rest of the evening drinking and playing cards. Around midnight, they telephoned the Franks' home and told Mr. Franks that he could soon expect a ransom demand for the return of his son. "Tell the police and he will be killed at once," they told Mr. Franks. "You will receive a ransom note with instructions tomorrow."

The next morning, the ransom note, signed with the name "George Johnson," was delivered to the Franks, demanding $10,000 in old, unmarked $10 and $20 bills. The money was to be placed in a cigar box that should be wrapped in white paper and sealed with wax. After its arrival, the Franks' lawyer notified the police, who promised no publicity.

Meanwhile, Leopold and Loeb continued with the elaborate game they had concocted. They took the bloody blanket to an empty lot, burned it, and then drove to Jackson Park, where Loeb tore the keys out of his stolen typewriter. He threw the keys into one lagoon in the park and the typewriter into another. Later in the afternoon, Loeb took a train ride to Michigan City, leaving a note addressed to the Franks in the telegram slot of a desk in the train's observation car. He got off the train at 63rd Street, as it returned to the city, and rejoined the waiting Leopold. Andy Russo, a yardman, found the letter and sent it to the Franks.

However, by the time the letter arrived, railroad maintenance men had already stumbled upon the body of Bobby Franks. The police notified Jacob Franks and he sent his brother-in-law to identify the body. He confirmed that it was Bobby and the newspapers went into overdrive, producing "extra" editions that were on the street in a matter of hours.

One of the largest manhunts in the history of Chicago began. Witnesses and suspects were picked up in huge numbers and slowly the "perfect crime" began to unravel. Despite their "mental prowess" and "high intelligence," Leopold and Loeb were quickly caught. Leopold had dropped his eyeglasses near the spot where the body had been hidden and police had traced the prescription to Albert Coe & Co., who stated that only three pair of glasses with such unusual frames had been sold. One pair belonged to an attorney, who was away in Europe, the other to a woman and the third pair had been sold to Nathan Leopold.

The boys were brought in for questioning and began supplying alibis for the time when Bobby had gone missing. They had been with two girlfriends, they claimed, "May and Edna." The police asked them to produce the girls but the killers could not. Leopold claimed that he had apparently lost the glasses at Wolf Lake during a recent bird-hunting trip. The detectives noted that it had rained a few days before but the glasses were clean. Could Leopold explain this? He couldn't.

Then, two novice reporters, Al Goldstein and Jim Mulroy, obtained letters that Richard Loeb had written with the stolen typewriter --- which had already been found in Jackson Park. The letters matched the type on the ransom note, which was a perfect match for the typewriter that Leopold had "borrowed" from his fraternity house the year before.

Loeb broke first. He said that the murder was a lark, an experiment in crime to see if the "perfect murder" could be carried out. He then denied being the killer and claimed that he had driven the car while Leopold had slashed Bobby Franks to death. Leopold refuted this. Finally, the boys were brought together and admitted the truth. Loeb had been the killer, Leopold had driven the car but both of them had planned the crime together --- they were both guilty of Bobby Franks' murder.

Leopold & Loeb (near center) on trial. Clarence Darrow is just left of the man in front with his head down.

(Right) Famous defense attorney Clarence Darrow

The people of Chicago, and the rest of the nation, were stunned. It was fully expected that the two would receive a death sentence for the callous and cold-blooded crime.

After the confession, Loeb's family disowned him but Leopold's father turned to Clarence Darrow, America's most famous defense attorney, in hopes that he might save his son. For $100,000, Darrow agreed to seek the best possible verdict that he could, which in this case was life in prison. "While the State is trying Loeb and Leopold," Darrow said. "I will try capital punishment."

Darrow would have less trouble with the case than he would with his clients, who constantly clowned around and hammed it up in the courtroom. The newspaper photographers frequently snapped photos of them smirking and laughing in court and the public, already turned against them, became even more hostile toward the "poor little rich boys."

Darrow was fighting an uphill battle, but he brought out every trick in the book and used shameless tactics during the trial. He declared the boys to be insane. Leopold, he said, was a dangerous schizophrenic. They weren't criminals, he railed, they just couldn't help themselves. After this weighty proclamation, Darrow actually began to weep. The trial became a landmark in criminal law. He offered a detailed description of what would happen to the boys as they were hanged, providing a graphic image of bodily functions and physical pain. Darrow even turned to the prosecutor and invited him to personally perform the execution.

Darrow's horrifying description had a marked effect on the courtroom and especially on the defendants. Loeb was observed to shudder and Leopold got so hysterical that he had to be taken out of the courtroom. Darrow then wept for the defendants, wept for Bobby Franks, and then wept for defendants and victims everywhere. He managed to get the best verdict possible out of the case. The defendants were given life in prison for Bobby Frank's murder and an additional 99 years for his kidnapping.

Ironically, after all of that, Darrow only managed to get $40,000 of his fee from Leopold's father. He got this after a seven-month wait and the threat of a lawsuit.

GHOST ALERT!

Sending Leopold and Loeb to prison, according to many people, did not bring about an end to this macabre case, thanks to two restless ghosts that continued to walk for many years afterward. The spirit with the most horrible connection to the case was that of Bobby Franks, who took nearly 50 years to find peace.

During this time, visitors to Rosehill Cemetery on the north side of Chicago often reported seeing the ghost of a young boy standing among the stones and mausoleums in the Jewish section of the graveyard. It is here where the Franks family mausoleum is located, although its location is not listed on any maps of the cemetery and employees are instructed not to point it out to curiosity-seekers. Even so, this tomb can be discovered within the confines of the beautiful burial ground and starting in the 1920s, maintenance workers and visitors alike encountered the ghostly boy. Many came to believe that it was the ghost of Bobby Franks, unable to rest in the wake of his bloody and violent death.

The boy was often seen wandering here but only from a distance. Whenever he was approached, the apparition would vanish. These sightings continued for years but eventually, they seemed to fade away. It's been noted that the encounters ended at nearly the exact same time that Nathan Leopold died in Puerto Rico. Could there be a connection between these two events? It certainly seems possible and perhaps Bobby Frank can now find peace on the other side.

The other ghost from this case was that of famous attorney Clarence Darrow. When Darrow died in 1936, his ashes were scattered over the lagoon at Jackson Park, just behind the Museum of Science and Industry. While standing on what has been named the Clarence Darrow Bridge, many people have somewhat regularly spotted what is likely Darrow's ghost on a veranda that spans the back of the museum. This wide stone area is at the bottom of the steps leading into the rear entrance of the museum. The ghost is reportedly seen dressed in a suit, hat and overcoat and bears a striking resemblance to the attorney. The figure is reported to stand and stare out across the water before disappearing.

Leopold and Loeb were sent to the Joliet Penitentiary. Even though the warden claimed they were treated just like all of the other prisoners, they each enjoyed a private cell, books, a desk, a filing cabinet and even pet birds. They also showered away from the other prisoners and took their meals, which were prepared to order, in the officers' lounge. Leopold was allowed to keep a flower garden. They were also permitted any number of unsupervised visitors. The doors to their cells were usually left open and they had passes to visit one another at any time.

Richard Loeb was eventually killed by another inmate, against whom he had been reportedly making sexual advances. The inmate, James Day, turned on him in a bathroom and attached him with a razor. Loeb, covered in blood, managed to make it out of the bathroom and he collapsed in the hallway. He was found bleeding by guards and he died a short time later. It was later discovered that Day had slashed him 56 times with the razor.

Loeb's mother rushed to the prison with the family doctor when she heard what had happened and Leopold waited anxiously by his friend's bedside. Loeb opened his eyes only one time. "I think I'm going to make it," he murmured and then moments later, he died.

When Clarence Darrow was told of Loeb's death, he slowly shook his head. "He is better off dead," the great attorney said, "For him, death is an easier sentence."

Leopold lived on in prison for many years and was said to have made many adjustments to his character and some would even say rehabilitated completely. Even so, appeals for his parole were turned down three times. Finally, in 1958, the poet Carl Sandburg, who even went as far as to offer Leopold a room in his own home, pleaded his fourth appeal. Finally, in March of that year, he was released.

He was allowed to go to Puerto Rico, where he worked among the poor and married a widow named Trudi Feldman Garcia de Quevedo, who owned a flower shop. He went on to write a book about his experiences called *Life Plus 99 Years* and continued to be hounded by the press for his role in the "perfect murder" that he had committed decades before. He stated that he would be "haunted" by what he had done for the rest of his life.

Nathan Leopold died of heart failure on August 30, 1971, bringing an end to one of the most harrowing stories in the history of the city.

THE MURDERS THAT FOREVER CHANGED CHICAGO

One of the most shocking and terrifying events in the history of Chicago took place in October 1955, when the bodies of the three boys were discovered in a virtually crime-free community on the northwest side of the city. The Schuessler-Peterson murders stunned the city and the horrific events --- which would remain unsolved for 40 years ---- changed the face of Chicago forever.

The terrifying events began on a cool Sunday afternoon in the fall of 1955 when three boys from the Northwest side of the city headed downtown to catch a matinee performance of a Walt Disney nature film called "The African Lion" at the Loop Theater. The boys made the trip with their parent's consent because in those days, parents thought little of their responsible children going off on excursions by themselves. The boys had always proven dependable in the past and this time would have been no exception, if tragedy had not occurred. Bobby Peterson's mother had chosen the film for him and his two friends, Anton and John Schuessler, and had

Newspaper photos that ran after the discovery of the bodies at Robinson Woods (Left to Right): Robert Peterson, John Schuessler & his brother, Anton

sent them on their way with $4 in loose change between them. It should have been plenty of money to keep them occupied for an afternoon and safely get them back home again.

What happened when the movie ended is a still shrouded in mystery.

The matinee ended that afternoon but for some reason, at around 6:00 that evening, the boys were reported in the lobby of the Garland Building at 111 North Wabash. There was no explanation for what they might have been doing there, other than that Bobby's eye doctor had an office in the building. It seems unlikely that he would have been visiting the optometrist on a Sunday afternoon but his signature did appear on the lobby registry for that day, so he was obviously there. The Garland did have a reputation in those days for being a hangout for gays, prostitutes and hustlers but if that had anything to do with the boys being there, no one knows.

Some have surmised that they only stopped long enough to use the restroom since Bobby knew there was one available on the ninth floor, where his optometrist's office was located. They may have hurried up to the ninth floor and then went right back out again because they were only believed to be at the Garland for less than five minutes.

Around 7:45 pm, the three entered the Monte Cristo Bowling Alley at 3226 West Montrose Ave. The establishment was a neighborhood eating place and the proprietor later recalled to the police that he remembered seeing the boys and that a "fiftyish-looking" man was showing an "abnormal interest" in several younger boys who were bowling. He was unable to say if this man had contact with the trio. They left the bowling alley and walked down Montrose to another bowling alley but were turned away   because a league had taken over all of the available lanes for the evening.

Out of money, but for some reason not headed toward home, the boys hitched a ride at the intersection of Lawrence and Milwaukee avenues. It was now 9:05 p.m. and their parents were beginning to get worried. They had reason to be, for the boys were never seen alive again.

Two days later, the boy's naked and bound bodies were discovered in a shallow ditch, near a parking lot and about 100 feet east of the Des Plaines River. A salesman, who had stopped to eat his lunch at the Robinson Wood's Indian Burial Grounds nearby, spotted them and called the police. Coroner Walter McCarron stated that the cause of death was "asphyxiation by suffocation." The three boys had been dead about 36 hours when they were discovered. He also declared that the killing had been a "sex crime" and the work of a "madman" or a "teen gang." It was, he stated, "the most horrible sex crime in years."

Bobby Peterson had been struck repeatedly and had been strangled with a rope or a necktie. Newspaper reports said that he had been slashed across the head 14 times with a knife or an ax. The Schuessler brothers, it appeared, had been strangled by hand and had been hit on their faces with what appeared to be the flat side of a knife. The killer had used adhesive tape to cover the eyes of all three victims. They had

The Schuessler-Peterson crime scene at Robinson's Woods.

then been dragged or thrown from a vehicle. Their clothing was never discovered.

The city of Chicago was thrown into a panic. Police officials reported that they had never seen such a horrible crime. The fears of parents all over the city were summed up by the shaken Anton Schuessler, Sr. who said, "When you get to the point that children cannot go to the movies in the afternoon and get home safely, something is wrong with this country."

Police officers combed the area, conducting door-to-door searches and neighborhood interrogations. Search teams combed Robinson's Woods, looking for clues or items of clothing. The killer (or killers) had gone to great length to get rid of any signs of fingerprints or traces of evidence. More than 100 officers, joined by 50 soldiers from the nearby Army anti-aircraft base, gathered near Robinson Woods at daybreak and walked in lines spaced four or five feet apart, looking for anything out of place. Divers were sent into the depths of the Des Plaines River for clues but they found nothing.

By this time, various city and suburban police departments had descended on the scene, running into each other and further hampering the search for clues. There was little or no cooperation between the separate agencies and if anything had been discovered, it would have most likely been lost in the confusion.

Away from the scene, patrolmen and detectives conducted a huge roundup of known "sex deviates," especially known to work in, or frequent, bowling alleys. They were convinced that this is where the boys had come into contact with the killer or killers. Most of the cops were convinced that a "gang" of some sort had been at work, finding it hard to believe that all three boys could have been killed otherwise. Coroner McCarron extended the possibility that they "fell into the hands of a group of older boys and were manhandled."

While the city remained in stunned shock, the investigation stumbled along under the leadership of Cook County Sheriff Joseph D. Lohman, who searched in desperation for some answers in the case. He even offered $2,500 from his personal bank account for information leading to an arrest. Lohman was over his head with this baffling case and he found himself under unwanted scrutiny by the newspapers, which sensationalized the murders, and the general public, which was collectively terrified.

Lohman was quoted in the press as stating: "Chances are, the attackers were persons close to the boys' own age, who might have known them." He also pointed to indications that the victims had been held captive before they were killed and may have been slain because something had "gone wrong" and the captors wanted to make sure they were not identified. He said that Bobby, who took the worst beating, might have been killed first.

Not to leave out any possible theories though, Lohman also went the other way and later, also surmised that the slayer was a "burly madman" or that two men had committed the crime. He noted that the "bodies had been thrown like bags of potatoes" and that this "would suggest that at least two persons or one very powerful person did it."

The first suspect picked up in the case was an unemployed schoolteacher, who was brought in for questioning early in the morning. He lived five blocks from the Schuessler home and had been named in an anonymous telephone call to the police. He was questioned vigorously, offering to take a lie detector test, but was soon released. He would not be the last "person of interest" to be questioned in the case but time after time, the men were interrogated and let go.

While investigators were coming up empty, newspaper reporters hounded the grief-stricken parents of the three boys. The press descended on their neighborhood of modest bungalow homes, a place where crime --- of any kind --- was rare. It was almost impossible for them to even fathom what had occurred. Murder was something that happened in the newspapers, not in their own homes.

Mrs. Schuessler, described as a "frail 37-year-old woman", rocked back and forth on her living room couch on the day the bodies were found, surrounded by friends and neighbors. Reporters pushed into the room, looking for comments but she only murmured things like, "My life... my arms... my legs... now gone." One she shrieked, "I want my boys! I want my...." before collapsing into hysterics.

Mr. Schuessler rushed into the room and fell to his knees in front of the couch where his wife was sitting. He shuddered with pain and apparent agony. "Mother, mother," he cried. "What kind of land do we live in?" He buried his face in her lap and sobbed.

The investigation continued with no results while the last days of Bobby Peterson and Anton and John Schuessler ended on a grim note. An honor guard of Boy Scouts carried the coffins of the three boys from the St. Tarcissus Roman Catholic Church to a hearse that would take them to St. Joseph Cemetery. The church was filled to capacity with an estimated 1,200 mourners and even more people joined the

The grieving parents of the Schuessler boys (Charleston Daily Main Photo)

families at the graveside service, numbering over 3,500. Reverend Raymond G. Carey told the gathering, "God has permitted sin, evil and suffering because He knows that He can bring good from the suffering."

No one present could see much in the way of good from the deaths of three innocent young boys, however. This marked the end of innocence in Chicago. it was now apparent to all that America had changed for the worse.

Years passed. As there is no statute of limitations for murder, the case officially remained open but there seemed to be little chance that it would ever be solved. The Schuessler-Peterson murders became sort of a cautionary tale in Chicagoland, painting a bloody picture of what happened when children talked to strangers.

Then, four decades later, and long after the principals in the case had passed away, a bizarre turn of events occurred that would finally offer closure for the cold case. In the middle 1990s, a government informant named William "Red" Wemette accused a man named Kenneth Hansen of the murders during a police investigation into the 1977 disappearance of candy heiress Helen Vorhees Brach.

In 1955, Hansen, then 22, worked as a stable hand for Silas Jayne, a millionaire from Kane County. Jayne himself was wild and reckless and had been suspected of many violent and devious dealings during his rise to power in the horse-breeding world. He went to prison in 1973 for the murder of his half-brother, George, and died of leukemia in 1987, escaping punishment for many of the crimes that were later laid at his doorstep.

Hansen had certainly committed plenty of crimes himself. The homosexual hustler would later admit to molesting as many as 1,000 young boys and investigators were easily able to build a case against him, thanks to the missing pieces filled in by Wemette. The renewed investigation resulted in his arrest in August 1994.

Cook County prosecutors showed jurors how Hansen had lured the Schuessler brothers and Bobby Peterson into his car under false pretenses around the intersection of Lawrence and Milwaukee avenues. They retraced the path of the killer to Silas Jayne's Idle Hour Stables in the 8600 Block of Higgins Road. His story was that he wanted to show the boys some prize horses that were being kept there. According to the testimony of several men that Hansen had bragged to, he molested and then killed Alton, John and Bobby one by one.

The boys were killed in the tack room when they tried to fight Hansen off and then he tied up the bodies and he and, allegedly, his brother dumped them at Robinson Woods. In the spring of 1956, the Idle Hours Stables burned to the ground. The week before the fire, the Cook County Coroner announced to the press that he planned to exhume the bodies of the three boys in a search for trace evidence. Silas Jayne, after seeing the newspaper report, became convinced that remnants of his stables might remain on the boys. Police detectives had previously visited the stable as they followed up on reports of boys' screams coming from the building at night and Jayne thought they might put it all together and Hansen's crime would bring him down. Out of fear, he torched the building to obliterate all of the evidence. The detectives never connected the arson to the murders and Hansen escaped from the long arm of the law for nearly 40 years.

As the case came to trial in 1995, four decades of silence were broken and many of Hansen's other victims came forward, recalling promises of jobs made to young men in return for sexual favors. He forced their silence with threats that included warnings that they might end up "like the Peterson boy." Even without evidence and eyewitnesses to corroborate the prosecution's allegations against him, a Cook County jury convicted Kenneth Hansen of the murders in September 1995. They deliberated for less than two hours and Hansen was sentenced for 200-300 years in prison.

But the case was not yet over. In May 2000, the Illinois Appellate Court overturned Hansen's conviction. Two of the three justices found that the judge in the case erred when he allowed evidence to be submitted that showed that Hansen regularly picked up hitchhikers and sexually abused them. Despite what some saw as a close call, Hansen was almost routinely convicted again and once more, he received the 200-300 year sentence. The Illinois Appellate Court affirmed the conviction in 2004 and Hansen later died behind bars - right where he belonged.

Bobby, John and Anton could finally rest in peace.

FAREWELL TO THE GRIMES SISTERS

On December 28, 1956, Patricia Grimes, 13, and Barbara Grimes, 15, left their home at 3624 South Damen Ave. and headed for the Brighton Theater, only a mile away. The girls were both avid fans of Elvis Presley and on that night were on their way to see his film "Love Me Tender" for the eleventh and final time. The girls were recognized in the popcorn line at 9:30 p.m. and then seen on an eastbound Archer Avenue bus at 11:00 p.m. After that, things became less certain, but this may have been the last time they were ever seen alive. The two sisters were missing for the 25 days, before their naked and frozen bodies were found along German Church Road, just outside the small town of Willow Springs.

The girl's mother, Loretta Grimes, expected the girls to be home by 11:45 p.m. but was already growing uneasy when they had not arrived 15 minutes prior to that. At midnight, she sent her daughter Theresa and her son, Joey, to

Patricia (top) and Barbara Grimes
(Wide World Photos)

the bus stop at 35th Street and Hoyne Avenue to watch for them. After three buses had stopped and had failed to discharge their sisters, Theresa and Joey returned home without them. They never saw the girls again, but strangely, others claimed to.

The last reported sightings of the two girls came from classmates who spotted them at Angelo's Restaurant at 3551 South Archer Ave., more than 24 hours after their reported disappearance. How accurate this sighting was is unknown, as a railroad conductor also reported them on a train near the Great Lakes Naval Training Center in north suburban Glenview around the same time. A security guard on the Northwest Side offered directions to two girls he believed were the Grimes sisters on the morning of the 29th, hours after they disappeared. On January 1, both girls were allegedly identified as passengers aboard a CTA bus on Damen Avenue. During the week that followed, they were reported in Englewood by George Pope, a night clerk at the Unity Hotel on West 61st Street, who refused them a room because of their ages. Three employees at Kresge believed they saw the girls listening to Elvis Presley songs at the record counter on January 3. The police theorized that the girls had run away, but Loretta Grimes refused to believe it. She was sure the girls had gone missing against their will but the authorities were not convinced. Regardless, it became the greatest missing persons hunt in Chicago police history. Even Elvis Presley, in a statement issued from Graceland, asked the girls to come home and ease their mother's worries. The plea went unanswered.

More strangeness would be reported before the bodies of the girls were found. A series of ransom letters, that were later discovered to have come from a mental patient, took Mrs. Grimes to Milwaukee on January 12. She was escorted by FBI agents and instructed to sit in a downtown Catholic church with $1,000 on the bench beside her. The letter promised that Barbara Grimes would walk in to retrieve the money and then leave to deliver it to the kidnapper. She and her sister would then be released. Needless to say, no one ever came and Mrs. Grimes was left sitting for hours to contemplate her daughters' fate. By that time, it's likely that the bodies of the two girls were already lying along German Church Road, covered with snow.

But if that's true, then how can we explain the two telephone calls that were received by Wallace and Ann Tollstan on January 14? Their daughter, Sandra, was a classmate of Patricia Grimes at the St. Maurice School and the Tollstans received the two calls around midnight. The first call jolted Mr. Tollstan from his sleep but when he picked up the receiver, the person on the other end of the line did not speak. He waited a few moments and then hung up. About 15 minutes later, the phone rang again and this time, Ann Tollstan answered it. The voice on the other end of the line asked, "Is that you, Sandra? Is Sandra there?" But before Mrs. Tollstan could bring her daughter to the phone, the caller had clicked off the line. Ann Tollstan was convinced that the frightened voice on the telephone had belonged to Patricia Grimes.

And that wasn't the only strange happening to mark the period when the girls were missing. On January 15, a police switchboard operator received a call from a man who refused to identify himself but who insisted that the girl's bodies would be found in a park at 81st and Wolf. He claimed that this revelation had come to him in a dream and he hung up. The call was traced to Green's Liquor Market on South Halsted and the caller was discovered to be Walter Kranz, a 53-year-old steamfitter. He was taken into custody after the bodies were found on January 22 --- less than a mile from the park that Kranz said he dreamed of. He became one of the numerous people who were questioned by the police and then released.

The search for the Grimes Sisters ended on January 22, 1957 when construction worker Leonard Prescott was driving south on German Church Road early one morning. He spotted what appeared to be two discarded clothing store mannequins lying next to a guardrail, a short distance from the road. A few feet away, the ground dropped off to Devil's Creek below. Unsure of what he had seen, Prescott nervously brought his wife to the spot, and then they drove to the local police station. His wife, Marie Prescott, was so upset by the sight of the bodies that she had to be carried back to their car.

Once investigators realized the "mannequins" were actually bodies, they soon discovered they were the Grimes Sisters. Barbara Grimes lay on her left side with her legs slightly drawn up toward her body. Her head was covered by the body of her sister, who had been thrown onto her back with her head turned sharply to the right. It looked as if they had been discarded there by someone so cold and heartless that he saw the girls as nothing more than refuse to be tossed away on a lonely roadside.

The officials in charge, Cook County Sheriff Joseph D. Lohman and Harry Glos, an aggressive investigator for Coroner Walter E. McCarron, surmised that the bodies had been lying there for several days, perhaps as far back as January 9. This had been the date of the last heavy snowfall and the frigid temperatures that followed the storm had preserved the bodies to a state that resembled how they looked at the moment of death.

The bodies discovered along German Church Road sent the various police departments into action. A short time after they were found, more than 160 officers from Chicago, Cook County, the Forest Preserves and five south suburban police departments began combing the woods -- and tramping all over whatever evidence may have been there. Between the officers, the reporters, the medical examiners and everyone else, the investigation was already off to a bad start.

And the investigation became even more confusing in the days to come. The bodies were removed from the scene and were taken to the Cook County Morgue, where they would be stored until they thawed out and an autopsy became possible. Before they were removed, though, both

Grimes Sisters Murder Site -- Then & Now
The site on German Church Road where the bodies of the Grimes Sisters were discovered & how the roadway looks today.

police investigators and reporters commented on the condition of the corpses, noting bruises and marks that have still not been adequately explained to this day. According to a newspaper article, there were three "ugly" wounds in Patricia's abdomen and the left side of her face had been battered, resulting in a possibly broken nose. Barbara's face and head had also been bruised and there were punctures from an ice pick in her chest. Once the bodies were moved, investigators stayed on the scene to search for clothing and clues but nothing was found.

Once the autopsies were performed the following day, all hope that the examinations would provide new evidence or leads was quickly dashed. Despite the efforts of three experienced pathologists, they could not reach agreement on a time or cause of death. They stated that the girls had died from shock and exposure but were only able to reach this conclusion by eliminating other causes. And by also concluding that the girls had died on December 28, the night they had disappeared, they created more mysteries than they managed to solve. If the girls had died on the night they had gone missing, then how could the sightings that took place after that date be explained? And if the bodies had been exposed to the elements since that time, then why hadn't anyone else seen them?

Barbara and Patricia were buried on January 28, one month after they disappeared. Their mystery was no closer to being solved than it had been in December.

The residents of Chicagoland were stunned and the case of the murdered girls became an obsession. The local community organized a search for clues and volunteers passed out flyers looking for information.

The Chicago Tribune invited readers to send in theories about the case and paid $50 for any they published. The

Loretta Grimes prays for the safe return of her daughters. Elvis Presley photographs decorate the walls above the girl's beds. (Chicago Daily News)

clergy and the parishioners from St. Maurice, where the Grimes family attended church, offered a $1,000 reward and sent out letters to area residents, hoping that someone might have seen the girls before they vanished. Even photographs were taken of friends of the girls wearing clothing that duplicated twhat the sisters wore on December 28 in hopes that it might jog the memory of someone who saw them. On the night they saw Love Me Tender for the last time, Patricia wore blue jeans, a yellow sweater, a black jacket with white stripes on the sleeves, a white scarf over her head and black shoes. Her sister reportedly wore a gray tweed skirt, yellow blouse, a three-quarter-length coat, a gray scarf, white bobby sox and black, ballerina shoes. The clothing, like the girl's killer, was never found.

The killer may have eluded the authorities, but it was not because no one was trying to find him. Investigators questioned an unbelievable 300,000 persons, searching for information about the girls, and 2,000 of these people were seriously interrogated, which in those days could be brutal. A number of suspects were seriously considered and among the first was the "dreamer," Walter Kranz, who called police with his mysterious tip on January 15. He was held at the Englewood police station for some time and was repeatedly interrogated and given lie detector tests about his involvement in the murders. No solid evidence was ever found against him.

The police also picked up a 17-year-old named Max Fleig as a suspect but the law at that time did not allow juveniles to be tested with a polygraph. Police Captain Ralph Petaque persuaded the boy to take the test anyway and in the midst of it, he confessed to kidnapping the girls. Because the test was illegal and inadmissible, the police were forced to let Fleig go free. Was he the killer? No one will ever know. Fleig was sent to prison a few years later for the brutal murder of a young woman but whether or not he had any connection to the death of the Grimes sisters remains a mystery.

In the midst of all of this, the police still had to deal with nuts and cranks, more so-called psychic visions and a number of false confessions, which made their work even harder.

Eager to crack the floundering case, Cook County Sheriff Joseph Lohman arrested a skid-row dishwasher named Edward L. "Benny" Bedwell. The drifter, who sported Elvis-style sideburns and a ducktail haircut, had reportedly been seen with the Grimes sisters in a restaurant where he sometimes washed dishes in exchange for food. When he was initially questioned, Bedwell admitted that he had been in the D&L Restaurant on West Madison with two girls and an unnamed friend but he insisted that the owners of the place were mistaken about the girls being the Grimes sisters.

According to the owners, John and Minnie Duros, the group had entered the diner around 5:30 a.m. on the morning of December 30. They described the taller girl, who Minnie Duros said was wearing a coat with the name "Pat" embroidered on it, as being either so drunk or so sick that she was staggering as she walked. The couples sat in a booth for a while, listened to Elvis songs on the jukebox, and then went outside. One of the girls came back in, laid her head on the table, and seemed to be sick. The two men eventually managed to get her outside and all of them left together. One of the girls told Minnie Duros that they were sisters.

Lohman found the story plausible, thanks to the unshakable identification of the girls by Minnie Duros, their respective heights, the fact that one of them said they were sisters and finally, Bedwell's resemblance to Elvis. Lohman believed this might have been enough to get the girls to go along with him. And then of course, there was Bedwell's confession, which related a lurid and sexually explicit tale of drunken debauchery with the two young women. He made and recanted three confessions and even re-enacted the crime for investigators on January 27.

Everyone doubted the story but Lohman. He booked Bedwell on murder charges, but the drifter's testimony was both vague and contradictory. On January 31, he testified that he had confessed out of fear of Lohman's men, who

Newspaper photo of the creepy Benny Bedwell

had struck and threatened him while he was being questioned. Lohman denied that Bedwell had been beaten and told newspapers that the drifter had lied when he contradicted his confession and added that he considered him the prime suspect in the case.

The case against Bedwell further unraveled when his "unnamed friend" was identified as William C. Williamson, who ended up in jail on charges of drunkenness soon after his meeting with Bedwell and the two girls at the Duros' diner. He admitted that he was with Bedwell and two girls but denied that they were the Grimes sisters.

State's Attorney Benjamin Adamowski ordered the drifter released. Bedwell later spent time in prison on a weapons charge and died at some point after he was released in 1986.

The dismissal of charges against Bedwell in the Grimes case set off another round of bickering between police departments and various jurisdictions and the case became even more mired in red tape and inactivity. It got even worse when coroner's investigator Harry Glos publicly criticized the autopsy findings concerning the time and cause of death. He shocked the public by announcing that Barbara and Patricia could not have died on the night they disappeared. He said that an ice layer around the bodies proved that they were warm when they were left along German Church Road and that only after January 7 would there have been enough snow to create the ice and to hide the bodies.

Glos also raised the issues of the puncture wounds and bruises on the bodies, which had never been explained or explored. He was sure that the girls had been violently treated prior to death and also asserted that the older sister, Barbara, had been sexually molested before she was killed. The pathologists had denied this, but the Chicago Police crime lab reluctantly confirmed it. However, they were angry with Glos for releasing the information.

The coroner, Walter McCarron, promptly had Glos fired and many of the other investigators in the case accused him of being reckless and of political grandstanding. Only Sheriff Lohman, who later

deputized Glos to work on the case without pay, remained on his side. He agreed that the girls had likely been beaten and tortured by a sexual predator who lured them into the kidnap car under a seemingly innocent pretense. Lohman remained convinced until his death in 1969 that the predator who had killed the girls had been Benny Bedwell.

Other theories maintain that the girls may have indeed encountered Bedwell, or another "older man," and rumors circulated that the reputation of the two girls had been polished to cover up some very questionable behavior on their parts. It was said that they sometimes hung around a bar on Archer Avenue where men would buy them drinks. One of the men may have been Benny Bedwell. Harry Glos, who died in 1994, released information that one of the girls had been sexually active, but later reports from those who have seen the autopsy slides say there is evidence that both of them may have been. It is believed that Coroner McCarron may not have released this because of religious reasons or to spare additional grief for the family.

Today, veteran detectives believe that there was much more to the story that met the eye. The general consensus seems to be that Barbara and Patricia may have been abducted by a front man for a "white slavery" ring and taken to a remote location in the woods surrounding Willow Springs. They are convinced that the girls were strangled after refusing to become prostitutes. It's also possible that the girls may have been lured into an involvement in the prostitution ring by someone they knew, not realizing what would be required of them, and they were killed to keep them silent.

Others refused to even consider this, and were angered by the negative gossip about the two girls. Some remain angry about this even today, maintaining that Barbara and Patricia were nice, ordinary, happy girls and were tragically killed on a cold night because they made the mistake of accepting a ride from a stranger. They didn't hang around in bars, these old friends maintain, they were simply innocent teenage girls, just like everyone else at that time.

Perhaps those old acquaintances were right. There are few stories as tragic as the demise of the Grimes sisters and perhaps it provides some cold comfort for us to believe that their deaths were simply a terrible mistake or the actions of deviant killer. It can provide us that comfort of knowing that the girls were simply in the wrong place at the wrong time and that such a thing could have happened to anyone. But does believing this make us feel better --- - or worse?

Now, 50 years later, the mystery of who killed the Grimes sisters remains unsolved. As there is no statute of limitations for murder, the case officially remains open, but hope of any closure has dimmed over the years and the murderer's trail has gone tragically cold.

BORN TO RAISE HELL

Richard Speck, the deviant & loser who killed 8 nurses on a Chicago summer night in 1966. Why did he do it? According to Speck, "it just wasn't their night". (UPI)

On the hot summer night of July 13, 1966, a brutal and dim-witted drifter butchered his way into the annals of Chicago crime with the murders of eight nursing students on the Southeast Side of the city. From that point on, the name of "Richard Speck" would strike terror into the hearts of young women living alone and few would ever forget the words inked onto his arm as a flaming tattoo.

"Born to Raise Hell," the tattoo read, and it was a fitting description of his life.

Richard Speck was born in Kirkwood, Ill., in December 1941, the seventh of eight children. Over the years, dozens have speculated about the reason behind Speck's brutal crimes and whether he turned evil somewhere along the way or if he was simply born bad -- as the tattoo scrawled on his arm claimed. Many have also wondered if perhaps things might have turned out differently in the lives of eight nursing students if Speck's father, whom he adored, had not died when Speck was only 6. Regardless, Speck was raised by his mother in a strict Baptist setting that forbade alcohol and worldly influences. She later married Carl Lindberg, a violent man with an arrest record, and they moved to Dallas, Tex., where Lindberg began taking out his drunken rages on his stepson. By this time, Speck was a slow-witted failure with schoolwork and on the fast track to nowhere. He started running with some older boys, drinking, fighting and getting into trouble.

In November 1962, Speck married Shirley Malone, and they had a daughter, Bobby Lynn, soon after. Their married bliss was short-lived, however, and Speck began abusing both his wife and his mother-in-law. According to Shirley's later accounts, he often raped her at knifepoint, claiming that he needed sex four to five times each day. Likely to Shirley's relief, Speck ended up in jail for theft and check fraud in 1963. He was paroled in January 1965 but after only four weeks was arrested again for aggravated assault. He was sentenced to serve another 16 months but was released after only six. Shirley filed for divorce in January 1966.

When Speck was arrested again for burglary and assault and he fled from Dallas with the help of his sister, Carolyn, and headed for Chicago. Speck showed up at the home of his sister, Martha, and his brother-in-law, Gene Thornton. Speck announced his intentions to search for work as a merchant seaman but after several days of doing nothing, Thornton got frustrated and drove his unwanted houseguest to the National Maritime Union Hall, located at 2315 East One Hundredth St. It was just a few doors away from three residential townhouses, including number 2319, which had been rented by the South Chicago Community Hospital for 24 of its 155 student nurses.

Thornton brought Speck to the Maritime Union Hall in hopes that there was still an open berth on a ship that was bound for Vietnam. The position went to a man with greater seniority, leaving Speck without a spot. Disappointed, but unwilling to take Speck back in, Thornton handed him $25 and wished him well. He then drove off and left his brother-in-law to fend for himself.

A short time later, Speck managed to get a position aboard an iron ore ship on the Great Lakes, where he was stricken with appendicitis and hospitalized in Hancock, Mich. When he returned to Chicago in mid-June, he was fired for being drunk and disorderly. He had been warned repeatedly about his drinking and violent behavior but he disregarded the threats. After that, he spent the next three weeks in cheap hotels, sleeping in the park and financing his liquor and his visits to prostitutes with whatever odd jobs he could find.

On July 13, a depressed and angry Speck was drinking heavily in the Shipyard Inn on the Southeast Side. After a volatile combination of pills and liquor, he suddenly got the urge to "raise some hell." He would later say that he remembered nothing after this point.

Speck left the bar with a hunting knife, a pocketknife and a borrowed .22 caliber pistol and walked over to one of the nearby student dormitories. For the past several weeks, the drifter had seen the women coming and going from the buildings, sunbathing in Luella Park and walking back and forth to their classes. He was familiar enough with their schedules to know that, at nearly 11:00 p.m., they would be home in bed.

Corazon Amurao, who shared a second floor bedroom with two other young women, answered a loud knock on the townhouse door. She found a tall, lean stranger standing on the doorstep. He smelled of liquor and had a knife in one hand and a gun in the other. He slurred that he was not going to hurt her. "I'm only going to tie you up," he said. "I need money to go to New Orleans."

A current view of the townhouse apartment on the southeast side where Speck committed his bloody crimes.

He shoved his way into the townhouse and ordered the three Filipino students, Valentina Paison, Merlita Garguilo and Corazon, into a bedroom at the back of the building, where Pamela Wilkening, Nina Schmale and Pat Matusek were getting ready for bed. Speck took the sheets from the beds and cut them into strips, which he used to bind the women by their wrists and ankles. At 11:30, a seventh nurse, Gloria Davy, returned home from a date and she was also tied up. Then, a half-hour later, Suzanne Farris and her friend, Mary Ann Jordan, came to the front door. Speck pulled them inside and led them into the back bedroom at gunpoint.

In the course of the hour, Speck had systematically tied and gagged each of the women. How he managed to do this with almost no resistance remains one of the great mysteries in Chicago crime. Why did none of the women try to escape? Why did they not try and overpower Speck as he was tying another victim? Why did none of the women in the other townhouses hear anything that was taking place? No one knows to this day.

By 3:30 a.m., Speck's lust was finally spent. One by one, he had taken the eight young women out of the bedroom and had killed them. Only one of them, Gloria Davy, had been raped but all were dead --- save for Cora Amurao, who had managed to roll under a bunk bed and cower there in fear and shock until Speck finally left. Amurao remained hidden, frozen in terror, until nearly 6:00 in the morning. When she finally emerged from her hiding place, she climbed out of the apartment window and, perched on a ledge, began to scream.

Her screams caught the attention of Judy Dykton, a student who lived across the street. She had gotten up early to study and was startled by the cries from outside. Snatching her robe, she ran over to find Cora shaking and crying on the window ledge. Judy entered the open door of the townhouse and stepped into the living room. She first discovered the naked body of Gloria Davy, her hands tied behind her and a strip of cloth wrapped tightly around her throat. Her skin had turned cold and a dusty blue color. She was obviously dead. Judy turned and fled to the apartment of the housemother, Mrs. Bisone.

The housemother woke up the other student nurses and ran from the house toward 2319. She brought Leona Bonczak with her, who entered the house. She first checked to see if Gloria showed any signs of life and then mounted the stairs and looked down the hall. In the bathroom, she found the body of Pat Matusek and then crept into the other bedrooms, where she discovered the rest of the students so drenched in blood that she was unable to recognize any of them, save for Nina Schmale. A pillow covered most of the girl's face but she lay on her back, hands tied behind her, a cloth around her neck, legs spread apart -- and a fatal knife wound to her heart.

Stunned, she went downstairs and numbly told Mrs. Bisone that everyone was dead. The housemother, shaking and sick, picked up the phone, called South Chicago Community Hospital, and told them that all of her girls had been murdered. When the hospital asked her who had been killed, she was unable to tell them. The only words she uttered were "send help!"

Someone on the street managed to flag down police officer Daniel Kelly, a young patrolman who had only been on the job for 18 months. He radioed in that there was trouble and then entered the house. He was shocked to discover the body of Gloria Davy in the living room. Kelly had once dated Gloria's sister. Upset, he drew his gun, searched the place, and found the other bodies. The townhouse looked like a charnel house and in places, the blood in the carpeting was so thick that it pooled over Kelly's shoes. He ran outside to his car radio and called it in. Soon, Kelly heard the comforting sounds of approaching sirens beginning to fill the air.

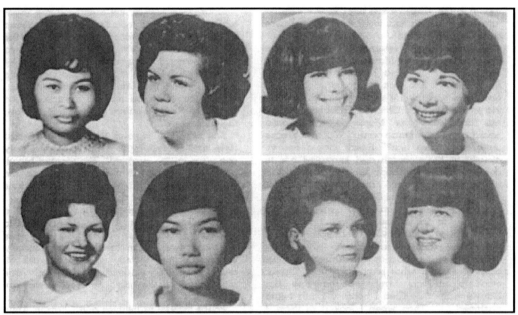

Speck's victims: (Top Row, Left to Right) Valentina Paison, Pamela Wilkening, Patricia Matusek, Suzanne Farris
(Bottom Row) Mary Ann Jordan, Merlita Garguilo, Gloria Davy, Nina Schmale (UPI)

The street outside filled with police cars and cops and people ran from door to door, alerting their neighbors of the horror found in 2319. The first detective on the scene was Jack Wallenda, who was shocked by the utter brutality of the killings. He entered the house and viewed the bodies one by one.

He found Gloria first. She was nude, belly down on the couch and tied with double-knotted bed sheets. He noticed what appeared to be semen between her buttocks and found buttons from her blouse strewn down the stairs. The killer had apparently torn them off her as he pulled her to the living room. Also tossed on the floor was a man's white t-shirt, size 38-40.

Wallenda then checked the upstairs bedroom and found the body of Pamela Wilkening. She had been gagged and stabbed through the heart. Suzanne Farris lay nearby in a pool of blood, a white nurse's stocking twisted around her neck. The detective counted 18 stab wounds to her chest and neck. He studied Mary Ann Jordan next. She had been stabbed three times in the chest and once in the neck.

In the northwest bedroom, he found Nina Schmale with her nightgown pulled up to her breasts and her legs pulled apart. She had also been tied and stabbed and it looked as though her neck might be broken. Valentina Paison was found under a blue cover, lying face down. Her throat had been cut. Tossed carelessly on top of her was the body of Merlita Garguilo, who had been stabbed and strangled.

Wallenda walked out the door and to the right and saw the legs of Patricia Matusek protruding from the bathroom. She was lying on her back with her hands bound behind her. She had been strangled with a piece of the bed sheet, double knotted, and her nightgown had been dragged up over her breasts. Her white panties had been pulled down to expose her pubic hair. Blood-soaked towels were strewn all over the bathroom floor.

Wallenda's hands were shaking as he left the townhouse. It was the worst crime scene that he had ever witnessed.

The police immediately went to work and, within hours, were on the trail of Richard Speck. Cora, although heavily sedated, had managed to give an excellent description of the killer and a nearby gas station attendant remembered one of his managers talking about a guy of the same description who had recently complained about missing a ship and losing out on a job. Police sketch artist Otis Rathel put together an uncanny likeness of Speck. Investigators took the sketch to the Maritime Union Hall and questioned the agent in charge. He remembered an irate seaman who lost out on a double booking -- two guys sent for one job -- and he fished the crumpled assignment sheet from the wastebasket. The sheet gave the name of Richard Speck.

State's Attorney Daniel P. Ward would later call the manhunt for Speck the "finest bit of police work" he had ever seen. Detectives were almost immediately on Speck's trail.

After the murders, Speck moved from bar to bar, drinking himself into oblivion, not knowing that the police were on his trail. Detectives had convinced the agent at the Maritime Hall to call Speck's last known telephone number, his sister's, to tell him that he was needed to ship out. The agent connected with Gene Thornton, who agreed to try and track Speck down. He managed to find him at the Shipyard Inn and told him that the union hall had a job for him. Speck called the union hall and was told to come down for an assignment on a ship that Speck knew had shipped out several days before. Suspecting a trick, he told the agent that he was up north and it would take him at least an hour to get there. He never showed up.

Immediately, Speck went upstairs, packed his bags and called a cab. While he waited in the tavern, playing pool, and three detectives came in looking for a tall blond man with a southern accent. The bartender was no help and Speck stayed quiet, listening and shooting pool just 10 feet away from them. When the cab arrived, he refused to give the driver an address and told him he wanted to go to his sister's house, which he said was in a poor and slummy section of town. The cabbie drove north and again asked Speck for an address. Clueless, he pointed to a building that turned out to be part of the Cabrini Green housing project. He got out of the cab and watched the cabbie drive away.

Speck started walking and ended up on Dearborn Street at the Raleigh Hotel, a flophouse that had once been a luxury apartment building. A desk clerk later recalled a drunken Speck coming in with a prostitute. Just before the elevator door closed, he heard the girl call him "Richard." A half hour later, the girl came back downstairs and told the clerk that her "date" had a gun. This prompted a call to the police and two officers from the 18th District police station showed up at the hotel at 8:30 a.m. Speck, still drunk, awoke to find two cops standing over him. He had the gun tucked into the waistband of his pants and when asked why he had it, told the officers that it belonged to the prostitute. When asked what his name was, he told them that it was Richard Speck. They checked his wallet and found his seaman's I.D. and passport but unfortunately, not all of the police had been notified of the identity of the student nurses' killer yet. He was questioned for 15 minutes and the officers confiscated the gun but never reported it. When they left the hotel, they told the desk clerk that he was "harmless."

Not realizing that Speck had narrowly

THE MYSTERY OF TERESITA BASA

In 1977, Teresita Basa, a 48-year-old woman who worked at Edgewater Hospital, was found on her bed in her Lakeview apartment, a butcher knife in her chest. She appeared to have been raped and murdered.

But the autopsy made a strange discovery - she had not been raped at all. In fact, she was a virgin. Something odd was clearly afoot. Why had she been murdered? Who was the killer?

The case was about to get stranger. The only clue they had was a note Teresita had left reading, "get tickets for A.S.," which was not a set of initials they could trace to any of her friends - though, when the case was near a standstill, they began to wonder if, just maybe, it referred to Allan Showery, an orderly at Edgewater Hospital.

Meanwhile, a doctor named Jose Chua worked at another nearby hospital. His wife had once worked with Showery at Edgewater. One day, Mrs. Chua began speaking in a voice that was not her own. The voice spoke in Tagalog, Basa's native dialect, with a strange Spanish accent. Dr. Chua, who was also from the Philippines, understood what it was saying when the voice through his wife's lips identified itself as Teresita Basa. The voice went on to state that she had been murdered by Allen Showery, who had come to her apartment and stabbed her.

The Chuas were, naturally, puzzled. Mrs. Chua remembered meeting Basa at an orientation meeting, but hadn't worked with her or known her well. When she began speaking in Teresita's voice again, she stated that Showery's motive had been to steal her jewelry. She went on to state that Showery had divided the jewelry between his wife and various girlfriends, and even told how to identify the jewelry. That jewelry had even been stolen was a part of the story that the police had not learned. On a third visit, the voice urged the Chuas to contact the Evanston police. When the police went to speak with Showery, they found the woman he was living with wearing the exact jewelry described by the mysterious voice. He was eventually booked for murder. He initially confessed, but then said he had been coerced into the confession and pleaded not guilty.

On the trial, The Chuas were put on the stand. Mrs. Chua, who claimed not to remember the "possession," was accused of murder herself, but the police were satisfied that the Chuas were entirely innocent.

However, the "voice from the grave" was the only real evidence that Showery had been the killer, not simply a receiver of stolen jewelry. The trial seemed headed for a mistrial when, in a move that shocked the press as much as the "voice" story itself, Showery suddenly changed his plea to guilty and was sentenced to a term in prison.

Today, some people hold up the Teresita Basa case as "scientific proof" of the afterlife, ghosts, possession, or, as often as not, whatever their own beliefs happen to be. But it's not proof of anything - it's only another story to indicate that there are things that happen in the world whose nature we may never fully understand. Even those who believe that the whole thing was a strange hoax must concede that it's one of the strangest cases in the history of the American legal system!

escaped capture, the police searched the South Side. They managed to track him from the Shipyard Inn to the cab company, and then to Cabrini Green. But while they canvassed the housing project, Speck drank himself into another stupor. Later in the afternoon, he ran into some old friends who suggested that he hop a freight train with them and head out of town. Speck went back to the Raleigh, packed his bags, and on his way out, told the manager that he was going to do some laundry. He never returned. Just 15 minutes after he walked out, two detectives came in and flashed a photo of Speck in front of the manager. Her eyes widened and he told the officers Speck had just left.

Oblivious, Speck then headed for the Starr Hotel, a rundown dive on West Madison Street that offered temporary refuge to winos and bums. The "rooms" were nothing more than cubicles that were portioned off by plywood and had "doors" made from chicken wire. For the rate of 90 cents per night, the occupant was provided with a cot, a wall locker, a metal stool and a 15-watt bulb that dangled from the ceiling on a wire. Here, losers could sleep off a drunk amidst the sounds of coughing and moaning and the smells of sweat, booze and vomit. It was the last rung on the ladder for the dregs of humanity.

Speck tossed his bags on a cot and went out to sell some of his belongings to raise money for another night of drinking. He picked up some wine at a local liquor store and saw several newspapers with his name and photo on splashed across them. Speck stumbled back to the Starr Hotel and finished off the entire bottle of wine. He then walked down the hall to the bathroom, smashed the wine bottle and then used the broken glass to cut his wrist and inner elbow. Blood splashed the wall and onto the floor and Speck wobbled down the corridor to his cubicle. He collapsed onto the bed, still bleeding badly and then called out to his neighbors for water and for help. They ignored him.

An anonymous call was made to the police but no patrol car was sent. Eventually, Speck was taken to Cook County Hospital. The ambulance drivers ignored Speck's cries for water and missed the police bulletin on their dashboard that had the injured man's photo on it. In the emergency room, Nurse Kathy O'Connor prepped Speck and first year resident Leroy Smith checked his wounds. He noticed something familiar about the man. He checked his arm, looking for a tattoo and saw it there, as he suspected, "Born to Raise Hell". He compared a newspaper photo with the man and realized that he had the killer on his table.

Speck pleaded with the young man for water but Smith grabbed him by the back of the neck and squeezed it as hard as he could. "Did you give water to those nurses?" he demanded. He dropped Speck's head back onto the gurney and called in a policeman who was guarding another patient down the hall. He told him that Richard Speck, the suspect in the murders, was there on the table. The stunned officer started making telephone calls and all hell broke loose.

Speck was in police custody a few hours later and William J. Martin, a young and hard-working state's attorney, was faced with putting together and trying the case. He based most of it on the sincere and compelling testimony of Corazon Amurao, who had to be persuaded to remain in the United States long enough to secure the conviction of the monster who had killed her friends. She was understandably unhinged from her ordeal and she wanted nothing more than to return to the Philippines to try and forget the horrific experience. Martin brought her mother and a cousin to Chicago for moral support and kept them in secret location away from the press. Her quiet testimony galvanized the courtroom and convinced the jury to convict Speck in just 49 minutes. He was given the death sentence for the murders.

Although sentenced to die in the electric chair, the Illinois Supreme Court voided the death penalty in 1971 and Speck was back in court again. This time, he was sentenced to 400 to 1,200 years at the Stateville Penitentiary in Joliet. It was the longest prison sentence ever given to an Illinois inmate.

During his incarceration, Speck never admitted his guilt in the murders. He died on December 5, 1991 from a massive heart attack. His autopsy showed that he had an enlarged heart and occluded arteries, having blown up to 220 pounds by the time of his death. No one claimed his body and he was cremated. His ashes were disposed of in an undisclosed location.

But unfortunately, in 1996, Speck was back.

In May of that year, television journalist Bill Kurtis went behind the walls of Stateville prison and came back with a secret videotape (originally filmed in the middle 1980s) that showed a bizarre Richard Speck with women's breasts -- apparently from hormone treatments -- wearing blue panties and having sex with another inmate. Segments of the video, which also showed sex and drug orgies, were shown on the program *American Justice* and it plunged the Illinois Department of Corrections into a major scandal. Viewers were as repulsed to see what had become of Speck as they were by his bloody crimes.

Even after death, he was still raising hell.

THE CLOWN THAT KILLED

To everyone who met him, John Wayne Gacy seemed a likable and affable man. He was widely respected in the community, charming and easy to get along with. He was a good Catholic and sharp businessman who, when not running his construction company, was active in the Jaycees and with community volunteer groups. When he was a Democratic Party precinct captain, he had his photo taken with then-First Lady Rosalynn Carter. He also spent much of his free time hosting elaborate street parties for his friends and neighbors, serving in community groups and entertaining children as "Pogo the Clown." He was a generous, hard working, friendly, devoted family man, everyone knew that -- but that was the side of John Wayne Gacy that he allowed people to see.

Underneath the smiling mask of the clown was the face of a depraved fiend.

John Wayne Gacy was born on St. Patrick's Day 1942 at Edgewater Hospital in Chicago and was the second of three children. The Gacy children were raised in the Church and all three attended Catholic schools on the North Side. Growing up, Gacy was a quiet boy who worked odd jobs for spending money, like newspaper routes and bagging groceries, and busied himself with Boy Scout activities. He

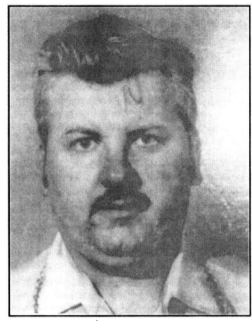

John Wayne Gacy

was never a particularly popular boy but he was well liked by his teachers, co-workers and his friends from school and the Boy Scouts. He seemed to have a normal childhood, except for his relationship with his father and a series of health problems that he developed.

When Gacy was 11, he was playing on a swing set and was hit in the head with one of the swings. The accident caused a blood clot in his brain that was not discovered until he was 16. Between the time of the accident and the diagnosis, Gacy suffered from blackouts that were caused by the clot. They were eventually treated with medication. At 17, he was also diagnosed with a heart ailment that led to him being hospitalized several times during his life.

In his late teens, he began to experience problems with his father, although his relationship with his mother and sisters remained strong. His father was an alcoholic who physically abused his wife and berated his children. He was an unpleasant individual, but Gacy loved him and constantly worked to gain his attention and approval. Gacy Sr. died before his son could ever get close to him.

His family problems extended into his schoolwork and after attending four high schools during his senior year and never graduating, Gacy dropped out and left home for Las Vegas. He worked part time as a janitor in a funeral home and saved his money to buy a ticket back to Chicago. Lonely and depressed, he spent three months trying to get the money together to go back home. His mother and sisters were thrilled to see him when he came back.

After his return, Gacy enrolled in business college and eventually graduated. While in school, he gained a real talent for salesmanship and he put these talents to work in a job with the Nunn-Bush Shoe Company. He excelled as a management trainee and he was soon transferred to a men's clothing outlet in Springfield, Ill.

While living in Springfield, Gacy became involved in several organizations that served the community, including the Jaycees, to which Gacy devoted most of his efforts. He was eventually voted vice-president of the local chapter and named "Man of the Year." Many who knew Gacy considered him to be ambitious and working hard to make a name for himself in the community. He was an overachiever who worked so diligently that he had to be hospitalized for nervous exhaustion on one occasion.

In September 1964, Gacy met and married a co-worker named Marlynn Myers, whose parents owned a number of Kentucky Fried Chicken restaurants in Iowa. Gacy's new father-in-law offered him a position with the company and soon the newlyweds were moving to Iowa.

Gacy began learning the restaurant business from the ground up, working 12 to 14 hours each day. He was enthusiastic and eager to learn and hoped to take over the franchises one day. When not working, he was active with the Waterloo, Iowa Jaycees. He worked tirelessly performing volunteer work and he made many friends. Marlynn gave birth to a son shortly after they moved to Iowa and not long after, added a daughter to the happy family. They seemed to have the picture perfect life, but trouble was already starting.

Rumors were starting to spread around town, and among Jaycees members, about Gacy's sexual preferences. No one could help but notice that young boys always seemed to be in his presence. Stories spread that he had made passes at some of the young men who worked in the restaurants but those close to him refused to believe it -- until the rumors became truth. In May 1968, a grand jury in Black Hawk County indicted Gacy for committing an act of sodomy with a teenage boy named Mark Miller. The boy told the courts that Gacy had tricked him into being tied up while visiting Gacy's home and he had been violently raped. Gacy denied the charges but did say that Miller willingly had sex with him in order to earn extra money.

Four months later, more charges were filed against Gacy. This time, he was charged with hiring an 18-year-old named Dwight Andersson to beat up Mark Miller. Andersson lured Miller to his car and then drove him to a wooded area, where he sprayed mace in his eyes and began to beat him. Miller fought back, breaking Andersson's nose, and managed to run away. He called the police and Andersson was picked up and taken into custody. He informed the officer that Gacy had hired him to attack the other boy.

Soon after, Gacy entered a guilty plea on the earlier sodomy charge. He received a 10-year sentence to the Iowa State Reformatory, the maximum time for the offence, and entered prison for the first time at the age of 26. Shortly after he went to prison, his wife divorced him on the grounds that he had violated their wedding vows.

Gacy was a model prisoner and was paroled after only 18 months. In June 1970, he made his way back to Chicago. He moved in with his mother and obtained work as a chef in a city restaurant.

Gacy lived with his mother for four months and then decided to move out on his own. She helped him to obtain a new house at 8213 West Summerdale Ave. in Norwood Park Township. Gacy owned one-half of the house and his mother and sisters owned the other. The new, two-bedroom ranch house was located in a clean, quiet neighborhood and Gacy quickly went about making friends with his neighbors, Edward and Lilla Grexa. Within seven months of moving in next door, Gacy was spending Christmas with the Grexas. They became close friends and often gathered for drinks and card games.

In June 1972, Gacy married Carole Hoff, a newly divorced mother of two daughters. Gacy romanced her when she was most vulnerable and she fell for his charm and generosity. She knew about his time in prison but believed that he had changed his life for the better. Carole and her daughters soon settled into Gacy's home and forged a close relationship with the Grexas. The older couple was often invited over to the Gacy's house for elaborate parties and cookouts. However, they were bothered by the horrible stench that sometimes wafted throughout the house. Lillie Grexa was convinced that an animal had died beneath the floorboards of the place and she urged Gacy to do something about it. He blamed the odor on a moisture buildup in the crawlspace under the house.

In 1974, Gacy started a contracting business called Painting, Decorating and Maintenance or PDM Contractors, Inc. He hired a number of teenage boys to work for him and lied when he explained to friends that hiring young men would keep his payroll costs low. In truth, Gacy's secrets were starting to catch up with him and it was starting to become very apparent to those who knew him, especially to his wife.

By 1975, Carole and Gacy had drifted apart. Their sex life had ended and Gacy's moods became more and more unpredictable, ranging from jovial to an uncontrollable rage that would have him throwing furniture. He had become an insomniac and his lack of sleep seemed to make his mood swings even worse. And if his personality changes were not enough, his choice of reading material worried her even more. Carole had started to find magazines filled with naked men and boys around the house and when confronted, Gacy casually admitted they were his. He even confessed that he preferred young men to women. Naturally, this was the last straw for Carole and she soon filed for divorce. It became final on March 2, 1976.

Gacy dismissed his marital problems and refused to let them hamper his need for recognition and success. To most people, Gacy was still the outgoing and hardworking man that he always had been and he always came up with creative ways to get noticed. It was not long before he gained the attention of Robert F. Matwick, the Democratic township committeeman for Norwood Park. As a free service to the committeeman, Gacy volunteered himself and his employees to clean up and repair Democratic Party headquarters. Unaware of the contractor's past and impressed by his sense of duty and dedication to the community, Matwick nominated Gacy to the street lighting commission. In 1975, Gacy became the secretary treasurer but his political career was short-lived. No matter how well he thought he was hiding it, rumors again began to circulate about Gacy's interest in young boys.

One of the rumors stemmed from an incident that took place during the time that Gacy was working on the Democratic headquarters. One of the teenagers who worked on the project was 16-year-old Tony Antonucci. According to the boy, Gacy made sexual advances toward him but backed off when Antonucci threatened to hit him with a chair. Gacy recovered his composure and made a joke out of it. He tried to convince Tony that he was only kidding and left him alone for the next month.

Several weeks later, while Antonucci was visiting Gacy's home, Gacy again approached the youth. He tricked the young man into a pair of handcuffs and then tried to undress him. Antonucci had made sure that he was loosely cuffed and when he slipped free, he wrestled Gacy to the ground and cuffed the older man instead. He eventually let him go when Gacy promised not to bother him again. That was the last time that Gacy ever made advances toward Antonucci and the boy remained working for the contracting company for almost a year after the incident. Tony Antonucci would not realize how lucky he had been that day.

Others would not fare as well.

Johnny Butkovich, 17, began doing remodeling work for Gacy's company in an effort to raise money for his racing car. He enjoyed the position, it paid well, and he maintained a good working relationship with Gacy until one pay period when Gacy refused to pay Johnny for two weeks of work. Angered that Gacy had withheld his pay, Johnny went over to his employer's house with two friends to collect what was rightfully his. When confronted, Gacy refused to pay and a loud argument erupted. Finally, he realized there was little that he could do and Johnny and his friends left. Butkovich dropped off his friends at home and drove away --- never to be seen again.

Michael Bonnin, 17, enjoyed working with his hands, especially carpentry and woodworking, and often had several different projects going at the same time. In June 1976, he had almost completed restoring an antique jukebox but, unfortunately, the job was never finished. He was on his way to catch a train to meet his stepfather's brother when he vanished.

Billy Carroll, 16, was a longtime troublemaker who had first been in trouble with the authorities at the age of 9. Two years later, he was caught with a gun and he spent most of his life on the streets of Chicago, making money by arranging meetings between teenage boys and adult men for a commission. Although he came from a very different background than Michael Bonnin and Johnny Butkovich, they all three had one thing in common -- John Wayne Gacy. Like the others, Carroll also disappeared suddenly. He left home on June 13, 1976 and was never seen alive again.

Gregory Godzik, 17, started working for PDM Contractors in order to finance parts for his 1966 Pontiac. The work that he did for Gacy paid well and he liked it. On December 12, 1976, Gregory dropped his date at her house and drove off towards home. The following day, the police found Gregory's Pontiac but the boy was missing.

On January 20, 1977, John Szyc, 19, also vanished. He had driven off in his 1971 Plymouth Satellite and was never seen alive again. Szyc had not worked for PDM Contractors but he was acquainted with Gregory Godzik, Johnny Butkovich and fatally, John Wayne Gacy.

On September 15, 1977, Robert Gilroy, 18, also disappeared. Gilroy was an avid outdoorsman and was supposed to catch a bus to meet friends for horseback riding. When he never showed up, his father, a Chicago police sergeant, immediately began searching for the boy. A full-scale investigation was launched but Robert was nowhere to be found.

Gacy's web of secrets began to unravel with the vanishing of a young boy named Robert Piest. The investigation into his disappearance would lead not only to the discovery of his body, but the bodies of Butkovich, Bonnin, Carroll, Szyc, Gilroy and 27 other young men who suffered similar fates. These discoveries would horrify not only Chicago, but all of America.

Robert, 15, disappeared mysteriously just outside the doors of the pharmacy where he worked. His mother, who had come to pick him up after his shift, was waiting outside for him when he vanished. He had told her that he would be back in just a minute because he was going to talk to a contractor who had offered him a job. He never returned. She began to get worried but as more time passed, her worry turned to terror. Finally, three hours after his disappearance, the Des Plaines police were notified. Lieutenant Joseph Kozenczak led the investigation.

The first lead to follow was the most obvious one and officers quickly obtained the name of the contractor who had offered Robert the job. Kozenczak went straight to Gacy's home and when the Gacy came to the door, he told him about the missing boy. He also asked him to accompany him to the police station for some questions. Gacy refused. He explained that there had been a recent death in his family and that he had to attend to some telephone calls but he agreed to come down later. Several hours later, Gacy arrived and gave a statement to the police. He said that he knew nothing about the disappearance and was allowed to leave with no further questioning.

Kozenczak decided to do a background check on Gacy. He was stunned when he discovered that he had done time for sodomy with a teenage boy. He quickly obtained a search warrant for Gacy's house and on December 13, 1978, a legion of police officers entered the house on Summerdale Avenue. Gacy was not at home at the time.

The police were shocked by what they found. Some of them items discovered in the search included a box containing two drivers licenses and several rings; a box containing marijuana and amyl nitrate pills; a stained section of rug; a number of books with homosexual and child pornography themes; a pair of handcuffs; police badges; sexual devices; a hypodermic needle and small brown bottle; clothing that was too small for Gacy; nylon rope; and other items. The police also confiscated three automobiles that belonged to Gacy, including a 1978 Chevrolet truck with a snow plow attached and the name "PDM Contractors" on the side, a van with "PDM Contractors" also painted on

Remains are removed from Gacy's home on West Summerdale Avenue

the side and a 1979 Oldsmobile Delta 88. In the trunk of the car were pieces of hair that were later matched to Robert Piest.

As the investigation continued, the police entered the crawl space under Gacy's home. They were discouraged by the rancid odor but believed it to be sewage. The earth in the crawl space had been sprinkled with lime but appeared to be untouched. They left the narrow space and returned to police headquarters to run tests on the evidence they had obtained.

Gacy was again called to headquarters and was told about the evidence that had been removed from his house. Enraged, he immediately contacted his attorney, who told him not to sign the Miranda waiver that was presented to him by detectives. The police had nothing to arrest him on and eventually had to release him after more questioning about the Piest disappearance. They placed him under 24-hour surveillance and over the next few days, his friends were called into the station and were also questioned. The detectives were unable to get any information from that connected him to Robert Piest and all of his friends insisted that Gacy simply was not capable of murder. Unable to gather other evidence, Gacy was finally charged with possession of marijuana.

Meanwhile, the police lab and investigators were coming up with critical evidence against Gacy from the items taken from his home. One of the rings found in Gacy's house belonged to another teenager who had disappeared about a year earlier, John Szyc. They also discovered that three former employees of Gacy's had also disappeared. Furthermore, a receipt for a roll of film that was found in Gacy's home had belonged to a co-worker of Robert Piest and he had given it to Robert on the day of the boy's disappearance. With this new information, the investigators suddenly began to realize the enormity of the case that was starting to unfold.

Under questioning, Gacy tearfully confessed that he had killed someone in self-defense and, frightened, had buried the body under his garage. Detectives and crime lab technicians returned to Gacy's house again. They decided to search the crawl space under the house, as well as the garage, and minutes after starting to dig, found the first corpse. Soon, a full-scale excavation was taking place.

On Friday, December 22, 1978, detectives confronted Gacy with the news that digging was being done under his house. With this, the monster finally broke down. He admitted to the police that he had killed at least 30 people and that most of their remains were buried beneath the house. The first murder took place in January 1972 and the second in January 1974, about a year and a half after he was married. He explained that his lured his victims into being handcuffed and then he would sexually assault them. To muffle their screams, Gacy stuffed a sock, or their underwear, into their mouths and would often kill them by placing a rope or board against their throats as he raped them. He also admitted to sometimes keeping the corpses under his bed or in his attic before burying them in the crawl space.

The police discovered two bodies during the first day of digging. One of these was John Butkovich, who was found under the garage, and the other was in the crawl space. As the days passed, the body count grew higher. Some of the victims were found with their underwear still lodged in their throats and others were buried so close together that investigators believed they had been killed, or at least buried, at the same time.

By December 28, the police had removed a total of 27 bodies from Gacy's house. Another body had also been found weeks earlier, not in the crawl space but in the Des Plaines River. The naked corpse of Frank Wayne 'Dale' Landingin had been found in the water but at the time, the police were not yet aware of Gacy and his crimes. It would not be until his driver's license was found in Gacy's house that he could be connected to the young man's murder.

The body of James Mazzara was also removed from the Des Plaines River. His underwear was found stuffed down his throat, linking him to the other victims. Gacy told the police that he had started disposing of bodies in the river because he was running out of room in his crawl space.

Much to the horror of the neighbors, the police were still excavating Gacy's property at the end of February. They had gutted the house but had found no more bodies in the crawl space. Bad winter weather had kept them from resuming the search but they believed there were still bodies to be found. While workmen began breaking up the concrete of Gacy's patio, another horrific discovery was made. They found the body of a man, still in good condition, preserved in the concrete. The following week, another body was found.

The 31st victim to be linked to Gacy was found in the Illinois River. Investigators were able to learn his identity thanks to a tattoo on his arm, which friends of the victim's father recognized while reading a newspaper article about the grim discovery. The victim's name was Timothy O'Rourke and he was believed to have been acquainted with Gacy.

Around the time that O'Rourke was discovered and pulled from the river, another body was found on Gacy's property, this time beneath his recreation room. It was the last body to be found on the property and soon after, the house was destroyed and reduced to rubble.

Although the death toll had now risen to 32, the body of Robert Piest was still missing. Tragically, his remains were discovered in the Illinois River in April 1979. The body had been lodged somewhere in the river but strong winds had worked it loose and carried it to the locks at Dresden Dam, where it was finally discovered. An autopsy report showed that Piest had been strangled by paper towels being shoved down his throat.

The most chilling image of Gacy of all -- as his "Pogo the Clown" character (Chicago Tribune)

Police investigators worked hard to identify Gacy's victims, using dental records and other clues, and eventually, all but nine of the young men were identified. A mass burial was held for these unknown victims on June 8, 1981.

John Wayne Gacy's murder trial began on February 6, 1980 at the Cook County Criminal Courts Building in downtown Chicago. The defense argued that Gacy was insane and not in control of his actions, but the prosecution refuted this, stating that the murders, and subsequent disposal of the bodies, had been carried out in a deliberate manner. In their closing statements, both sides emotionally argued their case but the jury took only two hours of deliberation to come back with a guilty verdict. Gacy had been convicted of the deaths of 33 young men and had the notoriety of being convicted of more murders than anyone else in American history. He received the death penalty and was sent to the Menard Correctional Center to await execution. After years of appeals, he was put to death by lethal injection on May 9, 1994.

His death brought an end to one of the most terrifying periods in Illinois' criminal history and the mere mention of his name still manages to send a chill through the hearts of many, even after all of these years.

8. WEIRD CHICAGO & THE UNEXPLAINED

Chicago has a strange metaphysical elegance of death about it.
Claes Oldenburg

It is human nature for us to love a mystery. We all love to be intrigued by the mysterious and tantalized by the idea of something that cannot be solved. For this reason, murder mysteries, courtroom dramas, and books about the paranormal have been immensely popular for decades. We love to question, to wonder and be baffled by those things that we believe to be unexplained. Of course, most fictional mysteries are usually solved by the intrepid detective in the closing pages of the book or the last reel of the film --- but what of mysteries that cannot be solved? What of real-life mysteries for which no explanation exists?

All of us at Weird Chicago have always been fascinated by anything that reeks of the unknown or the unsolved - from ghosts, to mystery creatures, to anything for which no hard, logical explanation exists. We have managed to track down Chicago reports of mysterious spook lights, religious apparitions, lake monsters, flying saucers, vanishing animals, mysterious happenings, and more. In each instance, though, we make no claim to know if the reports are true. We present them here for the approval of the individual reader and allow that person to judge for himself.

If you thought some of the earlier chapters of the book were weird ---- you ain't seen nothing yet!

THE RIDDLE OF THE FOOL KILLER SUBMARINE (OR "HEY KID.. YOU WANNA SEE A DEAD BODY?")

In the days following the *Eastland* disaster, a diver named William "Frenchy" Deneau was responsible for recovering around 250 bodies from the murky water. Four months later, in November 1915, Deneau was back in the river, working to lay cables beneath the Rush Street Bridge. While he worked, his shovel struck a large metallic object that turned out to be the wreck of a 40-foot long iron submarine. Deneau announced to the newspapers that he had found The *Fool Killer*, an "ancient, primitive submarine" that had been lost for at least eighteen years -- and possibly much longer!

At the time, submarines were in the papers almost daily. While attempts at submarine warfare had been made in both the Civil War and the American Revolution, using submarines as weapons had only recently become practical. Half a world away, Europe was in the grip of the world's first submarine war, submarine warfare being one of the deadly new types of battle introduced in the First World War. The discovery of the wreck of an old submarine in the Chicago River was an event noted by several regional papers throughout the country.

Initially, it was expected that the Chicago Historical Society would raise the odd vessel, but Deneau obtained permission from the federal government to raise the ship for "exhibition purposes." The next month, after boat traffic died down for the winter, he arranged to raise it up from the murky depths. Once it was ashore, a startling discovery was made: inside of the ship were several bones -- including the skulls of a man and a dog!

While police combed their records to identify the body, Deneau made preparations to put the odd craft on display. He appears to have enlisted the Skee Ball Company as investors. (Imagine the slogan: "Come for the *Fool Killer*, Stay for the Skee Ball!")

By the end of February, the ship was on display at 208 South State St. For a dime, customers could see the remains of the old ship -- and the remains of the dead guy and the dead dog! Admission also included a lecture and question-and-answer session by Deneau, a presentation on the history of submarines, and a chance to examine the interior of the *Fool Killer* itself (at the attendees' own risk). On Saturday mornings, groups of ten or more children could get in for half of the usual price!

The exact location where Deneau found the thing is a bit of a mystery. The newspapers first said it was near the Rush Street Bridge; then said it was at the Wells Street Bridge. A year or so later, while he was in World War I as a doughboy and speaking to reporters, Deneau said "Remember that old submarine, the *Fool Killer*, I found? I found it over by the Madison Street Bridge!" It also seems that in the process of raising it, workers had to drag it through the river a couple of miles to the Fullerton Street Bridge.

Two views of the Fool Killer being raised from the Chicago River

And the location of the wreck is only one of the mysteries. The list of unanswered questions about the submarine is a long one. Who built it? How long had it been in the river? Who the heck was the dead guy inside it, and what in the world possessed him to take his dog out on a submarine trip in the river? And whatever happened to the thing?

Research into these questions has proved frustrating. Stories and theories abound, but none can really be verified, and the newspaper reports seem to be full of hearsay, mistakes and contradictions.

Initially, the *Chicago Tribune* reported that the ship had been first launched in 1870 as a

floating craft and sank to the bottom of the lake the first time it was submerged. According to their first article on the sub's re-discovery, it was believed to have been built around 1890 by Peter Nissen, the accountant-turned-daredevil (see the Weird Chicago People chapter). Nissen sank it the first time he tried to use it. The next month, when the skulls were found, the Tribune reported that the ship had been purchased and raised in the 1890s by a man named William Nissen. Since then, most people have assumed that the skeleton onboard was his.

However, this is hard to verify. Census records indicate that there actually was a "William Nissen" in Chicago in the 1890s, but he was still alive as of the 1920 census, five years after the bones were discovered! This William Nissen seems to be no relation to Peter Nissen, leaving one to speculate that the report had been a typo, and that the reporter meant to say "Peter," not "William."

The fact that they called it the *Fool Killer* at all may indicate that the newspapers -- or Deneau -- had simply mistaken it for one of Peter Nissen's boats, which was an easy enough mistake to make. Nissen did build three experimental crafts, named the *Fool Killer 1*, *Fool Killer 2*, and *Fool Killer 3* and, although none of those crafts were submarines, buying, raising and testing a dangerous homemade sub sure seemed like the kind of thing Nissen would have done!

Further complicating the matter is the *Tribune's* statement that the ship had first sunk in 1870 then was raised again and sunk in either 1890 or 1897 (the date changes from story to story, indicating that it was all based on

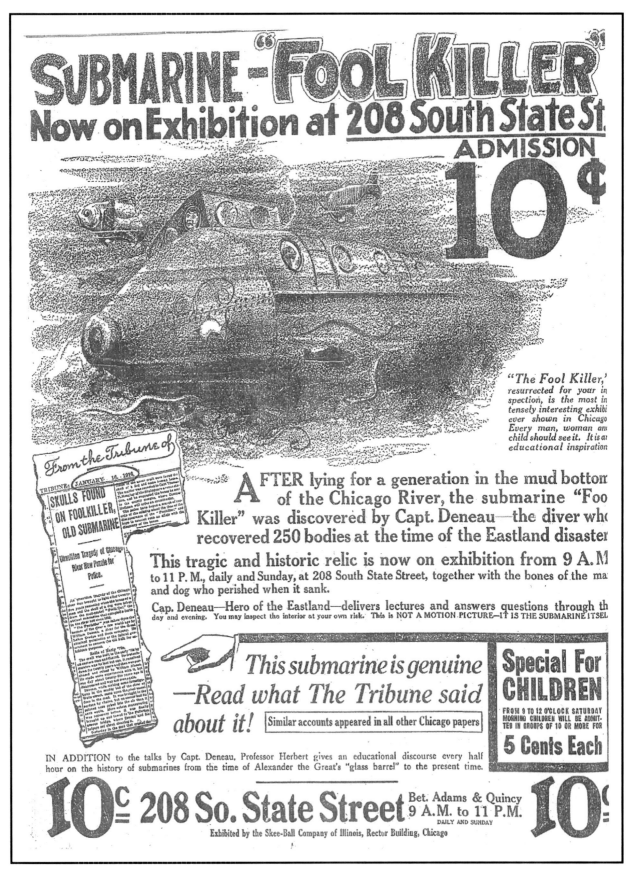

SUBMARINE-"FOOL KILLER"
Now on Exhibition at 208 South State St.

ADMISSION 10¢

"The Fool Killer," resurrected for your inspection, is the most intensely interesting exhibit ever shown in Chicago. Every man, woman and child should see it. It is an educational inspiration

AFTER lying for a generation in the mud bottom of the Chicago River, the submarine "Fool Killer" was discovered by Capt. Deneau—the diver who recovered 250 bodies at the time of the Eastland disaster

This tragic and historic relic is now on exhibition from 9 A. M. to 11 P. M., daily and Sunday, at 208 South State Street, together with the bones of the man and dog who perished when it sank.

Cap. Deneau—Hero of the Eastland—delivers lectures and answers questions through the day and evening. You may inspect the interior at your own risk. This is NOT A MOTION PICTURE—IT IS THE SUBMARINE ITSELF

This submarine is genuine —Read what The Tribune said about it! Similar accounts appeared in all other Chicago papers

Special For CHILDREN
FROM 9 TO 12 O'CLOCK SATURDAY MORNING CHILDREN WILL BE ADMITTED IN GROUPS OF 10 OR MORE FOR

5 Cents Each

IN ADDITION to the talks by Capt. Deneau, Professor Herbert gives an educational discourse every half hour on the history of submarines from the time of Alexander the Great's "glass barrel" to the present time.

10ᶜ = 208 So. State Street
Bet. Adams & Quincy 9 A.M. to 11 P.M. DAILY AND SUNDAY

10ᶜ

Exhibited by the Skee-Ball Company of Illinois, Rector Building, Chicago

From the Tribune of

TRIBUNE JANUARY 16, 1916

SKULLS FOUND ON FOOLKILLER, OLD SUBMARINE

Unwritten Tragedy of Chicago River New Puzzle for Police.

hearsay, not actual records). One report in the *Washington Post* even said that it had claimed a number of victims around the time of the World's Fair. However, if in fact the ship had sailed before, the paper saw no reason to mention it at the time, even though the launch of a submarine in the Great Lakes in 1870 would probably have been an event noticed by papers all over the world, as later submarine launches in the lake were. Furthermore, if the submarine had sunk in 1870 and raised after 20 years, who would be crazy enough to go sailing in it?

Most likely, all of the contemporary reports on the history of the craft were mistakes. No sources were ever given, and they seem to be the result of half-remembered stories of news items from decades before. Perhaps they were mistaking it for the submarine tested in Lake Michigan in 1892 by George C. Baker, which was about 40 feet long -- roughly the length of the *Fool Killer* -- or the model Louis Gatham tested in the lake the next year. The *Tribune* also initially said that it was built to float, but pictures of the Fool Killer make it clear that it was never built to be a floating vessel.

But the *Tribune* also once reported that the sub was first owned by an "Eastern man," and some have speculated that this might refer to Lodner Darvantis Phillips, a shoemaker from Michigan City, Ind., who also happened to be a submarine pioneer. There were only a very small handful of submarines ever known to be in the Great Lakes in the 19th century and Phillips just happened to build a few of them, including perhaps the only successful submarine built in its time.

Phillips appears to have designed at least four submarines in his lifetime. According to his descendants, his third model, built in 1851 and known as the *Marine Cigar*, was stable enough that he was able to take his family on fantastic underwater picnics (this was probably the one he lost in 1853 while trying to salvage the wreck of *The Atlantic* in Lake Erie. It's still lost in the lake today). A fourth model had torpedo mechanisms added. These third and fourth models were improvements on his earlier, less successful boats; the first, built in 1845, was a fish-shaped apparatus that sank in Trail Creek near Michigan City. The second just may have been the *Fool Killer.*

While actual details are scarce, family legend has it that Phillips' second model was a 40-foot cigar-shaped submarine that was built in the late 1840s (in an 1853 letter to the Navy, Phillips did mention building a sub in 1847). According to these family stories, the machine lacked a decent mechanism for propulsion and sank on a test run in the Chicago River. Phillips' family said decades later that the submarine found in the river was undoubtedly one of his.

That the *Fool Killer* was a Lodner Phillips creation seems to be backed up mainly by family legend, which is not always reliable. Another Phillips family legend states than when Phillips refused to sell one of his boats to the British Navy, they sank it, a story that is almost certainly more legend than fact. And the letter Phillips wrote to the Navy in 1853 indicates that the submarine he built in 1847 was a success. No mention is made of it sinking (though the letter was an attempt to sell his latest boat to the Navy, and talking about failed models wouldn't have been much of a selling point).

But that the *Fool Killer* was one of Phillips' subs is still the best explanation that has yet been offered for the origin of the mysterious submarine. No drawings or diagrams for his second submarine survive, but drawings of Philips' subs from the 1850s do strongly resemble the pictures of the *Fool Killer* that eventually came to light.

So, could the submarine have been beneath the river since the 1840s? It's entirely possible, especially if the reports about the ship being from 1870 are incorrect, as has been suggested. Some recent articles have stated that Phillips sold the submarine in 1871 to a man who promptly sunk it, explaining the early newspaper reports of the sub being from that era, but Phillips was busy being dead by this time.

Who, then, was the poor man who died onboard? Since Peter Nissen died onboard a different ship, not a submarine, and William Nissen seems to have been alive when the sub was raised, the identity of the ship's victim remains a mystery.

It's possible that the bones were, in reality, planted on the submarine when it was raised in 1915 as a publicity stunt to get more people to come see it on exhibition. After all, complete skeletons were not found -- just skulls and a few other bones. What happened to the rest of them? The Phillips' family legend about the sub sinking in the river doesn't include anything about anyone being onboard at the time. Also, Phillips first and third models were known to have escape hatches. Why wouldn't the second one have had one?

William Deneau does seem to have been a bit of a showman. In 1958, on the anniversary of the *Eastland* Disaster, Deneau told reporters that he had just been onboard the repaired *Eastland* -- which, he said, was still sailing under another name -- for a cruise from California to Catalina. In fact, the ship had been scrapped years before. Like most

Contrary to popular belief, the sub was not found during salvage missions after the *Eastland* Disaster, but four months later. This misconception probably stems from Deneau's involvement in both stories. Interestingly, both Deneau and Lodner D. Phillips held patents on diving suits!

great showmen, Deneau may have been willing to fudge the facts a bit in the name of a great story.

While it's likely that we'll never know the truth about the bones, many of the questions about the submarine and its origins could surely be answered today if anyone knew where the submarine was now. But unfortunately, this is another mystery.

In May of 1916, the submarine was listed in newspapers among the attractions at Parker's Greatest Shows, a traveling carnival run by Charles W. Parker, which had arrived for a weeklong engagement in Oelwein, Iowa. It was listed as "The Submarine or *Fool Killer*, the first submarine ever built," and was exhibited along with "Skee ball, a new amusement device," but it was merely listed among other top draws, including "The Electric Girl; The Vegetable King; Snooks, the smallest monkey in the world (the paper was especially enchanted with the monkey, who delighted crowds by sucking his thumb); the fat girl and the Homeliest Woman in the World." The *Fool Killer* was mentioned in the papers almost daily, although one can imagine that it didn't take much to make the papers in the town of Oelwein in 1916. In any case, it does not seem to have been as big a draw as the monkey. No mention was made of the bones, which may not have traveled on with the submarine.

By 1917, Parker's Greatest Shows had replaced the sub with a new submarine that could demonstrate maneuvers in a giant glass tank, leaving historians to speculate that Parker sold the old submarine for scrap, but no one really knows what happened to it. It could still be out there someplace today, as far as anyone knows!

We here at Weird Chicago are continuing our search for more information about the craft and what became of it -- but it's likely that the riddle of the *Fool Killer* will never truly be solved!

THE HAND OF DEATH

On the afternoon of Good Friday, April 18, 1924, the members of the Chicago Fire Department's Engine Co. 107 were going about their usual routine. Even though it was a holy day, it would be a day like any other to the firefighters who were on call. They still had to eat, clean and make sure their equipment and trucks were always ready. And cleaning the large firehouse seemed to be a never-ending task for the men. One of firefighters was a man named Francis X. Leavy and on this particular day, he had drawn the duty of cleaning the building's first floor windows.

Leavy was a good Irish family man who had been with the fire department for 13 years, after an eight-year tour with the Navy, which he had joined at age 14. He and his wife, Mary, were the parents of two children, Frank Jr. and a daughter, June. On this day, the usually jovial Leavy was strangely sullen and quiet. He couldn't seem to shake whatever was bothering him and this put his friends on edge.

Also troubling was the news that was coming over the telegraph system in front of the firehouse. A four-alarm fire had started in the Union Stockyards and even though Engine Co. 107 was too far away from it and not expected to respond, the idea that a large fire was burning just a few miles away bothered all of them. Leavy seemed to be lost in his own thoughts, keeping his attention on the window that he was washing. Then, for some reason that remains unknown, he paused in his work with his left hand resting against the pane of glass. He spoke aloud, announcing: "This is my last day on the fire department."

Leavy spoke to no one in particular, but several men heard the strange comment. This, along with his sudden change in personality, puzzled the others, including Edward McKevitt, who had been standing next to Leavy. He started to ask what his friend meant by this but, just then, the station received an alarm call. They were told to go to Fourteenth and Blue Island because the stations that normally covered that area were tied up with the stockyards fire. Just as the other men did, Leavy put on his helmet, coat and boots and jumped onto the back of the truck as it roared away from the station house.

The burning building they were sent to was Curran Hall, a 50-year-old brick structure that was located on South Blue Island, southwest of the Loop. During its heyday, it had been a popular dance hall, but had closed down because of Prohibition. Several small businesses were now operating out of it.

The fire crew stretched a hose up the fire escape and into the building's second story. They crawled through the smoke and fire to aim the water stream at the flames that were roaring inside. They had no breathing apparatus in those days and so the men had to crawl back and forth to a door or window, following the hose line, to get fresh air. They fought the fire for about a half hour before one of the building's outer walls suddenly buckled, knocking down the entire structure and trapping the firefighters inside. The collapse knocked out the electricity in the area and the remaining crew had to search for the buried men with flashlights. For hours, they dug by hand, ignoring the risk of another collapse, but it was not until cranes were brought in that the bodies of the eight men were discovered.

One of the dead men was Frank Leavy. His eerie prophecy had been fulfilled.

Edward McKevitt had been outside when Curran Hall collapsed and the following day, he told the other firefighters about Leavy's weird premonition at the window. As he told the story, he looked up at the window that

Frank had been cleaning and saw what appeared to be an unusual stain on the glass. It appeared to be in the same spot that Leavy had placed his hand when he made the dire prediction about his own future. McKevitt showed it to the other man and asked whether they thought it could be Leavy's handprint. They tried scrubbing it away and searched for ways to erase the print, but it was no use --- it seemed to be etched into the glass!

WHERE IS IT NOW?
The firehouse is long gone today, and no one seems to have taken a picture of the window while it was standing.

The story began making the rounds and firefighters from all over the city dropped in at the station to see the mysterious handprint. A number of suggestions were made as to how to remove the image, but it refused to come off. Not a single effort, including the use of ammonia and scraping the glass with a razor blade, ever succeeded. At one point, an expert from the Pittsburgh Plate Glass Company brought in a special solution, guaranteeing that it would remove the print, but it didn't work. It only succeeded in making the handprint more famous.

Hoping to dispel the story, a city official visited the station house after obtaining a copy of Frank Leavy's thumbprint. He planned to compare the print with that on the window and prove once and for all that this was only an anomaly and not the handprint of a dead man. Unfortunately for him, his plan failed for when the fingerprint comparison was concluded, it revealed that the two thumbprints matched perfectly. There was no doubt about the fact that the handprint on the window belonged to Frank Leavy.

But what could have caused it? Was it a supernatural occurrence that was left to remind the firemen of their own mortality? Or did the print have a scientific explanation? Some believe that Leavy's fear of a coming tragedy may have caused his body to create a chemical that left a permanent stain behind through his sweat.

No one will ever know for sure, though. The handprint continued to defy all explanation for the next two decades and provided an attraction for visitors to the firehouse. Then, on the morning of April 18, 1944, a careless paperboy tossed the morning edition at the firehouse and shattered the window where Frank's handprint had been. The glass was broken and the shards were scattered about on the ground, destroying not only the strange window but also any hope that the mystery of the handprint would ever be solved.

Even more eerie than the precise throw of an unknowing paperboy was the date on which the broken window occurred. It was April 18, 1944 --- exactly 20 years to the day of when Frank Leavy died!

THE VIRGIN MARY COMES TO CHICAGO

Mysterious visitations from angels, religious visions and the Blessed Mother are nothing new in the history of the world, although most believe that such events ended long ago. This may not be the case though, especially in Chicago, where the Virgin Mary makes regular appearances, where paintings, shrines and relics bleed and ooze and where trees, walls, windows and highway underpasses play host to miraculous forms that entrance the faithful -- and mystify everyone else.

THE QUEEN OF HEAVEN VISITATIONS

Several years ago, Mary also reportedly began appearing to six young people in the war-torn county of Bosnia. The events there have attracted more than 11 million people from over the world. One of the pilgrims who came to Bosnia was Joseph Reinholtz, a retired railroad worker from Hillside. Before journeying to Bosnia, he had been suffering from blurred vision and bouts with blindness. He traveled to the site of the apparitions to meet with one of the young people who had reported experiencing the Blessed Mother. She prayed over Reinholtz in 1987 and after his return to Illinois, his vision slowly returned to normal.

The Miracle Cross in Queen of Heaven Cemetery

Reinholtz returned to Bosnia in 1989 and met with the young woman again. She instructed him that when he returned home, he was to look for a large crucifix that was near a three-branched tree. She told him that this was a place where he was to go and pray. Reinholtz later discovered the location that she described at Queen of Heaven Cemetery in Hillside and he began making frequent visits to the site to pray. His determination was rewarded on August 15, 1990, when he experienced his first visitation from Mary. She returned to him again on November 1 and this time, he claimed, she was accompanied by St. Michael and three angels. Reinholtz spoke widely of what he was experiencing and soon thousands of people began flocking to the large cemetery cross. It wasn't long before complaints about the number of spectators caused the cemetery officials to move the crucifix to another location in 1992. Today, it is quite accessible and the cemetery has placed a paved parking lot next to it.

The visitations, apparitions and bizarre events reportedly continue today and occur every day but Tuesday, which is coincidentally the day of the week that the Archdiocese of Chicago placed a "restriction of obedience" on Reinholtz and asked that he not visit the cemetery. Sadly, Joseph Reinholtz suffered a stroke in February 1995 and was hospitalized, where the Blessed Mother continued to visit him. He passed away in December 1996 but his legacy continues in Queen of Heaven Cemetery, where the crucifix still stands.

Reinholtz has not been the only person to report miraculous visitations at the Queen of Heaven cross. There have been dozens of photographs trhere that purport to show angels and various types of light phenomena. Others claim that they have seen blood dripping from the cross and others have reported the scent of invisible roses in the air.

The site is almost always surrounded by the faithful, who are praying and passing out religious literature. Many "miraculous" photographs have been taken by pilgrims to the site and while some believe they are nothing more than sun glare and bad photography, there is no argument about the importance of these photos in the lives of the believers. No matter what the reader might believe in personally, a visit to Queen of Heaven will convince him that something wonderful is taking place here --- whether it be of this world or another.

OTHER RELIGIOUS VISITATIONS IN THE WINDY CITY

Along with sightings of the Blessed Mother, Chicagoland has also played host to other religious apparitions and few "miraculously" weeping statues and relics. Over the last three decades, there have been more than a dozen religious apparitions and unexplained happenings in the Chicago area. Each of them has attracted dozens, or even hundreds, of believers, skeptics, and news reporters, always on the lookout for an unusual story. The strange items and events have included statues, paintings and icons that appear to weep and bleed, as well as images, shapes and shadows that appear on windows, walls and even tree trunks.

One of the mysterious relics was a painting of the Blessed Mother that was hanging in the St. Nicholas Albanian Orthodox Church in 1986. One day, the painting suddenly began to weep, a phenomenon that continued over the next seven months. During this time, some sort of clear liquid that looked like water dripped from the eyes, and the fingers, of the painting. Hundreds of people came to witness the event but the icon abruptly stopped crying in July 1987. A year later, it began again but the weeping was short-lived this time. During this second incident, the tears produced by the painting were used to anoint 19 other icons in Pennsylvania and all of them began to weep too.

Another painting, this one an inexpensive rendition of Mary and Jesus, reportedly began to weep in April 1987. This one was not located in a church, however, but in the apartment of a retired tailor on West Devon Avenue in Chicago. The event made minor news in the city but still managed to attract crowds to the man's home.

Another barely remembered event took place at St. Adrian's Church on Chicago's South Side in May 1970. According to witnesses, a collection of remains of St. Maximina, which was a 1,700-year-old first-class relic, began to ooze watery blood. The bleeding lasted for a few months and then came to an end without warning.

In June 1984, a wooden statue of the Virgin Mary appeared to shed tears at the St. John of God Catholic Church on the Southwest Side. The Archdiocese of Chicago investigated the phenomenon for more than a year before announcing that it could not positively rule out natural causes for liquid oozing from the wood, despite the wood's age and composition. The faithful were not concerned and continued to gather at the church until the tears eventually came to an end.

Several icons at Apanacio and St. John on the North Side of the city reportedly began weeping in the early 1990s. The icons were stolen by an unknown thief, but were later returned. Once they came back, the tears no longer appeared. The church has since been disbanded.

An icon panel of the Blessed Mother at St. George's Antiochan Orthodox Church in Cicero began weeping oil at the beginning of Holy Week in April 1994. Eight orthodox bishops examined the tears and declared them to be genuine. Mary has continued to cry and the relic has since been renamed Our Lady of Cicero. An Orthodox bishop declared that an event was "an extension of the miracle of Our Lady of Cicero" in Schiller Park in May 1997. The event he referred to was when a tiny paper copy of the St. George Antiochian icon began to ooze oily tears. Moments later, the faithful who had gathered to see it claimed to see a life-sized image of the icon appear on a picture window behind the makeshift shrine that housed it. It was a one-time event but a breathtaking one to those who were present.

In November 1994, the owner of a religious gift store in St. Charles claimed that six plastic statues of Mary bowed their heads after being unpacked from a shipping box and having rosaries placed around their necks.

The Virgin of Guadalupe was said to have visited Hanover Park in July 1997, appearing on the wall of an apartment complex located at 2420 Glendale Terrace. The image appeared from shadows created by a security light that was angled at the building. When the light was turned off, the image vanished, but the faithful remained, convinced that a holy miracle had taken place. Today, at the southwest end of the parking lot, a tent has been erected next to the building where the apparition appeared. The tent contains hundreds of votive candles, offerings, rosaries and a statue of the Blessed Mother.

An image of the Virgin Mary that appeared in the window of a vacant house stopped traffic in Joliet in 1999.

In July 1999, another shadowy image of Mary appeared in Joliet. A young boy was playing in the street on the East Side of the city and looked up to the second story of a vacant house and saw the image in the window. News quickly spread and over the course of the next several weeks, thousands of people jammed tiny Abe Street, blocking traffic and trampling the lawns of those who lived nearby. They came to pray, stare, leave messages and to "soak up the sign from God." The police were forced to set up barricades to keep people on the sidewalks but it did no good and the crowds poured into the streets. The faithful remained here for most of the summer, leaving roses and candles, but not everyone who came was convinced. Most of the skeptical thought that the image looked "more like an owl."

In July 2001, the Blessed Mother dropped in again, this time in Rogers Park. This sighting was unique for Chicago as the Virgin reportedly appeared in an oval-shaped scar in the trunk of a tree. Despite the fact that skeptics insisted that the faithful were merely seeing "whatever they wanted to see," scores of people flocked to an area in the park near the corner of Honore and Rogers avenues and surrounded the tree with candles, rosaries and prayer offerings.

"It's very hard to describe it, but I can feel it's in there," said one man who came to visit the site."

Hundreds flocked to the site after the oddly shaped scar was first seen by a neighborhood woman on July 9. The alleged apparition appeared about 10 feet above the ground, inside the scar on the trunk. The scar looked like a medallion on a chain and the folds in the scar tissue created the image of cloaked person. As the story of the sighting spread, so many onlookers came to the park that Chicago police had to close the street to be able to handle the crowd.

Church officials were cautious about commenting on this most recent apparition. "People want to know 'is it authentic?' The scientific authenticity is not as important as does it cause an authentic response in faith by the people?" said the Rev. Patrick Lagges, vicar for canonical services of the Roman Catholic Archdiocese of Chicago. "We tend to put too much stock in the scientific proof of these things. If we're talking about a miracle, we're talking about something that is not measurable by science but is on the level of faith."

With that said, he sidestepped the suggestion that someone might want to look into the reality of the Virgin Mary in a tree a little more closely. Rev. Lagges added that in most cases where people report seeing the shape of the Virgin Mary in a tree trunk, window or wall, or see tears flow from a statue or picture, "the Archdiocese doesn't start any formal process to investigate them." (This proved to be accurate in the Rogers Park case as well for the church did not investigate the reports)

The Virgin Mary on the shell of a turtle. Not what the faithful have in mind?

He also said that no apparition of the Virgin Mary or incident where an icon or relic appeared to weep has been verified by the Vatican as an "official" miracle. He pointed out the fact that even though the case of Bernadette Soubrious in Lourdes, France, occurred in 1858, she was not declared a saint until 1933. This was even after thousands from all over the world came to seek out the curative waters of the grotto where the girl reportedly encountered Mary. Such events are only declared to be "miracles" after intense investigations and studies have been performed.

And that was not something that was not going to happen with a tree in Rogers Park...

OUR LADY OF THE UNDERPASS

Our Lady of the Underpass in 2005

One of the most recent alleged visitations by the Blessed Mother occurred in April 2005 when hundreds of people began gathering at a Fullerton Avenue underpass on the Kennedy Expressway to witness an image believed to be the Virgin Mary. Thousands who came to see the image quickly turned the spot into a shrine and dubbed the huge water and salt stain, which they believed formed into the shape of the Blessed Mother, "Our Lady of the Underpass." The faithful were convinced that it marked the recent passing of Pope John Paul II and noted that it closely resembled the Virgin of Guadalupe.

Word quickly spread and the image was widely reported on local, then national, news shows and in newspapers all over the country. Believers flocked to the underpass, tying up traffic and creating headaches for state troopers and city police officers. Those who gathered left behind candles, flowers, pictures and tokens, all offered with prayers and tears. Many of the people at the underpass were anxious to touch the image, presumably in the belief that it would bless or cure them, and some held their children out over the police barricades that were erected around the image to touch or kiss the stain.

The Chicago archdioceses had no immediate reaction to the image, due to more pressing issues such as the conclave in the Vatican City at the time to elect a new pope. When he returned from Rome after the funeral of Pope John Paul II and the selection of Pope Benedict XVI, Cardinal Francis George sidestepped the issue of whether the church believed the stain was legitimate. "If it's helpful in reminding people of the Virgin Mary's care and love for us," he said, "that's wonderful."

Within days, there was discussion about the city coming in and either painting over the image or power-washing it off the underpass due to the traffic congestion that it was causing. However, the area was actually under the jurisdiction of the Illinois Department of Transportation and officials there said that there were no plans to remove the image. As it turned out, someone took matters into his own hands.

On the night of May 5, 2005, a man used black shoe polish to scrawl the words "Big Lie" over the stain. Victor Gonzalez of Chicago was quickly arrested and charged with criminal damage to state-supported property. He told relatives that he believed visitors to the site were worshiping a graven image in violation of the Second Commandment. The graffiti did little to discourage the visitors and managed to make them angry instead. The following day, the Chicago police department directed transportation workers to paint over the image with brown paint for "safety reasons." Many of those who had gathered at the site wept as a coat of brown paint was rolled over the stain.

Many of the candles, flowers, pictures and other mementoes were left behind on the spot and as it turned out, this was for the best. Less than a week later, two car wash employees, Rosa Diaz and Anne Reczek, used a degreaser to clean off the wall on their lunch break, removing both the brown paint and the shoe polish that had been used to vandalize the stain. Onlookers were again "blessed" with the image of the Virgin Mary and the site remains intact, as of this writing. A visit to the site today finds fewer of the faithful gathered but it is still regarded as a sacred site.

The miraculous visions and visitations of Chicago are among the greatest oddities of the city and many are torn between belief and disbelief. What do you, the reader, make of these strange, and perhaps wonderful, sightings and experiences? If you are not a believer, you are apt to dismiss them as the fevered imaginings of a religious mind. Perhaps -- or perhaps not -- regardless, we'd prefer to leave that up to you to decide.

THE APPARITIONS AT ST. RITA'S

One of the most bizarre, mysterious, and controversial events ever to ever occur in a Chicago church is said to have taken place at the St. Rita of Cascia Church on All Souls Day, November 2, 1960. To this day, church officials deny that it ever happened and yet first-hand accounts, neighborhood stories and family recollections all insist that it did. The event has sparked debate among the faithful in Chicago for nearly 50 years now and has remained an incident of great interest for supernatural enthusiasts for nearly as long. Did an unexplained event really take place or is the whole thing, as one priest stated, merely "an old wives' tale?"

St. Rita's Church was established in 1905 by the Augustinian Fathers of Pennsylvania, who were invited to construct a church in Chicago by Archbishop James E. Quigley. They broke ground on the church and a college later that same year at 63rd and Oakley Avenue. As the parish grew, a new church was constructed north of 63rd Street, between Fairfield and Washtenaw avenues. The first mass was celebrated in this church in 1923. In 1948, the cornerstone of the present St. Rita's was laid, building over the old site at 63rd and Fairfield. It was in late 1960 that the church's most mysterious event allegedly occurred.

The last days of October and the first days of November are important dates on the calendar of the Catholic Church. Halloween is considered the eve of a holy day, All Saints' Day, when the faithful honor all of the saints of the church. All Souls' Day, November 2, follows, and this is the day when remembrance and prayers are offered for those who have died. It was on this day that a group of 15 to 17 parishioners gathered in the sanctuary of St. Rita's to offer prayers and devotions for their deceased loved ones. In the midst of this, a series of inexplicable events began and while they did not last long, they left an indelible mark on those who were present.

The events began with sounds from the church organ, which was located in a loft over the main doors. The instrument suddenly began to emit shrill tones, even though no fingers had been placed on the keys. The hands of the clock started to spin wildly in opposite directions. The commotion from the organ attracted the attention of those gathered in the church and when they turned in its direction, they were stunned to see six monk-like figures standing on either side of it. Three of the figures wore black robes and three wore white. For some reason that remains unknown to those of us who were not present that day, the parishioners were filled with terror. They scrambled from their seats and began to run toward the doors on the east and west sides of the church. However, when they reached the doors, they were unable to open them. They struggled to get out but the doors refused to budge, as if some invisible force were holding them closed!

Now, paralyzed with fear, the worshippers could only watch as the robed figures began to glide through the air from the organ loft. They settled just above the main floor, passing directly through pews and other solid objects as they traveled toward the front of the building. The organ blared once more and then a strange voice was heard, croaking in a rough whisper. It cried out: "Pray for me!"

Almost immediately, a strong wind blew through the sanctuary and the once-sealed doors burst open. The trapped congregation ran outside, fleeing in fear from the horrific scene.

What happened next remains as much a mystery as the event itself. According to some accounts, the church's pastor, Rev. Clement McHale, met privately with those who shared the bizarre experience and insisted that they not speak about it to anyone -- for the good of the church. Several of the unnerved parishioners were too frightened to even return to the church and the story did not remain a secret for long. In fact, it spread through the close-knit community like wildfire. For months after, few could refrain from talking about the terrifying afternoon at St. Rita's.

But what really happened that day? Supporters have long been split over what occurred, torn between a supernatural manifestation and a prank gone awry. There has been talk of devious altar boys, mass hallucinations brought on by fervent prayer and even the suggestion that the figures were real. Some believe that the day of the event was no coincidence in that some doomed spirit returned to the church to implore the parishioners to pray for his soul. Church officials weren't buying any explanation that reeked of the supernatural, however, and later pastors blamed their predecessors for allowing the story to continue for as long as it has. The late Reverend Francis Fenton grew so tired of the story that he actually denounced it from the pulpit.

But if the event never happened, then how did such a strange story get started in the first place? Was it merely a parable of good and evil (black and white) that became horribly misconstrued, or something else? No one knows, although St. Rita's has remained quiet ever since. There have been no return visits by the puzzling figures and each All Souls Day has passed without incident since 1960 -- making this Chicago mystery all the more mysterious.

THE DEVIL DANCED IN BRIDGEPORT

The town of Bridgeport, which was incorporated into the city of Chicago many years ago, got its start thanks to the building of the Illinois & Michigan Canal. Once the canal was completed, many of the Irish and German workers settled in Bridgeport, creating a thriving immigrant community that spawned not only many Chicago traditions, but a number of the city's mayors, as well.

Along Archer Avenue in Bridgeport in the early 1900s

One of the strangest stories connected to Bridgeport takes place along infamous Archer Avenue, which has long been considered one of the most haunted roadways in the Chicago area. Archer Avenue in Bridgeport passes through a fading collection of buildings that once marked a thriving business district. One building, a towering three-story structure at Archer and McDermott, blends into the background of the other brick and stone edifices here - but this building is different.

It plays host to one of the most famous legends of Bridgeport and has long been home to one of the region's longest-standing tales of diabolical delight. It was here, in the early part of the 20th century that the Devil came to Bridgeport one night!

The old building on Archer Avenue is still known today as Kaiser Hall, although the family who built it has long since passed on. The Kaisers came to Chicago's South Side from Wisconsin and opened the building with a butcher shop on the first floor, apartments on the second floor and a magnificent ballroom on the third. For many years, this third floor ballroom was the hub of community activity and saw frequent parties, neighborhood dances and events.

Tragically, the Kaisers both died young and the hall fell into a state of disrepair. In the 1940s, the ballroom was declared unsafe by the city and was closed down. The huge windows that looked out over Archer Avenue were boarded over and all of the furniture had to be removed from the top floor for safety reasons. The stories say that the grand piano, too heavy to be moved, had to be broken apart with an axe.

For years, the gloomy building was widely believed to be haunted. Reports claimed that the sound of music and dancing could often be heard coming from the abandoned ballroom on the third floor. Often, the sounds of shuffling feet could also be heard accompanying the music, as if some of those neighborhood dances from years gone by were still taking place. Eventually, the haunting began to fade but no one ever forgot the most vivid memory attached to Kaiser Hall --- when they Devil came here to dance.

This supernatural incident is said to have occurred one night during one of the many community dances held at Kaiser Hall. It was a night of laughter, revelry and music, much like

Kaiser Hall

the many others spent here by the young Irish people of the neighborhood. This night was only different because of the appearance of a handsome man that no one seemed to know. The stranger caught the attention of many of the women that night but one of them seemed to be particularly entranced by him. The dashing young man took her out on the dance floor and they spent hours whirling to the sounds of the upbeat fiddle tunes that could be heard for blocks away through the open windows at the front of the hall.

The attractive couple continued to dance, turning and stomping harder and harder, faster and faster until the young woman realized that the room was nothing but a blur. Then, she happened to glance down at her dance partner's flashing feet --- and her cries of pleasure turned to a shriek of horror!

Assuming that the stranger had made an inappropriate advance toward the girl, several of the men from the neighborhood angrily pursued the man, who ran across the room. He refused to fight with them and instead, backed away from their approach toward the large windows that looked out over Archer Avenue. Suddenly, he leapt up onto the window ledge and stepped off into the night. The man stunned everyone in the ballroom by managing to land on his feet three stories below! As the crowd pushed forward to look after him, they discovered him running away. He soon vanished into a dark alleyway between two buildings and that was the last time that he was ever seen.

However, the stranger's story did not end there. The dancers from the ballroom hurried down the staircase and followed the man outside. They soon were shocked again when they discovered the real reason that the young woman had screamed. Pressed into the concrete sidewalk, just where the stranger had landed, they found the unmistakable marks of hoof prints!

Could there be any truth to a story such as this? It may seem hard to believe to the modern reader but there can be no doubt that the story of the night the Devil came to Kaiser Hall has been a part of Bridgeport history of the better part of a century. Is this merely a legend, a piece of supernatural folklore that was told by Irish mothers to warn their daughters about what might happened to them if they got involved with the wrong sort of man? It's possible that this is the case for the stories of the "devil at the fiesta" were a part of Catholic, Mexican-American lore in Texas for many years. Perhaps the story, in a slightly different form, eventually made its way to Catholics in Chicago.

We will likely never know for sure but it certainly seems fitting that such a tale would find its home along the mysterious route of Archer Avenue.

THE MAPLE LAKE SPOOK LIGHT

Maple Lake is a tranquil reservoir that is located at the swampy north end of the Sag Ridge, tucked away in the Cook County Forest Preserve on the Southwest Side. By day, Maple Lake is a widely used recreational area but at night, long after the sun has gone down, it becomes home to one of the most famous "spook lights" in the region.

Stories of spook lights have been with us for centuries. Such a light is best defined as being a luminous phenomenon that, because of the way that it behaves, its location and regular manifestation, it's put into a separate category from ball lightning or from such supernatural phenomena as ghosts. However, most spook lights, especially those that appear regularly over a period of time and in one location tend to take on a supernatural air. Legends tend to grow around them concerning strange deaths and most often, a beheading from which a ghost returns looking for the severed head.

The shores of Maple Lake where the mysterious spook light appears

The spook light is most often said to be the light of a lantern that the spirit carries to assist him in the search.

According to stories, there have long been such lights in America. A book written in 1685 by a Nathaniel Crouch called *The English Empire in America* makes note of a remarkable flame "that appears before the death of an Indian or English upon their wigwams in the dead of night." Native American tales and early settler stories often told of such light appearing as a forewarning of death, perhaps hearkening back to similar tales from the Old World. Those stories told of "corpse candles" that would signify the presence of a spirit left behind by a death.

Spook lights appear in hundreds of places around the country and while most of them have an eerie legend or two attached to their appearance, few explanations can be reached as to why they appear. In the instances when the lights have been thoroughly investigated, the results have been inconclusive at best and at the worst, disappointing. In some cases, the mysterious lights turn out to be nothing more than the headlights of cars on distant highways or reflections of stars and lights that refract though layers of different air temperatures. But that's not always the case...

There are a number of locations where spook lights appear that manage to escape such explanations. These are locations where reports of the lights date back to well before the advent of the automobile and where claims of artificial lights in the distance just don't hold up. These are lights that serious researchers have been unable to debunk. And while it is the opinion of many with an interest in such things that spook lights are a natural part of our world for which we do not yet have an explanation, the most compelling ones still remain unsolved.

The Maple Lake Light is just such an anomaly. And not only is it a mysterious phenomenon, but it's likely that this weird light has less to do with beheadings and ghosts searching for missing body parts and more to do with a tragedy connected to a house that once stood nearby -- or most specifically, with the well that was to serve that house.

The land where Maple Lake now rests was once owned by an Irish immigrant named James Molony. He owned about 80 acres around 95th Street and Wolf Road. Members of the family owned this property from 1850 until it was taken over by the Forest Preserve District around 1920. At that time, the area from Archer Avenue southward was known as Maple Hill, thanks to the large number of sugar maple trees that were found there.

In 1924, the Forest Preserve contracted for the construction of a dam across a deep, narrow ravine that provided an outlet for a number of acres of swampland south of 95th Street and east of Wolf Road. The work was done in conjunction with the Cook County Highway Department, which was paving 95th Street from an intersection on Archer Avenue and up the hill to the east. The area that was submerged because of the dam came to be called Maple Lake.

Swimming became a popular pasttime along the south shore at the west end of Maple Lake. There was a bathhouse once located here, along with restrooms and a concession stand for the public. The biggest concern for some time was that the lake was overpopulated by fish, especially carp and bluegill. Eventually, a fish management program was started and rowboats were rented out to fishermen. In 1939, though, swimming was banned in the lake for reasons pertaining to public health, ending an era at Maple Lake.

In recent times, the lake has continued its appeal to picnickers, hikers, boaters and fishermen. The setting here is quiet and picturesque and offers much for outdoor enthusiasts during the daylight hours. At night, though, things look much different at Maple Lake. The towering trees that are so awe-inspiring during the daytime become foreboding and ominous in the darkness. The vast expanse of the lake, so clear and crystal blue in the sunlight, becomes a vast expanse of blackness after the sun sets.

Despite this eerie setting, there are those who come to Maple Lake after darkness falls. What attracts these nocturnal visitors to the lake are the accounts of the ghost light that is said to appear here. This light appears out over the water between 95th and 107th streets and can most often be seen along the northern edge of the water, across from the Maple Lake Overlook. It is from here that visitors have reported seeing a red light that moves slowly along the shoreline on the far side of the lake. The light is always round and burns a brilliant red. It is often so bright that it casts a glare down onto the water below it.

Debunkers have offered many explanations to disregard this light (and others like it) including swamp gas, foxfire, ball lightning, car lights and even the reflection of streetlights on the water. While swamp gas and foxfire could be possible in a marshy area like this, it seems improbable as the light appears to be red (which is unlike a naturally occurring glow given off by swamp gas) and it moves constantly, which these types of phenomenon never do. Ball lightning is even more difficult to believe as it is very rare and the chances of it occurring in the same spot over and over again during a lengthy period are next to impossible. Street lights reflecting on the water is another explanation that has been suggested, but once again, the light moves under its own power and gives off a reddish glow, which streetlights in the area do not.

The most popular debunking of the phenomenon is the suggestion that the light is nothing more than red taillights from an automobile. And while this seems plausible at first, it becomes less so when you realize that there are no through streets in the direction where the light is seen. The only other through street is 107th and it is on the other side of the ridge that runs between the road and the lake. No taillights could be seen through this wall of dirt and stone.

Ruling out the simple natural and artificial explanations for the spook light, we are now faced with the dilemma of confronting the supernatural. In the case of the Maple Lake lights, familiar legends come into play. The most common of these stories claims that a Native American was beheaded near the lake and is now seen as the ghost light, searching for his missing head. Another variation of the same story claims that the headless ghost is that of an early settler who was attacked and killed by Indians. The strange light is his lantern as he wanders the shoreline in a search for his head. Other explanations offered include the idea that the light is that of a man killed digging the nearby Illinois & Michigan Canal or the victim of gangland violence of the 1920s whose body was dumped nearby.

But in each case, no theory can point to a documented event that has taken place near Maple Lake that can explain the eerie light --- until now.

As mentioned earlier, the land where Maple Lake is now located was once owned by James Molony. He built a house on the property that is now forest preserve land surrounding Maple Lake. His home stood until about 1970 and was used by the Forest Preserve District until it burned down. The foundation is still visible today, just off the Bull Frog Lake parking lot, west of Maple Lake. However, this was not the first site where he planned to build his home. That location is now covered by the lake itself and Molony abandoned the site after a tragic event occurred here in 1858.

According to a 1923 edition of the *Palos in Autumn* magazine, Molony had come from Ireland in the 1850s and had been given the management of a small store that supplied the woodcutters who were clearing the path for the canal. He met, fell in love with and became engaged to a young woman named Ellen Connelly and Molony soon began seeking out a site on which to build a home for himself and his bride. He soon found a pleasant location and purchased it with his savings. A spot was chosen where the house would be built and as the first improvement of the land, Molony began digging a well.

He and the workmen that he hired had gone down about 80 feet but laid off work on the morning of October 8, 1858 to attend the christening of a baby boy named Michael Scanlon who had been born in the neighborhood. Festivities and drinking followed the gathering and during the party, Molony invited several of his friends to inspect his new well.

One of the men, named McGrade, climbed into the bucket that was being used by the workers and asked to be let down into the well. Before he had reached the bottom, he fell out, to the uproarious laughter of his friends. Having had too much to drink himself, John Roach quickly pulled the bucket back up and climbed in to go down and rescue McGrade. He also fell out of the bucket and splashed down into the mud and trickle of water at the bottom of the shaft. The men above called down to the pair below but there was no reply.

Thinking that perhaps his friends had imbibed too much at the christening, Molony pulled up the bucket and started to climb inside. Before he could do so, however, his friend Jim Butler stepped forward and grabbed him by the arm. He warned his friend not to go down, saying, "It might be the damps." The Irishmen was referring to an escape of gases that is sometimes experienced by miners working in swampy land. He offered to climb into the bucket and to call out if he noticed the gases, so the others could pull him back out. Butler stepped into the bucket, his eyes straining to see the men lost in the darkness below and his teeth clenched in case he had to cry out for assistance. He vanished into the shadows but was overcome by gases before he could call for help. Molony and the others pulled frantically on the rope but by the time Butler emerged into the sunlight again, he was dead.

Worried that other friends might still be alive and were somehow down below the area of the shaft where the gas had escaped, the men found a stray dog that roamed the neighborhood and tied him into the bucket. As fast as they could, they lowered the dog to the bottom of the well and then quickly pulled him back out again. But by the time he reached the top, the dog was also dead.

Resigned to the fact that their friends were lost, the men tracked down a heavy rope and a grappling hook and managed to snag and retrieve the bodies of the dead men, one at a time. The women gathered as the men worked late into the night, illuminating the area with candles and oil lamps. At last, by the dim glow of the lights, the corpses were laid out on the ground and a priest came to serve the final rites. The men were then buried a few days later in the cemetery at St. James-Sag Church.

After the horrific loss of his three friends, Molony had the well filled in and he built his house on one of the hills across the basin. He wanted nothing more to do with this cursed piece of ground.

If a paranormal explanation needs be found as to the cause of the Maple Lake spook light, this morbid incident certainly provides us with a real and terrible event that occurred where the light is now seen. Is this light natural or supernatural? None can say with authority but one thing is certain, if history does create modern day hauntings, then Maple Lake certainly has the history to go along with its ghost.

MYSTERY AIRSHIPS OVER CHICAGO

They have been up there since the beginning of recorded time ---- those strange objects that seem to have no explanation for being in the skies over our heads. Every civilization in history has told of things in the sky that create mysteries among the people. These bizarre objects have included burning wheels, fiery objects with wings and, during the late 1800s and early 1900s, mysterious cylindrical shapes that were constructed of weird metals and

shiny steel. Reports of these airships circulated around the country in those days, despite the fact that their construction, and very existence was an impossibility at the time. No aircraft, save for hot air balloons, flew under their own power before the Wright brothers left the ground at Kitty Hawk. So what were these strange ships, who had constructed them and perhaps strangest of all, who was flying them?

Reports of the cylindrical aircraft, which had vast metal wingspans and arrays of bright lights, first appeared in California in 1896. Hundreds of people saw the airships as they began what seemed to be a leisurely eastward tour across America. In addition to the ships, witnesses also reported encounters with the passengers of the airships, which were piloted and likely built, by human beings. They were not your average citizens, though. Most of them carried extraordinary messages to the people on the ground, while others seemed to have superior intelligence, odd skin colors and weird speech patterns.

One of the initial airship sightings took place in Sacramento, Calif., on November 22, 1896. A deputy sheriff named Walter Mallory first spotted a bright, white light in the sky and then noticed that the source was some sort of dark object. The next day, the object was seen in Tacoma, Wash., and in San Jose, Calif. On February 2, 1897, a giant airship was spotted in Nebraska and then on March 27, in Kansas.

The mysterious aircraft arrived in Illinois on April 3. The first sightings were in Evanston and in several other communities near Chicago. The local newspapers quickly spread the news that the airship was filled with "English spies." More than 500 people witnessed the ship when it was said to be in full view for over 45 minutes. One description stated that the airship was "composed of two cigar-shaped bodies attached by girders" and others claimed that it had wings and sails. Still others scoffed at the news. Professor G.W. Hough of the Dearborn Observatory admitted that he didn't even bother to look at the airship when it was over his headquarters in Evanston. He was sure that it was merely the star Alpha Orionis.

The airship reportedly stayed in the Chicago area for three days and was there long enough to be photographed by a newspaper dealer named Walter McCann. He was picking up his daily newspapers at the Northwestern Railway depot when he saw the ship coming toward him from the south. A short time before, his son had won a camera in a contest for getting newspaper subscribers and McCann ran into his store and snatched it up. He ran back outside and snapped a photo of the airship. He then ran down the railroad tracks and took another photo a few minutes later. After the plates were developed, McCann gave copies of the photos to all of the newspapers that requested them but he refused to sell the negatives. The staff artists and the etcher for the Chicago Times-Herald subjected the photos to acid tests and proclaimed them authentic. Sadly, though, the photos have since been lost.

After departing from Chicago, the airship began a tour across Illinois. It was spotted in dozens of cities and there seemed to be no rhyme or reason to its route. It appeared in both northern and southern Illinois, being in one region on one day and the other on the next. For instance, on April 5, it made an appearance in the southwestern Illinois town of Nashville and on April 8 was seen up north in Dixon, Rock Island and Sterling. The craft buzzed over Elgin, Jerseyville, Kankakee, Taylorville, East St. Louis, Edwardsville, Jacksonville, Ottawa, Quincy, Decatur, Lincoln, Hillsboro, Peoria and many other locations. Even if we discount many of the reports as being merely excitement or practical jokes that were generated by newspaper stories, there are still scores of credible and very similar accounts.

Several of the Illinois accounts from April 1897 stand out as even stranger than mere sightings of the airship itself. One of the encounters took place about two miles outside of Springfield, when two farmhands reported that the airship landed in a field where they were working. The occupants of the ship -- two men and one woman -- came out and told the field workers that they would make a report to the government about their journey "when Cuba is declared free." Modern readers who are confused about this should note that this period of history was marked by the Spanish-American War over the issue of Cuban independence. After their bizarre announcement, the occupants of the airship waved to them and climbed back into the craft. It lifted off again into the skies.

The aircraft was seen again near Mt. Vernon a few days after this. The city's mayor was looking at the sky with his telescope when the ship came into range. In addition to the airship, he also claimed to see one of the occupants of the craft hovering in the sky around it. He said that the man had some sort of device strapped to his back that allowed him to fly about and apparently make repairs to his ship.

The airship landed several more times over the next few days in Nilwood, Downs Township and Green Ridge, but the occupants always quickly climbed back aboard and lifted off when they were approached by witnesses. In two of the cases, the passengers were seen checking over some of the machinery on the airship before they departed. Could they have been experiencing some technical difficulties connected to the repairs that were taking place near Mt. Vernon?

How can we explain the mysterious airship that visited Illinois in April 1897? Was it a hoax, a case of mass hysteria? Perhaps, but this seems unlikely based on the unrelated and completely unconnected witnesses who spotted and reported it. Even before the airship was being widely reported in the Chicago area, hundreds of people were seeing it and describing it in almost exactly the same way.

If the ship were real, then who were the passengers? They had strange messages to pass along and seemed to be almost constantly at work on their vessel. During one earlier encounter that took place in Texas, an airship passenger actually asked for help in repairing his craft. He handed the witness current American money and asked him to get supplies from the local hardware store. But how could materials from the 1890s function in the baffling airships?

The mystery remains unsolved. The airship could not have been built by any mechanical means of the time period and yet it apparently existed. The passengers on the ship appeared to be normal humans, taking what seemed to them to be a normal trip, aboard a machine that could not exist - and yet did.

CHICAGO VS. THE FLYING SAUCERS

Aside from the weird airship sightings of 1987, most flying saucer reports from the Chicago area began at the dawn of the modern UFO age in 1947. Long before that time, strange shapes had been seen in the world's skies but it was not until two years after World War II that the public embraced the idea of "watching the skies" for mysterious visitors.

On June 24, 1947, a pilot named Kenneth Arnold told a widely publicized story of seeing nine, shiny objects in the skies over the Cascade Mountains in Washington state. They had flown at an estimated 1,600 miles per hour, in a skipping motion, as saucers would make if they were skipped across the water. The name "flying saucers" caught on and soon it was used by everyone, nearly everywhere, including in Chicago.

The news publisher to make the most out of Arnold's sighting was Ray Palmer of Chicago. He edited a number of pulp magazines like *Amazing Stories* and *Fantastic Adventures* and devoted pages and pages to the public's new interest in UFO's. As it happened, Palmer had his own UFO sighting a few years after he turned his attentions to the phenomenon. It happened on February 3, 1952 when Palmer saw an orange globe that emitted blue flashes speeding past his home at what be estimated to be 180 miles per hour. Palmer spent so much of the rest of his life circulating purportedly true UFO sightings that even he sometimes had trouble believing that he had seen one. Ray Palmer didn't invent the "flying saucer" but he undoubtedly invented the public's perception of it.

Those who saw flying saucers for themselves however, did not need Ray Palmer to convince them of their existence.

On June 25, 1947, Mrs. Nels Thor of South Forest Avenue in Chicago observed what appeared to be a moon-sized disk for 12 minutes as it hovered over Lake Michigan. She said that it glowed yellow and then drifted off into the clouds and vanished. The next morning, a woman named Mrs. J.M. Harrison, also of Chicago, looked out her window and saw a huge ball of fire that broke into two- or three dozen small disks that moved so quickly than an accurate count of them was impossible.

Sightings continued throughout Chicago for the entire summer and while many of the craft differed in size and shape, the majority of the encounters were reported by reputable people, including police officers, real estate salesman and World War II veterans.

Another flap of sightings began in the spring of 1952. On April 26, Victor Root reported seeing a flying disk in the skies over Chicago. On June 29, three Air Force police officers saw a bright silver, flat oval object that hovered in the sky, surrounded by a blue haze. It moved back and forth and up and down and remained within sight for nearly 45 minutes.

On July 3, Mrs. J.D. Arbuckle saw two bright green disks flying straight and level across the Chicago sky. On July 12, a U.S. Air Force captain, a weather officer, saw a red object with white lights on it make a sharp turn in the sky and disappear over the horizon. On August 22, two Air Force jet fighters, directed by ground observers, chased a yellow light over Chicago. It disappeared from sight and from radar at about the time the pilots began to close in on it. The pilots left the area and the UFO returned. It was spotted a few minutes later about 30 miles to the northwest. It hovered, blinked twice and then rose up and out of sight again.

There were dozens of other Chicago area witnesses, including a Mr. Turason, who saw a UFO on September 2. Turason was a radar tracker who worked ground control approach at Midway Airport and saw, during an eight-hour period, 40 different radar targets that were flying in several directions and at speeds up to 175 miles per hour. At one point, two of the objects lined up in formation with a DC-6 airliner.

On December 8, 1952, pilot Ernie Thorpe and his co-pilot, H.S. Plowe, saw a string of five or six white lights, and one blinking red light, flying alongside their plane as they flew over Chicago.

On April 8, 1954, Lelah Stoker saw a white, round-topped disk above Lake Michigan. She claimed that the craft skimmed the water with a human-shaped figure suspended beneath it. She watched as the craft landed and a figure in a green suit got out and walked around. After 30 minutes, it took off and vanished from sight. In August of that same year, a half-moon-shaped UFO was seen darting over Chicago.

On the night of October 3, 1962, Deputy Inspector of Weights and Measures Patrick McAley and his son were sitting outside their Chicago home and watching for a satellite to pass overhead. They looked up and saw a domed object cross in front of the moon. It tipped at an angle and seemed to be floating for a moment and then it disappeared.

U.S. district court reporter J.R. Betz saw three green crescent-shaped objects in the sky over Chicago on May 9, 1964. He stated that they looked to be the size of the half-moon and flew in a tight formation, from east to west, and were only in view for a few seconds before they zipped out of range.

Mrs. L. Drzonek of Bartlett, in the West Chicago suburbs, was driving with her relatives and the family dog on March 7, 1967 when the entire group saw a disk-shaped object descend into a wooded area. It was glowing bright red and Mrs. Drzonek slowed the car for a closer look. As they stared out the windows, they saw that the dog was pressed into the car's back window with his hackles raised in fright. After a few moments, the red glow turned into a brilliant white glare and the disk lifted out of the woods and soared into the sky. The terrified family quickly drove home.

On October 12, 1997, two children and an adult were driving home from a Cubs game in Chicago when they saw a circle of red light in the sky. It moved very fast, stopping, going back in the opposite direction and then hovering in place for about five seconds. Then, for several seconds, a white light came down from the craft and struck the ground. It shimmered for a moment and then the object flew out of sight.

A few weeks later, on November 20, three people driving in a rural area south of Chicago saw a fast moving, bright light appear from the northeast. They stopped the car to take a closer look and as they watched, the white light turned blue. It then flew straight upwards until disappeared.

In April 1998, an "invasion" began in northern Illinois. A few sightings took place earlier in the year, all in the same vicinity, but none of the earlier encounters were anything like the ones that took place starting on the afternoon of April 4.

The wave of sightings began in Bedford Park when a man left work and walked out his place of business to see a green shape, with a white trail behind it, streaking through the sky overhead. It soared past for some distance and then disappeared. Later on the next evening, at about 9:35, the same witness again saw the object while taking a walk with a friend. It headed west and then vanished again.

Two hours later, a student in Channahon saw a much different object. He had just left a friend's house, and dropped another friend off at his home, and then was driving alone when he saw three lights appear in the sky. The lights seemed to be hovering over a farm field and as he rounded a curve in the road to the right, he lost sight of them behind some trees. As he passed by a stand of woods, he saw the lights again and realized they were part of some sort of diamond-shaped aircraft. The ship was hovering over a local rock quarry. The UFO rotated clockwise and then it banked and turned, moving in the direction of the student's car. As it came closer to him, he sped off down the winding road, only to look back and see that the ship was keeping pace with him, flying alongside the roadway.

The road curved and he lost it in the trees again but a few moments later, as he stopped to turn left onto U.S. Route 6, he saw the lights were still with him. The UFO had banked so that the bottom of the aircraft was turned in the direction of the car. The student punched the accelerator and drove at high speed for several minutes without looking back. When he finally dared to look in the rearview mirror, the object had vanished.

On April 14, another bizarre encounter took place in Texico around 9:30 p.m. A woman and her two children were driving home when they spotted a bright light in the sky. It seemed to follow their automobile, growing brighter as they got closer to home. As they turned into their driveway and stopped, the object slowly passed over them. It traveled southward and then turned to the west, moving about another mile before it was lost from sight. The entire family, including the woman's husband, who had been alerted to the UFO when they pulled into the driveway, described it as being boomerang-shaped with numerous red, blue and white lights on the bottom of it. The ship itself was very dark in color, with no shine, and it moved with absolutely no sound whatsoever.

Four days later, in Glenview, a group of children saw another (or perhaps the same?) triangular craft. They stated that it was dark in color and had three white light lights at each corner. These lights were surrounded by smaller, orange lights. The ship hovered for a few moments and then sped off in a white blur.

Another sighting took place in Manito on April 25. Around 9:00 p.m., three friends saw a light, which broke into two disks. The disks then merged again and split into three disks. They merged once more and then disappeared with a white flash and a loud "shrieking" noise. A short time later, on May 6, the things in the sky came back to Manito. Two UFO's were spotted two miles north of town and then were seen again in the early morning hours of May 7.

On May 10, an observer saw a bright, circle-shaped object in the sky above Carpentersville. The disk was very bright and was able to reverse course very quickly, smoothly moving in opposite directions.

At 10:12 p.m. on the following day, a retired Illinois State Police officer and a licensed practical nurse were watching the sky outside of South Holland. They were not looking for UFO's but, rather, were watching the full moon. As they were sitting and relaxing, they saw four disk-shaped objects traveling in a V formation in a northeasterly direction. The objects gave off a slight glow and traveled in silence at an estimated 300 to 400 miles per hour. The witnesses saw the objects for about 30 seconds, until the reached the shoreline of Lake Michigan. As they flew out over the water, the lights changed course and disappeared from view.

On May 12, a man driving home through a heavy rainstorm in Chebanse spotted a light in the sky. The glowing ball flashed on for two or three seconds and then went out. The driver assumed that perhaps a plane had been struck by lightning and was concerned until he got home and his wife told him about a disk-shaped object that she had seen in the sky several minutes earlier. It had been in the same direction that her husband had been coming from and she described it as a bright flash and then a dark object with small lights on the bottom. It moved back and forth along the trees next to their house and then blinked out.

Two cousins who were camping in a barnyard near Woodstock spotted a large, green object in the sky on the night of May 30. They were talking and enjoying the evening and happened to see the light appear in the sky. When they saw the greenish glow emerge from the clouds, both of the boys panicked and ran for the nearby house. As they ran, the object sped away, leaving a yellow streak behind it. Moments later, the light appeared again, illuminating the entire yard and house. The UFO hovered for a few moments and then shot off into the sky again.

This brought an end to the spring "invasion" but the UFO's returned again in July. Sightings occurred in Round Lake Beach, over Chicago, and near Tinley Park before fading away again.

On March 11, 1999, the crew of an airliner that was coming into Chicago was allegedly burned by a UFO. Around 9:00 p.m., the pilot and co-pilot were watching a display of what they thought were the northern lights. As they began to prepare for landing, they were amazed to see the lights started to "stretch above and over the aircraft." There was a short pulse of green light and then the light turned into a bright ball, which approached the plane from the north, moving fast. According to later reports, the members of the cockpit crew began to experience a hot and tingling sensation on their faces as if they had been sunburned. As soon as the green light had vanished though, the burning sensation went with it. The next morning however, at least one of the crewmembers noticed that his skin was red and sore and arranged to see a doctor about his burns.

A few nights later, on March 19, another UFO was reported by a driver who was heading north from the Chicago area on Route 53. He spotted an object in the sky, moving fast, and first assumed that it must be an airplane thanks to the number of airports in the surrounding region. When the craft abruptly stopped and started zipping back in the opposite direction however, he knew that it was no ordinary aircraft. The object, which looked to be a silver-colored sphere, headed straight upward and vanished from his sight.

With each passing year, more and more UFO's are reported in the Chicago area. These reports were merely a sampling of the strange events that have occurred and there are literally hundreds of others. As strange and as bizarre as these have been however, there was at least one other UFO event that occurred in Chicago that was more dramatic -- and definitely much stranger --- than the rest of the others combined.

THE O'HARE AIRPORT UFO

One of the most recently reported UFO sightings in Chicago, and one of the most fascinating, occurred at O'Hare International Airport on Tuesday, November 7, 2006. At approximately 4:15 p.m., the Federal Aviation Administration (FAA) received strange reports from 12 employees of United Airlines. The ground crew of United Airlines was prepping flight 446 from Chicago to Charlotte, N.C., when a member of the ground crew and then the pilot, co-pilot and several others, spotted a spinning silver disc-shaped object hovering above gate C-17. The object stayed hovering at around 1,800 feet for nearly two minutes and then suddenly shot straight up through the clouds, allegedly leaving a huge gaping hole in the clouds that closed up after a few minutes. Although no one had any photographic evidence of the sighting, it was rumored that one of the pilots may have gotten off some shots with his digital camera. A minimum of 12 people (but quite possibly many more) witnessed the phenomena.

An article about this event was written on January 1, 2007 by John Hilkevitch of the *Chicago Tribune*. When questioned about the validity of what the people had witnessed, United Airlines and the FAA initially denied that anything out of the ordinary happened at O'Hare on that day. They maintained this story until the Chicago Tribune filed a Freedom Of Information Act request. Both the authorities at United Airlines and the FAA quickly reversed their previous statements when the FAA reviewed the control tower transmissions between a United Airlines supervisor and an FAA official about a "flying saucer" above gates C-17 and B-4.

Some reports made it to the mainstream media. They treated it like a fluff piece and made jokes, but shortly after the Freedom of Information Act request was filed by the *Tribune*, rumors about pictures and eyewitness interviews started coming out.

United Airlines employees allegedly had their jobs threatened if they continued to speak about the event and much was done by a variety of government agencies to stonewall any journalistic investigation into the matter. The official FAA stance had changed to explain that an unnamed "weather phenomenon" had caused the entire stir. United Airlines still says that nothing out of the ordinary happened at O'Hare.

Of course, those who saw the UFO say otherwise. Shortly after the event took place, an anonymous United Airlines employee posted a comment on the message board of the UFO website **www.abovetopsecret.com** He wrote:

> *I work for United like you guessed by now.*
>
> *We were ferrying a load of late bags for a 727 to F12 or 14, I don't remember now, when I saw what I thought was a widebody running off course out of the corner of my eye. When I looked up there it was just sitting there, a gray shiny thing pretty high up, more than 1000 feet.*
>
> *At first we thought it was really far away, because it was hard to focus on it, but it shifted left and right a couple times and that's when we knew it wasn't too far away. I looked up at the 727 cockpit and pointed to it then the crew saw it and was staring at it too. The pilot got on his radio and waving his arms like he was going nuts over what he was seeing. We figured it was a fat disc, like a M & M, about 20 feet wide but it was really hard to tell for sure because it was almost the same color as the clouds and if you looked away it was hard to find it and focus again. One of our crew ran to his locker to get his cell phone to take a picture.*
>
> *It hung there moving really slightly from side to side for about another minute when we all felt our hair stand on end, and it just shot straight up into the clouds faster than anything we ever seen. It disturbed the clouds, like it made a big shockwave and we could see sunlight for a bit. We never got a picture but I don't think it would have come out very good anyway.*
>
> *We could see a few other rats staring up at the hole and everyone was talking about it for a few days. Then the sups came and talked to all of us that we can't talk about this to anyone or we'd get fired. They said something about federal regulations and unauthorized reporting of false airspace breeches.*
>
> *Last week, the sups came down again and reminded everyone about the regulations. That's what made me think there's more to the story so I started searching online. I play pool with a buddy who told me about this website chat room so here I am.*
>
> *I always thought people who believe in aliens were crazy but I don't know what that thing was. We see lots of aircraft come in even the fancy stuff that stays in the air when the President lands, but this thing was like nothing none of us ever saw.*

ADAM SAYS:
While "weather phenomenon" strikes me as an even lamer excuse than the old reliable line about "swamp gas," I do like the phrase offered by union worker Craig Burzych: "To fly seven and a half million miles to O'Hare and then have to turn around and go home because your gate is occupied is simply unacceptable!" Why wouldn't they stick around? Were there no hillbillies who looked like good probe targets at the airport that day?

What really happened at O'Hare that day? No one can say for sure and, officially, no one is talking. Off the record, though, it seems pretty clear that something appeared in the sky over the airport and it was seen by both crewmembers and pilots for United Airlines - a group with absolutely no reason to lie about what they saw. Rumor has it that "Ghostbuster" Dan Akroyd (who is fascinated with the occult and UFOs, and is thought to be the only person who has actually seen the ghost rumored to haunt the U-505 WW II German submarine at the Museum of Science and Industry) plans to make a film about the O'Hare UFO event.

CHICAGO KANGAROOS

Although literally thousands of miles from their native habitat, reports of mysterious kangaroos were surprisingly widespread in Chicago in the 1970s. Strangely, there are sketchy records of kangaroos, or "hopping monkeys," in the Midwest that date back many years. However, it would not be until the middle 1970s that "kangaroo mania" would come to Chicago.

The event that started the Illinois kangaroo flap occurred in the early morning hours of October 18, 1974, when two Chicago police officers answered a call from a resident on the Northwest Side of the city. According to the caller, he claimed that a kangaroo was sitting on his front porch, peering into the window.

> If you see a kangaroo on your porch, call animal control at once. Do not try to box with it. The kangaroo will win!

Not surprisingly, the peculiar call was received with a good laugh by radio dispatchers, but it didn't seem so funny a few hours later when two officers who investigated the report had the five-foot high animal cornered in a dark alley. Patrolmen Leonard Ciagi and Michael Byrne approached the growling animal with caution and inexplicably thought that it would be a good idea to try and put handcuffs on it. Byrne gave this a try and the kangaroo suddenly started screeching and became vicious. It began punching the officers in the face and kicking them in the shins. Understandably, the officers backed away and short of using their guns, found that they had no way to subdue or capture the animal. A minute or two later, additional squad cars arrived and the kangaroo took off at high speed. It cleared a fence and vanished into the darkness, leaving some puzzled officers with sore shins behind.

The incident made the newspapers and became the first in a rash of sightings. Reports began to flood in from all over the Chicago area. On the same afternoon as the officer's early morning encounter, a four-and-a-half foot tall kangaroo was reported hopping down the street in Oak Park. The next afternoon, October 19, a young man who was delivering papers in the morning heard the screech of car brakes behind him. He turned to look and see what the trouble was and saw a kangaroo hopping across the intersection of Sunnyside and Mulligan streets. "He looked at me, I looked at him, and away he hopped," Kenneth Grieshamer recalled.

About an hour later, the kangaroo was reported again near Austin and Eastwood roads and later that evening, an anonymous call to the Chicago Police Department pinpointed the mysterious animal around Belmont and Mango avenues. The following morning, police dispatchers fielded a number of calls from concerned residents who had seen the kangaroo rummaging through their garbage cans.

On October 23, a kangaroo was seen roaming through Schiller Woods, near Irving Park Road, and this was the last sighting until November. For a short time, things stayed quiet in Chicago. The next sighting occurred on November 1 in Plano, west of the city. John Orr, an off-duty police officer, spotted the kangaroo on Riverview Road, just outside of town. The animal jumped about eight feet from the edge of a cornfield and landed in the middle of the road, directly in the headlights of Orr's car. "I'm positive that

THE LAKE MICHIGAN "SEA MONSTER"

At one point in the 1800s, Lake Michigan claimed to have a mystery inhabitant to rival the monsters of Loch Ness and various other bodies of water where long-necked beasts were believed to dwell. Hundreds of witnesses apparently observed the creature from both shore and from the water and an August 1867 issue of the Chicago Tribune even asserted, "that Lake Michigan is inhabited by a vast monster, part fish and part serpent, no longer admits of doubt."

The newspaper reported the crews of the tugboat, the *George S. Wood*, and the propeller boat, the Skylark, spotted the creature moving through the water just off Evanston. The crews reported that the monster was between 40 and 50 feet long, had a neck as thick as a person's and a body that was as big around as a barrel. A few days later, on August 6, a fisherman named Joseph Muhike had encountered the same, or a nearly identical, beast about a mile and a half from the Hyde Park section of Chicago.

The creature was seen off and on over the course of the next century but the sightings eventually dropped off and nothing has been heard from the "Lake Michigan Monster" in many years.

I saw him," Orr stated. "People don't believe you when you see things like that but I definitely know that it was a kangaroo. If I hadn't slowed down, I would have hit him. My cousin was in the car behind me and when she saw him, she just plain ran off the road." After pausing for a moment in front of the vehicles, the kangaroo hopped off into a wooded area and disappeared.

The next night, November 2, three young men named Jerry Wagner, Steve Morton and Shawnee Clark, were driving along Shafer Road in Plano when their headlights illuminated something in the middle of the road. As they swerved to the side, all of them got a good look at it and realized that it was a full-grown kangaroo. Startled, the animal hopped over a five-foot fence and took off into the woods. "I never believed the stories about people seeing a kangaroo around here," Jerry Wagner said the next morning, "but I do now."

After the sighting, the three men reported it to the Kendall County Sheriff's Office and at the same time, a similar incident was taking place with the same, or an identical kangaroo, about 50 miles away from Plano and back in Chicago.

A young couple named Cathy Battaglia and Len Zeglicz were out for a walk around 9:30 p.m. and spotted a strange creature hunched on the side of South New England Avenue. At first they thought it was a dog but when the animal turned and looked at them, and then rose up and hopped away, they realized they were looking at a kangaroo. Since it seems unlikely that a kangaroo could travel more than 50 miles in only a few minutes, one has to wonder just how many kangaroos were hopping around the Chicago area in November 1974?

On the morning of November 3, the kangaroo, or one like it, was spotted by Frank Kocherver near a forest preserve on Chicago's Northwest side.

The next day, November 4, a truck driver saw a deer and what he thought was a kangaroo near Plano. The driver pulled his rig over to the side of the road and followed the animal tracks into the woods. He easily recognized the trail left by the deer but the other animal was "definitely not a deer." The driver was sure the strange tracks belonged to a kangaroo.

The last Illinois sighting for 1974 occurred near Lansing when a truck driver was forced to swerve off the highway to avoid hitting one of the errant creatures. After a few more sightings in Indiana, kangaroos disappeared off the radar and the kangaroo flap of the 1970s came to an end in Chicago. However, this doesn't mean that the mysterious creatures have disappeared from the area for good. No one ever knew where the kangaroos came from, or where they went to ---- or when they might be back.

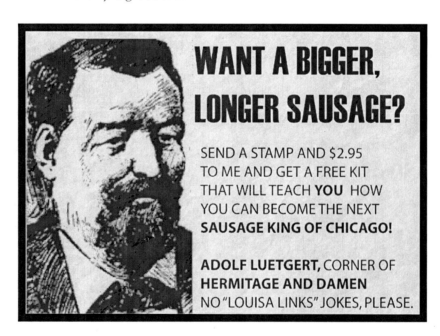

9. WEIRD CHICAGO GRAVEYARDS

Remember me as you pass by
As you are now, so once was I
As I am now, so you must be
Prepare for death and follow me
Early American Epitaph

I told you I was sick.
Epitaph of B.P. Roberts - Key West, Florida

The city of Chicago can boast some of the most beautiful cemeteries in the Midwest, and perhaps America. Those readers who have been fortunate enough to visit either Graceland or Rosehill Cemetery can attest to the glory of the open expanses, the shaded walkways and the incredible artwork that went into creating the monuments to the dead that cover the grounds. But it wasn't always this way; for years ago, cemeteries were a hellish and often frightening place.

Death, as they say, is the final darkness at the end of life. It has been both feared and worshipped since the beginnings of history. For this reason, our civilization has dreamed up countless practices and rituals to deal with and perhaps understand it. We have even personified this great unknown with a semi-human figure, the "Grim Reaper," and have given him a menacing scythe to harvest human souls with. Yet, death remains a mystery.

Maybe because of this mystery, we have chosen to immortalize death with stones and markers that tell about the people who are buried beneath them. We take the bodies of those whose spirits have departed and place them in the ground, or in the enclosure of the tomb, and place a monument over these remains that speaks of the life once lived. This is not only out of respect for the dead because it also serves as a reminder for the living. It reminds us of the person who has died -- and it also reminds us that someday, it will be our bodies that lie moldering below the earth.

The stone monuments became cemeteries, or repositories of the dead, where the living could come and feel some small connection with the one that passed on. The earliest of the modern cemeteries, or what is referred to as a "garden" cemetery, began in Europe in the 1800s.

Before the beginning of the garden cemetery, the dead were buried strictly in the churchyards of Europe. It soon became nearly impossible for the churchyards to hold the bodies of the dead. As towns and cities swelled in population during the 1700s, a chronic shortage of space began to develop. The first solution to the problem was simply to pack the coffins more closely together. Later on, coffins were stacked atop one another and the earth rose to the extent that some churchyards rose twenty feet or more above that of the church floor. Another solution was to grant only limited occupation of a gravesite. However, it actually got to the point that occupancy of a plot was measured in days, or even hours, before the coffin was removed and another was put in its place.

It became impossible for the churchyards to hold the dead and by the mid-1700s, the situation had reached crisis proportions in France. Walls of stone and dirt had been added around the graveyards in an attempt to hold back the bodies but they often collapsed, leaving human remains scattered about the streets of Paris. The government was finally forced into taking action. In 1786, it was decided to remove all of the bodies from the Cemetery of the Innocents and transport them to catacombs that had been carved beneath the southern part of the city. It was a massive undertaking. There was no way to identify the individual remains, so it was decided to arrange the bones into rows of skulls, femurs and so on. It has been estimated that the Paris catacombs contain the bodies of between 3 and 6 million people.

In addition to the catacombs, four cemeteries were built within the confines of the city. One of them Pere-Lachaise has become known as the first of the "garden" cemeteries. It was named after the confessor priest of Louis XIV and is probably the most celebrated burial ground in the world. Today, the walls of this graveyard hold the bodies of the most illustrious people in France and a number of other celebrities as well. The dead include Balzac, Victor Hugo, Colette, Marcel Proust, Chopin, Oscar Wilde, Sarah Bernhardt and Jim Morrison of the Doors (if you believe he's dead, that is).

Pere-Lachaise became known around the world for its size and beauty. It covered hundreds of acres and was landscaped and fashioned with pathways for carriages. It reflected the new creative age where art and nature could combine to celebrate the lives of those buried there. Paris set the standard and America slowly followed. In this country, the churchyard remained the most common burial place through the end of the 1800s. While these spots are regarded as picturesque today, years ago, they varied little from their European counterparts.

After the founding of the Pere-Lachaise Cemetery in Paris, the movement toward creating "garden" cemeteries spread to America. The first of these was Mount Auburn Cemetery in Cambridge, Massachusetts, which was consecrated in 1831. It was planned as an "oasis" on the outskirts of the city and defined a new romantic kind of cemetery with winding paths and a forested setting. It was the opposite of the crowded churchyard and it became an immediate success, giving rise to many other similar burial grounds in cities across the country. In fact, they became so popular that they served as not only burial grounds, but as public recreation areas as well. Here, people could enjoy the shaded walkways and even picnic on weekend afternoons. The garden cemetery would go on to inspire the American Park movement and virtually create the field of landscape architecture.

The idea of the garden cemetery spread across America and by the early 1900s was the perfect answer to the old, overcrowded burial grounds. Many of these early cemeteries had been established close to the center of town and were soon in the way of urban growth. Small towns and large ones across the country were soon hurrying to move the graves of those buried in years past to the new cemeteries, which were always located outside of town.

THE VANISHING CITY CEMETERY

Lincoln Park today was once the site of Chicago's City Cemetery

In Chicago, one burial ground actually created several garden cemeteries, and they came about thanks to the closure of the old Chicago City Cemetery around 1870. The City Cemetery was located exactly where Chicago's Lincoln Park is located today. Before its establishment, most of the early pioneers simply buried their dead out in the back yard, leading to many gruesome discoveries as the downtown was developed years later. Two cemeteries were later set aside for both Protestants and Catholics, but both of them were located along the lake shore, leading to the frequent unearthing of caskets whenever the water was high. Finally, the city set aside land at Clark Street and North Avenue for the Chicago City Cemetery. Soon, many of the bodies were moved from the other sites to this central and often troubling one.

Within 10 years of the opening of the cemetery, it became the subject of much criticism. Not only was it severely overcrowded from both population growth and cholera epidemics, but many also felt that poorly carried out burials here were creating health problems and contaminating the water supply. To make matters worse, both the city morgue and the local Pest House, a quarantine building for epidemic victims, were located on the cemetery grounds. Soon, local families and churches were moving their loved ones to burial grounds

For FAR more information on City Cemetery, see Pamela Bannos' web page at http://hiddentruths.northwestern.edu

considered safer and the City Cemetery was closed down in 1859. Little was done to enforce this prohibition, however, until 1866, when a final ban was put in place against more burials.

This ended the practice of the dead being carried to the City Cemetery, but the removal of bodies to other spots was a slow process. Monuments and slabs had to be moved, too, and the owners of lots had to have an exchange with lots in other cemeteries and some of those who wished to sell held out for high prices. This further prolonged the process and distressed the city planners, who hoped to turn the former cemetery into a park. One account describes the area at that time: "We saw countless open graves," wrote Mrs. Joseph T. Bowen, "with a piece here and there of a decayed coffin... the whole place looked exactly as if the Judgment Day had come."

Even forty years after the cemetery was moved, plenty of traces remained, including an empty tomb that was still in use as a tool shed. Today, the shed is gone, and only a couple of traces - the Couch Tomb (see next chapter), the boulder said to mark the burial place of David Kennison (see the Weird Chicago People chapter), which was placed there decades after the cemetery had closed. And of course the bodies.

Chicago has a long history of moving gravestones, but not the bodies buried beneath them. While all of the grave markers except for the Couch Tomb were moved from City Cemetery, countless sets of remains are still beneath the ground at Lincoln Park. Just how many former Chicagoans were never moved to new resting places remains a mystery but estimates range as high as 20,000. When the Chicago Historical Society dug out space for a new parking area on the south end of the park in 1998, eighty-one partial skeletons were uncovered, including an elaborate metallic coffin made by the Fisk Company that apparently contained a very well-preserved corpse. Digging of any sort - such as for water lines or sewers - in the area that was once City Cemetery (or the pauper's cemetery located directly south of it) tends to result in some unpleasant surprises.

THE COUCH TOMB:
THE MAUSOLEUM IN LINCOLN PARK

The Couch Tomb, built for Ira Couch in 1858, still stands in South Lincoln Park, right behind the Chicago Historical Society. It can easily be viewed when driving down Clark Street, North Avenue, or when taking the LaSalle Street exit off of Lake Shore Drive. It is one of the last standing reminders (above the ground, anyway) that the area now known as Lincoln Park was once the old City Cemetery.

There are two mysteries relating to it: why wasn't it moved when the other monuments of City Cemetery were moved -- and, more importantly, who's buried in Ira Couch's tomb?

That's a bit of a trick question. The Couch Mausoleum is an aboveground crypt, so nobody's technically buried in it (a bit of Weird Chicago humor.) But the question remains -- who's in there?

The Couch Mausoleum in 1903

Contrary to a rumor that's been going around, Ira Couch, the man for whom the crypt was built, is definitely interred in the crypt that bears his name. But who's in there WITH him, if anyone, and exactly why the crypt is still there to begin with, are a couple of the city's more enduring mysteries.

Ira Couch came to Chicago with his brother James in 1836 and opened a tailor shop in what would eventually be the Loop. Just a year later they opened the Tremont House, one of the city's first hotels. It was burned and rebuilt a couple of times, most notably in 1850, when they built an enormous version at Dearborn and Lake which came to be

known as "Couch's Folly" by people who thought he was wasting his money. The five-and-a-half story structure cost $75,000 to build. That version, though, was arguably the finest hotel in the city before it burned to the ground in the Great Fire of 1871. By then, Abraham Lincoln had spoken from the hotel's balconies, and John Wilkes Booth had maintained apartments there. After the fire, it was rebuilt yet again by James, who by this time was considered one of the city's great pioneers.

The Couch Tomb was built in 1858 by James Couch after Ira died in Cuba. It was designed by architects Osdell and Baumann and was constructed from 50 tons of stone imported from Lockport, N.Y. The cover alone required a team of eight horses to transport it through the city. The vault, which cost $7,000 to construct, contained a semi-circular opening in the center with niches for 11 bodies closed by marble slabs intended for inscriptions. When it was put in place in what was then City Cemetery, it was probably the finest tomb ever constructed in Chicago.

Stories as to why it remained in place after the City Cemetery was moved abound. Some reports have stated that it was the result of a "gentleman's agreement" between the Couch family and the Park District board members. Still others say that the family sued the city to keep it there, but no record of this has ever turned up. A variation on this story states that the Supreme Court had ruled that burial plots belonged to the dead, not the living, which prevented the city from moving the crypt. Most likely, though, it was kept in place due to the cost of moving it. Newspapers in 1877 reported that the city fathers let it stay after masons estimated that moving it to Rosehill Cemetery would cost the princely sum of $3,000, which was considered too much of an expense.

When James Couch died after stepping in front of a train at the age of 92 in 1892, the Couch family are said to have fought for -- and received -- permission to place his body in the vault along with his brother. However, according to an article written a few years later, the family found that the door was rusted shut, leaving it impossible for it to be opened without using dynamite. The family ended up burying James at Rose Hill.

By this time, there were already conflicting reports as to who, exactly, was inside the crypt. Records had been lost ages before, and the people who would have known for sure were dead. Stories and estimates vary. Some say that Ira Couch is the only person inside. Others, in the early 1900s, said that it was Ira and his father. As of the mid-20th century, descendants of the Couch family believed that there were seven people interred there -- Ira Couch, Ira Couch's father, wife, and children, and one person who was not related to them at all. They were certainly mistaken about Ira's wife, who is buried in Rose Hill, but the story that a non-relative is in the tomb is usually taken to be fact. Some have said that the extra person was a stranger who died at the Tremont House, but the more likely story is that it is a child of William H. Wood. According to old reports, Wood was married to Ira's sister-in-law, and, when one of their children died young, Mrs. Couch requested that the body be interred in the family crypt.

After nearly a century of neglect, by the late 20th century, the tomb was overgrown with bushes and surrounded by garbage. In the late 1990s, a massive renovation project was undertaken to clean up the site and rebuild the fence that had once stood around it. After the tomb was cleand up, it was even illuminated at night. The cost of the renovation was estimated to be over $100,000 - far more than the cost of moving it would have been in the first place! However, many felt it was well worth the cost to restore the oldest structure still standing in the region devasted by the Great Fire of 1871, a designation which seems to hold much more historic importance today than it would have in the 1870s.

But no one, throughout the renovation, seems to have attempted to get inside and find out, once and for all, who's interred in Ira Couch's tomb.

TALES OF GRACELAND CEMETERY

Graceland Cemetery came about because of the closure of the Old City Cemetery. The cemetery was started in 1860 by real estate developer Thomas B. Bryan and it was located far away from the city proper along North Clark Street. Over the years, a number of different architects have worked to preserve the natural setting of its 120 acres. Two of the men largely responsible for the beauty of the place were architect William Le Baron Jenney and another architect named Ossian Cole Simonds, who became so fascinated with the site that he ended up turning his entire business to landscape design. In addition to the natural setting, the cemetery boasts a number of wonderful monuments and buildings, including the cemetery chapel, which holds city's oldest crematorium, built in 1893.

There are a number of Chicago notables buried in Graceland, including John Kinzie; Marshall Field; Phillip Armour; George Pullman; Potter Palmer; Allan Pinkerton; Vincent Starrett, writer and creator of the Chicago chapter of the "Baker Street Irregulars," a group of Sherlock Holmes enthusiasts; architect Louis Sullivan, and many others.

Graceland is home to several different tales of the supernatural, including the ominous "haunted" monument that graces the final resting place of former hotel owner and businessman Dexter Graves. Created by Lorado Taft, the artist christened the design "Eternal Silence," but the brooding and menacing figure has become more commonly known as the "Statue of Death." The figure was once black in color but over the years, the black has mostly worn away, exposing the green, weathered metal beneath. Only one portion of it remains darkened and that is the face, which is hidden in the deepest folds of the figure's robe. It gives the impression that the menacing face is hidden in shadow and the look of the image has given birth to several legends. It is said that anyone who looks into the face of the statue will get a glimpse of his or her own death to come. In addition, it is said that the statue is impossible to photograph and that no camera will function in its presence. Needless to say, though, scores of photos exist of the figure, so

Eternal Silence, a.k.a. "Statue of Death". Impossible to photograph? Apparently not!

most people scoff at the threats of doom and death that have long been associated with "Eternal Silence."

But without a doubt, the most famous "haunted" sculpture of Graceland Cemetery is that of Inez Clarke.

According to local legend, Inez died in 1880 at the tender age of 6. Tradition has it that she was killed during a lightning storm while on a family picnic. Her parents, stunned by the tragic loss, commissioned a life-size statue of the girl to be placed on her grave. It was completed a year later, and like many Chicago area grave sculptures, was placed in a glass box to protect it from the elements. The image remains in nearly perfect condition today. Even in death, Inez still manages to charm cemetery visitors, who discover the little girl perched on a small stool. The likeness was cast so that Inez is seen wearing her favorite dress and carrying a tiny parasol. The perfectly formed face was created with just the hint of a smile. It is not uncommon to come to the cemetery and find gifts of flowers and toys at the foot of her grave. The site has become one of the most popular places in the cemetery, for graveyard buffs and curiosity seekers alike.

The stories say that the area around Inez Clarke's resting place is haunted. Not only are there stories of strange sounds heard nearby, but some claim the statue of Inez actually moves under its own power. The most disconcerting stories may be those of the disembodied weeping that is heard nearby, but the most famous tales are those of the statue itself. It is said that Inez will sometimes vanish from inside the glass box. This is said to take place during violent thunderstorms. Many years ago, a night watchman for the Pinkerton agency allegedly stated that he was making his rounds one night during a storm and discovered that the box that holds Inez was empty. He left the cemetery that night, never to return. Other guards have also reported it missing, only to find it back in place when they pass by again, or the following morning.

There are other tales that claim visitors to Graceland spot a little

The statue of "Inez Clarke"

girl playing in the cemetery. In other cases, children who accompany their parents to the burial ground have stated that they have met a little girl wearing old-fashioned clothes playing near the monument.

Of course, there is only one problem with these stories and accounts: no one named Inez Clarke is even buried in Graceland Cemetery! According to cemetery expert Al Walavich, there might have never been an Inez Clarke at all! One thing that he can state for sure: "Based on cemetery records there's no such person buried in that grave". He has also looked up U.S. Census records from the time and has found no indication that the child even existed.

Walavich also found a letter dated in 1910 from the woman who was supposed to have been Inez's mother that stated that the Clarkes had two daughters, both of whom were still living at the time. Perhaps the most damning bit of evidence against the existence of Inez Clarke is correspondence between the family and the cemetery, where the Clarkes were asked about the statue and the grave. They had no idea who Inez might be but noted that, "it was a lovely statue." Cemetery records show that an 8-year-old boy named Amos Briggs is buried at the site marked by the eerie monument.

So, why would the statue be placed at Graceland? Walavich believes that it may have served as an advertisement for a Scottish monument maker named Andrew Gage, who completed the statue in 1881. It may have been placed in a section of the cemetery that was particularly active at the time and was simply never removed, thus creating the legend.

The story became the most often-recounted bit of ghost lore about Graceland Cemetery. Scores of people were taken in by it over the years, mostly because they wanted to believe in the story. It was a tale that tugged at the heartstrings, a story of a little girl lost and one that captured the eerie presence of Graceland Cemetery in a way that no other tale could. It was a story that was so chilling that it was almost too good to be true --- of course, that's because it was.

But what about the tales that have surfaced over the last decade or so, claiming that people have encountered a ghostly little girl near this monument? Were these real accounts or fictional embellishments? Was it merely a case of wishful thinking on the part of those who swore they saw her? Perhaps, for there is one thing we can be sure of, they were not seeing the ghost of Inez Clarke --- because Inez Clarke never existed!

So, did someone purposely create the legend to fool legions of gullible Chicagoans? Despite what some might believe (including cemeteries with strict no-ghosts policies), probably not. The stories about the Inez Clarke statue have been around for quite a few years, although they have gained popularity in more recent times. Many have been fooled by the tales, perhaps wishing a little too hard for this particular Chicago ghost story to be true!

PHANTOMS OF ROSEHILL

Rosehill Cemetery began in 1859, taking its name from a nearby tavern keeper named Roe. The area around his saloon was known for some years as "Roe's Hill." In time, the name was slightly altered and became "Rosehill." After the closure of the "dreary" Chicago City Cemetery, Rosehill became the oldest and the largest graveyard in Chicago and serves as the final resting place of more than 1,500 notable Chicagoans, including a number of Civil War generals, mayors, former millionaires, local celebrities and early founders of the city.

There are also some infamous burials here as well, like that of Reinhart Schwimmer, the unlucky eye doctor and gangster hanger-on who was killed during the St. Valentine's Day Massacre. Another, more mysterious gravesite, is that of young Bobby Franks, the victim of "thrill killers" Nathan Leopold and Richard Loeb. After his death, Bobby Franks was buried at Rosehill with the understanding that his lot number would never be given out to the curious. To this day, it remains a secret, although visitors will sometimes find the site by accident among the tens of thousands of graves in the cemetery.

There are also a number of deceased Chicagoans who are apparently not peacefully at rest here and they serve to provide the cemetery with its legends of ghosts and strange happenings.

Perhaps the most famous ghostly site on the grounds is the tomb belonging to Charles Hopkinson, a real estate tycoon from the middle 1800s. In his will, Hopkinson left plans for his mausoleum to serve as a shrine to the memory of himself and his family. When he died in 1885, a miniature cathedral was designed to serve as the tomb. Construction was started and then halted when the property owners behind the Hopkinson site took the family to court. They claimed that the cathedral tomb would block the view of their own burial sites. The case made it all of the way to the Illinois Supreme Court, which ruled that the other families had no say over what sort of monument the Hopkinson family built and that they should have expected that something could eventually block the view of their site. Shortly afterward, construction on the tomb continued and was completed.

Ghost lore is filled with stories of the dead returning from the grave to protest wrongs that were done to them in their lifetime, or to continue business and rivalries started while they were among the living. Such events have long been a part of the lore of Rosehill's community mausoleum.

The Rosehill Cemetery Mausoleum was proposed in 1912 and the cemetery appealed to the elite businessmen of the city for the funds to begin construction. These men were impressed with the idea of a large and stately mausoleum and enjoyed the thought of entire rooms in the building that could be dedicated to their families alone and which also could be decorated to their style and taste. The building was designed by Sidney Lovell and is a massive, multi-level structure with marble passageways and rows upon rows of the dead. It is filled with a number of Chicago notables from the world of business and even architect Sidney Lovell himself.

One of the funding subscribers for the mausoleum was John G. Shedd, the president of Marshall Field's from 1909 to 1926 and the man who donated the wonderful Shedd Aquarium to Chicago. He guaranteed himself immortality with the development of what he dreamed would be the world's largest aquarium. Even though Shedd died four years before the aquarium would open, his directors remained loyal to his plans and created an aquatic showplace. A little of that extravagance can be found in the Rosehill mausoleum, as Shedd's family room is one of the most beautiful portions of the building. The chapel outside the room features chairs that are carved in images depicting shells and sea horses and the window inside bathes the room with a blue haze that makes the chamber appear to be under water. For this window, Shedd commissioned the artisan Louis Comfort Tiffany and made him sign a contract that said he would never create another window like it.

There have been no ghost stories associated with John Shedd, but there are others entombed in the structure who may not have found the peace that Shedd has found. Two of the men also laid to rest in the building are Aaron Montgomery Ward and his bitter business rival, Richard Warren Sears. One has to wonder if either of these men could rest in peace with the other man in the same structure, but it is the ghost of Sears who has been seen walking

through the mausoleum at night. The business pioneer has been spotted, wearing a top hat and tails, leaving the Sears family room and walking the hallways from his tomb to that of Ward. Perhaps the rivalry that plagued his life continues on after death?

Rosehill has been plagued with odd monuments and unusual stories connected to them. One of them is the tombstone of Mary Shedden, who was allegedly poisoned by her husband in 1931. Those who find the grave may have to use their imaginations a little but they will likely see two startling visions within the stone of the monument itself. One is the young and happy face of Mary Shedden --- and the other is her grinning and cadaverous skull! Skeptics dismiss the tale, saying that the illusion of 'faces' is nothing more than the stone's natural markings playing tricks on the eye, but others are not so sure.

One of the most famous mortuary statues in the cemetery, or at least one of the most visited, is the monument to Lulu Fellows, a young woman who died at age 16 in 1833. Visitors who come here often leave behind coins, toys and tokens to the girl whose monument bears the words "Many Hopes Lie Buried

Lulu Fellows

Here." A number of visitors claim that they have encountered the scent of fresh flowers around this life-like monument -- even in the winter, when no fresh flowers are present.

Another sad and tragic figure here is that of Philomena Boyington, the granddaughter of architect William W. Boyington, who designed the gothic gates that lead into the cemetery. According to the stories, people who sometimes pass by the cemetery at night will see the face of Philomena peering out at them from the window to the left and just below the bell tower of the Ravenswood gates. It has been said that the young girl often played near the site when the gates were being constructed back in 1864. She died of pneumonia not long after the structure was completed and she has haunted the place ever since.

THE ITALIAN BRIDE

Julia Buccola Petta's grave in Mount Carmel Cemetery

In Hillside, just outside of Chicago, is Mount Carmel Cemetery. In addition to being the final resting place of Al Capone, Dion O'Banion and other notorious Chicago mobsters, the cemetery is also the burial place of a woman named Julia Buccola Petta. While her name may not spring to mind as a part of Chicago history, for those intrigued by the supernatural, she is better known as the "Italian Bride." Julia's grave is marked today by a life-sized statue of the unfortunate woman in her wedding dress, a stone reproduction of the wedding photo that is mounted on the front of her monument. While a beautiful monument, there is nothing about it to suggest that anything weird ever occurred in connection to it. However, once you know the history behind the site, it's soon realized that this is one of the weirdest tales in Chicago's annals of the unknown.

Julia Buccola grew up on the West Side of Chicago and when she and her husband married, they moved to a more upscale Italian neighborhood. Eventually, she became pregnant with her first child but complications set in and she died giving birth to a stillborn child in 1921. Because of the Italian tradition that dying in childbirth made the woman a type of martyr, Julia was buried in white, the martyrs' color. Her wedding dress also served as her burial gown and with her dead infant tucked into her arms, the two were laid to rest in a single coffin

Julia's mother, Filomena, blamed her daughter's husband for the girl's death and she claimed the body and buried her with the Buccola family at Mount Carmel Cemetery. Shortly after Julia was buried, though, Filomena began to experience strange and terrifying dreams every night. In these nightmares, she envisioned Julia

GHOST ALERT

The stories of Julia Petta's "incorruptible body" have spawned takes of a woman in a bridal gown who haunts the portion of the cemetery where her grave can be found. Some of the stories come from students at Proviso West High School, which is located just east of the cemetery on Wolf Road. They have reported a girl walking in the cemetery at night and they are not alone. A number of people in a car traveling down Harrison Street were startled to see a woman passing through the tombstones one night. Thinking that it was simply a Halloween prank, they stopped the car for a closer look. They did not become unnerved until they realized that, even though it was pouring down rain, the girl was perfectly dry. They didn't choose to investigate any closer and immediately drove away!

telling her that she was still alive and needed her help. For the next six years, the dreams plagued Filomena and she began trying, without success, to have her daughter's grave opened and her body exhumed. She was unable to explain why she needed to do this; she only knew that she should. Finally, through sheer persistence, her request was granted and a sympathetic judge passed down an order for Julia's exhumation.

In 1927, six years after Julia's death, the casket was removed from the grave. When it was opened, Julia's body was found not to have decayed at all. In fact, it was said that her flesh was still as soft as it had been when she was alive. A photograph was taken at the time of the exhumation and shows Julia's "incorruptible" body in the casket. Her mother, and other admirers, placed the photo on the front of her grave monument, which was constructed after her reburial. The photograph shows a body that appears to be fresh, with no discoloration of the skin, even after six years. The rotted and decayed appearance of the coffin in the photo however, bears witness to the fact that it had been underground for some time. Julia appears to be merely sleeping. Her family took the fact that she was found to be so well preserved as a sign from God and so, after collecting money from other family members and neighbors, they created the impressive monument that stands over her grave today.

Julia in her grave after more than six years. Inexplicably, her body never decayed.

What mysterious secret rests at the grave of Julia Petta? How could her body have stayed in perfect condition after lying in the grave for six years? No one knows and to this day, the case of the "Italian Bride" remains one of Chicago's great unsolved mysteries.

THE MIRACLE CHILD OF CHICAGO

A grave that is located in the Chicago suburb of Worth, at Holy Sepulchre Cemetery, is said to have mysterious benevolent properties. In fact, it is said be able to heal the sick and the dying. Many people feel that this is a sacred place and is made so because the grave holds the final remains of a young girl named Mary Alice Quinn. Over the years, hundreds have claimed to experience miraculous healings at her gravesite, while others speak of strange occurrences that can only be paranormal in nature. Because of this, Mary's grave has been the site of visits by religious pilgrims and supernatural enthusiasts alike.

Mary was a quiet child who died suddenly in 1935, when she was only 14. Born in 1920, she was one of three children of Daniel and Alice Quinn. As a young girl, she was diagnosed with a heart condition and became devoutly religious, devoted to St. Theresa, who claimed to have a mystical experience when she saw a religious image appear on her wall. After that, she became known in her neighborhood for curing the sick. While on her deathbed, Mary told her parents that she wanted to come back and help people after her death. The faithful say that she has done just that. Soon after her death, she was said to have mysteriously appeared to a number of people in the Chicago area. Throughout the 1930s and 1940s, it was not uncommon to hear of new Mary Alice Quinn sightings.

On one occasion, a sick nun at Mary Alice's former school claimed that she was visited by an apparition of the girl and cured. Others who claimed to see her said that her apparition had a glowing veil over her face. This was attributed to being a "veil of grace," a supernatural manifestation that is found in cases of people who are saints. Witnesses also began to tell of the spectral scent of roses that surrounded the healings and the apparition sightings. This is noteworthy because of Mary Alice's devotion to St. Theresa, whose motto had been, "I will let fall from heaven a shower of roses." For years after their daughter's death, Daniel and Alice Quinn hoped that the numerous reports of healings and strange phenomena attached to their daughter would attract the attention of the Catholic Church and that the girl might someday be considered for sainthood herself. They distributed literature and holy

One of Chicago's most beloved shrines, the grave of Mary Alice Quinn

cards and helped to provide documentation for the few articles that were written about Mary Alice in Catholic journals.

And while there has been no official interest from the church, Mary Alice's following continues to grow among believers. Today, her healing powers are said to have taken on another manifestation, one that surrounds her grave marker. When she passed away, she was secretly buried in a cemetery plot that belonged to the Reilly family. It was thought that this might keep her burial place a secret and prevent the graveyard from being overrun by curiosity-seekers intent on finding her resting place. Word soon spread, though, and a gravestone was eventually cut with her name on it. Since that time, thousands have come to the site, many of them bringing prayer tokens, rosaries, coins and photos to leave as offerings and to ask that Mary intercede for them in prayer. Many claim to have been healed of their afflictions after visiting the grave and others have been healed by extension. They claim to have found relief from one of the many spoonfuls of dirt that has been taken from Mary's burial site.

Strangely, the phantom scent of roses has been reported filling the air around the gravestone, even when there are no roses anywhere around. The smell is said to be especially strong in the winter months, when the scent of fresh roses would be impossible to mistake. Many visitors are alleged to have noticed this smell over the years and some of them even say that it is overwhelming. The faithful claim that this unexplainable odor is proof that Mary's spirit is still nearby and interceding on their behalf. They say her love and charity continues, even decades after her death.

MYSTERIES OF ROBINSON WOODS

One of the last places in the busy city of Chicago that you would expect to find a Native American Burial Ground would be along a busy stretch of roadway, but that's exactly where you will find Robinson Woods - a mysterious site where the spirits of the dead are believed to linger behind.

Andrew Robinson was the son of an Ottawa Indian woman and a Scottish trader and may have been one of the most influential early leaders of Chicago. During the War of 1812, Robinson sided with the American troops and stayed hidden during the conflict, avoiding the local Indians and helping those who were sequestered inside Fort Dearborn when possible. He is credited with saving the lives of many of those who survived the massacre and was later rewarded for his efforts with land and a yearly stipend. Robinson became a permanent resident of Chicago in 1814 and cultivated good relationships with the mixed culture of the region. He was highly regarded both by the local tribes and by the white settlers who were beginning to arrive.

In 1826, Robinson married Catherine Chevalier and became the son-in-law of the Potawatomi chief, Shobonier. A short time later, after the death of the chieftain, Robinson assumed the role of chief, taking the name of Che-che-pin-quay, which means "winking eye."

The burial marker at Robinson's Woods

He worked as a translator for Chicago Indian agent Alexander Wolcott and continued to make friends among both the white residents and the Native Americans in the region. When the Potawatomi gave up a large portion of their land in the Treaty of Prairie du Chien in 1829, a large section was set aside for Robinson at Lawrence Avenue and River Road along the Des Plaines River. In addition, he was awarded a lifetime benefit of $200 per year, an amount that was later increased to $500.

ADAM SAYS:
The "our house is built on an Indian burial ground" story is one that we hear a lot. Normally, I'd tell people that they should have noticed that when they were digging out the basement. But there are a lot of burial grounds in Chicagoland, and plenty of landfills, so the stories aren't necessarily as unreliable as you might immediately think.

In 1830, Robinson opened a saloon in the city and five years later departed for Iowa. He lived away from Chicago for a few years and then returned with the departure of the remaining regional Indian tribes. He lived in Chicago until his death in 1872, signing away huge portions of land to the arriving settlers and attempting to make the transition of Chicago from a small settlement to a growing city a smooth one.

In the early 1900s, the remaining Robinson family continued to be a visible presence in the city. There were many stories about the Robinson house, located in the woods off of Lawrence Avenue, which told of wild living and unseemly parties. In spite of their reputation, the family continued to live in the house in the woods until 1955, when the structure burned to the ground.

A short time after the fire, another, more horrifying event took place here. In October 1955, the bodies of John and Anton Schuessler and Robert Peterson were discovered bound and naked in a ditch at the edge of the woods. The case stunned the city and would remain unsolved for almost 40 years. Not surprisingly, this event may have also left a dark stain on the atmosphere of Robinson Woods.

Several members of the family remained on the property until 1958, when the construction of O'Hare airport allowed the land to be annexed to Chicago as part of the link between the airport and the city. The last Robinson descendant died in 1972 and, while an agreement was made that would allow him to be buried on the remaining property with the rest of his family, the city later denied his wishes.

Robinson Woods still remain today, just off Lawrence Avenue. If you go there and leave the street, walking a short distance, you will see a large stone that serves as a burial monument to Andrew Robinson and his family. Their bodies lie here underneath the earth, where they rest peacefully... or do they?

Strange events have been reported here for many years and first-hand accounts claim the sightings of apparitions that look like Native Americans, along with odd lights that have been spotted in the woods by passing motorists. Other claims the sounds of drums beating and disembodied voices that seem to come from out of the air. A dozen paranormal experiments carried out here in 1974-1975 managed to pick up on audiotape some of the strange sounds that people reported hearing. What resulted sounded exactly like Indian tribal drums and the sounds of chopping wood. They were common sounds for the 1800s - but why would they still be heard today?

SHOWMAN'S REST

In the summer of 1918, one of the nation's largest circus companies, the Hagenbeck-Wallace Circus, was touring the Midwest. While this was still the heyday of the traveling circus, these were not good days for the company. World War I was in progress and governmental restrictions on the use of the railroads made moving three special trains filled with equipment, 22 tents, 1,000 employees and almost 400 animals a logistical nightmare. However, the show must go on and so plans were made, routes were mapped out --- and then mapped out again --- and the trains somehow managed to get from place to place, arriving in time to put on a great show.

In July, the circus was touring Indiana. After playing in Michigan City, the troupe packed up for its next stop in Hammond. By the time everything was loaded and the trains were underway, darkness had fallen. On board one of the trains, the exhausted performers caught up on their sleep as the train roared along through the night. The next day, July 22, would mark their arrival in

One of the many unknown performers graves at Showman's Rest

Hammond and a grand parade through town. But there would be no circus parade in Hammond that afternoon.

Just a few minutes before 4:00 a.m., on the edge of Hammond, the circus train was slammed from behind by a speeding troop train. The accident occurred when the circus train, which carried about 400 workers and performers, stopped on the tracks due to a mechanical problem. Although red lights were displayed and a flagman was sent out, the circus train was struck because the other train was unable to stop in time. The engineer of the troop train, A.K. Sargent, had fallen asleep at the throttle and caused the wreck. At his manslaughter trial, he claimed that he had been taking patent medicine pills. His defense was that he was overworked by the railroad for the war effort. The trial later ended with a hung jury.

The initial impact destroyed a portion of the Hagenbeck-Wallace train, which consisted mostly of the sleeping berths. The cars were crushed together or thrown from the tracks. The wreckage soon burst into flames. Many of the sleeping passengers never woke up and those who survived the crash were knocked unconscious in the jumble of debris. Many of them woke to find themselves trapped under heaps of broken wood and twisted steel. Broken gas lanterns caused the fire to spread even faster and many of the performers were burned alive. The night was quickly filled with the sounds of screams and cries for help.

There has never been a complete count of how many of the circus performers died that morning in the horrific crash. The Hammond Historical Society, which has carefully researched the disaster, believes the most accurate death toll stands at 86 but no one will ever be able to say for sure. The problem was that, in many cases, no accurate lists were kept of those who traveled with the circus and many of the worker's names were not recorded at all. The last sleeping car contained the roustabouts, temporary employees who were hired for day labor. Many of these men were drifters, with no present or past, and used assumed names or nicknames to identify themselves. The wreckage added to the problem as bodies were torn into pieces or burned beyond recognition. Dismembered body parts were scattered along the tracks and after the fires had gone out, an unidentified charred head was found beneath the cowcatcher on the locomotive. The wreck is still remembered today as one of the greatest disasters in American circus history.

The Showmen's League of America, founded by Buffalo Bill Cody, retains its headquarters in Chicago today. In early 1918, this benevolent organization purchased a large plot at Woodlawn Cemetery in Forest Park to be used as a final resting place for many of its members. On June 27, just five days after the accident, the plot was the scene of a mass burial. On that day, 56 of those killed in the wreck were buried at the same time. Tragically, only 13 of the bodies were positively identified. They were all buried with dignity, though, not in a common grave. Each of them had his or her own coffin and headstone. Most of the stones were marked with the word "unknown" but others included clowns and inscriptions like "Baldy" and "4 Horse Driver."

Since those first burials, hundreds of other circus and carnival showman have been buried at Showman's Rest. Five stone elephants were installed to watch over the silent graves of the plot, their trunks lowered in mourning. These majestic statues pay tribute to those who lost their lives in the 1918 disaster and also to the legion of performers who have followed them to the grave.

NO GHOSTS ALERT!

Rumors and legends have surrounded Showman's Rest since it was started in 1918. Contrary to the most popular story, there were no animals buried at Woodlawn Cemetery and no animals were killed in the train wreck. It's believed that these stories got started thanks to a tour guide in Chicago who circulated a story that the ghostly sounds of phantom animals could be heard around the cemetery at night. It was later proven that the "ghostly sounds" were actually coming from Brookfield Zoo!

CHICAGO'S MOST HAUNTED:
BACHELOR'S GROVE CEMETERY

Located near the southwest suburb of Midlothian is the Rubio Woods Forest Preserve, an island of trees and shadows nestled in the urban sprawl of the Chicago area. The rambling refuge creates an illusion that it is secluded from the crowded city that threatens its borders, and perhaps it is. On the edge of the forest is a small graveyard that many believe may be the most haunted place in the region. The name of this cemetery is Bachelor's Grove and this ramshackle burial ground may be infested with more ghosts than most can imagine. Over the years, the place has been cursed with more than 100 documented reports of paranormal phenomena, from actual apparitions to glowing balls of light.

The long vanished sign at Bachelor's Grove Cemetery
(Dale Kaczmarek)

There have been no new burials here for many years and as a place of rest for the departed, it is largely forgotten. But if you should ask any ghost hunter just where to go to find a haunting, Bachelor's Grove is usually the first place in Chicago to be mentioned!

The history of Bachelor's Grove has been somewhat shadowy over the years but most historians agree that it was started in the early part of the 1800s. Legend has it that the cemetery got its name because only men were buried here but it actually came from the name of a family who settled in the area. A nearby settlement from the 1820s consisted of mostly German immigrants from New York, Vermont and Connecticut. One family that moved into the area was called "Batchelder" and their name was given to the timberland where they settled. The settlement continued for some years as Batchelor's Grove, until 1850, when it was changed to "Bremen" by postmaster Samuel Everden in recognition of the new township name where the post office was located. In 1855, it was changed again to "Bachelder's Grove" by Postmaster Robert Patrick but the post office closed down just three years later. Officially, the settlement ceased to exist and was swallowed by the forest around it.

> Despite the legends, attempts to link the cemetery to the Batchelder family have not been conclusive, but there is some interesting speculation that the Batchelders in the area may have been related to the Batchelders who served as jurors and witnesses in the Salem Witch trials of the 1690s.

The cemetery itself has a much stranger history -- or at least a more mysterious one. The land was apparently first set aside to be used as a burial ground in 1844, when the first recorded burial took place here, that of Eliza (Mrs. Leonard H.) Scott. The land had been donated by Samuel Everden, and it was named "Everden" in his honor. The last burials to take place are believed to be that of Laura M. McGhee in 1965 and Robert E. Shields, who was cremated and his ashes buried in the family plot here in 1989.

The last caretaker of the cemetery was a man named Clarence Fulton, whose family were early settlers in the township. According to Fulton, Bachelor's Grove was like a park for many years and people often came here to fish and swim in the adjacent pond. Families often visited on weekends to care for the graves of the deceased and to picnic under the trees. Things have certainly changed since then!

Problems began in and around the cemetery in the early 1960s. Even before that, the cemetery had become a popular spot along a "lover's lane" and after a nearby road was closed, it became even more isolated. Soon it began to show signs of vandalism and decay and, a short time later, was rumored to be haunted.

The vandals first discovered Bachelor's Grove in the 1960s and, probably because of its secluded location, began to wreak havoc on the place. Gravestones were knocked

over and destroyed, sprayed with paint, broken apart and even stolen. Graves were opened and caskets removed. Bones were sometimes found strewn about the cemetery.

Was the haunting first caused by these disturbances? Most believe so, but others cite another source for the activity. Near the small pond that borders the cemetery, forest rangers and cemetery visitors have reportedly found the remains of chickens and other small animals that have been slaughtered and mutilated in a ritualistic fashion. Officers who have patrolled the woods at night have reported seeing evidence of black magic and occult rituals in and around the graveyard. In some cases, inscriptions and elaborate writings have been carved in and painted on trees and grave markers and on the cemetery grounds themselves. This has led many to believe that the cemetery has been used for occult activities.

There is no question that vandals have not been kind to Bachelor's Grove, but then neither has time. Roads leading to it were closed and people forgot about the place and allowed it to fade into memory, just like the poor souls buried there.

Today, the cemetery is overgrown with weeds and is surrounded by a high, chain-link fence, although access is easily gained through the holes that trespassers have cut into it. The cemetery sign is long since gone.

The first thing noticed by those who visit here is the destruction. Tombstones seem to be randomly scattered about, no longer marking the resting places of those whose names are inscribed upon them. Many of the stones are missing, lost forever and perhaps carried away by thieves. These macabre crimes gave birth to legends about how the stones of the cemetery move about under their own power. The most disturbing things to visitors, though, are the trenches and pits that have been dug above some of the graves, as vandals have attempted to make off with souvenirs from those whose rest they disturb.

Just beyond the rear barrier of the cemetery is a small, stagnant pond. This pond, while outside of the graveyard, is still not untouched by the horror connected to the place. One night in the late 1970s, two Cook County Forest Preserve officers were on night patrol near here and claimed to see the apparition of a horse emerge from the waters of the pond. The animal appeared to be pulling a plow behind it that was steered by the ghost of an old man. The vision crossed the road in front of the rangers' vehicle, was framed for a moment in the glare of their headlights, and then vanished into the forest. The men simply stared in shock for a moment and then looked at one another to be sure that had both seen the same thing. They later reported the incident and since that time, have not been the last to see the old man and the horse.

Little did the rangers know, but this apparition was actually a part of a legend connected to the pond. It seems that in the 1870s, a farmer was plowing a nearby field when something startled his horse. The farmer was caught by surprise and became tangled in the reins. He was dragged behind the horse and it plunged into the pond. Unable to

The stagnant pond outside of Bachelor's Grove

free himself, he was pulled down into the murky water by the weight of the horse and the plow and he drowned.

Even the road near Bachelor's Grove is reputed to be haunted. The Midlothian Turnpike is said to be the scene of vanishing "ghost cars" and phantom automobile accidents. No historical events can provide a clue as to why this might be, but the unexplained vehicles have been reported numerous times in recent years. People who are traveling west on the turnpike see the taillights of a car in front of them. The brake lights go on, as if the car is planning to stop or turn. The car then turns off the road. However, once the following auto gets to the point in the road where the first vehicle turned, they find no car there at all! Other drivers have reported passing these phantoms autos, only to see the car vanish in their rearview mirrors.

It remains a mystery as to where these phantom cars come from, and where they vanish to. Why do they haunt this stretch of roadway?

For those searching for Bachelor's Grove, it can be found by leaving the roadway and walking up an overgrown gravel track that is surrounded on both sides by forest. The old road is blocked with chains and concrete dividers and a dented "No Trespassing" sign that hangs ominously near the mouth of the trail. The burial ground lies about a half-mile or so beyond it in the woods.

It is along this deserted road where other strange tales of the cemetery take place. One of these odd occurrences is the sighting of the "phantom farmhouse." It has been seen appearing and disappearing along the trail for several decades now. The most credible thing about many of the accounts is that they come from people who originally had no idea that the house shouldn't be there at all.

The house has been reported in all weather conditions, both in the daytime and at night. There is no historical record of such a house existing here but the descriptions of it rarely vary. Each person claims it to be an old frame farmhouse with two-stories, painted white, with wooden posts, a porch swing and a welcoming light that burns softly in the window. Popular legend states that should you enter this house, you would never come back out again. As witnesses approach the building, it is reported to get smaller and smaller until it finally just fades away, like someone switching off an old television set. No one has ever claimed to have set foot on the front porch of the house.

Also from this stretch of trail come reports of "ghost lights." One such light that has been reported many times is a red, beacon-like orb that has been seen flying rapidly up and down the trail to the cemetery. The light is so bright, and moves so fast, that it is impossible to tell what it really looks like. Most witnesses state that they have seen a "red streak" that is left in its wake.

There have also have been many sightings of ghosts and apparitions within Bachelor's Grove Cemetery itself. The most frequently reported spirit is known by a variety of names from the "Madonna of Bachelor's Grove" to the "White Lady" to the affectionate name of "Mrs. Rogers." Legend has it that she is the ghost of a woman who was buried in the cemetery next to the grave of her young child. She is

THE FAMOUS BACHELOR'S GROVE GHOST PHOTOGRAPH

This famous photograph from Bachelor's Grove was taken by Jude Huff-Felz and during an investigation with Chicago's Ghost Research Society at the cemetery.

The photo was taken on infra-red film during a daytime excursion to the reputedly haunted graveyard. In the developed photograph, there appeared a semi-transparent figure of a woman seated on a tombstone within the cemetery grounds. She was not visible to anyone who was present and in fact, the image appeared in a much larger, almost panoramic view of the cemetery. The portion of the photo where the woman appears was enlarged when investigators noticed there was something out of the ordinary about it.

Skeptics declared the photo a hoax (as usual) but we have every reason to believe it is genuine. We had a copy of the photo examined by a number of professional photographers and while they would have liked to say that it was a fraud, they admitted that they were unable to. They ruled out the possibility of a double-exposure and the theory that it was a photo of a live woman who was made to appear like a ghost. One critic declared she was casting a shadow, but this is nothing more than the natural coloring of the landscape. Besides that, if she is casting a shadow in that direction, why isn't anything else?

reported to wander the cemetery on nights of the full moon with an infant wrapped in her arms. She appears to walk aimlessly, with no apparent direction and completely unaware of the people who claim to encounter her. There is no real evidence to say whom this woman might be but, over the years, she has taken her place as one of the many spirits of this haunted burial ground.

The Weird Chicago gang has visited, and investigated, Bachelor's Grove many times. In 2007, the series "Cringe," for which Troy Taylor is the executive producer, filmed an episode at Bachelor's Grove, spending the night among the toppled tombstones. In the course of the filming, much of the digital footage was inexplicably distorted and destroyed, something that a crew with many years of experience had never encountered before. Similarly, attempts to record a podcast there (a follow-up to the first episode of the Weird Chicago Podcast) were abandoned after equipment failures ruined the recording.

In 2006, Ken Melvoin-Berg, Weird Chicago's own psychic detective, accompanied a reporter from the *Chicago Tribune* to the old graveyard and encountered the spirit of a young boy. Soon after arriving at the cemetery, Ken heard a child's voice crying to him, telling him that he had lost something. A few moments later, Ken understood that it was money. According to the reporter, Ken appeared "to lose it himself" and he staggered out of the cemetery toward the adjacent, algae-filled pond. Wading into the murky water, Ken stopped, bent down, stuck his shaking hands into the muck, and pulled out a 1942 Walking Liberty half-dollar coin - exactly where the ghostly boy told him that it could be found.

Is Bachelor's Grove Cemetery as haunted as we have been led to believe? The reader has to decide that for himself - but, based on the stories, it seems to be one of the most haunted places in the Midwest.

But haunted or not, Bachelor's Grove is still a burial ground and a place that should be treated with respect as the final resting place of those interred here. It is first and foremost a repository for the dead and should be protected as such by those who hope to enjoy it, and possibly learn from it, in the years to come. It is also a piece of our haunted history that we cannot afford to lose.

ONE LAST TURN OF THE SPADE: A FEW OTHER HAUNTED CHICAGO GRAVEYARDS

"SEAWEED CHARLIE"

A mysterious figure haunts a stretch of roadway that leads into the gates of Calvary Cemetery, located along the North Shore in Evanston. This old Catholic Cemetery rests on the edge of Lake Michigan and is located between two large universities, Loyola in Chicago and Northwestern in Evanston.

According to the story, motorists following the "S" curve that passes between the cemetery on one side and Juneway Park and Beach on the other are often startled by a disheveled, wet and tired-looking figure as he pulls himself from the rocky water and staggers across the road to the graveyard. He often stumbles from the water and barely pulls himself across the road. In some reports, he even drags a strand of seaweed behind him, further adding to his drowned appearance.

Some believe that the phantom may be connected to a plane crash that occurred in nearby Lake Michigan in May 1951. An instructor from the Glenview Naval Air Station experienced engine problems and had to bail out of his aircraft. He landed in the lake just a short distance from Northwestern University. He was spotted alive and waving his arms as a signal for help, but unfortunately, he drowned before anyone could get to him. Two days later, his body was found washed up on the rocks near the cemetery. Could it be this lost soul who now haunts the roadway leading into the cemetery? Many local residents believe so and in fact, have dubbed the ghost "the Aviator" or "Seaweed Charlie."

BETHANIA CEMETERY

Another Chicago area burial ground, Bethania Cemetery in Justice, boasts at least three mysterious figures that haunt the grounds and the streets nearby.

One of the most common phantoms to appear here is seen on the 79th Street side of the cemetery. Just past the maintenance entrance to the grounds, motorists have often reported seeing the harmless figure of an elderly man as he rakes and burns leaves along the side of the road. These sightings normally occur during the fall, so it's not the time of year that it happens that seems so odd to the people who spot this scene -- it's the time of day! Those who are driving by are often puzzled as to why this old man would be out working in the cemetery between 2:00 and 4:00 in the morning. However, as the witnesses slow down to have a look in the rearview mirror, or even glance back in his direction, they discover that not only is the old man gone, but so is the pile of burning leaves. So far, no one has been able to provide an explanation as to why this odd figure is seen here, nor even who he might be.

Bethania's other phantom figure is more on the unnerving side. He haunts the far southwestern edge of the cemetery, located along Cork Avenue. Several reliable witnesses have said that they have seen a blood-covered man running across the street, waving a flashlight. He flees from the edge of the graveyard towards oncoming traffic, whirling the flashlight as he goes, as if trying to flag down one of the passing cars. Moments later, he vanishes. The identity of this strange figure also remains a mystery and no research has even been able to discover if a murder or accident occurred near here that might explain the horrific apparition.

Another ghostly figure is that of an old woman who stands inside the cemetery and screams at people who pass by. She has been reported here for many years and strangely, her identity may actually be known. According to her family members, the apparition may be that of Gertrude Kosary, who is buried in the cemetery. She was mean-spirited when she was alive and after her death in 1963, she reportedly began harassing those who passed by the graveyard.

ARCHER WOODS CEMETERY

Located in the woods near where Kean Avenue comes to a dead end just south of Archer Avenue, is another cemetery with a long connection to the supernatural. This secluded, and rather foreboding, burial ground is called Mount Glenwood Memory Gardens West, but most people know it by its original name of Archer Woods Cemetery.

There is no question that this graveyard is one of the most eerie burial sites in the region. The grounds have been poorly kept over the years and are broken and uneven, suggesting the presence of many unmarked graves. For many years, a female phantom has been reported along the edge of the grounds, wandering near Kean Avenue. She has been witnessed many times by those who have driven past the cemetery at night. These unwitting travelers are often greeted by the sound of a woman loudly weeping in despair. When they slow down, or stop their vehicles, to listen or get a look at where the sound is coming from, they see a woman in a white gown wandering in the edge of the graveyard. She is usually only seen for a very short amount of time and then she disappears.

Who is this mysterious woman? No one seems to know. She has been spotted at the cemetery for the past few decades but there has never been any explanation offered as to whom she might be or why she haunts the cemetery, weeping near the roadway. One story suggested that she was a suicide victim who was connected to a small roadhouse that once operated directly across the road from the cemetery's entrance but no real evidence has ever been produced to substantiate this tale. For now, the identity of this woman, and why she haunts this desolate stretch of road, remains a mystery.

ST. JAMES -SAG CEMETERY

St. James-Sag Church and burial ground dates back as far as the early 1830s and was started by men who settled in the area after the completion of the Illinois & Michigan Canal. The first church was constructed at the site in 1833. In 1850, it was replaced by the building that is still in use today. The pale yellow building, constructed from famous Lemont limestone, stands on top of the hill, just a short distance from the newer rectory and stands watch over the hundreds of graves scattered about on the hills below. It is a breathtaking scene and could easily be part of

the Irish countryside, rather than a landscape from the Southwest suburbs.

Supernatural events have been reported at St. James-Sag since around 1847. It was at this time when the first sightings of the "phantom monks" took place here. These stories continued for decades and there were many reliable witnesses to the strange activity. One of them, a former rector of the church, admitted on his deathbed that he had seen ghosts roaming the cemetery grounds for many years.

Perhaps the strangest account of the hauntings at the graveyard came from a cold night just before Thanksgiving in November 1977 when a Cook County sheriff's officer passed by the cemetery and happened to turn his spotlight up past the cemetery gates. He claimed to see nine hooded figures floating up the cemetery road toward the rectory. Knowing that no one was supposed to be in the cemetery, he stopped and yelled out the window at them to come back toward the road. If they did not, they would be arrested for trespassing. The figures simply ignored him and continued up the road toward the church and rectory.

Quickly, he grabbed his shotgun and ran around the gate and into the graveyard. He pursued what he first thought were pranksters into the graveyard but while he stumbled and fell over the uneven ground and tombstones, the monk-like figures eerily glided past without effort. He said that he nearly caught up with them when "they vanished without a trace." Unable to believe what had just happened, he searched the area for any trace of the figures but found no one. Finally, he returned to his squad car to write up his report. The paperwork that he filed merely stated that he had chased some trespassers through the cemetery but he always maintained that what he had seen was from beyond this world.

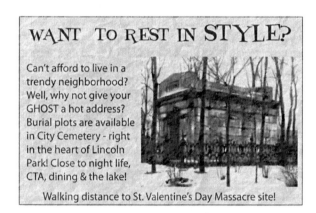

10. WEIRD CHICAGO GHOSTS & HAUNTINGS

Chicago is an October sort of city even in spring.
Nelson Algren

There are those who maintain that the only thing that keeps Chicago from being the greatest city in America is the weather. There seems to be something about blizzards and below zero wind chills that tend to put the damper on people's enthusiasms. But whatever Chicago might lack in this regard, it more than makes up for it with its history, legends, and lore -- and especially with its ghosts!

There are a number of American cities that make the claim of being "most haunted", but in my opinion, Chicago leads the pack. There is simply no other city that can boast the sheer number of haunts that Chicago can. The spirits here are simply a part of the city's culture and can be connected to Chicago's long, and often bloody, history. The history and the hauntings of the city go hand in hand and as it has often been said, the events of the past create the hauntings of today. In no place is such a statement as true as it is in Chicago. You see, ghost stories have always been a part of the history of Chicago. Tales of haunted graveyards, phantom figures and beautiful spirits who wander the area highways have always held great appeal for those with a taste for the unusual and the unknown.

In the pages ahead, we'll collect many of the hauntings that have not already been visited in the pages that have come before. In this case, we have saved the best of them for last, from tales of Chicago's most haunted house to the city's most famous ghost.

Read on - and be sure to keep a light burning on the table next to you. We guarantee that you'll be looking over your shoulder as you read, concerned about what may be sneaking up behind you!

JANE ADDAMS' HULL HOUSE

Hull House was constructed by Charles J. Hull at Halsted and Polk streets in 1856 at a time when this was one of the most fashionable sections of the city. After the Chicago Fire of 1871, the "better classes" moved to other parts of the city and the near West Side began to attract a large immigrant population of Italian, Greek and Jewish settlers. By the 1880s, Hull House was surrounded by factories and tenement houses, and, soon after, became one of the most famous places in Chicago. Although it was never intended to be known as a "haunted house," Hull House would not emerge from its heyday unscathed by stories of ghosts and the supernatural. Hull himself was interested in spiritualism, and it's likely that he conducted séances inside of the house around the time of the Civil War.

(Left) A young Jane Addams and her friend (Right) Ellen Starr Gates

Hull House would not achieve as its fame as a private home but rather as a pioneering effort of social equality that was started by a woman named Jane Addams and her friend, Ellen Starr Gates. They opened the house in 1889 at time when the overcrowded tenement neighborhoods west of Halsted Street were a jungle of crime, vice, prostitution and drug addiction. Jane Addams became the "voice of humanity" on the West Side, enriching the lives of many unfortunate people at the house.

Addams was born and raised in the village of Cedarville, the privileged daughter of a wealthy merchant. Jane was raised under pleasant surroundings and tragedy first came into her life with the death of her father, which occurred the same year that she graduated from the Rockford Female Seminary. She went into a deep depression and, unsure what to do with her life, she spent a portion of her inheritance traveling in Europe. It would be in London, in the terrible slums of Whitechapel, that she would find her calling.

In the company of her college friend and traveling companion, Ellen Starr Gates, Jane would spend time at Toynbee Hall, a settlement house for the poor. Here, young and affluent students lived and worked beside the poorest dregs of London, pushing for social reform and better standards of living. Jane was intrigued by the idea of it and after her return to Chicago, began making plans for such a place in the city. She soon discovered the run-down Halsted Street mansion and the terrible neighborhood around it. When she moved in, the house was bracketed by an Irish saloon and an undertaking parlor.

It was to the broken-down refugees and immigrants that Jane Addams' Hull House appealed. Jane and Ellen took control of the property in September 1889 and opened the settlement house. Addams was granted a 25-year, rent-free lease by Hull's confidential secretary, Helen Culver, and by the heirs to the Hull fortune, who were enthusiastic about Jane's efforts on behalf of the poor. They soon began turning the place into a comfortable house, aimed mostly at women, but affording food and shelter to the homeless and hungry, as well. The house also provided education and protection for many and the staff worked to better the lives of the local people for many years to come.

At the time when Jane Addams took over Hull House, several years had passed since the death of Mrs. Charles Hull, but this apparently didn't prevent her from making her presence known. She had died of natural causes in a second-floor bedroom of the mansion and, within a few months of her passing, her ghost was said to be haunting that particular room. Overnight guests began having their sleep disturbed by footsteps and what were described as "strange and unearthly noises."

Mrs. Hull's bedroom was first occupied by Jane Addams herself, who was awakened one night by loud footsteps in the otherwise empty room. After a few nights of this, she confided her story to Ellen, who also admitted to

Hull House in the early 1900s

Jane Addams went on to become one of America's leading social reformers, leader for women's rights, acclaimed speaker and author & one of the country's most noted suffragists.

experiencing the same sounds. Jane later moved to another room.

But she would not be alone in noticing the unusual happenings. Helen Campbell, the author of the book *Prisoners of Poverty*, reported seeing an apparition standing next to her bed (she took Jane up on the offer of staying in the "haunted room.") When she lit the gas jet, the figure vanished.

According to Jane Addams, earlier tenants of the house also believed the upstairs of the house was haunted. They had always kept a bucket of water on the stairs, believing that the ghost was unable to cross over it. Unfortunately, it was not the only "supernatural" legend connected to Hull House!

Hull House received its greatest notoriety when it was alleged to be the refuge of the Chicago "Devil Baby." This child was supposedly born to a devout Catholic woman and her atheist husband and was said to have pointed ears, horns, scale-covered skin and a tail. According to the story, the young woman had attempted to display a picture of the Virgin Mary in the house but her husband had torn it down. He stated that he would rather have the Devil himself in the house than the picture. When the woman had become pregnant, the Devil Baby had been their curse. After enduring numerous indignities because of the child, the father allegedly took it to Hull House.

After being taken in by Jane Addams, staff members of the house reportedly took the baby to be baptized. During the ceremony, the baby supposedly escaped from the priest and began dancing and laughing. Not knowing what else to do with the child, Jane kept it locked in the attic of the house, where it later died.

Rumors spread quickly about the baby and within a few weeks, hundreds of people came to the house to get a glimpse of it. How the story had gotten started, no one knew, but it spread throughout the West Side neighborhood and was reported by famous Chicago reporter Ben Hecht. He claimed that every time he tried to run down the story, he was directed to find the child at Hull House. Many people came to the door and demanded to see the child, while others quietly offered to pay an admission.

Each day, Jane turned people away and tried to convince them that the story was fabricated. She even devoted forty pages of her autobiography to dispelling the stories. Even though most of the poorly educated immigrants left the house still believing the tales of the Devil Baby, the stream of callers eventually died out and the story became a barely remembered side note in the history of Hull House. Or did it?

As the years have passed, some people still maintain the story of the Devil Baby is true -- or at least contains some elements of the truth. Some have speculated that perhaps the child was actually a badly deformed infant that had been brought to Hull House by a young immigrant woman who could not care for it. Perhaps the monstrous appearance of the child had started the rumors in the neighborhood and eventually led to Hull House.

Addams herself swore to the last that the story had no basis in fact, and that, except for a few variations of the story involving a red automobile, it could have been written a 1.000 years before. She began to see the story as a sort of sociological experiment that formed the basis of one of her books, The Long Road of Woman's Memory.

Regardless, local legend insists that at some point, there was a disfigured boy that was hidden away on the upper floors of the house. The stories also go on to say that on certain nights, the image of a deformed face could be seen peering out of the attic window and that a ghostly version of that face is still seen by visitors today.

Hull House has not been a settlement house for many years, but people still come here today. They are not just

MYTHS OF HULL HOUSE

There are plenty of strange stories about Hull House, but myths and misconceptions continue to plague the staff to this day. Among the more venerable myths that are still tossed around:

- There really was a "Devil Baby" that still haunts the place. (The rumors started in 1913 had, as far as we know, no basis in fact. While the house may be haunted, it's not the "Devil Baby" who does the haunting. Most of the photos said to show his ghostly white face on the second floor are, in reality, pictures of lamps.)

- The Devil Baby was the inspiration for the book and film *Rosemary's Baby* (It wasn't; when he wrote the book, Ira Levin knew nothing about Hull House).

- There's an abortion graveyard on the part of the grounds known as "The Garden of Evil" (There wasn't. Although there was an undertaking parlor near the garden site when Addams moved in, it had nothing to do with abortions. This was obviously a made-up story.)

- The Devil Baby is buried in the garden (Nope, and again, not an abortion graveyard either)

- There's a headless ghost that follows people home if they don't cross themselves before entering the garden (Nope-not even going to dignify this one with a comment.)

- There's an "Indian curse" on Hull House. (Not hardly -- and isn't the fact that Jane Addams helped thousands of people and won the Nobel Prize pretty much proof that the place isn't cursed?)

- While many strange pictures have been taken on the grounds, there are also a lot of false positives common to the site that one should be careful of. For instance, many shots said to be of a pale white face in the window are actually pictures of a lamp. Also, most of the "hooded figure on the stairs" pictures are actually showing a reflection of the photographer's ear!

tourists and historians, but ghost hunters, too. The eerie stories told by Jane Addams and the occupants of Hull House are still recalled when weird happenings take place in these modern times. It is common for the motion sensors of the alarm system to be mysteriously triggered. When security officers respond, they find the house is empty and there is no sign of a break-in or any disturbance. Officers state that no building on the University of Illinois Chicago campus (which maintains the house) has as many false calls as Hull House does. They have also answered reports about people inside the house, or looking out the windows, but the police have never found anyone in the place.

ADAM SAYS:

Please, please leave the people who work at Hull House alone. The Hull House organization is still active - and well-worth donating to - but the museum exists to promote Jane Addams' legacy. It's not a ghost hunting theme park.

CHICAGO'S FORGOTTEN HAUNTED HOUSES

No one knows how many haunted houses Chicago has -- or had. In 1886, the Society of Psychical Research stated that there were around 150 houses in Chicago that were sitting empty because no one would rent them on account of the hauntings! Plenty of allegedly haunted houses in the city remain, of course, but many formerly famous haunted houses have vanished into the sands of time. Some forgotten houses include:

THE PETER FANNING HOUSE

Standing on the Southeast corner of Taylor and Aberdeen, Peter Fanning, a stonecutter, purchased a huge lot on which he built a high stone wall and massive iron gates surrounding a huge stone foundation in the 1870s. The home he built there included a huge vault in which he planned to store his valuables. However, he died before the house was finished. His daughters built a much cheaper house on the foundations. The ghost of Peter Fanning haunted the place, and, when it was torn down for a commercial lot, the ghost put a curse on the property. It was said that no business on the site lasted for very long, and the owners of the businesses blamed Fanning's ghost.

On the site now: The curse must have worn off; Al's Italian Beef has been thriving there for years!

THE PETER SCHUTTLER MANSION

At Adams and Aberdeen, Peter Shuttler began building a mansion, but died of blood poisoning. His ghost was said to haunt the grounds, but by the time the house was torn down in 1911, the ghost had apparently been replaced by the ghost of a man said to have been kept prisoner in the house.

OTHER HAUNTED CHICAGO SPOTS

We sure as heck don't know every haunted place in Chicago -- no one does! There are lots and lots of places out there that have reported strange goings-on, though, in many cases, no story behind the haunting has ever been identified. In other cases, stories of suicides, mobster murders and Indian burial grounds have been tossed around but never verified. A few other places around town that are rumored to be haunted include:

Webster's Wine Bar - 1480 W. Webster: A former employee spoke of seeing the ghost of a man dressed as a pioneer on the second floor. Interestingly, outside of the restaurant is a "site of Fort Dearborn" plaque. Webster's Wine Bar is nowhere near the site of Fort Dearborn.

Chicago Board of Trade Building - 400 S. LaSalle : Apparitions and moans have been reported; they are said to be the result of a businessman who was killed outside of the place in the late 1970s.

Maggiano's - 516 N. Clark: People who work in the building report strange feelings that may be related to the ghost of Lucille Leonard, who was better known as Rae Wilson, a cabaret singer, who jumped (or was pushed) from a window of the building in 1917 when it was still The St. Regis Hotel.

22nd Place Block in Chinatown: Sometimes promoted as the "most haunted block in Chicago," lots of poltergeist-style activity was once reported on this block, though it's apparently quieted down now. No historical reason for it to be haunted has been determined.

Music Box Theatre - 3733 N. Southport: Poltergeist activity, including curtains falling on any organ player who misses a note, are blamed on the ghost of Whitey, a former owner.

Emmit's Irish Pub - 495 N. Milwaukee: Apparitions and strange feelings are reported in the basement, which still includes the vault from when the place was the Italian-American Bank.

On the site now: Parking lots and one-story buildings litter the area today.

THE SKATING POND GHOST

Somewhere near 35th and Cottage Grove stood a 19th century house where, according to legend, an old woman died. Her ghost was seen picking lilacs and wandering around on the skating pond that was formed in the sinkhole where the house used to be.

On the site now: Parks, but apparently no skating pond.

THE ELIZABETH MCCARTHY HOUSE

Right near the haunted skating pond at 3530 Cottage Grove Ave. stood a house build by Elizabeth McCarthy in the 1870s. Here, she spent her declining years sitting in her room, staring out the window. When she died, her daughters locked the room and left all of their mother's things in it. They tried to rent the house, but had a condition that the door to their mother's former room must be kept locked. There were no takers, and the building began to fall apart. The ghost was often seen staring out the window, just as she had in life.

On the site now: Parks and high rises. It's possible that this was the same ghost who haunted the skating pond.

ROBEY'S TAVERN

In the 19th century, Damen Avenue was known as Robey Street. The Robey farmhouse stood near the southeast corner of Robey and Washington streets, and, by 1900, had become Robey's Tavern, a bar with residences on the second floor. As of the turn of the 20th century, this was perhaps the most famously haunted house in all of Chicago. Many people said that they saw the ghost of Mrs. Robey wandering the premises wearing a black gown with a short waist, along with fine lace cuffs and a large lace collar. She was usually described as walking with folded hands, moaning and sighing. Some said that the city's first public "hanging bee" was held in front of the house. Newspapers used the term "hanging bee," to refer to the number of criminals hanged at the same time.

On the site now: a parking lot near the United Center. Not to be confused with the Frank Lloyd Wright-designed Robey House near the University of Chicago.

THE GHOST OF THOMAS WARD

During what must have been an awfully tense family reunion at 262 W. Polk St. (old address) in September of 1902, a man named Thomas Ward was beating his mother, who lived in the house, and threatening to kill her when his brother, Michael, shot him through the face and killed him. Thomas, who must have been a swell fellow, had already shot his mother in the arm earlier that year. The gunshot wound to the face didn't kill him - he ran out of the basement before collapsing and being carried back to the house, where he died in a chair. Barely two months later, his ghost was sighted sitting on an abandoned icebox on a rear porch. Screaming crowds gathered behind the house on Blue Island Avenue to see it, and, according to reports, were not disappointed. It was reported in the *Chicago Tribune* only once, but the comment of a bystander: "Tommy's on the icebox again," indicate that the ghost had been showing up for some time.

On the site now: 262 W. Polk St. was changed to 843 in 1909, but #843 no longer exists, as those portions of Polk Street and Blue Island are now covered by the University of Illinois campus. Our best estimate is that the house would have been in the middle of where the student center is now - right next to Hull House.

THE TAYLOR STREET VAULT

Near the former crossing of Taylor and Blue Island (which no longer intersect) stood an old house separated from the street by a small brick wall. It was said to have been designed not be a home but a mausoleum, and several people saw the ghost of an old man walking in and out of it. It was thought to be the ghost of a man who wanted to be buried there. Everyone in the neighborhood was said to know the story well, though not many actually saw the ghost.

On the site now: there is a house on the site now on the 1000 block of West Taylor that may be the original house, though the brick wall would have been rebuilt years ago.

THE GHOST OF SHAKY MORGAN

On East End Lane (now Hyde Park Boulevard), near 54th Street, stood the house where Shaky Morgan died. The family moved away, claiming that the ghost had driven them out of the house. The house was torn down and another rebuilt on the site, but the ghost of Shaky was seen there, too, especially on stormy nights.

On the site now: The exact location has not been ascertained, but one house in the area is thought to be the second house that Shaky haunted. No recorded sighting seems to have taken place in over a century, though.

OLD MAN LANE

Old Man Lane was a well-known figure around Hyde Park and lived at a house around 47th and Lark Park Avenue. After his death, his ghost drove several tenants out of the place, but one tenant, a Mrs. Mary Ford, seemed to like him. He used to give her advice as to exactly what sort of unusual blend of coal to use in the furnace. The coal deliveryman thought the combination to be ridiculous, but it seemed to work. Mrs. Ford never met Mr. Lane in life, but described him to neighbors perfectly and said she had several conversations with his ghost.

On the site now: Strip malls

OTHER HAUNTED CHICAGO SPOTS

Oak Street Beach (and other nearby spots): Ghostly black forms haven been seen floating along the lakeshore; some say that these are the ghosts of pioneers who died on the Great Lakes Trail. This, however, ignores the fact that the lakeshore would have been farther West in the days of the trail. What these forms are actually walking through is Cap Streeter's District of Michigan!

The Baton Club - 436 N. Clark: The apparition of a guy thought to be a mobster has been seen outside the front door.

Water Tower Place: Phantom shoppers are said to have shown up on security cameras.

The Hangge-Uppe - 14 W. Elm St.: The upper floor of this bar and dance club is allegedly haunted by a former manager who committed suicide in the building.

Betty's Blue Star Lounge - Grand and Ashland: Staff members say this place - below a former brothel - is haunted.

The Tribune Tower - Lots of unsubstantiated rumors abound, including the ghost of Jean Lalime. Others suggest that when the architectural antiques that are inlaid in the building were brought to Chicago, they brought ghosts with them.

Hooters -660 N. Wells: Waitresses working in the building have reported hearing phantom footsteps in the basement. They also claim to hear their names being called by disembodied voices. Phones and electrical equipment periodically have problems and malfunction and the jukeboxes turn themselves on and off.

And too many more to list!

THE OLD NATIONAL MEDICAL COLLEGE

The Old National Medical College building, at the present site of 17-19 West Erie St., was long thought to be one of the most haunted places on the near North side. Many cadavers had been delivered to the house when it was a medical college. Years later, neighbors would hear the sound of phantom carriages pulling up to the house, followed by the sound of coffins being unloaded. Some reports even stated that bones were found in the back yard!

On the site now: The actual spot, near Erie and State, appears to be parking today, but several old medical college buildings are still nearby, and the ghost WAS heard in the street, not the building itself!

THE HELM HOUSE

In the 1880s, a rickety frame house stood on the Northwest corner of Halsted and Lill, near Lincoln Avenue (very close to both the Biograph Theatre and The Tonic Room). The story went that sometime in the 1870s a man and his two children were found murdered in the house. The bodies were found on the first floor, but based on bloodstains found on the stairs they had apparently been dragged down from the attic. Chris Helm, who owned the ramshackle frame house in the 1880s, offered $5 to anyone who would spend the night in the attic, where the ghost seemed most active. He claimed that anyone who tried would be awakened by horrible screams and would open their eyes to find a woman in white, with eyes like saucers, holding out a handful of burning sulfur. Two people attempted to sleep there, and neither lasted more than an hour. Policemen on the beat claimed that they wouldn't go near the place, and Helm was still telling the same story 10 years later!

On the site now: A new brick building now occupies the spot.

THE GHOST OF LINCOLN STREET

In 1888, The *Chicago Tribune* reported that a ghost had been appearing in a shack on 21st and Lincoln Street (which is now Wolcott). The apparition was said to be the ghost of a Bohemian man who had committed suicide shortly after seeing the ghost of his murdered wife. Ever since then, the paper reported, his ghost had appeared nightly, and large crowds had come to see it and -- get this -- fire guns at it! When fired at, it would vanish and immediately re-appear 20 feet away. It seems to us that this story was probably invented by an awfully bored reporter!

HAUNTED CHICAGO POLICE STATIONS
A GHOSTLY GATHERING OF STRANGE TALES FROM 1907

Police stations, jails and prisons are not uncommon places to find ghosts. However, in late 1906 and early 1907, a number of police stations came to the Chicago public's attention as being infested with ghosts.

In 1907, six Chicago police stations, officials said, were definitely haunted. Ghosts had been seen at many stations from time to time, but those six stations were regularly haunted. In one of the stations, a patrol driver resigned his position rather than continue in the "ghost-besieged" headquarters where he was assigned to duty. In another station, a ghost attacked one of the patrolmen while he was sleeping in the off-duty quarters upstairs. He was so frightened that he fired his revolver at the phantom and left six bullet holes in the plaster wall. In still another station, a shadowy intruder so affected the

mind of a patrolman that he went insane and had to be taken away to an asylum.

The Stockyards, Hyde Park, Grand Crossing, Englewood, Des Plaines and New City stations were all reportedly haunted. The Stockyards station was said to be the most spirit-infested. Evidence of the spectral activity was vouched for by the commanding officer and the patrolmen. Desk Sergeant William Prindeville, who had been at the station since 1896, had seen so many ghosts in his time, he claimed, that he had become used to them and rather enjoyed their company.

THE STOCKYARDS

Stockyards Police Station (Chicago Daily News)

The first ghost made an appearance at the Stockyards station in the winter of 1902 and was seen on the night that followed his death in the basement of the building. The "old soldier," as the officers described him, was worn out after tramping through the snow all day, came into the station, and asked to be allowed to spend the night there. Sergeant Prindeville, who was on desk duty at the time, told the man to go down to the basement, where they often allowed "bojacks," as the homeless were known to the police, to spend the night. The old veteran made his way down to the warm basement and curled up on one of the bunks. Early the next morning, a number of "regulars" who had seen the old man come in the night before, found him dead on his bunk and reported it to the officers upstairs.

It the early morning hours of the following day, as Sergeant Prindeville was dozing in his chair and waiting for dawn to end the night watch and send him home for breakfast, he heard a slight rapping on the door. He first thought the wind had caused the door to rattle, but listening carefully, he realized that it was a sound made by someone knocking. He went over to the door and opened it. As he turned the knob, a flurry of snow whipped into his face and in the dim light, he saw the faint outline of the old soldier who had asked him for a place to sleep on the previous night. Knowing that the man had died, Prindeville quickly realized that he was facing a ghost. He hurriedly slammed the door and went back behind his desk, unnerved by what would turn out to be the first of many such encounters.

When the shift changed later that morning, Prindeville told the other officers what he had seen. Not surprisingly, they refused to believe him, insisting that the swirling snow must have been playing tricks on his eyes. After that, however, Prindeville began watching for the ghost, and so did some of the other men. Nearly everyone at the station saw the ghost at one time or another, because he returned every winter whenever the snow would fly. Each night following a storm, a knocking would come at the door and when answered, officers would find the old soldier standing outside. Prindeville stated that he often spoke to the ghost when it appeared, but he never received a reply.

HYDE PARK

Detectives at the Hyde Park Station (Chicago Daily News)

According to an account from 1907, Detective John Shea, one of the most reliable and trustworthy officers at the Hyde Park police station, nearly shot out the back wall of the station house one night when a ghost invaded his sleeping quarters. Shea had gone to sleep just after midnight in the dormitory on the third floor of the building. Just after 2:00 a.m., he reported, something began tugging on the bed covers, awakening him from a sound sleep. The room was pitch dark and Shea, who was only half awake, did nothing more at first than reach down and try and retrieve the disappearing blankets.

A few minutes later, the bed covers were again pulled from the bed and the police officer, now thoroughly awake, thought that somebody was trying to play a trick on him. He decided that he would wait until it happened again, and if anyone appeared, he would fire off his revolver into the ceiling to frighten them and show that he too enjoyed playing pranks. As he lay there with his finger on the trigger, he was horrified to see a phantom shape step out from behind a clothes locker and approach the bed.

Shea later stated that the ghost was shaped like a woman, except that it only had one eye, which shined with a blue sort of light. It slowly approached the bed until it was only about a foot away, and then it reached out a hand toward him. By this time, Shea was as cold as an icicle and his hand was gripping the butt of his revolver so tightly that his knuckles had turned white. Slowly, the ghost's fingers gathered up the corner of the bed quilts and gradually pulled them off onto the floor. Then, it seemed to draw backward, retreating to the place where Shea had first seen it, as it watched with its one blue eye as he pulled the bed covers back up again.

Shea declared that he stayed there looking at the ghost of nearly an hour. By that time, he said, his courage had returned to him and he raised the pistol in his hands and fired six times. The sound of the shots created a commotion downstairs, where some of the other night watch men were playing cards, and across the street at the Holland Hotel, where dozens of guests later reported hearing the sound of shots being fired. Shea's fellow officers crashed up the stairs and burst into the room. The lights were turned on to see what was happening and all of the men saw Shea sitting on the edge of the bed with sweat beaded on his brow and smoke curling from the barrel of his gun. He pointed to the wall on the south end of the room, where there were six large bullet holes.

He only uttered one word: "Ghost!"

GRAND CROSSING

Patrol wagon driver Thomas Murnane quit his job at the Grand Crossing station rather than put up with the ghost that he, and others, claimed haunted the place. For an entire year before Murnane resigned, the ghost appeared regularly at the station every night and found its chief delight in removing the harness from the patrol wagon horses. As required by the rules of the department, one team of horses had to be kept harnessed all night, and Murnane declared before he left service that the black figure of a man entered the barn every night and calmly removed the harness from his team.

A Chicago Police Patrol Wagon from the early 1900s
(Chicago Daily News)

Murnane and two other men who worked on the wagon with him always went to sleep between night runs. One night, Murnane was lying on his cot, not asleep but thinking, when he saw a man walk into the stall occupied by the team and remove the harness from the horses. In the darkness, Murnane thought it was one of the police officers and that he had been wrongly told to keep the horses harnessed all night.

The next morning, he told the other men what he had seen and they only laughed at him and told him that his night visitor was probably "Johnny Reeves." Murnane had never heard of the man, but not wanting to show his ignorance, he kept quiet and went on about his work. Later that day, though, he asked one of the police officers about Reeves and was told that he had been a tramp who had died one night while sleeping in the barn. Murnane became convinced after this that the figure he saw each night was that of a genuine ghost.

The sightings of "Johnny Reeves" continued and the patrol wagon driver, frightened out of his wits by the ghost, tried in vain to sleep as the other men did. Every night, he told them afterward, he lay in a cold sweat, watching the intruder. Finally, after he had worried himself sick, he wrote out his resignation, even though he knew that it meant never fulfilling his dream of being a police officer. Even that lifelong goal was not enough to convince Murnane to stay and brave the nightly visits from "Johnny Reeves."

ENGLEWOOD

According to police officials, Denny Lang, one of the detectives at the Englewood station was pushed out of bed by a ghost and then chased down Wentworth Avenue for several blocks one night in the summer of 1906. Lang had been told that the ghost of a Polish laborer, who had been killed by a switch engine on the Rock Island Railroad tracks just behind the station, had taken up residence in the sleeping quarters on the station's second floor. The ghost was said to carry a bag filled with bricks to attack anyone who came near it.

Lang didn't believe the story and laughed at his fellow officers who were too scared to sleep at the station house. He was determined to prove that he was no coward. One night, about an hour after he had climbed into one of the iron cots offered for use by men on reserve duty, Lang was startled by a heavy thumping on the floor under his bed. He looked around, trying to determine where the disturbance was coming from, and was terrified to see a ghost standing in the far corner of the room. He claimed that it had eyes that glowed like fire and a bag filled with bricks - just as the other men had described it.

Lang's courage immediately vanished and he ran from the room. He pounded down the stairs and kept running, out onto Wentworth Avenue and down the street. He reported that the ghost came after him, hurling pieces of bricks as it pursued him. Eventually, the ghost vanished but the experience was not lost on Lang and he never slept in the station house again.

A remodeling of the station in 1907 caused the ghost to appear less often than it had in the past. Even so, most of the men claimed they still wouldn't sleep there alone.

DES PLAINES STREET

The ghost that haunted the station on Des Plaines Street was said to be that of a tramp who had been killed there several years before. One night, two tramps were sleeping in Cell No. 3, having been given shelter from cold weather outside. They got into a fight that led to one of them choking the other to death. After that, men who slept in that cell, prisoners and tramps alike, claimed to be awakened by cold hands squeezing their throats. The cell was soon widely avoided and old timers, familiar with the story, stated that they would rather sleep on the cold Chicago streets than in Cell No. 3 at the Des Plaines station.

NEW CITY STATION

According to officers at the New City station, their resident ghost was that of a prisoner who died while trying to escape from his cell one night. After that, officers and prisoners were often aroused at night by an eerie sound like that of a file grating on an iron bar. They came to believe that the prisoner was still trying to escape from confinement, many years after his death.

Cops & prisoners at the Des Plaines Street Police Station (Chicago Daily News)

THE IRISH CASTLE

In the South Side neighborhood of Beverly stands one of the most unique of the reportedly haunted houses in Chicagoland. It has been known by several names over the years, from the Givens Mansion to the Irish Castle, although its present incarnation is the Beverly Unitarian Church. After the destruction of Palmer Potter's castle on Lakeshore Drive, this structure became designated as the only actual castle in the Chicago area. It is located on a slight hill at the corner of 103rd and Longwood Drive and has a strangeness about it that contrasts with the elegant homes nearby. If legends and lore about it are any indication, it certainly lives up to its odd appearance!

The man who erected the Irish Castle was Robert C. Givens, a Chicago real estate dealer of the 1880s. After working for some time with the realty firm of E.A. Cummings & Co., he decided to tour Ireland and Europe for a time and then returned to Chicago to establish his own real estate company. The firm prospered and soon Givens decided to construct his own home. The story goes that during his tour of Ireland, he became enamored of an ancient, ivy-covered castle on the banks of the River Dee. Possessing some

The famous Irish Castle in the Beverly neighborhood

amount of artistic ability, Givens sketched the castle and had plans drawn up for a home to be built on a bluff above Tracy Avenue (now Longwood). The neighborhood at that time was called Washington Heights. The castle was completed in 1886 and legend has it that Givens actually built the place for his wife. However, she died before she could ever live there.

Heartbroken, he moved into the house anyway and attempted to enjoy the structure that he had labored so long to be able to afford. He moved in a variety of Irish antiques and hung his collection of tapestries on the walls. Givens was never able to realize the quiet, retired life that he had hoped for in the castle, though, and he sold the house to John B. Burdett in 1908.

As time passed, the building went through a variety of owners. It was used by a manufacturer, a doctor and a girls' school before becoming a church. The house was sold to the Unitarian Church in 1942 and in the late 1950s new additions were constructed for classrooms. Later, plans were made to tear down the castle altogether for a new building, but these plans were discarded in 1972 and the church remains in the old castle today.

There have been a wide variety of strange happenings in the building. The source of the hauntings is said to be a previous occupant from the time when the castle was the Chicago Female College. According to the story, a young girl became ill with a serious case of influenza and died in the early 1930s. The legends say that her name is "Clara" and that she had never left this place.

The ghost was first encountered in the 1960s by a church custodian, who came upon a young girl in a long dress standing in one of the rooms. The two of them chatted for a few minutes and the young girl remarked that the place had changed much since she had lived there. The custodian left the room and then suddenly recalled that the church had been in the building for more than 20 years. Such a young girl couldn't possibly have lived there before that. She ran back to the room, but the girl had vanished! She then searched the entire building, only to find all the doors and windows locked. She even looked outside and discovered that a fresh layer of snow now blanketed the ground. There were no footprints leading in or out of the church.

Witnesses to the strange events have been numerous and even include a church pastor, who, shortly after she took over the position, saw two small arms embrace her husband's waist. While the pastor clearly saw this occur, her husband claimed to feel nothing.

Members of the congregation and visitors to the castle have also reported strange phenomena. Several attendees at a wedding reception discovered that a number of utensils mysteriously vanished, only to show up again later. Others have noted half-full wine glasses that have emptied when no one is around. There have also been a number of strange noises. Occupants of the building have described a "jingling" sound, like the tinkling of glasses and silverware at a dinner party. A former pastor, The Reverend Roger Brewin, stated that he often tried to track down the source of these mysterious sounds but he never could. He said that they seemed to come from everywhere, and yet nowhere, all at the same time.

Even the neighbors have seen odd things. They report seeing what appear to be candles drifting past the windows of the castle at night, even when no one is there. One woman also said that she saw a female figure walking across the grounds in the snow. The figure appeared to be solid and yet left no footprints behind. Some believe this spirit might be that of Eleanor Veil, who lived in the castle and maintained it through the Great Depression. It has been suggested that perhaps she loved the place so much she simply decided not to leave.

Who these ghosts are, or why they have remained here, remains a mystery but it seems certain that they are at peace in this place. There are no terrifying encounters that take place within the walls of this sanctuary and for this reason, officials at the church (who are more open-minded than most) are content to let the ghosts remain. The Irish Castle continues to appeal to not only the spirits of the past, but also the spiritual side of those who come here, as well. The restless spirits do not seem so restless here and perhaps have found comfort within these stone walls.

FATHER DAMEN & THE HAUNTING OF HOLY FAMILY

Located along Roosevelt Road on the South Side of Chicago, the magnificent spires of Holy Family Church point toward the sky -- or toward heaven, if you prefer. The gothic structure stands as the centerpiece of one of Chicago's oldest Catholic parishes and is a wonderful example of local and architectural history, as well as legend and lore.

According to church history, the parish that Holy Family Church serves was founded by Father Arnold Damen, a Jesuit missionary for whom Chicago's Damen Avenue was named. In 1857, the church was built over the running water of Red Creek, an ancient practice in Europe. The building's main altar is said to be positioned directly over the water. As an aside, tradition has it that the river received the name of "Red Creek" after an Indian battle that was fought here centuries ago caused the water to run red with blood. The site came to be considered sacred by the Native Americans, making it a perfect candidate for another holy site in years to come.

Holy Family Church & St. Ignatius School

Father Arnold Damen

The church saw what was considered to be its first miracle just a few years after it was constructed. On the east side of the main altar is a large, badly proportioned statue of Our Lady of Perpetual Help that was created by a local man sometime in the 1860s. It came to be considered the protective guardian of the church after a crack was discovered one day that threatened the very structure of the building. The crack had made its way down one wall of the church, from the ceiling to the floor. If it enlarged further, church officials were warned, a wall, or several walls, could collapse. Father Damen decided to place the church under the protection of Our Lady of Perpetual Help and he moved the large wooden statue so that it stood under the crack. Somehow, it held for many decades and was never repaired until a major renovation in the 1980s. For more than a century, despite years of water damage and decay from rain seeping through the fissure, parishioners were confident in the fact that the building was never in any real danger, thanks to the watchfulness of the church's protector.

Other miracles and strange happenings followed. Perhaps the greatest was the salvation of the church during the Great Chicago Fire of 1871. Although Mrs. O'Leary's cow never really kicked over a lantern, the fire did start near DeKoven and Jefferson streets, just a few blocks away from Holy Family. When the fire broke out, Father Damen was in New York, but he received a telegraph from Chicago that alerted him to the fact that the city was in flames and the church and the parish were in danger. There was little that he could do from so far away, other than to pray and to trust in God and Our Lady of Perpetual Help. Mysteriously, the fire somehow shifted away from the church and burned a path to the north instead, destroying the downtown business district, but sparing Holy Family. The parish was saved and the event was acknowledged as a miracle. When Father Damen returned home to Chicago, he ordered seven candles to be kept burning on a side altar to commemorate the event. After a few years, the candles were replaced by gas jets and then light bulbs, but they have burned brightly ever since.

Without a doubt, though, the most famous story of Holy Family also involves Father Damen and supernatural assistance of another sort. The legend has been referred to in parish histories of the church and it involves what many believe to be curious additions to the décor of Holy Family. These additions are two wooden statues that depict altar boys dressed in old-fashioned cassocks. The two young boys were said to be brothers who drowned together while on a parish picnic in 1874. No one had any idea at the time that they would return to play a very mysterious part in the history of this spiritual community.

According to the story, Father Damen was awakened one night around in the late 1880s, during a terrible snowstorm, by the insistent ringing of the bell at the rectory. When the porter opened the door, he found two young boys on the doorstep, shivering in the cold, anxiously asking for a priest to come and call on a sick woman who was not expected to live through the night.

Father Damen overheard their pleas and he told the boys that he would come with them immediately. Bundling up into his warmest coat and scarf, he followed the boys out into the night. They trudged for blocks through the nearly blinding snow to a dilapidated cottage on the far edge of the parish. As they reached the door, the boys told the priest that the sick woman had taken to her bed at the top floor of the house. He quickly opened the door and went inside and began climbing the rickety steps to the upper floor. As Father Damen turned to speak to the two boys, he realized that they were gone.

At the top of the steps, he entered a small room and found an old woman lying on a bed in the corner. She turned to look at him weakly but managed to smile when she saw that her caller was a priest. She thanked him for coming and he heard her confession and gave her the last rites of the church. The elderly woman was comforted and yet confused by his presence. She asked him how he knew to come to her, admitting that she was very ill and needed a priest, but that she had known no one to send for one.

Father Damen explained that two boys had awakened him and asked him to come. He assumed that they were neighbors, perhaps sent by their parents to fetch him. But the woman insisted that she had spoken with no one. She did not know her neighbors anymore and no one knew she had been ill. There had been simply no one for her to send to summon spiritual help.

"Have you no boys of your own?" Father Damen asked her.

"I had two sons many years ago, altar boys at the church," she replied. "But they have long since died."

Father Damen had the stunning revelation that the two vanished boys had been the woman's sons, returning to help her in her hour of need. He explained his feelings to the woman as she lay dying and when she passed away near morning, she did so with a smile on her face. She had found peace and believed that she would soon be reunited with her lost children. Father Damen was so moved by what had occurred that he commissioned two wooden statues of altar boys and had them placed high above the main altar of the church. They have been watching over the parish ever since.

Throughout modern times, reported hauntings at Holy Family seem to suggest that Father Damen still makes occasional appearances here, as well, watching over his beloved parish. During the latter part of the 1900s, clergy members and staff reported a figure wearing clerical dress, which passed through the church and patrolled the hallways of St. Ignatius College Preparatory High School next door. These sightings were especially prevalent during the 1990s, when the church and school were being renovated. Just a few years before, the Jesuits had considered destroying the aging landmark and selling off the empty lot, but donations and fund-raising had garnered the necessary funds to restore the place. Many believe that perhaps Father Damen returned because of the all the activity that was occurring in the building.

Since that time, he has still been occasionally seen, walking the hallways, dressed in his clerical garments. Those who have seen him as he has passed by know who he is -- Father Damen, still making his rounds.

THE HOUSE WITH NO SQUARE CORNERS

Near the tiny town of Bull Valley, Ill., is perhaps one of the strangest houses in the Chicago area. It was originally located far off the beaten path and remains secluded today along a quiet and mostly deserted country highway. George and Sylvia Stickney built this English country house in the middle 1800s. They chose such an isolated place for the peace and quiet and for their spiritualistic activities. Both of them were said to be accomplished mediums and they wanted to host parties and séances for their friends. The seclusion offered by the Illinois countryside made the perfect setting.

The house itself was very unusual in its design. It rose to a full two stories, although the second floor was reserved for a ballroom that ran the entire length of the building. During the Civil War, the house also served as quarters for Federal

The Stickney Mansion

soldiers and was home to the first piano in McHenry County. But this was not why the house gained its fame, or rather, its notoriety.

As devout practitioners of Spiritualism, the Stickneys insisted on adding distinctive features into the design of the house. These features, they assured the architect, would assist them when holding séances and Spiritualistic gatherings at the property. Since the séances would be held quite often, they specified that the house should have no square corners in it. They explained that spirits have a tendency to get stuck in these corners, which could have dire results. It has also been suggested that the Stickneys believed that corners attracted the attention of evil spirits as

MARY WORTH

In the 1970s, every child in the Western world suddenly knew some variation the story of "Bloody Mary," the evil woman who could be conjured up by saying her name in front of a mirror. Researchers were baffled - normally, when something like this, known as a polygenesis, happens, it can be traced to a book or a movie. No one had any idea, though, where the Bloody Mary story came from.

One of the few clues was a variation in which the ghostly woman was called Mary Worth - rather than chanting "Bloody Mary" in the mirror, one was supposed to say something like "I believe in Mary Worth." According to legend, Mary Worth was a woman in Lake County (the North Chicago suburban area) who ritualistically tortured and killed runaway slaves on her farm. When the locals found out about her activities, an angry mob burned her at the stake as a witch and buried her - either on her property or in St. Patrick's cemetery, depending on which version you believe (though several researchers have pointed out that few angry mobs would bury a witch in a Catholic cemetery).

Some say that the Worth farm - which is long gone - became haunted after a stone said to mark Worth's actual burial place was moved.

However, while there were several women named Mary Worth in the area in the 19th century, not a shred of evidence to support the story that Mary Worth, the witch, ever existed at all has ever come to light, and the stories are almost certainly just local legends. In fact, it's one of several stories that emerged to back up the story about chanting "Mary Worth" in a mirror - others have Mary as a car crash victim or axe murderess. Still, could this be the legend that spawned the Bloody Mary phenomenon?

well, a common belief in Spiritualist circles of the time.

During the time that the couple resided in the house, Sylvia Stickney gained considerable fame as a spirit medium. The upstairs ballroom was converted into a large séance chamber and people came from far and wide to contact the ghosts of their deceased loved ones and relatives.

According to legend, one corner of a room accidentally ended up with a 90-degree measurement. How this could have happened is unknown. Perhaps the architect either forgot or was unable to complete the room with anything but a right angle. Perhaps he thought that the Stickneys would never notice this one flaw. But they did notice! And here, the legend takes an even stranger turn.

The stories say that it was in this corner that George Stickney was discovered one day. He was slumped to the floor, dead from apparent heart failure, although no visible signs suggested a cause of death. Was he right about the square corners? Could an angry ghost, summoned by a séance, have been trapped in the corner?

Apparently this was not actually the case. This was a popular legend of the house, but it's not really true. George Stickney did not die the mansion, but passed away some time after moving out. However, it is thought that the house's single square corner did bring bad luck and misfortune to the Stickneys. They were plagued by tragedy and it's likely Sylvia's keen interest in Spiritualism was connected to the fact that seven of her children died over a short period of time. There are no records to say what the children died from but it must have come as quite a shock to the couple. As the Stickneys grew older, they moved to a smaller home a short distance away, perhaps realizing that the one square corner had been their downfall after all.

Time passed and despite the séances and the legend of a mysterious death being suffered by George Stickney, the house never really gained a bad reputation until the 1970s. It had always been considered a strange and unusual place, but it was never thought to be a bad one until a man named Rodrick Smith moved in. He lived in the house for several years and when he moved out, he began to claim that he had often heard strange noises in the place. He also added that his dogs were never comfortable there. This led him to believe that something was not right with the property. Smith's research led him to reveal that the house had become "tainted" by a group of "devil worshippers" who lived in it during the 1960s. He was convinced that their "black magic rituals" conjured up something unpleasant that now inhabited the house.

It later turned out that the so-called "devil worshippers" were actually a group of stoned-out hippies who painted the rooms in dark colors and built open fires on the floors of the house. When they departed, they left spray painted messages and drug paraphernalia in their wake. While it's unlikely that they worshipped the Devil, Smith was sure that they had changed the atmosphere of the Stickney Mansion.

He was certainly no help in getting the house sold, but neither was one of the real estate listings that came after his departure. A local antiques dealer claimed that he saw a real estate ad for the place in which a woman in a wedding gown could be seen pulling aside a curtain and peering out. The photographer who took the picture said that no one was in the house at the time. He also stated that he had seen no one at the window when he was snapping photos of the house. Was the woman a ghost?

Eventually, the house sold and the next owners claimed to experience nothing unusual in the place. They stayed on for several years but moved out when their plans to restore the mansion didn't pan out. Their occupancy leaves nothing to suggest that they were bothered by ghosts and apparently, neither are the current owners. The house is now the Bull Valley Village Hall and the local police department uses a portion of the restored house as their headquarters. They claim to experience nothing out of the ordinary. The official word is that, while the house was badly treated by vandals, it is not, nor was it ever, haunted.

So, who knows? Some area residents dispute the final word from the authorities. They say that ghostly things have been going on in the Stickney Mansion for many years, and continue to this day, whether the local officials want to admit it or not. What is the truth? No one seems to be able to say and the ghosts, if there are any here, are certainly not talking!

MYSTERIES OF THE SCHWEPPE MANSION

The north suburb of Lake Forest has become known over the years for its fabulous mansions and beautiful estates. This is a reputation that the area has gained over time, dating back to the early days of the last century when Chicago's millionaires began to leave the grime and bustle of the city in a search for more bucolic locales.

It was in Lake Forest that newlyweds Charles H. Schweppe and Laura Shedd were presented with a large Tudor Revival mansion as a wedding gift from the bride's father, John Graves Shedd, known in his day as the "Dean of Chicago merchants." Shedd was a partner in the Marshall Field Co. and after the death of Field in 1906 he became president of the firm until his retirement in 1922, when he took over as chairman of the board. Before his death, Marshall Field called Shedd "the best merchant in the United States." After the marriage of his daughter Laura to Charles Schweppe, the Shedds moved from their gothic mansion on Drexel Boulevard to Lake Forest, where Shedd also purchased a home for his daughter and his son-in-law.

THE GATE

Legend has it that if you are looking for a harrowing experience some summer evening, you should take a trip to see "The Gate," one of the most famous and bone-chilling locations on the North Side of Chicago. Located near Libertyville, The Gate can be found off the desolate and secluded River Road, which borders the Independence Grove Forest Preserve.

According to the legend, The Gate marked the entrance to a girl's finishing school back in the early 1950s. One night, the principal suffered a nervous breakdown and killed four of his young students. In a fit of madness, he planted the girl's heads on the metal posts of The Gate. There are other versions of the story, as well. According to some, The Gate did not mark the entrance to a school, but to a summer camp, or even an asylum. No matter what the version of the story, though, the end result is a tale of bloodshed, violence and horrific murder.

Each of the stories ends with local residents and officials razing the school, camp or hospital and trying to obliterate the remnants of the buildings. The murders, and even the very existence of the place, are erased from public record and when asked about it in the future, it is denied that the events ever occurred. And each of the stories also ends with The Gate being haunted.

There are those who claim to have visited The Gate during the early hours of the morning, only to find fresh blood dripping from the iron supports. Others say that on the anniversary of the murders, at the stroke of midnight, the phantom heads of the murdered girls appear on the fence posts, their mouths gaping in a silent scream. There are also those who claim to have seen a small boy staring out from behind the bars in the fence and countless tales of apparitions, phantom screams and mysterious sounds that cannot be explained. Did something terrifying really take place beyond the confines of "The Gate?"

Perhaps, but history of the site is hard to find. A little sketchy information has turned up and it does verify some of the elements of the legend. The Gate was once a part of an orphanage, the Katherine Dodridge Kreigh Budd Memorial Home for Children, which opened in 1925. It was shut down for unspecified reasons at an unknown date, but at some point in the late 1950s, the area was turned into the St. Francis Boys Camp. The camp also ceased operations and faded into oblivion some time ago. It has been surmised that perhaps whatever caused the orphanage to be shut down may have been what spawned the blood-soaked legends of The Gate but unfortunately we are likely to never know one way or another. What we do know is that The Gate will continue to entice nightriders and curiosity-seekers to consider the mystery for many years to come.

The Schweppe Mansion, as it came to be called, was the largest private residence in the region, boasting more than 20 acres of surrounding real estate, 20 bedrooms and 19 bathrooms. It had been constructed on a 90-foot bluff that overlooks Lake Michigan and was designed by prominent architects Frederick Wainwright Perkins and Edmund R. Krause, who had also created the Shedd Mansion in Chicago.

Thanks to the social standing of the family, Charles and Laura held lavish parties for Chicago friends and business contacts, as well as for important political and foreign visitors, including the Duke and Duchess of Windsor, Edward VII and Wallis Simpson. Sweden's Prince Gustavus Adolphus and Princess Louise stayed here as house guests for a time. They strolled through the luxurious house and gardens, admired the Italian statuary, the shimmering fountains and the fantastic view of Lake Michigan. But sadly, all good things must someday come to an end...

The Schweppe family fortune began to crumble after the stock market crash of 1929. Charles lost incredible amounts of money during the Depression and then in 1937, Laura died at the age of only 58. Charles sunk into deep despair, which only worsened when he learned that his wife had left him little in her will. She had inherited half of her father's vast fortune and even had a personal estate that was valued at nearly $6 million. She left nearly all of her money to her children, though, giving Charles a mere $200,000 with which to try and salvage the wreckage of his own career. He tried and failed and his financial future and physical health continued to decline. Schweppe began to suffer from chronic insomnia and he would wander through the vast house each night, pondering the loss of his fortune, stumbling about in his pajamas and robe. When friends insisted that he see a doctor, Charles began to be treated for a nervous condition, but it was too little, too late.

One dark night in 1941, the servants heard the crack of a single gunshot echo though the house. When they reached Charles' bedroom, they found his body thrown back across the blood-spattered bed. A small .32 caliber pistol lay on the covers beside him, his lifeless fingers curled just inches away from its trigger. A red hole could be seen in the center of his forehead, leaving a ghastly wound to the back of his skull that had erupted in blood, bone and pieces of his brain. Charles had taken his own life and had left a tortured suicide note scrawled out on the dresser next to the bed. "I have been awake all night. It is terrible," he had written, never bothering to sign this last missive.

For reasons that remain a mystery, the heirs to the Schweppe estate decided not to live in the house, nor to do anything else with the property. The servants were given their leave and the house was simply closed up and abandoned. The furniture had been left behind, the table still set for the breakfast that Charles Schweppe would never eat and the dust of time was left to gather for 46 years. Although the house and grounds were maintained by a caretaker, it remained 1941 inside the mansion for decades to come.

Not surprisingly, the period of decline spawned many ghost stories about the house. The dark history of the place and the feeling of decadent ruin about the estate were more than enough to attract the interest of ghost enthusiasts and the curious. Tales began to be told of phantom servants who still took care of the house, perhaps inspired by the legend of a pregnant maid who was found dead in the elevator years before. The story went on to say that the elevator always behaved erratically after that, coming to life on its own and moving up and down between floors.

Perhaps the most intriguing story, though, involved a mysterious window on the second floor. When the house had been constructed, beautiful leaded glass windows had been created for it but only one of them offered a clear view of the walk that led up to the front door of the mansion. Local lore had it that in the last days of Charles Schweppe, during the time when his mental health began to decline, he would often peer out of a lower frame of the window, nervously looking out at the front of the house. In the years that followed his death, curiosity-seekers who visited the estate were chilled to see that this same pane of glass in the old window -- and only this pane of glass -- managed to always stay clean. The rest of the windows had become weathered and covered with dirt and grime over the years but somehow, this single pane always looked polished and clean. According to legend, it was kept that way by the ghost of Charles Schweppe, still peering outside as he had done in his final hours.

The Schweppe Mansion had become Lake Forest's local "haunted house," that proverbial creature that spawns dark tales and eerie visits on cool October nights. Only this time, the reputation was well deserved.

In 1987, the fate of the Schweppe Mansion took another turn. The house was purchased by a woman who had restored and renovated four other historic properties. She paid a large sum for the property and planned to live here with her family as they tried to undo the damage that had been done to the mansion by time and neglect. The mansion is now known as Mayflower Place and the dust and dirt of decades past is gone. The house is once again a North Shore architectural gem and has also been placed on the National Register of Historic Places.

And unlike most cases of renovations, when ghosts seemed to be disturbed by the activity in the house, the renovations of the Schweppe Mansion have had an opposite effect -- they have actually laid the ghost to rest. During the work, the old leaded glass windows were temporarily removed to be restored. When it was no longer in place, the single pane that had looked out over the front walk became dirty just like all of the other glass. The ghost had no reason to keep it clean anymore and Charles Schweppe, if that is who this spirit was, passed on to the other side. There have been no ghostly happenings here since the restoration has been completed.

OLD TOWN TATU

A tattoo parlor may be the last place anyone would look for ghosts -- unless that tattoo parlor was Old Town Tatu, at 3313 W. Irving Park, one of the most haunted locations Weird Chicago has investigated.

When Old Town (then known as Odin Tatu) moved into the building in 2003, it had spent the previous 80 years as the Klemundt Funeral Home, which was built in 1923 by John Klemundt, supposedly over the foundations of an earlier funeral home that dated to the 1880s. No one knew it at the time, but the Klemundt family had believed the building to be haunted for years.

Soon after the tattoo parlor, then owned by Richie "Tapeworm" Herrera, moved in, strange things began to be reported. Some of it was simply what one would expect from moving into such a building. Many of the old furnishings were still in place. The woodwork, it was said, came from a long-demolished South Side mansion, and had been originally imported from an English country manor house. The gated doorway is said to have been salvaged from the German exposition of the 1933-34 World's Fair. In the attic, the new occupants found a gravestone, which was carried down to the front entryway and set up inside a mosaic fireplace. The tattoo artists said it made them nervous knowing it was up there, and they wanted to be able to keep an eye on it.

Odin Tatu when the sign still read Old Town Tattoo

One of the upstairs bedrooms (there was a residence/office suite on the second floor) had a "vibe" to it that made it impossible for anyone to get a good night's sleep there. Objects would fly off of the walls and across the room. Residents described nights when ashtrays would sail across the room off their own accord and land upside down -- but not a single ash would be disturbed when they were turned right side up. One particular Japanese mask had a tendency to fall off of the wall. But the poltergeist activity and strange "vibes" weren't all that was reported -- there were also several ghost sightings.

Several people, staff and customers alike, reported seeing and hearing the ghost of a little girl in old-fashioned saddle shoes in the front entryway. The general impression of researchers is that this was a residual haunting -- not a conscious entity, but the result of leftover mental energy. In fact, it's probably not even the ghost of a person who died in the place, but of a girl who was accidentally left in the funeral home, an experience that terrified her so much as to leave behind a "ghost."

Other ghosts described by the staff in 2006 included a man in a powder blue suit (apparently the ghost of some poor sap who died in the 1970s), a man in a brown suit, and one in a suit likened to a "zoot suit." A ghostly woman was seen in the vicinity of the front counter.

During the first investigation Adam and Ken conducted at the place, EVP (audio) recordings made in the old office picked up the sound of an organ, playing something that sounded like a funeral dirge. But the most clearly haunted part of the building -- that night, at least -- was the basement: the original foundation of the building, which may have been a funeral parlor as

The mosaic fireplace in the front entryway of the shop. Once part of the old funeral homes that existed here.

early as 1880.

Records on the building on the site prior to 1923 are spotty, though the foundations clearly predate the main part of the building. Still, a drainage area can clearly be seen, along with the former location of an incinerator. Near the basement, in fact, is a garage (formerly a stable) around which some 30 bodies were buried at one point. The tombstones are now long gone, but, this being Chicago, it's considered likely that the bodies are still there.

On the night of the first investigation, in June of 2006, cold spots were reported in one corner of the room, and investigators described feeling hands on their shoulders. When one investigator called out "what's your name?" the EVP recorder picked up a voice saying, "Walter."

But the story from that first investigation that has been retold most often was the story Tapeworm told of being attacked on the stairs.

Tapeworm, who had grown up in the neighborhood, said that he had always been superstitious about the funeral home -- and the staircase, which was visible from the street -- as a child. He said that since he had moved in, he had, on two occasions, felt as though someone was trying to push him down the stairs.

"And that freaks me out," he said, "because everyone knows you can't fight back with these cats!"

Richie "Tapeworm" Herrera

However, Tapeworm wasn't about to let them get the last word.

"Here's what I did," he told us. "The first time it happened, I just looked up and said 'Listen! If I die in this place, it is ON!'"

About three weeks after the first investigation, Tapeworm had a heart attack and died in the upstairs area of the building, not far from the staircase. He was 37.

His friends, renaming the place Old Town Tatu, kept it going in order to provide for Tapeworm's young son. After Tapeworm's death, the hauntings became even more pronounced. In early 2007, when Weird Chicago first returned to the place, a silhouette looking like Tapeworm was briefly seen in the basement. That summer, motion sensor cameras installed in the building began picking up strange blobs of light that would move across the room, approach the camera with a distinct sense of purpose, then move along. One of the members of the daytime staff said that picking up pennies that mysteriously appeared on one of the back staircases was a regular part of his morning duties.

On Halloween night of 2007, one of the employees noticed a strange thing on his cell phone -- he had

ADAM SAYS:
If there's ever been a ghost that I definitely believed in, it's the ghost of Tapeworm. Many times when I've been in the basement, I've distinctly felt like someone was flicking my ear or pulling my hair -- the way guys like Tapeworm pick on nerds like me. Maybe he's just still there in our hearts or something like that, but Tapeworm's there, all right!

missed a call from Tapeworm's old phone number. No message was left, and the number now belonged to a random person who had been asleep at the time.

Perhaps Tapeworm has joined the ranks of the ghosts who still call the old funeral parlor home!

THE CONGRESS HOTEL

Built in 1893 to accommodate tourists traveling to the World's Fair, The Congress Hotel was the very picture of elegance. The ballrooms, nightclubs and restaurants inside the hotel were among the finest in the city. The hotel was designed by Clinton Warren, a former employee of Burnham and Root, the firm entrusted with managing the construction of the fair.

Originally, the hotel was known as the Auditorium Annex, due to its proximity to the Auditorium Theatre across the street. At the time, a marble-lined tunnel beneath Congress Street known as Peacock Alley connected the hotel to the theatre. The tunnel is long-since closed off, but still exists below the hustle of the street above.

Over the years, the hotel was expanded. The south wing was constructed in 1902 and 1907, shortly before the name was changed to the Congress. Part of the new construction included the massive ballroom known as the Gold Room, which is still in place today and was the first ballroom in the city to be air-conditioned.

A floor above the Gold Room was the Florentine Room, a slightly smaller room decorated with reproductions of Italian paintings on the ceiling. This room became a favorite of politicians. It was in this room that Theodore Roosevelt jumped onto a table and announced, in June of 1912, that he was leaving the Republican Party, under which he had

A vintage view of the Congress Hotel
(Below) An early 1900s view of the Main Lobby

served as President from 1901-1909. Six weeks later, in August, Roosevelt was back in the Florentine Room, which served as his headquarters as he launched a bid for the presidency as the nominee of the Progressive Party, which, after a remark made by Roosevelt to reporters in the room, became known as the Bull Moose Party.

The Florentine Room eventually became a popular spot for women's suffrage meetings, as well as dances, skating parties, and banquets. In addition to this, the Elizabethan Room, another ballroom, was later renamed the Joseph Urban Room. Here, Benny Goodman played a six-month stand with his integrated orchestra in 1935-36, and, through a series of NBC broadcasts, introduced much of the nation to swing music. Some musical historians say that Goodman redefined American popular music during this engagement at the Congress Hotel.

Of course, the building has a dark side, as well. There seem to be as many hidden nooks and crannies around the Congress as there were the around the hotel H.H. Holmes built in the same era -- and there have probably been at least as many strange deaths there over the years. Just to name a few:

* Capt. Louis Ostheim, a U.S. Army officer, was found in his room with a bullet wound in his temple in 1900. He

had suffered from night terrors, and friends speculated that he had awakened and shot himself in the midst of a nightmare. He was to be married the next morning.

* In 1904, an elevator operator fell four stories down the elevator shaft to his death, an event witnessed by several guests.

* In 1908, there was a murder-suicide involving a love triangle just outside of the front door. A husband and wife, shot by a jealous lover, reconciled as they lay bleeding on the sidewalk. The wife's name was Ruby Pishzak - newspapers couldn't resist commenting on the "Ruby Red Blood of Ruby Pishzak" in headlines.

* Also in 1908, a man named Roy Gormely drank away every last dollar he had (and he had quite a few) in the Pompeiian room - where he had been drinking heavily nightly for some time. On one particular night, he insisted that the orchestra play "The Dead March from Saul." The conductor didn't have the music, so, instead, Gormley bought drinks for every musician - and paid for another round to be served the following Monday. Having enjoyed a drink with the band, he retired to his room and shot himself. A short while later, a woman (thought to be one with whom he'd recently separated) called the hotel to ask for him. When she was told that he'd killed himself, she said, "My God? Is that so?" and hung up.

* In 1919, a girl was poisoned during a party in the Pompeian room. She narrowly survived. The same year, opera singer Charlotte Caillies attempted to poison herself in her hotel room.

* In 1928, G.H. Palin, coiner of thousands of slogans including the venerable "Safety First," died in the hotel - of natural causes, not from a breach in safety.

* Jean Farrel, a showgirl, died of mysterious causes in the hotel in 1930.

* In 1932, a fifteen-year resident of the hotel named Hoyt Smith shot himself in his room.

* In 1938, a Czech refugee named Adele Langer who had been forced out of her homeland with her family when Hitler took over was driven to madness by the persecution she and her family had suffered. In a fit of what was determined to be temporary insanity, she threw herself out of a window - taking her sons Karel, 6, and Jan, 4, with her. The three were considered Czechoslovakian martyrs

* One man was suffocated in his room after an arsonist set four fires in the hotel in 1946.

And this is just a small sampling - the list of murders in the hotel is long, the list of suicides even longer, and the list of notables who died of natural causes in the hotel longer still. Many of the deaths and murders in the hotel never even made the newspapers.

Not surprisingly, there are numerous ghosts associated with the hotel. Rumor has it that Franklin D. Roosevelt, Theodore Roosevelt, Thomas Edison and Frank Lloyd Wright all haunt the place. These rumors appear to have no basis in fact, but the staff has plenty of stories of their own. Several staff members have told us that there are certain floors or rooms that they prefer to avoid at night.

Many customer reviews have mentioned televisions turning themselves off and on. This classic poltergeist activity is sometimes attributed to the ghost of "the Judge," one of the last elderly people to live in the hotel full time. In his declining years, the Judge would amuse himself by wheeling around in his wheelchair with a remote control, confusing people by turning their televisions off and on from the hallway outside.

There have been several reports of a little boy and girl running around. The boy is far more commonly seen than the girl, and is often spotted sprinting down hallways. He has been seen all over, including in the kitchen and at the foot of guests' beds in the middle of the night, but seems to be most active on the 12th floor of the north wing, which is commonly said to be the spookiest floor of them all. There are a couple of theories as to the boy's identity - some say that he may be the ghost of Karel Langer, the six-year-old who fell to his death along with his mother and brother in 1938. Another theory is that the boy and girl are Donald and Zudel Stoddard, two children who were killed in the Iroquois Theatre Fire. Their mother spent a frantic day searching for them before retiring, semi-conscious, to her room at the hotel, where she soon learned that their bodies had been found. Some say that the ghosts are her children coming to find her.

People who have seen the ghost say it looks like a slightly older version of Jan Langer when shown his picture, leading one to suspect that it's Karel, Jan's older brother. After all, sometimes ghosts seem to come about as a result of a lack of commemoration -- Karel's brother, mother and father were pictured in several newspapers as Czechoslovakian martyrs, but Karel's photo was not printed.

In a 2006 investigation, several staff members told us that there had been several recent calls from guests on the seventh floor of the south wing saying that a vagrant with a peg leg was lying in the hallway. Security would arrive and find no trace that a vagrant had ever been present. The ghost -- sometimes known as Peg Leg Johnny -- is thought to be that of a peg-legged hobo who is believed to have died in the hotel in the 1920s. Since then, he's been seen all over the place in the building - the peg leg apparently isn't slowing down his mobility much!

Another story involves a group of U.S. Marines who were scared out of their wits in the middle of the night by a "shadow figure" in their room. The shadow figure, with his connection to the military and to nightmares, is believed to be the ghost of Louis Ostheim, the U.S. Army veteran who shot himself after waking from a nightmare. The south wing, where the marines reported the figure, wasn't built yet at the time of Ostheim's death, but one would assume that a person who could come back from the dead could also figure out a way to walk down a hall! In fact, the shadow figure has been seen all over the hotel -- one security guard claims to have encountered it on the roof one night!

The Gold Room, the largest remaining ballroom, is not without ghosts of its own -- a phantom piano has been seen, and a well-dressed

In a closet near the balcony , we found the mysterious hand of "Drywall Dave." Protruding from the wall was a strange shape that some joked looked like a hand. It was behind too much rubble for us to get close, but an examination of the photo revealed four fingers and a thumb! Some say it was a glove that was plastered over by a prank-loving construction worker. Others, however, point to stories of a worker who was killed by being walled up in the hotel during construction. These stories are almost certainly fictitious, though.

Or could it be the ghost of Teddy Roosevelt, carrying his trademark "big stick?" In 2008, several somewhat whimsical EVP investigations were conducted to see if Roosevelt would endorse a candidate for 2008 (we here at Weird Chicago felt that the Colonel had been unfairly ignored by the mainstream media), but, if he's haunting the place, Roosevelt wasn't talking.

ghostly couple is sometimes spotted overseeing the ballroom from the balcony. Shadow figures sometimes show up in photographs taken of the southeastern corner.

As spooky as the Gold Room can be, it is the Florentine Room that the staff seems to regard as the scariest. At least three security guards have reported hearing old-fashioned music, likened to a calliope or music box, coming from the room in the middle of the night - some attribute this to music played in the room when it was used for roller skating parties years ago. Others have heard the piano in the room play of its own accord. Still others have reported seeing phantom dancers, and many have reported the feeling of a hand on their shoulder.

Regardless of who all of these ghosts might be, it's obvious that the Congress Hotel is one of the most haunted places in Chicago - a place where guests check in, and some of them never check out!

CHICAGO'S VANISHING HITCHHIKERS

The tale of the vanishing hitchhiker is truly an American ghost story. There is not a single part of the country that does not boast at least one tale about a pale young girl who gets a ride with a stranger, only to vanish from the car before they reach their destination.

Stories like this have been a part of American lore for many years and tales of spectral passengers (usually young women) are often attached to bridges, dangerous hills and intersections and graveyards. Folklorist Jan Harold Brunvand calls the vanishing hitchhiker "the classic automobile legend" but stories of these spirits date back as far as the middle 1800s, when men told stories of ghostly women who appeared on the backs of their horses. These spectral riders always disappeared when they reached their destination and would often prove to be the deceased daughters of local farmers. Not much has changed in the stories that are still told today, outside of the preferred method of transportation.

"SCREAMING LIZZIE"

A tragic murder occurred at streetcar stop at Carmen & Lincoln Avenue on November 18, 1905, when a young woman named Lizzie Kaussehull was killed by a crazed stalker named Edward Robhaut, who had been pursuing her for three months. During that time, Robhaut had tried unsuccessfully to win Lizzie's heart. He constantly bothered her, wrote her letters, sent her flowers, and simply refused to accept her rejection. Neighbors later recalled that he frequently waited around the corner of Lincoln and Carmen, waiting for the streetcar that would bring Lizzie home from her job at Moeller & Stange's grocery store, located farther south on Lincoln. Lizzie did her best to ignore him but he followed her home every night.

Lizzie became so fearful for her life that her family reported Robhaut's behavior to the police, including the fact that he told Lizzie that he would kill her if she would not marry him. Robhaut was arrested and a restraining order (called a "peace bond" in those days) was filed against him on November 11, but it had no effect on his actions. He continued to follow her home from the streetcar stop each afternoon, begging her to marry him and threatening to kill her if she did not.

On November 18, Lizzie finished her shift at Moeller & Stange's and, as always, rode the streetcar north on Lincoln. When she reached her stop, she stepped off with several girlfriends, all of them laughing and talking. Then, suddenly, she saw Robhaut leaning against the wall of a nearby storefront. Lizzie's friends froze and Lizzie shakily put up a hand and stammered in his direction that the peace bond was still in place against him. Robhaut suddenly ran toward her and Lizzie began to scream.

Robhaut sprang upon her and plunged a knife into Lizzie's chest. She staggered back away from him, but Robhaut attacked again, stabbing her three more times. Finally, her dress soaked with blood, she fell to the sidewalk. Robhaut looked down at the woman that he claimed to love so much that he had to kill her because he couldn't have her, drew a revolver, placed the barrel into his mouth, and pulled the trigger. The back of Robhaut's skull blew out in a red spray of gore and his body collapsed on top of Lizzie's. They were finally together – in death.

But this was not the end of the story. According to legend, Lizzie's ghost has haunted the intersection at Lincoln and Carmen for more than a century now. The stories claim that, on nights of the full moon, Lizzie returns to the former streetcar stop and can be heard screaming – just as she did when she saw Edward Robhaut lurching toward her on the day that he ended her life.

Today, such tales are usually referred to as "urban legends." They are stories that have been told and re-told over the years and in most every case have been experienced by the proverbial "friend of a friend" and have no real basis in fact -- or do they?

Are all of these stories, as some would like us to believe, nothing more than folklore? Are they simply stories that have been made up and have been spread across the country over a long period of time? Perhaps this is the case, or perhaps not. One has to wonder how such stories got started in the first place. Could any of them have a basis in truth? What if an incident occurred --- perhaps an encounter with a vanishing hitchhiker --- actually happened somewhere and then was told, and re-told, to the point that it lost many of the elements of truth? As the story spread, it was embraced by people all over the country until it became a part of their local lore. It has long been believed that people provide an explanation for something that they cannot understand. This is usually done by creating mythology that made sense at the time. Who knows if there may be a very small kernel of truth hidden inside of the folk tales that sends shivers down your spine?

Tales of phantom hitchhikers can be found all over the world but in no city are they as prevalent as they are in Chicago. There are a number of mysterious phantoms to be found in the region, from the typical vanishing hitchers of legend and lore to what some have dubbed "prophesying passengers" -- strange hitchhikers who are picked up and then pass along odd messages, usually involving the end of the world or something almost as dire.

One Chicago story tells of a prophesying nun. A cab driver once told of a strange and unsettling fare that he had picked up in December 1941. He was cruising the downtown streets in his cab one night and he pulled over to let in a nun who was dressed in the traditional garb of a Catholic order. She gave him the address that she wished to be taken to and they drove off. The radio was on and the announcer was discussing the events that had taken place at Pearl Harbor a short time before and the preparations that the United States was making for war.

The nun suddenly spoke up from the back seat. "It won't last more than four months," she said and then didn't speak again for the rest of the ride. When the cabbie reached the address, he got out to open the door for the sister. He was surprised to discover that she wasn't there! Afraid that the little old lady had forgotten to pay her fare, the driver climbed the steps of the address she had given him and discovered that it was a convent. He knocked on the door and was brought to the Mother Superior. He explained his predicament to her but she told him that none of the sisters had been downtown that day. She asked the driver what the nun had looked like.

As the driver began to describe her, he happened to look up at a portrait that was hanging on the wall behind the Mother Superior's desk. He pointed to the picture and in an excited voice, told her that the woman in the portrait was the nun he had brought to the convent house. He probably thought that he was going to get his fare after all --- but he couldn't have been more wrong. The Mother Superior smiled and quietly said, "But she has been dead for 10 years."

And the nun, like those passengers who tell of the end of the world, was incorrect in her prediction about the short end to World War II. If these beings are truly supernatural, then perhaps they should consider another source from which to get their information about upcoming events!

Another passenger from the Windy City had her own strange prediction to make.

During Chicago's Century of Progress Exposition in 1933, a group of people in an automobile told of a strange encounter. They were traveling along Lake Shore Drive when a woman with a suitcase, standing by the roadside, hailed them. They invited her to ride along with them and she climbed in. They later said that they never really got a good look at her because it was dark outside.

As they drove along, they got into a conversation about the exposition and the mysterious woman oddly told them: "The fair is going to slide off into Lake Michigan in September." She then gave them her address in Chicago and invited them to call on her anytime. When they turned around to speak to her again, after this doom-filled warning, they discovered that she had disappeared!

Unnerved, they decided to go to the address the woman gave them and when they did, a man answered the door. They explained to him why they had come to the house and he merely nodded his head. "Yes, that was my wife. She died four years ago," he said.

THE FLAPPER GHOST

Another ghostly hitchhiker haunts the roadways between the site of the old Melody Mill Ballroom and Waldheim Cemetery, which is located at 1800 South Harlem Ave.

The cemetery, once known as Jewish Waldheim, is one of the more peaceful and attractive graveyards in the area and is easily recognizable from the columns that are mounted at the front gates. They were once part of the old Cook County Building, which was demolished in 1908. This cemetery would most likely go quietly through its existence if not for the tales of the "Flapper Ghost," as the resident spirit has been dubbed.

The story of this beautiful spirit tells of her earthly existence as a young Jewish girl who attended dances at the Melody Mill Ballroom, formerly on Des Plaines Avenue. During its heyday, the ballroom was one of the city's favorite venues for ballroom dancing and played host to dozens of popular big bands from the 1920s to the middle 1980s. The brick building was topped with a miniature windmill, the ballroom's trademark.

This young woman was a very attractive brunette with bobbed hair and a penchant for dressing in the style of the Prohibition era. In later years, witnesses would claim that her ghost dressed like a "flapper" and this is how she earned her nickname. Legend has it that this lovely girl was a regular at the Melody Mill until she died of peritonitis, the result of a burst appendix.

The girl was buried at Jewish Waldheim and she likely would have been forgotten, to rest in peace, if strange things had not started to happen a few months later. The events began as staff members at the Melody Mill began to see a young woman who looked just like the deceased girl appearing at dances at the ballroom. A number of men actually claimed to meet the girl here (after her death) and also to have offered her a ride home. During the journey, the young woman always vanished. This fetching phantom was also known to hitch rides on Des Plaines Avenue, outside the ballroom, and was also sometimes seen near the gates to the cemetery. Some travelers who passed the graveyard also claimed to see her entering a mausoleum that was located off Harlem Avenue.

Although recent sightings have been few, the ghost was most active in 1933, during the Century of Progress Exhibition. She became active again 40 years later, during the early 1970s, and stayed active for nearly a decade.

In the early 1930s, she was often reported at the ballroom, where she would dance with young men and ask for a ride home at the end of the evening. Every report was basically the same. A young man agreed to drive the girl home and she would give him directions to go east on Cermak Road, then north on Harlem Avenue. When they reached the cemetery, the girl always asked for the driver to stop the car. The girl would explain to them that she lived in the caretaker's house (since demolished) and then get out of the car. One man stated that he watched the girl go towards the house but then duck around the side of it. Curious, he climbed out of the car to see where she was going and saw her run out into the cemetery and vanish among the tombstones.

Another young man, who was also told that the girl lived in the caretaker's house, decided to come back during the day and to ask about her at the house. He had become infatuated with her and hoped to take her dancing again on another evening. His questions to the occupants of the house were met with blank stares and bafflement. No such girl lived, or had ever lived, at the house.

More sightings took place in the early 1970s and one report even occurred during the daylight hours. A family was visiting the cemetery one day and was startled to see a young woman dressed like a "flapper" walking toward a crypt, where she suddenly disappeared. The family hurried over to the spot, only to find that the girl was not there and there was nowhere to which she could have vanished so quickly.

Since that time, sightings of the "Flapper" have been few, and this may be because the old Melody Mill is no more. The days of jazz and big bands were gone by the 1980s and attendance on weekend evenings continued to slip until the place was closed down in 1985. It was later demolished and a new building was put up in its place two years later. Has the Flapper Ghost simply moved on to the other side since her favorite dance spot has disappeared? Perhaps -- and perhaps she is still kicking up her heels on a dance floor in another time and place, where it's 1933 every day!

THE LITTLE HITCHHIKER OF EVERGREEN PARK

Another phantom hitcher haunts the roadways near Evergreen Cemetery in Evergreen Park, a Chicago suburb. For more than two decades, an attractive girl who has been described as a young teenager has been roaming out beyond the confines of the cemetery in search of a ride. A number of drivers claim to have spotted her and in the 1980s a flurry of encounters occurred when motorists in the southern and western suburbs reported picking up this young girl. She always asked them for a ride to a location in Evergreen Park and then mysteriously vanished from the vehicle at the cemetery.

According to the legends, she is the spirit of a child buried within the cemetery, but there is no real folklore to explain why she leaves her grave in search of travelers to bring her back home again. She is what some would call the typical "vanishing hitchhiker" but there is one aspect to this ghost that sets her apart from the others. In addition to seeking rides in cars, she is resourceful enough to find other transportation when it suits her.

In recent years, encounters with this phantom have also taken place at a bus stop that is located directly across the street from the cemetery. Many have claimed to see a dark-haired young girl here who mysteriously vanishes. On occasion, she has also climbed aboard a few Chicago Transit Authority buses.

One evening, a young girl climbed aboard a bus and breezed right past the driver without paying the fare. She walked to the back of the vehicle and sat down, seemingly without a care in the world. Irritated, the driver called out to her but she didn't answer. Finally, he stood up and walked back toward where she was seating. She would either pay, he thought, or get off the bus. Not surprisingly though, before he could reach her, she vanished before his eyes!

According to reports, other shaken drivers have had the same eerie experience at this bus stop. The other drivers have also seen this young girl and every single one of them has seen her disappear as if she had never been there in the first place.

THE NAKED HITCHHIKER

One of the most intriguing of Chicago's phantom hitchers was the spirit dubbed the "Kennedy Road Phantom" around Christmas time in 1980. This mysterious female ghost was first seen around Byron during the frigid months of December and attracted so many curiosity-seekers that traffic was often bumper-to-bumper along Kennedy Road. Our guess would be that many of these would-be ghost hunters were male -- for this slender young woman was allegedly dressed, despite the cold weather, in very little clothing!

The sightings continued for several weeks and a number of reliable witnesses came forward to police officers and newspaper reporters, all claiming to have seen the phantom. One witness, Dave Trenholm, stated that he was driving along Kennedy Road with Guy Harriett of Oregon at about 9:00 p.m. on the night of January 2, 1981. He told the Chicago Tribune that he saw the girl step out from behind some bushes at the side of the road and that he had to look twice because he was so shocked by her appearance. He couldn't believe his eyes! He described her as being "tall, slender, nice-looking, about 20. All she was wearing were some black panties and some kind of scarf around her neck." The woman seemed to be unaffected by the cold weather (it was about 10 degrees that night) and after she spotted the car, she turned and ran towards a nearby farmhouse --- and then vanished.

There were a number of theories as to who the woman might be, ghostly or otherwise. Some thought that she was a lost mentally handicapped girl who had been reported missing by her parents around Christmas. This turned out not to be the case and after all of the standard theories of pranksters were dismissed (for what woman would go to the length of standing on the side of the road nearly naked in December for a joke?), many ideas turned to the supernatural.

Initial thoughts were that she was a car accident victim who had been killed along Kennedy Road and had now come back to haunt the highway. Others speculated that she was the ghost of a woman who had been buried in a nearby abandoned cemetery, which had been destroyed.

Regardless of who she was, additional sightings continued through January and began to include reports in which the phantom varied her clothing and description. Other witnesses stated that she was wearing a pair of light-colored shorts and a sweatshirt; shorts and a light jacket; and even a skimpy halter-top. Again, this was the dead of winter and a remote rural roadway so it didn't seem to be a joke or a hoax, so what was going on?

In late January 1980, the Rockford Register-Star published a report that a mysterious woman was run over by an Ogle County Sheriff's car around 8:00 p.m. The woman had suddenly appeared in the middle of the road and the squad car had slammed into her. According to the officers, the woman was pulled beneath the car and they heard her bones crunch and felt the impact of the tires rolling over the body. Needless to say, they quickly came to a stop and jumped out of the car to investigate and to assist her if possible. But when they ran back up the road, they found no woman lying there. A police lieutenant called the story "crazy and untrue" but the stories and the strange sightings continued.

By the end of January, the stories started to die out and finally, despite many people still looking for her, the ghostly woman had faded out of existence. Does she still haunt this lonesome stretch of road? No one knows for sure but even though she has not been seen in quite awhile, we have a feeling that many male ghost hunters are still keeping an eye out for her!

RESURRECTION MARY

Chicago is a city filled with ghosts, from haunted houses to ghostly graveyards. But of all of the tales, there is one that rises above all of the others. Her name is "Resurrection Mary" and she is Chicago's most famous ghost.

According to legend, the story of Resurrection Mary began with the death of a young woman who was killed while hitchhiking on Archer Avenue in the middle 1930s. This is the popular version of the story and has all of the elements of Chicago's greatest haunting --- a beautiful blonde, a lonely highway, a popular big-band ballroom and, of course, a hitchhiking ghost.

Many would dismiss this story as nothing more than an urban legend gone awry, a bedtime story that has taken on a life of its own over the years. Others would argue this and recount the most widely told version of the tale, never wavering from the idea that they believe the story to be true. Unfortunately though, the story of Resurrection Mary is filled with mystery --- and myth --- and nothing about it is simple. It's a complicated tale of two young women and a single legend that became, without question, American's greatest ghost story.

The legend of Resurrection Mary began at the Oh Henry Ballroom (now known as the Willowbrook Ballroom), a popular place for swing and big band dancing during the middle 1930s. The ballroom is still located today on the south stretch of Archer Avenue in Willow Springs. Many years ago, this was a somewhat secluded place, nestled among the trees in a small town with a "wide open" reputation for booze, gambling and prostitution. Young people from all over the south side came to the Oh Henry Ballroom for music and dancing and owner John Verderbar was known for booking the hottest bands in the Chicago area and the biggest acts

The Willowbrook Ballroom, which was the Oh Henry back when the story of Resurrection Mary began

Resurrection Cemetery on Archer Avenue

that traveled around the country.

The story goes that Mary came to the Oh Henry one night with a boyfriend and they spent the evening dancing and drinking. At some point, they got into an argument and Mary stormed out of the place. Even though it was a cold winter's night, she decided that she would rather face a cold walk home than another minute with her obnoxious boyfriend. She left the ballroom and started walking up Archer Avenue. She had not gotten very far when she was struck and killed by a passing automobile. The driver fled the scene and Mary was left there to die.

Her grieving parents buried her in Resurrection Cemetery, wearing her favorite party dress and her dancing shoes. Since that time, her spirit has been seen along Archer Avenue, perhaps trying to return to her grave after one last night among the living. Motorists started picking up a young woman on Archer Avenue, who offered them vague directions to take her home, who would then vanish from the automobile at the gates to Resurrection Cemetery.

But is there any truth to this legend? Did a young woman actually die after leaving the Oh Henry Ballroom and then begin haunting Archer Avenue? Many say that none of this ever happened. They speculate that "Mary" never existed at all. They dismiss the idea of bothering to search for her identity and believe she is nothing more than an "urban legend" and a piece of fascinating folklore. She is, they say, nothing more than Chicago's own version of the "vanishing hitchhiker".

While the story of Resurrection Mary does bear some resemblance to the classic bit of American highway lore that we call the "vanishing hitchhiker", the folklorists have forgotten an important thing about Mary's story that other versions of the don't have --- credible eyewitness accounts, places, times and dates. Many of these reports are not just stories that have been passed from person to person and rely on a "friend of a friend" for authenticity. In fact, some of the encounters with Mary have been chillingly up close and personal and remain unexplained to this day.

In addition, the story of Mary includes something that the urban legends leave out --- physical evidence of her presence. And Mary, unlike our highway legends, springs from real-life counterparts for whom evidence remains about their lives --- and deaths. We confess that, in the pages ahead, you will not find evidence that any of the "Marys" in question died after leaving the Willowbrook Ballroom but you will find some pretty compelling evidence that Mary still haunts Archer Avenue to this day.

Old Archer Avenue

ARCHER AVENUE

The story of Resurrection Mary is a part of Illinois and Chicago history --- but she is also an essential part of Archer Avenue history, too. This ghost could not exist without Archer Avenue and it's unlikely that this haunted highway would have found its fame without Mary.

Archer Avenue, which runs along the southwest side of Chicago, following the route of the old Illinois & Michigan Canal, seems to be the perfect place for a haunting. It is not just Resurrection Mary who prowls the shadowy sections of this highway. There are many locations along this road --- from homes to cemeteries to businesses - that boast more than their share of ghosts.

But what makes Archer Avenue so haunted? In the early days of Chicago, the road was an Indian trail that stretched all of the way from Fort Dearborn and the old mouth of the Chicago River to what are now the southwest suburbs. The pathway linked to the Saucunasi trail that led south and to the Joliet trail that led to the southwest. An Indian village was located just north of the trail's end, across from what would be the Illinois & Michigan Canal and along Mud Lake. Some have suggested that the original inhabitants forged a path here because of some mystical, magnetic force that connected it to the next world. They say that paranormal energies would also be attracted to this magnetism and this would explain the hauntings in the area.

Some have also suggested that Archer Avenue is connected to magnetic lines that run beneath the earth. Many believe these so-called ley lines cross the entire world and that locations where the lines cross are especially energy-filled. This might explain what seems to attract such a large number of hauntings to the vicinity of Archer Avenue.

It has also been theorized that this area is so haunted because of its proximity to water. Archer Avenue is nearly surrounded by water sources like the Cal-Sag Channel, the Des Plaines River, the Illinois & Michigan Canal, the Chicago Sanitary and Shipping Canal and even Maple Lake, which reportedly is the scene of "ghost lights" activity.

Others (like most of the Weird Chicago gang) believe that the hauntings reported along this old roadway manifest because of the history that has imprinted itself on the land. Archer Avenue is one of Chicago's most historic roads and its use, as an Indian trail, dates back to long before the white explorers and settlers ever came to Chicago. After that, it followed the Illinois & Michigan Canal and became the main thoroughfare to move men and materials along the construction site. After that, it was known as one of the best roads for travelers to come into Chicago from the southwest. The road is a place filled with history and as most ghost enthusiasts know, it's the events of the past that create the hauntings that are experienced today.

But no matter what the reason turns out to be, there seems to be little debate about the fact that Archer Avenue is the most haunted road in the Chicagoland region!

The Indian trail was turned into a roadway in the 1830s when Irish workers were brought in to build the Illinois & Michigan Canal. It was named for Colonel William B. Archer, one of the promoters of the canal. Irish settlements sprang up along the road, anchoring in Bridgeport and Lemont, at what became the opposite ends of Archer Avenue, or Archer Road, as it was called at the time.

In the years that followed, hauntings have appeared along the length of the roadway, from a ballroom that has become home to one of Chicago's longest-standing tales of diabolical delight to one of the region's oldest haunted cemeteries - all of which have been recounted in these pages already. This leaves us with only one story to include - Chicago's greatest ghost story, Resurrection Mary.

THE JERRY PALUS ENCOUNTER

The first accounts of Resurrection Mary on Archer Avenue came about in the spring of 1934 and we'll explore those accounts a little later on in the chapter. At that time, a number of drivers who passed Resurrection Cemetery at night began to report strange occurrences with a girl who tried to flag down rides from them and, sometimes, tried to climb onto the running boards of their cars.

Aside from the harried motorists who encountered Mary along Archer Avenue were those who came face-to-face with her under other conditions. One of these people was a young man named Jerry Palus. His experience with Mary took place in 1939 but would leave such an impression that he would never forget it until his death in 1992. Palus remained an unshakable witness and appeared on a number of television shows (including Unsolved Mysteries) to discuss his night with Resurrection Mary. He never doubted the fact that he spent an evening with a ghost!

Palus met the young girl, who he described as a very attractive blond, at the Liberty Grove & Hall, a music and dancing venue that was near 47th Street and Mozart in the Brighton Park neighborhood. As it happens, this dance hall, which was a "jumping spot" on the South Side for many years, was located not far from the homes of both the women who are usually believed to have been the girl who became Resurrection Mary. However, because of his description of the girl as an "attractive blond," we're reasonably sure that we know which of the two Jerry Palus met that night.

That night at the Liberty Grove & Hall, Jerry asked the girl to dance. He had been watching her for some time that evening, although he admitted in later interviews that he never saw her come into the place. She spent a couple of hours sitting by herself, since she didn't seem to know anyone, and Jerry finally gathered the courage to take her out onto the dance floor. The girl accepted his invitation and they spent several hours together. Strangely, she seemed a little distant and Palus also noticed that her skin was very cold, almost icy to the touch. When he later kissed her, he found her lips were also cold and clammy.

At the end of the evening, the young woman asked Jerry for a ride home. He readily agreed to give her a lift. When they got to his automobile, she explained that she lived on South Damen Avenue but that she wanted to take a ride down Archer Avenue first. Jerry shrugged and told her that he would be happy to take her wherever she wanted. By this time, he was infatuated with the girl and likely wanted to extend the night for as long as he could. He knew that it would be quite some distance out of the way to drive down Archer Avenue but he didn't mind, so he put his car into gear and drove off.

To reach Archer Avenue from the Liberty Grove & Hall, Jerry only had to travel west on 47th Street. Once he made it to the old roadway, they traveled southwest to Summit and then on to Justice. It was a dark, dimly lit road in those days but Jerry was somewhat familiar with the area, so he just followed the course of the road, heading eventually, he thought, towards Willow Springs.

But as they approached the gates to Resurrection Cemetery the girl asked him to pull over. She had to get out here, she told him. Jerry was confused, unable to understand why she would want to get out at such a spot, but he pulled the car to the side of the road anyway. He agreed that he would let her out, but only if she allowed him to walk her to wherever she was going. There was a row of houses to Jerry's right, about a block off Archer Avenue, and he assumed that she was going to one of them. He wanted to be sure that she made it there safely.

The beautiful young girl refused to allow this, though. She turned in her seat and faced Palus. She spoke softly, saying, "This is where I have to get out, but where I'm going, you can't follow."

Jerry was bewildered by this statement but before he could respond, the girl got out of the car and ran --- not in the direction of the houses but across Archer Avenue and toward the gates of Resurrection Cemetery. She vanished before she reached them --- right before Jerry's eyes! That was the moment when he knew that he had danced with a specter.

Determined to find out what was going on, Palus visited the address the girl had given him on the following day. The woman who answered the door told him that he couldn't have possibly been with her daughter the night before because she had been dead for years. However, Palus was able to correctly identify the girl from a family portrait in the other room.

Needless to say, Jerry was stunned by this revelation but apparently the address and identity of the woman were forgotten over the years. Sometime later, when Palus was contacted again about his story (when the passage of time had renewed interest in the elusive ghost) he was unable to remember where he had gone on the day after his encounter. Despite this memory lapse, Palus' story remains one of the most credible of all of the Resurrection Mary encounters.

DANCING WITH MARY.....

This was only the beginning for Mary and, starting in the late 1930s, she began making regular appearances on Archer Avenue. Stories like the one told by Jerry Palus became almost commonplace over the years as other young men began to tell of picking up a young woman, or meeting her at a local ballroom, only to have her disappear from their car.

The majority of the reports seemed to come from the cold winter months, like the account passed on by a cab driver who picked up a girl who was walking along Archer Avenue one night in 1941. It was very cold outside, but she was not wearing a coat. She jumped into the cab and told him that she needed to get home very quickly. She directed him to go north along Archer and, a few minutes later, he looked back and she was gone. He realized that he was passing in front of the cemetery when she disappeared.

The stories continued but starting in the early 1970s, the number of "Mary sightings" began to increase. People from many different walks of life, from cab drivers to ministers, claimed they picked her up and gave her rides. They encountered her in local nightspots and saw her vanish from the passenger seats of their automobiles.

It was during this period that Resurrection Cemetery was undergoing some major renovations and perhaps this was what caused her restlessness. There are others who believe that Mary's grave was disturbed many years before that. It is thought that she was buried in the single grave section of the cemetery and just after World War II, the graveyard needed more space. Some of the graves were moved to other locations, while others, according to the relatives of some who had loved ones buried in the cemetery, were reportedly bulldozed under the earth. Whatever the cause of the increased activity, there is no denying that things on the Southwest Side started getting very interesting!

In 1973, Mary was said to have shown up at least twice at a nightclub called Harlow's, which was located at 8058 South Cicero Ave., almost directly east of Resurrection Cemetery. Bob Main was the night manager at Harlow's at the time and he is perhaps the only person to ever encounter Resurrection Mary on two different occasions. He saw her on a Friday night that spring and then saw her again about two weeks later on a Saturday.

He described her: "She was about 24 to 30 years-old, five foot eight or nine, slender with yellow-blond hair to the shoulders that she wore in these big spooly curls coming down from a high forehead. She was really pale, like she powdered her face and her body. She had on this old dress that was yellowed, like a wedding dress left in the sun. She sat right next to the dance floor and she wouldn't talk to anyone. She danced all by herself, this pirouette-type dance. People were saying, "Who is this bizarre chick?"

When Main and some of the other staff members tried to talk to the young woman, and make sure that she was okay, the woman only shook her head. Main described her expression as though she "seemed to look right through you."

Bob had no idea who the girl might have been and while he doesn't dismiss the idea that it could have been some sort of prank, or even a mentally disturbed woman, he did add something rather disconcerting to the story: "The strangest thing was, even though we carded everyone who came in there ---- I worked the door and there were waitresses and bartenders and people there --- nobody, either night, ever saw her come in and they never saw her leave."

He added that he never would have assumed the woman was Resurrection Mary until he read a newspaper article about her a few years later. After that, it was the only thing that really made sense.

Other types of accounts began to surface around this same time and now, Mary was being reported running out into the middle of Archer Avenue and being struck by passing cars. These reports, although unknown to most of those who submitted them, hearkened back to the early 1930s and they had an eerie similarity to the very first Mary stories from that time.

In these new accounts, drivers began to report a young woman with light brown hair, wearing a white dress who ran out in the front of their automobiles. Sometimes, the girl would vanish just before colliding with the car and at other times, they would feel the impact and see her crumple and fall to the road as if seriously injured. When the motorist stopped and went to help the girl, she would either disappear or no sign of her body would be found.

On August 12, 1976, Cook County Sheriff's Police officers investigated an emergency call about an apparent hit-and-run victim near the intersection of 76th Street and Roberts Road. The officers found a young female motorist in tears at the scene and they asked her where the body was that she had allegedly discovered beside the road? She pointed to a wet grassy area and the policemen could plainly see a depression in the grass that matched the shape of a human body. The girl said that just as the police car approached the scene, the body on the side of the road vanished!

In May 1978, a young couple was driving north on Archer Avenue when a girl suddenly darted out in the road in front of their car. The driver swerved to avoid her but knew when he hit the brakes that it was too late. As they braced for impact, the car passed right through the girl! She then turned and ran into Resurrection Cemetery, melting right past the bars in the gate. Another man was on his way to work in the early morning hours and spotted the body of a young girl lying directly in front of the cemetery gates. He stopped his truck and got out, quickly discovering that the woman was apparently badly injured, but still alive. He jumped into his truck and sped to the nearby police station, where he summoned an ambulance and then hurried back to the cemetery. When he came back, he found that the body was gone! However the outline of her body was still visible on the dew-covered pavement.

The burned and scorched bars of Resurrection Cemetery (Dale Kaczmarek)

In October 1989, two women were driving past Resurrection Cemetery when a girl in a white dress ran out in front of their car. The driver slammed on the brakes, sure that she was going to hit the woman, but there was no impact. Neither of the women could explain where the apparition had gone. They had seen the young girl clearly though and described her as having light brown, curly hair.

THE RESURRECTION CEMETERY GATE

The strangest account of Resurrection Mary occurred on the night of August 10, 1976. This event has remained so bizarre after 30 years because on this occasion, Mary did not just appear as a passing spirit. It was on this night that she left actual evidence behind!

A driver was passing by the cemetery around 10:30 p.m. when

A close-up of the burned bars. (Dale Kaczmarek)

he happened to see a girl standing on the other side of the gates. He said that when he saw her, she was wearing a white dress and grasping the iron bars of the gate. The driver was considerate enough to stop down the street at the Justice police station and alert them to the fact that someone had been accidentally locked in the cemetery at closing time. A patrolman named Pat Homa responded to the call but when he arrived at the cemetery gates, he couldn't find anyone there. He called out with his loudspeaker and looked around with his spotlight, but there was no one to be seen. He finally got out of his patrol car and walked up to the gates for one last look. As far as he could tell, the cemetery was dark and deserted and there was no sign of any girl.

But his inspection of the gates, where the girl had been seen standing, did reveal something unusual. What he saw there chilled him to the bone! He found that two of the bronze bars in the gate had been blackened, burned and --- well, pulverized. It looked as though someone had taken two of the green-colored bars in his or her hands and had somehow just squashed and twisted them. Within the marks was what looked to be skin texture and handprints that had been seared into the metal with incredible heat. The temperature, which must have been intense, blackened and burned the bars at just about the spot where a small woman's hands would have been.

The marks of the hands made big news and curiosity-seekers came from all over the area to see them. In an effort to discourage the crowds, cemetery officials attempted to remove the marks with a blowtorch, making them look even worse. Finally, they cut the bars out of the gate and installed a wire fence until the two bars could be straightened or replaced.

The cemetery emphatically denied the supernatural version of what happened to the bars. In 1992, they claimed that a truck backed into the gates while doing sewer work at the cemetery and that grounds workers tried to fix the bars by heating them with a blowtorch and bending them. The imprint in the metal, they said, was from a workman trying to push them together again.

While this explanation was quite convenient, it did not explain why the marks of small fingers were clearly visible in the metal or why the bronze never reverted back to their green, oxidized state.

As mentioned, the bars were removed to discourage onlookers but taking them out actually had the opposite effect. Soon, people began asking what the cemetery had to hide. The events allegedly embarrassed local officials, so they demanded that the bars be put back into place. Once they were returned to the gate, they were straightened and left alone so that the blackened area would oxidize to match the other bars. Unfortunately though, the scorched areas continued to defy nature and the twisted spots where the handprints had been impressed remained obvious until 2002, when the bars were finally removed for good. At great expense, Resurrection Cemetery replaced the entire front gates and the notorious bars vanished for good.

THE CAB DRIVER'S STORY

Just a few minutes after midnight, in the early morning hours of Friday morning, January 12, 1979, a taxicab driver had an unsettling experience with Resurrection Mary. It was a cold winter's night and at the time the driver picked up his unusual passenger, a major blizzard was just hours away from hitting the southwest side of Chicago. As he traveled along Archer Avenue, rain and sleet pelted the windshield. The driver reached over to crank the heater up one more notch. It is the kind of night, he thought, that makes your bones ache.

He was returning to the city after dropping off a fare in Palos Hills. His route took him past the Old Willow Shopping Center, located at the intersection of Archer Avenue and Willow Springs Road, just a short distance away from the Willowbrook Ballroom. As he passed the collection of stores at the shopping center, a pale figure, blurry through the wet and icy glass of the window, appeared along the road. The driver craned his neck and saw a woman standing there alone. He later recalled: "She was a looker. A blond. I didn't have any ideas or like that. She was young enough to be my daughter."

The young woman was strangely dressed for such a cold and wet night. She was wearing only a thin white cocktail dress. The girl never stuck out her thumb or anything. She just stood there, looking at the cab, but the driver pulled over and stopped the car. The girl stumbled as she walked toward him and he rolled down the window to speak to her. She was beautiful, the driver saw, despite her disheveled appearance. Her blond hair was damp from the weather and plastered to her forehead.

Old Willow Shopping Center

He invited her into the cab and she opened the passenger door and slid into the seat. The cabbie looked over at her and asked her what was wrong. Had she had car trouble or something? The girl didn't answer, so he asked her where she wanted to go and offered her a free ride. It was the least that he could do in that weather, he told her.

The girl simply replied that he should keep driving north on Archer Avenue, so the cabbie put the car into gear and pulled back onto the road. He noticed that the young woman is shivering so he turned up the heater again. He commented on the weather, making conversation, but she doesn't answer him at first. She stared at out the window in such a vacant way that he wondered if she might be drunk. Finally, she answered him, although her voice wavered and she sounded almost fearful. The driver was unsure if her whispered words were directed to him or if she was speaking to herself. "The snow came early this year," She murmured. After that, she was silent again.

The cabbie agreed with her and attempted to make some more small talk but he soon realized the lovely young girl was not interested in conversation. "Her mind was a million miles away," he said.

Finally, the girl spoke, but when she did, she shouted at him. She ordered him to pull over to the side of the road. She needed to get out!

The startled driver jerked the steering wheel to the right and stopped in an open area in front of two large, metal gates. He looked across the road, searching for a house or a business where this girl might need to go. He knew there was nothing on the right. She couldn't get out there --- it was a cemetery.

He looked back at the girl and realized what had just occurred. "And that's when it happened. I looked to my left --- like this --- at this little shack. And when I turned back she was gone. Vanished! And that car door never opened. May the good Lord strike me dead, it never opened," he insisted.

The beautiful young girl had simply disappeared.

At the time of this encounter, the driver (a 52-year-old working guy, father, veteran, churchgoer and Little League coach) had no idea that he had just had a brush with the region's most enigmatic and sought-after ghost. He wouldn't find out until a friend put him in touch with a newspaper columnist, who began looking into the story for himself.

After looking into the story of Resurrection Mary, his trail led him to the Willowbrook Ballroom, which was once known as the Oh Henry. He discovered that the cab driver had picked up the young girl just about 10 minutes after midnight, a few blocks from the Willowbrook on Archer Avenue. Was this merely a coincidence? The reporter didn't think so, especially based on the strange occurrences connected to Mary that had taken place at the Willowbrook Ballroom over the years.

The site of the ballroom in Willow Springs, right on Archer Avenue, started as a beer hall that was operated by the Verderbar family in 1920. In 1929, the original structure burned down and was replaced by an elaborate ballroom. They called it the Oh Henry but the name was later changed to the Willowbrook. Starting in the 1930s, the ballroom gained a reputation as one of the best dance clubs in Illinois and attracted customers from all over the area. The Oh Henry, and later the Willowbrook, developed a strong following and today, it is one of the last of the old-time ballrooms in Chicago. Times and musical tastes may have changed but a visit to the Willowbrook is like taking a trip back in time. The old dance floor, the tables, the cocktail bar and even the restrooms are just as they were back in the days when Mary reveled here. It's a place where the big band sound can still be heard and a time capsule of another era.

In 1998, the Verderbar family decided to sell the ballroom to Birute and Gedas Jodwalis, who decided to keep the Willowbrook just the way that it was. Longtime customers likely breathed a little easier when they found out the big bands would still be coming to the ballroom - and likely so did the ghost buffs and Resurrection Mary enthusiasts. If the big bands kept coming, then likely Mary would too!

The Oh Henry Dance park was started by John Verderbar in 1920. After a fire, the ballroom was constructed and by the 1930s was considered one of the hottest night spots on the southwest side.

(Below) The Willowbrook Ballroom in the 1930s

Since the 1930s, Mary has been encountered numerous times on the dance floor by customers and employees alike. Commonly, reports tell of an attractive young woman in a white party dress who is seen from the opposite side of the ballroom. Occasionally, she is dancing and at other times, just standing at the edge of the floor, watching people with a slight smile on her face. At times, she vanishes without warning and on other occasions, she has disappeared whenever someone tries to approach her.

Aside from the white dress, the descriptions of the girl vary just a little. She is always beautiful but some have stated that she was a blond and others say that she was a brunette with curly hair. Each time, she disappeared --- leaving little doubt that she was a ghost --- but also leaving behind the question as to which Mary the witness actually saw!

There is one thing that each of these sightings have in common, no matter what the girl looked like. That one thing is that Mary has never been reported by anyone who actually went to the Willowbrook with the intention of seeing her. Every sighting seems to come from someone who had a chance encounter with the phantom.

Don't let that discourage you from spending an evening at the Willowbrook Ballroom, though. Even if you don't get to meet Mary face-to-face, you will still get a chance to experience a place that is uniquely a part of Archer Avenue history and an integral part of the roadway's most famous haunt!

Sightings of Mary continued into the 1980s and the 1990s, and even though Mary sightings and first-hand encounters have slacked off in recent years, they still continue to occur today. While many of the stories are harder to believe these days, as the tales of Mary have infiltrated our culture to such a degree that almost anyone with an interest in ghosts has heard of her, some of the stories still appear to be chillingly real.

IN SEARCH OF THE "REAL" RESURRECTION MARY

Because of Troy's interest in Resurrection Mary (he has written an entire book on the subject!), people often ask him about her. They are filled with questions: when she was most recently seen? Does he believe people who tell him they have seen her? Does he think she is still haunting Archer Avenue? And there are many more. Needless to say, though, the one question that he is asked most often is --- who was Mary when she was alive?

Troy searched for the answer for years, searching through evidence and first-hand accounts, until he began to form his own ideas as to who Mary might have been. During his research, he began tracking down not only accounts of Resurrection Mary but details about dance halls around Archer Avenue, deaths of young women, and much more.

Over the years, there have been many who have searched for the earthly counterpart of Resurrection Mary and a number of candidates have emerged. Some are more likely than others. One of the options is Mary Duranski, who was killed in an auto accident in 1934. Another is a 12-year-old girl named Anna Norkus, who died in another tragic accident in 1936. That same year marked the date of another accident that some believe spawned Resurrection Mary. In this case, a farm truck collided with an automobile and three of the four passengers in the sedan were killed. One of the victims, a young woman, may have become Resurrection Mary. Others believe Mary can be traced to another accident near Resurrection Cemetery that occurred in the 1940s. In this case, a young Polish girl had taken her father's car to meet her boyfriend in the early morning hours. She died in an accident and was buried in the nearby cemetery. Most believe this to be little more than a neighborhood "cautionary tale" told by protective parents, but it certainly adds another element to the legend.

It's possible that any one of these young women could still haunt Archer Avenue and may have contributed to the Resurrection Mary legend. However, we believe there that the majority of the sightings that have occurred can be connected to two young women who, ironically, lived only a few blocks away from one another in life. You could say they have become "sisters" in death....

THE "ORIGINAL" RESURRECTION MARY

The first reports of Resurrection Mary began to appear in the late spring of 1934. It was at this time that motorists on Archer Avenue, passing in front of Resurrection Cemetery, began telling of a young woman who would appear on the roadway, as if trying to hitch a ride. On some occasions, she became frantic as cars passed her by and many times, actually desperate. Motorists told of the woman running toward them across the road, trying to climb onto the running boards of their automobiles and sometimes, even trying to climb into the open back windows! They all described her in the same way, wearing a light-colored dress and having curly, light brown hair that reached to her shoulders.

A photograph of Mary Bregovy from 1934

What made matters worse is that many of the people in these automobiles, who were residents of the Southwest Side, actually recognized this young woman. Her name was Mary Bregovy and some of these motorists were her friends. They laughed with her, drank with her, and often danced with her at their favorite spot, the Oh Henry Ballroom. Of course, that had been in the past because when they began seeing Mary trying to flag them down on Archer Avenue --- she had been dead for several weeks!

Mary Bregovy was 21 in March 1934. She had been born on April 7, 1912 and attended St. Michael's Grammar School, a short distance from her home. She lived in a small home at 4611 South Damen Ave., which was in the stockyards neighborhood of Bridgeport. She was of Polish descent and was employed at a local factory, where she worked hard to help support her mother, father and two younger brothers, Steve and Joseph, during the early days of the Great Depression.

Friends would later remember her as an extremely fun-loving girl who enjoyed going to parties and loved to go out dancing, especially to the Oh Henry Ballroom, which was her favorite place. Her friend LaVern Rutkowski, who grew up with Mary on the southwest side and lived just two houses away from her, recalled in a 1984 interview, "She was personality plus. She always had a smile and you never saw her unhappy."

Mrs. Rutkowski, or "Vern" as she was commonly known, spent Mary's final day with her on March 10, 1934. The two of them spent a lot of time together and years later, Vern would vividly recall going out with Mary to dance halls all over the Southwest Side. Ironically, Mary's parents had forbidden her to go out on the night of March 10 and Mary might have listened to them if she and Vern had not met a couple of young men earlier that day. These two men, who are believed to have been John Reiker and John Thoel, were in the car that night when Mary was killed.

Mary and Vern spent that Saturday afternoon shopping at 47th Street and Ashland Avenue

Mary's last day was spent shopping with her friend, Vern Rutowski, at a shopping area located at 47th & Ashland. The area is marked today by an abandoned Goldblatt's store that was undoubtedly visited by the girls in 1934.

The Bregovy home was located here in this row of modest homes in the Back of the Yards neighborhood.

and it was in one of the stores located here that they met the two men. After getting into their car to go for a ride, Vern took an instant dislike to them. "They looked like wild boys and for some reason I just didn't like them," she said. Vern added that they drove recklessly, turning corners on two wheels and speeding down narrow streets. Finally, Vern demanded to be let out of the car a few blocks from home. She asked Mary if she planned to go out with the young men that night and Mary said that she did. Vern urged her to reconsider, not only because she didn't like the boys but also because Mary's parents had already told her that she couldn't. Mary shrugged off her friend's warnings. She simply replied, "You never like anyone I introduce you to."

Vern stood watching on the street corner as Mary and the young men roared away in the car. It was the last time that she would ever see her friend alive.

No one knows how Mary Bregovy spent the rest of the day but a few clues have emerged from family members over the years. The wife of Mary's younger brother, Steve, reported in 1985 that she had received a letter from a friend of Mary's years before that stated Mary planned to attend a novena at church before she went out dancing that night. The Bregovys were devout Catholics and this would not have been out of the ordinary for Mary to do. She also said that she believed Mary had been going to the Oh Henry Ballroom that night.

But did she ever arrive there? No one knows for sure but tradition holds that Mary and her new friends, who now included a young woman named Virginia Rozanski, did go dancing at the Oh Henry Ballroom that night. After the ballroom closed, it is believed that they drove into the city, where most of the clubs stayed open much later. In the early morning hours, they were leaving downtown, traveling along Wacker Drive, likely headed for Archer Avenue, which would take Mary home to Bridgeport, when the deadly accident occurred. One has to wonder if alcohol, combined with the reckless driving described by Vern Rutkowski, combined to cause the crash.

A short piece in the March 11 edition of the Chicago Tribune described the accident:

Girl Killed in Crash

Miss Marie Bregovy, 21 years old, of 4611 South Damen Avenue, was killed last night when the automobile in which she was riding cracked up at Lake Street and Wacker Drive. John Reiker, 23, of 15 North Knight Street, Park Ridge, suffered a possible skull fracture and is in the county hospital. John Thoel, 25, 5216 Loomis Street, driver of the car, and Miss Virginia Rozanski, 22, of 4849 South Lincoln Street, were shaken up and scratched. The scene of the accident is known to police as a danger spot. Thoel told police he did not see the "L" substructure.

The accident occurred along Wacker Drive, just as it curves to the south and away from the Chicago River. At the point where Wacker crosses Lake Street, there is a large, metal support for the elevated tracks overhead. If a driver was coming along Wacker too quickly, it could be easy to not make a complete turn and collide with the support column, which is almost in a straight line around the curve. This is apparently what happened to John Thoel that night.

When the automobile collided with the metal column, Mary was thrown through the windshield and instantly killed. She was also badly cut up by the glass. Before her funeral, the undertaker had to sew up a gash that extended all of the way across the front of her throat and up to her right ear. Tragically, Mary was not even supposed to be sitting in the front seat when the accident occurred. Her parents would later learn that she had switched places with Virginia Rozanski because Virginia didn't like John Thoel, next to whom she had been sitting in the passenger's seat. She had asked Mary to sit in front with Thoel and Mary had agreed. Unfortunately, her good-natured personality would turn out to be fatal for her.

Vern Rutkowski accompanied Mary's mother and her brother, Joseph, to the morgue to identify the body. Mary was taken to the Satala Funeral Home, located just a couple of blocks from the Bregovy home, to be prepared for burial. The owner at the time, John Satala, easily remembered Mary. In 1985, he recalled, "She was a hell of a nice girl. Very pretty. She was buried in an orchid dress. I remember having to sew up the side of her face."

Mary was buried in Resurrection Cemetery and this is where some of the confusion about her story comes along. According to records, Mary was buried in Section MM, Site 9819. There was a Mary Bregovy buried here, but it was not the young woman who was killed in March 1934. A search for this gravesite revealed that the Mary Bregovy laid to rest here was a 34-year-old mother who was born in 1888 and died in 1922. This is a different Mary Bregovy altogether!

Family members of Mary Bregovy said that Mary was actually buried in a term grave and never moved. After World War II, when space was needed for more burial sites at Resurrection Cemetery, some of the term graves were moved but others, like Mary's, were simply covered over. For this reason, according to Mrs. Steve Bregovy, the

The Satala Funeral Home, where Mary Bregovy was prepared for burial

location of Mary's grave is unknown. Could this be one of the reasons that her spirit is so restless?

The stories of Mary Bregovy's ghost began a very short time after her death. In April 1934, a caretaker at Resurrection Cemetery telephoned funeral home director John Satala and told him that he had seen the barefooted ghost of a young girl walking around the cemetery. She was a lovely girl with light brown hair and she was wearing a pale, orchid-colored dress. The caretaker was positive that the ghost was the woman that Satala had recently buried. Satala later said that he recognized the description of the girl as Mary Bregovy.

Soon after, other reports began to appear, like the earlier-mentioned accounts of a woman matching Mary's description who was trying to hitch rides in front of the cemetery. These Archer Avenue sightings also included reports from people who actually recognized the ghost as Mary Bregovy.

We're convinced that these reports were the beginning of the Resurrection Mary legend. These were the first stories of a young woman hitching rides on Archer Avenue and thanks to the destination of many of these motorists, combined with the fact that the Oh Henry Ballroom was Mary's favorite dance spot, the story began to grow. We believe that many of the reports of a ghostly woman being seen around Resurrection Cemetery can be traced to Mary Bregovy --- the "original Resurrection Mary."

But Mary Bregovy does not haunt this stretch of Archer Avenue alone...

"RESURRECTION MARY WAS MY BABYSITTER..."

Mary Bregovy may have started the legend of Resurrection Mary but she was not the only phantom haunting Archer Avenue and the area around it. The stories of a "beautiful blond" don't physically match Miss Bregovy, who was certainly beautiful, but definitely not a blond. She had naturally curly, light brown hair, which means that she is not the same spirit so frequently being picked up by motorists and spotted on the side of the road.

However, thanks to a letter that Troy received in 2005 (and the interviews that followed it), he believes that he may have the identity of the second woman who has contributed to the legend of Resurrection Mary --- who may also be the same woman that Jerry Palus met at the Liberty Grove & Hall in 1939.

The name of Mary Miskowski is a familiar one to Resurrection Mary buffs. There have been numerous brief mentions of her in ghostly literature, listing her as a possible candidate for the identity of the legendary ghost. Little has been known about her except for the fact that she was killed in October 1930 by a hit and run driver. She was allegedly crossing the street while on her way to a Halloween costume party.

In July 2005, Troy received a vague letter from a woman who promised him information about Resurrection Mary, claiming that the real-life counterpart of Mary had once been her mother's babysitter when she was a child. If he was interested, he could call her and get more information. Her mother was still alive and would be happy to speak with me about it.

He read the letter with interest, but with a lot of skepticism, too. This was not the first time that he received information of this sort but, out of curiosity, he decided to give the woman a call. She gave him a few details of the story and then gave him the telephone number of her mother, who was 85 years old, and urged him to contact her. The next afternoon, he called the number and was soon speaking with Mrs. Martha Litak, who grew up on South Damen Avenue on Chicago's southwest side. He told her why he was calling and asked her what she could tell him

The home of Mary Miskowski on South Damen Avenue, just a few blocks away from Mary Bregovy's home

about the story of Resurrection Mary.

Her answer surprised him. She laughed and said: "Resurrection Mary was my babysitter!" According to Mrs. Litak, Mary Miskowski had lived just down the street from her family when she was a child. Mary's house was located at 4924 South Damen Ave. (interestingly, just three blocks away from Mary Bregovy, so it seems possible these two women could have known one another) and she often watched neighborhood children to earn extra money. Mrs. Litak was not sure if Mary had a regular job or not. She lived with her parents but she was old enough to be out of school.

Martha remembered Mary very well. "She was a very pretty girl. She had light blond hair with just a little bit of curl to it. It was cut short, just a little below her ears. All of the boys in the neighborhood were in love with her. I do remember that she liked to go on dates but I don't recall that she had any one boyfriend in particular," she said.

Martha said she had spoken with her younger brother, Frank, after her daughter told her that Troy might get in touch. She had asked him if he could remember anything about their old babysitter, Mary Miskowski. Frank was only 7 at the time Mary died but he recalled what she looked like and remembered some of his older cousins talking about Mary after she had been killed. The cousins said that Mary loved to go out dancing, including to the Oh Henry Ballroom, which had opened in 1921. Her favorite place, though, was the Liberty Grove & Hall, which was located only about 12 blocks from her home.

Troy couldn't help but wonder if Mary Miskowski might have been the ghost that Jerry Palus encountered at the dance hall that night. She certainly matched the description that Palus (and many others over the years) later gave of the young woman that he met and who vanished from his car in front of Resurrection Cemetery.

There is also no question that Mary Miskowski had long since passed away by that time. Martha Litak confirmed that Mary had been killed by a hit-and-run driver in October 1930. A car had struck her as she was crossing 47th Street and had sped away. Whoever the driver was, he was never caught. Martha surmised that perhaps this incident was how the story got started about Resurrection Mary being run over by a car and left for dead on Archer Avenue. With the Oh Henry Ballroom, and later the Willowbrook, being so closely tied to the legend, she was not surprised that the accident had been moved to a location that was closer to the dance hall. Mrs. Litak also confirmed that Mary had been on her way to a costume party that night. She had been dressed as a bride, wearing her mother's old wedding dress. Martha didn't know what Mary had been buried in but she did believe that perhaps the white dress that so many people reported Resurrection Mary wearing could have been this dress from the early 1900s.

Mrs. Litak further connected Mary Miskowski to the legend by adding that she had been buried in Resurrection Cemetery. We have been unable to confirm this but Martha and Frank were both sure this was the case. They told Troy that she had been buried in a term grave (just like Mary Bregovy) but she did not know the ultimate location of the site.

If any of this is accurate, it may explain the Resurrection Mary encounters that don't match the description and behavior of Mary Bregovy. Could the presence of Mary Miskowski explain the sightings of a pretty, blond phantom that hangs out in dance halls and vanishes from cars? And could she be the ghost who is seen running across the road in front of the cemetery where she is buried, perhaps re-enacting her final moments over and over again as she is stuck by a passing automobile?

It's possible, perhaps even likely. It's a fascinating and compelling story --- compelling enough that it prompted our theory that Resurrection Mary is not one ghost, but two or maybe even more.

KEEP YOUR EYES ON THE SIDE OF THE ROAD!

So, who was Mary? And does she really exist?

We believe that she does and we also believe that we know the identities of at least two of the girls who have created her enduring legend. But there are many other theories that also exist. Mary Bregovy and Mary Miskowski may be just two of the girls and there may be many more. Only one thing seems to be certain --- that she could have only achieved her legendary status on a roadway like Archer Avenue. Whether it's the road's mysterious connections to the next world or merely its long and haunted history, Archer Avenue has certainly earned a unique spot in the annals of the paranormal in America.

But what about Mary?

Does she really exist? Many still remain doubtful about her, but we have found that their skepticism doesn't really seem to matter. Whether these people believe in her or not, people are still seeing Mary walking along Archer Avenue at night. Motorists are still stopping to pick up a forlorn figure that seems inadequately dressed on cold winter nights, when encounters seem to be the most prevalent. Curiosity-seekers still come to see the gates where the twisted and burned bars were once located and some even roam the graveyard, hoping to stumble across the place where Mary's body was laid to rest.

We still don't know for sure who she really is but that has not stopped the stories, tales and songs from being circulated about her. She remains an enigma and her legend lives on, not content to vanish, as Mary does when she reaches the gates of Resurrection Cemetery. You see, our individual belief, or disbelief, does not really matter. Mary lives on anyway --- a mysterious, elusive and romantic spirit of the Windy City.

RESURRECTION MARY GOES ON RECORD:

Mary's influence has been so great that a number of songs have been recorded about her, including:
"Resurrection Mary" by Ian Hunter
"Resurrection Mary" by Rich Ingle
"The Ballad of Resurrection Mary" by Guy Gilbert
"Resurrection Mary" by Ron Randolph
And even a rap song called "Rez Mary" and a band from Arizona that uses "Resurrection Mary" as its name.

There are likely others as well, but none of them have become as famous as Dickey Lee's song, "Laurie." The song was inspired by a short story written by a 15-year-old girl named Cathie Harmon. She penned a "vanishing hitchhiker" story, which was based on Resurrection Mary, for a Memphis, Tenn., newspaper in 1965. A psychologist and songwriter named Milton Addington read the story and turned it into a song for Dickey Lee called "Laurie (Strange Things Happen in this World.)" Dr. Addington credited Cathie Harmon for the story and he shared the royalties that he earned from the song with her. Here are the lyrics from the song:

Artist: Dickey Lee
Song: Laurie (Strange Things Happen in this World)

Last night at the dance I met Laurie,
So lovely and warm, an angel of a girl.
Last night I fell in love with Laurie -
Strange things happen in this world.

As I walked her home,
She said it was her birthday.
I pulled her close and said
"Will I see you anymore?"
Then suddenly she asked for my sweater
And said that she was very, very cold.

I kissed her goodnight
At her door and started home,
Then thought about my sweater
And went right back instead.
I knocked at her door and a man appeared.
I told why I'd come, then he said:

"You're wrong, son.
You weren't with my daughter.
How can you be so cruel
To come to me this way?
My Laurie left this world on her birthday -
She died a year ago today."

A strange force drew me to the graveyard.
I stood in the dark,
I saw the shadows wave,
And then I looked and saw my sweater
Lyin' there upon her grave.

Strange things happen in this world.

BIBLIOGRAPHY & RECOMMENDED READING

Abbott, Karen - Sin in the Second City (2007)
Adler, Jeffrey S. - First in Violence, Deepest in Dirt (2006)
Appelbaum, Stanley - The Chicago World's Fair of 1893 (1980)
Asbury, Herbert - Gem of the Prairie (1940)
Beck, Frank - Hobohemia (1956)
Bernstein, Arnie - Hollywood on Lake Michigan (1998)
Binder, John - The Chicago Outfit (2003)
Bolingbrook Historical Society
Brannon, W.T. - Album of Famous Mysteries
Brundage, Slim -- From Bughouse Square to the Beat Generation (1997)
Burroughs, Brian - Public Enemies (2004)
Caren, Eric C. Collection - Crime Extra: 300 Years of American Crime (2001)
Casey, Robert J. - Chicago, Medium Rare (1952)
Chicago Public Library
Chicago Historical Society
Chicago Historical Society - The Great Chicago Fire (notes by Paul M. Angle) (1946)
Cowdery, Ray - Capone's Chicago (1931)
Cromie, Robert - The Great Chicago Fire (1958)
Davis, James E. - Frontier Illinois (1998)
Demaris, Ovid - Captive City (1969)
Drabek, Paul - Old Chicago Website
Drury, John - Old Chicago Houses (1951)
Drury, John - Old Illinois Houses (1948)
Ehhigian, Mars, Jr. --- After Capone (2006)
Enright, Laura - Chicago's Most Wanted (2005)
Everett, Marshall - The Great Chicago Theater Disaster (1904)
Fliege, Stu - Tales & Trails of Illinois (2002)
Franke, David - The Torture Doctor (1975)
Goulart, Ron - Line up Tough Guys (1966)
Halper, Albert - The Chicago Crime Book (1967)
Hansen, Harry - The Chicago (1942)
Harris, Patrica A. Gruse -- The Great Lakes' First Submarine : LD Phillips Fool Killer (1982)
Hatch, Anthony P. - Tinder Box (2003)
Helmer, William & Rick Mattix - The Complete Public Enemies Almanac (2007)
Helmer, William - Public Enemies (1998)
Helmer, William & Arthur J. Bilek - The St. Valentine's Day Massacre (2004)
Humble, Ronald D. - Frank Nitti (2008)
Johnson, Curt - Wicked City (1994)
Keefe, Rose --- Guns and Roses (2003)
Keefe, Rose - The Man who Got Away (2005)
King, Jeffery --- Rise and Fall of the Dillinger Gang (2005)
Kobler, John --- Ardent Spirits: The Rise & Fall of Prohibition (1973)

Kobler, John - Capone (1971)
Kogan, Herman & Lloyd Wendt - Lords of the Levee (1944)
Lait, Jack & Lee Mortimer - Chicago Confidential (1950)
Larson, Erik --- Devil in the White City (2003)
Lesy, Michael - Murder City (2007)
Lewis, Lloyd & Henry Justin Smith - Chicago: The History of its Reputation (1929)
Lindberg, Richard - Chicago by Gaslight (1996)
Lindberg, Richard - Return to the Scene of the Crime (1999)
Lindberg, Richard - Return Again to the Scene of the Crime (2001)
Loerzel, Robert - Alchemy of Bones (2003)
Long, Megan - Disaster Great Lakes (2002)
Lowe, David - Lost Chicago (1975)
Lunde, Paul --- Organized Crime (2004)
Mark, Norman - Mayors, Madams & Madmen (1979)
Matera, Dary - John Dillinger (2004)
Miller, Donald - City of the Century (1996)
Nash, Jay Robert - Bloodletters and Bad Men (1995)
Nash, Jay Robert - The Dillinger Dossier (1970)
Nash, Jay Robert - Murder, America (1980)
Nash, Jay Robert - Open Files (1983)
Nash, Jay Robert - People to See (1981)
Nickel, Stephen & William J. Helmer - Baby Face Nelson (2002)
Northwestern University - The Chicago Historical Homicide Project
O'Gorman, Thomas & Lisa Montanarelli - Strange But True Chicago (2005)
O'Shea, Gene --- Unbridled Rage (2005)
Palos in Autumn Magazine (1923)
Parrish, Randall - Historic Illinois (1905)
Paulett, John & Ron Gordon - Forgotten Chicago (2004)
Pinkwater, Daniel - Fish Whistle (1990)
Pohlen, Jerome - Oddball Illinois (2000)
Quaife, Milo - Chicago Highways Old and New (1923)
Rath, Jay - I-Files: True Reports of the Unexplained in Illinois (1999)
Rosemont, Franklin -- The Rise and Fall of the Dil Pickle Club (2003)
Rothert, Otto - Outlaws of Cave-in-Rock (1924)
Sann, Paul - The Lawless Decade (1957)
Schechter, Harold - Depraved (1994)
Sifakis, Carl - Encyclopedia of American Crime (1982)
Smith, Henry Justin - Chicago: A Portrait (1931)
Stead, William T. - If Christ Came to Chicago (1894)
Taylor, Troy - Bloody Chicago (2006)
Taylor, Troy - Dead Men Do Tell Tales (2008)
Taylor, Troy - Haunted Alton (2000 / 2003)
Taylor, Troy - Haunted Chicago (2003)
Taylor, Troy - Haunted Decatur (2006)
Taylor, Troy - Haunted Illinois (2004)
Taylor, Troy - No Rest for the Wicked (2003)
Taylor, Troy - Resurrection Mary (2007)
Taylor, Troy - Weird Illinois (2005)
Toland, John - Dillinger Days (1963)
Waskin, Mel - Mrs. O'Leary's Comet (1985)
Wendt, Lloyd & Herman Kogan - Big Bill of Chicago (1953)
Wright, Sewell Peaslee - Chicago Murders: True Crimes and Real Detectives (1947)

Personal Interviews and Correspondence

Magazines, Newspapers & Periodicals
Chicago American (Illinois)
Chicago Daily Herald (Illinois)
Chicago Daily News (Illinois)
Chicago Globe (Illinois)
Chicago Herald (Illinois)
Chicago Herald & Examiner (Illinois)
Chicago Inter-Ocean (Illinois)
Chicago Mail (Illinois)
Chicago Sun (Illinois)
Chicago Sun-Times (Illinois)
Chicago Times (Illinois)
Chicago Daily Tribune (Illinois)

Above Top Secret Website: www.abovetopsecret.com
Jazz Age Chicago Website: www. chicago.urban-history.org
Wikipedia Website: www.wikipedia.org

Note: Although Whitechapel Press, the authors, and all affiliated with this book have carefully researched all sources to insure the accuracy and completeness of all information contained here, we assume no responsibility for errors, inaccuracies or omissions.

Special Thanks to:
Jill Hand (Editing & Proofreading)
Lindsey Harper
Rich Vitton
Dale Kaczmarek
Jim Gracyzk
Martha Itak
Willowbrook Ballroom Staff
Tom & Michelle Bonadurer
Kathy Richardson
Eddie & Marianne Schaeffer
Mike & Sandra Schwab
Jay Robert Nash
John Winterbauer
Wendy Jones
Donna Dozeman
Richie "Tapeworm" Herrera
Jeff Jeske
Deborah Sacks
Seth Kleinschrodt
Jim Card
The CW Parker Museum
Hector Reyes
The Newberry Library
Katie Jacobson
Willie Williams
& Haven Taylor

I've reported murders, scandals, marriages, premieres and national political
conventions. I've been amused, intrigued, outraged, enthralled and exasperated by
Chicago. And I've come to love this American giant, viewing it as the most
misunderstood, most underrated city in the world. There is none other quite like my
City of Big Shoulders.
Irv Kupcinet,

WEIRD CHICAGO TOURS

THE ULTIMATE TOUR OF CHICAGO'S GHOSTS, GANGSTERS & GHOULS - AVAILABLE YEAR ROUND! CALL 1-888-GHOSTLY FOR RESERVATIONS! WWW.WEIRDCHICAGO.COM

Printed in the United States
220501BV00001B/61/P